Praise for *Food for the Soul*

"Peter Kreeft is a most gifted theologian, but more importantly, he is a man of faith. With this latest book of reflections on the Scripture readings for Mass, he is sharing with us the lights born of a life of prayer and faithful discipleship. It is truly an expression of what Hans Urs von Balthasar called *kniende Theologie*, 'theology on the knees.' In addition to the solid content, Peter Kreeft's artfully expressed thought never fails to inspire."

—**Cardinal Seán O'Malley**, Archbishop of Boston

"Peter Kreeft has no equal with respect to making the deepest truths shine forth with aphoristic brilliance. He is the perfect person to place in the pulpit. Kreeft on the readings for Mass is a match made in heaven."

—**Joseph Pearce**, Editor of the *St. Austin Review* and author of *Wisdom and Innocence: A Life of G.K. Chesterton*

"Reading this series is like joining the masterful Peter Kreeft for coffee after Mass to talk about the readings. It's a wonderful resource that Catholics can pick up and return to again and again throughout the liturgical year, full of wisdom from one of the top guiding lights of our era in the Catholic world."

—**Dr. Edward Sri**, theologian and author of *A Biblical Walk through the Mass*

"Unfortunately, we have written records of only seven of C.S. Lewis' sermons. But thank God we now have dozens of reflections from Peter Kreeft, the modern C.S. Lewis, based on the Mass readings throughout the liturgical year. Kreeft's decades of reading Scripture, teaching students, and loving wisdom shine forth in this compendium, which deserves wide readership by priests and laypeople alike. With his characteristic wit and wisdom, Kreeft offers an invaluable resource in understanding the Scriptures proclaimed in the liturgy. I hope Kreeft's book finds its way into the hands of every Catholic eager to better understand the readings of Sunday Mass."

—**Christopher Kaczor**, Professor of Philosophy, Loyola Marymount University, and Fellow of the Word on Fire Institute

"More than a help, this book is a gift to the Church, and the gift is an encounter with Christ, the Word. Not only for priests—although I encourage this book to be used by priests and hopefully also in seminary formation—this book is also for laity and religious. It is for anyone who is seeking to know God more profoundly through prayer and reflection on his Word, helping us in our journey to know him and discern this message of love."

—**Sr. Josephine Garrett**, Sister of the Holy Family of Nazareth

"Preaching is among the most important tasks of the Church. It is the premiere form of catechesis for the average parishioner and a surefire way to inspire the hearts of God's people. Today, the faithful are hungering for substantial homilies informed by the Scriptures and Sacred Tradition. This collection of Peter Kreeft's biblical reflections provides Catholics with a trustworthy and insightful resource in response to this need. With his usual clarity, Kreeft guides the reader in a stirring series of reflections that will prove a valuable asset to any layperson, religious, seminarian, deacon, or priest."

—**Fr. Blake Britton**, author of *Reclaiming Vatican II: What It (Really) Said, What It Means, and How It Calls Us to Renew the Church*

"Peter Kreeft's reflections are challenging yet simple, piercing right to the soul with his wit, charm, and heart. If you're wondering whether or not you need another book offering reflections on the Mass readings, I offer a resounding yes! These reflections show how deeply God loves us through the Word and the Church, ultimately reminding us of the simple fact that the point is not the homily or the prose—the point is Jesus."

—**Rachel Bulman**, author, speaker, and Fellow of the Word on Fire Institute

FOOD

for the

SOUL

FOOD
for the
SOUL

REFLECTIONS ON THE MASS READINGS

———

CYCLE B

PETER KREEFT

Published by Word on Fire, Elk Grove Village, IL 60007
© 2023 by Peter Kreeft
Printed in the United States of America
All rights reserved

Cover design, typesetting, and interior art direction by Katherine Spitler,
Cassie Bielak, and Clark Kenyon

First printing, October 2023

ISBN: 978-1-68578-034-0

Library of Congress Control Number: 2021922577

CONTENTS

INTRODUCTION

Why this book?

Because one of the things we Catholics can learn from Protestants is to sing, from experience and from the heart, this old hymn by Edwin Hodder:

> Thy Word is like a garden, Lord, with flowers bright and fair;
> And everyone who seeks may pluck a lovely cluster there.
> Thy Word is like a deep, deep mine; and jewels rich and rare
> Are hidden in its mighty depths for every searcher there.
>
> Thy Word is like a starry host: a thousand rays of light
> Are seen to guide the traveler and make his pathway bright.
> Thy Word is like an armory, where soldiers may repair
> And find, for life's long battle day, all needful weapons there.
>
> O may I love Thy precious Word, may I explore the mine,
> May I its fragrant flowers glean, may light upon me shine!
> O may I find my armor there, Thy Word my trusty sword,
> I'll learn to fight with every foe the battle of the Lord.

Who is this book for?

I wrote this book for three classes of people: enterprising priests, lazy priests, and laity.

It's for enterprising priests who want a "homily helper" that does to their homilies what "Hamburger Helper" does to boring hamburgers.

It's also for lazy priests who want to use my poor brains instead of theirs. I'm practical enough to know that this second category is pretty large. Laziness affects all of us, and we laity don't hold it against you priests very much. So

I think it's okay to take the easy way out and simply draw from my words, though I think it's much better for your people to hear your own words rather than mine. Besides, they're not even very original. Their origin is not in my mind but in the long and deep tradition of the Church. The Church is in the business of farming. Her words are seeds, meant for scattering on many mental soils. Whoever you are, dear reader, both of us are only links in the chain of God's mail delivery.

And this book is also for a third class of people: for the laity who are hungry for more of "the bread of life."

What is a homily?

Protestants have sermons; Catholics have homilies. One difference between them is that sermons are usually doctrinal or topical, while homilies are biblical. They are supposed to be expositions of the biblical texts assigned for Mass, which are the good soul-food that Mother Church puts on the plate of our high chair each Sunday at Mass. (Do you resent that insult? Most two-year-olds do. That just shows how old you are.)

A homily is to the Bible what a slave is to his master, what money is to the things that money can buy, or what ears are to hearing. Its whole, single, simple purpose is to "break the bread" of the Bible as the Mass breaks the bread of Christ's Body. Both the Bible and Christ are called the "Word of God." The Bible is the Word of God on paper; Christ is the Word of God in flesh, and on wood (the wood of the cross). Paper is made out of wood; wood is not made out of paper.

The purpose of a homily depends on the identity of the Bible, which is the master it serves. There are two radically different answers to the question of what the Bible is. Nonbelievers (some of whom call themselves Catholics) believe it is man's words about God; believers believe it is God's Word about man. Believers call it "the Word" in the singular because it is a singular book, the only one that has the authority of divine revelation.

Nonbelievers see the Bible as human wisdom about God; believers see it as divine wisdom about man. They differ not about the book but about the author. Obviously, men wrote it, but were they God's instruments or not? If so, it has "author-ity" from its primary Author. Like Christ, it has two natures: human and divine. It is the Word of God in the words of men. Fundamentalists deny its human nature and modernists deny its divine nature, just as in the early Church, Docetists denied Christ's human nature and Arians denied his divine nature.

Both Protestants and Catholics believe that the Bible is divine revelation, but Protestants believe that it is the only infallible divine revelation. (If it's divine, it has to be infallible; God may be mysterious and obscure but he makes no mistakes.) Catholics believe that there is also a divinely authorized Church that is to the Bible what a teacher is to a textbook and that the New Testament is part of a larger and earlier Sacred Tradition ("tradition" literally means "hand down"), which Christ handed down to his Apostles, and that he gave them his authority to teach in his name and to appoint their successors (the bishops) through whom they passed on this authority to future generations. The Bible itself says that. Thus, faithful Catholics always interpret the Bible according to the Sacred Tradition of the Church, and vice versa.

A Catholic homilist, then, serves four masters: (1) God, (2) God's Christ, (3) Christ's Church, and (4) the Church's Bible—the Bible because of the Church, the Church because of Christ, and Christ because of God.

Catholics do not skip the third link in that chain—the Church. As St. Augustine said, "I would not believe the Bible unless I believed the Church." For the apostolic Church was the Teacher that (1) authored (wrote) this Book, (2) authorized it (the word "author" is in "authorize"), (3) defined its canon (why these twenty-seven New Testament books and not others?) and (4) continues to interpret it, to break its bread and feed it to us. That is why Catholic homilies are always founded on the Bible.

Homily helpers

Another more obvious difference is that sermons are long (typically between fifteen minutes and an hour), while homilies are short (typically between three and ten minutes). Yet Catholics complain more about their priests' short homilies than Protestants do about their preachers' long sermons. The reason is obvious: homilies are almost always boring. They put us to sleep instead of waking us up, surprising us, shocking us, or challenging us. They are full of platitudes. They are sometimes also insults to our intelligence. They do not tell us anything we did not already know, feel, believe, or appreciate. They make the Church Militant sound like the Church Mumbling. They make the Mystical Body of Christ look like Mister Rogers' Neighborhood. They make Jesus sound like Joel Osteen or Oprah.

But they do have a certain power: they are effective sleeping pills. And unlike other sleeping pills, they cost nothing and are always safe. In fact, they are excruciatingly safe.

Preaching is one of many things we Catholics can learn from Protestants of the old-fashioned kind. (I do not waste my wind on the windy ones, the worldly ones who are so current that they swim with the current, not against it, like dead fish instead of live ones, and who identify religion with the platform of either political party—worshiping either the elephant or the donkey.)

One reason Protestants usually preach better sermons is that they usually know the Bible better than Catholics do. They love it and revere it and are passionate about it. The cynical Catholic's explanation for this is that that's all they've got: sola scriptura. No infallible creeds, no ecumenical councils, no authoritative Sacred Tradition, no Mystical Body, no Real Presence, no Mass, no canonized saints, no mystics, no attention paid to Mary or to the angels, no pope, no purgatory, no seven sacraments, no icons, no incense, no holy water, no exorcisms, no Latin, no Gregorian chant, etc. Protestants find Catholicism far too fat. Catholics find Protestantism far too skinny. But though their religion is skinny, their sermons are fatter. Imagine a Mass that ended with the homily, that had nothing more substantial or supersubstantial than the homily. The homily would have to be bigger and better. But, of course, to a Catholic, that Protestant service would be like an egg without a yolk, or a target without a bull's-eye.

Okay, so somebody should improve our homilies. Somebody should market a "homily helper" to do to homilies what Hamburger Helper does to hamburgers.

But why me? I'm an absent-minded philosophy professor, not a priest or a deacon. I have never preached a homily in a Catholic church. I do not teach biblical theology or homiletics. I am not professionally qualified to write this book.

But I know, from observation, how many people fall asleep during homilies; and I know, from experience, how many Catholics are exercising heroic charity toward their priests in being polite and patronizing and pretending as they endure their mild weekly purgatory.

There are some priests who are very good homilists, but they are very rare. My parish priest preaches excellent homilies, but that is because he was trained and ordained as a Protestant (Anglican) before he became a Catholic.

So the need is clear. How much this book can help, if at all, is not clear. But just maybe it can. And the situation can't get much worse. My friend actually heard an Easter homily in which the priest said that the message Christ was trying to get across to us from the pulpit of the cross was "I'm OK, you're OK." This is not a joke from *Monty Python's Life of Brian*.

For priests only

If you are a priest, I have one and only one piece of advice for you if you plan to draw from these words of mine. As someone who is not a shepherd (a priest, a deacon, or an expert in homiletics) but just one of the sheep, here is my primary bleat to my shepherds. It does not matter what we think of you, whether you are a good speaker or not, intelligent or not, eloquent or not, or even whether or not you are wise and competent in anything else in this world. The one and only thing that will give your homily power is your heart's passion, your love, both of Jesus Christ the shepherd and of us his sheep who desperately need him in our lives.

We're not impressed by your head or your mouth or your hands, but we can't help being impressed by your heart. And you can't help showing it; you can't help wearing your heart on your sleeve. You can't fake your heart, as you can fake your head or your hands. You can't give us what you don't have yourself. If you don't believe this stuff, stop pretending and go back to the school of prayer and ask God for the gift of faith to believe it. If your hope is dim and dull and sleepy, go back and ask God to put that hope in your heart so you can give it to your people. If you don't have a passionate, all-consuming love for Jesus Christ the good shepherd and for every one of his needy, bleat-y sheep, go back and ask God to light a bonfire in your heart. We can be fooled by fake light, but we can't be fooled by fake heat. We can tell how much you mean every word you say. We're still little kids that way. We have surprisingly good baloney detectors. We can read our spiritual fathers just as we can read our biological fathers. Let us see your heart. Don't be afraid or embarrassed. We're not your judges—God is. If you're afraid to be embarrassed in front of us now, you're going to be embarrassed in front of him at the Last Judgment.

The heart of your target as a homilist is the heart of each person who hears your homily. God aims at the heart, which is the center of the soul and the source of its life just as the physical heart is the source and center of the life of the body.

So your homily should be heart to heart. "Heart speaks to heart"—that was St. John Henry Newman's personal motto because he knew it was God's. (But as Newman knew well, that does not decrease the importance of the mind and intelligence but increases it. The mind is the heart's closest counselor.)

Christ is the one who sews hearts to God and to each other. Therefore, like the Scriptures they "unpack," homilies should be centered on Christ. If there is one thing we Catholics need always to be reminded of by Evangelical Protestants, it is Christocentrism. And since Christ is both the historical Jesus and the eternal "Logos," the "Word" or "language" of God, the light of truth who "enlightens everyone" (John 1:9), Christians defend the "logocentrism" that "deconstructionists" denounce. Their logophobia is really a Christophobia.

Scripture uses the term "Word of God" both for itself and for Christ. The Bible is the gold mine and Christ is the gold. Therefore, St. Jerome says that "ignorance of Scripture is ignorance of Christ." Christ is the central point of Scripture and also the "big picture" or frame surrounding it. So if homilies are to be faithful to the scriptural bread that they break open, Christ must be both the center and the surrounding frame for every homily. They are to be looked along, not looked at. They are pointing fingers, words of men that point to the Word of God.

The content of the book

Some of these reflections try to connect the different readings for each Sunday Mass—the Old Testament reading, the epistle, and the Gospel—and some do not. The readings were put together, in the mind of the Church, for a reason. However, to be perfectly frank, sometimes the reason and the connection is not clear, at least not to me. So I don't always "push the envelope" and strain to see a unity I don't really see very well. But even then, the main point of each of the separate readings is clear, and one arrow is enough to pierce a heart.

The reason God sent his Son into our world, the reason he founded his Church and instituted the Mass, the reason for everything he has done for us, is to consummate our spiritual marriage to him: a living, personal, joyful, faithful, hopeful, and love-full relationship with God that is totally encompassing, both individual and social, both private and public, both body and soul, both invisible and visible, both spiritual and sacramental, both through hierarchy and through equality, both intellectual and moral, both rational and mystical, both in this world and in the next. That is the reason for everything he has done, from banging out the Big Bang to my writing and your reading these tiny little pops that are its remotest echoes.

Use them, choose them, and lose them as you will. Some will "work" better, some worse. My words as well as my ideas are given to you for God's glory, not mine or yours.

ADVENT

FIRST SUNDAY OF ADVENT

FIRST READING
Isaiah 63:16b–17, 19b; 64:2–7 _____

You, Lord, are our father,
  our redeemer you are named forever.
Why do you let us wander, O Lord, from your ways,
  and harden our hearts so that we fear you not?
Return for the sake of your servants,
  the tribes of your heritage.
Oh, that you would rend the heavens and come down,
  with the mountains quaking before you,
while you wrought awesome deeds we could not hope for,
  such as they had not heard of from of old.
No ear has ever heard, no eye ever seen, any God but you
  doing such deeds for those who wait for him.
Would that you might meet us doing right,
  that we were mindful of you in our ways!
Behold, you are angry, and we are sinful;
  all of us have become like unclean people,
  all our good deeds are like polluted rags;
we have all withered like leaves,
  and our guilt carries us away like the wind.
There is none who calls upon your name,
  who rouses himself to cling to you;
for you have hidden your face from us
  and have delivered us up to our guilt.
Yet, O Lord, you are our father;

3

we are the clay and you the potter:
we are all the work of your hands.

(I am going to offer two reflections, not just one, on this passage. You can use either or both, in either order. The first centers on the most pressing problem of our lives, if we are believers—namely, the problem of evil: Why does the good God allow so much evil? The second is less philosophical and more "pastoral" and textual.)

Reflection 1

Twice the prophet Isaiah calls God our Father. What does that mean?

Everything true of a father is true of a mother also. A father, with the cooperation of a mother, procreates children. Procreation is part of God's image in us, since God is our Creator. He gives us our very existence.

A father gives more than just existence. A builder gives existence to a building, and an author gives existence to a book, but a father (and a mother) gives something more: life. God gives us life.

A father gives us not just any kind of life but *human* life, human nature. Human fathers give their children human life, and that is an image of the fact that God gives us a human and finite share in his divine life, through Christ, so that we become adopted children of God by faith and Baptism.

A father gives his children protection and care and guidance and wisdom and education and time. He shares his lifetime with his children.

A father loves his children. What is love? Love is the gift of your very self to another. What is the clearest proof of love? The proof of love is sacrifice. God the Father sacrificed the dearest and most precious thing he had for us, to save us from sin and eternal death: his own infinitely beloved Son.

Human fathers, and all these gifts that they give to their children, are all imperfect. But God is perfect.

Why, then, in light of this amazing and wonderful fact that the perfect God is our Father, are we in such dire straits? Why does such a good and perfect God allow us to harden our hearts to him? Of course, he does not himself harden our hearts—none of his works are evil—but he does allow us to harden our own hearts, so that we no longer fear him.

"The beginning of wisdom is fear of the Lord," says the Bible in many places (see Prov. 9:10). That fear is not servile fear, a slave's fear of cruelty from a wicked master whom he hates, but filial fear, a child's fear of disappointing his good father whom he loves.

So if the fear of the Lord is the beginning of wisdom, why does God not give us the grace to fear him more? He *could*. Grace is a gift. It is freely given. It is not automatic and necessary, like our essential nature. We cannot ever *not* have human nature, but we can and do often *not* have divine grace—and then, in contrast, we do have it when God gives it, but not before. The question, then, is why not before? Why not always? Why not perpetually?

God does not lack the power to do that. Isaiah confesses that God is the potter and we are the clay, the work of God's hands. He is omnipotent. Why are the clay pots all crackpots? God does not make crackpots. Why does he let us crack? Why are our best deeds like polluted rags? God is not a polluter.

The origin of evil is our own free choice, of course, not God. God chose to create children, not robots, and the children rebelled, and continue to rebel. But when Isaiah asks God why he allows us to sin, he is not asking that question as a philosopher or theologian wondering how to rationally reconcile God's infinite power and goodness with human sin. He knows that we, not God, are the ones who choose to sin. He is not philosophizing; he is praying—and he is both confessing and complaining, and agonizing over our sins. He is not *wondering why* God does not "rend the heavens and come down" and fix things: he is asking him to *do* that. He is praying, not philosophizing. He wants a miracle, not an answer. And he will get what he is praying for, but in God's good time: he will get Jesus Christ, the incarnate Savior. He will get more than an answer: he will get the Answerer. That's the reason Job was satisfied in the end. God didn't give him answers: he gave him himself.

But we do need an answer to the great question of why God allows so much evil in his world, both physical evil and moral evil, both sufferings and sins. His power is so great that he could minimize or even eliminate both. Why doesn't he?

We need *three* answers to that question, not just one: one in our heads, one in our hearts, and one in our hands. That is, we need an answer in our thought, in our faith, in our theology; and also one in our will, in our choices, in our loves; and also one in our actions, in our deeds. In other words, one in light, one in love, and one in life, the three things we need the most.

The answer in thought is that God is all-wise, and he knows what is best for us, and he makes no mistakes. He knows that, given what we are—always somewhat foolish and sinful and selfish—it is best for us to learn from experience, to suffer and even to be allowed to sin, so that we can profit from our failures even more than we could profit only from our successes. God always knows and wills the greatest good for us, although we don't usually see this, because we are not God. (Duh!)

That is the answer to our heads. The answer to our hearts and our wills is even more important than the answer to our heads and our minds. God cares most of all for our hearts. He gives truth to our heads, gives us divine revelation, not just for our heads but also for our hearts, not just to satisfy our curiosity but also to instruct our hearts. Our hearts have an even greater need of truth than our heads do. For our hearts are the heart of the matter. For the heart is where love comes from, and, as St. John of the Cross said, "In the evening of our lives, we will be judged on our love." And the reason for that is that we will be judged by the God who *is* love, as St. John the Evangelist said, in perhaps the profoundest sentence ever written. Because God, our judge, is love, we will be judged according to our loves.

Our hearts are essentially our wills, not just our feelings. Our feelings come *to* us, passively, but our choices come *from* us, actively, by our free will. We are not responsible for our feelings, but we are responsible for our choices. Our choices are free.

But they are not wholly free, because we are addicts. We are not all alcoholics, but we are all sinaholics. We are addicted to our own selfishness. We love to sing "I did it my way." So one of the things we do with our free will is forge the chains of our own slavery to sin with the strength of our freedom. The other thing we do with our free will is the opposite: we freely choose freedom by choosing God's way. God gave us this terrible power to freely choose either slavery or freedom, either "My will be done" or "Thy will be done."

So the central answer to the problem of evil is in our own will, our free will. Our wills are freer than our minds. Our minds can't not-know that 2 + 2 = 4 or that the sky is blue, but our will can not-love, can refuse love and refuse God and prefer selfishness to love.

The answer to the problem of evil is in three places: in our heads, our hearts, and our hands. We have more power over our hearts than over our heads, but we have the most power over our hands. In fact, what I have called "the answer in our hands" is literally *in our hands*. God has put the solution to the problem of evil in our own hands. We can "solve" the "problem of evil" most adequately not just by thinking and choosing but above all by *doing* good, by doing God's will, by becoming saints.

Our hands move in obedience to our hearts (that is, our loves, our desires, our wills); and both our hearts and our hands can act only on what they know from our heads (that is, on what we know or believe). So the foundation and beginning of the answer to the problem of evil must be in our heads, and the center and heart of it is in our hearts, and the final and definitive answer to the problem of evil is in our hands.

We need three things, the three things Christ is: light, love, and life. These correspond to the needs of our heads, our hearts, and our hands: light for our heads, love for our hearts, and life for our hands. The light must come first because nothing can be freely loved with our hearts or lived with our hands without light for our heads, our minds. The answer in our hearts must come next, and centrally; that is the answer in love. But the answer in our hands must come last, and that is the answer in our lives. The final answer to the problem of evil is in our own hands. It is to become saints. Saints are the solution to the problem of evil. Be one!

Reflection 2

Isaiah speaks like a young child to God as his father. A child trusts his father. (By the way, I say "his" and "he" instead of "his or hers" and "he or she" just as every single person who wrote or spoke the English language did for hundreds of years, not to exclude women but to exclude a superfluous "or she" after each inclusive "he," or a dehumanizing "it.") A child trusts his father but does not wholly understand him. That's why he has to trust him (or distrust him—that is the child's basic choice): precisely because he does not understand him. And we are always children in relation to God. We grow, but we never grow equal to God. Even in heaven, when we see him face to face in the beatific vision, there will still be the child's trust in his always infinitely wiser Father.

A child needs especially two things from his father: wisdom and help. Freud, the founder of modern psychology, who was an atheist, said that we invented God because all children need these two things—wisdom and protection, deliverance from ignorance and deliverance from fear and suffering—and when children realize that their father, who supplied these two things throughout their childhood, will die, they invent an invisible heavenly Father because they cannot live without hope that these two things will still come to them from somewhere. Freud was totally wrong about God, but he was not totally wrong about human psychology and human needs. We cannot live without hope.

So Isaiah says to God, in his prayer, "You, LORD, are our father, our redeemer" (that is, our savior, our helper, our hope). Yet he goes on to say, "Why do you let us wander, O LORD, from your ways, and harden our hearts so that we fear you not?" Why does our Father let us wander so far away from him in our hearts and lives?

God, of course, does not do anything evil, and hardening any heart is an evil work, so God does not harden anyone's heart. But he does allow us to harden our own hearts. And Isaiah complains about that to God. He says, in effect, Why don't you stop us? Why don't you interfere? Why don't you give us more grace? More miracles? Why don't you appear to us miraculously, as you did to our ancestors, when you saved your people from their slavery in Egypt by miracles—the ten plagues, and the pillar of fire, and the pillar of cloud, and the parting of the Red Sea, and the manna in the wilderness?

So Isaiah pleads to God to "return for the sake of your servants, the tribes of your heritage." His complaint is a good one! It stems from faith. He says to God, We are your children, your own people, your special, personal heritage. Why do you seem to be neglecting your children?

Isaiah is not asking "Why?" as a philosopher or a scientist would ask "Why?" He is not looking for an explanation; he is looking for a miracle. If you or someone you dearly love is dying, what you want from your doctor is not an explanation of what they are dying of! You want a cure, or at least a medicine that will actually help, not just an explanation of why the doctor is not giving you a cure or a medicine. Isaiah is not complaining about his head; he's complaining about his heart. His heart is broken by God's absence, and he asks God to break the heavens themselves and come and save him: "Oh, that you would rend the heavens and come down, with the mountains quaking before you, while you wrought awesome deeds." Isaiah knew that God did that in the past. He saved Israel from slavery to Egypt, and now Israel faces slavery from her Babylonian conquerors. Why isn't God fixing that?

And there is a far worse slavery that Isaiah complains about than slavery to Babylonians: slavery to sins. When the horrible sin of slavery polluted America, the slave masters were in a far worse slavery than the slaves, because the slaves' souls were innocent and pious, and full of faith and hope, while the masters' souls were full of pride, contempt, and arrogance. They were the real slaves: slaves to their own desires. The slaves were interiorly free, free of need for the masters, while the masters were interiorly enslaved, enslaved to their need for their slaves.

Isaiah confesses that Israel has sinned and deserves her punishment of defeat in war and captivity in Babylon, so he is not complaining about God's just punishments. He is not asking God why he allowed the Babylonians to justly punish the Jews but why he allowed the Jews to sin and deserve those punishments. He says, "Behold, you are angry, and we are sinful." God is rightly and justly angry—the lack of rightful anger at sins and injustices is itself unjust and sinful, and God has no sin, and so God is therefore rightly angry.

Isaiah confesses that "all of us have become like unclean people, all our good deeds are like polluted rags." We had some good deeds, but even in our good deeds we had mixed motives, bad motives, polluted motives.

He says, "We have all withered like leaves." Sin does harm not only to others but to the sinner: it withers his soul; it takes the life out of his soul; it detaches his soul from God, as the cold autumn wind detaches a dead, withered leaf from a living tree. He says, "Our guilt carries us away like the wind." *Living* leaves are not carried away by the wind because they are stuck onto the living tree. But once the leaf dies to the living sap of the tree, it becomes withered and passive, the victim of the wind. The leaf here is us, and the tree is God, and the sap is the very life of God in the soul, and the separation of the leaf from the tree is sin, and the wind is all the other forces in the world that become our Lords and masters, that move our souls once they are separated from God: forces like the media, or our own hates and prejudices, or "the spirit of the times," or ideologies, or our own hunger for money, sex, and power, greed and lust and pride.

So Isaiah is not bargaining with God and not complaining that God is unjust or unfair. He is confessing the terrible truth that God's abandonment of Israel to defeat is fully deserved. He says, "You have . . . delivered us up to our guilt." Guilt is not a mere feeling, any more than faith or hope or love are mere feelings. Guilt is a fact. The prisoner does not have the right to complain to the judge about a verdict of guilty that he doesn't *feel* guilty.

Guilt is a truth. But it's not the whole truth. There's a "but," and it's a big "but." (I don't know whether or not Isaiah was fat, but I know he had a big "but.") Here it is: "But you are our father, Lord" (GNT). The father of the prodigal son is still the son's father and still loves him, even after his son left him. He did not imprison his son and prevent him from leaving him and going into the far country to make some horrible mistakes and suffer their consequences. He allowed it. He did not approve it, but he allowed it to happen—because the son was not a robot or a machine or a possession but an individual with free will. The only way the son could learn the hard lesson was by experience. He had to repent and return of his own free will. The father could have forced his son's *body* to come home—he could have sent soldiers out to capture him—but he could not force his *soul* to come home. Even God cannot force a choice of our free will. God does not take back his gift of free will even when we abuse it.

Yet God is in control all the time. Isaiah says, "We are the clay and you the potter: we are all the work of your hands." All of history is his-story, and all of us are part of his story, and this divine author, this storyteller, knows every detail of what he is doing. But we do not. That's why we have to live in hope and faith and trust.

But the redemption comes. God acts. In his good time, he comes and redeems us. That is what we will celebrate on December 25. Now, in Advent, we stand with Isaiah in the darkness and wonder why God does not come sooner. We will get our answer, but only in God's good time.

And when we get the answer, when he does come, it will be far greater, far better, than we could have hoped or desired or imagined. It will be "what eye has not seen, and ear has not heard, and what has not entered the human heart" (1 Cor. 2:9). It will be God himself, God incarnate, God in the flesh giving us his own flesh and blood, his own life, for our salvation.

Today we celebrate both our present Advent and our future Christmas. We celebrate Advent with Isaiah as we confess that we stand in the same sin and darkness as ancient Israel. But our Advent is not just a complaint but also a celebration, because we stand in hope. We also celebrate our hope for Christmas today. In fact, Christmas will come to us sooner than December 25. It will come to us in the Mass, which is the answer to Isaiah's prayer, when God literally rends the heavens and comes down, when the Son of God descends into the darkness of our sinful world and even into our death, and then rises to dispel our darkness and destroy our death and swallow our sins.

RESPONSORIAL PSALM

PSALM 80:2–3, 15–16, 18–19_____

R. (4) **Lord, make us turn to you; let us see your face and we shall be saved**.

O shepherd of Israel, hearken,
    from your throne upon the cherubim, shine forth.
Rouse your power,
    and come to save us.

Once again, O LORD of hosts,
    look down from heaven, and see;
take care of this vine,
    and protect what your right hand has planted,
    the son of man whom you yourself made strong.

May your help be with the man of your right hand,
    with the son of man whom you yourself made strong.
Then we will no more withdraw from you;
    give us new life, and we will call upon your name.

_____

What today's Psalm asks God for is the same thing Isaiah asked for in today's Old Testament reading, and it is also different: it is something more.

Isaiah prayed, "Oh, that you would rend the heavens and come down," and the Psalmist prays, "From your throne upon the cherubim, shine forth. Rouse your power, and come to save us." They are asking God for the same thing—his presence, his power. But there is a difference: the Psalmist adds something very important to this basic prayer. He goes on to say, "Give us new life, and *we will call* upon your name."

In other words, he prays: Please send your grace into our lives not only from without but also from within; not only from you yourself, acting unilaterally, but also from us, acting in cooperation with your grace. Save us not only from our captors, the Babylonians, our enemies, but also from our far worse enemies, ourselves, our sins, the enemy within.

God responds to that prayer because God inspired that prayer. What principle is God teaching us by those words "give us new life, and we will call"? The principle is that divine grace, supernatural grace, does not bypass human nature, or substitute for it. Grace turns nature on, not off. And especially human nature. And since human free will is an essential dimension of human nature, divine grace turns our human free will and free choice on, not off. The more grace, the more nature. The more grace, the more freedom. The more God, the more us. It's like the relation between light and colors: the more light there is, the more each color shines.

The principle is clear, but the practice is paradoxical. The Psalmist, in praying, is turning to God. That is what prayer essentially is: turning to God. And he is turning to God to ask for something. For what? That God would turn to us, and "take care of this vine, and protect what your right hand has planted." All right, but what is the Psalmist asking God to do to the vine or the vineyard, which of course is God's people, us? He is asking God to turn us to him: "Give *us* new life, and we will call upon *your name*." So he is turning to God to ask God to turn to us and turn us to turn to him!

So he is answering his prayer in the very act of praying; he is getting exactly what he asked for in the very act of asking for it. He is asking God, as the disciples asked Christ, to teach us to pray. And that very asking is prayer. So we get the answer to our prayers, or at least the beginning of that answer, by the very first act of praying.

And that very first act of ours, that very first turning to God in prayer, was itself inspired by something that came before it: by God's own act of grace that inspired our asking for grace. God's action, God's grace, comes first, not second. Then it turns on our human nature and our free choice, the choice to pray. God's will activates our will. And that thing that we will, what we pray for—what is that? God's grace. God's grace to do what? To turn our hearts to him, to turn our hearts and wills from sin to sanctity, from selfishness to godliness.

What comes first *in our experience* is our need, our desire, our love, our heart, our will. We will to pray: that's why we pray. So our will to pray, our desire to pray, our desire to be in God's presence, is the first thing, *for us*. And God's response to our prayer seems to be the second thing, *for us*. Jesus says to us, "Ask and it will be given to you; seek and you will find; knock and the door will be opened to you" (Matt. 7:7). First ask, then receive. And yet in fact, in reality, it is always God who comes first, who first inspires that thing that seems first to us—namely, our desire to pray. We cannot take credit for that; we do not act first—God does. If we are the question and God is the answer, the answer always comes before the question. If we are the need and God is the supply, the supply always comes before the need.

There is an old Protestant hymn that expresses that paradox. It goes like this:

> I sought the Lord, and afterward I knew
> he moved my soul to seek him, seeking me.
> It was not I that found, O Savior true,
> no, I was found of thee.

It's tempting for us to use that fact as an excuse for not praying: "I guess God just isn't inspiring me to pray today. It's all up to him, after all." No it isn't! It's all up to you, because the very first thing God did to you is give you free will, free choice. And when God does move you, he will not move you *instead of* yourself, or in spite of yourself. He will move you to freely move yourself. The time to give God all the credit for your prayers and good works is *after* they are done, not before; when they are past, not future; when they are actual, not just potential. Trace your good works back far enough and you will see the face of God. But you can do that tracing only after you do the works and prayers. Only after you freely do a good work can you honestly thank God for having inspired it.

The principle is that we simply cannot divide up the responsibility between God and ourselves and say that God does 50% and we do 50%, or God does 100% and we do 0%, or we do 100% and God does 0%, or even that God does 99% and we do 1%. God does 100% and so do we. It's not like procreation, where the man and the woman each contribute half the chromosomes. It's more like writing, where the hand and the pen each do all the writing, not half. We do not do any of the writing without the pen, and the pen does not do any of the writing without us. Pens without hands don't write, and neither do hands without pens. We can't do it without God, and God won't do it without us.

Actually, that analogy of the hand and the pen is not totally correct because sometimes God does do his work without us, when he performs miracles. And miracles really happen, and are much, much more common than we think, especially if we are so foolish as to get all our information from our secular media. I think most of the people reading this can honestly say that they have received at least one miracle in their lives, one clearly supernatural intervention of God. But usually God uses human agents, as we use pens or pencils.

The clearest example of the 100%/100% principle, the principle that there is no dividing up a good between divine grace and human nature, divine grace and human free will—the clearest example of that is Jesus Christ, who is 100% God and 100% man, wholly divine and wholly human. Everything he did, including being born of Mary (also by her totally free cooperation) and living and dying and resurrecting and ascending to heaven—all these things were done by God *and* by man. Christ is one person, not two—one that is divine and another one that is human. Everything he does is done by man, and everything he does is done by God. In him, God and man are totally united.

There are two authors of every book in the Bible: man and God, the human author and the divine author—for example, Isaiah and God, or David and God. And the divine author knows and intends much more than the human author understood at the time. This Psalm has a prophetic reference to Christ, which was, of course, not clearly understood by the Psalmist one thousand years before the Incarnation. But divine providence arranged for the Psalmist to write these words, which we today can see as clearly predicting and foreshadowing Christ, when the Psalmist prays for "the man of your right hand" and "the son of man whom you yourself made strong." God the Father is the eternal source and strength of God the Son, and since the Father holds nothing back, but gives all of himself, God the Son eternally possesses all the attributes of divinity in himself.

Like Christ, the Bible is also fully human and fully divine. Both Christ and the Bible are called "the Word of God." The Bible is the Word of God in the words of man. Christ is the Word of God in the flesh of man: "the Word was made flesh." Both Christ and the Bible are 100 percent divine and 100 percent human.

The same is true of our prayers. They are truly done by us and by God. They are done by us because they are done by our free choice, for which we are truly responsible. And they are really done by God, whose Holy Spirit is the one who moves us and inspires us and turns us to pray. So we must pray as if it all depended on us, because it truly does, and also we must pray as if it all depended on God, because it truly does.

We are totally dependent on God. Christ tells us, "Without me you can do nothing" (John 15:5). Yet we are also totally responsible for our choices, including our choice to pray or not to pray, to love or not to love, to sin or not to sin. Because when God moves us, when he shines his light on us, we ourselves shine. When we look back on any good we have done, we must look beyond ourselves to God, because he is really there as the first cause of every good, including our own good choices.

Ultimately, everything is divine grace, especially our choosing to pray for divine grace. Everything is God's grace, but that does not mean that nothing is our choice, because grace turns our free will on, not off.

The truths we've been exploring here are not easy to wrap our minds around. But we don't have to understand it to do it. You don't have to understand the chemistry of water before you can drink, or the physics of electricity before you can turn on a light, or the astronomy of the sun before you can enjoy its light and heat. But we do have to act—to drink, or to flip the switch, or to go out into the sun. If we waited until we understood the science of hydration before we drank, we'd all die of thirst. That's how foolish we are if we don't pray because we don't really understand how it works. Because our souls are like plants, and prayer is their water, their very life.

So the practical point of this very complex reflection is very simple. It's a single syllable: pray.

But how? The answer to that question is this: just do it. You don't first learn it and then do it—you learn it by doing it. It's not science or technology. Don't wait until you master some spiritual technique or spiritual technology. There is no technology for faith and hope and love. Just do it. Because prayer is your soul's life, your soul's water, and if you don't drink the water until you master the chemistry, you will die.

Does a baby have to understand how to smile before he can smile? You are God's baby. God is your Daddy. Smile up at him! See him smiling down at you. That's prayer. So just do it already.

SECOND READING
1 CORINTHIANS 1:3–9 _____

Brothers and sisters: Grace to you and peace from God our Father and the Lord Jesus Christ.

I give thanks to my God always on your account for the grace of God bestowed on you in Christ Jesus, that in him you were enriched in every way, with all discourse and all knowledge, as the testimony to Christ was confirmed among you, so that you are not lacking in any spiritual gift as you wait for the revelation of our Lord Jesus Christ. He will keep you firm to the end, irreproachable on the day of our Lord Jesus Christ. God is faithful, and by him you were called to fellowship with his Son, Jesus Christ our Lord.

We are apt to smile sleepily at these familiar phrases, thinking subconsciously: That's nice. That's appropriate. That's churchy language. That puts a sleepy smile on my face and closes my eyes and my mind. The words are like a magic formula, like a password: God, Lord, Jesus, Christ, grace, peace, fellowship. And vague, old-fashioned words that we don't use much any more like "testimony" and "confirmed"—the words are not supposed to make you think. It's a sleeping pill. It works like counting sheep to go to sleep. It works because it's so boring: a kind of comfortable buzz, like a sound machine.

Let's do something different, something dangerous. Let's actually look at the words to see what they mean. Let's make the radical assumption that they're supposed to wake us up instead of putting us to sleep.

In this passage, St. Paul mentions several gifts of God—in the past, in the present, and in the future.

First, he says that we have God's grace. "Grace" means "a gift that is given freely because it's not owed by the giver and not deserved by the receiver."

Our very existence is a grace from God. God freely chose to create us. He did not owe us anything at all, because we did not *exist* before he created us. We could not deserve to be created because only something that exists can deserve anything.

And our redemption, our salvation, is also a gift, because we did not deserve that. No one deserves to go to heaven or to share God's own supernatural life. We are all fallen and foolish, selfish and stupid, sinful and shallow. No matter who you are, that's the one thing we all are, the one thing all human beings have in common. If you think you're not that, then that proves that you are. There are only two kinds of people: saints, who know they're sinners, and sinners, who think they're saints; the wise, who know they're fools, and the fools, who think they're wise.

Another thing St. Paul tells us is that God is the origin of our peace. Peace with God is another name for salvation.

What, exactly, is peace? It's not just the absence of war. We can be at peace within even if we are fighting a war without—if it is a good and just and necessary and honorable war—because peace means first of all peace with God, peace with God's will, peace with what God wants us to be, our true selves, not split in half with one half of us saying yes to God and the other half saying no.

Thomas Merton wrote, "We are not at peace with others because we are not at peace with ourselves, and we are not at peace with ourselves because we are not at peace with God." Just think about those very simple words for a while and you will see that they are true. Saints are happy, and happy people don't fight wars with other people. The three kinds of peace always go together, as do the three kinds of war. Merton's formula is true by definition of the three words in it, like "two plus two equals four equals half of eight." "Saints" *means* "people who are at peace with God," and "happy people" *means* "people who are at peace with themselves." That's why saints are happy. And peaceful people don't fight wars with other people, either individually or collectively. They know who their enemies are: not flesh and blood but evil spirits and evil deeds. Our worst enemies are always our own sins.

Another thing St. Paul tells us is that God has given us every "spiritual gift." God gave us the three most important gifts in the world: faith and hope and charity. God gave us seven sacraments that give us grace in life's seven different stages or areas or vocations. God gave us his wisdom in the Bible and in the Church. He gave us truth and goodness and beauty in our theology and morality and liturgy, our creeds and commandments and Catholic culture. God gave us souls with the power of reason to know the true and the power of conscience to know the good and the power of wonder and appreciation to know the beautiful. God gave us saints and angels surrounding us to help us. God gave us families and friends—they, too, are God's inventions. The family is his invention of the "pay it forward system." We can't possibly pay back the gifts our parents have given us, so we pay it forward to our children. Even the material universe is God's spiritual gift because the universe is both the greatest masterpiece of art and the greatest masterpiece of science. And above all we have Jesus Christ, the fullness of all these gifts of God because he is God himself in the flesh. And Christ has given us his whole self, Body and Blood, Soul and Divinity, on the cross for our salvation and in the Eucharist for our sanctification and glorification. That's a pack of gifts that makes Santa's sack look like a lump of coal.

If we are Christians, we already have all these gifts. And we have even more gifts to look forward to in the future. And that's the gift of hope. St. Paul mentions three aspects of our hope.

What do we hope for? First, and most fundamentally of all, we "wait for the revelation of our Lord Jesus Christ"—that is, his second coming in glory and triumph. We await not just more of the gifts but more of the Giver.

What we know now about Christ is only a tiny part of what he is. He revealed much more of himself in the New Testament than in the Old, but he will reveal even more in his second coming, which will make even the New Testament look as incomplete as the Old Testament looks to us now. He says, "Behold, I make all things new" (Rev. 21:5). All things! New heavens and a new earth. New truths, new joys, new loves, new relationships, new understandings, new *everything*. It will be like being born into a larger world, one that will make this universe look like a confining little womb. It has not been revealed yet, so it can only be described in terms of what we do *not* yet know. In St. Paul's words, "What eye has not seen, and ear has not heard, and what has not entered the human heart, what God has prepared for those who love him" (1 Cor. 2:9).

And as we wait and hope for this glorious future, God gives us another gift in the present—namely, his faithfulness and firmness to keep *us* faithful and firm and "irreproachable." We need to be faithful to this hope, and we can do that only because God is faithful to his promise.

The gift of hope for the future makes Christians the most progressive people in the world, and the gift of fidelity makes Christians the most conservative people in the world. Hope is like a spreading sail that catches the wild winds, and fidelity is like a strong, secure anchor that keeps the ship safe. We need both in this life in order to reach the next. Christians are both more radically progressive than any political progressives and more radically conservative than any political conservatives.

Another gift of God that St. Paul mentions is the perfecting of our "fellowship," or friendship, both with God and with each other. That's the most important gift of all: not just a whole new, perfected world, or even the new, perfected self, but new, perfected relationships, new and perfected loves, friendships, fellowships.

That love and friendship is the meaning of life, after all, and we all know it, deep down. Our world is important, but our selves are more important, and our loves are the most important of all. There's more happiness between two lepers in love in Kolkata than there is between two millionaires fighting in a posh resort in Hawaii.

You see, Scripture is like an enormous old treasure chest. There's more there than appears on the surface. But you have to open it and dig into it.

GOSPEL

MARK 13:33–37 _____

Jesus said to his disciples: "Be watchful! Be alert! You do not know when the time will come. It is like a man traveling abroad. He leaves home and places his servants in charge, each with his own work, and orders the gatekeeper to be on the watch. Watch, therefore; you do not know when the lord of the house is coming, whether in the evening, or at midnight, or at cockcrow, or in the morning. May he not come suddenly and find you sleeping. What I say to you, I say to all: 'Watch!'"

You can almost hear the exclamation points when Jesus says, "Watch! Be watchful! Be alert!" But watch for what?

Watch for him. He is the Lord—the active Lord, who does not sit and wait for us like a book on a shelf but actively hounds us, like the Hound of Heaven, seeking us like the shepherd seeking his lost sheep.

But when and where does Jesus come?

In three different times. He comes to earth in his first advent, his first coming, the Incarnation. That is what we celebrate now. The Incarnation really happened nine months *before* Christmas, on March 25, when Mary said yes to God's angel and Christ was conceived in her womb. Our Lord was "born of the Virgin Mary" but "conceived by the Holy Spirit." But we celebrate Christmas nine months later because that is when he appeared to the world, when he was born.

He will come a second time, at the end of the world, the end of time, the end of history. This is his "second coming," and it will end all time and all chances to repent and be saved. He gives us plenty of time between his first coming and his second, but everything in time has to end eventually. Only eternity has no end.

He will come to the whole world at the end of time, the end of the world; but he will come to each one of us at our own death, which is for us the end of our world and our time. So when Jesus says, "Watch!" he is not just speaking to the last generation, the generation that will see his second coming, but to all generations. He himself says that explicitly: "What I say to you, I say to all: 'Watch!'"

But Jesus also comes to us in a third time, the present. He comes to us many times each day. He comes in each opportunity to choose him, to love him, to do his will by doing good to others, by sacrificing self-will for his will.

He comes in many disguises. For instance, right at this very moment, he is coming to us in a form that does not look very special: in the opportunity to honestly face him and confess that we have missed many opportunities in the past to welcome him, and to confess that we know that he sees us now and knows everything about us now and is offering one more opportunity to say yes to his will with our whole heart and our whole mind and our whole soul and our whole strength, which includes our whole body and its actions, no matter how tired we are, and no matter how unholy we feel, and no matter how bored we are by these unoriginal words that you have probably heard many times, and no matter how much we feel like going to sleep and turning away from him and switching off the light of the world who is Jesus.

I know that's what you are thinking because that's what I'm thinking too. I'm thinking: Jesus, if I could see you in your heavenly glory, as Peter, James, and John saw you on the Mount of Transfiguration, I would not be tired or bored. I would thrill to your glory. But I *see* no glory now and *feel* no glory now.

And Jesus is saying to me, in response to that—he is saying this to me right now in my own conscience, as he is saying it to you too—You know I am here. Even though you do not see me or feel me, you know I am here. You see me with the eyes of faith, not feeling. It doesn't matter what you feel. It matters what you believe and what you love. Don't feel guilty about not feeling holy. I don't usually come into your life through the door of feeling. But I always come through the door of faith, your free choice to believe in me and trust me and love me no matter what you feel.

Would you rather have the *feeling* of my presence but not my *real* presence, or would you rather have my real presence even without the feeling of it? My presence is me; your feelings are you; what do you most want, me or you? Who is your Lord, me or you?

That's how Jesus comes to each of us many times every day. And he is very patient and does not expect us to catch the football he passes to us every single time he throws it. But he does expect us to try—to reach out and try to catch it, in faith. He is very hard to satisfy, but he is very easy to please. That is a good description of a good father, and Jesus is the full revelation of God the Father.

But he is not the Godfather. The Godfather makes you an offer you can't refuse. God the Father makes you an offer you can refuse, and you do, again and again. But not every time. Not when you pray.

Jesus summarizes the point of today's Gospel in a single word: "Watch!" And he identifies his audience with the single sentence that comes right before it: "What I say to you, I say to all."

He expanded this point, this one-word lesson, in his parable of the five wise virgins who watched for the coming of the Bridegroom and the five foolish virgins who did not, and who had no oil for their lamps. The point is put with power and beauty in a nineteenth-century translation of the Greek Orthodox hymn "Behold the Bridegroom Cometh":

Behold the Bridegroom cometh in the middle of the night,
And blest is he whose loins are girt, whose lamp is burning bright;
But woe to that dull servant whom the Master shall surprise
With lamp untrimmed, unburning, and with slumber in his eyes.
Do thou, my soul, beware, beware, lest thou in sleep sink down,
Lest thou be given o'er to death and lose the golden crown;
But see that thou be sober, with a watchful eye, and thus
Cry, "Holy, holy, holy God, have mercy upon us!"
That day, the day of fear, shall come; my soul, slack not thy toil,
But light thy lamp, and feed it well, and make it bright with oil;
Who knowest not how soon may sound the cry at eventide,
"Behold the Bridegroom comes! Arise! Go forth to meet the bride."
Beware, my soul; beware, beware, lest thou in slumber lie,
And like the five, remain without, and knock, and vainly cry;
But watch, and bear thy lamp undimmed, and Christ shall gird thee on
His own bright wedding-robe of light—the glory of the Son.

"Beware" does not mean "Be in fear." It means "be aware," "be awake," "be awatch." Be ready. For he is surely coming. He is coming for *you*.

SECOND SUNDAY OF ADVENT

FIRST READING

Isaiah 40:1–5, 9–11 _____

Comfort, give comfort to my people,
    says your God.
Speak tenderly to Jerusalem, and proclaim to her
      that her service is at an end,
      her guilt is expiated;
indeed, she has received from the hand of the Lord
      double for all her sins.
        A voice cries out:
In the desert prepare the way of the Lord!
      Make straight in the wasteland a highway for our God!
Every valley shall be filled in,
      every mountain and hill shall be made low;
the rugged land shall be made a plain,
      the rough country, a broad valley.
Then the glory of the Lord shall be revealed,
      and all people shall see it together;
      for the mouth of the Lord has spoken.

Go up on to a high mountain,
    Zion, herald of glad tidings;
cry out at the top of your voice,
    Jerusalem, herald of good news!
Fear not to cry out
    and say to the cities of Judah:

Here is your God!
Here comes with power
   the Lord GOD,
     who rules by his strong arm;
here is his reward with him,
   his recompense before him.
Like a shepherd he feeds his flock;
   in his arms he gathers the lambs,
carrying them in his bosom,
   and leading the ewes with care.

When we hear the sound of these beautiful words, we cannot help remembering the sounds of Handel's *Messiah* that showed us their beauty by setting them to music. It is almost impossible to invent music that does justice to those words, but Handel did it. If you've never heard the *Messiah*, drop everything and listen. It's for everybody. If you love Jesus Christ, it's dangerous to really listen to Handel's *Messiah* because when you do the plumbing in your eyes will suddenly leak.

The words are beautiful because they announce the Gospel, the Good News, the best news we have ever, ever heard: that God's power and love have opened the door to heaven and shut the door to hell for all who trust him and love him and accept his incredible gift of himself. The good news is that God has done the best thing anyone ever did in all of time; that he has overcome the worst thing anyone ever did in all of time: our sin, our rebellion, our "no" to him. In the words of Edwin Markham's famous little poem "Outwitted," we drew a circle that shut him out, but he drew a circle that took us in. Here are the four little lines of Markham's poem. I think he meant it to be spoken by God:

> He drew a circle that shut me out—
> Heretic, rebel, a thing to flout.
> But Love and I had the will to win:

We drew a circle that took him in!

J.R.R. Tolkien, the author of *The Lord of the Rings*, says of the Gospel that "there is no tale ever told that men would rather find was true. . . . But this story has entered history. . . . This tale is true. . . . The Gospel has not abrogated legends [myths], it has hallowed them." C.S. Lewis called it "myth become fact."

Jesus says, in the book of Revelation, "Behold, I make all things new" (Rev. 21:5). St. John, the writer, puts these words in the context of Christ's second coming, when he will complete his redemption of the world in glory; but Mel Gibson, in *The Passion of the Christ*, put these words in Jesus' mouth on the *via dolorosa*, the Way of the Cross, as Jesus, whipped and tortured and almost dead, is carrying his cross to Calvary, and his mother, Mary, in agony, asks him why he has to do all this, and he answers her: "See, mother, I make all things new."

Jesus began the world's greatest work in his first coming, and he will complete it in his second.

And that work is total. All obstacles will be overcome. "Every valley shall be filled in, every mountain and hill shall be made low." The valleys of despair and the mountains of pride will both disappear. Nothing will be the same after the tsunami of God's love fills the whole world with life as Noah's flood filled it with death. Nothing can stand against God, in the end, any more than a flea can stand up against a tornado, or an ice cube can hold out against the sun.

Reread this beautiful prophecy of Isaiah three times, once for the past, once for the present, and once for the future. Read it first in light of the first coming of Christ, the Incarnation. These words may have been among the actual words the angels sang to the shepherds on the first Christmas Day. Read it second in light of Christ's coming into your life today, at this very moment. The angels may be speaking these words to you today as an invitation to open all the doors of your heart and all the doors of your life to Christ. For they are *his* angels, after all! And read it a third time in light of Christ's glorious second coming at the end of the world and at the end of your life, as the words he will speak to you, or his angels will speak to you, as your welcome to heaven.

The Gospel is your invitation to that wedding feast—to *your* wedding feast, to your own spiritual wedding to him. He is proposing marriage to your soul: he longs to give you nothing less than eternal, infinite, incomprehensible, unimaginable, unending joy. Be sure you RSVP to him with a yes. Say that most powerful of all words, the word that Mary said to his angel: "Yes. *Fiat.* Let it be done. Be it done unto me according to your word." Pray to your heavenly mother that she teach you how to say that word to God.

RESPONSORIAL PSALM

PSALM 85:9–10, 11–12, 13–14 _____

R. (8) **Lord, let us see your kindness, and grant us your salvation.**

I will hear what God proclaims;
    the LORD—for he proclaims peace to his people.
Near indeed is his salvation to those who fear him,
    glory dwelling in our land.

Kindness and truth shall meet;
    justice and peace shall kiss.
Truth shall spring out of the earth,
    and justice shall look down from heaven.

The LORD himself will give his benefits;
    our land shall yield its increase.
Justice shall walk before him,
    and prepare the way of his steps.

_____

(There are two reflections here, on two separate parts of this Psalm. They can be combined, but they do not have to be.)

Reflection 1

The Psalm for today praises those who "fear" the Lord; and the Bible often repeats the principle that "the beginning of wisdom is fear of the Lord" (Prov. 9:10). But the critics of religion use this as an argument against it: the argument is that religion is based on fear, which is a bad thing, or at least a very primitive thing, and turns believers into slaves, with God as their slave master.

I want to explore what David the Psalmist says about this "fear": what it is and what it produces as its effects in us, its fruits. The most practical man who ever lived once said, "By their fruits you will know them" (Matt. 7:20).

There are two kinds of fear: servile fear and filial fear. Servile fear is the fear of a slave to his master, of a victim to his victimizer, or of an unfree citizen to a tyrant. It is the fear of being harmed and being made unhappy in some way. Filial fear is the fear of a *filius* or *filia*, a son or daughter, to his or her parent. It is the fear of harming the parent, who is loved and respected; the fear not of receiving unhappiness but of giving it. That fear is based on love.

When the Bible praises "the fear of the Lord," it is the second kind of fear, filial fear, that it praises, not the other kind, the servile fear. In fact, servile fear is a heresy, because it assumes that God is a slave master and a tyrant; that we are his victims and he is the victimizer. The God of the Bible, the God of the Church, the God of the saints, is the exact opposite of that. We are *his* victimizers, and he is our victim. We did not sacrifice our body and blood for him; he did that for us. His sins did not put us on the cross; our sins put him there.

This good fear of the Lord, this fear of disappointing our heavenly Father, this fear that is based on love, has good fruits. Three of those fruits are mentioned by the Psalmist in this passage. They are, in three words that rhyme, "hear," "near," and "here": he invites us to "hear" him; he is "near"; and his glory is "here," "dwelling in our land."

The Psalm begins with the words "I will hear what God proclaims." Notice that hearing is an active choice of the will. When a loud machine, like a leaf blower, interrupts your concentration, you have no free choice to hear it or not; but when another person tells you something personal, you must *choose* to hear it in your heart, and you can choose to refuse to hear it. That's true no matter what it is: trivia, gossip, praise, blame, forms of love, or forms of hate.

Whatever we choose by free choice of the will, we must have some reason for, some motivation for. So let's look for that motivation. *Why* does the Psalmist choose to hear the voice of God? Because God proclaims peace, peace in three places: peace above us, in his relation with us; and peace within us, that comes from that peace above us; and peace around us, that comes between us and others, who are our spiritual siblings, God's other children.

The Psalmist next mentions a second reason for fearing God: that "near indeed is his salvation to those who fear him." The fear of the Lord does exactly the opposite of what its critics say it does: it does not push God away from us and us away from God but brings us nearer, closer, willingly closer, voluntarily closer. No one voluntarily wants to get closer to an abuser, a tyrant, or a slave master.

But this effect of nearness to God is not imposed but chosen. It is a gift of God, and gifts must be freely given and freely received. God's gifts are always freely given, and they are intended for everyone. But not everyone gets them because not everyone freely chooses to believe in them and receive them. God's graces and mercies and love and forgiveness are "near" only to those who "fear," those who choose this holy fear, which is a form of love.

What form of love is this "fear of the Lord"? It is adoration. It is far deeper than "respect." We "respect" even harmful things like hurricanes and polar bears, and neutral things like money. The fear of the Lord is more than respect. It is awe and adoration, wonder and worship. That is a kind of love, in fact the highest kind of love, though it is not a kind of easy, cheap, cozy, comfortable love. Love takes many forms. Adoration is the highest.

Finally, the Psalmist proclaims that the God who is the object of this holy fear is not only near but already here. The glory of God, says the Psalmist, is "dwelling in our land." It is not only true and good and beautiful but *glorious*: gloriously true, not trivially true; and gloriously good, not conventionally good;

and gloriously beautiful, not just comfortably beautiful. For God's greatest glory is his love, a love that is so beautiful that it breaks your heart. But if we do not have the basic attitude of "the fear of the Lord," we do not hear the glory of the Lord; we do not see that it is so near that it is already here.

This "glory" that the Psalmist speaks of is a frequent theme in Scripture. Both the Old Testament and the New use the word "glory" hundreds of times. It's a word we hardly ever use anymore. Pity us, because if we don't use the word, that means we don't know the reality that it names. How do we see it? How do we return to it? By "the fear of the Lord." The Psalmist sees God's glory not just in heaven but also here on earth. He calls it "glory *dwelling in our land.*" He sees patches of God-light in the dark woods of our human experience. He has the eyes to see it, which are the eyes of faith and trust, the eyes of an unusually wise child who trusts his parents and therefore sees love even in their laws and even in their refusals of his foolish requests and even in their just punishments of his sins.

God's glory will be manifested to us in heaven in a form we cannot even imagine now. We probably could not endure it if we saw it now. We need dark glasses to look at the sun without going blind. But even now we see God's glory in a thousand different visible forms: in the light of the day and in the darkness of the night, in nature and in history, in others' lives and in our own, in our talents and in those we admire in other people, and in a providence that divinely delivers us from dozens of dangers and diseases and darknesses—and even damnation.

God's definitive revelation of his glory is his Son. His angel told Joseph, "You are to name him Jesus (which means "Savior"), because he will save his people from their sins" (Matt. 1:21). Jesus saves us from many things, but above all from the three worst things of all, sin and death and hell. He shows us the glory of God in the opposites of sin and death and hell: sanctity instead of sin (he turns sinners into saints), and resurrection to eternal life instead of death, and heaven instead of hell.

Who is this God whom we "fear"? It is Jesus. When we see him, we see the face of our heavenly Father.

Reflection 2

There is a verse in today's Psalm that is puzzling when we first look at it and rewarding when we think more deeply about it. (Those are the two reactions we get to many passages of Scripture. The first, the puzzle, always turns into the second, the reward, if we persist and dig more deeply into the rich soil of the Scriptures. There are many hidden treasures there as well as treasures on the surface.)

The verse says: "Kindness and truth shall meet; justice and peace shall kiss. Truth shall spring out of the earth, and justice shall look down from heaven." What does that mean?

It means what its author meant it to mean. And Scripture has not just one but two authors: the divine author and the human author, whose humanity and human limitations were providentially used by the divine author as his instruments. So we can always ask those two questions about any passage of Scripture: "What did its human author mean us to learn from it?" and "What did the divine author mean us to learn from it?"

What God means is always more than what his human instruments meant because God always knows and means far more than we do. And the most important application of that principle is how we as Christians understand God's Old Testament revelations as hints and prophecies and foreshadowings of what we see as their total fulfillment in Christ. Because we live after the Incarnation, we are able to see Christ in many places in the Old Testament Scriptures. The whole purpose of the Old Testament is to set up Christ, to point to Christ, to prepare the way for Christ, who is the final and definitive and perfect divine revelation. He is a divine person, who has no limitations and who knows everything; but he was written about by many human persons, who all have human limitations and who do not know all that God knows. Christ is "the Word of God," but he is written about in the words of men. He is the one single Word of God in the many different words of many different men who wrote the Scriptures. So the Bible is like Christ in that way: it has two natures, human and divine.

That's why we should read the New Testament in light of the Old and the

Old Testament in light of the New. The title "Christ" means "Messiah," or "anointed one," or "promised one," and so we look at him when he appears in the New Testament in terms of the Old Testament promises and prophecies; but we also look at the Old Testament prophecies in terms of Christ as their fulfillment.

So what does God mean when he inspires the Psalmist to write, "Kindness and truth shall meet; justice and peace shall kiss"? And how is Christ the answer to that question?

To understand that answer, remember that there are two absolute goods, two absolute values, two things we should never compromise. They are truth and goodness, the object of our mind and the object of our will, the mental ideal and the moral ideal. No one wants to be in error and darkness, even if they are so wicked as to want others to be in error and darkness; and no one wants cruelty and injustice done to them, even if they are so wicked as to want that done to others. We all want to know the truth, and we all want both the good of justice and the good that goes beyond justice—namely, love and kindness and mercy and peace. Justice fights a just war against injustice, but kindness and mercy seek peace rather than war.

Our ongoing problem is that these two things seem very different and often seem at odds with each other. Truth is impersonal and hard and unyielding, like a rock or a bone. Kindness is soft and compassionate, like flesh. Our bodies need both bone and flesh, and in our bodies there is cooperation, not competition, between the hard bone and the soft flesh; but in our minds and in our souls we often see competition and contradiction between the hard bones of truth and justice on the one hand and the soft flesh of mercy and peace on the other hand, between the hard virtues and the soft virtues.

Justice fights against injustice. Peace wants to end fighting. So justice and peace seem to be opposites, and so do justice and mercy. Justice demands payment of just debts; mercy does not demand payment and forgives debts. Justice cannot simply forgive and forget, and mercy cannot simply forget justice. Justice has a strong claim: the claim of moral truth, objective truth. Mercy has a strong claim: the claim of personal love, subjective love. We cannot ignore either claim, but they seem to contradict each other, like the two sides of a seesaw.

We tend to specialize in virtues, to practice one set at the expense of the other set. Our ancestors were probably much stronger on the hard virtues than we are, virtues like courage and honesty and justice and honor and heroism. But they were not as strong on the soft virtues as we are: kindness and mercy and sensitivity and compassion and forgiveness. By our standards, they were more unfeeling and cruel than we are; but by their standards, we are more self-indulgent and decadent and soft and spoiled than they were.

The Psalmist prophesies that these two opposing goods will meet and kiss and reconcile with each other; that the opposition between them will be overcome. Notice that he speaks in the future tense, not the present. This reconciliation is a prophecy. In fact, it is a messianic prophecy. It came true only in Christ. When? Most especially on the cross, when he did the most important deed ever done, saving us from sin and death and hell by offering his own body and blood to God.

Why did he have to do that? For two equally necessary reasons: to satisfy God's love and to satisfy God's justice. He paid for our sins, and that was love, but it was also justice. God is just, so he could not simply say: "Forget justice! Throw justice and truth out the window. I just snap my fingers and pardon you all. It doesn't matter that Hitler tortured and murdered six million of my beloved children. He can go to heaven side by side with the saints that he murdered." God can't do that because it isn't true; it isn't true to what-is—namely, that evil exists and evil is not good, and no one but a blind fool can pretend that good and evil are the same and treat them in the same way. And God is not a blind fool. He cannot lie. Justice and truth, especially moral truth, are his very nature, his very unchangeable essence.

But love is also his essence, and love demands kindness and compassion and forgiveness and mercy; and mercy goes beyond justice. For us, it's an either/ or: if we are just, we punish the criminal; if we are merciful, we revoke the just punishment. If we are just, we flunk the failing student, because it is true that he failed; if we are merciful, we pass him, because we love him. If we are just, we demand repayment of the debt for stolen goods; if we are merciful, we forgive the debt.

But we can't *merely* forgive the debt, because when we forgive a debt, if no one pays it, the victim suffers. If I'm the president, and I forgive a criminal for robbing the treasury of millions of dollars in owed taxes, every citizen is cheated because that money has to be repaid out of their innocent pockets. And if I'm the victim of a robbery, and you robbed me, and I forgive your debt to me, I still have to pay my creditors out of my own money, so I'm the loser. Forgiving a debt isn't like waking up from a bad dream, from something that isn't true. The debt is true. If *you* don't have to pay it, somebody else does. If somebody else doesn't, you do.

So what God did in Christ is forgive our debt to him, thus satisfying mercy; but he paid it himself on the cross, thus satisfying justice. The judge declared that the convicted criminal before him had to pay the price for his crime, and then the judge paid it himself.

So on the cross, God satisfied both justice and mercy by exchanging places with us. We deserved justice, not mercy, but we got mercy instead of justice. He paid our fine himself. He set us free by freely choosing to take our place—like St. Maximilian Kolbe, the saint and martyr in Auschwitz who volunteered to take the place of the man who had to be executed.

So Christ reconciled justice and peace, truth and love, righteousness and kindness, the hard values and the soft values. And he also reconciled us to God, "vertically," so to speak, so that the hard values of truth and justice could come out of the earth, out of Mary's human womb, as well as from heaven, and so that the soft values of mercy and forgiveness could come out of heaven, from God the Father, from the divine nature, as well as from man, from human nature. This joining of the horizontal and the vertical was like the joining of the two bars of the cross.

This joining, this universal reconciliation, could not be done by any mere human being. I can forgive you for your sins against me, but I cannot forgive you for your sins against others. Only God can do that, because God is the only one who is sinned against in all sins.

So the second part of the quotation from the Psalm, about justice coming both down from heaven and up from earth, explains how the first part worked, the part about justice and mercy reconciling. It worked only by the Incarnation; it could be done only by the same person, Christ, being both God and man, both divine and human. The first verse says that truth, or justice, or righteousness, is reconciled with kindness, or mercy, or peace. And the next verse tells us how—by truth and justice coming from both places at once, earth and heaven, humanity and divinity: "truth shall spring out of the earth, and justice shall look down from heaven." Justice and mercy are reconciled by heaven and earth being reconciled. Truth and love are reconciled by God and man being reconciled in Christ.

Think of a cross, with God and heaven at the top and man and earth at the bottom. Think of the hard values of justice and truth as the right half of the crossbar, and think of the soft values of mercy and love as the left half of the crossbar. Christ is where the two planks of the cross cross. He reconciles the good of the "right" (the hard bones of truth and justice) with the good of the "left" (the soft flesh of love and mercy), and he also reconciles God with man, heaven with earth. Christ is the center of all things, the place where opposites cross and combine.

SECOND READING
2 PETER 3:8–14 _____

Do not ignore this one fact, beloved, that with the Lord one day is like a thousand years and a thousand years like one day. The Lord does not delay his promise, as some regard "delay," but he is patient with you, not wishing that any should perish but that all should come to repentance. But the day of the Lord will come like a thief, and then the heavens will pass away with a mighty roar and the elements will be dissolved by fire, and the earth and everything done on it will be found out.

Since everything is to be dissolved in this way, what sort of persons ought you to be, conducting yourselves in holiness and devotion, waiting for and hastening the coming of the day of God, because of which the heavens will be dissolved in flames and the elements melted by fire. But according to his promise we await new heavens and a new earth in which righteousness dwells. Therefore, beloved, since you await these things, be eager to be found without spot or blemish before him, at peace.

(Again, I give you two reflections: one practical, one textual; one a single simple point, the other with a number of points in the text.)

Reflection 1

Our epistle for today is from the Second Letter of Peter, our first pope. It was written to all Christians, a circulating papal letter, the first papal "encyclical."

The point of the passage in today's reading is that since the entire universe, both this earth and the "heavens," that is, the rest of the universe, is doomed to death, like our own bodies, therefore we must prepare for this inevitable and undeniable fact by becoming the kind of persons we want to be when we die and face God in the Last Judgment.

Behind this obvious point is the principle that what we choose, what we do with ourselves and our lives, must be based on our knowledge of reality, our knowledge of the facts. St. Peter begins with this most practical of all principles: "Do not ignore this one fact, beloved." We cannot change facts. We cannot change objective truth. We can only choose to either ignore the truth or admit the truth and live according to the truth that we admit. And if we ignore the truth, we cannot plead ignorance, because that ignorance was our own fault: we created our own ignorance by deliberately ignoring the truth that we knew.

The truth, in this case, is death. Everyone and everything must die. The whole world will die, either by a cosmic catastrophe, like the sun exploding or a large asteroid crashing into the earth; or by a divine miracle; or simply by old age, when the sun becomes cold and the whole universe runs down, billions of years from now. Entropy is the scientific word for that. All energy tends to dissipate and homogenize, like a hot cup of coffee gradually losing its heat into the air around it. The old saying is half true: the only two certainties are death and taxes. You can cheat on your taxes, but you can't cheat death. You can choose to avoid your taxes, but you cannot choose to avoid your death, or the death of the whole world. You can only ignore it.

But that ignoring is not ignorance but insanity. If you ignore the fact that you are not Superman and cannot fly by jumping off a cliff, you will not, as some silly philosophers say, "create your own reality," but you will create your own unreality instead, your own death.

And if you ignore the fact that you are not God but God's creature, and therefore that you are infallibly destined to be infallibly judged by the infallibly wise God who is infallible truth—well, I have shocking news for you: you are *not* God, and therefore you are not infallible.

And if you think time will go on forever and never end, if you think that God is so patient that he will always keep giving you more and more time, more and more opportunity for repentance and conversion, more and more second chances—if you think that will go on forever, you are not only stupid: you are insane. You are not living in reality, in the real world, the world of facts rather than fancies and fictions and fantasies.

The Church is unpopular because the Church tells the truth. The Church announces the facts. The Church is an alarm clock that tells you that it is time to wake up and face the facts. God is real, and the will of God is real, and the law of God is real, and your own sins are real, and the need for you to change, to repent and turn back to God and start over again, is real. The need for you to go to Confession with a sincere and honest heart is real, as real as the fact that you will one day no longer have time to do that, the fact that one day will be your last day under the sun, and God will take the place of the sun and shine the total light of truth on you and you will no longer be able to hide or ignore anything at all. That is a fact, and your attitude toward that fact no more changes the fact than your feelings about the sun change the sun.

The God who you will meet when you die is pure love, but also pure truth. God's love is true love, not fake love or false love or pretend love or any kind of love that ignores the truth.

There are two false gods that many people believe in. One is the god who is truth but not love, and the other is the god who is love but not truth.

The god who is truth but not love is like a cold scientist. He is impersonal, like "the Force" in *Star Wars*, or like the light from the sun. He is like a judge in court. He simply announces the truth about what you deserve. He is abstract justice.

The god who is love but not truth is a sweet swamp of feel-good fantasies. He does not care about truth or justice or objective reality. He is a dream.

The true God is neither abstract, impersonal truth and justice nor a dreamy feeling or fantasy. The god of truth without love has a mind but not a heart, and the god of love without truth has a heart but not a mind, but neither of those two false gods has a will. Unlike both of those false gods, the true God has a will as well as a mind and a heart. And St. Peter tells us that what he wills for all of us is both truth and love together, and that's why he wills our repentance and salvation. He writes that God is not willing "that any should perish but that all should come to repentance." He wills our salvation, but he does not will salvation without repentance, because that would be love without truth. He wills salvation through repentance, because he wills truth as well as love. And so he gives us the two continuing sacraments of Confession and the Eucharist for our repentance and salvation.

I hope to see all of you frequently in both of those two sacred places. They are the two places the devil hates and fears above all others.

Reflection 2

Jesus promised us that he would return "soon." It has been almost two thousand years so far. Has he forgotten his promise?

No. Why not? Because, as St. Peter says in today's reading, "with the Lord one day is like a thousand years and a thousand years like one day." Einstein was once asked what his theory of relativity meant when it claimed that time is relative, and he replied, "When you're with the one you love, a lifetime feels like one minute, and when you're sitting on a hot stove, one minute feels like a lifetime."

Love does not count time by quantity but by quality, not by matter and molecules but by spirit and purpose. And since God is love, that is how God counts time. Christ tells us that he is coming again "soon" (Rev. 22:7; "quickly" in KJV). All the years between Christ's first coming and Christ's second coming are short, or "soon," or "quickly," because they are trivial compared to those two world-shattering events when Eternity touches time.

A second answer St. Peter gives to the complaint that God seems to be delaying his promise is that "he is patient with you, not wishing that any should perish but that all should come to repentance." Once Christ comes again, the time that is measured by matter and the movements of the earth will end, and there will be no more opportunity for repentance and conversion and salvation.

And even if he does not come again for the whole world for another ten thousand years, he will come for you and your whole world and your whole life very soon. That's why the most practical man who ever lived warned us in these words: "We have to do the works of the one who sent me while it is day. Night is coming when no one can work" (John 9:4). God gives us many second chances, but death is the end of second chances. The Bible says, "It is appointed that human beings die once, and after this the judgment" (Heb. 9:27).

St. Peter's third answer is that we do not know when that will be, either for the life of the whole world or for our own life. As Peter says, "The day of the Lord will come like a thief."

And, he goes on to say—and this is his fourth answer—then "the earth and everything done on it will be found out." All hiding and evading will become impossible. All excuses will sink like paper boats. Every thought of our hearts will be exposed, every little secret revealed. Jesus said, "I tell you, on the day of judgment people will render an account for every careless word they speak" (Matt. 12:36). Our souls will be stripped naked, for God is total truth as well as total love. As the Letter to the Hebrews says, "No creature is concealed from him, but everything is naked and exposed to the eyes of him to whom we must render an account" (Heb. 4:13). St. John writes: "I saw the dead, the great and the lowly, standing before the throne, and scrolls were opened. . . . The dead were judged according to their deeds, by what was written in the scrolls" (Rev. 20:12).

What is the *sane* reaction to this fact? The *insane* reaction is denial. That's like a man who is falling off a cliff ignoring the rocks below and merely smelling the roses on the face of the cliff as he's falling, and planning for a good night's sleep. The *sane* reaction is, in Peter's words, "Since everything is to be dissolved in this way, what sort of persons ought you to be, conducting yourselves in holiness." The meaning of life, the meaning of every single person's life, is to become a saint, to become one who welcomes that judgment, who is blessed and blissed by the truth of who they are, because who they are is someone who loves God and God's other children, someone who can call God "our Father," someone whose reaction to this prophecy is joy because "Daddy's coming."

Of course, we are all sinners, but if we have repented and believed, God has forgiven our sins because of Christ and has adopted us as his children; and therefore, we have nothing to fear and everything to hope for in the Last Judgment. If we have accepted him by faith and Baptism, if our hearts most deeply want not sin but sanctity, if we truly want him and what he is—namely, truth and love, justice and mercy—then that is what we will get, that is what we will find, Jesus assures us. "The one who seeks, finds" (Matt. 7:8). If we seek God, if we want God, we will find him; and if we seek ourselves apart from God, we will find that. That's the difference between heaven and hell.

And that is why our first pope, St. Peter, tells us the good news that even though "the heavens will be dissolved in flames and the elements melted by fire," yet "according to his promise we await new heavens and a new earth in which righteousness dwells." This righteousness, this holiness of God, this supernatural goodness, will be terrifying only to the wicked, who hate it. It will be supreme comfort and satisfaction and happiness to us who love it.

For in the end all will get what they most deeply want, what they most deeply love. As the great saint and mystic St. John of the Cross says, "In the evening of our lives, we will be judged on our love." That's why it's so important to educate our loves, to make our loves true loves, holy loves.

GOSPEL
MARK 1:1–8 _____

The beginning of the gospel of Jesus Christ the Son of God.
As it is written in Isaiah the prophet:
  Behold, I am sending my messenger ahead of you;
    he will prepare your way.
  A voice of one crying out in the desert:
    "Prepare the way of the Lord,
    make straight his paths."
John the Baptist appeared in the desert proclaiming a baptism of repentance for the forgiveness of sins. People of the whole Judean countryside and all the inhabitants of Jerusalem were going out to him and were being baptized by him in the Jordan River as they acknowledged their sins. John was clothed in camel's hair, with a leather belt around his waist. He fed on locusts and wild honey. And this is what he proclaimed: "One mightier than I is coming after me. I am not worthy to stoop and loosen the thongs of his sandals. I have baptized you with water; he will baptize you with the Holy Spirit."

Today's Gospel reading introduces John the Baptist and his baptism by contrast to Jesus and Jesus' baptism. All four Gospels do that, and the contrast is the same: John baptizes with water for repentance while Jesus baptizes with fire and the Holy Spirit.

Both baptisms are total. The Greek word for baptism means literally "immersion" or "sinking," as when a ship sinks totally into the sea. That's why the most complete symbolism for Christian baptism has traditionally been dunking, or total immersion, although pouring water is just as effective and valid, though not as strikingly symbolic. Baptists still baptize only by total immersion, which is good, but they do not baptize infants, as all other Christians have always done, which is not good.

The whole of the Old Testament is like John the Baptist: a preparation for Christ. John is the opening band; Jesus is the main event. John is the road; Jesus is the car. John is the old paint scraper; Jesus is the new paint. John is the house cleaner; Jesus is the guest. John is spring training; Jesus is the baseball season. John is the rehearsal; Jesus is the play.

The reason all four Gospels begin with John the Baptist is that Jesus does not just pop into history like magic when God snaps his fingers. He is the fulfillment of a long preparation, throughout Old Testament history. And in John the Baptist all the Old Testament comes to a point, like the point of an arrow, and Jesus is the target of that arrow. So the Gospels first present the arrow, then the target.

John the Baptist is a prophet. Jesus says that there has been no greater prophet than John. A prophet is not essentially a fortune-teller, a predictor of the future. The word "prophet" means literally "one who speaks forth," or "one who speaks for another." Prophets speak God's word, reveal God's mind and will. And this prophet, John the Baptist, summarizes the fundamental message of all the Old Testament prophets in one word: Repent. Turn. Convert. Say no to sin and yes to God instead of saying no to God and yes to sin.

That is the first thing we need to do to be saved. That's the negative thing. And the other thing, the positive thing, is to accept Jesus Christ as our Savior and our Lord. We accept him as our Savior by our faith and hope in him, and we accept him as our Lord by our obedience to his will, by our good works, the works of love.

These two things are mentioned and distinguished from each other in today's Gospel as two baptisms. John the Baptist's baptism is a baptism only of water; it is a baptism of repentance. It does not put God into our soul; it only expresses our repentance from sin and our desire for God to come into our soul. In contrast, Jesus' baptism is a baptism of fire, the fire of the Holy Spirit; it is a baptism of salvation. It is not just an expression of what is in us; it is a transaction, a receiving of a gift from God to us. It is not like a song we sing or a speech we make to express ourselves; it is like a heart operation, or a rescue, or a pregnancy: something objectively real that we receive from God.

It is our free choice to accept his gift, but the gift itself is a finite, human share in God's infinite, divine life. That life is not merely a "lifestyle," an ideology, a set of principles, any more than our natural human life that we get from our parents is merely a lifestyle. Jesus explicitly compares it to being born and calls it being born again, or being born from above. It's spiritual, not physical, though it's mediated by physical water and words in the sacrament of Baptism; but it's a real, concrete thing, not a thought or a feeling or an abstract set of rules or principles. It's not concrete in the way that cement is concrete—it's not made of molecules—but it's concrete in the way that you and God are concrete persons, not just ideas. It's God himself who enters our souls.

We need both baptisms. We need John's baptism of repentance as well as Jesus' baptism of faith; we need both the no to sin and the yes to God, because sin and God are like darkness and light: they cannot exist together. Sin is separation from God, and God is separation from sin. Each one casts the other one out. So we need both baptisms: we need both to turn away from sin and to turn to God. That's the literal meaning of the word "conversion": "turning." Both baptisms are conversions. First we turn away from the dark, and then we turn to the light. First we clean the garbage out of the kitchen, and then we eat the banquet. First we go to Confession, and then we go to Holy Communion. God provides for all our needs.

THIRD SUNDAY OF ADVENT

FIRST READING

ISAIAH 61:1–2A, 10–11 _____

The spirit of the Lord GOD is upon me,
    because the LORD has anointed me;
he has sent me to bring glad tidings to the poor,
    to heal the brokenhearted,
to proclaim liberty to the captives
    and release to the prisoners,
to announce a year of favor from the LORD
    and a day of vindication by our God.

I rejoice heartily in the LORD,
    in my God is the joy of my soul;
for he has clothed me with a robe of salvation
    and wrapped me in a mantle of justice,
like a bridegroom adorned with a diadem,
    like a bride bedecked with her jewels.
As the earth brings forth its plants,
    and a garden makes its growth spring up,
so will the Lord GOD make justice and praise
    spring up before all the nations.

What is the prophet Isaiah prophesying here? The answer is in this passage from the Gospel of Luke:

He came to Nazareth, where he had grown up, and went according to his custom into the synagogue on the sabbath day. He stood up to read and was handed a scroll of the prophet Isaiah. He unrolled the scroll and found the passage where it was written: *The Spirit of the Lord is upon me, because he has anointed me to bring glad tidings to the poor. He has sent me to proclaim liberty to captives and recovery of sight to the blind, to let the oppressed go free, and to proclaim a year acceptable to the Lord.* Rolling up the scroll, he handed it back to the attendant and sat down, and the eyes of all in the synagogue looked intently at him. He said to them, "Today this Scripture passage is fulfilled in your hearing." (Luke 4:16–21)

Jesus quotes today's passage from Isaiah word for word and applies it to himself. His congregation was familiar with the words. These words had been their faith and their hope, their dream—and now the dream was speaking to them; the dream had become true; the Word had become flesh; the fairy tale had become literal, historical fact.

What was the effect of those words? You can hear the sound that Jesus' words produced in that synagogue. It was the sound of silence. Everybody stopped breathing for a few seconds.

So Isaiah's prophecy was messianic, and Jesus is the Messiah, so it is about Jesus. But what, exactly, did the prophecy say about the Messiah?

Most of the Jews in Jesus' day did not accept Jesus' claim to be the Messiah, for two reasons.

First, and most centrally, it was his claim about himself. He claimed to be not just a prophet, a sage, or a saint but the Son of God. If that was not true, it was the most blasphemous claim any human being ever made.

Second, they thought the Messiah would bring to Israel, which was now under the tyrannical dictatorship of Rome, the power and prosperity and riches and freedom that Rome had stolen from her and that she had not enjoyed since the time of David and Solomon. But Jesus was apolitical. He did not make the poor richer. He did not free Jewish prisoners from Roman jails. He did not free Israel from Rome's oppressive and tyrannical taxation. He did not give Israel political freedom. To many of the Jews of Jesus' day, that disqualified his claim to be the Messiah. It was like a so-called messiah and savior entering Auschwitz and not destroying the gas ovens.

The prophecy also spoke of the Messiah as healing the blind. And Jesus did heal a few blind men, but it was only a few. He left many more unhealed, of blindness and leprosy and lameness and every other illness. He healed the whole world of its blindness about God, but that was not what most of the Jews were looking for. They thought they already had that, and they were looking for worldly wisdom and success. But Jesus said, "My kingdom does not belong to this world" (John 18:36).

Why did Jesus come? Was it to solve our medical problems? Was it to solve our economic problems? Was it to solve our political problems? If so, then Jesus was a fake and a failure. We still get sick and die. We still have grinding poverty. We still have politics that are corrupt and divisive and radically imperfect everywhere in the world. What did Jesus give the world that it did not have before?

The name "Jesus" means "Savior"; what did Jesus save us from? Isaiah's prophecy said that the Messiah would save us from blindness and imprisonment and poverty and oppression. Jesus didn't do that. Therefore, Jesus was not the Messiah. Right?

Wrong. Jesus did do that. He did save us from enemies, but our enemies were not the Romans, or even the Nazis. Our enemies were our own sins. Jesus saved us from the worst poverty of all, spiritual poverty.

Mother Teresa understood that when she said that America is not a rich country but a poor country, a terribly poor country. Any country where parents kill one-third of their babies before they can be born is a terribly poor country. Spiritual poverty is the worst poverty.

Jesus also saved us all from the worst blindness, spiritual blindness, the blindness that makes us think we are our own gods, the makers of our own values and our own identity and destiny, the blindness that makes us worship idols, especially the most popular idol of all, our own selves and our own will. He healed a few blind men as signs or symbols of that deeper healing.

Jesus also saved us from the worst oppression from our worst enemies, which is oppression not by Caesar or even Hitler but by Satan. Jesus gave us the most essential freedom, which is not political freedom but spiritual freedom, freedom from sin and death and hell, not freedom from Democrats and socialism or freedom from Republicans and capitalism.

Jesus also saved us from the worst diseases, the most crippling diseases, which are our addictions to our own favorite sins, whatever they are, which cripple our souls and which make our souls diseased and subject to not just physical death but eternal death.

So what did Jesus give the world that it did not have before? God. Jesus gave us God. Because Jesus gave us himself, and he is God. Jesus put God into our hands. "The Son of Man is to be handed over to sinners" (Mark 14:41)—that describes both the Crucifixion and Holy Communion.

The opposite of God is not Romans or Nazis or Democrats or Republicans or political oppression or poverty or disease or blindness or imprisonment or slavery. The opposite of God is sin, which is spiritual oppression and spiritual poverty and spiritual disease and spiritual blindness and spiritual imprisonment and spiritual slavery. Jesus went to the heart of the matter. He was called "Jesus," or "Savior," because he saved us from our sins.

Of course, all these other things matter too, and Jesus is relevant to all these other things too. No one who knows Jesus can be indifferent to all these physical and political wrongs. But Jesus was not just our Super Social Worker or our Perfect Political Pundit or our new CEO for the Centers for Disease Control. He left us to work out all those details. And Christians have been doing that for the last two thousand years, in different human ways.

Islam has a detailed program for social and political perfection, a set of laws called Sharia. Islam is a very political religion, where the church and the state are one. Christianity does not have a detailed political program like that. And many Christians still today, like the Jews of Jesus' time, think that's a mistake, that Jesus made a mistake in not being political, and they're trying to correct his mistake. But Jesus doesn't make mistakes; we do. We are his children, not his mistakes, but our biggest mistake is to forget him.

Social justice is important. In fact, it is a moral imperative. But it is not the essence of Christianity. Every religion preaches social justice, and so do most atheists. We all have reason and conscience, no matter what religion or nonreligion we believe, and on that basis of human equality we can all work together for social justice. But Jesus is not the equal of anyone else. He is the only one who gives us God, the only man who was God, and who is God. That is why we go to Mass, in a church, every sabbath day, every holy day, at a place and time that is set apart: to worship him, not ourselves or our own social or political programs.

That's one part of the truth: that Jesus is our Savior from sin, not from political incorrectness. The other part of the truth is that there are social and political sins too, and we are responsible for repenting of them and correcting them. But social sins are not sins against ideology but against people, against our fellow men and against God. Christianity has something to say about politics too, and one of the most important things is that politics is to serve persons; persons are not to serve politics or parties. Our Lord is neither the donkey nor the elephant but the Lamb, the Lamb of God who alone takes away all the sins of the world.

RESPONSORIAL PSALM
Luke 1:46–48, 49–50, 53–54 ⎯⎯⎯⎯⎯⎯⎯⎯⎯⎯⎯⎯⎯⎯⎯

R. (Isa. 61:10b) **My soul rejoices in my God.**

My soul proclaims the greatness of the Lord;
   my spirit rejoices in God my Savior,
for he has looked upon his lowly servant.
   From this day all generations will call me blessed:

The Almighty has done great things for me,
    and holy is his Name.
He has mercy on those who fear him
    in every generation.

He has filled the hungry with good things,
    and the rich he has sent away empty.
He has come to the help of his servant Israel
    for he has remembered his promise of mercy.

Our Psalm for today is not from the Psalms of David. It is the one and only Psalm we have from Mary, the Mother of God. Mary's Psalm, which is both a song and a prayer, is even holier than David's Psalms, even though both were inspired by God. The only holier prayer than Mary's prayer is the one prayer Jesus himself gave us, the "Lord's Prayer." So this prayer of Mary, the "Magnificat," stands between the prayer of Jesus and the prayers of David and the other inspired Psalmists. We cannot get closer to the mind of God than praying these three divinely inspired prayers.

Protestants often reproach Catholics for paying too much attention to Mary; they say it detracts from the focus on Christ. But if you look at all the things Mary says and does in Scripture, you can see that that is the exact opposite of the truth because Mary herself forces us to focus on Christ; in fact, that is the only thing she ever does and the one thing she is all about: him. This can be seen in her first recorded words, and in her last recorded words, and in all her words in the middle.

Her first recorded word was *fiat*: "May it be done to me according to your word" (Luke 1:38). That was her response to the angel of God when God asked her permission to have his Son be born of her. It is her first yes to Christ.

Her very last word in Scripture, her command to the waiters at the wedding feast at Cana, was "Do whatever he tells you" (John 2:5). That is her one and only command to all of us at all times. That is the meaning of life in five words. And because the waiters obeyed, they got his first miracle, turning water into wine.

And today's Psalm is in the middle, between Mary's first and last words. It is called the "Magnificat" after its first word. In it she says nothing about herself alone but only about Christ.

She says that "all generations will call me blessed," and that sounds pretty self-centered and arrogant, until you remember the reason she gives for that: "for he has looked upon his lowly servant."

She does not call herself holy; she calls his name holy: "for holy is his name."

She does not say she will do great things for him; she says he "has done great things for me."

She does not say God gives her justice but that "he has mercy on those who fear him."

She does not say God gives his grace to her alone but that "he has mercy on those who fear him in every generation."

The angel hails her not as full of her own virtue but as full of grace. Grace is a purely undeserved gift.

This is why we Catholics love and honor Mary: because she helps us to love and honor Christ more than any other human being who ever lived. The more we pay attention to her, the more we pay attention to Christ. The more we love her, the more we love Christ.

No one ever loved Jesus more than Mary did, and we cannot do better than to follow in her footsteps. No one ever loved Mary more than Jesus did, and we cannot do better than to follow in his footsteps.

If you don't love Jesus enough—and you don't—then ask Mary to help you love him more. I guarantee you that she wants to do that for you and that no one can do that better than she can. She is the Queen of Heaven and the Queen of Angels. The angels obey her bidding!

If you don't love Mary enough, ask Jesus to help you love her more. I guarantee you that Jesus wants to do that for you, and that he will. He will send angels to help you. They are his angels, after all!

SECOND READING
1 THESSALONIANS 5:16–24 _____

Brothers and sisters: Rejoice always. Pray without ceasing. In all circumstances give thanks, for this is the will of God for you in Christ Jesus. Do not quench the Spirit. Do not despise prophetic utterances. Test everything; retain what is good. Refrain from every kind of evil.

May the God of peace make you perfectly holy and may you entirely, spirit, soul, and body, be preserved blameless for the coming of our Lord Jesus Christ. The one who calls you is faithful, and he will also accomplish it.

_____

Today's short epistle describes the universal vocation of all Christians, which is to become saints, to become holy.

Holiness is not for monks and mystics or canonized saints alone. It is God's demand for all of us. The formula is repeated many times in the Old Testament: "Be holy, for I, the LORD, your God, am holy" (Lev. 19:2). Jesus says, in his most famous sermon, the Sermon on the Mount, "Be perfect, just as your heavenly Father is perfect" (Matt. 5:48). Holiness is not our *ideal*; it is our obligation. It is a demand. God will not rest until we are holy. That's why for most of us there needs to be a purgatory, where the process that began here on earth is completed before we are pure enough to enter heaven, to endure heaven, to enjoy heaven. The Church clearly and consistently says, in line with all its saints and teachers, that there is a "*universal* call to holiness."

What does that look like? It looks like God. "Be holy, *for I, the LORD, your God, am holy*." So the principles of God's law, the principles of morality, show us not only who we are meant to be but also who God is. Those are the two things that Christ shows us: since he is both perfect man and perfect God, he shows us who we are meant to be, as well as who God is.

St. Paul lists ten Ds in his account of our holiness: three dos, three don'ts, three dimensions, and one definition.

He begins with three dos, which seem impossible. Then he gives three don'ts, which seem easy. Then he shows us the three areas or dimensions of holiness. And then he sums it all up in one definition of holiness, one principle, one rule.

The three dos are "Rejoice always. Pray without ceasing. In all circumstances give thanks."

We all admit that we should rejoice, that we should pray, and that we should give thanks. And there are times we all find that easy. And there are times when we don't find it easy. But St. Paul adds the shocking qualifiers "always," "without ceasing," and "in all circumstances."

But how can we rejoice when we feel suffering or see evil? How can we pray when we have to concentrate on our work? How can we give thanks when we have lost our job, our health, or a friend or family member? Is St. Paul just exaggerating here? Perhaps he doesn't mean it; perhaps he is just "gushing." Is he commanding us to do the impossible? That's not productive. That produces only guilt and despair.

Let's take the three dos one by one.

First, "rejoice always." We do not feel joy always. In fact, we feel joy very rarely. We feel contentment quite frequently, especially if our hopes and desires and ideals are fairly modest—for instance, in taking a hot bath or eating tasty food. And we feel happiness less frequently than contentment, because happiness is deeper and more precious than contentment; but we all do have moments of happiness—for instance, when we have completed a job that is both worth doing and well done, whether it's cleaning the whole house or getting a full recovery from a disease or seeing our children or our friends in a loving, happy marriage. But just as happiness is deeper and rarer and higher than contentment, joy is even deeper and rarer and higher than happiness. We probably remember only a few moments of deep joy. Joy is always surprising, which shows how rare it is. How can we feel that joy, that "high," always? We can't. It's psychologically impossible, isn't it?

Yes, that's true if joy is only a subjective, personal feeling. But what if joy is another person? What if Jesus *is* our joy? Then, if we have Jesus always, we have joy always, whether we feel it or not. We have it by faith, not by feeling.

St. James says, at the beginning of his epistle, "Consider it all joy, my brothers, when you encounter various trials" (James 1:2). He does not command us to *feel* a trial as joy (that's impossible) but to *count* it as joy, to *reckon* it as joy, to *know* it as joy, to know it by faith, to *believe* it as joy. Which would you rather have: a false joy that feels like joy, or a true joy that does not? A joy that feels like joy but that you know or believe is fake, or a joy that does not feel like joy but that you know or believe is true joy? Would you rather really be in hell and worship the devil but feel good about it, or go to heaven and worship God but not feel anything? Do you worship your own feelings, or do you worship God, and therefore truth, because God *is* truth?

Can we have joy even in sorrow? Of course we can! Jesus himself gives us an example of that both in words and in deeds: in words when he gives us the example of a woman in labor (John 16:21), and in deeds when he is on the cross. Hebrews 12:2 says of Jesus that "for the sake of the joy that lay before him he endured the cross." Joy does not always remove sorrow. Just as you can love and hate the same person at the same time, you can have joy and sorrow at the same time, like a mother in labor. And you can also be at peace and at war at the same time. You can have peace in your heart even while you rightly fight a just war with your hands.

A Christian's joy is not a fleeting thing, like a cloud or a rainbow. It is a certain and permanent thing, like an anchor that holds even while the surface of the sea is full of turbulence. This is because Jesus *is* our joy, and he is real and true and solid and secure and forever.

The next "do always" is prayer. How can we pray always? That's a little easier to understand than joy always. Prayer can exist in the subconscious mind always, even though it can't be in the conscious mind always. There are things that are very much alive and real in us all the time even when we don't consciously attend to them, like our relationships with our family, or our gender, or our age. When you hug your kids, for instance, you're not consciously thinking, "Those are my kids," but you hug them differently than you'd hug your spouse, or other people's kids. Take another example: When you try to find the right words to use to talk to your boss about a problem at work, they're not the same words you'd use with your kids or your spouse or a stranger, but that relationship with your boss is not the thing you are consciously thinking about right now, even though it's subconsciously influencing every word you choose.

That's how you can pray always. If you make a Morning Offering every day to God (I certainly hope you all do: it takes only one minute!), and if you really mean it, that makes everything you do that day into a prayer, because you know that even when you forget God, God never forgets you, so you are always in that relationship to God that is called prayer and adoration, even when you are not thinking about it.

Let's assume that when you say to God "Thy will be done," you mean it, because you believe that everything in your life is willed by God, either positively willing you good things or negatively permitting bad things for good reasons. If you have that relationship with God, however foggy and weak it is, then that prayer of yours, "Thy will be done," is attached to everything that happens to you every day, even when you're not consciously praying. When you give money to your children to spend as they wish, that freedom to spend is attached to every dollar, every choice, and every purchase they make, as a kind of blessing from you. And when a robber steals your money and spends it as he wishes, not as you wish, your non-blessing on that money, your curse, is attached to every dollar.

What about the third do, "in all circumstances give thanks"? That's the easiest one of all. You can give thanks even when you don't feel thankful, like "Thanks, I needed that" after a rude shock or a rude awakening that you don't enjoy but you know you need, like a loud alarm clock going off early in the morning. Thanksgiving is a giving, an action, an act of will. It is not a feeling. Feelings are passive; they come over you. We are not commanded to feel or not feel things; we are commanded to do or not do things—and giving thanks is a doing; giving thanks is a choice. It's a choice that enlarges your heart whenever you do it and that narrows and constricts and squeezes the life out of your heart when you refuse to do it, both to other human beings and above all to God. If you pray and mean the most fundamental of all prayers, "Thy will be done," then it necessarily follows that you are saying "thanks" to God for everything, even the pains; that you are saying to God about them, even before they happen, "Thanks, I needed that." Because God infallibly knows what you do really need for your own good. God makes no mistakes; that's why we can pray "Thy will be done" always.

The fact that we *can* do this does not mean that it's easy, of course. But it's right, and it's good. And it's always possible. God does not command the impossible.

Then come three don'ts. "Do not quench the Spirit," "Do not despise prophetic utterances," and "Refrain from every kind of evil."

How do we quench the Spirit? The Holy Spirit's inspirations are mainly those of conscience. But we often forget that conscience gives us dos as well as don'ts, and some of the dos are not *obligations* but *invitations* to overcome our fears and take risks, even risks of doing something embarrassing, like singing in church even if you don't have a great voice. (That's probably just about the last and hardest thing most Catholics would ever do.) When St. Paul says, "Quench not the Spirit," he's not talking about our spirit but God's Spirit, the Holy Spirit. We often *should* quench our own spirit when it tells us to do something foolish, but we should never quench or turn away from or disobey what we honestly believe is God's Holy Spirit. We need to distinguish those two very clearly; that's why St. Paul adds, "Test everything; retain what is good." We need to be critical, rational, judgmental—not of people but of ideas. In the words of Christ, we need to be wise as serpents as well as harmless as doves. Not an easy combination, but an absolutely necessary one.

What is meant by the second don't, "Do not despise prophetic utterances"?

Prophets are not primarily foretellers but forthtellers. A prophet is simply one who speaks forth God's word and God's will. The Church is God's public prophet to the world, so we are not to despise what she says even when we are tempted to. We are tempted to despise it because we have no desire to obey it, and we have no desire to obey it because we have no understanding of it, and we have no understanding of it because we listen to what the secular media say it means instead of listening to what the Church herself says it means. The primary example of this today is what the Church says about sexual morality. Less than 1 percent of Catholics who despise the prophet Pope St. Paul VI's *Humanae Vitae* have ever read it, or Pope St. John Paul II's explanation of it in his beautiful "theology of the body."

St. Paul's third don't, "Refrain from every kind of evil," summarizes half of all morality. The other half is "do every kind of good, every kind that you can." All don'ts imply dos, and all dos imply don'ts. The two always go together.

Then comes Paul's definition of holiness. Old Aristotle said that a complete definition of anything includes four factors, which philosophers call "the four causes": the essence of the thing, its contents, its origin, and its end or fulfillment or consummation. St. Paul gives us these four parts of a definition of holiness in his last words: the essence, the contents, the origin, and the end.

First, he tells us that the *essence* of holiness is to be like God, when he says, "May the God of peace make you perfectly holy." God defines holiness; holiness does not define God. Holiness is godliness, peace with God, right relationship with God, faith and hope and love to God.

Second, the *contents* of holiness are all three parts or aspects or dimensions of human life. St. Paul says, "May you entirely, spirit, soul, and body, be preserved." These are the three dimensions of human nature in which we are called to be holy: spirit, soul, and body. "Spirit" here probably is used to mean that aspect of the soul by which we relate to God, while "soul" here, when contrasted to "spirit," means our relations with other human beings and ourselves, while our "body" is part of the material world and thus the agent of our relationship with all material things, including money and all the things money can buy, and our attitude toward our own body and other people's bodies. We relate to the material things beneath us, the human souls around us and within us, and the God above us. That's simply everything. Being holy is not a narrow, specialized thing; it's everything. It's simply being a complete human being.

Third, St. Paul also tells us the *origin* or cause of holiness when he says that "the one who calls you is faithful, and he will also accomplish it." God is the first cause of this accomplishment of holiness in us; our role is to accept it and cooperate with it. We can block it; we can say no to it; we can say no to God. But we can also say yes to God. But when we say yes to God, God is the first cause of that free choice of ours to say yes to him. Divine grace comes first; our cooperation with it comes second. But it really does come, because God's grace does not substitute for our free choice; it turns our free will on, not off. He promises to do this, and he is faithful to his promises, and therefore he will accomplish it.

Finally, St. Paul also gives us the end of holiness when he says, "May you . . . be preserved blameless for the coming of our Lord Jesus Christ." Here he points to the payoff, the consummation, the reward, of holiness. Christ's second coming will consummate and complete and perfect our holiness, and therefore also all the ingredients in it: our rejoicing always, our praying without ceasing, our giving thanks in all circumstances, our not quenching the Spirit, our not despising prophecies, our testing everything and retaining only what is good, and our refraining from every kind of evil.

All believers can become perfect saints. Even you. Even your spouse and your kids. Hard to believe? No. Hard not to believe, because God promises this, and God is absolutely faithful to his promises. He does not promise that the road will be short or easy, but he does promise that the road will lead to a heaven that is so unimaginably good and great that, as St. Paul describes it, "eye has not seen, ear has not heard, nor has it entered into the heart of man, the things God has prepared for those who love him."

GOSPEL
JOHN 1:6–8, 19–28 _____

A man named John was sent from God. He came for testimony, to testify to the light, so that all might believe through him. He was not the light, but came to testify to the light.

And this is the testimony of John. When the Jews from Jerusalem sent priests and Levites to him to ask him, "Who are you?" he admitted and did not deny it, but admitted, "I am not the Christ." So they asked him, "What are you then? Are you Elijah?" And he said, "I am not." "Are you the Prophet?" He answered, "No." So they said to him, "Who are you, so we can give an answer to those who sent us? What do you have to say for yourself?" He said:

"I am *the voice of one crying out in the desert,*
'make straight the way of the Lord,'
as Isaiah the prophet said."

Some Pharisees were also sent. They asked him, "Why then do you baptize if you are not the Christ or Elijah or the Prophet?" John answered them, "I baptize with water; but there is one among you whom you do not recognize, the one who is coming after me, whose sandal strap I am not worthy to untie." This happened in Bethany across the Jordan, where John was baptizing.

_____

(Again, I offer a choice between two reflections that cover pretty much the same material. The first is more personal and practical, the second is more historical and theological.)

Reflection 1

In one way John the Baptist is more of a model for what we are all called to be than Jesus is, and in another way he is less.

How is John more our model? How are we called to be more like John than like Jesus? In our job description. We are not the Messiah. We are not the saviors of the world. We are only his forerunners, his messengers, his servants.

Of course, if we are sane, we admit that this is our place, playing second fiddle; but something in us also rebels against that. We all naturally tend to play God. We see everything from our own "I" perspective. We are the center of our world, as the sun is the center of our solar system. We naturally think this way. You are in front of me, or behind me, or to my right, or to my left; I am not behind you, or in front of you, or to your left, or to your right. But this is an illusion. We even think of God as the object of our religious experience rather than thinking of us as objects of God's religious experience. But God is the sun, and we are only planets. We are totally relative to him; he is not relative to us.

So, because of this innate illusion of perspective, we have to keep reminding ourselves that we are not God, or the Messiah, which is what many of the Jews thought John was, God's anointed and promised Savior. Others thought he was the great prophet Elijah, sent back to earth. Still others thought he was the mysterious figure they called simply "the Prophet," the one whom Moses promised God would send after his death to be the new Moses, and whom they mistakenly distinguished from the Messiah. John the Baptist confesses that he is none of these great figures. He is smaller than people think. He is a tiny planet compared to Christ the true sun, the Son of God. In fact, John says he is not worthy to untie the sandal strap of the one his whole job is to prepare for and to point to. Untying the sandals of a traveler, and then washing his feet, was the job of the lowest servant. That's John's position. It is also ours, if we want to enter Christ's kingdom. Christ showed us our entrance requirement and our job description when he washed his disciples' feet.

There is a famous Zen Buddhist saying: "A finger is useful for pointing at the moon, but woe to him who mistakes the finger for the moon." We, like John, are pointing fingers, pointing others to Christ by our words and our good works, our faith and our love. We cannot save the world. We are not the saviors of the world. We are not God's great gift to the world. We are not what our commencement speakers always tell us we are, especially when they tell us one of the world's stupidest but most beloved lies, that "you can be whatever you want to be." No. You cannot be Superman, or an angel, or an ape. If God made you a man, you cannot be a woman, and if God made you a woman, you cannot be a man, because you are not God. You are not your own creator and designer. Sorry to be the bearer of that shockingly bad news.

We humans are not wizards or elves, or even kings; we are hobbits. Christ himself did not come as a wizard or a king or an elf or an angel but as a poor peasant, a humble, homely hobbit.

John says of Christ, "He must increase; I must decrease" (John 3:30). We must say the same. For when we decrease, when we stop pointing to ourselves and start pointing to Christ, that's when we fulfill our vocation and really increase. We are never taller than when we kneel, both to pray and to obey. And we are never shorter than when we strut, never lower than when we look down from on high with a sneer.

But in another way, John is *not* our model—Jesus is. Jesus is the model for all of us; John is the model only for those few who have not only the vocation to point to Christ, which is the vocation of all of us, but also the special vocation from God to be a prophet, the last of the Old Testament prophets. And even more specific than that, not just any kind of prophet but a troublemaking prophet, a public prophet denouncing a decadent world. John is rough and tough. He lives as a hermit in the desert. He eats locusts and wild honey. He wears clothing of camel hair. He uses fiery language, accusing people of sin and demanding repentance. He calls respectable sinners "You brood of vipers!" (Matt. 3:7). He threatens us with fear of divine judgment. He says that God "will clear his threshing floor and gather his wheat into his barn, but the chaff he will burn with unquenchable fire" (Matt. 3:12). He preaches hellfire and damnation. He was so uncompromising in denouncing the sexual sins of King Herod that the king had to put him in prison. And King Herod's lust for his brother's wife and for Salome the dancing girl cost John his head.

We are not all called to be hermits, ascetics, hellfire preachers, public denouncers of kings, and martyrs. We *are* all called to be just as tough and courageous as John, but in a different way for most of us. Courage takes different forms. A woman's courage, though just as real and just as valuable and just as strong as a man's courage, manifests itself differently, just as a man's compassion manifests itself differently than a woman's. John the Baptist is our model only for the hard virtues; Christ is our model for all the virtues, the soft virtues like kindness and compassion and sensitivity and mercy and forgiveness as well as the hard and courageous virtues like self-control and justice and truth and honesty and the fighting spirit of spiritual warfare. All the virtues, both the hard ones and the soft ones, are summed up in love, in charity; but there is a need for both tough love and tender love. It is a great defect to lack either one.

Jesus said that no prophet was greater than John, because his purpose was most clearly to lead us to Jesus. Jesus also gave us Mary, his own mother, for that purpose: to lead us to Jesus. Her last words recorded in Scripture were the words she spoke to the waiters at the wedding feast at Cana, when she knew Jesus would turn the water into wine: "Do whatever he tells you" (John 2:5). John and Mary are very different: John is very loud; Mary is very quiet. But they tell us the very same thing. They both say, with their words and with their hearts and with their lives, "Look at him. Look at Jesus."

Reflection 2

To understand today's Gospel, it's helpful to know that there were four predictions or prophecies in the Old Testament about mysterious figures who would appear at the time when God would do his greatest work and set up on earth his own kingdom, the kingdom of God or kingdom of heaven. Most of God's chosen people misunderstood what that kingdom would be. They thought it would be a political kingdom that would free the Jews from their Roman masters and tyrannical oppressors militarily. That's one reason why so many did not accept Jesus: because he was not political. Even today, many Christians are more passionate about politics than about religion and secretly wish Jesus had hung around for two thousand more years so he could run for president.

John the Baptist claimed to be one of those four figures, the least important one, the one Isaiah called "the voice of one crying out in the desert, 'Make straight the way of the Lord.'" John said he was *not* the most important one, the "Christ," which is a title that means the Messiah, or anointed one, or promised one, who would be the King of this new kingdom. That was Jesus, of course.

Jesus said that among all the prophets there was none greater than John, yet John said that he was not worthy to untie the sandal strap of the true Messiah, because John only baptized with water for repentance, but the Messiah would baptize with the Holy Spirit. John was only sweeping the floor in preparation for Jesus to take possession of the house. John was only making a road to the palace of the kingdom; Jesus would build the palace. John was only a pointing finger; Jesus was the one he pointed to.

The other two Old Testament figures referred to in today's Gospel are Elijah and the one called simply "the Prophet."

Elijah did not die but was taken up to heaven in a chariot of fire, and God promised, through the prophet Malachi, that "I will send you Elijah, the prophet, before the day of the LORD comes, the great and terrible day" (Mal. 3:23). This did happen, in fact, but in two different ways. Jesus said (in Matt. 11:14) that John the Baptist was indeed Elijah. But that was because John had the fiery spirit of Elijah. John was not Elijah personally. Jews did not believe in reincarnation, as Hindus and Buddhists do. So John said he was not Elijah literally. But Elijah himself did come back to earth literally and personally a little later, on the holy mountain at the Transfiguration, together with Moses, and spoke with Jesus in sight of his disciples Peter, James, and John.

The other figure, called simply "the Prophet," was probably the one promised by God to Moses, who was the greatest of all prophets. Deuteronomy says that "since then no prophet has arisen in Israel like Moses, whom the LORD knew face to face. He had no equal in all the signs and wonders the LORD sent him to perform in the land of Egypt" (Deut. 34:10–11). God said to Moses, "I will raise up for them a prophet like you from among their kin, and will put my words into his mouth" (Deut. 18:18). Acts 3:22 and 7:37 identify Jesus as that prophet.

Jesus is more than a prophet, but he is a prophet too, and a priest and a king, the three offices God appointed in Israel. But Jesus is more than a prophet who only speaks the words of God: Jesus *is* the Word of God. And he is more than a priest: he is *the* priest, the offering as well as the offerer. And he is more than an earthly king: he is the King of the universe and the King of heaven.

We naturally wonder why God spoke in such riddles, in such mysterious ways. Why didn't he specify exactly and literally what would happen, so that there was no mystery and no possible misunderstandings and misinterpretations? If you were God, and you knew all that you now know about Christ and his kingdom and the Church, you could have inspired an Old Testament that was much clearer than the one we have. God is certainly not more muddleheaded and confused than you are, so he must have *deliberately* left many things ambiguous. Why?

It must be for our sake, for our greater good. That's why he does everything, including the things that puzzle us and disappoint us, like the sufferings that seem to do no good but only harm, and the ignorance that leads us to serious mistakes, both theologically and morally and practically, in all areas of our life and in our relationship with him and our relationships with each other.

So what good does it do us to have a divine revelation that is unclear and needs interpretation instead of one that gives us all the answers clearly? The answer is that it tests us. It's like the tests we got in school. If the teacher gave us all the answers to the questions, we'd all get As but we wouldn't learn as much because we wouldn't need to expend much effort. Like a good teacher, God gives us just enough light to motivate us to move in the right direction, so that if we really want to learn, we will; if we really want to find him, we will; but we have to seek and search. Jesus promises, "The one who seeks, finds" (Matt. 7:8), but that implies that those who do not seek, will not find. So he is testing our hearts, our loves, our desires, our wills. The very first thing Jesus says to his prospective disciples in John's Gospel is "What are you looking for?" (John 1:38). In other words, what kind of Messiah are you looking for? A political and military hero who will save you from political tyranny and economic oppression? If so, do not come to me. A mere miracle worker who will manipulate the material world to take away all your pains and diseases and inconveniences and give you a painless utopia on earth but do nothing for your souls and your selfishness and your sins, who will change your external world but not your hearts? If so, don't come to me. Wait two thousand years until modern technology comes along.

But if what you want is salvation not from politics or poverty or pain but from sin, then come to me. My name is "Jesus," which means "Savior," and God's angel chose that name for a reason. He said to Joseph, "You are to name him Jesus, because he will save his people from their sins" (Matt. 1:21).

John the Baptist fits into this divine strategy of testing us. Do we hate sin the most? Do we want forgiveness of our sins? Do we repent of our sins? If so, come to him and be baptized in clean water as a symbol of that cleanness of heart that we most desire. And then, if we come to John, he will point us to Jesus. To be saved, we need to repent and believe. John preaches repentance, and Jesus preaches faith. Repentance leads to faith, as John leads to Jesus.

But we should not come to Jesus and believing without first coming to John and repenting. Jesus serves us the spiritual meal, but John cleans the kitchen. Jesus is the dining room, and John is the bathroom. Jesus fills us with God's Holy Spirit, and John exorcises us of our own evil spirits. Jesus comes to live in our spiritual house, and John is the exterminator who gets rid of the cockroaches. To be saved, we need both of those two things: to repent and to believe; to say no to sin and yes to God. John is there to remind us of that. He summarizes the whole Old Testament preparation for the Messiah, the whole message of all the prophets, in that one word, "repent." "Turn." "Convert." Swallow your pride and ignore your false prophets who tell you to simply accept yourself exactly as you are and to proudly sing "I did it my way," which is the song they all sing as they enter hell.

That's a tough message. But it's tough *love*. Love has to be both tough and tender. It's the two-part message all good parents give to their kids. The second half, the positive half, the do, the yes, is far more important than the first half, the negative half, the don't, the no. But both halves are necessary. Because evil and good, darkness and light, can't coexist. Each one drives out the other. You can't drive a car in two opposite directions at once. We have to not just drive but drive in the right direction.

So let's remember to frequently examine our conscience and use the sacrament of Confession, which is something like John the Baptist continuing his work in a much fuller, sweeter, more merciful way. Confession and repentance are necessary because truth is necessary as well as love. In fact, honesty with truth is the heart of true love.

Jesus tells us to love our neighbors as ourselves, which presupposes that we do love ourselves. And we *should* love ourselves, but in the right way—that is, honestly and with tough love as well as tender love. And tough love means kicking out all the enemies of true love. If you truly love your body, you don't love your cancers and corns and cholesterol, your hemorrhoids and hernias and herpes. If you truly love your soul, you don't love your sins. Your sins are your waste products. Get rid of them. Don't get spiritual constipation. Flush your sins down the toilet in the sacrament of Confession, which is like the bathroom, and then go on to eat the bread of angels in the dining room with clean hands. Fast from sin so you can feast on salvation and sanctification.

FOURTH SUNDAY OF ADVENT

FIRST READING

2 SAMUEL 7:1–5, 8B–12, 14A, 16 _____

When King David was settled in his palace, and the LORD had given him rest from his enemies on every side, he said to Nathan the prophet, "Here I am living in a house of cedar, while the ark of God dwells in a tent!" Nathan answered the king, "Go, do whatever you have in mind, for the LORD is with you." But that night the LORD spoke to Nathan and said: "Go, tell my servant David, 'Thus says the LORD: Should you build me a house to dwell in?'

"'It was I who took you from the pasture and from the care of the flock to be commander of my people Israel. I have been with you wherever you went, and I have destroyed all your enemies before you. And I will make you famous like the great ones of the earth. I will fix a place for my people Israel; I will plant them so that they may dwell in their place without further disturbance. Neither shall the wicked continue to afflict them as they did of old, since the time I first appointed judges over my people Israel. I will give you rest from all your enemies. The LORD also reveals to you that he will establish a house for you. And when your time comes and you rest with your ancestors, I will raise up your heir after you, sprung from your loins, and I will make his kingdom firm. I will be a father to him, and he shall be a son to me. Your house and your kingdom shall endure forever before me; your throne shall stand firm forever.'"

_____

This incident from the Old Testament has many lessons to teach us.

The first lesson is that even saints and prophets make mistakes. David is a saint, a lover of God. God describes him as "a man after his own heart" (1 Sam. 13:14). Yet this great saint was mistaken in his pious and unselfish and well-intentioned desire to build God a temple. The prophet Nathan was also mistaken in his initial approval of David's plan, and God corrected him, and, through him, corrected David. Individual saints and prophets are not infallible. God speaks infallibly through Christ and the Apostles whom he chose and authorized to teach in his name and with his authority and to ordain successors, the bishops and popes of his Church, even though they are often not as holy as his saints and are sometimes even wicked, like Judas Iscariot and some of the Renaissance popes. God has established a visible, public, universal Church to teach with his authority. He has not left it up to us to judge the holiness of the teachers and to proportion our faith to our own fallible judgement of their holiness.

We can see from this incident of David the king and Nathan the prophet that sometimes even piety, as well as impiety, makes mistakes, and God has to correct them, though not usually as quickly as he did this time, that very night.

You remember that this great saint David made more serious mistakes than this. He committed two great sins, adultery and murder: adultery with Bathsheba and the arranged murder of Bathsheba's husband Uriah by David's generals, who left him undefended in battle to be killed by the enemy so that David could legally have his wife Bathsheba. Even today those two sins often go together: the most frequent reason innocent, defenseless unborn babies are murdered by abortion is so that their unmarried parents can continue to have sex without consequences. Abortion is backup contraception, and contraception is the demand for sex without babies. If babies came from storks, abortion clinics would have no customers. I am sorry if the truth offends anyone, but nothing I just said is untrue. It is also true that God is infinitely merciful, loving, and forgiving. No sin, however great, is greater than God's love and forgiveness. We see that with David.

There are two opposite mistakes we can make here. One is to ignore or deny God's love and mercy and forgiveness. That is really to deny that God is God. The other mistake is to ignore or deny God's truth and law and justice, and to deny that sin is sin. These two mistakes are equally tempting, equally popular, and equally disastrous, both in this life and in the next.

(You may want to omit the previous two paragraphs from your homily, for a number of possible reasons, but please make sure that your honest motive for doing so is not to avoid being a prophet and being hated and criticized and to preserve your own good status in the eyes of your parishioners at the expense of God's divine and infallible truth as revealed by the Church whose divine revelations you solemnly promised to teach and defend. It is wrong for any man to judge and condemn any man, but there is one thing that is even more wrong, and that is to be judged and condemned by God for refusing to preach the truth, the whole truth, and nothing but the truth. Truth and love are both absolutes.)

A second, related lesson from our Scripture reading is that God always has a good reason for correcting us, for not approving what seems good to us, or for not answering our prayers or desires as we think he should. Sometimes God tells us the reason, as he did to David, and sometimes he does not. And when he does not, sometimes we can come to see God's reason in this life and sometimes we cannot. But even then, we will see it after death. God always knows what he is doing.

A third lesson is that we have an active role to play even when God's response to our plans or his answer to our prayers is no. Both David and Nathan had to choose to hear and heed and obey God's word. God said to Nathan, his servant, "Go, tell my servant David, 'Thus says the LORD . . .'" That was Nathan's active role: to preach. David's active role was to believe and to obey. Nathan and David were both God's active servants, not his passive slaves.

A fourth lesson here is that in obeying and serving God, David also served and did what was best for all his people, even if David did not see how this was so. That is implied in God's promises to David. The promises were not just personal, for David, but also public and political, for the whole nation. There is never a conflict between individual and social morality, between serving God and serving God's people, between love of God and love of neighbor, even when sometimes there may seem to be. True religion and true social justice are always allies, never enemies.

A fifth lesson in this narrative is an implicit philosophy of war that repudiates both militarism and pacifism. David is not allowed to build the temple because he is a man of war. That does not imply that fighting a war is always and everywhere sinful—God *commanded* some wars—but it does imply that peace is better, and that the arts of peace are higher and holier than the arts of war, even if the war is just and necessary and honorable. A war is like an amputation or a painful punishment: sometimes necessary to prevent greater evil. Not that it is a "necessary evil"—that is a self-contradictory term—but when it is good, it is always less good than peace, and its goal is to abolish itself and create a just peace. Peace is a gift of God and a blessing; war is not.

Here is a sixth lesson: God tells David, "It was I who took you from the pasture and from the care of the flock to be commander of my people Israel." In light of the previous point about war and peace, this promotion from shepherd to warrior was not a step up to a higher vocation, because shepherds make peace and warriors make war. But it was a step up in another sense because David's flock as king was higher and holier than David's flock as shepherd, because people are higher than animals.

But being a king is not essentially being a warrior but essentially being a shepherd, not of sheep but of people. Fighting is not the main business of either kind of shepherding. Shepherds do fight wolves, but that's not their end; that's only a means to their end, which is protecting the sheep: and warrior kings also fight wars only for the sake of protecting their people.

A seventh lesson is that God is "with" David as a warrior just as he was with David as a shepherd. For God, too, is a warrior and a shepherd. He is a warrior against sins and demons, not against human beings, and he is a shepherd of human beings. But since he is our good shepherd, that means that God, too, must be a warrior against the wolves that are the enemies of the sheep.

God is the only perfect and innocent warrior. No human war ever begins without sin and blame on the part of one or both parties. David is not a perfect and innocent warrior, and David was far from an innocent and perfect human being—he was guilty of adultery with Bathsheba, theft of Uriah's wife, and conspiracy to murder Uriah. Yet David repented, and God blesses David and says, "I have been with you wherever you went." Being with God, as God is with us—this is the whole meaning of life. It is a distant foretaste of the spiritual marriage that will be our eternal happiness in heaven.

A final lesson concerns God's promise to be with David's descendants "forever." He said: "I will raise up your heir after you, sprung from your loins, and I will make his kingdom firm. I will be a father to him, and he shall be a son to me. Your house and your kingdom shall endure forever before me." But Israel's peace and unity and holiness were broken just two short generations after David, and idolatry, civil war, military defeat, and captivity and slavery ensued for both Judah and the rest of Israel. And the line of David's descendants as kings ended.

Yet God kept his promise, for the Messiah was literally David's descendent, and that was David's true kingdom—not the state but the Church; not statesmen but saints. God kept his promise to David's family, but his family was not his political family. It was not less literal than that, but more literal than that. It was his biological family. Mary was David's great-great-great-great (etc.) granddaughter, and that made David Jesus' great-great-great-great (etc.) grandfather. That was an infinitely greater privilege than being Israel's greatest king. Sometimes we misinterpret God's prophecies not because we are too literal but because we are not literal enough.

God blessed Solomon, David's biological son and heir, but Solomon's reign ended in idolatry and failure, and his sons split Israel forever and plunged her into civil war. But the "heir" of David that God spoke of was not Solomon but Christ. God said, "I will be a father to him, and he shall be a son to me," and God was the eternal Father to Christ, the Son of God.

That is the most literal fatherhood, not a mere symbol or image. Biological fatherhood is an image of that divine fatherhood, not vice versa, because we are made in God's image, not vice versa. Thus, St. Paul speaks of God as "the Father, from whom every family in heaven and on earth is named" (Eph. 3:14–15).

The collapse of Israel's peace and independence shortly after David's reign shows us that God's promises are fulfilled perfectly and completely only when *we* are perfect and complete, in the next life. Good triumphs over evil in this life only temporarily, and the evil of death always seems to eventually triumph over the good of life and to have the last word, for all nations as well as for all individuals.

But things are not merely what they seem. There is more. There is more to this life than this life. And there is more to death than death: there is resurrection. Reality is always more than appearance. As Shakespeare wrote, in *Hamlet*, "There are more things in heaven and earth than are dreamt of in your philosophy." That's because heaven and earth are designed by the God who is infinite power, infinite wisdom, and infinite love.

RESPONSORIAL PSALM
PSALM 89:2–3, 4–5, 27, 29

R. (2a) **For ever I will sing the goodness of the Lord.**

The promises of the LORD I will sing forever;
    through all generations my mouth
        shall proclaim your faithfulness.
For you have said, "My kindness is established forever";
    in heaven you have confirmed your faithfulness.

"I have made a covenant with my chosen one,
    I have sworn to David my servant:
Forever will I confirm your posterity
    and establish your throne for all generations."

"He shall say of me, 'You are my father,
    my God, the Rock, my savior.'
Forever I will maintain my kindness toward him,
    and my covenant with him stands firm."

Let's try to dive more deeply into five important words in this short poetic passage: "promises," "covenant," "sing," "kindness," and "forever."

First, *promises*. Promises are the single most important glue that holds together all levels of society and all kinds of societies, from families to nations. If we cannot trust each other to keep our promises, *all* human relationships fall apart.

This is true "vertically" or supernaturally, in our relationship with God, as well as "horizontally" or naturally, in our relationships with each other. The theological virtue of hope is one of the three strands of the rope that attaches us to God, the other two being faith and charity; and hope's object is God's promises. Hope is not a wish or a vague optimism but an absolute assurance, a guarantee that God will be faithful to all his promises.

A *covenant* is a solemn, public promise between two parties. Another word for a covenant is a "testament." The "Old Testament" is not first of all a book or a series of books but a real historical event, an act of God in history, a covenant that God established with Israel—followed by a New Covenant, or "New Testament," that God established with all of humanity through Christ and the "catholic," or universal, Church that Christ established and gave his authority to. Like the books we call the Old Testament, the books we call the New Testament are filled with promises from God that are part of the New Covenant, the new relationship with God that Christ made for us.

Marriage is the closest and most complete of all human, horizontal images of this divine, vertical covenant. That is why it is sacred, and by far the single most important promise we can make with each other. It is by far the most important foundation of all human relationships, and the fact that it is today in a far greater crisis than ever before in history means that we are approaching history's greatest crisis. For if we cannot trust each other to keep our single most sacred, solemn, and serious covenant promise, how can we trust each other to keep any lesser promises? If we lie about our promise to the most important person in our life during the marriage vow, why shouldn't we lie in newspapers, social media, universities, political speeches, law courts, international treaties, and friendships?

The Psalmist promises that he will be faithful to God's promises. More than that, he will *sing* them. He has freely chosen with his will to give faith, hope, and love to God and his promises, but then there is more: his heart also cannot help *rejoicing* in them. How can we do anything less than overflow with joy when we understand what God has promised us? It is nothing less than an eternally faithful spiritual marriage to him who is the source of all joy, all beauty, and all happiness.

The Psalmist does not tell us to take music lessons or become professional opera singers: he tells us simply to "make a joyful *noise* unto the Lord" (Ps. 100:1 KJV). It is the heart that sings, not first of all the lungs and the lips. Corpses don't sing even though they have lungs and lips, because they don't have hearts and souls. Don't act like corpses; it's not Halloween. Have a heart—sing!

What do we sing? The Psalmist says he will sing God's *kindness* forever. Kindness goes beyond justice, beyond the minimum that is morally required and necessary. It is freely given. It is God's free choice to be kind and merciful to us, and that is not necessary and eternal and to be taken for granted; it is news, incredible good news. It does not have to be. There are things God has to be. God has to be real, and all-knowing, and all-just, and all-powerful, but he does not *have* to be kind and loving and merciful and compassionate to us. But he is. That God exists is not news; that is as necessary as 2 + 2 = 4. God's justice and God's knowledge and God's power are not news; those, too, are eternal and necessary, and good philosophical reasoning can prove all those things. But God's kindness and mercy are up to God's free choice and are not provable by reason alone; we have to believe it and trust it. It's a free gift. That's the Good News, the Gospel, and that's the news the Psalmist sings. He celebrates God's faithfulness to his covenant promises, which are promises not just of justice and truth but of kindness and mercy and forgiveness and love. God has to be just, but justice does not demand that he loves us, because we sinners and rebels do not justly deserve his love. But he does. That's the news that makes us sing for joy. God is faithful forever, not only to his necessary nature, his being and his knowledge and his justice and his power, but also to his freely chosen promises of love and mercy and forgiveness and kindness that he made to us in his covenant, his spiritual marriage, with us. The incredible good news is that God loves us so much that he wants to marry us to himself, spiritually, forever!

That's what we sing. That's why we sing. The word *forever* or "everlasting" occurs literally hundreds of times in the Old Testament. Belief in life after death was not a late development in Judaism, as many modern scholars claim, but it was part of God's revelation from the beginning. Jesus himself proved this to the Sadducees, who denied the resurrection, when he quoted from the first and oldest books in the Jewish Scriptures to prove it. (Look it up, in Matt. 22:23–33.)

Life in this body is not forever. Life on this earth is not forever. This whole universe is not forever. Eventually, everything in it dies, including all the galaxies, stars, and planets. But God is forever, and God made us in his own image, with souls that live forever, either with him in heaven or without him in hell, whichever we choose. Since God is forever, his promises are also forever, and therefore the people he makes those promises to also must live forever if the promises are to last forever. God does not make forever promises to dewdrops or mayflies or even galaxies but to us. When all the galaxies grow old, we shall still be eternally young. In the words of the last stanza of the great old hymn "Amazing Grace," "When we've been there ten thousand years, bright shining like the sun, we've no less days to sing his praise than when we'd first begun."

SECOND READING
ROMANS 16:25–27

Brothers and sisters: To him who can strengthen you, according to my gospel and the proclamation of Jesus Christ, according to the revelation of the mystery kept secret for long ages but now manifested through the prophetic writings and, according to the command of the eternal God, made known to all nations to bring about the obedience of faith, to the only wise God, through Jesus Christ be glory forever and ever. Amen.

These are the last lines of St. Paul's Letter to the Romans, his longest and most important letter. The central theme of the letter is the Gospel, the Good News, the deed God did in Christ to save the world. That is what he here calls "the revelation of the mystery kept secret for long ages but now manifested . . . made known to all nations."

But why did God do this? What is its purpose? And what are we supposed to do about it to fulfill that purpose? Paul's answer is "to bring about the obedience of faith."

Faith in this Good News, faith in this Gospel, faith in Christ, is identified as a kind of *obedience*. The Jews all agreed that God was to be obeyed. God is totally good and totally just and totally true and totally trustable, totally trustworthy, worthy of all trust, and therefore he ought to be trusted and obeyed. That was not controversial. What was controversial was Christ. Did this obedience to God entail faith in Christ as God's Messiah? Was he the Savior from sin? Was he the Son of God, as he claimed to be? Was he the Lord? Jews and Christians agree about obedience but not about faith. They obey the same God and the same divine law, but they do not share the same faith in Christ.

St. Paul, in using the phrase "the obedience of faith," is joining the Old Testament with the New, joining Judaism and Christianity, joining obedience to God with faith in Christ. He is arguing that the Jewish premise entails the Christian conclusion; he is deriving this new faith in Christ from the old obedience to God and his will. For St. Paul, faith is not just an opinion or a mental belief but above all an obedience. It begins in the will. It is a choice, a work, a deed. It is the second stage of our obedience to God, the first stage being the Old Covenant or Old Testament.

When the Jews asked Jesus, "What can we do to accomplish the works of God?" Jesus answered, "This is the work of God, that you believe in the one he sent" (John 6:28–29). In other words, to obey God, to do his will, is to believe in Christ. There should be no conflict between faith and works because faith is our first good work.

When St. John ended his Gospel, he asked the same question that St. Paul is asking here at the end of his Letter to the Romans. The question is: What is the bottom line for us? What are we supposed to do about it? What is the point? Why are you preaching? Why did you write this book? What is its purpose? And John's answer was: "These are written that you may [come to] believe that Jesus is the Messiah, the Son of God" (John 20:31). Christ is God's gift to us, and faith means accepting that gift. And that is the most important deed, the most important choice, the most important work, that we can do in our lives. That's the simple point of our whole religion. That's where it all comes to a point. That's the single sharp tip at the end of the long arrow. It's so simple that a child could understand it. Only a professional theologian could possibly miss it.

GOSPEL
LUKE 1:26–38

The angel Gabriel was sent from God to a town of Galilee called Nazareth, to a virgin betrothed to a man named Joseph, of the house of David, and the virgin's name was Mary. And coming to her, he said, "Hail, full of grace! The Lord is with you." But she was greatly troubled at what was said and pondered what sort of greeting this might be. Then the angel said to her, "Do not be afraid, Mary, for you have found favor with God.

"Behold, you will conceive in your womb and bear a son, and you shall name him Jesus. He will be great and will be called Son of the Most High, and the Lord God will give him the throne of David his father, and he will rule over the house of Jacob forever, and of his kingdom there will be no end." But Mary said to the angel, "How can this be, since I have no relations with a man?" And the angel said to her in reply, "The Holy Spirit will come upon you, and the power of the Most High will overshadow you. Therefore the child to be born will be called holy, the Son of God. And behold, Elizabeth, your relative, has also conceived a son in her old age, and this is the sixth month for her who was called barren; for nothing will be impossible for God." Mary said, "Behold, I am the handmaid of the Lord. May it be done to me according to your word." Then the angel departed from her.

Today's Gospel narrates the event we call the "Annunciation," when God sent his angel to ask Mary permission for him to send his Holy Spirit to miraculously conceive his Son in her womb, and she said yes. Next to Christ's death and Resurrection, that event was the most important event that ever happened in the whole history of the world. It is because of Mary's choice that the whole human race has the hope of heaven. God would not save the world unilaterally, without our cooperation; he is such a gentleman that he first sent his angel to ask Mary's permission to come into her womb, and he waited until she freely said yes; and only then, at that moment, the Incarnation happened: the Word became flesh, God became a human being, conceived in her womb as a zygote, then grew into an embryo, then a fetus, then a newborn, then a boy, then a teenager, then a man. (Imagine that! God became a teenager! This one teenager didn't just think he was God—he actually was God!)

God is teaching us crucially important lessons through every sentence of this divinely inspired Scripture passage. Here are just a few of them.

"The angel Gabriel was sent from God to a town of Galilee called Nazareth, to a virgin betrothed to a man named Joseph, of the house of David, and the virgin's name was Mary." Notice all the humility in this passage. First of all, angels are spectacular, yet they are humble and obedient: they do nothing and say nothing but what God himself commands them to do and say. Second, this angel, Gabriel, was not sent to Jerusalem or Rome but to a humble little town,

Nazareth, in the humblest and most remote of the areas of Israel, Galilee. Third, he was sent to Mary and Joseph, who were humble peasants, even though they were descended from King David. Jesus was literally and biologically descended from David, and even though no literal political kingdom lasts forever, Jesus' kingdom lasts forever. Fourth, Joseph was so humble that not a single word of his is ever recorded in Scripture. He was a carpenter, an honest but humble occupation. Fifth, Mary, like God, chooses humble places to appear. For the next two thousand years, all of the many miraculous public appearances of Mary, including those approved by the Church, have been to humble, poor, ordinary persons. The three most well known were to Juan Diego in Mexico, to Bernadette at Lourdes, France, and to the three peasant children at Fatima, Portugal. If God himself is so consistently humble, how dare we be proud?

"And coming to her, he said, 'Hail, full of grace! The Lord is with you.'" The "Hail Mary" prayer, the prayer prayed more times by more people throughout the world than any other prayer in all of human history, begins here, with the angel's own words. The greeting is high and holy: "Hail, full of grace," not "Hi there, kid."

And she is hailed as full of grace, full to the brim, having as much grace as any merely human being ever had or ever can have. There has never been and never will be in the history of the human race any merely human being as high and holy and totally full of divine grace as Mary.

Yet her highness is in her lowliness, her humility. When she has to refer to herself, she identifies herself as "the handmaid of the Lord" and says, "May it be done to me according to your word," not her own. When she heard the angel say to her, "The Lord is with you," she was "*greatly troubled* at what was said." Why was Mary troubled? Not because she was afraid of God or his angel, but because she was too humble to think of herself as special. The saintlier you are, the less self-centered you are. Mary could hardly believe the Lord would pick her, of all people. It's not that she thought of herself as worthless or wicked; that's not what humility does: in fact, thinking of yourself as very, very wicked is a form of pride, not humility. Humble people don't think of themselves as very good *or* as very bad; they just don't think of themselves at all. They think of God and other people.

That's why Mary knew God much better than we do: because of her humility, her total openness to God. Her deep knowledge of God is evident in her "Magnificat," when she said that "he has shown the strength of his arm, and has scattered the proud in their conceit. He has cast down the mighty from their thrones and has lifted up the lowly" (Luke 1:51–52). God seems to turn us upside down when he is really turning us right side up. The world calls humility folly and humble saints "losers." But God says it's the world that is upside down. Which of the two do you think most likely sees things as they really are? The infallible Creator or the fallen and fallible creature?

Mary is the most saintly and sinless woman who ever lived. In the "Hail Mary," we address her with the words of her cousin Elizabeth: "Blessed are you among women, and blessed is the fruit of your womb" (Luke 1:42). Notice that Elizabeth does not say merely that Mary is blessed but that she is blessed *among women*. Is that sexism or genderism or whatever the fashionable insult is today? Is that either an implied male chauvinism or a female chauvinism? Exactly the opposite. Jesus is the most blessed man who ever lived, and Mary is the most blessed woman who ever lived. Jesus and Mary are the only two perfectly sinless human beings, like Adam and Eve before the fall. Jesus chooses to reverse Adam's curse by involving Mary, whom the earliest Christian writers call "the new Eve." Where Eve said no to God and yes to the devil, Mary said yes to God and no to the devil. She reversed Eve's role in the fall. God arranged for both genders, male and female, to play a role in both the fall and the Redemption. God is not a sexist. He is an equal opportunity employer.

The blessings and graces of Jesus and Mary are different, of course, for Jesus is the divine *giver* of graces and blessings, while Mary is the *receiver* of them. But it was an active receiving, a free choice. It was both totally free and totally dependent on God, received from God. Mary's perfection, Mary's sinlessness, Mary's Immaculate Conception, Mary's being conceived without original sin, is God's gift, God's grace: she is full of God's grace, not full of herself. Mary's greatness is totally relative to Christ. That's why the angel does not say how great Mary will be but how great Christ will be: "He will be great and will be called Son of the Most High, and the Lord God will give him the throne of David his father, and he will rule over the house of Jacob forever, and of his Kingdom there will be no end."

Protestants object to our Catholic devotion to Mary because they think it detracts from our adoration of Jesus. In fact, it is exactly the opposite: the more we love Mary, the more we love Jesus, and the more we love Jesus, the more we love Mary. How could the most perfect man and the most perfect woman possibly be rivals for our love? How could they be competitive, in a kind of zero-sum or either/or relationship? Mary gave us Jesus, in consenting to be his mother, and Jesus gave us Mary, when he said to St. John, the only disciple who stayed with him at the cross, "Behold, your mother" (John 19:27). So if we, like John, want to be Jesus' disciples, if we want to be close to Jesus, as John was there at the cross, then we must be close to Mary, because Jesus gave us Mary. He gave us Mary as our mother in heaven as well as giving us God the Father as our Father in heaven by making us his children.

Here is a poem entitled "Jesus and Mary" that uses many different images and analogies for that relationship:

> Body of Christ, from Mary's body;
> Blood of Christ, from Mary's blood.
> Jesus the bread, Mary the yeast;
> Mary the kitchen, Jesus the feast.
> Mary the mother by whom we are fed;
> Mary the oven, Jesus the bread.
> Mary the soil, Jesus the vine;
> Mary the wine maker, Jesus the wine.
> Jesus the Tree of Life, Mary the sod;
> Mary our God-bearer, Jesus our God.
> Mary the silkworm, Jesus the silk;

Mary the nurse, Jesus our milk.
Mary the stem, Jesus the flower;
Mary the stairway, Jesus the tower.
Mary and Jesus, our castle entire;
Mary the fireplace, Jesus the fire.
Mary God's ink, Jesus God's name;
Mary the burning bush, Jesus the flame.
Mary the paper, Jesus the Word;
Mary the nest, Jesus the bird.
Mary the artery, Jesus the blood;
Mary the floodgate, Jesus the flood.
Mary and Jesus, our riches untold;
Mary the gold mine, Jesus the gold.

CHRISTMAS TIME

THE NATIVITY OF THE LORD (CHRISTMAS): VIGIL MASS

FIRST READING

Isaiah 62:1–5 _____

For Zion's sake I will not be silent,
    for Jerusalem's sake I will not be quiet,
until her vindication shines forth like the dawn
    and her victory like a burning torch.

Nations shall behold your vindication,
    and all the kings your glory;
you shall be called by a new name
    pronounced by the mouth of the LORD.
You shall be a glorious crown in the hand of the LORD,
    a royal diadem held by your God.
No more shall people call you "Forsaken,"
    or your land "Desolate,"
but you shall be called "My Delight,"
    and your land "Espoused."
For the LORD delights in you
    and makes your land his spouse.
As a young man marries a virgin,
    your Builder shall marry you;
and as a bridegroom rejoices in his bride
    so shall your God rejoice in you.

When I first read this glorious passage, I thought it was the prophet Isaiah speaking and that he was speaking of the nation of Israel ("Zion" and "Jerusalem"), God's "chosen people." A lesson from the past. Then I realized that it was God speaking, and that he was speaking to us, who are also his "chosen people," and that he is speaking in the present. That made the whole passage like an electric shock from a defibrillator to a heart that had been only half alive. What does God think of us? What does he have in store for us? The answer to those questions, from God himself through his prophet in the words of this passage, is almost too amazingly wonderful to believe. But the concrete proof of it is Christmas—Christ's Mass, Christ's Incarnation, Christ himself.

God does not simply speak here; he shouts and sings to get our attention. He cannot be polite and hold himself back: "For Zion's sake I will not be silent, for Jerusalem's sake I will not be quiet." Why?

Because his love is not a mild, proper philanthropy. His passion and persistence will not shut up until the "vindication" of his beloved (us!) "shines forth like the dawn and her victory like a burning torch."

It is "her" victory that he longs for; we are not just his friends or his children but his passionately beloved bride. It is a disastrous fantasy to imagine God's love as something less volcanic than our most powerful sexual passions. The purer love is, the stronger it is. St. Thomas Aquinas says that God's passionate love makes him a "zealot." That is why God cannot, like us, fall in love: he is love. He can no more fall in love than the sea can get wet.

The other side of the coin of theology is always anthropology. Because "God is love," man, made in his image, must become love. This is our destiny: not merely justification and sanctification but also glorification—in fact, a share in the divine glory! What is that glory? The greatest glory of God is his love.

Look at the words the Apostle uses for this glory: when he writes, "Her vindication shines forth like the dawn," the words actually shine forth like the dawn. The words are sacramental: they effect what they signify. They do not merely describe things: they change things; they make a difference. God tells us, "You shall be called by a new name pronounced by the mouth of the

Lord" (see Rev. 2:17). When God makes a new name, he makes a new thing. His words are creative. Our man-made names can only label and describe the old, that which was or is; God's names create new worlds, both without and within, both "new heavens and a new earth" (Isa. 6:17; see Rev. 21:1), and also a new heart—as in Psalm 51:10, where the Psalmist asks God not to merely improve him or reform him but to "create" in him a new heart. He uses the unique Hebrew word *bara*, which always has God as its subject. "Behold, I make all things new," says the Word of God incarnate (Rev. 21:5).

The definitive refutation of the complaint of old Ecclesiastes, that "nothing is new under the sun" (Eccles. 1:9), is Christmas. How is Jesus new? Before he came, there were wars, sufferings, corruption, poverty, disease, and death; and now, two thousand years later, there are still wars, sufferings, corruption, poverty, disease, and death. What did Jesus change? What did he give us that we did not have before? The answer is very simple: he gave us God. He brought God down to earth so that we could go up to heaven.

That is the most amazing thing that ever happened. And the reason he did this, his motive in destining and demanding this new thing in us, our justification and sanctification and glorification, is also amazing: he "delights in" us. God enjoys us! Did you think God was joyless?

And we can contribute to that joy! Do you think we make no difference to him? Christ's definitive name for him is the "Father," and he tells us to call him "Our Father"; do you think any good father could not "rejoice in" the happiness and holiness of his children? Does a good father enjoy his children or not?

And then comes still another amazing revelation: God's plan for us is to be even more than our Father. "Your Builder shall marry you; and as a bridegroom rejoices in his bride so shall your God rejoice in you." "Your husband is your Maker" (Isa. 54:5). God wants—God passionately longs, and thirsts—to marry us, to share his very life, his divine nature, with us. Our first pope, St. Peter, was probably thinking of this passage when he wrote that we are to "come to share in the divine nature" (2 Pet. 1:4).

Truly this is a destiny that "eye has not seen, and ear has not heard, and

. . . has not entered the human heart," for we cannot imagine "what God has prepared for those who love him" (1 Cor. 2:9). If anyone but God ever told us this, we would label him insane or blaspheming. This idea—that God wants to marry us—is either the most Satanic sacrilege and descent into darkness or the summit of divine revelation and light. The one thing it cannot possibly be is boring.

SECOND READING
Acts 13:16–17, 22–25 _____

When Paul reached Antioch in Pisidia and entered the synagogue, he stood up, motioned with his hand, and said, "Fellow Israelites and you others who are God-fearing, listen. The God of this people Israel chose our ancestors and exalted the people during their sojourn in the land of Egypt. With uplifted arm he led them out of it. Then he removed Saul and raised up David as king; of him he testified, 'I have found David, son of Jesse, a man after my own heart; he will carry out my every wish.' From this man's descendants God, according to his promise, has brought to Israel a savior, Jesus. John heralded his coming by proclaiming a baptism of repentance to all the people of Israel; and as John was completing his course, he would say, 'What do you suppose that I am? I am not he. Behold, one is coming after me; I am not worthy to unfasten the sandals of his feet.'"

_____

St. Paul, in this short sermon, summarizes God's long preparation for the coming of the Messiah, by means of "our ancestors" (Abraham, Isaac, Jacob, Joseph), the Exile in Egypt, the miraculous Exodus, King David and the messianic promise to his dynasty, and all the prophets, culminating in John the Baptist. All these nearly two thousand years of preparation were a means to the end of the event we celebrate today, the coming of Jesus Christ, the Messiah, the agent of God's final and definitive work in this world and in the human race, the Savior from sin and death and hell.

Jesus is "what it's all about" from God's point of view, and therefore he must become "what it's all about" from our point of view as well. And that "point of view," if it is true, is simply realism, living in truth, living in the real world, which is the world as God sees it. How radically does that change our lives? As radically as waking up from sleep.

Christianity is a historical religion in the sense that the object of our faith is not a platitude or a principle or an idea but a historical fact, a historical event: Jesus Christ—his birth, life, teaching, Passion, Death, Resurrection, Ascension, and Second Coming. But Christianity is not merely a historical religion based on past events, but it is also a life-transforming religion that alters everything in our present life and world. And it is also a forward-looking religion that puts us on the path to a future glory that is so ecstatic that it is inconceivable and incomprehensible to the capacities of our present human intellect. And yet it is believable and receivable by faith and hope and love for this amazing God, the God of supreme surprises.

GOSPEL
MATTHEW 1:1–25 _____

The book of the genealogy of Jesus Christ, the son of David, the son of Abraham.

Abraham became the father of Isaac, Isaac the father of Jacob, Jacob the father of Judah and his brothers. Judah became the father of Perez and Zerah, whose mother was Tamar. Perez became the father of Hezron, Hezron the father of Ram, Ram the father of Amminadab. Amminadab became the father of Nahshon, Nahshon the father of Salmon, Salmon the father of Boaz, whose mother was Rahab. Boaz became the father of Obed, whose mother was Ruth. Obed became the father of Jesse, Jesse the father of David the king.

David became the father of Solomon, whose mother had been the wife of Uriah. Solomon became the father of Rehoboam, Rehoboam the father of Abijah, Abijah the father of Asaph. Asaph became the father of Jehoshaphat, Jehoshaphat the father of Joram, Joram the father of Uzziah. Uzziah became the father of Jotham, Jotham the father of Ahaz, Ahaz the father of Hezekiah. Hezekiah became the father of Manasseh, Manasseh the father of Amos, Amos the father of Josiah. Josiah became the father of Jechoniah and his brothers at the time of the Babylonian exile.

After the Babylonian exile, Jechoniah became the father of Shealtiel, Shealtiel the father of Zerubbabel, Zerubbabel the father of Abiud. Abiud became the father of Eliakim, Eliakim the father of Azor, Azor the father of Zadok. Zadok became the father of Achim, Achim the father of Eliud, Eliud the father of Eleazar. Eleazar became the father of Matthan, Matthan the father of Jacob, Jacob the father of Joseph, the husband of Mary. Of her was born Jesus who is called the Christ.

Thus the total number of generations from Abraham to David is fourteen generations; from David to the Babylonian exile, fourteen generations; from the Babylonian exile to the Christ, fourteen generations.

Now this is how the birth of Jesus Christ came about. When his mother Mary was betrothed to Joseph, but before they lived together, she was found with child through the Holy Spirit. Joseph her husband, since he was a righteous man, yet unwilling to expose her to shame, decided to divorce her quietly. Such was his intention when, behold, the angel of the Lord appeared to him in a dream and said, "Joseph, son of David, do not be afraid to take Mary your wife into your home. For it is through the Holy Spirit that this child has been conceived in her. She will bear a son and you are to name him Jesus, because he will save his people from their sins." All this took place to fulfill what the Lord had said through the prophet:

Behold, the virgin shall conceive and bear a son,
  and they shall name him Emmanuel,
which means "God is with us."

When Joseph awoke, he did as the angel of the Lord had commanded him and took his wife into his home. He had no relations with her until she bore a son, and he named him Jesus.

The most popular book of the twentieth century, Tolkien's *The Lord of the Rings*, begins with hobbits, a very traditional people, rooted in the earth, who loved mushrooms, simple tools, bright colors, and genealogies—that is, lists of their ancestors. The same was true of other races in this tale about the early days of Middle-earth: elves, dwarves, and men. Tolkien put these lists into the appendix to the long book because he knew readers would be bored by the lists of names. Matthew's Gospel begins with a long genealogy that traces Jesus back to Abraham through forty-two generations. Of all the passages in the Bible, the genealogies probably elicit the least interest and attention from most of us today. But they elicited the most from most of our ancestors. Why?

There is a moving passage from Hemingway's novel about the Spanish Civil War, *For Whom the Bell Tolls*. His protagonist is spiritually exhausted and convinced that the war's passion and propaganda on both sides has eviscerated all meaning from language. He contemplates the names on gravestones in a cemetery and muses that these are the only words that have not lost their meaning: proper names, the names of persons—not abstractions like "causes" or "values" or "rights," but only the concrete individuals who were the dead, the victims of the war.

Why is a list of your ancestors important? Because they were concrete individuals, like you. If any one of your ancestors had not existed, neither would you. Every one of the ancestors of Jesus helped make his Incarnation possible. These names are sacred. *All* names are sacred. Proper names are unique; they are the most precious private property of all, for they name not things or events or abstractions but persons, eternal souls. And they invoke the presence of those persons who own those names. The names of the dead in our cemeteries evoke only a spiritual presence, but when God speaks your name at Judgment Day, you will obey his voice and "come forth" physically, just as Lazarus did.

In his movie *The Gospel According to St. Matthew*, Paolo Pasolini, though he was an atheist who portrayed Jesus as an angry proto-Marxist, got Mary beautifully right. In the first scene described in today's Gospel, Joseph learns that Mary is pregnant, though not by him; and he, "since he was a righteous man, yet unwilling to expose her to shame, decided to divorce her quietly" (i.e., end the solemn engagement that was the promise of marriage). Pasolini shows the gentle sorrow on the face of Mary, standing at the front door as Joseph leaves her house and walks away downward to his own home. But there is also a hint of hope and confidence on her face. (Pasolini was a master of faces, especially their subtleties.) When night falls, we see an unearthly light around Joseph's house. It is the angel Gabriel, the angel of the Annunciation who had announced the coming miracle of the Incarnation to Mary, now announcing the same miracle to Joseph. And because Joseph, like Mary, believed and accepted and obeyed the voice of God, we see Joseph the next morning walking back up the hill to Mary's house. She is still standing in the doorway, and when she sees him, we see that mysterious little Mona Lisa smile appear on her face.

THE NATIVITY OF THE LORD (CHRISTMAS): MASS DURING THE NIGHT

FIRST READING

Isaiah 9:1–6_____

The people who walked in darkness
    have seen a great light;
upon those who dwelt in the land of gloom
    a light has shone.
You have brought them abundant joy
    and great rejoicing,
as they rejoice before you as at the harvest,
    as people make merry when dividing spoils.
For the yoke that burdened them,
    the pole on their shoulder,
and the rod of their taskmaster
    you have smashed, as on the day of Midian.
For every boot that tramped in battle,
    every cloak rolled in blood,
    will be burned as fuel for flames.
For a child is born to us, a son is given us;
    upon his shoulder dominion rests.
They name him Wonder-Counselor, God-Hero,
    Father-Forever, Prince of Peace.
His dominion is vast
    and forever peaceful,
from David's throne, and over his kingdom,

which he confirms and sustains
by judgment and justice,
    both now and forever.
The zeal of the LORD of hosts will do this!

If we look at the details of this passage, we will find not just a vague, comforting, uplifting feeling but definite promises that have a structure and a specificity—and also a surprise.

The passage makes four points: (1) the three things we are oppressed by and need deliverance from, (2) God's surprising response to these needs, (3) the visible results of this divine response, and (4) the cause or force that will bring those results about.

The first thing we all need is the first thing God created: light, the light of truth. For the thing all individuals and all cultures have in common is not light but darkness, the darkness that comes from sin and selfishness, for sin makes us stupid. Isaiah announces that "the people who walked in darkness [which is the whole world] have seen a great light." That light is the man who said, "I am the light of the world" (John 8:12).

The second thing we all need is the joy that comes from that light, to replace the gloom of darkness. So the prophet announces that "upon those who dwelt in the land of gloom a light has shone. You have brought them abundant joy." This second thing, joy, depends on the first thing, truth. For joy in untruth is not true joy.

The third thing we all need is freedom from slavery and oppression, freedom from "the yoke that burdened them." And this yoke is not only external and physical, "the pole on their shoulder, and the rod of the taskmaster," but first of all internal and spiritual. It is the sin and selfishness that invented the pole and the rod and the slavery. It is our addiction to power and control and getting our own way at the expense of others: in other words, sin. Civilization's sinful outer structures, like slavery and tyranny, always come from sinful inner choices. We are enslaved and addicted to our own selfish desires; thus, our Savior must save us not only from others but also from ourselves.

God's response to this sinful demand for power over others is a paradox and a surprise: the birth of a baby, the most vulnerable thing in human life. "Upon his [baby] shoulder dominion rests." And his dominion is "vast and forever peaceful." In this world of human affairs, war is typically stronger than peace, for it is much easier to destroy than to create, to kill than to heal; but his peace, unlike the world's peace, is stronger than war. "Every boot that tramped in battle, every cloak rolled in blood, will be burned" by his peace, because his peace is peace with God and self and neighbor, not with the world, the flesh, and the devil; a peace that embraces poverty, chastity, and obedience rather than greed, lust, and pride. As light is stronger than darkness and as joy is stronger than gloom, so this peace is stronger than war. The baby is stronger than the warrior. The Lamb is stronger than the Beast.

The result is a peace and a justice that the world cannot give. Human nature aspires to peace and justice, but human nature cannot deliver it. Our history never has and never will abolish war and injustice. Visible peace and justice are this-worldly, but their only effective origin is otherworldly, or supernatural. Millennia of history prove that all merely human aspirations for peace and justice have failed and will always fail, because they misidentify the enemy as external and political. They deal with the symptoms, not the disease. The disease is sin, the inherent selfishness of the human heart, which God created and only God can re-create.

Those who sincerely devote themselves to "peace and justice" are not wrong, but as Augustine says, "Seek what you seek, but it is not where you seek it." Where is it to be found, then? Where we least expect it: in the birth of a baby in the poverty of a stable, the chastity of a virgin, and the obedience of a foster father who obeyed God's angel. Only that baby can save us because he alone can change our hearts and therefore our destiny. For he is both human and divine; he is both one with us and one with God; he is both the son of Mary and the Son of God. Only "the zeal of the Lord of hosts will do this" (Isa. 9:6), not human zeal.

SECOND READING

TITUS 2:11–14 _____

Beloved: The grace of God has appeared, saving all and training us to reject godless ways and worldly desires and to live temperately, justly, and devoutly in this age, as we await the blessed hope, the appearance of the glory of our great God and savior Jesus Christ, who gave himself for us to deliver us from all lawlessness and to cleanse for himself a people as his own, eager to do what is good.

We need grace. Grace is defined by three things: it is a free gift, it is undeserved, and it is from God. God's grace is actually the very presence of God among us. The giver is himself the gift.

St. Paul says something startling about this grace: that "the grace of God has appeared." It became very, very concrete, in time and space and matter and history. It appeared to our senses and our bodies, and even designed a sacrament in which we are to eat the Body of the God who gives grace. Grace is not a hope or a dream or an ideal or a value; it is a fact, as concrete as a rock. If you celebrate Christmas, you know his name.

St. Paul also mentions the second coming of this grace of God when he says that "we await the blessed hope, the appearance of the glory of our great God and savior Jesus Christ." Grace will then become glory. On Christmas, he came in poverty and disguise, to suffer and die; when he comes again, he will come in glory and triumph and joy."

And that second coming will be as concrete and visible as the first. Christianity is centered on something that to those who prefer "spirituality" to religion seems embarrassingly and crudely literal: visible historical facts, past and future facts about Jesus Christ in this world, facts that are as concrete as a stone wall. It is this Christ who makes us an offer that is as unavoidable and nonnegotiable and demanding as a marriage proposal. It is a marriage proposal.

If we accept it, St. Paul reminds us how we are to live in the present between

Christ's two comings, one past and one future, and because of both of them—both because of what God has already done and because of what God will do. God's grace is presently "training us to reject godless ways and worldly desires and to live temperately, justly, and devoutly in this age."

In all ages, faith, hope, and love are the three "theological virtues" that glue us to God. The special virtue needed before Christ's first coming was hope, hope for the coming Savior to appear; the special virtue needed now is faith in the God who has appeared; and the perfection of love will be the only one of the three theological virtues that will be needed after his second coming and in eternity.

It's spring training now, and the real season will begin soon. We'd better get busy rehearsing for the show, for "the show must go on."

GOSPEL
LUKE 2:1–14 _____

In those days a decree went out from Caesar Augustus that the whole world should be enrolled. This was the first enrollment, when Quirinius was governor of Syria. So all went to be enrolled, each to his own town. And Joseph too went up from Galilee from the town of Nazareth to Judea, to the city of David that is called Bethlehem, because he was of the house and family of David, to be enrolled with Mary, his betrothed, who was with child. While they were there, the time came for her to have her child, and she gave birth to her firstborn son. She wrapped him in swaddling clothes and laid him in a manger, because there was no room for them in the inn.

Now there were shepherds in that region living in the fields and keeping the night watch over their flock. The angel of the Lord appeared to them and the glory of the Lord shone around them, and they were struck with great fear. The angel said to them, "Do not be afraid; for behold, I proclaim to you good news of great joy that will be for all the people. For today in the city of David a savior has been born for you who is Christ and Lord. And this will be a sign for you:

you will find an infant wrapped in swaddling clothes and lying in a manger." And suddenly there was a multitude of the heavenly host with the angel, praising God and saying:

"Glory to God in the highest

and on earth peace to those on whom his favor rests."

In the familiar and beloved hymn "O Little Town of Bethlehem," we address the town itself when we sing, "The hopes and fears of all the years are met in thee tonight." In this poor, humble, ordinary place, our hope of heaven was born on earth.

God chose Bethlehem for two very specific reasons, as St. Thomas Aquinas notes. First, it was "the city of David," the town David was born in, and the prophets had promised that the Messiah would be "of the house and family of David" (Luke 2:4). Second, the word "Bethlehem" means literally "house of bread," and Christ was to be our bread of life, of eternal life, in the Eucharist. He himself said, "I am the living bread that came down from heaven; whoever eats this bread will live forever; and the bread that I will give is my flesh for the life of the world" (John 6:51).

The most striking thing about today's familiar Gospel passage is so big and obvious that we might miss it, like the names of the continents on a map when we are squinting at the cities. It is the contrast between the first paragraph and the second. It is the contrast between how the event looked from the perspective of earthly eyes and how it looked from the perspective of heaven.

The first paragraph is about the earthly appearance of the most incredible thing that ever happened, the birth of God. Everything about it seemed to go wrong. The tyrant Caesar demanded that everyone in the empire be enrolled in his empire-wide census, so Joseph and Mary, who was nine months pregnant, had to make a long, hard journey on foot from Nazareth to Bethlehem. No one traveled for "vacationing" in those days, especially the poor. When they got there, the baby was about to be born, most inconveniently. But the inn was full, so Mary had to give birth outdoors in a stable, probably a cow barn, and put the baby in a manger, which was a feeding trough for animals. I used to live half a block from a cow barn when I was a kid. I remember smelling it at night when the wind was up. That's one reason why they wrapped Jesus tight in swaddling clothes: so he wouldn't play with cow pies. That was his maternity ward.

And then, in the second paragraph, heaven opens up and "the angel of the Lord" appears to poor shepherds working the night shift, and with the angel appears the *shekinah*, that unique unearthly light which is "the glory of the Lord" himself. The shepherds' reaction was not comfortable smiles; it was "great fear." Then comes the Gospel, the Good News, the angel's words, heaven's "Fear not." And then many, many more angels drop down through a hole in the sky like shooting stars, echoing the first angel's solo in earth-shattering choruses of glory that would make our greatest operas and symphonies sound like a kid's kazoo by comparison.

Every baby's birth is a little like that. Two stages. First, the exhaustion, the pain, the strain—and then comes something with a "Made in Heaven" label on its tiny tush, like the small angel announcing the greatest news, the greatest event that ever happened. It's not a new regime or a new emperor or even a new world, but something much greater: a new image of God, destined for unspeakable ecstasy forever, long after all merely mortal things like nations and empires and civilizations and worlds die.

A similar contrast would characterize Christ's final accomplishment of what he came to this earth for, on Calvary. What happened there appeared to earthly eyes to be simply horror: blood and gore, torture, agony, failure, loss, and death. Yet that was heaven's triumph over hell, over sin, and over death forever. We dare to call that Friday "Good."

THE NATIVITY OF THE LORD
(CHRISTMAS):
MASS AT DAWN

FIRST READING

Isaiah 62:11–12 _____

See, the LORD proclaims
  to the ends of the earth:
say to daughter Zion,
  your savior comes!
Here is his reward with him,
  his recompense before him.
They shall be called the holy people,
  the redeemed of the LORD,
and you shall be called "Frequented,"
  a city that is not forsaken.

_____

There are two important words in this short passage that we may overlook. They are the two imperatives, the two commands: "see" and "say." "See, the Lord proclaims to the ends of the earth: say to daughter Zion, your savior comes!"

In times like ours, times of fear of domestic terrorism and gun violence, we are told by the custodians of our safety, "If you see something, say something." In times of grace and glory and joy we are told the same thing.

Railroad crossings without gates used to have this sign on them: "Stop, look, and listen." Seeing and hearing, looking and listening, are the two senses we depend on the most. Many other people depend on what we see and hear; this is why we should speak. And before we speak, we should look and listen.

But in order to look and listen, we must first stop. It is in silence that we hear, and this is true for supernatural things as well as natural things. Do we do most of the talking when we pray, or do we stop all other concerns and look at God and listen and open our hearts and minds to God, even though he usually speaks in whispers?

Because we live in communities, and first of all in families, life is like a relay race. We pass on the baton of life that we received from our parents. Because we cannot repay our debt to our parents—life itself—we "pay it forward" to our children. Our job here is to pass on all that we have received to others. And this, too, is true of supernatural graces just as it is of natural gifts. Receiving it is called faith in divine revelation—that is, Sacred Scripture and Sacred Tradition—and passing it on is called evangelization, which is done by deeds of love and words of wisdom, as well as deeds of wisdom and words of love.

What is the message the prophet Isaiah sees and says in this passage? It is Christ, barging into history: "Your Savior comes!" And what does he bring? What is his "reward with him" and his "recompense before him?" Two things: first, that "you shall be called 'Frequented' [RSV: 'Sought out']," not "forsaken," and therefore, second, that "they shall be called the holy people." God will make us holy, will make us saints, will sanctify us by the gift of his Holy Spirit because he has sought us out and saved us, justified us, by the gift of his Son. He has justified us in order to sanctify us. God never gives up on us. Thus, St. Paul writes, "I am confident of this, that the one who began a good work in you will continue to complete it" (Phil. 1:6).

These two reasons, justification and sanctification, explain each other. On the one hand, we will be holy not by our own efforts but only because we have been "frequented" and "sought out" rather than "forsaken" by God, the God who demands and promises that "you shall make and keep yourselves holy, because I am holy" (Lev. 11:44). And on the other hand, we have been frequented and sought out by God only because we are to be his children, the children of the Holy One, and are destined to reign as kings in holiness and glory.

SECOND READING

Titus 4:3–7 _____

Beloved: When the kindness and generous love of God our savior appeared, not because of any righteous deeds we had done but because of his mercy, he saved us through the bath of rebirth and renewal by the Holy Spirit, whom he richly poured out on us through Jesus Christ our savior, so that we might be justified by his grace and become heirs in hope of eternal life.

What is the essential meaning of Christmas? It's all here in this very short passage.

When St. Paul writes, "When the kindness and generous love of God our savior appeared," what does he mean by "appeared"? He means appeared to our senses, to our bodies. He means the Incarnation, the coming of Christ. The kindness and love of God is an eternal truth, but its appearance in Christ is a catastrophic event that changed everything.

What brought him down? Was it our "righteous deeds"? No, St. Paul says he "appeared not because of any righteous deeds we had done but because of his mercy." Christ is the incarnation of God's mercy.

How did he get into us? How did we obtain a new heart, "renewal by the Holy Spirit"? Because the Spirit is, as St. Paul says, the one "whom he richly poured out on us through Jesus Christ our savior." It is Christ who sends the Spirit to complete our sanctification.

Notice, incidentally, that the Spirit is not a "which" but a "whom," a divine person, not a "Force," as in *Star Wars*. Thus, elsewhere St. Paul says, "Do not grieve the holy Spirit of God" (Eph. 4:30). You can't grieve a force, only a person.

What was God's purpose and end and goal in sending his Son and his Spirit here? "So that we might be justified by his grace and become heirs in hope of eternal life." It is Christ who saves us by both justifying us, by his cross, in the past, and sanctifying us, by his Spirit, in the present, and glorifying us, at his Second Coming, in the future.

Christ is literally everything for us. That is why Christmas is our favorite holiday. Our Mass is our participation in Christ's Mass, our life is our participation in Christ's life, our joys are our participation in Christ's joys, our sufferings are our participation in Christ's sufferings, and our glory is our participation in Christ's glory.

GOSPEL
LUKE 2:15–20 _____

When the angels went away from them to heaven, the shepherds said to one another, "Let us go, then, to Bethlehem to see this thing that has taken place, which the Lord has made known to us." So they went in haste and found Mary and Joseph, and the infant lying in the manger. When they saw this, they made known the message that had been told them about this child. All who heard it were amazed by what had been told them by the shepherds. And Mary kept all these things, reflecting on them in her heart. Then the shepherds returned, glorifying and praising God for all they had heard and seen, just as it had been told to them.

God is incomparably and inexpressibly strange! As his greatest poet said, "He has cast down the mighty from their thrones, and has lifted up the lowly. He has filled the hungry with good things, and the rich he has sent empty away" (Luke 1:52–53). For God, the greatest earthly darkness is only an opportunity for a far greater heavenly light. "Where sin increased, grace overflowed all the more" (Rom. 5:20).

Look at all the movement words in today's Gospel. We move our bodies to go where we want our souls to go: nearer to those we love. The angels had come from heaven to earth to sing of the glory of Christ's Incarnation to the shepherds, and, through them, to the whole world, and to us. That was quite a distance to move through: much farther than the next galaxy.

The first verse of today's passage says, "When the angels went away from them to heaven, the shepherds said to one another, 'Let us go, then, to Bethlehem.'" The horizontal travel of the shepherds was their response to the vertical travel of the angels.

Ours must be the same. We, too, must go in spirit to Bethlehem, "the house of bread," to see and eat "the living bread that came down from heaven" (John 6:51).

The passage continues, "So they went in haste, and found Mary and Joseph and the infant." We, too, must go in haste, not the haste of worry but the haste of passion and love. And if we do, we, too, will find Christ. All who seek him will find him. He promised that.

And when we find him, we will also find, with him, surrounding him, his mother Mary, whom he left to us as *our* mother just before he died on the cross. And we will also find his foster father St. Joseph, to be our model of fatherhood as Mary is our model of motherhood.

Christmas is the time for generous gifts, and God gave us not only the most generous of all gifts, his own divine Son, but also our two primary parental models in Mary and Joseph. It is not polite to ignore great gifts!

What happens next? When the shepherds saw Jesus and Mary and Joseph, "they made known the message that had been told them about this child." They went out and evangelized. And we must follow this travel directive too; we must spread the good infection. We, too, must be angels (the word means "messengers"), for most of the people in our post-Christian culture have no idea how new and how newsworthy this message is.

Mary is the only one in the story who does not travel. The passage says, "Mary kept all these things, reflecting on them in her heart." (The Greek word is actually stronger and more active than "reflecting"; it is "pondering." Mirrors can reflect, but only persons can ponder.) Mary stays at home because her home is wherever Christ is, and now Christ is confined to swaddling clothes and a manger, a feeding trough for animals. Later, Mary will travel with Christ to the cross, and she will eventually be taken up to heaven to be with him and with his intercessory work there forever.

The passage concludes, "Then the shepherds returned, glorifying and praising God." We, too, now travel once more: we, too, return to our daily work, whatever it is, whether sheep or cars or daycare or insurance policies, but we can never forget the new light of heavenly glory that now shines over our whole world. Only the eye of faith can see that light. But it is really there. The light is Christ himself, the one who said, "I am the light of the world" (John 8:12). Though really, truly, personally, and fully present here in the Eucharist, he now *hides* behind the appearances of bread and wine. And he continues to hide in a different way, in the souls of his people, who look so ordinary. But no one can be merely ordinary anymore, now that God has been born not only among us but also in us.

THE NATIVITY OF THE LORD (CHRISTMAS): MASS DURING THE DAY

FIRST READING

Isaiah 52:7–10

How beautiful upon the mountains
    are the feet of him who brings glad tidings,
announcing peace, bearing good news,
    announcing salvation, and saying to Zion,
    "Your God is King!"

Hark! Your sentinels raise a cry,
    together they shout for joy,
for they see directly, before their eyes,
    the LORD restoring Zion.
Break out together in song,
    O ruins of Jerusalem!
For the LORD comforts his people,
    he redeems Jerusalem.
The LORD has bared his holy arm
    in the sight of all the nations;
all the ends of the earth will behold
    the salvation of our God.

When the prophet Isaiah wrote these beautiful words, he could not possibly have seen the coming of Christ specifically and clearly and concretely, as we have done. Absolutely no one expected what happened when Christ came: not good people, not evil people, not believers, not unbelievers, not Jews, not Gentiles, not the angels, not the demons. These beautiful messianic prophetic promises were accepted by faith, a faith that saw only "indistinctly, as in a mirror" (1 Cor. 13:12), as through a foggy telescope. But we who have seen the fulfillment of this prophecy in Christ now understand it with a concreteness and literalness that would have amazed, stunned, and shocked Isaiah.

Isaiah, like all religious Jews, knew the truth that he announced, that "your God is King," King of the universe. But he could not have known that God the King would become a man, and not only a man but a tortured, unjustly convicted, and crucified criminal. How could the eternal God be born in time? How could the Creator of all life die?

So what did Isaiah mean when he wrote, "Your sentinels raise a cry, together they shout for joy, for they see directly, before their eyes, the Lord restoring Zion"? He is predicting something visible, and he knows that it is from the invisible God and for God's visible people, but when he speaks of the Lord "restoring Zion" he probably means restoring the political glory and success of David and Solomon's kingdom, which were now lost in the remote past to Isaiah's time.

But the true meaning of this good news, though it was indeed visible and literal, was not any political or military or even moral revolution. God did not "restore Zion" simply by repeating the good things of the past, but by a deed so much newer and greater that the "restoration" was a new creation and the Zion restored was not just Israel but the whole of humanity.

Why was this prophecy to be interpreted literally? Because it specifically says it is visible, not invisible. "Literal" usually means "physical and visible." So the simplest way to tell whether something is to be interpreted literally or symbolically is whether you can see it. Eyewitness descriptions are literal.

So when Isaiah wrote that "all the ends of the earth will behold the salvation of our God," he probably thought of a visible kingship, but certainly not of a king who was both God and man, and who reigned from the throne of a cross by giving us his sacred body and blood. God had surprises in store that never entered into the heart of man. As Isaiah prophesied elsewhere, "From now on I announce new things to you, hidden events you never knew. Now, not from of old, they are created, before today you did not hear of them, so that you cannot claim, 'I have known them.' You never heard, you never knew, they never reached your ears beforehand" (Isa. 48:6–8).

And he still has more surprises in store for us. He has more, always more, infinitely more, for he is infinite goodness and infinite wisdom. One thing we can be quite certain about regarding heaven: it will not be boring or predictable.

SECOND READING
Hebrews 1:1–6 _____

Brothers and sisters: In times past, God spoke in partial and various ways to our ancestors through the prophets; in these last days, he has spoken to us through the Son, whom he made heir of all things and through whom he created the universe, who is the refulgence of his glory, the very imprint of his being, and who sustains all things by his mighty word. When he had accomplished purification from sins, he took his seat at the right hand of the Majesty on high, as far superior to the angels as the name he has inherited is more excellent than theirs.

For to which of the angels did God ever say:
You are my son;
this day I have begotten you?
Or again:
I will be a father to him,
and he shall be a son to me?
And again, when he leads the firstborn into the world, he says:
Let all the angels of God worship him.

Of all the epistles, Hebrews is the most comprehensive and systematic. Its central point is the same as that of all the other books of the Bible, Old Testament as well as New: namely, Jesus Christ as the Alpha and Omega of the whole creation, as Christ himself labels himself in Revelation, the last book of the Bible.

There are ten basic points made in today's epistle, in the introduction to the book by its anonymous author (who may have been, but probably was not, St. Paul):

1. Christ is the fulfillment of all the many "partial and various" ways in which God "spoke . . . to our ancestors through the prophets." The completest interpretation of all these words (in the plural) that God "spoke" (that is, revealed) in former times is in Christ, the divine person who is the (singular) Word of God incarnate. Just as the New Testament is fully understood only in terms of the Old, as the fulfillment of the Old, so the Old Testament is fully understood only in terms of the New, in terms of Jesus Christ.

   This is why Jews who become Christians do not leave one religion for another but find themselves as "completed Jews," as more Jewish, not less. It is also why Christians cannot confine their telling of the Good News of the Gospel only to the rest of the world but not to the Jews. That would be truly not only discrimination but anti-Semitism.

2. This final and complete revelation of God, Jesus Christ, is not only God's Word but also God's "Son," co-eternal and co-divine, "God from God, Light from Light, true God from true God . . . consubstantial [that is, one in being] with the Father."

3. Christ is also the one "whom he [God] made heir of all things." He is the Omega, the final end and good and purpose and point and meaning and fulfillment, not just of religion or morality or spirituality but of "all things." What does that mean? "All" means all! Jesus Christ is the ultimate meaning and end and goal and point and perfection and fulfillment of every grain of sand on earth and of every galaxy in the universe and every photon of light and every subatomic particle in all the galaxies.

4. He is the Alpha as well as the Omega, the absolute beginning as well as the absolute end, for he is the one "through whom he [God] created the universe." Genesis 1 tells us that God created by speaking his Word: "And God said . . . and it was." Christ, the final cause or end, is also the efficient cause or beginning, of all things, all matter and all spirits, "all things visible and invisible."

5. Christ is "the refulgence of his [God the Father's] glory." "Refulgence" means more than simply "reflection." It includes glory, a kind of overplus of being, a "shine." God not only exists but "shines" in Christ. Alas, our gray culture has such low ideals and aspirations that it almost never uses those words. It never speaks of "glory" because it seldom sees it or thinks of it or hopes for it. Its lightweight shoulders cannot bear the "weight of glory" (2 Cor. 4:17) that is Christ. Its image of Christ has been thinned out from "the meaning of the whole universe" and "the glory of God" to "Mister Nice Guy" or "Super Social Worker," or even Ned Flanders on *The Simpsons*. The brightness of the colors on our stained-glass windows have been blurred into beige. No wonder our young people simply "drift away" from their faith. No one who met Jesus Christ ever simply "drifted away" from him. You don't "drift away" from a tsunami.

6. Christ is also "the very imprint of his [the Father's] being." For "in him all the fullness of God was pleased to dwell" (Col. 1:19). Once you know Jesus, you know everything, every goodness, truth, and beauty that there is anywhere. There is no more in God the Father than there is in God the Son. When Philip said to Christ, "Show us the Father and we shall be satisfied," Jesus replied, "Have I been with you for so long a time and you still do not know me, Philip? Whoever has seen me has seen the Father" (John 14:8–9).

7. He "sustains all things by his mighty word." That word not only created the universe 13.7 billion years ago, but even now continues to utter the command to all things to "be." If God withdrew that command, that word, all things would cease to exist.

That is why the being of all things is holy: because God is the one who wills them to be. It is not only stupid but sacrilegious to misuse anything in creation. What makes that misuse sacrilegious is the holiness of nature—of the energy in the atom, of the human body, of the energy in our sex drives, and above all of our free will, all of which are willed to be and held in being by their Creator at every moment. The existence of all things, not just in general but in particular, in each individual entity from atoms to archangels, is a finite participation in the infinite power of existence that is God himself.

Because God is in all things, all things are holy, not only in their effects or their appearances or their properties but down to their very existence.

8.   Christ the Co-Creator is also the Redeemer. When Christ said, on the cross, "It is finished" (John 19:30), "he had accomplished purification from sins." The only thing that can separate anything from God is not death or suffering but sin, and Christ conquered sin. The Lamb of God "took away" the sins of the world.

9.   And in his triumphant Ascension, "he took his seat at the right hand of the Majesty on high." His last words to us were, "All authority in heaven and on earth has been given to me" (Matt. 28:18). He is Christ the King. It is prudent to protect ourselves from the finite, fallible, fallen, and often foolish authority of kings in earthly politics by preferring democracy. But to try to protect ourselves from the authority of Christ the King, and from his Mystical Body, the Church that he authorized to teach in his name and with his authority; to try to contracept his regenerative work in our souls—this is worse than imprudent. It is fatal.

10.   Finally, the point the author of this letter goes on to make in detail is that Christ is infinitely superior even to the angels, who themselves are as immensely superior to us in intelligence and power as we are to newborn kittens. That is why, in Scripture, when angels appear to men, they experience fear and trembling and are often tempted to worship them. And the angels always have to say not only "fear not" but also "worship

God alone." Christ is God. They are his angels. Thus, the author of the epistle says, "Let all the angels of God worship him."

GOSPEL
JOHN 1:1–18 _____

In the beginning was the Word,
    and the Word was with God,
    and the Word was God.
He was in the beginning with God.
All things came to be through him,
    and without him nothing came to be.
What came to be through him was life,
    and this life was the light of the human race;
the light shines in the darkness,
    and the darkness has not overcome it.

A man named John was sent from God. He came for testimony, to testify to the light, so that all might believe through him. He was not the light, but came to testify to the light. The true light, which enlightens everyone, was coming into the world.

He was in the world,
    and the world came to be through him,
    but the world did not know him.
He came to what was his own,
    but his own people did not accept him.

But to those who did accept him he gave power to become children of God, to those who believe in his name, who were born not by natural generation nor by human choice nor by a man's decision but of God.

And the Word became flesh
and made his dwelling among us,
and we saw his glory,
the glory as of the Father's only Son,
full of grace and truth.

John testified to him and cried out, saying, "This was he of whom I said, 'The one who is coming after me ranks ahead of me because he existed before me.'" From his fullness we have all received, grace in place of grace, because while the law was given through Moses, grace and truth came through Jesus Christ. No one has ever seen God. The only Son, God, who is at the Father's side, has revealed him.

Today's Gospel contains the profoundest words ever written. It is the story of the greatest miracle that ever happened, the Incarnation, when God became man, the Good News of the Gospel, the event that changed the meaning of everything.

The story had been told from earth's point of view in the other three Gospels. Here, St. John tells the story from God's point of view, from heaven's point of view.

That same device had been used in Genesis to tell the story of God creating the world. Chapter 1 tells the story from the Creator's point of view, and chapter 2 tells the same story from the creation's point of view, from man's point of view.

That device was also used in the book of Job. The first and last chapters tell the story from God's point of view, framing it, so to speak. The middle chapters tell the story from Job's point of view. The drama of the story is vertical, not horizontal: it is the contrast between the two points of view. And that was God's answer to Job in the end: that he did not have the divine point of view.

The same device was used in pagan literature, which often mingles and contrasts the two points of view, that of the gods and that of men, as in Sophocles'

Oedipus the King, in Homer's *Iliad*, and in Vergil's *Aeneid*. Of course, the divine point of view in pagan literature was only human guesswork, riddled with fallacies, fables, and follies—man's word about God rather than God's word about man.

That's what Christ is: God's word about man, God's divine word about who man is and who God is. These two things are the two things we need to know the most. St. Augustine composed a series of imagined dialogues between God and himself, in which God asks him what he wants to know, and Augustine replies, "Only two things: who you are and who I am." God asks, "Nothing more?" and Augustine replies, "Nothing more." For those are the two persons we most need to know, since we will never be able to escape either one of them for a single second, either in time or in eternity. And to both of those questions, Jesus Christ is the only adequate and total and final and definitive and infallible and perfect and absolute answer.

FEAST OF THE HOLY FAMILY OF JESUS, MARY, AND JOSEPH

FIRST READING
Sirach 3:2–6, 12–14

God sets a father in honor over his children; a mother's authority he confirms over her sons. Whoever honors his father atones for sins, and preserves himself from them. When he prays, he is heard; he stores up riches who reveres his mother. Whoever honors his father is gladdened by children, and, when he prays, is heard. Whoever reveres his father will live a long life; he who obeys his father brings comfort to his mother.

My son, take care of your father when he is old; grieve him not as long as he lives. Even if his mind fail, be considerate of him; revile him not all the days of his life; kindness to a father will not be forgotten, firmly planted against the debt of your sins—a house raised in justice to you.

The Decalogue, or Ten Commandments, is divided into three commandments about our relation to God and seven about our relation to each other. As the first commandment in the first half is to worship God alone, the first commandment of the second half of the Decalogue is "Honor your father and mother." The Latin word for "piety," *pietas*, means both reverence to God and reverence to parents and ancestors. The two always go together in every culture in history, and so does their absence.

St. Paul notes that "this is the first commandment with a promise" (Eph. 6:2). The promise has been fulfilled throughout human history. For the primary cause of the happiness, peace, and longevity of a society, throughout history, has been the divinely invented and authorized institution of the family. The five most stable, lasting, and successful cultures in history all had great respect for the family: Jewish, Confucian, Roman, Christian, and Islamic. The devil could not have picked a more crucial institution to attack in our day and our culture.

In our Old Testament reading for today, Sirach the sage reminds us that it is God who "sets a father over his children, a mother's authority over her sons." That is why "whoever honors his father atones for sins" and "he stores up [supernatural] riches who reveres his mother."

"Authority" and "obedience" are correlative. Both words are unfashionable today; yet no society can survive or thrive without the reality they properly designate. "Authority" is not the same as power; it is not that "right makes might." Authority is the might of right, not the right of might. And obedience to authentic authority is not demeaning but fulfilling, not oppressive but liberating, and not blind but wise. All authority comes ultimately from God, and God is not a tyrant but a loving and merciful Father.

Submission and obedience to him and therefore also to those that he has set in authority over us, especially parents in the family and rulers in the state ("Let every person be subordinate to the higher authorities" [Rom. 13:1]), is *sub-missio*, which means literally coming "under the mission" of those whom God has set in authority. We must respect their divine mission even if we do not like the persons who are entrusted with that mission. As they say in the army, you salute the uniform, not the man.

We are to submit to their mission, which is their submission. They are set over us only because they have been set under God and because they themselves are "under" their "mission," under higher authority. It's like the centurion in Matthew 8:8–9: he had authority over one hundred soldiers because he was under the authority of Caesar, and when his soldiers heard him they heard Caesar, Lord of the world. And this centurion asked Jesus to restore his dying servant because he recognized that Jesus had authority over death itself because he was under the authority of his Father, who was the Lord of life. God himself submits to the authority of his Father; how can we do less?

Not only in the natural order of human history but also in the supernatural order of the Last Judgment, obedience to the commandment to honor parents counts for many merits and offsets many demerits. Not only human societies in this world but also human souls in the next reap great benefits from our obedience to this commandment of respecting parents (and grandparents, and whatever is good in one's ancestry and tradition). Thus, Sirach says that "whoever honors his father atones for sins" and that this honor "will be firmly planted against the debt of your sins—a house raised in justice to you." Everything counts. Nothing in this world is forgotten in the next.

These missions and duties are different but reciprocal between parents and children, husbands and wives, citizens and rulers. Sirach mentions three duties of children to parents: honor, kindness, and care, especially in old age. Although we still respect kindness and care, "honor" is a word conspicuously missing from our vocabulary and therefore from our life. For words are the places where ideas live, and if an important word disappears from our vocabulary, that means it disappears from our minds. Honor today seems to have devolved into "fame" or "number of likes on social media." How can we give our parents honor if we no longer know what it means? Only in the Deep South and in the military do we even hear honoring phrases like "Yes, ma'am" or "No, sir." As we speak, so we think, and as we think, so we live. That's also why the second commandment is about language: not to take the name of the Lord in vain.

SECOND READING
COLOSSIANS 3:12–21
(OR COLOSSIANS 3:12-17) _____

Brothers and sisters: Put on, as God's chosen ones, holy and beloved, heartfelt compassion, kindness, humility, gentleness, and patience, bearing with one another and forgiving one another, if one has a grievance against another; as the Lord has forgiven you, so must you also do. And over all these put on love, that is, the bond of perfection. And let the peace of Christ control your hearts, the peace into which you were also called in one body. And be thankful. Let the word of Christ dwell in you richly, as in all wisdom you teach and admonish one another, singing psalms, hymns, and spiritual songs with gratitude in your hearts to God. And whatever you do, in word or in deed, do everything in the name of the Lord Jesus, giving thanks to God the Father through him.

Wives, be subordinate to your husbands, as is proper in the Lord. Husbands, love your wives, and avoid any bitterness toward them. Children, obey your parents in everything, for this is pleasing to the Lord. Fathers, do not provoke your children, so they may not become discouraged.

In the first paragraph of this reading, St. Paul exhorts us to practice thirteen important virtues that are perhaps the least controversial virtues in our world today, at least in thought and theory, though not in practice, which is more demanding: compassion, kindness, humility, gentleness, patience, tolerance, forgiveness, love, peace, unity, thanksgiving, wisdom, and gratitude. Although many other virtues, such as chastity, courage, honesty, and honor (we may call them the "hard virtues") may be drying up today, these thirteen (we may call them the "soft virtues") are still spoken of highly.

So we like this paragraph. But then when we read the next paragraph, we become embarrassed or even angry. In fact, the next paragraph has been dropped entirely from the optional "short form" of this epistle because it is probably the most controversial and hated passage in the entire Bible today because it is so misunderstood. (Perhaps it is not only hated because it is misunderstood but also misunderstood because it is hated; for hate always blinds our eyes, as love opens them.) It exhorts wives to be subject, or submissive, or subordinate, to their husbands. To many or most Catholics today, this feels similar to a call for the restoration of the Spanish Inquisition or the burning of witches.

Those who feel this way forget at least six things in St. Paul's writings.

First of all, St. Paul also exhorts husbands and wives to "be subordinate to one another out of reverence for Christ" (Eph. 5:21); and, as Pope St. John

Paul II has reminded us, the command to wives to submit is half of, and must be interpreted in the context of, St. Paul's more universal and generic command to both husbands and wives to submit, surrender, and be subject to each other. Husbands must respect, listen to, and surrender to the wisdom of their wives just as wives must respect, listen to, and surrender to the wisdom of their husbands. God designed men and women to learn from each other, not to boss each other around.

Second, this is not addressed to all men and women but only to husbands and wives. It is not because she is a woman but because she is married to her husband that she must surrender to him, not to all men; and it is because he is married to his wife that he must surrender to her, not to all women. Their authority over each other comes from the institution of marriage, not merely from their gender.

Third, the husband has his own reciprocal duty to love and respect his wife, and love excludes all oppression, force, and tyranny. In fact, this love the husband is told to give to his wife is even more demanding than the love the wife is told to give to her husband, for in Ephesians 5:25, St. Paul says he must love her *as Christ loved the Church*, who is his Bride. What kind of love is that? What did Christ do for his Bride? He gave himself up for her. He gave his whole self for her. He sacrificed himself. He died for his Bride. If the husband is a kind of king, it is a Christlike kingship, and his crown is a crown of thorns, not of gold.

There are two possible motives for getting married: to get happiness or to give it. If the motive of either or both is to get it rather than to give it, the odds are that the marriage will fail. If the motive of both is to give it, it will almost certainly succeed.

Fourth, the wife's task is "submission," but this means literally "sub" (under) the "mission" of her husband. What mission is that? It is described in the above two paragraphs.

Fifth, it is true that St. Paul also says that the husband is the "head" of the wife (Eph. 5:23) and not vice versa, but in what sense? What does that headship mean? His answer is "as Christ is the head of the Church, his body." We are his Body, and he died for us. The head exists for the body. Only a seriously deranged "head" sees himself outside his body, manipulating it like a machine. As St. Paul goes on to say: "He who loves his wife loves himself. For no one hates his own flesh" (Eph. 5:28–29).

Sixth, and most simply, the rule that colors everything else is "Whatever you do, in word or in deed, do everything in the name of the Lord Jesus." No one, husband or wife, man or woman, can oppress or abuse (or use rather than love) another in the name of Jesus. Surrender to him is the secret of the highest human happiness.

GOSPEL
Luke 2:22–40
(or Luke 2:22, 39–40) _____

When the days were completed for their purification according to the law of Moses, they took him up to Jerusalem to present him to the Lord, just as it is written in the law of the Lord,

Every male that opens the womb shall be consecrated to the Lord,
and to offer the sacrifice of
a pair of turtledoves or two young pigeons,
in accordance with the dictate in the law of the Lord.

Now there was a man in Jerusalem whose name was Simeon. This man was righteous and devout, awaiting the consolation of Israel, and the Holy Spirit was upon him. It had been revealed to him by the Holy Spirit that he should not see death before he had seen the Christ of the Lord. He came in the Spirit into the temple; and when the parents brought in the child Jesus to perform the custom of the law in regard to him, he took him into his arms and blessed God, saying: "Now, Master, you may let your servant go in peace, according to your word, for my eyes have seen your salvation, which you prepared in sight of all the peoples, a light for revelation to the Gentiles, and glory for your people

Israel." The child's father and mother were amazed at what was said about him; and Simeon blessed them and said to Mary his mother, "Behold, this child is destined for the fall and rise of many in Israel, and to be a sign that will be contradicted—and you yourself a sword will pierce—so that the thoughts of many hearts may be revealed." There was also a prophetess, Anna, the daughter of Phanuel, of the tribe of Asher. She was advanced in years, having lived seven years with her husband after her marriage, and then as a widow until she was eighty-four. She never left the temple, but worshiped night and day with fasting and prayer. And coming forward at that very time, she gave thanks to God and spoke about the child to all who were awaiting the redemption of Jerusalem.

When they had fulfilled all the prescriptions of the law of the Lord, they returned to Galilee, to their own town of Nazareth. The child grew and became strong, filled with wisdom; and the favor of God was upon him.

Today's Gospel is the Fourth Joyful Mystery of the Rosary, the Presentation in the Temple. Scripture tells us almost nothing about Jesus' life between this event and the next mystery of the Rosary, the Finding in the Temple at the age of twelve when Jesus was lost to his parents for three days (the Fifth Joyful Mystery of the Rosary). After Luke narrates that event, he tells us the only thing we know about Jesus' life until the beginning of his public ministry at age thirty, his baptism in the Jordan by John the Baptist, the first of the five Luminous Mysteries of the Rosary. Luke summarizes those eighteen silent years with a single sentence: "Jesus advanced in wisdom and age and favor before God and man" (Luke 2:52).

Six points stand out for our consideration and profit.

First, Mary and Joseph obeyed the law of God in presenting their baby in the temple. They do not contrast their spirituality with "organized religion," as so many do today. In fact, they do not separate those two things; they identify them. Their obedience to God is both private and public because it is the same God who demands both. And they teach their son this double obedience too; that is why Jesus is so attracted to the temple. He is obedient both to them, in the Holy Family, and to God the Father, in the eternal family of the Trinity. Religious piety and family piety always stand together or fall together. In fact, in most ancient languages the very same word, the word translated "piety," refers to both. It is literally true that "the family that prays together stays together," as Fr. Peyton's famous slogan says.

A second point is that, in presenting her child to God in the temple, Mary was giving God permission to take Jesus from her and give him to us by his Crucifixion. Our Father in heaven and our spiritual mother on earth both gave up their only son for our salvation. Mary in the temple repeated to God her *fiat*, her "yes," her "May it be done to me according to your word and according to your will, not mine," the "yes" that she had said to God's angel nine months earlier, the "yes" that brought about the Incarnation and our hope of salvation. Both Christ's Father and his mother, both his divine parent and his human parent, freely gave him up to us.

No person, human or divine, ever loved any other person, human or divine, more than God the Father loves God the Son, yet he sacrificed him for our salvation. But our mother in heaven also sacrificed her son for us, when she presented him in the temple, and no human person ever loved any other person more than Mary loved Jesus.

A third point: God arranged for Mary and Joseph to find Jesus in the temple twelve years later after they had lost him for three days. They got him back in the temple because twelve years earlier, in today's Gospel, the Fourth Joyful Mystery of the Rosary, the Presentation, they had given him up to God's care in the temple. God's Church, the true Temple, is like a spiritual bank where we invest our true wealth, which of course is far greater than money or anything money can buy. It is the First Supernatural Bank and Trust Company, and God invites us to trust our whole fortune there, everything we have both in time and in eternity, and he always gives back our deposits with infinitely compounded interest.

A fourth point is about the two prophets that Mary and Joseph met in the temple, Simeon and Anna. God prepared many prophets, all of whom were forthtellers and some of whom were foretellers, to prepare the way for Christ. The Old Testament prophets were the first ones, and John the Baptist was the last one; Simeon and Anna were doing the same thing as John the Baptist in a different way. God not only does all things well but also patiently and prudently prepares them well, like a good artist. No person in history fulfilled more prophecies than Jesus.

A fifth point is about Simeon's prophecy. It says the same thing about God that Mary's "Magnificat" had said to her cousin Elizabeth at the Visitation (the Second Joyful Mystery of the Rosary): that God lays low the proud and raises up the humble and the fallen; that God turns us upside down and reorders our lives. Simeon says that this child is destined for the rise and fall of many, and that he will be "a sign that will be contradicted," hated and feared as well as loved. More than anything else in history, Christianity has always produced not only the most saints but also the most martyrs. Like Christ himself, Christ's Church has provoked the world both to love it and to hate it more than anything else in the world.

A sixth point: Simeon prophesies that Mary's soul will be pierced with a sword, that she will share Christ's sorrows. The traditional "seven sorrows of Mary" are (1) this prophecy; (2) the flight into Egypt; (3) losing the child Jesus for three days in the temple, foreshadowing losing him later for the three days between his death and Resurrection; (4) meeting Jesus on the *via dolorosa*, the Way of the Cross, the road to Calvary; (5) his Crucifixion and death; (6) receiving his dead body from the cross (depicted by the most famous and beloved sculpture in the world, the *Pietà*); and (7) his burial.

This was much too much for any ordinary mother to bear. But Mary was no ordinary mother. She was the mother of God, the God who is love; and love alone can bear great suffering because love also bears great gifts, great joys. Love always multiplies both our sorrows and our joys. Both are "blessings," because both are willed or permitted by the God of infinite love. God's loving providence provided to Mary the greatest sorrows any merely human being ever had, but also the greatest joys.

A seventh point in this passage is about the silent years in Jesus' life. Most of his days growing up in the Holy Family, the wholly human family, were like most of the days of our lives: unspectacular and ordinary. Yet those years were as necessary as the three years of miraculous events that they prepared him for. Good painters always spend more time preparing the surface than painting it. They were "the silent years," but words and deeds that come out of silence are always the deepest and most lasting and most powerful.

Silence teaches us patience. God is not measured by clock time. The Bible says that with God, one day is like a thousand years and a thousand years are like one day. God is incredibly patient. He waited 13.7 billion years after creating the universe in the Big Bang before there could be a relatively short story of human history on this planet. And even most of that history is silent prehistory, as most of Christ's life was silent preparation. Yet every second of the history of time is part of his plan: all the long preparation, in the growth of the universe and in the growth of humanity and in the growth of Jesus himself, for the greatest deed ever done, Christ's salvation of the world, and then the deed itself, and then all the fallout of it, all the consequences of it in the lives of billions. The long preparation was like the long shaft of an arrow, and the sharp *point* of the arrow was Christ. And the target that God shoots that arrow into is our hearts: not to kill but to save.

He who is the point of that arrow is also the point of our lives. We will meet him, suddenly, face to face, at death. Our whole lives are preparation for that. So let's not undervalue those ordinary days of our lives. Because those ordinary times are an essential part of the most extraordinary stories ever told, the stories that we are. That's why we tell stories: because we *are* stories. And if we are Christians, if we have been baptized into his Body, we are not only human stories but also divine stories, parts of his story. Every one of us makes history every day.

SOLEMNITY OF THE
BLESSED VIRGIN MARY,
THE MOTHER OF GOD

FIRST READING
NUMBERS 6:22–27 _____

The LORD said to Moses: "Speak to Aaron and his sons and tell them: This is
how you shall bless the Israelites. Say to them: The LORD bless you and keep
you! The LORD let his face shine upon you, and be gracious to you! The LORD
look upon you kindly and give you peace! So shall they invoke my name upon
the Israelites, and I will bless them."

Why does the Church give us this liturgical formula for invoking God's blessing
for today's feast of the Solemnity of Mary, the holy Mother of God?

The formula is for Israel. "This is how you shall bless the Israelites." And
all of Israel comes to a sharp point in Mary, like the point of an arrow, at the
Annunciation. God is about to bless Mary with the gift of his own Son, and
through Mary all of Israel, and through Israel the entire world. This blessing
sums up all of Judaism. Mary is the total Jewish mother. She is God's chosen
instrument for the greatest of all blessings to the widest of all recipients, the
whole human race. God prepared her, by her Immaculate Conception, to
be his own Son's perfect, sinless human mother and assumed human nature
through her and her alone.

All the formulas of this blessing refer to the same thing: God's grace. And
God's angel announced to Mary not just that she was the recipient of grace
but that she was "full of grace" (Luke 1:28). Listen again to the words of this
blessing and apply them to Mary:

"The LORD bless you" (as he blessed Mary, and as he blessed us all through Mary, who is our greatest merely human blessing, our greatest saint and model) "and keep you" (as Mary "kept" God's Word in her heart and in her womb).

"The LORD let his face shine upon you . . ." (God smiled on Mary because he was totally pleased with her, as with no other human creature. Because of Mary's *fiat*, which allowed the Lamb of God to come to take away the sins of the world, God now smiles on us with total pleasure because he sees us not in our sinful selves but in his Son's Mystical Body, which would not have existed if Mary had not said her *fiat* with her body as well as her will.)

"And be gracious to you." (Being "gracious" means giving grace. No one ever received more graces than Mary, and no one ever channeled more graces than the "Mediatrix of All Graces.")

"The LORD look upon you kindly . . ." (What is kindness? What does kindness do? It reaches down with compassion to save us from our greatest dangers and our worst enemies, which are our own sins.)

"And give you peace." (Through Mary we receive the Prince of Peace, who gives us eternal peace with God. And that is the incomparably truest, strongest, and most necessary peace, and the source of all other peace. As Thomas Merton said, with admirable summary, "We are not at peace with others because we are not at peace with ourselves, and we are not at peace with ourselves because we are not at peace with God.")

SECOND READING
GALATIANS 4:4–7 _____

Brothers and sisters: When the fullness of time had come, God sent his Son, born of a woman, born under the law, to ransom those under the law, so that we might receive adoption as sons. As proof that you are sons, God sent the Spirit of his Son into our hearts, crying out, "Abba, Father!" So you are no longer a slave but a son, and if a son then also an heir, through God.

What is meant by the phrase "the fullness of time" in St. Paul's first sentence, "When the fullness of time had come, God sent his Son, born of a woman"?

It means, first of all, that God had providentially prepared human history for this, the greatest event of all time, the Incarnation, by mysterious foreshadowings, hints, and longings in pagan mythology; by the wisdom and clarity of Greek philosophy; and by the system of laws, political order, roads, and language that had united the world under the Pax Romana, the Roman Peace.

It means, second, that God had prepared his little chosen nation of Israel for two thousand years, through both successes and failures, her saints and her sinners, through learning the easy way and learning the hard way. Israel had been trained to be God's collective prophet to the world. She revealed to the world the nature of the true God and of his will, summarized in his Law.

But most concretely, it meant that God had prepared Mary, in whom was concentrated the best of humanity and the best of Judaism. "The fullness of time" was another name for Mary.

For what did Mary do? She affirmed and enabled and co-operated with God's supreme act, "to ransom those under the law." And why? To what end? "So that we might receive adoption as sons."

St. Paul says "sons" generically, as including, not excluding, daughters. In the ancient world, "sons" meant legally "those who inherit from their parents." What we inherit from our Father in heaven is not only eternal life and salvation from sin but incorporation into God's family, so that we can now truly pray to him as "Our Father." The term is not meant biologically, but it is meant literally. "So you are no longer a slave but a son, and if a son, then also an heir."

That's what Mary did. God the Father gave us Mary, so that Mary could give us God incarnate, God the Son. And then God the Son gave us Mary, from the cross, to be our heavenly Mother as he is our heavenly Father. The circle is completed with her.

GOSPEL

LUKE 2:16–21 _____

The shepherds went in haste to Bethlehem and found Mary and Joseph, and the infant lying in the manger. When they saw this, they made known the message that had been told them about this child. All who heard it were amazed by what had been told them by the shepherds. And Mary kept all these things, reflecting on them in her heart. Then the shepherds returned, glorifying and praising God for all they had heard and seen, just as it had been told to them.

When eight days were completed for his circumcision, he was named Jesus, the name given him by the angel before he was conceived in the womb.

Circumcision was the functional equivalent of Baptism for the Jews. It was their God-ordained sacred rite of initiation into God's holy people, a people apart from all others. It was done eight days after birth. The child was also given his name at that time, because the name was thought of as much more than a mere humanly chosen label; it was a divinely chosen identity, and it was the child's destiny to live into his name. Thus, observant Jews were forbidden to change their name, since it was their God-given destiny. When Jesus changed Simon's name to Peter, he was doing something God alone could rightly do. It was God who had changed Abram's name to "Abraham" and Jacob's name to "Israel." When God changes your name, he changes your life and your destiny. According to the book of Revelation, we all will get a new name in heaven, a name that no one knows but you and God (Rev. 2:17).

Names are not things but signs—signs that signify things. They are meanings. The name "Jesus" means "Savior" or "God saves." Luke points out that this name was "the name given him by the angel before he was conceived in the womb." This was a divine name in two senses: in its content and in its origin. Its content was divine because only God saves. No one else can save us from our sins. Its origin was also divine, for angels speak only the words that God tells them to speak.

Why does the Church give us this Gospel reading on the feast of Mary, God's mother? Because when Mary said to the angel Gabriel, "May it be done to me according to your word," she accepted God's word and God's will (Luke 1:38). She had the power to say no instead of yes, since she had free will. She was immaculate and sinless, but she was not a robot. And if she had not freely consented to be the Mother of God incarnate, then God would not have come through her to save humanity. He will not save humanity without humanity's free consent.

And the *name* "Jesus," or "God saves," is part of what Mary consented to. Or rather, it was the whole of what she consented to. For that name is the whole *meaning* of Jesus' life, death, and Resurrection: what they mean is that God is saving us from sin and death and hell. So what those events *mean* is what they actually *do*. They are like the sacraments in that way. A sacrament is a sacred rite instituted by Christ that actually accomplishes what it signifies. For instance, the physical water of Baptism not only signifies or symbolizes spiritual washing from sin but also actually accomplishes the removal of original sin. The Eucharist both symbolizes and really accomplishes and re-presents (that is, makes really present again) Christ's offering of his own body and blood on the cross for our salvation. So Mary's word *fiat*, or "may it be done," actually did what it said: it opened her will and her womb to Jesus, who is God's salvation for all of us. Mary's will was like a faucet handle, and Christ was the saving water. She is the place, the locus, of our salvation, for in her Christ appears in our world.

In the God-designed temple in Jerusalem, the Holy of Holies was the place that only the high priest could enter, and only once a year. It contained the ark of the covenant, which contained the two stone tablets of the Law, the Old Covenant, the Ten Commandments, that God gave to Moses. Mary is the new Holy of Holies, and her womb is the Ark of the New Covenant, for it contained God's greatest gift to man: himself.

SECOND SUNDAY AFTER THE NATIVITY (CHRISTMAS)

FIRST READING
SIRACH 24:1–2, 8–12

Wisdom sings her own praises and is honored in God, before her own people she boasts; in the assembly of the Most High she opens her mouth, in the presence of his power she declares her worth, in the midst of her people she is exalted, in holy fullness she is admired; in the multitude of the chosen she finds praise, and among the blessed she is blessed.

"The Creator of all commanded and said to me, and he who formed me chose the spot for my tent, saying, 'In Jacob make your dwelling, in Israel your inheritance, and among my chosen put down your roots.'

"Before all ages, in the beginning, he created me, and through all ages I shall not cease to be. In the holy tent I ministered before him, and in Zion I fixed my abode. Thus in the chosen city I have rested, in Jerusalem is my domain. I have struck root among a glorious people, in the portion of the LORD, his heritage; and in the company of the holy ones do I linger."

The words of Sirach the sage praise wisdom, and that is not surprising. For without wisdom, without light, without truth about the most important things, nothing can be done. As Solomon said, "The beginning of wisdom is: get wisdom; whatever else you get, get understanding" (Prov. 4:7). But it is surprising that wisdom is described as an actual, concrete person, not just an ideal, abstract value; as the subject rather than the object of verbs like "sings" and "boasts" and "declares." Wisdom speaks, as a "me" and an "I."

This could be simply the literary device of personification, which means treating what is not a person as if it were, so that the concrete imagination can symbolize an abstract value or principle, since we remember concrete images much more readily than abstract concepts. But as Christians, we know that it is more than that, because the New Testament (especially the beginning of John's Gospel) identifies the Logos, or eternal truth and wisdom, the wisdom sought by all the sages and philosophers, with the concrete person of Christ, the second person of the Holy Trinity, God the Father's eternal, complete, and perfect expression and knowledge of himself.

That is why the Incarnation could happen. An abstract essence or nature or ideal or value or principle like justice or wisdom cannot become incarnate and take on a human nature, but a divine person can. And that is what Christ did in the Incarnation. Without losing his divine nature, he added human nature to his person. It is a person who has a nature; it is not an abstract nature that "has" a person. A person is concrete, even when that person is divine and spiritual; a nature is abstract. Human nature does not love or hate, get born and die; human persons do.

A divine person can take on human nature—that is what Christ did—and a human person can also take on a finite participation in the divine nature, and that is what Christ enables us to do, as Scripture tells us (2 Pet. 1:4). In fact, that is the ultimate reason he assumed the whole of our human nature: not only to die on the cross to save us from sin but also so that we could receive a finite but real share in his divine nature when we are "born again" by faith and Baptism. God came down so that we might go up.

And since Christ is the fullness of divine wisdom, this means that insofar as we are "in" Christ we are "in" divine wisdom itself, not merely on the outside looking in from a distance. Imagine a child on the beach looking at the sea with wonder and longing but remaining dry. The sea is the largest thing we can see on earth, and a natural image of the infinite. We are like that child not just looking at the sea but actually in it, splashing around in the water. Of course, he is only in the shallows of the sea. But it is the same sea, the same water. It has waved at us, and its wave has come to us and flooded our dry land and made us wonderfully wet with a wisdom that did not come simply from us.

Where did this wisdom, this Gospel, come from, after all? Did anyone on earth ever expect God—the God who is perfect in every way and who has no more need for us than a dog has need for fleas—did anyone on earth ever expect this God to love us so crazily that he would become man and die for our sins so that we could live with him forever in heaven as his children, his family, in fact as his Bride, in a spiritual marriage? Did you ever think that this whole incredible story could possibly have been the invention of such sinful, shallow, selfish, silly fools as us? We might be so arrogant as to think ourselves the equals of God, but how could God be so humble as to become the equal of us? Such a thought could never have come from our hearts. This "Good News" of the Gospel seems far too good to be true. Yet when we hear this "far too good to be true" Good News, our hearts recognize that it is true, that Jesus Christ is indeed "the way and the truth and the life" (John 14:6).

SECOND READING
Ephesians 1:3–6, 15–18 _____

Blessed be the God and Father of our Lord Jesus Christ, who has blessed us in Christ with every spiritual blessing in the heavens, as he chose us in him, before the foundation of the world, to be holy and without blemish before him. In love he destined us for adoption to himself through Jesus Christ, in accord with the favor of his will, for the praise of the glory of his grace that he granted us in the beloved.

Therefore, I, too, hearing of your faith in the Lord Jesus and of your love for all the holy ones, do not cease giving thanks for you, remembering you in my prayers, that the God of our Lord Jesus Christ, the Father of glory, may give you a Spirit of wisdom and revelation resulting in knowledge of him. May the eyes of your hearts be enlightened, that you may know what is the hope that belongs to his call, what are the riches of glory in his inheritance among the holy ones.

Today's epistle is about predestination. St. Paul tells us that God "chose us in him [that is, in Christ], before the foundation of the world, to be holy," that he "destined us for adoption to himself through Jesus Christ." Our lives have a destiny, a purpose, an end, a meaning, a goal. And the goal is already there before we know it and before we accept it or reject it. We did not invent it; God did. God knew us before we knew him. He chose us before we chose him. He believed in us before we believed in him.

He loved us before we loved him. In fact, God loved us before we even existed. He loved us into existence.

This concept of destiny or predestination is a very mysterious one, but it is an important one because it concerns everything in our lives, so I'm going to try to stretch your minds to think into it just a little bit here.

Life is a story. And every good story contains destiny or predestination. And this predestination does not exclude free will but includes it in every good story. The free will of the characters is one of the things that is destined, or predestined, by the author. And God is the author, the Creator, of everything, not just of the material universe but also of the story of our lives. It is he who gives us the real freedom to choose between good and evil, between that which leads to God and that which moves in the other direction, away from God and his will and his law.

The "pre" in "predestination," however, is not our temporal "pre," since God has no past or future, as we do. Most of the time in our lives is in the forever-dead past or in the not-yet-real future, but God is timelessly present, present to all our moments of time. He does not gaze into a crystal ball to predict our future or read history books to remember our past. All of him is present all at once, in perfect order and understanding.

People often catch a glimpse of this divine timelessness at the moment of death, or near death, when they say they saw their whole life pass before their eyes with perfect clarity and perfect order in a split second, all at once.

St. Paul, in today's epistle, is asking us to take account of this divine pre-destination and see our present temporal lives of faith and hope in light of that destiny, when he says, "May the eyes of your hearts be enlightened, that you may know what is the hope that belongs to his call, what are the riches of glory in his inheritance among the holy ones." If we saw our future heavenly destiny, if we saw the glorious and joy-filled saint that God destines us to eventually become in heaven, we would probably be strongly tempted to fall down and worship it.

We must direct our worship to Christ, the source of that glorious light, for we are told that in the end, "we shall be like him, for we shall see him as he is" (1 John 3:2). When we see God face to face, we will be transformed into perfect saints, unable to be tempted by any lesser lights. The best thing we can do in this world is to get closer to that vision by practicing the presence of God in prayer, in the faith that sees God now, but only "indistinctly, as in a mirror" (1 Cor. 13:12), in the hope for this transforming vision that God himself has promised us, and in the love that seeks only his perfect will in all things, in all our prayers, works, joys, and sufferings of every day and every moment in this world. That, and nothing less, is what we have been predestined for. That, and nothing less, is the meaning of human life.

GOSPEL

JOHN 1:1–18 _____

This magnificent poem was used for the Mass for Christmas during the Day, above.

THE EPIPHANY OF THE LORD

FIRST READING

Isaiah 60:1–6 _____

Rise up in splendor, Jerusalem! Your light has come,
   the glory of the Lord shines upon you.
See, darkness covers the earth,
   and thick clouds cover the peoples;
but upon you the LORD shines,
   and over you appears his glory.
Nations shall walk by your light,
   and kings by your shining radiance.
Raise your eyes and look about;
   they all gather and come to you:
your sons come from afar,
   and your daughters in the arms of their nurses.

Then you shall be radiant at what you see,
   your heart shall throb and overflow,
for the riches of the sea shall be emptied out before you,
   the wealth of nations shall be brought to you.
Caravans of camels shall fill you,
   dromedaries from Midian and Ephah;
all from Sheba shall come
   bearing gold and frankincense,
   and proclaiming the praises of the LORD.

_____

When Isaiah's audience heard this glowing, glorious prophecy, some five or six centuries before Christ, most of them probably thought it was prophesying a visible, material, this-worldly triumph of the nation of Israel rather than the invisible, spiritual, supernatural "Good News" that was in fact not just better than that but infinitely better than that because it gave us not just temporal but eternal "success." But only three wise men from outside Israel were wise enough to recognize the fulfillment of this prophecy in a baby in a feeding trough in an animal barn, whose parents were poor peasants who could not find a room indoors for the birth.

Isaiah's vision of the whole world making pilgrimage to Jerusalem to worship the true God, bearing "the wealth of nations" and "caravans of camels . . . bearing gold and frankincense" certainly seemed to be a vision of visible, this-worldly political success. Yet the nation of Israel, the great temple, and the central religious act of Judaism, the liturgical sacrifices mandated by the Mosaic Law, were to end forever when the Romans destroyed Jerusalem and the temple in AD 70. Hardly a success story! The success was spiritual. Nearly half the world came to believe in the God of the Jews because of Christian missionaries.

The prophecies said that when the Messiah came, God would establish his kingdom, and the whole world would come to know the true God. That's why Jews don't send out missionaries: they believe the Messiah is yet to come. And that's why Christians do: because they believe he has already come, and fulfilled the prophecies. He has established his kingdom here, and he is its king, but his throne is not a gold chair in a palace. His throne is in your heart, in your faith and hope and love.

Why didn't God inspire his prophets to make things clearer? God could have overcome this natural misunderstanding of his kingdom as a political kingdom. It was probably the main reason why most of the Jews of Jesus' day didn't accept him as the Messiah. When they came to make him king, he ran away. Instead of running for office, he ran from it. Why didn't God make that clear in the Old Testament prophecies of the Messiah? Why did God deliberately inspire his prophets to speak so ambiguously?

Because God is love, and what love wants is not first of all minds but hearts. The obscurity of mind is a test of the heart. God gives us enough light to enlighten us so that if we want to find him, we will, and if we don't, we won't. "The one who seeks, finds" (Matt. 7:8). But those who do not seek, do not find. He is testing us, because he is love and therefore he wants hearts first of all, not minds. We don't get into heaven by passing a theology exam but by loving God and neighbor. He is testing our hearts, our loves.

That's why the very first words out of Jesus' mouth to his prospective disciples in John's Gospel are "What are you looking for?" (John 1:38). Those whose hearts were set on worldly comfort and success would interpret God's promises, such as today's passage from the prophet Isaiah, according to that love of their hearts, and thus misinterpret them. And those whose hearts were set on God and on what God is, which is love, righteousness, justice, and mercy, would rightly interpret them, and they would find Jesus as their Messiah. He would give them what their hearts longed for the most. He would not do that to those whose hearts were set on worldly success.

The heart always influences the head. Orthopraxy leads orthodoxy. Right living educates right thinking. If you love, you will see. "Blessed are the clean of heart, for they will see God" (Matt. 5:8). Jesus said to those who doubted him, "Whoever chooses to do [the Father's] will shall know whether my teaching is from God or whether I speak on my own" (John 7:17). That's why the saints know God better than the theologians: because the best interpreter of Love is love.

The messianic prophecies are prophecies of salvation. The Messiah would be our Savior. But salvation from what? Military defeat? Poverty? Suffering? Lack of social enlightenment? Zechariah prophesied that this baby "would save us from our enemies" (Luke 1:71). But who are our enemies? Not the Romans but our own sins. The angel announced that "you are to name him

Jesus [which means 'Savior,' or 'God saves'], because he will save his people from their sins" (Matt. 1:21).

That job description explains why his crown is not of gold but of thorns. The most beautiful thing about him is his wounds, for they are the wounds of God's love, and nothing is more beautiful than God's love.

SECOND READING

EPHESIANS 3:2–3A, 5–6 _____

Brothers and sisters: You have heard of the stewardship of God's grace that was given to me for your benefit, namely, that the mystery was made known to me by revelation. It was not made known to people in other generations as it has now been revealed to his holy apostles and prophets by the Spirit: that the Gentiles are coheirs, members of the same body, and copartners in the promise in Christ Jesus through the gospel.

The "mystery" that St. Paul speaks of in today's epistle is God's plan, from the beginning, to prepare his chosen people the Jews not for themselves but for the world, as his collective prophet or mouthpiece.

The purpose and goal of Jewish exclusivism was global inclusivism. In a world fallen into both sin and the ignorance of idolatry and polytheism, God hammered into the hard heads of this one people for almost two millennia the truth that he was one and unique and that he was righteous and holy and good (both just and merciful), while the rest of the world remained in darkness. And he did this concentrated and exclusive revelation to his chosen people for the sake of eventual inclusivism, for the sake of the rest of the world.

St. Paul says that the ultimate purpose of this divine strategy has now finally been revealed in Christ, who made the Gentiles coheirs with the Jews of God's covenant of spiritual marriage. He did this by his command to his disciples to "go into the whole world and proclaim the gospel to every creature" (Mark

16:15). God did not tell the Jews to send out missionaries to the Gentiles, until Christ the Messiah came. The coming of the three wise men from the east at the Epiphany was the beginning of this new stage in God's strategy to save the whole world.

Critics often question what they call "the scandal of particularity" in God choosing just one people to reveal himself to. But the whole purpose of this particularity and exclusivism was an eventual universality and inclusivism.

The two ways the world gets this wrong are (1) the exclusivist's idea that exclusivism is the end rather than the means and (2) the inclusivist's idea that inclusivism is attainable without any exclusivism. Jesus is the exclusive Savior, but he is the Savior for everyone. Even now, today, when Christians have been converting the world for two thousand years, we are divided into these two camps, each teaching a half-truth, the first insisting, rightly, on the purity and distinctiveness of revealed doctrine, and the second insisting, rightly, on non-judgmental "big tent" inclusiveness of mission and service. All the saints insist on and practice both. The differences are only in emphasis (e.g., St. Thomas Aquinas and St. Francis of Assisi).

God used this strategy from the beginning. Adam and Eve were a single man and woman, but God dealt with the whole human race in them as concrete individuals, when the whole human race was in potentiality in their reproductive systems, rather than waiting until the population was spread out and then dealing with humanity in general, in a vague, collective crowd. He did the same thing with Christ, whom St. Paul calls "the second Adam," and Mary, whose earliest title, in the writings of the Church Fathers, was "the second Eve." God knows that we learn best through concrete individuals rather than through generalized abstractions. We are like targets that are pierced by arrows that come to a single sharp point rather than by an enveloping, universal cloud. So he prepared Mary, who was the point of the Jewish arrow, and sent his angel Gabriel to ask her, not the whole of the chosen people, to say her yes to his plan to save all humanity by his Son, the one, concrete, unique, exclusive Lamb of God who inclusively takes away all the sins of all the world.

The "exclusivist" Jews who opposed St. Paul's missionary activity saw this inclusivism and universalism of evangelization and service as one kind of scandal, and the "inclusivists" of our own time see its doctrinal and creedal exclusivism as the opposite kind of scandal. We must transcend both and have what St. Paul calls "the mind of Christ" (1 Cor. 2:16), "living the truth in love" (Eph. 4:15), since both orthodoxy and orthopraxy, truth and love, are equally absolute demands of the single Gospel.

The ultimate reason truth and love are one is in the eternal nature of God himself. The Son is the whole truth of the Father, so real that it is a person, eternally begotten by the Father, and the Holy Spirit is the love between Father and Son, so real that it is a person, eternally proceeding from both.

GOSPEL
MATTHEW 2:1–12 _____

When Jesus was born in Bethlehem of Judea, in the days of King Herod, behold, magi from the east arrived in Jerusalem, saying, "Where is the newborn king of the Jews? We saw his star at its rising and have come to do him homage." When King Herod heard this, he was greatly troubled, and all Jerusalem with him. Assembling all the chief priests and the scribes of the people, he inquired of them where the Christ was to be born. They said to him, "In Bethlehem of Judea, for thus it has been written through the prophet:

And you, Bethlehem, land of Judah,
  are by no means least among the rulers of Judah;
since from you shall come a ruler,
  who is to shepherd my people Israel."

Then Herod called the magi secretly and ascertained from them the time of the star's appearance. He sent them to Bethlehem and said, "Go and search diligently for the child. When you have found him, bring me word, that I too may go and do him homage." After their audience with the king they set out. And behold, the star that they had seen at its rising preceded them, until it came and stopped over the place where the child was. They were overjoyed at seeing the star, and on entering the house they saw the child with Mary his mother. They prostrated themselves and did him homage. Then they opened their treasures and offered him gifts of gold, frankincense, and myrrh. And having been warned in a dream not to return to Herod, they departed for their country by another way.

Today's Feast of the Epiphany celebrates Christ's "epiphany" or "showing" to the world. The three wise men from the east were the first people in the world to come to worship him. Billions have followed them in the last two thousand years, as they followed the star. The Epiphany reveals something about God's providential plan for the rest of the world, with its many other religions. God has not abandoned or forgotten them. "He did not leave himself without witness" there (Acts 14:17), for nature bears witness to his goodness and wisdom and conscience bears witness to our sinfulness and foolishness (Rom. 1:19–23).

The practical takeaway from today's Gospel is summarized on the bumper sticker "Wise men still seek him."

The "magi" or wise men from the east were scholars, philosophers, astronomers, and astrologers. They may have been Zoroastrians, from Persia, who believed in a single God who was all good and all wise, unlike most of the Gentiles of that day. They were not Jews, but they must have heard of the similarly monotheistic and moral religion of the Jews, so different from the polytheism and immoralism around them, for they made a long and hard journey simply to see what they had heard about—"the newborn king of the Jews"—and to do homage to him. God must have spoken to them in a dream or a vision and guided them by an unusual star.

The star may have been a fast-moving comet, or perhaps it was a very rare conjunction in the sky of three bright planets, which actually happened in 4 BC. (Our calendars are "off" by three or four years.)

God providentially deals with and cares for all people at all times, in different ways, then as well as now. Those ways are always mysterious, surprising, and unpredictable, now as well as then. As the classic old hymn says, "God moves in a mysterious way his wonders to perform." If a Christian is one who confesses, in the words of the oldest and shortest Christian creed, that "Jesus is Lord," then these wise men were the world's first Christians—outside of his mother and foster father—for they were the first to worship Christ, though they were Gentiles from a culture very far away.

The wise men looked at the star in the same way as we should look at everything in God's creation: not merely as a *thing* but as a *sign*. What did it signify? What did it mean? They looked *along* it, not merely at it. And that is why they followed it, as we follow street signs or printed words on paper. They sought God by means of this miraculous sign. It was like a word written in the sky, a "word of God" in nature that led them to the one who is the one eternal Word of God in person.

Why were these "wise men" wise? Not because they had the best answers but because they had the best question. They were seekers of the truth. Christ promised that "the one who seeks, finds" (Matt. 7:8). All who truly seek the true God, the God whose essence is not power but goodness and love, will find him—if not in this life, then in the next. For us, the clearest division seems to be the visible one between atheists and theists, unbelievers and believers, between those who have found God and those who have not. But for God, the deepest division is the invisible one between seekers and non-seekers. For seeking is done with the heart, and God alone knows the secrets of every heart.

THE BAPTISM OF THE LORD

FIRST READING

Isaiah 42:1–4, 6–7 _____

Thus says the Lord:
Here is my servant whom I uphold,
    my chosen one with whom I am pleased,
upon whom I have put my spirit;
    he shall bring forth justice to the nations,
not crying out, not shouting,
    not making his voice heard in the street.
A bruised reed he shall not break,
    and a smoldering wick he shall not quench,
until he establishes justice on the earth;
    the coastlands will wait for his teaching.

I, the Lord, have called you for the victory of justice,
    I have grasped you by the hand;
I formed you, and set you
    as a covenant of the people,
    a light for the nations,
to open the eyes of the blind,
    to bring out prisoners from confinement,
    and from the dungeon, those who live in darkness.

_____

Baptism is the beginning of the Christian life, which is not merely the imitation of Christ but the very life of Christ himself in the human soul and in a human life. That life is supernatural and divine, though it is received into fallen, fallible, and foggy earthly minds and hearts. Christ's earthly ministry also began with a baptism, but of course Christ could not receive as something new his own eternal divine life.

When Christ was baptized in the Jordan River, God did not use the water to infuse a new power into him, but he infused a new power into water, all the water in the world: the power to be God's instrument in our Baptism. When Christ was baptized, the water did not baptize him; he baptized the water.

When Isaiah wrote, "Thus says the LORD: Here is my servant whom I uphold, my chosen one with whom I am pleased," those were prophetic words because they were the very words God spoke from heaven when he parted the skies at Jesus' baptism.

Isaiah's prophecy goes on: "Upon whom I have put my spirit." John the Baptist baptized only with water, but Jesus baptizes with the Holy Spirit. That is the formula John the Baptist himself used, according to all three of the synoptic Gospels: "I am baptizing you with water, for repentance, but the one who is coming after me is mightier than I. I am not worthy to carry his sandals. He will baptize you with the Holy Spirit and fire" (Matt. 3:11; see Mark 1:8; Luke 3:16).

Isaiah continues, "He shall bring forth justice to the nations." Christ did that. He gave us not just political justice but justification with God, reconciliation with God. Christ fulfilled justice as well as mercy on the cross, offering to the Father the death that justice required as punishment for our sin and rebellion.

Isaiah further describes him as "not crying out, not shouting, not making his voice heard in the street." Jesus never even protested or complained about his Crucifixion, for that was what he had come to earth for in the first place. Every other baby comes into the world to live; Jesus came into the world to die.

Then Isaiah continues, "A bruised reed he shall not break, and a smoldering wick he shall not quench." His wisdom and compassion are so great that when he sees human souls bruised by sin almost to the point of breaking, he will not bruise them any further, and when he sees the tiniest hint of fire still smoldering in the candle wick of a human soul, a fire that is almost totally gone out, he will not let the fire go out completely but will bend down and carefully blow it into a flame, restoring even the most desperately sick soul. The more we need him, the more he heals us; the less we deserve him, the more grace he gives us. That is not the usual meaning of human justice. The innocent one dies for the guilty. It is the great exchange: he gets what we deserve so that we can get what he deserves.

This is the hidden, spiritual meaning of what must have seemed to most of Isaiah's readers to refer to visible political success: that the Messiah would be "a light for the nations, to open the eyes of the blind, to bring prisoners out of confinement, and from the dungeon those who live in darkness." Jesus did literally open the eyes of a few dozen blind men, but he opened the spiritual eyes of the whole world.

He physically brought St. Peter out of prison, as narrated in the Acts of the Apostles, but he brought the whole world out of the infinitely worse prison of sin and its consequences by blocking our road to hell and opening our road to heaven.

God always surprises us by doing more, not less, than we think. As St. Francis of Assisi said to one of his monks, Brother Juniper, "Brother, which do you think is the readier: God to give us grace or we to receive it?"

SECOND READING

ACTS 10:34–38 _____

Peter proceeded to speak to those gathered in the house of Cornelius, saying: "In truth, I see that God shows no partiality. Rather, in every nation whoever fears him and acts uprightly is acceptable to him. You know the word that he sent to the Israelites as he proclaimed peace through Jesus Christ, who is Lord of all, what has happened all over Judea, beginning in Galilee after the baptism that John preached, how God anointed Jesus of Nazareth with the Holy Spirit and power. He went about doing good and healing all those oppressed by the devil, for God was with him."

What Isaiah had prophesied some six centuries earlier, the Apostles observed with their own eyes: the "epiphany" or "showing" or "revelation" of God in a final and definitive and total way in Christ, not just to the Jews, whom God chose as his prophetic instrument, but now to the whole world. St. Peter realized this when God gave him the vision of a great sheet full of animals that were both clean and unclean by Jewish law, telling him to eat them all. At the same time, God gave to the godly pagan centurion Cornelius a vision of an angel who told him to summon St. Peter to come to his house and share the Good News of Christ with him. If the three wise men at the Nativity were the first Gentiles to receive the Gospel, Cornelius and his household were the second.

This extraordinary and miraculous interference by God was necessary because it was such a shock to the Jews that their privileged knowledge of God was only a means to the end that the whole world now come to the knowledge of the true God, now fully revealed in Christ.

We moderns, in contrast to the ancient Jews, are no longer shocked by the universality of this new revelation, but by the specificity and concreteness and particularity of it. This one man, Jesus, is the one man for all mankind because he is divine, the Word by whom God created the whole world and all the human race. Being God, he is not just one being among others, but the meaning of everything that exists. In the words of St. Paul in his Letter to the Colossians, "All things were created through him and for him. He is before all things, and in him all things hold together. . . . For in him all the fullness [of God] was pleased to dwell" (Col. 1:16–19).

GOSPEL
MARK 1:7–11

This is what he proclaimed: "One mightier than I is coming after me. I am not worthy to stoop and loosen the thongs of his sandals. I have baptized you with water; he will baptize you with the Holy Spirit."

It happened in those days that Jesus came from Nazareth of Galilee and was baptized in the Jordan by John. On coming up out of the water he saw the heavens being torn open and the Spirit, like a dove, descending upon him. And a voice came from the heavens, "You are my beloved Son; with you I am well pleased."

When John the Baptist says that he is not worthy to stoop and loosen the thongs of Jesus' sandals, he is making the most extreme comparison between himself and Christ. But it is totally justified by the reason he gives: John baptizes people with only water, as a symbol of repentance and cleansing, but Jesus will baptize with the Holy Spirit, who is God himself! Jesus will give us a participation in the very life of God. Because of him, God will actually live in our souls (and even in our bodies, by the Eucharist).

God made this invisible spiritual truth known clearly to his people by miracles. Here is the first recorded miracle in Jesus' life, even before the miracle at Cana, where he changed water to wine. The sky was ripped open like a piece of paper, and the voice of God spoke in audible human words identifying Jesus as the Son of God, not just a son of man; as the Father's beloved; and as the one with whom the Father was totally pleased—that is, as our only perfect model and our divine, infallible authority.

God stooped to our needs in performing miracles in the natural world of visible matter. Our knowledge naturally begins with sense experience, so God descended there. But our knowledge does not end there; our mind "x-rays" our senses and interprets what we see. So God sent us unmistakable signs (the word "miracle" literally means "sign") for us to read. We must look along them, not just at them.

LENT

FIRST SUNDAY OF LENT

FIRST READING
GENESIS 9:8–15 _____

God said to Noah and to his sons with him: "See, I am now establishing my covenant with you and your descendants after you and with every living creature that was with you: all the birds, and the various tame and wild animals that were with you and came out of the ark. I will establish my covenant with you, that never again shall all bodily creatures be destroyed by the waters of a flood; there shall not be another flood to devastate the earth." God added: "This is the sign that I am giving for all ages to come, of the covenant between me and you and every living creature with you: I set my bow in the clouds to serve as a sign of the covenant between me and the earth. When I bring clouds over the earth, and the bow appears in the clouds, I will recall the covenant I have made between me and you and all living beings, so that the waters shall never again become a flood to destroy all mortal beings."

_____

The point of the story of Noah and the ark comes at the end. The whole story is dramatic and memorable, but we often forget its point, as we also do with other stories in the Bible.

For instance, the point of the story of Abraham and Isaac and the sacrifice on Mount Moriah is not the point at the beginning of the story—that God seems to be asking for human sacrifice, the ultimate test of faith, and that faithful Abraham is willing to do it—but rather that God is offering a substitute, the ram, or the sacrificial lamb, and that the religion he is establishing with Abraham, unlike all pagan religions, is the worship of a God who created mankind in his own sacred image and who does *not* want human sacrifice. That point comes only at the end of the story.

The point of the story of Job is also at the end, not at the beginning. The point is not the "problem" of evil and how Job and his three friends wrestle with that problem; rather, the point is what God says to Job at the end of the story: that he, not Job, has the answer to this problem.

The point of the story of Jesus is also at the end. The point is not first of all Jesus' long and dramatic ministry with all the miracles and teachings, great as they are, or even his sufferings and death, but his Resurrection and triumph over death and the devil, which is also our resurrection and triumph.

The story of the last book of the Bible, Revelation, is not so much about the spectacular events leading to the end of the old world, but the establishment of a new world, God's kingdom coming finally and eternally.

Human life itself, every individual life, is a story, and the point of the story always comes at the end: that the apparent end, death, is really the beginning of eternal life.

Every story ever told has those two aspects: the problem and the solution, the war and the peace, the dramatic conflict and its resolution, the challenge and the response, the suffering and the deliverance. If we ask, "Why does the good God allow the righteous to suffer?" the answer is the essential nature of every story: there is always first the night and then the day, first the valley and then the mountain, first the prison and then the escape, first the suffering and then the deliverance.

To be more exact and complete, every story has three stages, not just two. A situation has to be set up first in order to be upset and then reset. Nothing is evil in the beginning. Evil is always the corruption of some good. So the three stages of the story of humanity are the creation, the fall, and the redemption. That's why we always find some version of that three-stage process in all the stories we tell: because that's the story we're in.

So the main point of the story of Noah's flood and Noah's ark is not the flood itself or the ark or the animals. The main point is the covenant that God makes with us after the flood is over; that is, the divinely guaranteed, infallible promise of God to protect mankind and *not* to allow a universal flood, a universal catastrophe. If you read the text carefully, you will see that it says that the promise is not just to Noah or even to all mankind but to "all living beings," that is, to plants and animals also, since mankind cannot live without them.

The story of Noah and the ark may be symbolic, a parable rather than literal history. The Church does not definitively tell us which it is, though it reminds us that a symbolic truth, like a parable, is still a revealed truth from God. But there is no symbolism in God's covenant itself. That is literal. The symbol or sign of the covenant is the rainbow. We are to interpret the rainbow symbolically and the covenant literally. The rainbow is a sign that God promises that "never again" will that universal catastrophe happen.

One obvious lesson of the Noah story is faith and trust in the God who saves us, even when the rest of the world laughs at us and laughs at God. The ark is a symbol of Christ and Christ's Body, Christ's Church, the ark of salvation. That's how St. Peter interprets it in his first letter, in the New Testament.

And one aspect of that new, Christian interpretation is about death. The flood means death, death by drowning. The ark saves Noah's family from death. As there is life after the flood, there is life after death. The point of God's "never again" promise is not just about what will happen to others in the remote future of the world but about what will happen to each one of us when we die. Death seems to be a universal catastrophe, the loss of all things forever. But it is not. There is life after the flood of death. That flood happens only once, and then comes a deathless eternity, if we are in the ark of salvation that God provides for us.

RESPONSORIAL PSALM
Psalm 25:4–5, 6–7, 8–9 _____

R. (cf. 10) **Your ways, O Lord, are love and truth to those who keep your covenant.**

Your ways, O Lord, make known to me;
    teach me your paths,
Guide me in your truth and teach me,
    for you are God my savior.

Remember that your compassion, O Lord,
    and your love are from of old.
In your kindness remember me,
    because of your goodness, O Lord.

Good and upright is the Lord,
    thus he shows sinners the way.
He guides the humble to justice,
    and he teaches the humble his way.

The few short verses from the Psalm today mention God's "way" or God's "ways" or God's "paths" no less than four times. What does this mean?

Instinctively and intuitively, we know the answer to that question. We know it from the old hymn that sings,

> God's way is the best way, though I may not see
> Why sorrows and trials oft gather 'round me. . . .
> God's way is the best way; my path He hath planned
> I'll trust in him always while holding his hand.

That's the hymn we will sing when we enter heaven. The song they sing as they enter hell is the opposite song: "I did it my way."

That's the most important takeaway from this Psalm: trust. Even if the point is not wholly clear, it can be wholly dear and wholly near. We don't have to make it clear to our mind before we make it dear to our heart and near to our life.

But it would help to make it clear. The more we understand the one we love, the more reasons we have to love him. So let's try to focus more clearly on that word "way."

Literally interpreted, it is a road or a path that is laid out before us for us to walk down. The image of life as a road is the single most common and popular image for life in all of our literature. An image is a particular concrete thing that somehow suggests or symbolizes an abstract general idea, like "life is a love story" or "life is war" or "life is a bowl of cherries" or "life is a box of chocolates."

We all know that life is a road. What does this tell us that we don't know? Why is this part of divine revelation? What does this image of a road tell us about God?

It tells us that God has planned and designed our life, as an author designs the life stories of his characters. Life is not an impenetrable jungle without any roads, so that we have to make all the roads. There are already roads through life—good ones and bad ones. There is good, and there is evil. There is a road that leads to God, and there is another road that leads away from him. That is the single most important fact about human life. That is God's road map through life for us.

Of course, we move from one road to another many times. People and their choices and their lives are mixtures of good and evil. "There's a little bad in the best of us and a little good in the worst of us." But though people are mixtures, roads are not. There's no badness in goodness, and there's no goodness in badness. People are mixed paints, like the color gray, but roads are either black or white. The relativism of gray makes no sense without the absolutism of black and white. There's both black and white in gray, but there's no black in white and there's no white in black.

We can get confused about that in an age of moral relativism, and we need to keep reminding ourselves of the simple truth of the goodness of goodness and the badness of badness. The very first Psalm tells us that. It is about two roads, good and evil, and they lead to two opposite destinations. We all know that, deep down, instinctively. But it is good to remind ourselves, because we are all very spiritually absentminded. We all have a serious attention deficit disorder when it comes to God.

There is a total identity between God and goodness, and therefore between God's way and the best way. But what, exactly, is meant by God's "way" or God's "ways"?

The first and most obvious answer is that God's way is the way God wants us to live. It is an image for God's will, which is revealed to us very clearly in God's law. That law may be hard to obey, but it's not hard to understand. We like to pretend it's hard to understand because that makes it easier to obey. We like to make it vague and foggy because our souls and our character and our lives are vague and foggy. But that's a rationalization, a pretense, a dishonesty. And our conscience knows better.

In the Old Testament there are three levels of God's law. There are no fewer than 613 specific laws or commandments from God, most of them having to do with either civil laws for the public life of ancient Israel, about what we would classify as social and political details, or liturgical laws about the details of public worship and liturgical sacrifice that God mandated for his chosen people. The civil laws are no longer in force because today's Israel is a secular political entity that lives in a very different world, a very different time, than Old Testament Israel, and the liturgical laws are no longer in force because the temple no longer exists and the liturgical sacrifices of food and animals that God mandated in the Old Testament have not been carried out since AD 70, when the Romans destroyed Jerusalem and the temple.

A second level of the law, or the way, is the Ten Commandments. Properly interpreted, these encompass all our moral obligations, and they are for all times, all cultures, and all people, forever, both individually and collectively. Every civilized society knows them. There is no society in history that believes that piety to God and reverence to family are evil or that murder, robbery, adultery, lying, greed, and lust are good. This moral law is not only "out there" in ten written commandments, on tablets of stone or pages of paper, but also "in here," in the heart, in the conscience, and cannot be erased. They are things we can't not know. We can't rip up our moral motherboard, no matter how we try. We can only rip up the laws we make, not the laws God makes. When the Supreme Court ruled against public funding for displays of the Ten Commandments, the ruling took place inside the Supreme Court building, and inscribed in stone on the facade of that building were—the Ten Commandments!

The third and deepest level of God's law is the summary of the Ten Commandments that Jesus quoted from the Old Testament: "You shall love the LORD, your God, with all your heart, with all your soul, and with all your mind. . . . You shall love your neighbor as yourself" (Matt. 22:37–39). That is the heart of the matter because that is the matter of the heart. We all know that. No one thinks selfishness and hate are good or that unselfish love and charity are evil.

So the first meaning of "God's way" is God's commandments, which tell us God's will for us. They are not the same kind of laws as the laws of physics or mathematics, which are always obeyed by the universe, not freely but necessarily. The number three can never choose to become an even number, and triangles can never have four sides, and gravity never repels, and energy always flows from higher concentrations to lower concentrations. Moral laws, in contrast, can be disobeyed because they are addressed to our will, our free choice. Our physical heart cannot choose to stop circulating blood, but our spiritual heart can choose to stop circulating love. That's because God is not like the Godfather, who makes you an offer you can't refuse. He is God the Father, who makes you an offer you *can* refuse. Why? Because that is what love does, and God is love.

That leads us to a second level of meaning in the image of God's "ways." It is God's personality, God's character, God's nature. God has a personality. He is not everything. There are things he is not. He is good, not evil; just, not unjust; wise, not foolish; merciful, not cruel; loving, not selfish. He is *infinitely* good and just and wise and merciful and loving, but "infinite" does not mean "everything in general and nothing in particular." God is not like a tapioca pudding, and we are not just lumps of tapioca. God is not a blob of being. God is not a "what" but a "who." And he invites us to get to know him, as we get to know a friend or a spouse or a parent.

How do we get to know him? By practicing his presence by prayer and by deliberate obedience to his will. When the Jews asked Jesus how they could understand his teaching with their minds, he responded by saying something about their will: he said, "Whoever chooses to do his will shall know whether my teaching is from God or whether I speak on my own" (John 7:17). In other words, we get to know God in the same way we get to know each other: by loving him. Love is not essentially a feeling; it is a willing that is also a knowing. The heart does not just feel; it knows. It opens *eyes*. An open heart is the source of an open mind.

And this is the single ultimate reason for all of God's commandments: he repeats this reason many times in the Old Testament when he is giving Israel all her many laws. He says, "Be holy, for I, the LORD, your God, am holy" (Lev. 19:2). He does not say we must obey him because he is the boss; he says we must obey him because he is holy. We worship God not because he is almighty but because he is all-holy.

We *should* be holy, because God *is* holy. Holiness is not just an ideal; it is a fact. It is the nature of ultimate reality, the nature of God. We must be holy because to be holy is to conform to the nature of ultimate reality. Holiness is realism. We must be holy because we must live in the real world. We must be saints because we must be sane. Sanctity is sanity.

And this brings us to a third meaning of the image of the road, or the way. Like God himself, God's way is a person, the Son of God, God the Son, the one who came to earth and said not merely, like all other human teachers, "I teach the way" but "I AM the way." The Way is not an *it*; it is a *he*. There is no more perfect definition of the good man than the God-man. There is no better definition of the way we are to be and live and think and love than Jesus Christ himself. He is not just the *best example* of the way; he *is* the way. He is perfect God and perfect man.

So if anyone asks you what is the meaning of life, pull out your Rosary and point to the crucifix.

SECOND READING

1 PETER 3:18–22 _____

Beloved: Christ suffered for sins once, the righteous for the sake of the unrighteous, that he might lead you to God. Put to death in the flesh, he was brought to life in the Spirit. In it he also went to preach to the spirits in prison, who had once been disobedient while God patiently waited in the days of Noah during the building of the ark, in which a few persons, eight in all, were saved through water. This prefigured baptism, which saves you now. It is not a removal of dirt from the body but an appeal to God for a clear conscience, through the resurrection of Jesus Christ, who has gone into heaven and is at the right hand of God, with angels, authorities, and powers subject to him.

There are many important points in today's epistle, but there are a few that may surprise us, and that we might miss. I want to point them out. They are all connections among four real events. One event is Jesus' descent into the world of the dead on Holy Saturday; another is Noah's ark; the third is our baptism; and the fourth is Jesus' Resurrection. You are probably familiar with all four events, but you probably don't realize how closely they are connected.

Let's begin with Jesus' whereabouts between his death and his Resurrection. Peter says that in the Spirit he "went to preach to the spirits in prison." This is not an earthly prison but the place of the dead, something like purgatory, where the spirits, or souls, of the dead who had been disobedient, back in the days of Noah, were waiting for him as their only hope of salvation. This place, or state, or condition, is what is meant by the Apostles' Creed when it says that Jesus "descended into hell." The Greek word that is translated "hell" there is not the word for the place of eternal torment for the damned and for demons but simply the place of the dead. They are called "spirits" because their bodies are dead. Christ came to "preach" to them the Good News of their salvation. They are neither already in heaven nor in the hell of the damned, nor are they alive on earth, so they must be in purgatory. What Christ did on Calvary thousands of years later saved them retroactively, so to speak. For Christ saved not only those who died after him but also those who died before him. Christ's act of salvation on the cross worked not only forward, applying to all who came after him and believed and hoped in the Savior who came, but also backward, to all who believed and hoped in the Messiah, the promised Savior to come. There is only one Savior, even though there are different relationships to him in time.

But Peter focuses on those who were alive during the days of Noah because he sees the ark as a symbol of Christ and Christ's Church—as "the ark of salvation" from the flood of sin. The flood of water that God brought about in Noah's day cleansed the sinful earth so that it could begin again. Peter sees this as a natural sign and symbol of Baptism, which uses water to cleanse not the body but the soul by removing original sin.

He goes so far as to say that Baptism "saves you." It is not just a symbol, as most Protestants believe; it actually effects what it symbolizes: it really changes you and puts into your soul the supernatural life of God. All the Gospels contrast Jesus' baptism with that of John the Baptist this way: John baptized only with water, symbolizing repentance, but Jesus baptizes with fire and with the Holy Spirit. Christian Baptism, Baptism in the name of the Father and the Son and the Holy Spirit, actually puts the life of God, the Spirit of God, the Holy Spirit, into our souls.

Man did not invent the sacraments; God did. The Church did not invent the sacraments; Christ did. The Church received them from Christ's chosen Apostles, who received them from Christ. In establishing the sacraments, Christ used natural, material, visible means like water, wine, and bread to do his supernatural, spiritual, invisible work: water in Baptism, chrism oil in Confirmation, bread and wine in the Eucharist, words in the sacrament of Reconciliation or Confession and in the sacrament of Matrimony, the laying on of hands in the sacrament of Holy Orders, and oil in the sacrament of Extreme Unction or Anointing of the Sick.

God's life, God's invisible, spiritual, eternal, supernatural life, is the food of our souls; and the visible, material sacraments are like food delivery services. But God delivers only when we ask him to. The sacraments do not work like machines, like technology, or like magic, impersonally and automatically. We have to believe in them and choose them, want them, ask for them. But our faith does not make them work; God makes them work. Our faith is our opening the door of our souls to let the food in. God himself is the food of our souls.

Why does Peter mention Christ's Resurrection in this connection, saying that Baptism works "through the resurrection"? Because none of the sacraments would work without the Resurrection. We can't be saved by a dead Savior. It is Christ's Resurrection that gives life to the sacraments because they all give us not just a symbol of Christ or a reminder of Christ but Christ himself, "alive and kicking." Christ is the actor in the sacraments. He really does things to us in them. We meet him there.

We also meet him in prayer and in moral choices, and in every act of genuine human love, but we meet him in the most powerful way in the sacraments that he himself gave to us. They are not merely ceremonies or symbols or beautiful works of art. They change us. Baptism is like a maternity ward; and Confirmation is like a workout gym; and the Eucharist is like a dining room; and Confession is like a bathroom; and Anointing of the Sick is like a hospital, or like hospice; and Holy Orders is like a kitchen; and Marriage is like a bedroom. They are seven aspects of our lives, like seven rooms in our house. They are holy places, the holiest places on earth. They are where earth and heaven meet and touch.

The devil hates and fears them all, especially the two ongoing sacraments of the Eucharist and Confession. He will do anything he can to keep you away from them, to starve your soul of their food, because he's always fighting against you, and if you are starving you cannot fight very well. Life is a war; it is spiritual warfare. It is also like an election: God always casts a vote for you, and the devil always casts a vote against you, and you cast the deciding vote. So the sacraments are like ballot boxes where you vote for God. Vote for the Lamb, not for the donkey or the elephant. They can't save you.

GOSPEL
MARK 1:12–15 _____

The Spirit drove Jesus out into the desert, and he remained in the desert for forty days, tempted by Satan. He was among wild beasts, and the angels ministered to him.

After John had been arrested, Jesus came to Galilee proclaiming the gospel of God: "This is the time of fulfillment. The kingdom of God is at hand. Repent, and believe in the gospel."

_____

The title of a famous spiritual classic, by Thomas à Kempis, is *The Imitation of Christ*. That is one way to describe our lives as Christians. Lent fits into that pattern because the forty days of the Lenten fast are our imitation of Jesus' fast of forty days in the desert.

This fast was not his own idea; the Gospel says that "the Spirit drove Jesus out into the desert." This same Spirit, the Holy Spirit, moves us, in a gentler way, into the much gentler desert of our Lenten fast in imitation of Jesus. Since he is our model, we, too, are moved by the same Holy Spirit, both through our individual conscience and also through the Church, for the Holy Spirit is the soul of the Church.

The Gospel says that Jesus was alone there in the desert, with no other human beings, only wild beasts, angels, and demons. He fasted for forty days not only from food but also from human friendship, which is even more basic than food. It would be worse to be the last person alive on earth forever, even if you were surrounded by plenty of food, than to be hungry but surrounded by friends. Animals and angels are both good and important—in fact, both are much more important to us than we usually think—but even good friends above us and below us are not human friends. We are neither animals nor angels. Animals have no spiritual souls, and angels have no mortal bodies.

And these animals in Jesus' desert were not cute, cuddly pets; they were "wild beasts." Some animals help us, either as our food or as our pets, but some animals harm us, like wasps or lions or poisonous snakes. Similarly, some spirits help us: the good angels, who guard us and guide us; but some try to harm us: the evil spirits who tempt us. Jesus is suspended among all these forces, alone.

He was led there by the Holy Spirit to toughen up his humanity, so to speak, like basic training in the Army; to prepare for his three years of spiritual warfare in his public ministry, which would culminate in his Passion and Death and Resurrection. He prepared for this for the first thirty years of his life, the silent years, but especially during these forty days.

Lent is like a desert because it is a time of fasting. Fasting is not only about food but also about many other deliberate sacrifices of little innocent good things that make our lives soft or pleasant or convenient, like sugar or desserts or parties or alcohol or games or TV shows or extra sleep.

People today rarely talk about fasting. They talk about dieting. But dieting is a dull compromise, while feasting and fasting are parts of a drama. Fasting and feasting are like black and white; dieting is like gray. Fasting and feasting is like white and red; dieting is like pink: a compromise. There are areas of life where we need compromise, but we appreciate things best by contrast.

Fasting and feasting give us the contrast, the drama; dieting gives us no contrast. Dieting may be a good thing, especially since too many of us are overweight and unhealthy, but dieting is not really a form of fasting, even though it is expressed in the same physical actions of not eating certain foods. Dieting is only for yourself and your body, while fasting is for others and for your soul. It is for others because it can be offered up as a prayer for God's greater graces for those you love. And it is for your soul because it makes your soul stronger, and we need the hard virtues, like courage, just as much as we need the soft virtues, like compassion.

God gave us fasting for the sake of the feasting, not the feasting for the sake of the fasting, just as he allows suffering for greater joy in the end, not joy for suffering. The Gospel is fundamentally the Good News, not the Bad News. But to appreciate the good, we need to know the bad. The height of the mountain is measured by the depth of the valley. It is the Church who gives us fasts, but it is the Church who also gives us feasts. She gives us Easter at the end of Lent, and Christmas at the end of Advent.

Fulton Sheen used to say that there are two philosophies of life: one says, "First the fast, then the feast," and the other says, "First the feast, and then the fast." Selfishness, self-indulgence, and addiction demand the feast first, and that never works; it always backfires and ends in unhappiness. Self-control and self-discipline and self-sacrifice and self-giving, on the other hand, if they are reasonable and prudent, always end in happiness and the satisfaction of a job well done. Playing first and working later spoils both play and work, because if we have not yet done the work we know we ought to do, we will worry about that while we play, and that nagging knowledge that our work is unfinished will spoil our play. And then the work will also be spoiled because it will be hurried and sloppy since we have wasted too much time on play. But if we work first and then play, both the work and the play will be better. The work will be done better because we put it first, and it will be done with more happiness and hope and anticipation of play as our reward. The play will also be done better because it will not be haunted by worry about the work that is yet to be done; the play will be done with the happiness and satisfaction and self-congratulation of a deserved reward.

So in the end, our fasting makes for our greater enjoyment. Try it; you'll like it. It's not a kill-joy thing; it's a make-joy thing.

SECOND SUNDAY OF LENT

FIRST READING

Genesis 22:1–2, 9a, 10–13, 15–18 _____

God put Abraham to the test. He called to him, "Abraham!" "Here I am!" he replied. Then God said: "Take your son Isaac, your only one, whom you love, and go to the land of Moriah. There you shall offer him up as a holocaust on a height that I will point out to you."

When they came to the place of which God had told him, Abraham built an altar there and arranged the wood on it. Then he reached out and took the knife to slaughter his son. But the Lord's messenger called to him from heaven, "Abraham, Abraham!" "Here I am!" he answered. "Do not lay your hand on the boy," said the messenger. "Do not do the least thing to him. I know now how devoted you are to God, since you did not withhold from me your own beloved son." As Abraham looked about, he spied a ram caught by its horns in the thicket. So he went and took the ram and offered it up as a holocaust in place of his son.

Again the Lord's messenger called to Abraham from heaven and said: "I swear by myself, declares the Lord, that because you acted as you did in not withholding from me your beloved son, I will bless you abundantly and make your descendants as countless as the stars of the sky and the sands of the seashore; your descendants shall take possession of the gates of their enemies, and in your descendants all the nations of the earth shall find blessing—all this because you obeyed my command."

_____

What is the point, what is the lesson, of this shocking story of God testing Abraham by commanding him to kill his innocent son Isaac? Is it that the moral law does not really bind us? That's not what the rest of the Bible teaches. Is it that God is arbitrary? Is it that, since God is the boss, anything goes as long as it pleases him? That's not the God of the Bible; that's an irrational tyrant. And is God testing Abraham because he does not know how strong Abraham's faith is and this is how he finds out? That's not the God of the Bible either. All three of those interpretations contradict the rest of the Bible.

When God gives his laws to his chosen people Israel, he repeatedly says that the reason for them is this: "Be holy, for I, the LORD, your God, am holy" (Lev. 19:2). The moral law reflects God's character. It describes what God is like. And God is not a murderer or an irrational tyrant, or an uncertain experimenter. So the point of this story is not that. What is it, then?

God is not arbitrary or irrational. He is mysterious to us, but that is not because he is less than rational but because he is more than rational. God says to his prophet Isaiah, "Come now, and let us reason together" (Isa. 1:18 KJV). God invented reason and intelligence; it is part of his image. God is not irrational. God is truth itself.

Nor is the lesson that God is simply the boss, omnipotent, all-powerful. He is, but that's not why we worship him. It's because he's *good*. His power is used for his goodness. It's not that for God "might makes right." It doesn't, either for God or for us. Power is to be judged by a higher standard of moral good and evil. That's the message of all the prophets.

Nor is God performing a kind of laboratory experiment in order to find out whether Abraham's faith and obedience are total. God does not need to find out anything. God is never ignorant of anything. God knows everything, including the secrets of every human heart, and also including what to us is the future. It's not God but Abraham who has to learn who Abraham is and also who God is.

So what is the lesson then? There are two. The obvious lesson that the text itself spells out is total trust, total faith and obedience. Abraham's faith is tested and approved by God. Abraham trusts God completely and absolutely, and therefore obeys completely and absolutely.

That interpretation is right as far as it goes. But it lacks two things. First, it reveals who Abraham is—faithful—but what does this story reveal about who God is? And second, the interpretation that emphasizes Abraham's trust and obedience reveals what religion is, what our right relation to God is, but what does it reveal about morality, about our right relation to our neighbor and to moral laws like "Thou shalt not murder"?

It *seems* to reveal that God is less moral than Abraham because Abraham loves God but God does not seem to love Abraham. It seems to reveal that God is selfish because he asks Abraham to give him back the son he miraculously gave Abraham when his wife was way past menopause. And it seems to reveal that God does not want Abraham to love his neighbor, even his closest neighbor, his own son, because he tells Abraham to kill Isaac, and of course killing someone is not an act of love.

But in fact, it reveals the exact opposite of these shocking things that it seems to reveal. It reveals that God, unlike the gods of pagan religions, does *not* want human sacrifice but animal sacrifice instead, and it also reveals that God is so unselfish that he himself gives up his own son for us.

In the Jewish tradition, this story is interpreted as God not approving human sacrifice but forbidding it. That's the new lesson God's chosen people had to learn: that the true God created man in his own image and that therefore human life is sacred. No other people knew that. Every other culture approved human sacrifice, usually only as an emergency measure but sometimes as an everyday, ongoing thing, as with the Aztecs in Mexico and the Canaanites in Palestine. Both cultures worshiped the demon gods that ruled their cultures by ritually murdering one-third of all their children by either cutting out their hearts or making them walk into the fire or both.

(By the way, one-third is close to same proportion of our children that we kill. The only difference is that we do it before they are born rather than after, and that the name of the evil god that we obey when we abort our own children is not Moloch or Baal but our own sexual freedom and autonomy.)

All other cultures in the world in Abraham's time practiced human sacrifice. The idea that the true God was only one God, not many, was rare, but not unknown. There were a few countercultural nonconformists in polytheistic pagan cultures who knew there was one god, like Socrates or Akhenaten. Also, although the gods of Gentile cultures were no more moral than we, since we created them in our image, yet a few people, like Socrates, thought the true God was wholly good. But no one ever came up with the idea that God created us in his own image, that he made us his adopted children, and that human life was therefore sacred. That truth was radical and revolutionary, and its origin is here in this story. The lesson God planned to teach Abraham from the beginning came at the end of the story, not the beginning: that he did *not* want human sacrifice; that man is not just another animal, as many of our modern pagans say.

The Christian interpretation adds another layer to this Jewish one. The ram that God provided for Abraham to sacrifice instead of his son Isaac represented the Lamb of God, God's own Son whom he himself would provide to suffer the punishment due to us for our sin. That was what all the divinely instituted sacrifices of lambs in the temple for the next two thousand years would signify. The full meaning of the story of Abraham and Isaac would not be known until the Messiah came.

God does not act without our consent. Abraham's unqualified yes to God's will was like Mary's *fiat* to the angel. Abraham's total faith brought about the Jewish preparation for our salvation, the liturgical symbol of our salvation, the Lamb of God; Mary's brought about the thing signified, the Lamb himself. That's what faith does: it's not just belief, and it's not just about us; it opens the door for God to act as he will in our lives. And his will is our salvation.

RESPONSORIAL PSALM
PSALM 116:10, 15, 16–17, 18–19 _____

R. (116:9) **I will walk before the Lord, in the land of the living.**

I believed, even when I said,
  "I am greatly afflicted."

170

Precious in the eyes of the LORD
 is the death of his faithful ones.

O LORD, I am your servant;
 I am your servant, the son of your handmaid;
 you have loosed my bonds.
To you will I offer sacrifice of thanksgiving,
 and I will call upon the name of the LORD.

My vows to the LORD I will pay
 in the presence of all his people,
In the courts of the house of the LORD,
 in your midst, O Jerusalem.

This beautiful Psalm-prayer can be prayed by anyone who believes in the true God, the God who is not just a limited pagan deity who helps us with a few of our problems but the one and only God who designed and created us and who is pure love and goodwill toward us, even in our afflictions, so that we can trust him totally and say, "I believed, even when I said, 'I am greatly afflicted.'" That is the God worshiped by Jews and Muslims as well as by Christians. But Christians can see a deeper dimension in this prayer, as in most of the Psalms.

In fact, there are at least seven uniquely Christian points or aspects in these few verses.

First, the Christian can say "Precious in the eyes of the LORD is the death of his faithful ones" because Christ's Resurrection has defeated death, so that our death, like his, is a door to higher life.

Second, the Christian can say "O LORD, I am your servant; I am your servant, the son of your handmaid" because it is Mary, the Mother of God, who showed us the vocation of all Christians when she said, "Behold, I am the handmaid of the Lord. May it be done to me according to your word"

(Luke 1:38)—and that was not just piety but power, because at that moment the Word became flesh and dwelt among us.

Third, the Christian can say to God "You have loosed my bonds" because the worst bonds are not suffering or disease or death or even slavery but sin, and Christ has loosed those bonds, those chains, by his death on the cross.

Fourth, the Christian can say to God "To you will I offer sacrifice of thanksgiving" because that is what the Mass is: thanksgiving not just for all the blessings of this life but above all for the salvation God has wrought in Christ.

Fifth, the Christian can say "I will call upon the name of the LORD" because Christ revealed the name of God as our Father by making us his adopted children.

Sixth, the Christian can say "My vows to the LORD I will pay in the presence of all his people" because the Mass is public, collective worship, the worship of the Body of Christ. All of the Bible's descriptions of heavenly worship are communal.

Seventh, the Christian can say "In the courts of the house of the LORD, in your midst, O Jerusalem" because the holy city for Christians does not depend on any earthly city or building, like Jerusalem or Mecca or Rome. The city of God is the Church of Christ, the Mystical Body of Christ, the true Jerusalem. All holy cities on earth are symbols of that heavenly city. Heaven is where God is, and God is in his people; therefore, the Mass is the worship of heaven. Angels and saints join with us, literally, not because the *building* is the holy city but because we are, and that is true only through Christ.

The more Christian our minds and hearts are, the more Christian meanings we will find in the Old Testament, especially the Psalms. Jesus prayed them, because he is the eternal Word of God whose Spirit inspired them. Many of them are messianic. We are not imposing an alien, external interpretation on them by interpreting them in this Christ-centered way. The God they address is the God who designed them that way, the God who knew from the beginning that he would send his Son and who prepared the way for him in many ways and in many places in the Old Testament. When Christ came, his claim was not to replace or to override the Law and the prophets but to fulfill them.

The Jesuits have a great saying: that we can and should "find God in all things." "Jesuits" means literally "Jesus people," and for Jesus people, finding God everywhere means finding Jesus everywhere. That takes many different forms, in many different places; and the first and most obvious place is in the Holy Scriptures. Jesus is the lens through which we most truly see all of the divinely inspired Scriptures of the Old Testament. And he is also the lens through which we most truly see the ultimate meaning of all the events of our present lives.

SECOND READING
Romans 8:31b–34 _____

Brothers and sisters: If God is for us, who can be against us? He who did not spare his own Son but handed him over for us all, how will he not also give us everything else along with him?

Who will bring a charge against God's chosen ones? It is God who acquits us. Who will condemn? Christ Jesus it is who died—or, rather, was raised—who also is at the right hand of God, who indeed intercedes for us.

To get the most out of this passage, there is no need for cleverness or scholarship or subtlety or hidden wisdom. In fact, they all divert and distract from the point, which is right on the literal surface. "If God is for us, who can be against us?" If almighty God, the Creator and Lord of the universe, takes our side; if God's wisdom and power and love make all things in our lives, even the bad things, even the tragedies, to work together for our greater good; if the God of power is also the God of love; if God loves us far more than we love the dearest person in our lives—why, then, nothing can harm us, in the long run. Nothing! Not Satan and all his evil spirits. Not hell itself. The gates of hell will not prevail against the People of God, which is what Christ's Church is. It is people, not just principles and practices and values and laws and creeds. It is a visible institution, but it is also an invisible spiritual organism, a Body—Christ's Mystical Body. It is God's gift to us.

Nothing and no one can defeat God, and therefore insofar as we are with God, in Christ, because we are members of his Body, organs in his body, nothing can defeat us in the end. Nothing can defeat our divine protection, not even our own stupid sins, if only we sincerely repent of them.

Thus, as St. Paul says, God makes all things work together for good for those who love him, those who are called according to his providential purposes. Not all things are good, but all things work together for good for those who are characters in God's novel, because our Author loves every last one of us. In fact, he loves us so dearly that if we felt that love in all its fullness without blinders, without shadows, and without ignorance—if the divine sun shone directly on our eyes without any clouds between—we would go blind; we could not possibly endure it.

But God does not *have* to love us. Love is a free choice. That's why it's news: "the Good News." It sounds too good to be true. How do we know it's not just our desperate desires plus our fairy-tale imaginations that invented this story, this incredible good news of the God who loves us? God's love can't be proved, even if God's existence and wisdom and power can be proved, because it depends on God's free choice. You don't choose to exist, or to have wisdom or power, but you choose to love. How do we know God chose to love us?

Because of Jesus. Because Jesus is the complete revelation of God, the Word of God, and the Son of God, and God gave up his own only begotten Son, the one he loved *infinitely*, for us. He gave him up to death to save us from death, which is the necessary punishment for sin. St. Paul writes, "The wages of sin is death, but the gift of God is eternal life in Christ Jesus our Lord" (Rom. 6:23). *Wages* and *gifts* are opposites. Wages are necessary; gifts are free. Wages are demanded by justice; gifts are chosen by love. Wages are deserved; gifts are not. We don't *deserve* God, or heaven, or salvation. What ridiculous arrogance it would be to think that we did! To think that when we die and meet God we could say to him, "You have to let me into your eternal, infinite, incomprehensible joy; you have to adopt me into your heavenly family; you have to let me share your very life, because I deserve it." If you think that, you are not only stupid and arrogant, you are morally insane.

The incredible news, the Good News, the Gospel, is that God freely chose to love us and spared nothing to save us from the just punishment that our sins deserved—namely, exclusion from himself and his life and his heaven. He spared nothing, not even the life of his own dearly beloved Son. If you want concrete *proof* that God loves you, look at a crucifix. If you want to know *how much* God loves you, look at a crucifix.

Look at his arms. They are not held close to his sides; they are extended out to the opposite ends of the earth. They embrace everybody. They are opened out and pointed in every direction without limit. Nothing limits his love, not even your own sins. Your sins limit not his love but only your reception of his love.

Look at his five wounds; look at the blood pouring out of his feet and his hands and his side. Each of the five wounds in Christ's body is a mouth, and the spilled blood that comes out of those mouths is a word, and the word is love.

St. Paul's argument is unanswerable because it is not an abstract argument but a historical fact: the fact of Christ; that Christ is what God did for us—not argued for us, not proved for us, not preached to us, but *did* for us—that "he who did not spare his own Son but handed him over for us all, how will he not also give us everything else along with him?"

Will God deny us little goods after he has given us the greatest good? If God gave us *everything* in giving us Christ, how could there be anything more than that? How could anything be more than everything? If God did not hold back the greatest gift he could give, how could there be any other good gift that he still holds back from us? He has conquered sin and death and hell and Satan for us; how could any lesser evil ever possibly conquer him and his love for us?

But, you say, all sorts of bad things happen. God lets us fall into terrible tragedies. Yes, he does. And he delivers us from them all. There are two acts to his drama, as there are in every good story we tell. The first act is the tragedy, and the second act is the comedy, the deliverance. That's the plot of every great love story. If there was no lovelessness and loneliness, there could be no conquest of it by love; love would have nothing to conquer. If there was no suffering, there could be no joy of deliverance from suffering. If there was no death, there could be no resurrection. If there was no tragic misunderstanding and alienation, there could be no tears of joy in reconciliation. If there was no losing, there could be no finding.

And the joy of the finding is far greater than the misery of the losing. Think of your favorite love story, the one that broke your heart and gave you the great gift of tears. Remember the tears you shed when the story came to that point of reconciliation and reunion and acceptance and forgiveness. You remember those tears that you shed at the end of the story more than you remember the tears you shed in the rest of the story, the tears at all the tragedies and sufferings. Cherish that memory. Cherish those tears. Those tears of joy are the truth, the truth of all the great love stories we tell. Those tears, that joy, are the truth of the stories we invent because they are the truth of the story we're in, the story God is telling. Our fictions are not facts, but God's fictions are. The story he tells is our fact. And the heart of that story, in a single word, is Christ. All the words of that story are summed up in a single word. Christ is not just one or some of the words of God, in the plural, but the Word of God, in the singular. It is Christ who proves the truth of the incredible good news that "God is love."

In a great story, everything works together for good in the end. But the characters don't see the end until they get there. But even when they don't see it, they can believe in it—even before they get to the end. Even as they "walk in the dark valley," they can fear no evil, because they know that God is with them (Ps. 23:4). Evil is real, but God delivers us from evil, both the evil of suffering and the evil of sin. But it takes time, and we are in time, and God is not done with us yet. He's a fisherman, and he plays the fishing line with patience and infinite wisdom. He knows exactly what he's doing. He makes no mistakes. *We* do, of course, many, many times. But he lets us make all those mistakes because he knows that that's the way we fools learn—the hard way. But we do learn, and that's his plan, his perfect plan for our lives. And it's very mysterious, of course, because God's infinite wisdom is bound to look mysterious to our finite minds. If it didn't, we'd be as wise as God. And we're not. I realize that's a terrible shock—to realize that we're not as wise as God—but it should be an even more terrible shock to realize that we're so foolish that we have to be reminded of that fact. Fortunately for us, God is very, very patient with his severely brain-damaged children, and he has an incredible sense of humor.

If we never suffered, we could have no compassion for those who suffer. If we had no fear, we could have no courage to face fear. If we had no poverty, no unmet needs, we could have no gratitude for gifts that filled our needs and overcame our poverty. And without compassion, without courage, and without gratitude, no one can be wise, or good, or even happy.

Jesus promised us two things: first, he said, "In the world you will have trouble," and second, "Take courage, I have conquered the world" (John 16:33).

That applies not only to the sufferings of our life but also to death. The Bible calls death our "last enemy" (1 Cor. 15:26) and says that God did not invent death (Wis. 2:23–24). When someone we love dies, we should not say that "God took him" but that death took him, but God took death.

Sufferings are little deaths. So when someone we love is suffering, including ourselves, we should not say that God wants them to suffer but that God wants to give them the joy that they cannot attain without suffering.

That joy, that future joy, that hoped-for joy, that promised joy, that joy that God sees coming from our sufferings and that we can only believe in and trust in and hope for, that joy that we do not yet see coming but God does—that joy is the joy that is meant when the Bible says that "rejoicing in the LORD must be your strength!" (Neh. 8:10).

We are all like women in childbirth. Our hope for the incomparably great joy of birthing a child does not take away the pains of childbirth, but it wraps it in a new light, so that when we accept the whole package, the whole plan of God, we, like God, say yes to the pain, not because it is pain but because it is part of his plan, part of his wisdom and power and love. His wisdom is unlimited and makes no mistakes. His love for us is unlimited, not even by our sins. And his power is unlimited and meets no obstacles that he cannot conquer.

Christ did not come to take away our sufferings but to transform them, to give them a new meaning, a great and wonderful meaning. Our pains, and even our death, can now be part of Christ's pains, and our death can be part of Christ's death. We embrace our crosses because they are splinters of his cross. We embrace his cross not because it is a cross but because it is his cross, because he is there.

And as he transforms our sufferings, he transforms our joys and makes them so great that they are too big to enter into us, to fit inside of us, so we have to enter into them. When we enter heaven, we will hear his welcoming words: "Come, share your master's joy" (Matt. 25:21).

GOSPEL
MARK 9:2–10 _____

Jesus took Peter, James, and John and led them up a high mountain apart by themselves. And he was transfigured before them, and his clothes became dazzling white, such as no fuller on earth could bleach them. Then Elijah appeared to them along with Moses, and they were conversing with Jesus. Then Peter said to Jesus in reply, "Rabbi, it is good that we are here! Let us make three tents: one for you, one for Moses, and one for Elijah." He hardly knew what to say, they were so terrified. Then a cloud came, casting a shadow over them; from the cloud came a voice, "This is my beloved Son. Listen to him." Suddenly, looking around, they no longer saw anyone but Jesus alone with them.

As they were coming down from the mountain, he charged them not to relate what they had seen to anyone, except when the Son of Man had risen from the dead. So they kept the matter to themselves, questioning what rising from the dead meant.

This heavenly vision of Christ that Peter, James, and John had on the mountaintop is called the Transfiguration. They were so dazzled with his light and beauty that they were struck speechless. So of course it was Peter who spoke. Mark, whose Gospel came from Mark's close friendship with Peter, inserts these words, which were very probably Peter's own interpretation: "He hardly knew what to say." Peter was totally honest but usually confused; he had the habit of speaking first and thinking later, and of putting his foot in his mouth (he had foot-in-mouth disease); so he babbled out some nonsense plans about building three tents on the site. If that had been done, they probably would have made a lot of money by selling tacky, overpriced souvenirs, more money than they were making selling fish.

Peter's apparently pious plan was stupid for two reasons. First, if the Apostles had only listened to Jesus and understood what he had been teaching them for years, they would have known that what God wants first and most of all is not tents or temples made from the building materials of the world but temples in our souls and in our lives, temples made of faith and hope and, above all, charity. Peter was not wrong to want to build something beautiful for Christ; he was wrong about the building materials. Temples of brick and mortar, or of stained glass and stainless steel, are great and beautiful things if they are the expressions of that faith and hope and love, but they all eventually decay and collapse. They are no substitute for the interior temples that last forever. The cathedrals of the Middle Ages were the most beautiful buildings in the history of the world, buildings that almost miraculously transcended the primitive technology of the time. What explains them? Only that they were built with great faith and hope and love, to glorify the God who was really present on their altars in the Eucharist. They were built *by* love and *for* love, to glorify the God who is love itself and who died on the cross out of love for us and who loves us so completely that he instituted the Eucharist so that he could be present with us forever, until the end of time, hiding behind the appearances of bread and wine, on the altars of our churches. That's why Catholics built cathedrals.

The second reason Peter's reaction was stupid is that the three tents were to be for Jesus, Moses, and Elijah, not for the Father and the Son and the Holy Spirit, because at this point Peter and the others did not yet understand that Jesus was more than a great human prophet, not equal to Moses and Elijah but divine, equal to the Father and the Spirit.

It is a telling and precious little detail that Mark, the most simpleminded and practical of the four evangelists, describes the dazzling light in terms of chlorine bleach: "His clothes became dazzling white, such as no fuller on earth could bleach them." We see the same simple, childlike, honest peasant mind at work here as we see in Peter.

This vision was not a dream. The Apostles were awake and had their eyes open. It was not an imagining but a seeing, a vision of what was really there. Jesus always had this heavenly glory, but to protect our eyes he had kept his glory hidden from us until this moment—just as he does in the Eucharist, where he actively hides behind the appearances of bread and wine, like a child at Halloween hiding behind a costume.

The Transfiguration is the same kind of vision as one had by the servant of the prophet Elisha in the Old Testament. In that story, Elisha and his servant are surrounded by Elisha's enemies, a ring of soldiers with chariots, horses, and weapons, sent by a wicked king to kill Elisha; and Elisha's servant does not understand why his master is not afraid of them. So Elisha prays to God to open his servant's eyes. And God does, so that the servant now sees another army surrounding the first one, an army of horses and chariots made of fire, like the chariot of fire that had carried Elisha's great predecessor Elijah up to heaven: God's army of angels (see 2 Kings 6:17).

They are always there, but we do not see them. God did not put a vision *into* the eyes of Elisha's servant, or into the eyes of Peter and James and John on the Mount of Transfiguration; he simply removed the hiding, the disguise, the protective blinders on their eyes, so that they could see what was really there all the time but invisible most of the time.

We do not usually receive such striking visions, yet we are in exactly the same situation as Peter and James and John, and Elisha's servant, because we, too, are surrounded by the divine glory of Christ and his angels, 24/7; we just don't see it with the eyes of the body as they did.

But we see it with the eyes of faith! Faith is not a feeling; it is a seeing.

Our faith comes either from God's mind or from our own minds. If it comes from our own minds, then it's the world's biggest fantasy. If it comes from God's mind, then it's the world's biggest fact. We can be sure it's true because *God* has revealed it, and God can neither deceive nor be deceived.

We know we are surrounded by angels not because we see them as Elisha's servant did but because Jesus says so. Remember, when he blessed the little children, he said that "their angels even now see the face of the Father in heaven."

We know that Jesus shines with a heavenly radiance and beauty that is far greater than that of the angels, wherever he is really present—and he is really present in the Eucharist—even though we do not see it with the eyes of our body. We know this is so for a very simple reason: because the Church Jesus established to teach in his name and with his divine authority says so.

We see his glory with the eyes of our faith. Faith is like a telescope. It's another set of eyes. Remember what Jesus said to "Doubting Thomas" when Thomas finally saw the resurrected Jesus with his own bodily eyes: "Have you come to believe because you have seen me? Blessed are those who have not seen and have believed" (John 20:29).

When we need faith the most; when, to the eyes of the body alone, things seem to fall apart in us or in our lives; when our trust in the total wisdom and power and love of God is the hardest; when the appearances do not look like God's love and power and wisdom; when our senses show us winds and waves on the surface of our lives—that is when the anchor of faith is the most necessary, and also the most precious to God as well as to ourselves, and also the most powerful, because it trains the muscles not of our bodies but of our souls, the muscles of the eyes of faith.

Jesus gave to us, through St. Faustina, the shortest and most practical prayer of faith in the world, and we should pray it many times every day. It's just five words: "Jesus, I trust in you." That's what faith essentially means: trust.

It means belief in the truth of everything he says, because we trust the person who says it. We trust the words of Jesus because Jesus is the Word of God.

And Jesus promises us, in his own words, "If you believe you *will* see" (John 11:40). The skeptical world says, "Seeing is believing." The Christian replies that believing is also seeing.

Atheists often call themselves "the smarts," implying that believers are "the stupids." We are indeed stupid, and like Peter and the Apostles we all make mistakes—but not the mistake of being so arrogant that we call ourselves "the smarts." We're all stupid compared to God, stupid in different ways; but the stupidest mistake of all is to deny that we're stupid.

We often struggle to believe. Faith is not easy. Even when we believe, we often misunderstand, like Peter on top of the mountain. And even after that, after the mountaintop vision, when they were coming down the mountain, Mark shows us how stupid they were when he writes that Jesus told them to keep this vision secret until he "had risen from the dead," and their reaction was to wonder what rising from the dead meant! They did not know that what rising from the dead meant was—rising from the dead. On a number of other occasions Jesus clearly told them, "I'm going to Jerusalem and the chief priests are going to kill me, and on the third day I'm going to rise from the dead." And they wondered what he could possibly mean by that. It couldn't possibly be really, literally true, could it?

Some Catholics today still wonder what the Church really means by saying that Jesus is really, truly, objectively present, fully present, personally present, in the Eucharist, Body and Blood, Soul and Divinity. Like Jesus, she means exactly what she says. Her Magisterium, her teaching authority, is Jesus' mouth, and her Eucharist is his Body.

At Holy Communion, we freely choose to receive his Body into our mouths because we have freely chosen to believe—that is, to receive and accept his words from his mouth. Our bodies will receive his Body because our minds have received his mind, by faith. Faith and good works are one thing, not two.

Faith always works, and receiving our Lord in the Eucharist is the first and greatest work of faith.

THIRD SUNDAY OF LENT

The readings given for Year A may be used in place of these.

FIRST READING

Exodus 20:1–17

(or Exodus 20:1–3, 7–8, 12–17) _____

In those days, God delivered all these commandments:
    "I, the LORD, am your God,
      who brought you out of the land of Egypt, that place of slavery.
You shall not have other gods besides me.
You shall not carve idols for yourselves
      in the shape of anything in the sky above
      or on the earth below or in the waters beneath the earth;
      you shall not bow down before them or worship them.
For I, the LORD, your God, am a jealous God,
      inflicting punishment for their fathers' wickedness
      on the children of those who hate me,
      down to the third and fourth generation;
      but bestowing mercy down to the thousandth generation
      on the children of those who love me and keep my commandments.
"You shall not take the name of the LORD, your God, in vain.
For the LORD will not leave unpunished
      the one who takes his name in vain.
"Remember to keep holy the sabbath day.
Six days you may labor and do all your work,
      but the seventh day is the sabbath of the LORD, your God.
No work may be done then either by you, or your son or daughter,
      or your male or female slave, or your beast,
      or by the alien who lives with you.

In six days the LORD made the heavens and the earth,
>   the sea and all that is in them;
>   but on the seventh day he rested.

That is why the LORD has blessed the sabbath day and made it holy.

"Honor your father and your mother,
>   that you may have a long life in the land
>   which the LORD, your God, is giving you.

You shall not kill.

You shall not commit adultery.

You shall not steal.

You shall not bear false witness against your neighbor.

You shall not covet your neighbor's house.

You shall not covet your neighbor's wife,
>   nor his male or female slave, nor his ox or ass,
>   nor anything else that belongs to him."

The Ten Commandments are about the ten most important dimensions of every human life: religious worship, language, work and rest, family, life and death, marriage, property, oaths, money and the things money can buy, and sex. That is why idolatry, blasphemy, oppression, family breakdown, murder, adultery, theft, lying, greed, and lust are ten of the most pervasive and destructive evils in every human life.

The Ten Commandments are the most well-known and well-tried and true prescriptions for social order in the history of the world. They are to the moral dimension of life what the creation in Genesis is to the physical dimension. They bring order out of chaos. They foster harmony and peace, and they deter strife and war. They are proved true not by argument but by facts, by history, both positively and negatively, both by the happiness of the individuals and cultures that believe them and obey them and by the unhappiness of the individuals and cultures that disbelieve them and disobey them.

This is not only the Law of God but also the law of human nature itself, the natural moral law, naturally known by reason and conscience. Every society in history acknowledges them. There has never been a society that believed that worship, reverence, rest, family, life, marriage, property, honesty, unselfishness, and self-control were evil and that felt guilty about protecting these goods; and there has never been a society that believed that idolatry, blasphemy, oppression, family breakdown, murder, adultery, theft, lying, greed, and lust were good and that felt a moral obligation to practice these evils. You could not even imagine such a society! It is simply a lie that the basic moral laws are socially and culturally relative, that what is morally right in one culture is morally wrong in another, that the Ten Commandments are just Jewish, not Gentile; or Western, not Eastern; or medieval, not modern; or white, not black; or "conservative," not "liberal." That is as clearly a lie as that the earth is flat. Yet this cultural moral relativism is taught by the most influential anthropologists, historians, sociologists, and psychologists in most of our modern secular universities.

St. Paul writes, "Through the law comes consciousness of sin" (Rom. 3:20). Without some version of the moral law, without a real, universally binding moral law, there is no definition of sin, because sin means disobeying that law. And without the knowledge of sin, there is no possibility of repentance for sin. And without repentance for sin there is no salvation. Therefore, a denial of the moral law, if this denial is one's deepest and truest conviction, makes salvation impossible. If the patient denies that he is ill, he will not ask for healing. The road to hell is not paved with good intentions; it is paved with stones that say, "I'm okay, you're okay." That is why modern moral relativism is an absolute disaster: not only does it make human moral health and happiness impossible in this world, but it also makes eternal salvation impossible if it is not abandoned and repented of. It is one of the devil's most powerful and successful inventions.

Fortunately, conscience was designed in heaven, not in Hollywood or Harvard. Even those who deny the absolute obligation to obey the moral law still have a conscience, even when they are suppressing it. For instance, they seldom say that Hitler was simply lacking in self-esteem, or that sadism and torture are not really evil for everyone, or that deliberate dishonesty and disobedience to your own individual conscience is sometimes right rather than always wrong. Moral obligation is something we can't really *not* know.

But we can deny what we know. We all know the moral law, and we all disobey it quite often, but some of us acknowledge it and some do not. Religion is by far the strongest thing that does acknowledge it. Every religion in the world takes morality very seriously. That's why religion is by far the solidest, surest, and most universal foundation for morality. There are abundant facts and statistics to prove that. Every religion in the world, even though they differ very widely in theology, has essentially the same morality, because human nature is essentially the same everywhere and everywhen.

If you deny the close relationship between morality and religion, ask yourself this question. Imagine you are walking alone at night on a deserted city street. Suddenly you see a very large man walking toward you, carrying something in his hand. You are afraid it is a weapon of some kind. Then, as he comes closer, you see what it is: it is a Bible. Does that make you feel more afraid of him, or less?

RESPONSORIAL PSALM
PSALM 19:8, 9, 10, 11 _____

R. (John 6:68c) **Lord, you have the words of everlasting life.**

The law of the LORD is perfect,
    refreshing the soul;
The decree of the LORD is trustworthy,
    giving wisdom to the simple.

The precepts of the LORD are right,
    rejoicing the heart;

The command of the LORD is clear,
   enlightening the eye.

The fear of the LORD is pure,
   enduring forever;
The ordinances of the LORD are true,
   all of them just.

They are more precious than gold,
   than a heap of purest gold;
Sweeter also than syrup
   or honey from the comb.

When we think of the law, we usually think of protection. The law protects the innocent from the guilty, the good from the evil. It threatens evil persons, potential criminals, with punishment; it deters them. It is a kind of force, or at least a threat of force, against evil, so that it works like a shield, or like a fence that surrounds a kids' playground in a busy downtown neighborhood to prevent the kids from running out into the street. The fence is the moral law. It's good; in fact, it's necessary.

That's pretty obvious. What may be puzzling is that the Psalmist sees it not just as good and necessary but also as beautiful. A fence doesn't have to be beautiful. No one writes romantic poetry about a fence or compares it to refreshing water, heartfelt rejoicing, precious gold, or sweet honey, but that's exactly what the Psalmist says about the law, the moral law, as summarized in the Ten Commandments.

So the law is more than just a fence for protection. The Psalmist praises the law as "refreshing the soul" and "rejoicing the heart," as "more precious than gold" and "sweeter also than syrup or honey." Elsewhere, in many other Psalms, David writes of how he *loves* the law, and how "blessed" is the man who "meditates on his law day and night" (Ps. 1:2). When you ask yourself the question "What is it that I love to meditate on all day and night?" the answer you probably think of first is the face of the person you have just fallen in love with, the person who is so beautiful to you that you just can't get her out of your mind. So why does the Psalmist treat the law more like a face than a fence? And why don't you?

I think there are at least two answers. The first is that the law, for the Jews, did for them what Christ does for Christians: it was their connection, their link, their umbilical cord, with God, the God of all meaning and goodness and hope. They not only looked *at* the Law, they also looked *along* the Law, as we look along a sign, or a word; and when they looked along the Law they saw not a fence but a face, the face of God, and God's love for them and God's beauty and goodness and adorable character. For pious religious Jews, reading the Law was like reading a love letter from their beloved. Love asks the beloved: "What do you want? What do you desire? What do you love? I want to fulfill your desire because I love you." And God, their beloved, answers that question with the Law, the Ten Commandments. "This is what I love: these values, this kind of person, this kind of life. Being that kind of person and living that kind of life is what would make me proud of you and happy. Give this to me; give me your will and your heart and your love, by trusting me and obeying me." They were eager to do that because they were God's lovers.

The love of God did not begin with Christianity; it began with Judaism. Love is not a new invention of the New Testament. It is the eternal nature of God, and it is the first and most fundamental of all the Old Testament commandments. It is the only one of the 613 commandments in the Old Testament that demands *everything*: "You shall love the LORD, your God, with all your heart, and with all your soul, and with all your strength" (Deut. 6:5). Jesus did not invent that, nor did he change it. It is the essence of Judaism as well as the essence of Christianity.

The Law was their intimate love letter from God. How far we are from this wisdom when we see it as a chain to imprison us, control us, or oppress us! That's like seeing healthy food as poison.

All ten of the Ten Commandments, not just the first three but also the last seven, which tell us how to treat our neighbors, are first of all about our relation with God. The Law was not just social but religious, not just natural but supernatural, not just horizontal but vertical. Even the natural, social, human parts of it are rooted in God, in God's will, in God's nature. After each of the many laws God gave to his chosen people in Leviticus, the book of the laws, he added, "Be holy, for I, the LORD, your God, am holy" (Lev. 19:2). The very nature of God was revealed in the Law. That's why the Jews loved it: because they loved God.

The Jews loved the Law because they saw God's law not as a set of external rules imposed by the Boss in the Sky to restrict and control their behavior, like prison guards, but as truths, as accurate maps through human life, so that all who follow the straight roads become not only obedient but also genuinely happy because those laws of God were based not only on God's will but also on God's nature and therefore also on human nature, because God created human nature in his own image and likeness. God's commandments are based on universal human needs; that's why the supernatural moral law coincides with the "natural moral law."

The two dimensions of human life, supernatural and natural, divine and human, religious and social, love of God and love of neighbor, religious piety and social justice, faith and works, principles and practice, orthodoxy and orthopraxy, are two dimensions of the very same law. The Jewish Scriptures, like the Christian Scriptures, do not separate these two things and ignore one of them to concentrate on the other, as we tend to do today. For instance, both the left and the right in today's politicized climate tend to emphasize morality, either social or individual, and tend toward either socialism or individualism, collectivism or libertarianism.

These two dimensions of the moral law, the vertical and the horizontal, the religious and the human, the theological and the social, are distinguished but joined in the Ten Commandments: the first three commandments are about our relations with God and the last seven about our relations with each other. But both come from the same God and lead back to the same God.

And Jesus repeated this unity when he summarized the whole moral law in just two great commandments: love God with our whole heart, mind, soul, and strength and love our neighbor as ourselves. These two dimensions, the divine and the human, the supernatural and the natural, the vertical and the horizontal, are joined like the two lines in a plus sign, or like the two wooden planks of a cross—of Christ's cross. For Christ, as both fully divine and fully human, is at the center of both together at once. So as Christ says, whatever we do to other people, who are his family, we do to him. That's not my exaggeration; those are Christ's words. When we snub or scream or sneer at others, we are snubbing Christ, screaming at Christ, sneering at Christ.

All Christians are members of Christ's Body. What you do to my body, you do to me. When you kick my butt, you kick me, because my butt is part of me. When you slap my face, you slap me, because my face is part of me. What you do to my body part, you do to me. And what we do to Christ's body parts, we do to him. And all Christians are members of his Body, not as individuals are members of clubs or political parties but as your organs are members of your body. The Church is not essentially an organization but an organism. He is the Head of that Body not as Bill Gates is the head of Microsoft but as that hairy ball between your shoulders is the head of your body.

Even our non-Christian neighbors are Christ's beloved children, Christ's family. He identifies with them even if they don't identify with him. When you harm a child, you harm the child's parents, as long as they love their children. And Christ loves his children infinitely. We harm the lover when we harm the ones he loves. And we make the lover happy when we do good to the ones he loves.

We can make Christ sad, and we can make Christ happy. He is a divine person, but he has a human nature too, a complete and perfect human nature, and therefore human feelings. If you want to make Jesus happy, if you love Jesus, obey his commandments.

That's what he says: "If you love me, you will keep my commandments"

(John 14:15). The greatest thing in life is not law but love, but the commandments of the law are the specific roads of love, the map of how to love.

SECOND READING
1 Corinthians 1:22–25 _____

Brothers and sisters: Jews demand signs and Greeks look for wisdom, but we proclaim Christ crucified, a stumbling block to Jews and foolishness to Gentiles, but to those who are called, Jews and Greeks alike, Christ the power of God and the wisdom of God. For the foolishness of God is wiser than human wisdom, and the weakness of God is stronger than human strength.

Athens and Corinth were the two largest, most famous, and most well-educated cities in Greece. When St. Paul's missionary journeys brought him to Athens, he interacted with the Stoic and Epicurean philosophers there, and he quoted some of their own poets in his brilliant sermon. But he made only a few converts, and we know nothing of the early Christian Church in Athens. St. Paul never wrote an epistle to the Athenians. But he wrote two long epistles to the Corinthians, because he made many more converts there. Why? Because when he went to Corinth, he says he decided to focus differently. He says he claimed to know nothing "except Jesus Christ, and him crucified" (1 Cor. 2:2).

Both cities were sophisticated and proud and famous and had many philosophers and poets in them, and St. Paul appealed to them in Athens to build a bridge between the wisdom the Athenians already had and the greater wisdom of the Gospel. That was not wrong, and some were converted by this broad appeal. But in Corinth he had a sharper and narrower focus, like laser light: Christ himself. He realized that the primary obstacle to faith was not ignorance but pride, and he directly challenged the Corinthians' pride in their human wisdom, contrasting it with the wisdom of God in Christ.

When Jesus appeared in Israel, many of the Jews believed that he was the promised Messiah. But what did that mean? There were at least two main opinions about who the Messiah would be. The most popular one was that he would be a new King David, a warrior who would free Israel from her Roman tyrants by military power. Some said it would be by the power of miracles, as Moses freed Israel from Egyptian slavery by the miracles of the ten plagues and the parting of the Red Sea. Another, less common interpretation was that the Messiah would bring wisdom rather than power; that he would be a great prophet and teacher, a rabbi, the greatest scribe or writer or scholar or philosopher. But the real Messiah did not fulfill either of these two expectations. As for the first one, Jesus did have the power to perform miracles, but they were only signs, pointing beyond themselves; and he did not use them to free Israel politically or militarily from Rome. As for the second expectation, he did teach with unparalleled wisdom, but his claim was not about his teachings but about himself and his work, which was first of all to die on the cross to save us from sin. Philosophers and sages said to us, "This is my mind," but Jesus saved us by saying, "This is my Body."

That did not seem like either power or wisdom. Yet, as St. Paul says in today's passage, that was the supreme power and the supreme wisdom, the power of God that seemed like the supreme weakness (for we are never weaker than when we die) and the wisdom of God that seemed like the supreme folly or foolishness (to apparently lose everything, to lose the whole world, by dying).

Whenever anyone meets the true God, they are shocked. He is always more than we expect, more than we possibly could have expected. The true God is always shocking. If he always fulfilled our expectations, he would not be the true God at all but a figment of our own imaginations.

Discovering the nature of the real world is always surprising, and often shocking, to our expectations and assumptions and prejudices: how big it is, how old it is, how complex it is, how little its mechanisms and forces resemble what we can see on the surface.

In a similar way, discovering the nature of real people, discovering what is in the personality and feelings of others, is always able to surprise us, even with those we know best, those in our own family. There is always more in their minds and feelings and imaginations and desires than we can know in our own minds, because they are not just carbon copies of us.

And the things that happen to us in our lives are never exactly what we anticipated. No one reading this is exactly who and what and where they thought they would be twenty or thirty or forty years ago.

Only our own dreams and fictions match our expectations, because they are no more than our own minds and imaginations. Reality is always more, as Shakespeare's Hamlet says to Horatio: "There are more things in heaven and earth, Horatio, than are dreamt of in your philosophy." That's what God says to us all the time, both in the nature of the universe and in the nature of other people, and even in our own lives. The real world is always shocking to our expectations. Sometimes it's shockingly worse, and sometimes it's shockingly better.

St. Paul presented to the Corinthians the greatest shock of all, the shock of Jesus Christ. Nobody expected that; nobody expected that kind of Messiah. Nobody expected that he would be God himself, or that God himself would die on the cross, or that that would be the strongest and wisest thing ever done.

When Jesus was dying on the cross, the unbelieving Jews said, "Let him come down from the cross now, and we will believe in him." He had performed miracles before; why not now? They taunted him: "He saved others; he cannot save himself" (Matt. 27:42). They did not realize the wisdom of their words: it was precisely by not saving himself that he saved others. He himself said, "Do you think that I cannot call upon my Father and he will not provide me at this moment with more than twelve legions of angels?" (Matt. 26:53). That would prove his divine power to everyone, wouldn't it? So why didn't he do that?

If Jesus had done that, and never died, and hung around for two thousand years, and performed miracle after miracle to save the world from every disaster and death, so that nobody ever suffered or died again, wouldn't that have proved to everybody that he was God so that there would be no unbelievers left, and wouldn't that have turned this world into heaven on earth? Jesus could have used his power to abolish all disease and poverty and war and suffering and death itself. Instead, he died.

Yes, he also rose, but he first died and kept his wounds in his resurrected body. He did not avoid death; he suffered it. It was the dead man who rose. And he did not prevent our death: he made us go through it too before we can rise from it, so that, like Christ, we can experience both death and resurrection, both suffering and deliverance, both sorrow and joy.

Even now there are some very clever people called "transhumanists," mainly in Silicon Valley, California, who are working on artificial immortality by genetic engineering. Some of them are serious scientists who actually believe they can do this. They probably can't, but if they do, they will not create heaven on earth but hell on earth. If you want to see what kind of world that would be, just leave a dozen eggs out on your kitchen table for a year and then smell them. As C.S. Lewis said, "We are like eggs at present. And you cannot go on indefinitely being just an ordinary, decent egg. We must be hatched or go bad."

The same is true of the soul as is true of the body: there has to be a death before there can be a resurrection into a transformed body and a transformed world. If your soul has never been broken, if your heart has never been broken by suffering love, by the coming together of love and suffering; if you have avoided life's greatest suffering by avoiding life's greatest joy, loving another person with your whole heart, then you are not a complete human being. The only whole heart is a heart that has been broken, because only a broken heart can experience life's supreme joy. Only a heart that has experienced failure can experience success. Only the heart that has given itself away by loving others can find itself. As Jesus said, only the grain of wheat that falls into the ground and dies can bring forth new life.

We should be able to understand the mistake the Jews who didn't believe in Jesus made about him: not understanding that the Messiah's supreme power, the power to save the world, was in dying. The Muslims make the same mistake. The Quran says that Jesus, as a true prophet of God, could not have really died on the cross because God would never allow his prophet to fail and suffer public disgrace. It's a shock to discover that the supreme power is weakness. As St. Paul wrote, "When I am weak, then I am strong" (2 Cor. 12:10). To be really strong is to be good, and to be good is to be loving, and to be loving is to be vulnerable, and to be vulnerable is to be apparently weak; therefore, to be really strong is to be apparently weak.

St. Paul says, "Jews demand signs and Greeks look for wisdom" (1 Cor. 1:22), but God's answer to both is Christ, the wisdom of God and the power of God. But this wisdom is not philosophy but the Gospel, which seems absurd—God becomes a man and dies out of love for us rebellious, selfish sinners. And this greatest kind of power is not miracles—Jesus' *refusal* to save himself from the cross by miracles is the greatest of all miracles. But it's shocking. It's not what anyone expected.

No one meets the true God without being shocked. When our little minds meet God's great mind, we are shocked into humility and awe. When our selfish wills meet God's unselfish will, we are shocked into repentance and conversion. We all need those mental and moral corrections; we need to conform our minds to God's mind and our wills to God's will, not vice versa.

Jesus is the total, supreme, final, complete revelation of God. St. Paul preached only Jesus to the Corinthians because he realized that we see God most truly and most completely not when we try to look beyond Jesus but when we look at Jesus. And Jesus is the supreme shock—the supreme power that looks like weakness, and the supreme wisdom that looks like folly.

Let's all learn from St. Paul, so others can learn from us. For we are all missionaries, whether we know it or not, and whether we like it or not. We are like books, and everybody reads us, reads what we are both by what we do and by what we say, just as we read and understand characters in a novel. As many books are misunderstood, we will often be misunderstood. We will often be thought of as naïve instead of wise and thought of as "losers" instead of "winners." Just as Jesus was.

And that's fine, that's okay, because, as Mother Teresa so often said, "God did not put me in this world to be successful; he put me in this world to be faithful." That's essentially what Jesus said too; that's why he carried his cross, faithfully, and that's why we have to carry ours too, because if we are in him and he is in us, then our crosses are tiny splinters of his cross.

That is a tremendous privilege! The most precious relics in the world are the literal splinters from the true cross. They are put into gold, airtight containers called reliquaries, and they can be found in various places around the world, and you may have seen some of them, in cathedrals or at the Vatican; but no one reading this owns them. They are literally priceless, and it is strictly forbidden to sell these tiny crosses.

Yet *everybody* reading this has one of them, in a more important way than possessing one in a reliquary. We have little crosses in our lives, and if we are in Christ by Baptism, if we are many tiny parts of his Body, then they are many tiny parts of his cross. They are more precious in God's eyes than the ones in reliquaries. Offer yours to him right now, and again when you meet him in the most complete and intimate way when you receive him in Holy Communion.

GOSPEL
JOHN 2:13–25 _____

Since the Passover of the Jews was near, Jesus went up to Jerusalem. He found in the temple area those who sold oxen, sheep, and doves, as well as the money changers seated there. He made a whip out of cords and drove them all out of the temple area, with the sheep and oxen, and spilled the coins of the money changers and overturned their tables, and to those who sold doves he said, "Take these out of here, and stop making my Father's house a marketplace." His disciples recalled the words of Scripture, *Zeal for your house will consume me.* At this the Jews answered and said to him, "What sign can you show us for doing this?" Jesus answered and said to them, "Destroy this temple and in three days I will raise it up." The Jews said, "This temple has been under construction for forty-six years, and you will raise it up in three days?" But he was speaking about the temple of his body. Therefore, when he was raised from the dead, his disciples remembered that he had said this, and they came to believe the Scripture and the word Jesus had spoken.

While he was in Jerusalem for the feast of Passover, many began to believe in his name when they saw the signs he was doing. But Jesus would not trust himself to them because he knew them all, and did not need anyone to testify about human nature. He himself understood it well.

This is the only time we know of when Jesus, the "prince of peace," used physical violence. It shows that Jesus no more practiced strict pacifism than he preached it. Jesus said that among the prophets there was no one greater than John the Baptist, and when John the Baptist was asked by soldiers what to do, he did not tell them to leave the army but told them not to misuse their power to bully people. Might does not make right, but might can be used honorably in the service of right.

Jesus also never *condemns* pacifism or pacifists, by the way. And he stopped the shortest and most just war in history when he was arrested in the Garden of Gethsemane and St. Peter took out his sword to defend the most innocent man who was ever attacked and cut off the high priest's servant's ear, and he told St. Peter, "Put your sword back into its sheath, for all who take the sword will perish by the sword" (Matt. 26:52). And then he healed the war's only casualty other than himself.

God was not asleep when he inspired John to put this incident of Jesus cleansing the temple by overturning the money tables into his Gospel. It's there to teach us something. But what?

It's not that money and markets and marketplaces are evil, or that making money is evil. Like alcohol, gambling, and football, it can be dangerous and addictive, but it's not evil. It's a great invention; in fact, it's a necessity, even a human need. The abuse of a good thing does not make it a bad thing. Jesus is not a Woodstock hippie, an anarchist, or a communist any more than he is a strict pacifist.

So what does this incident teach us? The money was for buying animals to sacrifice: could it be that Jesus wants the Jews to stop killing animals for religious sacrifices in the temple? No. God himself commanded that in the Old Testament, through his prophet Moses. It was Jesus' eternal Father who commanded that, and Jesus never disagrees with his Father. Jesus does not believe animals have human rights. He is not a vegetarian or a vegan, though he does not condemn that either.

Nor is it economic injustice or oppression of the poor that Jesus is protesting here. The Mosaic law, the same law that mandated animal sacrifices, provided that rich people were to sacrifice oxen, middle-class people sheep, and poor people birds. If there are to be animal sacrifices, there must be animals; and they must be purchased with money, and that requires money changers.

But not in the temple area. Modern life requires telephones too, but not in church. The church is not a place for anybody to make money but a place to give money, to sacrifice it. The Jewish temple was not a place to breed animals and buy them but a place to sacrifice them: a place to give, not to get.

Economics and politics have some moral principles that are clear, but they also have gray areas that are not. The same is true of religion. The temple itself had a gray area, an area inside its outer walls but outside its inner walls. That's why the text says Jesus was in "the temple *area*" rather than "the temple." But even this gray area of the holy temple was holy, just as the gray areas of politics are political.

Jesus' point here is not about money, or animals, or economic or political justice. The point is very clear, in his own words: "Stop making my Father's house a marketplace." Turning God's house into a marketplace is as wrong as turning a marketplace into God's house. You don't change money in church, and you don't say Mass in a bank. Making money out of God is as wrong as making a god out of money. Trying to buy God's favor with your money is as wrong as worshiping money as your god.

If Jesus were alive today, he would have the same anger against our confusion between religion and politics, against either making a religion out of your politics or making political profit out of your religion. Too many people today have religious passion for politics but not for religion. When you lose your religion, you have to have something to fill the void, and all too often it's politics. Or economics. Or even your little iPhone. You can make anything an idol, a false god. Whatever you can't part with that's less than yourself is your idol.

The mistake of the money changers in the temple was not just a theological confusion. Jesus would pity that. But he does not pity the sheep sellers or the money changers; he gets angry at them. In fact, he uses the violence of a whip that he makes with his own hands to drive them out.

There are no whips in heaven. A whip, like a sword, is not a nice thing. It is a weapon. But it is at least an honest weapon. What you see is what you get. It's not like a bomb, or a gun, or even an arrow. There is no distance between you and your enemy. You are totally and exclusively responsible for what you do with it. There is no safety, no distance, no impersonality, no hiding behind your weapon.

Wrongly directed anger, or irrational anger, is a dangerous sin. But anger itself is not a sin. Jesus got angry many times, although this is the only time we know of when he used physical rather than verbal violence. Anger is often wrong, but it is sometimes right; it's often unrighteous, but sometimes it's righteous anger. If you have no anger at the crooked lawyer who blackmailed the judge and got the drug dealer declared innocent so he could go out again into the street and sell more drugs and ruin many other people's lives—if you have no anger at that, then you're not a complete human being; you're a wet noodle and a wimp.

After Jesus drives the money changers out of the temple area, the Jews challenge him by asking him what "sign" he will do. Notice that they do not ask what sign he will show them, or speak of, but what sign he will "do." That's because the word "sign" in the New Testament (*semeion* in Greek) usually means "miracle." Miracles are signs of divine authority. The Jews did not believe that might made right, but they did believe that right makes might; that divine right and authority could and often did prove itself by miracles, because miracles are acts that only God can do. The point of Jesus' miracles was not to point to themselves but to what they signified, what they were signs of—namely, his identity as God and as Savior. Jesus' healing of bodies was a sign that he is the healer of souls.

His answer to their demand for a sign was: "Destroy this temple and in three days I will raise it up." They thought this meant the physical temple they were standing in, but John says he meant the temple of his body, which they would indeed destroy, on the cross, and which he would raise up again three days later. (The Romans did the physical deed, but the Jews got them to do it: Judas and the high priest and the Pharisees.)

Jesus' body was indeed the true temple. So are ours. St. Paul writes, "Do you not know that your body is a temple of the Holy Spirit?" (1 Cor. 6:19). Christ's body is holier than our cathedrals. In fact, the cathedrals were built, at immense cost and effort, only to house the true Holy of Holies, his Body in the Eucharist. But *our* bodies are also holier than our cathedrals. They, too, are God's house.

The "sign" or miracle that Jesus says he will do is his act of saving us from sin by dying on the cross. A sign can be misread, and this one was radically misread by Jesus' enemies because it was paradoxical. It seemed to be a sign of weakness, and it really was power. After all, what looks weaker than dying? Yet this was the most powerful deed ever done. It conquered sin and death and hell. That is the paradox St. Paul speaks of in today's epistle, where he says that the folly of God is wiser than the wisdom of man and the weakness of God is more powerful than the power of man. Nothing seems more foolish and more of a failure than to be crucified as a criminal. Yet no deed ever done had more wisdom and more power than that one.

Jesus' words about the temple of his body were a deliberate paradox and puzzle because they were a test, a test of faith. His disciples eventually understood it, but only after they came to believe. "Doubting Thomas" refused to believe until he saw. He said, in effect, "Seeing is believing." But Jesus said, instead, that "believing is seeing" because he said, "If you believe you will see" (John 11:40).

But seeing often takes time. It was only later, after Jesus' Resurrection, that his disciples understood the meaning of what he said. Similarly, only after Jesus came to fulfill "the law and the prophets" did the disciples fully understand the law and the prophets of Judaism. Only after the Resurrection did they understand what the Passover meant. Only after the Lamb of God came did they understand the meaning of the sacrifice of lambs in the temple. Only after Christ fulfilled all the prophecies did they understand the prophets.

When Jesus said, "Destroy this temple and in three days I will raise it up," his enemies said to him, "This temple has been under construction for forty-six years, and you will raise it up in three days?" But since the temple he meant was the temple of his body, they were off by thirteen years, since he was thirty-three years old when he died; so it took thirty-three years, not forty-six, to build the true temple.

That is the same temple that we enter in Holy Communion. We enter into his Body when he enters into ours. And that is also a paradox: it seems to enter into us, but we really enter into it, into him. When we eat ordinary food, we transform it into the molecules and organs, the organic parts, of our human body; but when we eat this heavenly food, we let him transform us into the molecules, the organic parts, the organs, of his Mystical Body. And it is that Body, of which he is the Head and we are the members, that is the full and complete Temple of the Holy Spirit.

FOURTH SUNDAY OF LENT

The readings given for Year A may be used in place of these.

FIRST READING

2 CHRONICLES 36:14–16, 19–23 _____

In those days, all the princes of Judah, the priests, and the people added infidelity to infidelity, practicing all the abominations of the nations and polluting the LORD's temple which he had consecrated in Jerusalem.

Early and often did the LORD, the God of their fathers, send his messengers to them, for he had compassion on his people and his dwelling place. But they mocked the messengers of God, despised his warnings, and scoffed at his prophets, until the anger of the LORD against his people was so inflamed that there was no remedy. Their enemies burnt the house of God, tore down the walls of Jerusalem, set all its palaces afire, and destroyed all its precious objects. Those who escaped the sword were carried captive to Babylon, where they became servants of the king of the Chaldeans and his sons until the kingdom of the Persians came to power. All this was to fulfill the word of the LORD spoken by Jeremiah: "Until the land has retrieved its lost sabbaths, during all the time it lies waste it shall have rest while seventy years are fulfilled."

In the first year of Cyrus, king of Persia, in order to fulfill the word of the LORD spoken by Jeremiah, the LORD inspired King Cyrus of Persia to issue this proclamation throughout his kingdom, both by word of mouth and in writing: "Thus says Cyrus, king of Persia: All the kingdoms of the earth the LORD, the God of heaven, has given to me, and he has also charged me to build him a house in Jerusalem, which is in Judah. Whoever, therefore, among you belongs to any part of his people, let him go up, and may his God be with him!"

Today's Old Testament reading summarizes the pattern of three stages of Jewish history, a pattern that would be repeated many times: first their rebellion against God and their infidelity to their covenant with him, then their punishment by military defeat and captivity, and finally their return to the promised land after years of purgatorial suffering and purification.

This is a familiar pattern in the life of every nation and every individual, through many changing details of time and place. But even while God's chosen people change radically in going through these three very different stages of rebellion, repentance, and restoration, or sin, sorrow, and salvation, which are like hell, purgatory, and heaven—even as we, like the Old Testament Jews, go through these radical changes in our relationship with God, God himself does not change.

But when one of two parties in a relationship changes and the other does not, the relationship between them does. It's like a pendulum. Think of the ball and the hinge as the two parties in the relationship, and the arm as the relationship itself. The ball of the pendulum changes and swings from one extreme of its arc to the other, and therefore the arm that connects the ball to the hinge changes too, but the hinge does not. God is like the hinge, and we are like the ball, and the arm is like our relationship with God. As we change, our relationship with God changes, but God does not.

God is love, totally and infinitely and eternally and unchangeably. But that love manifests itself very differently to us depending on our relationship to it, our attitude toward it. When we gradually sink deeper and deeper into sin, God seems to gradually lose patience with us. But that is an illusion of perspective. It's like staying out in the sun without sunblock: we gradually get burnt, and it seems as if the sun is getting hotter and hotter, but it is really only we who are getting hotter and hotter.

When we crack and come to a crisis in our rebellion, God seems to crack and come to a crisis too: when we declare divorce to him, he seems to declare divorce to us. But that, too, is an illusion of perspective. When we hate God, God does not hate us, only our sins. He always hates our sins and always loves us. When we love our sins, he does not follow us and also love our sins. He hates our sins always, because he loves us always. That's the only reason he hates our sins: because he loves us, as a surgeon hates a cancer only because he loves his patient. (If he hated his patient and wanted him dead, he would *love* his cancer.)

When we love our sins, we are not really loving ourselves but hating ourselves; so when God seems to get angry at us and hate us, he is really loving us and having mercy on us. If he changed and stopped having mercy on us, he would not punish us for our sins; he would not teach us and rehabilitate us, and make us learn the hard way when we refused to learn the easy way; he would let us sin away until we utterly destroyed ourselves.

He gives us our purgatories, our Babylonian captivities, our punishments for our sins, because he cannot and will not stop loving us; and love has to be tough when it deals with rebels. The very same love that says yes to our yes must say no to our no. That's true of families and tribes and races and cultures and nations and civilizations and the world and the Church, just as it is true of individuals. The Old Testament's history of Israel is there for our instruction, both as individuals and as a people. It is easier to see sin in the life of others and in the larger public realm than it is to see it in ourselves, where it is not as visible.

It looks like God's mercy changes and fluctuates, but that is not so. God's mercy is as eternal and unchangeable as his justice. Punishments are mercies too, just as much as rewards are. God's rewards and his punishments are equally his mercy and his blessings, just as they are also equally his justice. In God there is no difference between his mercy and his justice. His justice *is* his mercy, and his mercy *is* his justice. Our justice and mercy are different, and often we have to choose one at the expense of the other. But God is not like that. God is the unchanging hinge of the pendulum. He seems to change only because we change and therefore our relationship with him changes, like the arm of the pendulum.

The practical point of this theology is that when we sin, we *must* be punished, and that's because of God's mercy, not just because of his justice. The Babylonian captivity of the Jews was God's mercy to them. It was their purgatory. Yes, it hurt; it was a suffering, as our purgatory is too, both in its beginnings in this life and in its completion in the next life. But it's needed, and it's necessary, and it's love. From the standpoint of justice, it is punishment, but from the standpoint of mercy and love, it is purifying and perfecting and blessing.

Most of us will probably need some purgatorial purifying before we can enter heaven and enjoy it; we are not saintly enough to go to heaven directly, nor are we hopelessly rebellious and unrepentant enough to go to hell. But if we are wise, we see God's punishments for our sins, both here and in purgatory, as expressions of his love and mercy, not his hate or his cruelty. He has no hate; he is pure love. What seems hateful and cruel is in us, not in him.

Some of the saints even go so far as to say that it is the very love of God that tortures the souls in hell, because they hate that love and want to escape from it, but they can't. They want darkness, but the sun can't stop shining on them. They want to live a lie, but they can't hide anymore from the truth. It's truth that tortures them, truth and love, the two things that God eternally is and cannot change. If you do not love what God is, which is love and truth; if you hate what God is, which is love and truth; then you cannot go to heaven because you would not enjoy heaven, because heaven is full of what God is: love and truth.

That is the only reason there is a hell. Some think hell does not really exist. They are certainly wrong. Hell really exists; Jesus repeatedly says so. Do you really think you know better than he does about such things? Are you arrogant enough to correct the teachings of God incarnate? But it exists not because God is hate rather than love—it exists only because some of us are hate rather than love.

On one occasion, Jesus' disciples asked him, "Lord, will only a few people be saved?" His answer was *not* "Most will be saved," *nor* was it "Most will be damned," but it was "Strive to enter through the narrow door" (Luke 13:23–24). In other words, stop speculating about what road others are on and be sure you know the way to heaven. Jesus not only *teaches* the way, he *is* the way, and the truth, and the life—the life eternal.

RESPONSORIAL PSALM
PSALM 137:1–2, 3, 4–5, 6 _____

R. (6ab) **Let my tongue be silenced, if I ever forget you!**

By the streams of Babylon
    we sat and wept
      when we remembered Zion.
On the aspens of that land
    we hung up our harps.

For there our captors asked of us
    the lyrics of our songs,
And our despoilers urged us to be joyous:
    "Sing for us the songs of Zion!"

How could we sing a song of the LORD
    in a foreign land?
If I forget you, Jerusalem,
    may my right hand be forgotten!

May my tongue cleave to my palate
    if I remember you not,
If I place not Jerusalem
    ahead of my joy.

Imagine you are one of the Jews who was captured and enslaved by Babylon's invasion and conquest of Israel. You had been free all your life, and now you are a captive and a slave in a foreign country. Worst of all, it is a country that does not know God. Jerusalem was your home, your holy home, and the great temple of Solomon was the spiritual center of the world, the one place on earth where God had instituted the true worship of the true God. This was your pride and joy.

St. Augustine defines a city as a community united by love, not just by buildings or space or time or laws or even biology but by agreement about what is loved, by loving the same thing, loving the same God and his revelation and his law. The holy city of Jerusalem was the closest thing to heaven on earth. It was not just some beautiful buildings; it was *your identity*. You were not merely an isolated, uprooted, autonomous individual, like most people in modern societies. You were a part of your people, God's chosen people. You had been miraculously freed from slavery in Egypt by God, the God who was the whole meaning of your life. And now your God had allowed you to sink back into a second Egypt, a second slavery to pagan people. You had been married to God, and now God has apparently divorced you, or rather your people have divorced him. The Babylonian Captivity is God's necessary purgatorial punishment for the infidelity and apostasy of his covenant bride, his chosen people Israel. You are in exile—not just from your land but from your identity, your joy, your home, and your marriage to God.

And now these Babylonians have the arrogance to ask you to entertain them by singing some of the songs of Zion, the songs that gave you such joy when you sang them together with thousands of your people, in the great Jerusalem temple. "Entertain us. Sing us your songs." And your only possible response is "How can I sing the songs of joy in the middle of this sorrow? How can I sing love songs to amuse my enemies? How can I sing songs of God's friendship and intimacy for the entertainment of God's enemies? My tears are my only comfort now, my tears of remembering my lost joys. I cannot forget you, O Jerusalem. May my tongue cleave to my palate, may I be unable to speak forever if I forget you, Jerusalem, my only true joy, my only true love."

There are two aspects of your Babylonian exile. One is this external situation of exile from your land and your freedom. The other, deeper exile is internal: the exile from your former relationship with God. God seems to have forsaken you. You feel like Christ on the cross when he prayed, "My God, my God, why have you forsaken me?" You *know* God has not totally forsaken you; you have not lost your faith, or your love for God, but you have lost everything else, and it certainly *feels* like total forsakenness.

That is a description of the heart out of which this Psalm of lament came. It was a broken heart, and you can feel the sorrow, the sorrow that only love can cause. If you want to avoid life's deepest sorrows, don't ever give your heart away to anyone; don't ever love anyone or anything very deeply. The price you have to pay for not having that sorrow, life's deepest sorrow, is that you will also never have life's deepest joy. And to live that way, to never give your heart away in love so that you can avoid that sorrow, is not to live a foretaste of heaven but to live a foretaste of hell. A heart that cannot be broken also cannot be healed and made whole. The only whole heart is a heart that has been broken by love.

St. Augustine famously prayed, "You have made us for yourself, and therefore our hearts are restless until they rest in thee." Our hearts are made to rest in God and nothing less. They are too big to be totally filled with anything less. There is a God-sized and God-shaped hole in our hearts. We are all in exile here; only heaven is our heart's home.

We all have an innate longing for something more than this world can ever give us, even though we can't imagine it or define it. (That's why there has never been a good movie or novel about heaven: it's much more and much better than we can possibly imagine.)

We are not literally ancient Jews, God's chosen people, exiled in Babylon. But that is exactly what we are spiritually. All Christians are God's chosen people, and we are all exiled here in this fallen world. The question this Psalm poses to us is this: Have we lost that hunger? Have we stifled our hearts? Have we become dumb and incapable of song? Has our tongue cleaved to our palate because we have forgotten Jerusalem, forgotten our home, our chief joy, our marriage covenant with God?

Nothing in human life is capable of giving us more sufferings *and* more joys than marriage, because it is the most total and most intimate and most vulnerable of all human relationships. And God offers spiritual marriage to us. That's what the Christian religion is: a marriage proposal. And that marriage proposal comes with this challenge: there will be great joys but also great sufferings, great intimacies but also great exiles. The bitter and the sweet always go together. We do not have the option of the sweet without the bitter; our only two options are to accept both or to accept neither—to never give our whole hearts to anyone, either our spouse or our God, and thus avoid the bitterest of bitters but also the sweetest of sweets.

So we have to honestly ask ourselves: Are we afraid of accepting God's marriage proposal, with all its inevitable sufferings and exiles as well as joys and intimacies? Are we more afraid of love, because of its sufferings, than we are afraid of lovelessness? Are we afraid to love God with our *whole* heart and soul?

Of course we are. That's why we're not saints. We're afraid of their sufferings and maybe also afraid of their joys. We're afraid of the heights as well as the depths. We want security and safety and dull, level places. We have anesthetized our souls so that they do not feel the pain. If we are honest with ourselves, we have to ask: Are our spiritual hearts even still beating? Have our hearts disappeared into our screens and our smartphones?

Society cannot answer that question for you. You have to answer it for yourself. Modern Western society has largely lost faith and hope and love for God. It used to be called Christendom, Christian society. It is no longer called that. It is no longer married to God; it is divorced. It is in exile, in Babylon, not in Jerusalem.

But that's not the greatest tragedy, because Western society is not eternal, but you are. American culture is not going either to heaven or hell, but you are. Modern civilization does not have a heart, but you do. "Society" is not a person. It cannot take your place. Society cannot have faith or hope or love.

Only you can. No one and nothing can take your place. Society is not another person, a single very large person. It is only a large series of relationships between persons.

So what can we do, here beside the waters of Babylon, in the Tower of Babel, surrounded by pagan babble? Even here in Babylon we can choose what the Psalmist chose: to remember Zion, to remember Jerusalem, to remember God, to remember our spiritual marriage with God, to remember the echoes of the Garden of Eden that still reverberate in our hearts, that make us restless with our godlessness, like Augustine, that make us desire and hope for something more, here in this Babylonian exile, this valley of the shadow of death. Even here we can still choose what the Psalmist chooses—namely, the beautiful love that gives us the beautiful sorrow.

In another Psalm, the Psalmist imagines God collecting his tears in a bottle (Ps. 56:8). The tears are offerings. They are one of four offerings every one of us should make every morning when we pray our morning offering: "O my God, I offer you all my prayers, works, joys, *and sufferings* of this day." Our sufferings are not worthless, any more than our joys are. They are precious. They are jewels. Let your heart teach you how to produce those jewels, how to weep as well as rejoice here in our exile. Those tears are more precious than diamonds, because what they express is the holiest thing in the world. Its name is love. St. John says, "God is love, and whoever remains in love remains in God and God in him" (1 John 4:16).

SECOND READING

EPHESIANS 2:4–10 _____

Brothers and sisters: God, who is rich in mercy, because of the great love he had for us, even when we were dead in our transgressions, brought us to life with Christ—by grace you have been saved—, raised us up with him, and seated us with him in the heavens in Christ Jesus, that in the ages to come he might show the immeasurable riches of his grace in his kindness to us in Christ Jesus. For by grace you have been saved through faith, and this is not from you; it is the gift of God; it is not from works, so no one may boast. For we are his handiwork, created in Christ Jesus for the good works that God has prepared in advance, that we should live in them.

Martin Luther started the Protestant Reformation, the most serious split the Church ever lived through, primarily over the issue raised in this passage from Ephesians—"For by grace you have been saved through faith, and this is not from you; it is the gift of God; it is not from works, so no one may boast"—and a parallel passage in Romans that says, "We have been justified by faith" (Rom. 5:1). Luther interpreted this to mean that we are justified, or saved, by faith alone and not by good works, the works of obedience to God's moral law. But the word "alone" is not in that verse, and the Bible also says, in the Letter of James, that "we are justified by works and not by faith alone," and that "faith without works is dead" (James 2:24, 26). The Bible teaches, and the Church has always taught, that Luther is right in what he affirmed and wrong in what he denied. We are not saved by good works alone—Luther is right there—but it's also true that we are not saved by faith alone. We are saved by the faith that produces good works, the works of love. Faith and hope and love are not three different things but three different dimensions of one and the same thing.

Think of an orange tree. It has three parts. The first part that grows is the roots. They grow underground, invisibly. Without the roots, the tree dies. Faith is like the roots. It is the absolutely necessary beginning. The second part is the trunk and the branches, which reach upward from the roots, like arms stretched out in prayer to heaven. Hope is like that. The third part, the most precious part, is the fruits, the oranges. Those are like the works of love.

It's unlikely that Protestants never hear any homilies about faith, or that Catholics never hear any homilies about love, about good works. But it's more likely that we Catholics don't hear the part Luther rightly reminded us of; it's likely that many Catholics think that the only thing that matters is good works, that as long as you do enough good works you will be saved and go to heaven. If they thought about that, they'd question it; they'd wonder where the cutoff point was. Do you have to do 1000 good works to get to heaven, so that if you only do 999 you go to hell? Or is it just 10? Whatever the cutoff point is, it's clearly neither just nor loving for God to send someone to hell and someone else to heaven just because the second person did just one more good work than the first one did.

What's wrong with that picture is not just the problem of the cutoff point but also that it assumes that we can save ourselves. We can't. No matter how many good works we do, we can't deserve heaven. It's a free gift of grace, not a payment of justice. It's not wages that are deserved. St. Paul says in Romans that "the wages of sin is death, but the gift of God is eternal life in Christ Jesus our Lord" (Rom. 6:23). We're all sinners; we're all rebels; we've all divorced ourselves from God, and only God can save us. We've sold ourselves into sin, into slavery, and we have no money left to buy our freedom back. God's grace alone can save us. Faith is our free acceptance of that grace, that gift.

But faith is not just a set of beliefs. St. James says, "You believe that God is one. You do well. Even the demons believe that and tremble" (James 2:19). Our *beliefs* are only an act of our *minds*, but our *faith* is more than that; it is also an act of our *wills* and our hearts, and includes our hope and our love, and the works of love. So when St. Paul says that it's faith that saves us, he means by "faith" not just one but all three of those dimensions of it, belief and hope and love, the roots and the branches and the fruits. And when St. James says that faith alone does not save us, he means by "faith" just the intellectual dimension of it, the beliefs.

Since most of us probably know St. James' point pretty clearly but perhaps are not quite so clear about St. Paul's point, we need to go more deeply into St. Paul's point. Why is it important to realize that we are saved by faith and not just by good works?

Because the object of faith is God and his grace, while the object of good works is other human beings. Other human beings can't save us any more

213

than we can save ourselves. If we believed we were saved by our own good works, we'd think we *deserved* heaven, as wages, as justice. That's what the Pharisees believed—that their good works made them deserve heaven. But Jesus shocked them when he told them they were on their way to hell! Why? Because they lacked the very first virtue, humility, the humility to confess and repent. Jesus said to them, "Those who are well do not need a physician, but the sick do. I did not come to call the righteous but sinners" (Mark 2:17). Jesus is saying: If you admit that you are sick and come to me as your soul's doctor, if you knock on my door, I will open it; but I will not force myself on you. You need heart surgery, and you will die without it, but you have to acknowledge that and ask me for the healing I alone can give you. All who ask, will receive, but *only* those who ask."

There is a famous painting of Jesus knocking at our door, the door of our hearts and lives. There is no knob on the outside of the door. The knob is on the inside. Jesus does not ignore our free will and knock the door down. The door has to be opened from the inside, by us.

Our part is to let the doctor in. His part is to give us a healing operation, a heart transplant. The Psalmist prays, "A clean heart create for me, O God" (Ps. 51:12). Only God can create something radically new. And we need a new heart. Our fallen and foolish and selfish hearts would not be able to endure God's heaven, God's full presence. And clearly we can't perform heart surgery on ourselves. Only God can do that work. But he won't do it without our consent.

We are saved by faith because faith is our consent to his operation, our free choice to accept the gift, the offering of his grace, the offering of his own life that he gave us from the cross and communicates to us in his sacraments. It's like a blood transfusion. It is the injection of his own life into us. That's what happens in Baptism and in Holy Communion. Jesus is the exact opposite of Dracula. Dracula drinks your blood, takes your blood, your life. Jesus *gives* you his Blood, his life, to drink.

At the end of the book of Revelation, Jesus says, "Behold, I make all things new" (Rev. 21:5). The first thing he makes new is our hearts, our souls, our selves. And the first beginning, the root of all subsequent growth, is faith.

If we were saved simply by our own good works, we would have the right to be proud and to boast. But if we're saved by *God's* good work, on the cross, we can only be humble and grateful. Cinderella didn't deserve to live in the palace; she wasn't born a queen. The prince fell in love with her and married her. Jesus is the prince, and we are his Cinderella bride. That's the incredibly good news of the Gospel.

GOSPEL
JOHN 3:14–21

Jesus said to Nicodemus: "Just as Moses lifted up the serpent in the desert, so must the Son of Man be lifted up, so that everyone who believes in him may have eternal life."

For God so loved the world that he gave his only Son, so that everyone who believes in him might not perish but might have eternal life. For God did not send his Son into the world to condemn the world, but that the world might be saved through him. Whoever believes in him will not be condemned, but whoever does not believe has already been condemned, because he has not believed in the name of the only Son of God. And this is the verdict, that the light came into the world, but people preferred darkness to light, because their works were evil. For everyone who does wicked things hates the light and does not come toward the light, so that his works might not be exposed. But whoever lives the truth comes to the light, so that his works may be clearly seen as done in God.

(Note: The first of the two reflections on John 3:14–21 centers on its central point, which is also the central point of the whole Gospel, summarized in John 3:16. That central point has been made many times in other reflections here, so if you think it unnecessary and superfluous, use the second reflection. But many today simply have not understood, or have not even heard, this most central point, so it is probably worth another try. The second reflection, instead of focusing on this single point, explores all the verses of today's Gospel, and some of the ones immediately preceding it.)

Reflection 1

The Bible is the most popular, most well-known, and most loved book in the world. The New Testament is the most loved part of the Bible. The Gospels are the most loved books in the New Testament. John's Gospel is the most loved Gospel. And chapter three, verse 16 is its most loved verse. So John 3:16 is the most loved sentence in the world. You often see it scribbled on bridges and on cardboard signs held up at ball games. It says that "God so loved the world that he gave his only Son, so that everyone who believes in him might not perish but might have eternal life." That is the essence of the Good News of the Gospel, the essence of Christianity.

The first thing to notice about it is that it is *news*. It is a historical event, not a timeless abstract principle. It really happened. It is the most amazing, wonderful, stunning, incredible thing that ever happened: God sent his divine and infinitely beloved Son into our world to offer his life, his body and blood, on the cross, to save us from our sins and give us a share in his own eternal life.

That is absolutely astonishing. Imagine you kept ants as pets, in an ant farm. They had free choice between the food you gave them, which would give them life and happiness forever, and an alternative food, which was really poison for them. They chose to mistrust you and take the poison instead. And your response to this rebellion was not to leave them alone to die, which would be what they deserved, but to save them, by becoming an ant yourself and entering their ant farm to give them your own body and blood as the only antidote to their poison, and the only alternative food that would save them. You gave this undeserved gift to any ants that would trust you and take it. You knew the ants would kill you if you came into their world, but you did all that anyway, just because you loved those undeserving, rebellious little ants that much. You got nothing out of it. You didn't need them at all. But they needed you. You did it out of pure altruistic love.

What a ridiculous story! Hard to believe, isn't it? That is the great mystery of our religion: why should God love us that much? And the only answer is: because that's what God is. God is pure love, and love gives everything.

When he came, he gave us everything, all of himself, all twelve pints of his blood, on the cross. Divine blood is so infinitely powerful that just one drop of it could have saved the whole world, a drop he shed at his circumcision. Why did he give us twelve pints instead of one drop? Because he had twelve pints to give. That's what love does: it gives everything.

And what do we have to do to get it? Do we have to qualify? How could anyone qualify for that? Do we have to be good enough to deserve it? Impossible. Is this gift only for saints? No, it's for sinners, and saints are the first to admit that they are sinners. It's only sinners who think they are saints.

So where is the cutoff point? Who gets saved and who doesn't? Who gets eternal life and who doesn't? There is no cutoff point. It's for everyone. It's free. Nobody can buy it, not even with the biggest pile of good works. It's a gift, and you can't buy a gift, because a gift is given out of love, and you can't buy love.

So how do you get eternal life, or divine life, or the life of heaven? Do you go to heaven if you're good enough and to hell if you're bad enough? No. You get it if you want it, choose it, accept it, trust it, believe it. You *receive* it if you *believe* it (see John 1:12). Because this "it" is a "him"; it's Jesus Christ himself, the eternal Son of God.

All you need to do is one thing. The one thing has two parts, one negative and one positive. The negative part is to be honest enough to confess your sins and repent. The positive part is to believe, to say yes, to trust this gift and this giver, because this divine giver is himself the gift. It's not merely an idea that you believe; it's a person. Faith is not just an *opinion*, inside you, in your mind: it's a *relationship*; it's *between* you and God; it's like marriage. God proposes an eternal spiritual marriage to you, and it's up to you to say yes or no to him.

And if you say yes, he impregnates you with his divine life, which is the life of self-giving love, and then the works of love begin to come out of you like children out of a married woman.

If you object to that image and that analogy as being "sexist," you are setting yourself against God himself, who invented sex and marriage and who continually, down through the centuries, inspired his Scriptures and his Church and all her saints to use that image. If you don't like sexual imagery, that proves that you are not a Catholic but a puritan or a Victorian who thinks of sex as dirty or animalistic or unholy. In other words, you are a typical modern secularist. You need some radical rethinking. I suggest you read Pope St. John Paul II's "theology of the body," which is the Church's positive alternative to both the playboy philosophy of the so-called sexual revolution that reduces the reproductive system to the entertainment system, and the puritan, Victorian heresy that sees sex as dirty and embarrassing.

The spiritual marriage is the link between faith and salvation. The Bible says, in many places, such as today's Gospel, that those who believe are saved and those who do not believe are not saved. Why? What is the causal *link* between faith and salvation, or eternal life, or heaven? The link is Jesus Christ. Christ is the object of our faith and the cause of our salvation. We are Juliet, and Christ is Romeo, and he proposes marriage to us, and faith is our acceptance of his proposal. If we accept his proposal, he gives us new life, makes us spiritually pregnant; but he comes only when he is welcomed. That's why faith is necessary for salvation. It's not that God gives you a theology test at the gates of heaven and lets you in only if you pass his test by getting sixty out of one hundred answers right. Faith is necessary for salvation not in the same way that right answers are necessary for passing a test but in the same way that mutual love and trust are necessary for welcoming a new baby.

In the first chapter of his Gospel, St. John equates two words: "believe" and "receive." He writes, "To those who did accept him he gave power to become children of God, to those who believe in his name, who were born not by natural generation nor by human choice nor by a man's decision but of God"

(John 1:12–13). In the verses immediately preceding today's Gospel, Jesus told Nicodemus that in order to enter the kingdom of God, or the kingdom of heaven, or the divine family, we have to be "born again," spiritually (John 3:3). That's what faith does: it is not just a private change of mind but a real transaction between you and God that gives you the beginning of spiritual life, just as sexual intercourse and conception gave you the beginning of your physical life.

It begins with baptism. Faith and baptism are always joined in the mind of God—we often find them mentioned together in the Bible—just as personal love and trust is always joined to sex in the mind of God. Faith is not merely spiritual, and baptism is not merely physical, just as love is not merely an inner, private, spiritual attitude, and sex is not merely a very pleasant physical, biological act. Baptism is like the honeymoon night, and Holy Communion is like subsequent acts of intercourse. All this made sense for thousands of years, when sex was still connected with both procreation and God. Today, when contraception has separated sex from procreation and reduced the reproductive system to the entertainment system, we have to make a great effort to get ourselves back into that way of thinking—that is, back into the mind of God, God's wise and loving intention for human health and happiness, which usually contradicts ours and surprises ours, but is always better than ours.

Reflection 2

Today's Gospel comes from Jesus' sermon to Nicodemus, the inquiring Pharisee who came to him secretly, by night, for fear of scorn and stigma from the other Pharisees. Nicodemus suspected that Jesus was the Messiah who would institute the kingdom of God, or the kingdom of heaven, so he had these three questions in his mind: Who is Jesus? What is the kingdom of heaven? And how do I enter it?

There are at least six ironies or paradoxes, and plays on words, in this short narrative.

First, Nicodemus came to Jesus "by night" for fear of the Pharisees. But the night was really in Nicodemus' soul rather than in his world. When Jesus told him he had to be born again, he said, "How can this happen?" (John 3:9), and Jesus replied, "What! You are a rabbi and you don't even know that? How ironic! That's the heart of your whole religion!"

Second, Nicodemus came as representing many of the Jews who were wondering about Jesus, so he used the pronoun "we" instead of "I" when he addressed Jesus. He said, "Rabbi, we know that you are a teacher who has come from God, for no one can do these signs that you are doing unless God is with him." And Jesus answered him with his own "we," saying, "Amen, amen, I say to you [the rabbinic formula for "take these words as seriously as possible; do not weaken them or dance around them with little nuances"], we speak of what we know and we testify to what we have seen, but you people do not accept our testimony" (John 3:2, 11). Jesus' "we" refers to the Trinity. If the witness of even one divine person trumps all human persons, then the witness of three divine persons certainly does.

The third wordplay is on the word *ruah* in Hebrew, *pneuma* in Greek. Both have the triple meaning of "spirit," "breath," and "wind." So Jesus uses the analogy of the physical *wind*, which blows wherever it wishes so that we can neither see it nor see where it comes from nor where it is going, to symbolize the *breath*, the breath of *life*, which is more than just air, which in man is more than biological life because it is *spirit*. So the same word means first, physical air molecules, or wind; and second, organic biological life, or breath; and third, the life of the spirit or human soul, the inner life. The first is a symbol of the second, and the second is a symbol of the third.

The fourth wordplay is on the word "born." Jesus says, "You must be born from above" (John 3:7). Nicodemus replies, in effect, "That's ridiculous. How can a grown man enter back into his mother's womb?" But Jesus is talking about spiritual rebirth, where God becomes our heavenly Father and we receive a share in his own divine life by Baptism and faith—so he says "born by water and the Spirit," because Baptism is by water and faith comes by the inspiration of the Holy Spirit and allows the Holy Spirit to live in our soul.

Fifth, Jesus says, "If I tell you about earthly things and you do not believe, how will you believe if I tell you about heavenly things? No one has gone up to heaven except the one who has come down from heaven, the Son of Man" (John 3:12–13). Being "born again" is an "earthly thing" because it happens here on earth, not in heaven. There is a double meaning of the word "heaven": the spiritual place where God lives and the physical atmosphere, the sky. The sky is a natural symbol of the real heaven. Jesus knows he came from the real heaven and that he will ascend back to heaven, through its mere symbol, the sky.

Sixth, Jesus says, "As Moses lifted up the serpent in the desert, so must the Son of Man be lifted up, so that everyone who believes in him may have eternal life." We physically "lift up" kings and queens and heroes and flags and banners to express our mental and spiritual admiration and reverence and "high" regard for them; but Jesus will be lifted up on the throne of the cross, wearing a crown of thorns, not jewels, and naked, not robed in royal purple. He will be ugly, like the bronze snake that God told Moses to erect to heal the people's snakebites, if only they looked up to it in faith and trust. The bronze serpent functioned as Jesus functioned. A snake is not high, like a bird, but low and ugly. The snake is used to symbolize the devil in the Garden of Eden story. Yet this low beast is what God told Moses to raise high on a pole to heal the people from snakebites. Jesus took the lowest place, the place of the snake, the sinner, the evil one, when he was crucified and died so that we could live and be saved from Satan's snakebite. It's the supreme irony.

Jesus, the Word of God, uses words in the most supreme and rich and even ironic, almost humorous, way to describe the holiest and highest things.

(The following explanation might add to the points above, or might distract from them. Use your own judgment as to whether to include them.)

The most beloved verse in the Bible is in this passage, during Jesus' talk with Nicodemus: John 3:16. "God so loved the world that he gave his only Son, so that everyone who believes in him might not perish but might have eternal life." That's the Gospel, the Good News: that God comes down to us, in the person of Jesus, out of love, and we have to go up to him out of faith in that love.

Faith and love always go together, because you can't have faith and trust in someone you don't love, and you can't love someone you can't trust.

Faith does not mean simply mental belief in a set of ideas; it means personal trust in this divine person, the trust that accepts his gift of himself, of his own divine life.

The objective aspect of our salvation is that God gives us eternal life in Christ, and the sacraments of Baptism and Holy Communion are like the hose that gets that water to us. The subjective aspect is that we receive it through our faith and trust and openness and desire and love for it and for its divine Giver.

Gifts have to be both freely given and freely received—freely given out of love and freely received out of faith and trust. That explains hell as well as heaven, damnation as well as salvation. For God sends no one to hell. The Bible says that God is "not wishing that any should perish but that all should come to repentance" (2 Pet. 3:9). In his conversation with Nicodemus, after explaining how salvation works, Jesus also explained how damnation works when he said: "And this is the verdict [or this is how the judgment works], that the light came into the world [Jesus said, "I am the light of the world"], but [some] people preferred darkness to light, because their works were evil." Here Jesus gives us the motive for unbelief: not ignorance, or misunderstanding, but sin. Criminals prefer darkness to light.

We are all criminals. None of us would feel comfortable if every hidden thought and desire of ours for the last twenty-four hours were broadcast on public television for the whole world to see. As the great Russian novelist Solzhenitsyn wrote, "The line separating good and evil passes not through states, nor between classes, nor between political parties either—but right through every human heart." We are all torn between a desire for light and a desire for darkness, between a desire to stand in the light of truth and a desire to hide from truth, from the God who is light and truth. If our deepest, most fundamental desire is darkness, that is what we will get, forever, in hell. (If that's not true, then Jesus is a liar, because he clearly taught us that hell is real.) But if our deepest, most fundamental desire is light, then that is what we will get, forever, in heaven, even though most of us will probably have to get to heavenly joy through purgatorial pain, which begins in this life, through painful confession and repentance and learning the hard way.

All who seek God will find him, Jesus solemnly assures us in his famous Sermon on the Mount. God casts no one into hell against his will; you have to choose it yourself. Mere ignorance of the Gospel does not damn you, nor does misunderstanding. It's not the knowledge in your head that saves you but the love in your heart. In the Last Judgment, God will read your heart, your deepest heart, and if he sees that what you love most is the light, the truth, especially the truth of love, the truth that the meaning of life is genuine, unselfish love, God will give you that thing that you want most. If your deepest love is a love of God, a love of what God really is—namely, light and love—then that is what you will get. If your deepest love is for the opposite, then that is what you will get.

How can Jesus save non-Christians? When non-Christians die and meet God, they will learn that Jesus is indeed "the way and the truth and the life" for everyone, that Jesus is the universal Savior. And if that is what they most fundamentally sought in their lives, then that is what they will find. And if what they most deeply sought was not honesty and truth but darkness and lies and hiding, and if what they most deeply sought was not unselfish love but selfish pleasure and privilege and power, then they will get what they loved: simply themselves, and not God, who is the source of all life and light and love and joy. Another name for that is hell.

If we are so shallow that we think that physical fire and torture are more terrible than the absence of all hope for light and life and love, then we need to believe that hell is fire and torture. If we are not that shallow, we can take the fire and torture as mere symbols of something far worse.

It is not at all clear *how many* will be saved. But it is very clear who will save them. It is not clear *how much* we have to know about the Savior in order to be saved. But it is very clear how much he knows about us: he knows everything. He knows our deepest hearts, much better than we do. When Jesus' disciples asked him how many would be saved, Jesus' answer was, in effect, that they were asking the wrong question. They were asking about other people; they should have been asking about themselves. His answer to their question about how many will be saved was "Strive to enter through the narrow door" (Luke 13:24). In other words, "Be one of them." Join the saints who will go marching in to heaven singing "God's way is the best way," not the sinners who go marching in to hell singing "I did it my way." The populations of heaven and hell are not predetermined by God alone, unilaterally. He gives each of us a vote. He casts his vote for us, and the devil casts his vote against us, and we cast the deciding vote.

FIFTH SUNDAY OF LENT

The readings given for Year A may be used in place of these.

FIRST READING

JEREMIAH 31:31–34 ⎯⎯⎯⎯⎯⎯⎯⎯⎯⎯⎯⎯⎯⎯⎯⎯⎯

The days are coming, says the LORD, when I will make a new covenant with the house of Israel and the house of Judah. It will not be like the covenant I made with their fathers the day I took them by the hand to lead them forth from the land of Egypt; for they broke my covenant, and I had to show myself their master, says the LORD. But this is the covenant that I will make with the house of Israel after those days, says the LORD. I will place my law within them and write it upon their hearts; I will be their God, and they shall be my people. No longer will they have need to teach their friends and relatives how to know the LORD. All, from least to greatest, shall know me, says the LORD, for I will forgive their evildoing and remember their sin no more.

Today's reading from the Old Testament is a prophecy of the greatest revolution in history. There have been many revolutions in world history: the mastery of fire, of farming, of animals, and of diseases; revolutions against many political tyrants, and against slavery. There have also been evil as well as good revolutions, such as the Nazi revolution and the communist revolution. But the first and foremost revolution was the revolution against God, the fall of the whole human race in Adam and Eve, our first parents.

But these are not the greatest revolutions. They are all man-made revolutions, but the greatest revolutions are always the ones God made. Creation was the first: a revolution against nothingness. Creation makes the difference between nothing and something. That's the most revolutionary difference of all. The difference between oppression and freedom is great, of course, and so is the difference between the fear of fire and the control of fire, but they are only relative differences; but there is an absolute difference between nothing and everything in the universe.

The creation of the human soul was the second revolution, because the difference between a human soul and a body is another absolute difference. There is a great difference between the human body and the animal body, between human biology and animal biology, but it's only relative. Ninety-five percent of our DNA we have in common with monkeys; and we have even more in common with them in our politics. But there is an absolute difference between an animal and a person with a spiritual soul, with reason and conscience and free will and a relationship with God.

Once he created mankind, God made a series of covenants with them: with Adam; with Noah; with Abraham, Isaac, and Jacob; with Moses; with David; and with his chosen people collectively. Then, in the greatest revolution of all, God became man. After revealing himself as their transcendent Father and Creator, he revealed himself also as their incarnate brother. The divine Son of God the Father became a human being, Jesus Christ, to suffer and die to save us from eternal death. The Incarnation was the greatest revolution and also the greatest covenant, the New Covenant, or New Testament. "Covenant" and "testament" are synonyms. The book we call the New Testament is about the reality we call the New Covenant.

Marriage is the primary example in human life of a covenant, a solemn promise; that is why, when marriage is in good shape, all other human relationships are also, and when marriage is in bad shape, as it clearly is today, all other human relationships are corrupted. If we cannot trust the most solemn and binding promise a person makes to another person who he claims is the most important person in the world to him, then what other promises that he ever makes can we trust? None. When marriage falls apart, everything in society falls apart.

A 50 percent divorce rate, which is what we now have, is like a 50 percent suicide rate, because divorce is a kind of suicide, the suicide of the family, of the new "one flesh" reality created by marriage. We have a 50 percent divorce rate, which is a 50 percent suicide rate among families. Suppose you found a society with a 50 percent suicide rate among individuals? How healthy and happy would you think that society is?

Marriage is the most important covenant. Covenants are solemn promises. God made promises of a kind of spiritual marriage to us in three stages. In the Old Testament, he promised to be with us as our heavenly Father and to send a Messiah (the name means "the promised one," or "the anointed one") to be with us even more intimately, as our incarnate brother, fully human as well as fully divine. Finally, this Messiah promised his disciples that after he went back to heaven, he would send the Holy Spirit to live in their hearts and lives and to guide them from within, as the final stage of intimacy of his spiritual marriage to us.

All three revelations, of the Father and of the Son and of the Holy Spirit, were motivated by love, for God *is* love, and love always seeks more and more intimacy; thus, the Father is God with us by being above us, God the Son is God with us by being beside us, and God the Holy Spirit is God with us by being inside us. The Old Testament reveals God as our Creator; the New Testament reveals God as our Savior, our justifier; and the Church reveals God as our sanctifier, our saint-maker, by the Holy Spirit.

In today's passage from the Old Testament, the prophet Jeremiah prophesies this final stage, the final revolution in his relationship with us. We are now in the last phase of this divine love affair. The era we are now living in is indeed "the last days," as the New Testament calls them, no matter how near or far away the end of the world is, whether it comes tonight or ten thousand years from now. God has come among us to live not only alongside us but also within us forever.

His name is "Emmanuel," which means "God with us." "Withness" is the very essence of love: to love someone is to be with them and to want to be with them more and more completely. The model for that is the Trinity, in which each of the three divine persons is totally with the others, totally one with the others, totally affirming of the others, totally *in* the others by perfect love.

Jeremiah describes in detail how revolutionary this last covenant is. First, he says that this New Covenant will not be like the covenants in the Old Testament, which God's people repeatedly violated and had to be punished for. There will be no divorce from this final spiritual marriage. That spiritual divorce, that rebellion, is what sin is. In the heavenly perfection of the New Covenant, sin will cease to exist. That's what we are rehearsing for now, training for now, learning to do.

And the reason why sin will cease is the second detail that the prophet mentions: God's law, which is the expression of God's will, will be not just outside us but inside us, in our hearts. We will obey not out of fear but out of love.

The third detail is that we will all be taught directly by God, not just indirectly through our leaders and friends. (Like the other two details, we are not quite there yet, of course; we still need guides and teachers and authorities in every field, especially the knowledge of God.) But in this final era, God himself will lead us and teach us and guide us and speak to us in our hearts, not just partially and intermittently, as he already does, but perfectly, so that all of us, from the greatest to the least, will know God—know him not just as one knows a distant stranger but as one knows one's most intimate friend and lover. Sin will be not only forgiven but not even remembered. Sin will be abolished.

These promises will come true completely only in heaven, of course. But even here and now they begin and they grow, like any living thing, from plants to human relationships. If it's not growing, it's dying.

If we do not have this heaven in our hearts now, at least as a tiny but real seed, it cannot be transplanted into perfect pots, resurrection bodies, or heavenly fields after death in heaven.

This prophetic description of heaven that God revealed to his prophet Jeremiah—the presence and intimacy of God in us and his will in our will and his mind in our mind—already exists in us as a kind of spiritual embryo. It will come out of the womb of this world and into the greater world of heaven when we die. We did not begin our life at birth, you know; we began it nine months before we were born. Then, in Baptism, we were "born again" into the life of God. Finally, at death, we will be born a third time and emerge from the womb of this universe into the larger world of heaven.

What will we be like in heaven? Asking that is almost like an unborn baby asking what he will be like in the world outside the womb. C.S. Lewis wrote that if any one of us ever met any one of these human creatures who had already been perfected and glorified in heaven, we would probably be tempted to fall down and worship it. Yet that is what every one of us who is now in the state of grace is destined to become, in the end.

Of course, we progress only slowly and fitfully to that end, and the road may well be long and hard and twisty. But God is immensely pleased with every little step we take in that direction, as a loving father is pleased with the first halting steps of his toddler. God is very easy to please and also very hard to satisfy. But in the end, as Jesus told us, he will say, "Well done, my good and faithful servant. . . . Come, share your master's joy" (Matt. 25:21). That's ultimately what Jeremiah's prophecy is about.

RESPONSORIAL PSALM
Psalm 51:3–4, 12–13, 14–15 _____

R. (12a) **Create a clean heart in me, O God.**

Have mercy on me, O God, in your goodness;
    in the greatness of your compassion wipe out my offense.
Thoroughly wash me from my guilt
    and of my sin cleanse me.

A clean heart create for me, O God,
    and a steadfast spirit renew within me.
Cast me not out from your presence,
    and your Holy Spirit take not from me.

Give me back the joy of your salvation,
 and a willing spirit sustain in me.
I will teach transgressors your ways,
 and sinners shall return to you.

Our Psalm verse today is from the Psalm that is the favorite of many of the saints. It is the sinner's Psalm; and the greater the saint, the greater his knowledge of his sins, while the greater the sinner, the greater the illusion he has that he is a saint. No sin is more dangerous than pride, self-satisfaction, and impenitence; no virtue is more necessary than the honesty and humility that leads us to repentance, which brings us forgiveness and salvation.

David asks God not for justice but for mercy. Both justice and mercy are good, and necessary; but mercy is greater, and better.

God is mercy before he is justice; for justice means deservingness, and we could not possibly deserve even to exist, for we were created by God, and what is not yet created and does not yet even exist cannot possibly deserve anything at all.

We who have received the gift of having been created have all misused that gift, the gift of our being, and disobeyed God's law. Our conscience tells us that, and so does God's Word. Our hope is totally dependent on God's grace and mercy rather than justice. Justice is the hope of the innocent, but we are not innocent, and our hope is not justice but mercy.

Chesterton wrote that little children love fairy tales in which the villains all get punished exactly as they deserve, but adults prefer stories in which the villains repent and escape, because little children are relatively innocent, and love justice, whereas adults are all guilty, and prefer mercy.

This Psalm is the classic plea for mercy. David prayed it after his great sin with Bathsheba, which was actually a fivefold sin of lust, lying, theft, adultery, and murder. First, he demanded the satisfaction of his lust for the beautiful Bathsheba, who was Uriah's wife. To that end, he contrived to have Uriah killed in battle, so he was the agent of Uriah's murder. He then stole Uriah's wife and took her for his own, which was both theft and adultery. Finally, he lived this lie until, through the prophet Nathan, God exposed it—not just out of justice but out of mercy and compassion, to bring David to repentance and to save his soul. Often, the most important kind of mercy and love we can give to someone is the "tough love" of telling them the hard truth. This is especially true when that someone is ourselves.

Notice that David's repentance was not just a private feeling inside himself but a transaction with God. He needed not just to forgive himself but to ask for and receive forgiveness from God. Repentance and forgiveness are not just pop psychology. They're religion. They're relationship with God. They're reality, for God is the ultimate reality. They're much more than feelings. Imagine a criminal, found guilty by the judge, arguing, "But judge, I don't *feel* guilty!" I don't think the judge would have mercy on *that*.

Mercy does not abolish justice and truth: it presupposes them. If you do not believe in justice and truth, if you do not believe that right and wrong are objective, universal, and absolute, you cannot believe in mercy or forgiveness or salvation. Because salvation means salvation from something. From what? From sin. From real guilt, not just from guilty feelings. Psychologists can take away your guilty feelings, but only God can take away your guilt.

Notice also that David asks God not merely for freedom from the just *punishments* that his sins deserve but for freedom from sin itself. He's not satisfied being a sinner saved from punishment; he wants to be an ex-sinner saved from sin. He wants to be a saint. He asks God to create in him a clean heart. In theological terms, he asks God for not only justification but also sanctification.

Notice also the word "create." It is a word that existed in only one language in the ancient world—Hebrew. Because no other people knew of a God who could literally create everything out of nothing. None of the gods of the Gentiles could do that. Each of them had power over a part of the universe, but none of them had power over the whole universe, and none of them created the very existence of the universe itself. And now David is asking God to use his unique, divine power to do something God alone can do: to create a new heart, a new motive, a new love, in David; to give him the kind of love that only God has by nature, the love that is divine and supernatural, the love that the New Testament calls *agape*, the love that is total, the love that is the gift of the whole self. We must seek the same thing David did, no matter how small or how great our sins are. We must seek not just repentance but also reform.

Notice also that David asks for the "full treatment" from God. He mentions no less than six things. First, to create in David this new heart. Second, to keep this new spirit "steadfast" and constantly renewed. Third, to never abandon David or cast him away from his divine presence. Fourth, not to deprive David of the gift of his Holy Spirit, which gives supernatural life to David's soul. Fifth, to restore to David not just his salvation but also the joy of that salvation, the joy that David had before he had abandoned God. For God is the source of not only all holiness but also of all joy.

Finally, David asks God to sustain "a willing spirit" in him. He recognizes that God wants David himself to freely will and choose and desire and love the holiness that he asks for. In order to receive God's grace, we must want it. We are receptive but active, like a catcher in baseball. We are radically dependent on divine grace, as the catcher is dependent on receiving the pitch from the pitcher; but the pitcher will not deliver the ball unless the catcher is ready and willing to catch it. God will not give grace to us unless we want it and ask for it. He is always more ready to give than we are to receive. Jesus says, "Ask and you will receive" (Luke 11:9). If in our heart we long for and ask for a new heart, a clean heart, God will give it to us.

Of course, he will give it to us in his patient time and in his mysterious way, not in our impatient time and our simple and obvious way. He is our lover, not our washing machine. Becoming a saint is not a work of engineering; it is a work of romance.

SECOND READING
HEBREWS 5:7–9_____

In the days when Christ Jesus was in the flesh, he offered prayers and supplications with loud cries and tears to the one who was able to save him from death, and he was heard because of his reverence. Son though he was, he learned obedience from what he suffered; and when he was made perfect, he became the source of eternal salvation for all who obey him.

In the early Church there were two opposite heresies about Jesus. One group, the Arians, denied his full divinity, and the other group, the Docetists and the Gnostics, denied his full humanity. The Arian heresy was much more widespread, popular, lasting, and damaging, but both were heretical.

The word "heretic" means literally "one who chooses for himself" what to believe rather than accepting the authority of God, through his Son and his Church, to reveal the truth. The fashionable term today is no longer "heretics" but "cafeteria Catholics," who treat God's revelation as a cafeteria where the customers choose which of the foods to eat—that is, to act as editors and correctors of God's mail rather than faithful mail carriers.

Both heresies about Jesus still exist today, and the one that denies his divinity is still the more popular one. Jesus is often accepted as "the man for others" or "the ideal man" or "Jesus the super social worker" but not as the supernatural miracle worker and Savior of souls. Most Catholics who are faithful to the Church's *laws* and so come to Mass every Sunday are also faithful to the Church's *teachings* about Jesus. So most of you reading this are probably not the kind of heretic that denies Jesus' full divinity. But perhaps we faithful, believing, orthodox Catholics often tend more than we realize to the other, opposite danger, the denial of his full humanity. Today's epistle might be a good opportunity to check on that.

The first thing in today's epistle that speaks of Jesus' humanity is the word "flesh." That means not just *skin*, or even just the *body*, but all of fallen, mortal, weakened human nature. In the Incarnation, Jesus did not assume the perfect human nature of unfallen Adam, but the wounded and weakened human nature of the fallen Adam. He had no sin, but he had the *consequences* of sin in his human nature, both body and soul. His body was mortal, and subject to pain. His human soul was dependent on his human body, and he had to learn from experience. Today's epistle says that he "learned obedience from what he suffered." He was obedient to Mary and Joseph (see Luke 2:51). He experienced fears and weaknesses and temptations, just as we do, though he did not succumb to temptations as we do. He was not in the state of a constant mystical experience, a heavenly "beatific vision" of God his Father. All that is part of the meaning of "the flesh." St. Paul says he was like us "in every way, but without sin" (Heb. 4:15).

Like us, Jesus was dependent on his Father. He prayed to him, and his prayer was not only a prayer of adoration that expressed the joy of union with the Father but also a prayer of "supplication"—that is, petition—that expressed human needs and pains, which the Father does not have. In fact, the text says, "He offered prayers and supplications *with loud cries and tears.*" He wept over Jerusalem, and in the Garden of Gethsemane he shed tears, sweat, and blood. Jesus was not a Stoic. He experienced and expressed every human emotion we have, and every human weakness.

Those weaknesses included being subject to temptations. The New Testament says he is "not unable to sympathize with our weaknesses" because he is "one who has similarly been tested in every way, yet without sin" (Heb. 4:15). Jesus was genuinely tempted by the devil in the wilderness. That was real; that was not a fiction or a play-acting, a fake stage performance. Jesus felt the pull of all the temptations that we have, but he resisted; he said a total no to Satan and a total yes to God the Father.

And those human weaknesses included not just temptations but also fears. He feared the Crucifixion and asked his Father, in the Garden of Gethsemane, to spare him from it if it was possible (see Luke 22:42).

He also shared our human ignorance. He did not pop out of Mary's womb speaking perfect Hebrew. He told his disciples that he did not know when the Father would send him back for his second coming at the end of the world (see Matt. 24:36).

Another aspect of Jesus' humanity in our epistle today is that it says that when Jesus prayed, "he was heard because of his reverence." Jesus had to have reverence for his Father. Jesus had to obey his Father. He had to learn that. He had to learn how to obey his human foster father Joseph too. When he was twelve, after staying behind in Jerusalem for three days in the temple and finally being found by his parents, Luke says, "He went down with them and came to Nazareth, and was obedient to them" (Luke 2:51). Today's epistle says that he "learned obedience from what he suffered." That is how we learn it too: the hard way.

Finally, the epistle says that he "became the source of eternal salvation for all who obey him" only after he "was made perfect." He had to be *made* perfect. "Perfect" means "complete." He was innocent and sinless but not complete as a baby. He had to learn. That took 90 percent of his lifetime. He did not begin his three-year-long public ministry until he was thirty. And even then, he was planning on more preparation, for when his mother Mary, at the wedding feast at Cana, presented him with the problem that there was no more wine, he protested to his mother that "my hour has not yet come" (John 2:4). He changed his plans because of her prayer. That's not incompatible with perfection. Being flexible enough to change your plans when unforeseen needs arise is not an imperfection but part of human perfection.

Jesus was flexible—not in his principles but in applying them to different persons and different needs and different situations. He was flexible not in his love but in the many different and creative ways to express that love. Too many of us are flexible and compromising in our principles and, even worse, in our loves, or else we are stubborn and narrow-minded and inflexible in applying them, or, worst of all, both.

We who rightly insist on being faithful and uncompromising to the laws and principles and to the truths and teachings that our Lord gave us should also be flexible in practicing them and applying them, as our Lord was. We need to stay rooted, but we also need to sprout and grow. We need an anchor, but we also need a sail. If some so-called progressives deny the need for an anchor, we should not respond by denying the need for a sail. We need to both keep our essential identity and also grow, and change, in our souls as well as in our bodies. In fact, that growth will not stop even in heaven. There will always be something new to learn. We will not be bored. We will not be frozen, or static. We will be completely human, like our Lord.

Pope St. John Paul II loved to quote this sentence from the documents of the Second Vatican Council: "Only in the mystery of the incarnate Word does the mystery of man take on light." Jesus shows us not only perfect divinity but also perfect humanity, not only who God is but also who we are when we are complete; in knowing Christ, we know the two most important realities in our life, the true God and our true selves. These are the two things we most need to know—who God is and who we are—because they are the only two realities we will never, ever be able to escape or avoid for a single second either in time or in eternity.

GOSPEL
JOHN 12:20–33

Some Greeks who had come to worship at the Passover Feast came to Philip, who was from Bethsaida in Galilee, and asked him, "Sir, we would like to see Jesus." Philip went and told Andrew; then Andrew and Philip went and told Jesus. Jesus answered them, "The hour has come for the Son of Man to be glorified. Amen, amen, I say to you, unless a grain of wheat falls to the ground and dies, it remains just a grain of wheat; but if it dies, it produces much fruit. Whoever loves his life loses it, and whoever hates his life in this world will preserve it for eternal life. Whoever serves me must follow me, and where I am, there also will my servant be. The Father will honor whoever serves me.

"I am troubled now. Yet what should I say? 'Father, save me from this hour'? But it was for this purpose that I came to this hour. Father, glorify your name." Then a voice came from heaven, "I have glorified it and will glorify it again." The crowd there heard it and said it was thunder; but others said, "An angel has spoken to him." Jesus answered and said, "This voice did not come for my sake but for yours. Now is the time of judgment on this world; now the ruler of this world will be driven out. And when I am lifted up from the earth, I will draw everyone to myself." He said this indicating the kind of death he would die.

Today's Gospel seems puzzling at least five times.

First, some Greeks want to see Jesus, and Jesus' answer to them is to speak of his forthcoming death. How is that an answer? The connection is probably this: they want to learn from him and understand him, and they think they can do that only while he is alive, but they suspect that the religious leaders' plot to kill him will succeed in the next few days, so they are desperate to get to him before it's too late. His answer, in speaking of his death, is, in effect, that to understand him they must look at his death, not just his life, because that's what he came into the world for. Thus, Jesus prays aloud so that he can be heard by the Greek visitors as well as the Jews and his disciples: "I am troubled now. Yet what should I say? 'Father, save me from this hour'? But it was for this purpose that I came to this hour."

These Greeks wanted to know the true God. They suspected, rightly, that the best way to do that was to know Jesus. What they did not know was that to know Jesus most truly was not to know him simply as a teacher, a rabbi, a wise man, and a sage, or even as a miracle worker, but as a martyr, as one who gave his life for others, for *all* others, including them, out of love, because that is the very essence of God. "God is love," and the essence of love is the gift of yourself to others.

The second puzzle is this: when Jesus speaks of his death, he uses the analogy of the grain of wheat giving itself up to the ground and only in this way fulfilling its destiny to be a living plant. He says this to teach them that only by death can we keep on living; that the human self was designed by God to die in two ways: first, to actively die to itself, to its own natural selfish egotism, and only thus come to life spiritually; and second, that each of us also has to literally, physically die in order to enter our heavenly life and fulfillment. C.S. Lewis put it this way: "We are like eggs at present. And you cannot go on indefinitely being just an ordinary, decent egg. We must be hatched or go bad."

Artificial immortality by genetic engineering, which some mad scientists are actually working on right now, would be the worst thing that could possibly happen to the human race. We would all become rotten eggs that would never hatch. Death is hatching; death is being born, just as our birth was a kind of hatching from the egg of the womb.

Jesus explicitly interprets his analogy of the grain of wheat by saying that to love your life and insist on keeping it, to grasp it, to hold on to it, to refuse to give it away to others, is to lose it; and that the only way to keep it, to preserve it, is to give it away, to lose it—in fact, he says, to "hate" it. The word translated "hate" here does not mean the emotion of despising your life but the choice to give it up, to sacrifice, to turn away from the temptation to idolize it and make your own life your god.

We all know by experience that the most deeply joyful moments in our lives have been moments when we simply forgot all about ourselves, when we lost ourselves in something or someone else that was so beautiful that it took our breath away. Literally. When you see something so stunningly good or true or beautiful that you stop breathing for a minute, and suddenly get all silent inside, that's a foretaste of heaven.

That unselfconsciousness, that self-forgetfulness, is one of the things Jesus meant when he said that unless we became like little children we could not enter into his kingdom of heaven. Little children are usually happy because they are not self-conscious. They are honest enough to say what they think even if adults laugh at them.

A third paradox in today's Gospel is that Jesus speaks of his Crucifixion as his *glorification*. But crucifixion was the most grimly *in*glorious, terrifying, painful, ugly, degrading invention in the long and terrible human history of torture. When people saw a line of crosses erected anywhere in the Roman Empire, they knew that there would be dying bodies on them. The crosses were public warnings posted by a cruel and tyrannical empire to terrify its subjects and deter any opposition to its power.

Yet after his Resurrection, when Jesus appeared in his new, glorious, immortal resurrection body, it still had its wounds from his Crucifixion! Why? Because they were now part of his glory. They were like badges of honor, like purple hearts or congressional medals of honor. That's why we put gold on our crucifixes. It's shocking. It's like wearing pretty gold electric chairs around our necks. It's like putting gold nooses on top of our cathedral spires.

Why are his wounds glorious? Because they were wounds of love, and love is glorious. Love transforms sufferings into glories. The same is true of our sufferings if they are united with Christ's.

Our post-Christian culture encourages people who are old and feeble and suffering to ask for physician-assisted suicide because they value what they call "death with dignity." This is a profound mistake, not just about ethics but about dignity. Dignity does not mean the absence of suffering. A martyr does not lose his dignity when he is martyred. Nothing has more dignity and more glory and more spiritual beauty than love, and love is shown most strongly in sacrifice, in actively accepting suffering out of love and its two sisters, faith and hope.

A fourth paradox in today's Gospel is that what seems to be the supreme triumph of the devil, whom Jesus calls "the ruler of this world" (John 12:31)— namely, getting Jesus killed—is how Jesus says he will drive the devil out. Jesus beat the devil by a kind of spiritual judo: using the enemy's own force against him. It works because it is the essential nature of evil to be self-destructive. That's why mass murderers usually also kill themselves.

A fifth paradox is what Jesus means when he says that he will draw everyone to himself. He says that the way he will do this, the way he will win the world and attract us to himself, the way he will make us fall in love with him and imitate him and want to be like him, is by being "lifted up from the earth." But what he means by this is not being lifted up on a throne to become the world's king or emperor or Caesar, or even his own future glorious Ascension into heaven, but by being lifted up on the cross. How can this attract us? How can torture and agony attract anyone except a masochist?

It's not the suffering that attracts us but the love, the love that is so great that it goes the extra mile and meets the supreme test of self-sacrifice. When love does not suffer, it is still good and powerful; but when love suffers, it gains not only immense goodness but also immense power. Suffering also gains power when it is joined with love. The power of a loveless tyrant is fragile and external; the power of love to motivate the beloved is irresistible.

Today there are many strong powers in the world that lack love, such as Islamic terrorism, which will suffer and die not for love but for hate. Opposing this suffering without love is what we usually find in America: love without suffering, love that is not willing to suffer. Neither will win the world. But suffering love will win the world, Christian love, the love that is willing to suffer. That is how Christ won heaven for us on the cross. If we tap into that power, we will win the world again for Christ.

HOLY WEEK

PALM SUNDAY OF THE LORD'S PASSION: READINGS AT THE MASS

GOSPEL AT THE PROCESSION WITH PALMS

(First option) Mark 11:1–10 _____

When Jesus and his disciples drew near to Jerusalem, to Bethphage and Bethany at the Mount of Olives, he sent two of his disciples and said to them, "Go into the village opposite you, and immediately on entering it, you will find a colt tethered on which no one has ever sat. Untie it and bring it here. If anyone should say to you, 'Why are you doing this?' reply, 'The Master has need of it and will send it back here at once.'" So they went off and found a colt tethered at a gate outside on the street, and they untied it. Some of the bystanders said to them, "What are you doing, untying the colt?" They answered them just as Jesus had told them to, and they permitted them to do it. So they brought the colt to Jesus and put their cloaks over it. And he sat on it. Many people spread their cloaks on the road, and others spread leafy branches that they had cut from the fields. Those preceding him as well as those following kept crying out:

"Hosanna!
   Blessed is he who comes in the
      name of the Lord!
   Blessed is the kingdom of our father
      David that is to come!
Hosanna in the highest!"

(Second option) John 12:12–16 _____

When the great crowd that had come to the feast heard that Jesus was coming to Jerusalem, they took palm branches and went out to meet him, and cried out:

"Hosanna!

Blessed is he who comes in the name of the Lord,

the king of Israel."

Jesus found an ass and sat upon it, as is written:

"Fear no more, O daughter Zion;

See, your king comes,

seated upon an ass's colt. "

His disciples did not understand this at first, but when Jesus had been glorified they remembered that these things were written about him and that they had done this for him.

Here are some lessons from today's Processional Gospel.

Here's Lesson One. Jesus had arranged for the colt on which he rode into Jerusalem on Palm Sunday to be available for him, and his disciples found it exactly as he said they would. Whether Jesus arranged this by ordinary human means or by a supernatural miracle is not the point: the point is that Jesus takes care of every single little detail of our lives. He is the Son of God, and "like father, like son," and God our Father is not a deadbeat dad; he is not absent but present. He is not absent from anything. When he created the universe, he knew perfectly the exact movement of every atom, every animal, and every thought that would ever happen in the whole of time.

The lesson here, then, is to find God in all things, as the Jesuits love to say. Because he *is* in all things. Our God takes care of all the details of our lives, the little things as well as the big things, the means as well as the ends.

Here's Lesson Two. Great kings and conquerors, who loved and attained great military, economic, or political success, always rode large horses in their parades of conquest and glory. Jesus rode the colt of an ass, a baby donkey. His conquest is humility. His glory is the humility of love. A few days later, his crown of thorns would make the same paradoxical point: that his kingship is not one of power but of love, love that endures even suffering, which is the severest test of love. The humility, meekness, kindness, and suffering of that love is our conquest too. Do you want to conquer the world? Jesus tells you how: "Blessed are the meek, for they will inherit the land" (Matt. 5:5). Believe it. He said it, and he is the only human being who can never, never lie.

Here's Lesson Three. It's an animal lesson. What animal did Jesus choose to do the most important work any animal ever did: to carry him into Jerusalem to do the essential job he came for, to die to save us all from sin and death and hell? He chose a jackass. He keeps choosing the same animals to do his work today. His Church is full of jackasses. You don't have to go to the zoo to see one: just look in the mirror.

Here's Lesson Four. On Palm Sunday, the crowds gave up their cloaks to make Jesus' saddle on the colt, and they made a red carpet out of the green palm branches for him to ride on. They didn't throw gold at Jesus because they didn't have gold. They gave him what they had. Jesus accepts the humblest and poorest of gifts, as long as we give them out of love. In the popular Christmas song, the little drummer boy had nothing but his drumming to give to Jesus, so that's what he gave. That was his prayer.

When you pray, give everything you have. That's the essential prayer, the prayer of trusting love, the love that entrusts everything, without exception, everything in your life, to the God who loves you. Our trust in each other is very good and necessary too, but it can never be *total*. We're not God. But God is! And our trust in God can never be *less* than total—unless we are pagans, and polytheists, and have many gods, one for each part of life, instead of the one God who designed and created all things and who providentially rules over absolutely everything in our lives.

The only way to keep anything is to give it up to the one who it really belongs to. Make your life a red carpet for Jesus to ride on.

Here's Lesson Five. The crowds did not understand Jesus. Even his Apostles did not understand him. They thought he would be the new King David and rule the world. When he was crucified, they were devastated. But we do not have to fully understand him in order for us to trust him and love him and give ourselves wholly to him. In fact, nobody fully understands him, not even the greatest saint or the greatest mystic. He is God. He is infinitely wise, and we are not. But we can still love him and trust him and praise him, as these ordinary people did. They said of him, "Blessed is the kingdom of our father David that is to come!" and they spoke the truth, even though they did not understand it. They remembered the prophecy that their king would come riding on an ass' colt, and they saw that prophecy fulfilled with their own eyes, and they were right to trust him and believe in him even though they did not understand what kind of king he would be or what kind of kingdom he would have.

We can do the same to him: we can trust him and love him even when we do not understand him. When a baby looks up into its mother's eyes and smiles with total love and trust, does the baby have to understand what a mother is before it can do that? Well, then, neither do we. Let's not forget that great wisdom we once had when we were babies. Remember, Jesus said that only if we become as little children can we enter his kingdom, the kingdom that all these people around him on Palm Sunday were truly praising even while they were not fully understanding it.

Here's Lesson Six. These people were sincere in their praises. Yet it was the same people, at least some of them, who, only five days later, on Good Friday, at Jesus' trial, would be using their same loud voices to cry out "Crucify him!" Human nature is terribly fickle and unstable and persuadable by demagogues. Our demagogues are not charismatic speakers like Hitler but respected experts and media and political parties. Don't trust the elephant or the donkey; trust the Lamb, the Lamb of God who takes away the sins of the world.

Jesus was not a starry-eyed optimist or a utopian idealist. Here is what the Bible says he thought about human nature: "While he was in Jerusalem for the feast of Passover, many began to believe in his name when they saw the signs he was doing. But Jesus would not trust himself to them because he knew them all, and did not need anyone to testify about human nature. He himself understood it well" (John 2:23–25).

Jesus loves us totally, but he does not trust us totally. Love and trust don't always go together. We trust banks with our money, but we don't love banks. We love our families unreservedly, but we don't trust them unreservedly, because we don't trust ourselves unreservedly either. We know ourselves too well for that. God is the only one we can both love unreservedly and unconditionally and also trust unreservedly and unconditionally.

Don't make an idol of any human being, especially yourself. Don't put divine expectations on human shoulders. Those shoulders will eventually break. Be grateful when they don't break, and don't be surprised when they do. That applies equally to the ones you love and to yourself.

Here's Lesson Seven. Don't be like the fickle crowd. Be loyal. Stick by Jesus both on days of sunlight like Palm Sunday and on days of the eclipse of the sun like Good Friday. (The eclipse of the sun that happened on that day was an eclipse of the sun in a double sense: the sun of the solar system and the Son of God. But in both cases it was only a temporary eclipse; the sun rose again, and so did the Son.)

There are more Palm Sundays than Good Fridays in our lives, more sunny days than dark days, but dark days always come. At least death always comes. But it's not the end. It's just an eclipse.

It's easy to be with Jesus on Palm Sunday, with the great crowds there shouting "Hosanna!" But on Good Friday only four remained by the cross, and three were women. John was the only one of the twelve Apostles who had the courage to stay by Jesus even as he was dying on the cross; the others all ran away, including Peter, whom Jesus chose as the first pope. (Yet Jesus makes no mistakes.)

In the Rosary, there are five joyful mysteries and five luminous mysteries and five glorious mysteries but also five sorrowful mysteries. The Rosary is like life, because it's about the life of Christ, and Christ reveals to us not only the true nature of divinity but also the true nature of humanity and human life. We will always find some people who say "Hosanna" to us (though in a more polite and mild way than those passionate peasants), and some people who say "Crucify him!" to us (though also in a more polite and mild way), and sometimes they will be the same people.

Love them anyway. Give them your heart, because if you don't, then you don't love them. And give them the power to break your heart, because if you don't, then you're not giving them your heart. Always remember Mother Teresa's philosophy of life, the one that made her so cheerful: "God did not put me in this world to be successful. He put me here to be faithful."

GOSPEL
Mark 14:1–15:47
(or Mark 15:1–39) _____

The Passover and the Feast of Unleavened Bread were to take place in two days' time. So the chief priests and the scribes were seeking a way to arrest him by treachery and put him to death. They said, "Not during the festival, for fear that there may be a riot among the people."

When he was in Bethany reclining at table in the house of Simon the leper, a woman came with an alabaster jar of perfumed oil, costly genuine spikenard. She broke the alabaster jar and poured it on his head. There were some who were indignant. "Why has there been this waste of perfumed oil? It could have been sold for more than three hundred days' wages and the money given to the poor." They were infuriated with her. Jesus said, "Let her alone. Why do you make trouble for her? She has done a good thing for me. The poor you will always have with you, and whenever you wish you can do good to them, but you will not always have me. She has done what she could. She has anticipated anointing my body for burial. Amen, I say to you, wherever the gospel is proclaimed to the whole world, what she has done will be told in memory of her."

Then Judas Iscariot, one of the Twelve, went off to the chief priests to hand him over to them. When they heard him they were pleased and promised to pay him money. Then he looked for an opportunity to hand him over.

On the first day of the Feast of Unleavened Bread, when they sacrificed the

Passover lamb, his disciples said to him, "Where do you want us to go and prepare for you to eat the Passover?" He sent two of his disciples and said to them, "Go into the city and a man will meet you, carrying a jar of water. Follow him. Wherever he enters, say to the master of the house, 'The Teacher says, "Where is my guest room where I may eat the Passover with my disciples?"' Then he will show you a large upper room furnished and ready. Make the preparations for us there." The disciples then went off, entered the city, and found it just as he had told them; and they prepared the Passover.

When it was evening, he came with the Twelve. And as they reclined at table and were eating, Jesus said, "Amen, I say to you, one of you will betray me, one who is eating with me." They began to be distressed and to say to him, one by one, "Surely it is not I?" He said to them, "One of the Twelve, the one who dips with me into the dish. For the Son of Man indeed goes, as it is written of him, but woe to that man by whom the Son of Man is betrayed. It would be better for that man if he had never been born."

While they were eating, he took bread, said the blessing, broke it, and gave it to them, and said, "Take it; this is my body." Then he took a cup, gave thanks, and gave it to them, and they all drank from it. He said to them, "This is my blood of the covenant, which will be shed for many. Amen, I say to you, I shall not drink again the fruit of the vine until the day when I drink it new in the kingdom of God." Then, after singing a hymn, they went out to the Mount of Olives.

Then Jesus said to them, "All of you will have your faith shaken, for it is written:

I will strike the shepherd,
and the sheep will be dispersed.

But after I have been raised up, I shall go before you to Galilee." Peter said to him, "Even though all should have their faith shaken, mine will not be." Then Jesus said to him, "Amen, I say to you, this very night before the cock crows twice you will deny me three times." But he vehemently replied, "Even though I should have to die with you, I will not deny you." And they all spoke similarly.

Then they came to a place named Gethsemane, and he said to his disciples, "Sit here while I pray." He took with him Peter, James, and John, and began to be troubled and distressed. Then he said to them, "My soul is sorrowful even to death. Remain here and keep watch." He advanced a little and fell to the ground and prayed that if it were possible the hour might pass by him; he said, "Abba, Father, all things are possible to you. Take this cup away from me, but not what I will but what you will." When he returned he found them asleep. He said to Peter, "Simon, are you asleep? Could you not keep watch for one hour? Watch and pray that you may not undergo the test. The spirit is willing but the flesh is weak." Withdrawing again, he prayed, saying the same thing. Then he returned once more and found them asleep, for they could not keep their eyes open and did not know what to answer him. He returned a third time and said to them, "Are you still sleeping and taking your rest? It is enough. The hour has come. Behold, the Son of Man is to be handed over to sinners. Get up, let us go. See, my betrayer is at hand."

Then, while he was still speaking, Judas, one of the Twelve, arrived, accompanied by a crowd with swords and clubs who had come from the chief priests, the scribes, and the elders. His betrayer had arranged a signal with them, saying, "The man I shall kiss is the one; arrest him and lead him away securely." He came and immediately went over to him and said, "Rabbi." And he kissed him. At this they laid hands on him and arrested him. One of the bystanders drew his sword, struck the high priest's servant, and cut off his ear. Jesus said to them in reply, "Have you come out as against a robber, with swords and clubs, to seize me? Day after day I was with you teaching in the temple area, yet you did not arrest me; but that the Scriptures may be fulfilled." And they all left him and fled. Now a young man followed him wearing nothing but a linen cloth about his body. They seized him, but he left the cloth behind and ran off naked.

They led Jesus away to the high priest, and all the chief priests and the elders and the scribes came together. Peter followed him at a distance into the high priest's courtyard and was seated with the guards, warming himself at the fire. The chief priests and the entire Sanhedrin kept trying to obtain testimony against Jesus in order to put him to death, but they found none. Many gave false witness against him, but their testimony did not agree. Some took the stand and testified falsely against him, alleging, "We heard him say, 'I will destroy this temple made with hands and within three days I will build another not made with hands.'" Even so their testimony did not agree. The high priest rose before the assembly and questioned Jesus, saying, "Have you no answer? What are these men testifying against you?" But he was silent and answered nothing. Again the high priest asked him and said to him, "Are you the Christ, the son of the Blessed One?" Then Jesus answered, "I am; and 'you will see the Son of Man seated at the right hand of the Power and coming with the clouds of heaven.'" At that the high priest tore his garments and said, "What further need have we of witnesses? You have heard the blasphemy. What do you think?" They all condemned him as deserving to die. Some began to spit on him. They blindfolded him and struck him and said to him, "Prophesy!" And the guards greeted him with blows.

While Peter was below in the courtyard, one of the high priest's maids came along. Seeing Peter warming himself, she looked intently at him and said, "You too were with the Nazarene, Jesus." But he denied it saying, "I neither know nor understand what you are talking about." So he went out into the outer court. Then the cock crowed. The maid saw him and began again to say to the bystanders, "This man is one of them." Once again he denied it. A little later the bystanders said to Peter once more, "Surely you are one of them; for you too are a Galilean." He began to curse and to swear, "I do not know this man about whom you are talking." And immediately a cock crowed a second time. Then Peter remembered the word that Jesus had said to him, "Before the cock crows twice you will deny me three times." He broke down and wept.

As soon as morning came, the chief priests with the elders and the scribes, that is, the whole Sanhedrin, held a council. They bound Jesus, led him away, and handed him over to Pilate. Pilate questioned him, "Are you the king of the Jews?" He said to him in reply, "You say so." The chief priests accused him of many things. Again Pilate questioned him, "Have you no answer? See how many things they accuse you of." Jesus gave him no further answer, so that Pilate was amazed.

Now on the occasion of the feast he used to release to them one prisoner whom they requested. A man called Barabbas was then in prison along with the rebels who had committed murder in a rebellion. The crowd came forward and began to ask him to do for them as he was accustomed. Pilate answered, "Do you want me to release to you the king of the Jews?" For he knew that it was out of envy that the chief priests had handed him over. But the chief priests stirred up the crowd to have him release Barabbas for them instead. Pilate again said to them in reply, "Then what do you want me to do with the man you call the king of the Jews?" They shouted again, "Crucify him." Pilate said to them, "Why? What evil has he done?" They only shouted the louder, "Crucify him." So Pilate, wishing to satisfy the crowd, released Barabbas to them and, after he had Jesus scourged, handed him over to be crucified.

The soldiers led him away inside the palace, that is, the praetorium, and assembled the whole cohort. They clothed him in purple and, weaving a crown of thorns, placed it on him. They began to salute him with, "Hail, King of the Jews!" and kept striking his head with a reed and spitting upon him. They knelt before him in homage. And when they had mocked him, they stripped him of the purple cloak, dressed him in his own clothes, and led him out to crucify him.

They pressed into service a passer-by, Simon, a Cyrenian, who was coming in from the country, the father of Alexander and Rufus, to carry his cross.

They brought him to the place of Golgotha—which is translated Place of the Skull—. They gave him wine drugged with myrrh, but he did not take it. Then they crucified him and divided his garments by casting lots for them to see what each should take. It was nine o'clock in the morning when they crucified him. The inscription of the charge against him read, "The King of the Jews." With him they crucified two revolutionaries, one on his right and one on his left. Those passing by reviled him, shaking their heads and saying, "Aha! You who would destroy the temple and rebuild it in three days, save yourself by coming down from the cross." Likewise the chief priests, with the scribes, mocked him among themselves and said, "He saved others; he cannot save himself. Let the Christ, the King of Israel, come down now from the cross that we may see and believe." Those who were crucified with him also kept abusing him.

At noon darkness came over the whole land until three in the afternoon. And at three o'clock Jesus cried out in a loud voice, *"Eloi, Eloi, lema sabachthani?"* which is translated, "My God, my God, why have you forsaken me?" Some of the bystanders who heard it said, "Look, he is calling Elijah." One of them ran, soaked a sponge with wine, put it on a reed and gave it to him to drink saying, "Wait, let us see if Elijah comes to take him down." Jesus gave a loud cry and breathed his last.

Here all kneel and pause for a short time.

The veil of the sanctuary was torn in two from top to bottom. When the centurion who stood facing him saw how he breathed his last he said, "Truly this man was the Son of God!" There were also women looking on from a distance. Among them were Mary Magdalene, Mary the mother of the younger James and of Joses, and Salome. These women had followed him when he was in Galilee and ministered to him. There were also many other women who had come up with him to Jerusalem.

When it was already evening, since it was the day of preparation, the day before the sabbath, Joseph of Arimathea, a distinguished member of the council, who was himself awaiting the kingdom of God, came and courageously went to Pilate and asked for the body of Jesus. Pilate was amazed that he was already dead. He summoned the centurion and asked him if Jesus had already died. And when he learned of it from the centurion, he gave the body to Joseph. Having bought a linen cloth, he took him down, wrapped him in the linen cloth, and laid him in a tomb that had been hewn out of the rock. Then he rolled a stone against the entrance to the tomb. Mary Magdalene and Mary the mother of Joses watched where he was laid.

Today's Processional Gospel begins by showing Jesus riding into Jerusalem in triumph with people strewing palm branches on his path like a red carpet made of greens; and then in this Gospel reading, a few days later, after the Last Supper and just before his arrest and trial and Crucifixion, we see Jesus in terrible agony in the Garden of Gethsemane. We like to look at the triumph and not at the agony, of course; but there are precious lessons we can learn from the agony if we look carefully at it. Let's dare to do that.

By the way, isn't it fascinating that the very same thing—tears—express both our highest joys and our deepest sorrows? Those who shouted their hosannas to Jesus as their Messiah and King on Palm Sunday probably wept with joy; and Jesus wept with agony in the Garden of Gethsemane so deeply that he sweat blood as well as shed tears.

Jesus said, "My soul is sorrowful even to death." Jesus prayed to his Father asking if there was any other way to do the Father's will and save the world, any way that would avoid the terrible sufferings to come, the Crucifixion. Crucifixion was perhaps the most exquisitely terrible form of torture ever invented. Jesus prayed two things, two petitions. First, "Father, all things are possible to you. Take this cup away from me." Second, "But not what I will but what you will." The first petition was conditional on the second, which was absolute.

Luke, who was a physician, and the most sensitive of the four Gospel writers, adds that an angel had to come from heaven to comfort him, and that "he was in such agony and he prayed so fervently that his sweat became like drops of blood falling on the ground" (Luke 22:44).

Jesus was completely human in all things except sin, so of course he was terrified of the unimaginable pain of having his flesh ripped off his body with a leather whip with sharp metal attached and then having nails put through his hands and feet and then hanging for many hours in excruciating agony on the cross until he slowly died. (The very word "excruciating" comes from the word *crux*, which means "cross.") But I think there was something even more terrifying to him, and even more unendurably painful, that threw him into such agony in the Garden of Gethsemane. Let's dare to think about this even more terrifying thing, because it helps us to understand our Lord.

What is the greatest suffering that you can imagine? What is the very worst thing that could ever happen to you in your life here on earth? I think the answer is very clear. Who is the person you love the most? It's probably either a child or a spouse or a parent. Now imagine the worst thing you can imagine entering the life of that person whom you love the most. That suffering most breaks your heart.

I can imagine three such "worst things." The first is death. The more you love someone, the more their death breaks your heart. But that's expected, and inevitable, and universal. It happens to everyone. We all are destined to lose someone we love, and never in this world to recoup that loss, even if we could search every place in the world and every planet in the universe for a million years.

Yet that's not the very worst thing that could ever happen to you. There are things worse than death. You could see someone you dearly and deeply love destroying themselves, either by suicide or by drugs or by despair. If you truly love them, there is nothing that can hurt you more than that: the dying of their soul, and their hope, not just their body. And the more you love them, the more they can hurt you.

Now imagine something even worse. Imagine this person you love more than you love yourself hates you. Imagine your spouse or parent or child responding to your love for them by saying to you: "I don't love you. I hate you. I want you out of my life forever. I never want to see you again. I hope you die. I want you dead. I'd love to kill you. You no longer exist for me." I don't think you can imagine a more terrible thing than that.

Why? Because the deepest suffering can come only from the deepest love. The more you love, the more vulnerable you are to suffering. The only way to avoid the worst kind of suffering is not to give the best kind of love. The only way to keep your heart safe is to lock it up, not to give it up. But those who choose that way of life, those who refuse to love anyone else very deeply because they want to avoid life's greatest suffering, also avoid life's greatest joy. If you don't open your heart with love, you can't open your heart to receive it either. That's true even about loving God. If you don't give God your heart, you can't receive his heart. If your fist is clenched tightly around yourself, it's not opened to receive his gift of himself. That's why Jesus clearly says that if we do not forgive, we cannot and will not be forgiven. It's not a deal, a contract, a treaty; it's a psychological necessity. Only a heart open to giving love can receive love. The heart valve of free will must open in order to let the blood of life pass through in either direction, the arteries or the veins.

And the more you love, the more you can suffer. The more of your heart you give away, the more others can hurt you. Now how much did Jesus love? Infinitely more than we do. And how many people did he love? Every single one. They are all his infinitely beloved children. To have children is to give hostages to heartbreak, and Jesus has billions of children.

That's why I think it's likely that the thing that caused Jesus to sweat blood in Gethsemane, and to ask his Father if there was some other way, was a vision of all the people who would reject him and his love and end up in hell, beginning almost certainly with Judas Iscariot, despite his love for them and despite his gift of his own life for them. For a gift has to be freely accepted as well as freely given.

Perhaps God the Father allowed the devil to tempt Jesus one more time in the Garden by showing him all his children, each one of whom he loved infinitely, who would reject him and his love and end up not in heaven but in hell. That would be a far greater suffering than the cross, because on the cross Jesus experienced only his own suffering, but in Gethsemane he experienced the hopeless despair of all the lost children that he loved with infinite love. We don't know how many, and it doesn't matter, because he loved each one infinitely.

Jesus was not a coward. What made him terrified in the Garden was not just the fear of his own physical pain, however extreme that would be. There are worse things than physical pain. The spirit can have far greater and deeper joy than the body can, but it can also suffer much more than the body can.

That's why, when people are in unendurable spiritual agony, they often distract themselves from the greater spiritual pain by inflicting physical pain by banging their head against the wall or tearing their hair out.

How great were Jesus' sufferings? The answer to that question is the answer to this question: How great was Jesus' love? You can see the answer to that question when you look at a crucifix. His outspread arms give you the answer: "This much." There is no limit. The arms point away; they do not close in on themselves like a fist. The four arms of the cross, the crossbeams, point in all four directions at once unlimitedly. A circle is perfect but limited and enclosed. It is a natural symbol of selfishness and safety. In contrast, a cross is a crisis, a conflict, a contradiction, but it is unlimited and open. It is a natural symbol of self-giving love.

"God is love" (1 John 4:16). Jesus is the total, complete, perfect manifestation of God's love, even for those who refuse it—especially for those who refuse it, because love always goes out to those who need it the most.

And that loving is what we are called to do too. When we see Jesus' love, we want to respond to it, and we wonder how, and here is his answer to our question of how to do that: "Amen, I say to you, whatever you did for one of these least brothers of mine, you did for me" (Matt. 25:40).

HOLY THURSDAY

FIRST READING

EXODUS 12:1–8, 11–14 _____

The LORD said to Moses and Aaron in the land of Egypt, "This month shall stand at the head of your calendar; you shall reckon it the first month of the year. Tell the whole community of Israel: On the tenth of this month every one of your families must procure for itself a lamb, one apiece for each household. If a family is too small for a whole lamb, it shall join the nearest household in procuring one and shall share in the lamb in proportion to the number of persons who partake of it. The lamb must be a year-old male and without blemish. You may take it from either the sheep or the goats. You shall keep it until the fourteenth day of this month, and then, with the whole assembly of Israel present, it shall be slaughtered during the evening twilight. They shall take some of its blood and apply it to the two doorposts and the lintel of every house in which they partake of the lamb. That same night they shall eat its roasted flesh with unleavened bread and bitter herbs.

"This is how you are to eat it: with your loins girt, sandals on your feet and your staff in hand, you shall eat like those who are in flight. It is the Passover of the LORD. For on this same night I will go through Egypt, striking down every firstborn of the land, both man and beast, and executing judgment on all the gods of Egypt—I, the LORD! But the blood will mark the houses where you are. Seeing the blood, I will pass over you; thus, when I strike the land of Egypt, no destructive blow will come upon you.

"This day shall be a memorial feast for you, which all your generations shall celebrate with pilgrimage to the LORD, as a perpetual institution."

For the liturgy for Holy Thursday, the Institution of the Lord's Supper, the Church gives us the account of God instituting the Passover meal when his people were in slavery in Egypt. She does this not only to remember and commemorate the ancient rite whose full meaning was revealed in Christ instituting the Eucharist, but also, much more, to actually bring about what happened in the old Passover, when the angel of death who slew the firstborn son of every Egyptian household passed over the houses of the Jews because their doorposts were sprinkled with the blood of the lamb. On Holy Thursday, the Lamb of God who was symbolized by the lamb of the old Passover gave us his own Body and Blood, gave us himself, for our salvation, not just from temporal death but from eternal death, and to free his people, not just from physical slavery in Egypt but from the spiritual slavery of sin.

The Old Testament account of the institution of the Jewish Passover and the New Testament account of Christ's institution of the Eucharist explain each other. The meaning of each event is found in the other event. Christ is fulfilling the Old Covenant and showing its ultimate meaning by instituting the New Covenant, the new spiritual marriage between God and man. He is giving us, in this sacrament, his own Blood, his own life, to free us from sin and its consequence, eternal death. As St. Paul wrote, "The wages of sin is death, but the gift of God is eternal life in Christ Jesus our Lord" (Rom. 6:23). That's the bad news and the good news all in one sentence.

Every detail of the Exodus account is fulfilled on Holy Thursday. Holy Thursday is not a symbol of the old Passover; the Passover was a prophetic symbol of Holy Thursday.

Symbolically, Egypt is the land of slavery. Sin is the worst slavery.

The Pharaoh is the enslaver, the tyrant, and our enslaver is in fact Satan.

God saves and frees his people from physical death in Egypt by the blood of the slaughtered lamb, who symbolized the true Lamb of God who takes away not just physical death but spiritual death—that is, sin, the separation from God.

The lamb had to be young and alive and without any blemish, as Christ was perfect, sinless, and innocent.

But faith was also required to receive this salvation; if the Jews did not believe and obey God and put the blood on their doorposts, they were not spared.

The Jews were to actually eat of the flesh of the sacrificial lamb, as Christians eat the flesh of Christ in the Eucharist. It was not just a symbol but a sacrament, which is a sacred rite instituted by God that actually effects what it signifies, actually brings about salvation and the new life, the supernatural life, the eternal life, the divine life in our souls.

Thus, Christ said, "Do not think that I have come to abolish the law or the prophets [that is, the Old Covenant with its Passover]. I have come not to abolish but to fulfill [in the New Covenant]" (Matt. 5:17).

God told the Jews they were to eat their Passover meal "with your loins girt, sandals on your feet and your staff in hand" for an any-moment exodus. The symbolism here is clear: when Christians receive the Eucharist, they are reminded that their destiny is not in this world but, through an any-moment exodus from it, in the Promised Land, because their Lord has conquered death itself.

SECOND READING
1 Corinthians 11:23–26 _____

Brothers and sisters: I received from the Lord what I also handed on to you, that the Lord Jesus, on the night he was handed over, took bread, and, after he had given thanks, broke it and said, "This is my body that is for you. Do this in remembrance of me." In the same way also the cup, after supper, saying, "This cup is the new covenant in my blood. Do this, as often as you drink it, in remembrance of me." For as often as you eat this bread and drink the cup, you proclaim the death of the Lord until he comes.

In today's Old Testament reading, we read about God instituting the Passover feast and commanding that it be handed down through the generations by Sacred Tradition, a tradition that God, not man, originated. In our New Testament epistle, we have its meaning and fulfillment, in St. Paul's account of the sacred tradition instituted by Christ, the new Passover, the Eucharist.

To the ears of our modern, post-Christian culture, the word "tradition" connotes something artificial, man-made, and oppressive, something to be "liberated" from and to "progress" out of. In other words, our culture exchanges and confuses Egypt, the place of slavery, and the Promised Land, the place of freedom. It reverses the Exodus.

The Eucharist and the Mass is the most sacred tradition in the world because what it "hands down" (the literal meaning of "tradition") is nothing less than God incarnate, our only hope of salvation and eternal life and joy. The Mass is a kind of time machine that makes us contemporary with Christ, by making Christ contemporary with us—literally, bodily as well as spiritually. It makes Christ not a distant ideal two thousand years in the past for us to admire and try to imitate from afar but our very present Savior and Lord who humbles himself to enter into us and into our lives, both body and soul, here and now: in our churches, in a little Host in a little building, and now, at this very present hour of our lives. It's not just a symbol. He does stuff to us when we receive him in faith.

If this is not true, if that is only bread and wine and not the Body and Blood of Christ, then the heart and soul of Catholic Christianity is a monstrous idolatry and a ridiculous lie. But if it is true, it is our greatest privilege and the most real and complete union with the One who is our eternal joy that is possible on this earth.

GOSPEL
JOHN 13:1–15 _____

Before the feast of Passover, Jesus knew that his hour had come to pass from this world to the Father. He loved his own in the world and he loved them to the end. The devil had already induced Judas, son of Simon the Iscariot, to hand him over. So, during supper, fully aware that the Father had put everything into his power and that he had come from God and was returning to God, he rose from supper and took off his outer garments. He took a towel and tied it around his waist. Then he poured water into a basin and began to wash the disciples' feet and dry them with the towel around his waist. He came to Simon Peter, who said to him, "Master, are you going to wash my feet?" Jesus answered and said to him, "What I am doing, you do not understand now, but you will understand later." Peter said to him, "You will never wash my feet." Jesus answered him, "Unless I wash you, you will have no inheritance with me." Simon Peter said to him, "Master, then not only my feet, but my hands and head as well." Jesus said to him, "Whoever has bathed has no need except to have his feet washed, for he is clean all over; so you are clean, but not all." For he knew who would betray him; for this reason, he said, "Not all of you are clean."

So when he had washed their feet and put his garments back on and reclined at table again, he said to them, "Do you realize what I have done for you? You call me 'teacher' and 'master,' and rightly so, for indeed I am. If I, therefore, the master and teacher, have washed your feet, you ought to wash one another's feet. I have given you a model to follow, so that as I have done for you, you should also do."

The brilliant and famous author Ralph Waldo Emerson asked a good question about today's Gospel, where Jesus washes the feet of his twelve Apostles. Emerson was not a Catholic and did not believe in sacraments. He asked, How do you Christians know that Jesus wanted Baptism and the Lord's Supper to be perpetuated as sacraments, but not foot washing? Jesus said almost the same thing about what he did when he washed their feet as he said about what he did at the Passover meal when he instituted the Eucharist: "Do you realize what I have done for you? . . . I have given you a model to follow, so that as I have done for you, you should also do." If those words were meant symbolically, not literally—if washing each other's feet was meant not literally but only to symbolize any and all lowly services to others—then why were the words "This is my Body" and "This is my Blood" and "Do this in remembrance of me" meant literally and not symbolically? And if the Eucharist was meant literally, and if the command to repeat it was meant as a continuing sacrament, why isn't foot washing meant literally and to be repeated as a continuing sacrament?

There is only one clear answer to this question: that this is what the Church has always both taught and practiced from the beginning—the Church Christ himself established and gave his authority to when he said to his Apostles, "Whoever listens to you listens to me" (Luke 10:16). And Christ ordained his Apostles to ordain successors, who were called "presbyters" or bishops, to carry out and carry on this commission of Christ with the authority of Christ to all succeeding generations. That is the meaning of "apostolic succession." One of the four marks of the true Church of Christ mentioned in the Nicene Creed is "apostolic."

Denying this apostolic "deposit of faith" passed down by Sacred Tradition is the meaning of "heresy." The word "heretic" means simply "one who picks and chooses for himself." There have always been many serious disagreements about doctrine in the history of the Church, but only Catholics have a teaching authority that can judge which doctrine is heretical and which is not. And only the Catholic Church, among all human institutions, has always taught the same doctrine and morality for two thousand years consistently, without ever contradicting any of its previous authoritative teachings and interpretations. That is why the Church has always been unpopular and countercultural, like Christ himself. The Church is not a democracy but a theocracy because it was founded not by man but by God. It has often failed to practice what it preaches, sometimes in horrible and spectacular ways, but it has always preached the same thing.

The essence of all Catholic doctrines are in the Bible, the Church's primary teaching document; but as we saw in the example of Ralph Waldo Emerson, the Bible itself does not solve every controversy about how to interpret it. The Church is the living teacher, and the Bible is her textbook. Both have an authority in matters of religion that is infallible because it is from God himself. If that is not true, the Catholic Church is not simply one of many Christian denominations but is the most arrogant false prophet of all. Similarly, if Jesus' claim to divinity is not true, he is the most arrogant false prophet who ever lived. And yet no one sees Jesus as an arrogant tyrant. And no one who knows the saints and meets in them what the Bible calls "the beauty of holiness" can look at their mother and teacher, their Church, as a tyrant. She has been humbly washing the feet of sinners and fools and poor "losers" consistently in a symbolic way just as she has been celebrating the Real Presence of Christ in the Mass and the Eucharist in a more-than-symbolic way.

The world, which absolutizes secular politics and classifies everything into "conservative" and "progressive," wants to contrast and separate and divorce her social service, her "foot washing," from her theology, morality, and liturgy, but this is impossible because both express the same love from the same God.

If you believe in the Real Presence but are skeptical about social justice and love of the poor, read this passage again and pray about it. If you believe in the "foot washing" of social justice but not the Real Presence, do the same with John 6:52–72 and 1 Corinthians 11:23–30. The same Lord revealed both.

GOOD FRIDAY OF THE LORD'S PASSION

FIRST READING

Isaiah 52:13—53:12 _____

See, my servant shall prosper,
    he shall be raised high and greatly exalted.
Even as many were amazed at him—
    so marred was his look beyond human semblance
and his appearance beyond that of the sons of man—
    so shall he startle many nations,
because of him kings shall stand speechless;
    for those who have not been told shall see,
    those who have not heard shall ponder it.

Who would believe what we have heard?
    To whom has the arm of the Lord been revealed?
He grew up like a sapling before him,
    like a shoot from the parched earth;
there was in him no stately bearing to make us look at him,
    nor appearance that would attract us to him.
He was spurned and avoided by people,
    a man of suffering, accustomed to infirmity,
one of those from whom people hide their faces,
    spurned, and we held him in no esteem.

Yet it was our infirmities that he bore,
    our sufferings that he endured,
while we thought of him as stricken,

as one smitten by God and afflicted.
But he was pierced for our offenses,
   crushed for our sins;
upon him was the chastisement that makes us whole,
   by his stripes we were healed.
We had all gone astray like sheep,
   each following his own way;
but the LORD laid upon him
   the guilt of us all.

Though he was harshly treated, he submitted
   and opened not his mouth;
like a lamb led to the slaughter
   or a sheep before the shearers,
   he was silent and opened not his mouth.
Oppressed and condemned, he was taken away,
   and who would have thought any more of his destiny?
When he was cut off from the land of the living,
   and smitten for the sin of his people,
a grave was assigned him among the wicked
   and a burial place with evildoers,
though he had done no wrong
   nor spoken any falsehood.
But the LORD was pleased
   to crush him in infirmity.

If he gives his life as an offering for sin,
   he shall see his descendants in a long life,
   and the will of the LORD shall be accomplished through him.

Because of his affliction
   he shall see the light in fullness of days;

through his suffering, my servant shall justify many,
    and their guilt he shall bear.
Therefore I will give him his portion among the great,
    and he shall divide the spoils with the mighty,
because he surrendered himself to death
    and was counted among the wicked;
and he shall take away the sins of many,
    and win pardon for their offenses.

The prophecy of Isaiah that we heard today is about the coming Messiah, and he is not what Israel expected. That's why, when the true Messiah appeared, many of the Jews did not accept him. They expected a glorious, conquering king who would restore Israel's this-worldly greatness and power and riches and free them from the Roman tyrants who, they thought, were their enemies. For the prophets foretold that the Messiah would save Israel from her enemies. They did not realize that their real enemies were their own sins, which were more serious tyrants than the Romans because they were addicted to them. All sins are addictions and take away our inner freedom. Most of the Jews did not accept Jesus because their hearts were set on worldly success, and Jesus, far from showing them his political and this-worldly power, was apolitical and died not in power but in total weakness, on the cross.

The prophecy begins in a familiar way: "He shall be raised high and greatly exalted." Not raised in the way they expected—as a king—but raised on a cross to die. And not greatly exalted because of his worldly success but because of his love that led him to die for his people. God raises high the humble and humbles the high and mighty.

Isaiah says that "many were amazed at him—so marred was his look." A tortured and crucified man does not look like a king. Isaiah foretold that "so shall he startle many nations, because of him kings shall stand speechless." He also prophesied that most would not believe him: "Who would believe what we have heard?" For "there was in him no stately bearing to make us look at him, nor appearance that would attract us to him." (He didn't look like the King of kings and Lord of Lords, there on the cross.) "He was spurned and avoided by people, a man of suffering, accustomed to infirmity, one of those from whom people hide their faces, spurned, and we held him in no esteem." Like the sick, the dying, the poor, the homeless, the deformed, the physically disabled, the mentally disabled. Isaiah goes on to prophesy: "We thought of him as stricken, as one smitten by God." He was like Job, suffering horribly; and Job's three friends all saw this as proof that he must have deserved it, that he was wicked, that God was punishing him. Their argument seemed sound because its premise is true and repeated many times in the Bible: God is just, and punishes the evil and rewards the good.

Their premise was correct: God is just, and punishes the evil and rewards the good. But their conclusion was wrong, because it was not because of his own sins that Jesus suffered. He suffered for our sins, not his own. Isaiah says: "But he was pierced for our offenses, crushed for our sins; upon him was the chastisement that makes us whole, by his stripes we were healed. We had all gone astray like sheep, each following his own way; but the LORD laid upon him the guilt of us all." We committed the crimes, and he took our punishment. God deserved and demanded perfect obedience from man, and man refused that offering, so Jesus offered it in our place, offered his own perfect life and perfect obedience for us. Isaiah says, "He gives his life as an offering for sin." He was the sacrificial lamb, the innocent dying in place of the guilty.

For thousands of years the Jews, at God's command, had sacrificed lambs and other innocent animals in place of guilty human beings. All other ancient religions practiced human sacrifice, usually only in great emergencies but sometimes routinely, like the Canaanites and the Aztecs. It is estimated that those two cultures killed one-third of their children—a statistic eerily similar to our present abortion rate. God forbade human sacrifice—that was the whole point of the Abraham and Isaac story—and provided a substitute, a sheep, instead. It was only a symbol: animal sacrifices did not really take away human sins; but it was a true symbol of the Lamb of God who really does take away the sins of the whole world. But they didn't "get it"; his own chosen people didn't get the main lesson. As John said, "He came to what was his own, but his own people did not accept him" (John 1:11).

Do we get it? We have more than just prophets who foretell it in mysterious, symbolic ways: we have seen it and been taught it explicitly in the New Testament. St. John opens his first epistle with these words: "What was from the beginning, what we have heard, what we have seen with our eyes, what we looked upon and touched with our hands" (1 John 1:1). The Jews had a fairly good excuse for not getting it. If we don't get it, we have far less excuse than they did.

When don't we get it? When we don't confess that we are sinners that don't deserve heaven; when we don't confess and repent and fight against our sins; when we trust not the Lamb of God but the psychology of man and our own self-help programs to conquer our sins. When don't we get it? When we ask God for justice. When do we get it? When we ask him for mercy.

But why should he give us mercy? By definition we don't deserve mercy. Justice means giving exactly what is deserved. Mercy goes beyond that. Why should God go beyond justice? Why would he enact the Great Exchange and take our place so that we could take his place? Why would the prison chaplain choose to go to the electric chair in place of the convicted murderer?

Because God is love. And that's what love does.

Yes, it is amazing. It sounds crazy—to love the unlovable. Love is crazy, and God is love, so God is crazy with love for us. It's almost unbelievable. Almost, but not quite. Two billion Christians throughout the world profess to believe it.

Do you? And if you do, what difference does that make to your life?

Look at a crucifix. Jesus is "the Word of God"; what word is Jesus saying to you personally from his cross? He's saying: "This is what I did for you. Now what will you do for me?"

SECOND READING
Hebrews 4:14–16, 5:7–9 _____

Brothers and sisters: Since we have a great high priest who has passed through the heavens, Jesus, the Son of God, let us hold fast to our confession. For we do not have a high priest who is unable to sympathize with our weaknesses, but one who has similarly been tested in every way, yet without sin. So let us confidently approach the throne of grace to receive mercy and to find grace for timely help.

In the days when Christ was in the flesh, he offered prayers and supplications with loud cries and tears to the one who was able to save him from death, and he was heard because of his reverence. Son though he was, he learned obedience from what he suffered; and when he was made perfect, he became the source of eternal salvation for all who obey him.

_____

The author of the Letter to the Hebrews sees Christ's Passion and Death on Good Friday as a work of his priesthood. What is the essence of a priest? Just as a prophet is someone appointed by God to be a mediator of God's truth, God's word, and God's will to man, a kind of mouthpiece (the very word "prophet" means "one who speaks forth"), so a priest is also a mediator appointed by God (or "called"—the literal meaning of the word "vocation") to mediate God's love and grace and salvation to mankind.

God instituted three offices in ancient Israel: prophets, priests, and kings. Prophets mediate God's truth and wisdom, priests mediate God's love and salvation, and kings mediate God's authority and power.

Christ fulfilled all three offices. He is our ultimate prophet, the very Word of God. He is our priest, our Savior and mediator. And he is Christ the King—the king of our lives and of the whole created universe.

These three offices are not only biblical but secular as well. Many of our secular epics have three heroes who do these three works. For instance, in *The Lord of the Rings*, Gandalf the wizard is the wise prophet, Frodo the hobbit is the priest who saves Middle-earth by carrying the Ring, symbolic of evil and destruction, to its death, and Aragorn is the king who returns to his rightful rule.

A priest mediates between God and man. Christ is our perfect priest, our perfect mediator, because he is both perfect God and perfect man. That God should become man, in the Incarnation, was shocking and unexpected to everyone in the world. But this was necessary for him to be our Savior and mediator.

He had to be fully divine in order to have the authority and power to take away our sins, and he had to be fully human in order to bear the punishment for our sins. Human nature alone cannot atone for sins, and the divine nature alone cannot suffer for sins.

In assuming our human nature, Christ assumed all our weaknesses, our temptations, our sufferings, and our death. Sometimes it is harder for us to believe in Jesus' total humanity than his total divinity. If we do that, we keep him at a safe distance, so that he cannot really touch us and we cannot touch him. But he went all the way down into our weaknesses so that he could bring us all the way up into divine strength and power. He had all the activity and power of God and all the passivity and passions of man. He turned death itself, which is our ultimate passivity, into a freely chosen act. He said: "I lay down my life in order to take it up again. No one takes it from me, but I lay it down on my own. I have power to lay it down, and power to take it up again" (John 10:17–18).

Jesus had the full range of all human experiences and emotions. Our epistle tells us that "we do not have a high priest who is unable to sympathize with our weaknesses, but one who has similarly been tested in every way, yet without sin." Jesus shared not only all our pains and our mortality but also all our emotional as well as physical weaknesses, all our fears and even our temptations. (Temptation is not sin; yielding is sin.)

Jesus fully understands all our temptations and sympathizes with all our weaknesses, because he experienced all of them. If he were not fully human, he would not be able to identify with us. Being fully human, and in time, he had to grow not just in body but also in soul. Scripture says that "he had to learn obedience from what he suffered" so that in all things he could be our example. Luke's Gospel tells us that after his three days of being lost in the temple and found by his parents, he "came to Nazareth, and was obedient to them . . . and Jesus advanced in wisdom and age and favor before God and man" (Luke 2:51–52). Jesus had to grow in every way, just as we do. He began as a zygote, then an embryo, a fetus, an infant, a child, and a teenager!

He was not an alien but a member of our species, our brother. And on Good Friday, he shared our ultimate vulnerability and passivity, our death. He brought God all the way down so that he could bring man all the way up.

GOSPEL
JOHN 18:1–19:42 _____

Jesus went out with his disciples across the Kidron valley to where there was a garden, into which he and his disciples entered. Judas his betrayer also knew the place, because Jesus had often met there with his disciples. So Judas got a band of soldiers and guards from the chief priests and the Pharisees and went there with lanterns, torches, and weapons. Jesus, knowing everything that was going to happen to him, went out and said to them, "Whom are you looking for?" They answered him, "Jesus the Nazorean." He said to them, "I AM." Judas his betrayer was also with them. When he said to them, "I AM," they turned away and fell to the ground. So he again asked them, "Whom are you looking for?" They said, "Jesus the Nazorean." Jesus answered, "I told you that I AM. So if you are looking for me, let these men go." This was to fulfill what he had said, "I have not lost any of those you gave me." Then Simon Peter, who had a sword, drew it, struck the high priest's slave, and cut off his right ear. The slave's name was Malchus. Jesus said to Peter, "Put your sword into its scabbard. Shall I not drink the cup that the Father gave me?"

So the band of soldiers, the tribune, and the Jewish guards seized Jesus, bound him, and brought him to Annas first. He was the father-in-law of Caiaphas, who was high priest that year. It was Caiaphas who had counseled the Jews that it was better that one man should die rather than the people.

Simon Peter and another disciple followed Jesus. Now the other disciple was known to the high priest, and he entered the courtyard of the high priest with Jesus. But Peter stood at the gate outside. So the other disciple, the acquaintance of the high priest, went out and spoke to the gatekeeper and brought Peter in. Then the maid who was the gatekeeper said to Peter, "You are not one of this man's disciples, are you?" He said, "I am not." Now the slaves and the guards were standing around a charcoal fire that they had made, because it was cold, and were warming themselves. Peter was also standing there keeping warm.

The high priest questioned Jesus about his disciples and about his doctrine. Jesus answered him, "I have spoken publicly to the world. I have always taught in a synagogue or in the temple area where all the Jews gather, and in secret I have said nothing. Why ask me? Ask those who heard me what I said to them. They know what I said." When he had said this, one of the temple guards standing there struck Jesus and said, "Is this the way you answer the high priest?" Jesus answered him, "If I have spoken wrongly, testify to the wrong; but if I have spoken rightly, why do you strike me?" Then Annas sent him bound to Caiaphas the high priest.

Now Simon Peter was standing there keeping warm. And they said to him, "You are not one of his disciples, are you?" He denied it and said, "I am not." One of the slaves of the high priest, a relative of the one whose ear Peter had cut off, said, "Didn't I see you in the garden with him?" Again Peter denied it. And immediately the cock crowed.

Then they brought Jesus from Caiaphas to the praetorium. It was morning. And they themselves did not enter the praetorium, in order not to be defiled so that they could eat the Passover. So Pilate came out to them and said, "What charge do you bring against this man?" They answered and said to him, "If he were not a criminal, we would not have handed him over to you." At this, Pilate said to them, "Take him yourselves, and judge him according to your law." The Jews answered him, "We do not have the right to execute anyone," in order that the word of Jesus might be fulfilled that he said indicating the kind of death he would die. So Pilate went back into the praetorium and summoned Jesus and said to him, "Are you the King of the Jews?" Jesus answered, "Do you say this on your own or have others told you about me?" Pilate answered, "I am not a Jew, am I? Your own nation and the chief priests handed you over to me. What have you done?" Jesus answered, "My kingdom does not belong to this world. If my kingdom did belong to this world, my attendants would be fighting to keep me from being handed over to the Jews. But as it is, my kingdom is not here." So Pilate said to him, "Then you are a king?" Jesus answered, "You say I am a king. For this I was born and for this I came into the world, to testify to the truth. Everyone who belongs to the truth listens to my voice." Pilate said to him, "What is truth?"

When he had said this, he again went out to the Jews and said to them, "I find no guilt in him. But you have a custom that I release one prisoner to you at Passover. Do you want me to release to you the King of the Jews?" They cried out again, "Not this one but Barabbas!" Now Barabbas was a revolutionary.

Then Pilate took Jesus and had him scourged. And the soldiers wove a crown out of thorns and placed it on his head, and clothed him in a purple cloak, and they came to him and said, "Hail, King of the Jews!" And they struck him repeatedly. Once more Pilate went out and said to them, "Look, I am bringing him out to you, so that you may know that I find no guilt in him." So Jesus came out, wearing the crown of thorns and the purple cloak. And he said to them, "Behold, the man!" When the chief priests and the guards saw him they cried out, "Crucify him, crucify him!" Pilate said to them, "Take him yourselves and crucify him. I find no guilt in him." The Jews answered, "We have a law, and according to that law he ought to die, because he made himself the Son of God." Now when Pilate heard this statement, he became even more afraid, and went back into the praetorium and said to Jesus, "Where are you from?" Jesus did not answer him. So Pilate said to him, "Do you not speak to me? Do you not know that I have power to release you and I have power to crucify you?" Jesus answered him, "You would have no power over me if it had not been given to you from above. For this reason the one who handed me over to you has the greater sin." Consequently, Pilate tried to release him; but the Jews cried out, "If you release him, you are not a Friend of Caesar. Everyone who makes himself a king opposes Caesar."

When Pilate heard these words he brought Jesus out and seated him on the judge's bench in the place called Stone Pavement, in Hebrew, Gabbatha. It was preparation day for Passover, and it was about noon. And he said to the Jews, "Behold, your king!" They cried out, "Take him away, take him away! Crucify him!" Pilate said to them, "Shall I crucify your king?" The chief priests answered, "We have no king but Caesar." Then he handed him over to them to be crucified.

So they took Jesus, and, carrying the cross himself, he went out to what is called the Place of the Skull, in Hebrew, Golgotha. There they crucified him, and with him two others, one on either side, with Jesus in the middle. Pilate also had an inscription written and put on the cross. It read, "Jesus the Nazorean, the King of the Jews." Now many of the Jews read this inscription, because the place where Jesus was crucified was near the city; and it was written in Hebrew, Latin, and Greek. So the chief priests of the Jews said to Pilate, "Do not write 'The King of the Jews,' but that he said, 'I am the King of the Jews.'" Pilate answered, "What I have written, I have written."

When the soldiers had crucified Jesus, they took his clothes and divided them into four shares, a share for each soldier. They also took his tunic, but the tunic was seamless, woven in one piece from the top down. So they said to one another, "Let's not tear it, but cast lots for it to see whose it will be," in order that the passage of Scripture might be fulfilled that says:

They divided my garments among them,
and for my vesture they cast lots.

This is what the soldiers did. Standing by the cross of Jesus were his mother and his mother's sister, Mary the wife of Clopas, and Mary of Magdala. When Jesus saw his mother and the disciple there whom he loved he said to his mother, "Woman, behold, your son." Then he said to the disciple, "Behold, your mother." And from that hour the disciple took her into his home.

After this, aware that everything was now finished, in order that the Scripture might be fulfilled, Jesus said, "I thirst." There was a vessel filled with common wine. So they put a sponge soaked in wine on a sprig of hyssop and put it up to his mouth. When Jesus had taken the wine, he said, "It is finished." And bowing his head, he handed over the spirit.

Here all kneel and pause for a short time.

Now since it was preparation day, in order that the bodies might not remain on the cross on the sabbath, for the sabbath day of that week was a solemn one, the Jews asked Pilate that their legs be broken and that they be taken down. So the soldiers came and broke the legs of the first and then of the other one who was crucified with Jesus. But when they came to Jesus and saw that he was already dead, they did not break his legs, but one soldier thrust his lance into his side, and immediately blood and water flowed out. An eyewitness has testified, and his testimony is true; he knows that he is speaking the truth, so that you also may come to believe. For this happened so that the Scripture passage might be fulfilled:

Not a bone of it will be broken.

And again another passage says:

They will look upon him whom they have pierced.

After this, Joseph of Arimathea, secretly a disciple of Jesus for fear of the Jews, asked Pilate if he could remove the body of Jesus. And Pilate permitted it. So he came and took his body. Nicodemus, the one who had first come to him at night, also came bringing a mixture of myrrh and aloes weighing about one hundred pounds. They took the body of Jesus and bound it with burial cloths along with the spices, according to the Jewish burial custom. Now in the place where he had been crucified there was a garden, and in the garden a new tomb, in which no one had yet been buried. So they laid Jesus there because of the Jewish preparation day; for the tomb was close by.

This passage is far longer than a reflection would be, and infinitely more powerful. No words should follow it. All heaven's angels bow their heads and shut their mouths in awe and adoration at these events; that is their homily on it. We cannot improve on that. Only fools rush in where angels fear to speak.

EASTER TIME

EASTER SUNDAY: THE RESURRECTION OF THE LORD: AT THE EASTER VIGIL IN THE HOLY NIGHT OF EASTER

Nine readings from Scripture are assigned for this Mass, seven of them from the Old Testament. Those who designed this Mass, which is more than twice as long as the Mass for other Sundays, obviously did not intend it to include also reflections on each passage or on any one of them.

If a (very brief) reflection is thought to be needed, there is none better than 1 Corinthians 15:12–20.

EASTER SUNDAY: THE RESURRECTION OF THE LORD: THE MASS OF EASTER DAY

FIRST READING

Acts 10:34A, 37–43

Peter proceeded to speak and said: "You know what has happened all over Judea, beginning in Galilee after the baptism that John preached, how God anointed Jesus of Nazareth with the Holy Spirit and power. He went about doing good and healing all those oppressed by the devil, for God was with him. We are witnesses of all that he did both in the country of the Jews and in Jerusalem. They put him to death by hanging him on a tree. This man God raised on the third day and granted that he be visible, not to all the people, but to us, the witnesses chosen by God in advance, who ate and drank with him after he rose from the dead. He commissioned us to preach to the people and testify that he is the one appointed by God as judge of the living and the dead. To him all the prophets bear witness, that everyone who believes in him will receive forgiveness of sins through his name."

The Acts of the Apostles reports Peter, the first pope, preaching at least seven sermons: in chapter 2, at Pentecost; in chapter 3, after healing the blind man; in chapter 4, to the council that accused him; in chapter 5, to Ananias and Sapphira and then again to the council; and in chapter 8, to Simon the Magician. All of them center on Jesus and his Resurrection from the dead. The last one, in chapter 10, our reading for today, is his longest. It summarizes the Gospel, and its repeated claim is that the Apostles and many others are literal eyewitnesses to the amazing events of Jesus' life, Crucifixion, and Resurrection.

The essence of Christianity is not a set of abstract truths, laws, principles, or values, though it includes all of these. It is a series of actual, visible, physical, historical events that actually and literally happened, here on this planet, and were seen by eyewitnesses. These men who testified to having seen Jesus after his Resurrection either were liars or truth tellers. There is no third alternative. When someone tells you they actually saw something happen, they do not leave open the option for you to interpret their story symbolically, like a parable or a myth or a fable.

Peter makes the same claim about Jesus' miracles in his second letter. He writes: "We did not follow cleverly devised myths when we made known to you the power and coming of our Lord Jesus Christ, but we had been eyewitnesses of his majesty. For he received honor and glory from God the Father when that unique declaration came to him from the majestic glory, 'This is my Son, my beloved, with whom I am well pleased.' We ourselves heard this voice come from heaven while we were with him on the holy mountain" (2 Pet. 1:16–18).

How do we know whether to interpret an event literally or symbolically? It's really very simple: if the narrator claims to have seen it, he means it literally; if not, not. Santa Claus can be interpreted as a mere myth, a mere symbol for charity and gift giving, but "I saw Santa Claus come down our chimney last night" is literal, not meant as a symbolic truth—it's a literal lie.

Some of the stories in the Old Testament are borderline cases that may be historical events, or they may be meant as myths or fables or parables, like the Tower of Babel or Noah's ark or Jonah's whale. But the events in the Gospels are not like that. Concrete and specific names, dates, places, and people are mentioned. The eyes of the witnesses were open, not closed in a dream or a vision.

So here, Peter claims: "We are witnesses of all that he did both in the country of the Jews and in Jerusalem. They put him to death by hanging him on a tree. This man God raised on the third day and granted that he be visible . . . to us, the witnesses chosen by God in advance, who ate and drank with him after he rose from the dead."

And the upshot, the bottom line, the difference this historical fact about the past makes to our lives now and in the future, is eternal. For "he is the one appointed by God as judge of the living and the dead . . . that everyone who believes in him will receive forgiveness of sins through his name." If Jesus didn't really live and die and rise, then our sins are not really forgiven.

So when you die and you meet God and God asks you why he should let you into heaven, please do not speak of how well or how poorly you understood and obeyed some abstract principles, important as they are. What saves you is a person, not a principle. Your answer should not begin with the word "I" but with the word "Jesus." As they say even about life in this world, it's not what you know, it's who you know.

SECOND READING

COLOSSIANS 3:1–4
(OR I CORINTHIANS 5:6B-8) _____

Brothers and sisters: If then you were raised with Christ, seek what is above, where Christ is seated at the right hand of God. Think of what is above, not of what is on earth. For you have died, and your life is hidden with Christ in God. When Christ your life appears, then you too will appear with him in glory.

_____

In our first reading, from the Acts of the Apostles, we found St. Peter's sermon centering on the fact of Christ's Resurrection. The consequences of this fact are explored in our second reading, from St. Paul's Letter to the Colossians.

The consequences of this past event are present. What we confess is not merely that "Christ rose" in the past but that "Christ is risen," in the present. The present consequences of Christ's Resurrection are not simply that our souls live on after death. That is not news; that was true from the beginning, when God created human souls that are spiritual, not physical. What is new is that God put us into Christ and Christ into us, so that we now share both Christ's death and Christ's Resurrection.

How do we share Christ's death? We're not dead yet, are we? Well, here's the surprise: we are! St. Paul tells us, "You have died, and your life is hidden with Christ in God." I know of a holy person who suddenly realized what that verse meant and responded, "Thank God! I'm dead! I'm dead!" That sounds crazy, but it's true: if we are in Christ, our old sinful nature is dead; we are dead to sin. Baptism killed original sin in us, and sin is spiritual death. But sin is no longer our essential nature. It is still a great bother, like a large, heavy albatross around our neck, but it's dead, and it's not our identity. Our identity is in Christ. We are reborn, transformed, regenerated, given new life, supernatural life, divine life, in Christ. Christ is both divine and human, and so are we, although our share in divine life is presently only like an embryo, or a seed.

Christ's Resurrection did not give our souls life after death for the first time; that was done by God creating our spiritual soul at the moment of our conception. That was only our human nature. What Christ's Resurrection gave us was supernatural—our divine nature, our share in God's own very life, which is the life of *agape* love: ecstatic, self-forgetful, self-giving love. It's far from pure and perfect in us yet, but it's really there. When we choose to love in this way, we are choosing to let God act in us and through us.

That is what St. Paul means when he says, "If then you were raised with Christ, seek what is above, where Christ is seated at the right hand of God." He does not mean "speculate about the details of what your life in heaven will be after you die," but rather "Live now as if you knew who you are. Who you are is whose you are. God is your Father. You are God's children; you are the King's kids. Stop living like you are King Kong's kids; stop aping the apes." "Your life is hidden with Christ in God." Your identity is hidden, but it is really there. It is disguised very well by your fallen human nature and your remaining sinful habits, but it is glorious, with the glory of God. St. Irenaeus of Lyon famously said, "The glory of God is a man fully alive." By "fully alive," he did not mean merely "alive with human natural life" but "alive with God's own supernatural life, given to you in Christ."

There are two Greek words for "life." *Bios* means simply natural life, soul as well as body. A related word is *sarx*, or the "flesh," which means not just the body but all of fallen, sinful human nature. The other kind of life is *zoe*, which is supernatural life. Your faith and Baptism have given you that life. You have died to your old life as your true identity. You are now a cell in the Mystical Body of Christ. That is what the Church is: it's Christ's people. It's not a human organization; it's a divine organism.

This point about our new identity comes up again and again in the letters of St. Paul, and yet most of us keep missing it again and again. That's why we have to remind ourselves again and again, as I've tried to do in these reflections on the epistles—because we all have spiritual attention deficit disorder.

We keep forgetting the two most important things in the world: who God is, and who we are. God is love; God is *agape*; and we are his kids; we are the fools Jesus Christ has made his Father the Father of.

God and yourself—those are the only two realities you will never, never be able to escape or avoid for a single moment, either in time or in eternity. And it is Jesus Christ who shows us those two things.

We know this now by faith, not by sight. But St. Paul reminds us that "when Christ your life appears, you too will appear with him in glory." The glory of God that is hidden in us will shine forth in all its glory when Christ comes again to reveal not only his own glory but also ours. That is our destiny, the finish line of the race that is human life. St. Paul is telling us not to be distracted from that most final, fundamental, and foundational truth, our ultimate end and goal and destiny. As they say in the Olympics, keep your eyes on the prize.

GOSPEL
JOHN 20:1–9 _____

On the first day of the week, Mary of Magdala came to the tomb early in the morning, while it was still dark, and saw the stone removed from the tomb. So she ran and went to Simon Peter and to the other disciple whom Jesus loved, and told them, "They have taken the Lord from the tomb, and we don't know where they put him." So Peter and the other disciple went out and came to the tomb. They both ran, but the other disciple ran faster than Peter and arrived at the tomb first; he bent down and saw the burial cloths there, but did not go in. When Simon Peter arrived after him, he went into the tomb and saw the burial cloths there, and the cloth that had covered his head, not with the burial cloths but rolled up in a separate place. Then the other disciple also went in, the one who had arrived at the tomb first, and he saw and believed. For they did not yet understand the Scripture that he had to rise from the dead.

Every little detail of this event is significant.

Begin with the last line: "For they did not yet understand the Scripture that he had to rise from the dead." Nobody—not Mary Magdalene, not Peter, not John, nobody—could believe it was possible that Jesus would literally rise from the dead, even though Jesus had repeatedly told his disciples that he would. They thought he must have meant something symbolic and spiritual, not something literal.

The Resurrection was certainly not a case of wishful thinking, of mistaking a dream for a reality, for the Apostles were not tender-minded dreamers. Doubting Thomas would not believe the others even when they swore that they had literally seen the resurrected Christ, until he himself had touched Christ's wounds with his own hands. That's how literal the Resurrection was.

The first line of our Gospel says: "On the first day of the week, Mary of Magdala came to the tomb early in the morning, while it was still dark." That impatience shows her love. The next few verses show John getting to the tomb before Peter, but Mary got there before all of them. The women come out on top again, just as they did at the Crucifixion, when John was the only man who stayed with Jesus at the cross; the rest were all women. The Gospels were not written by male chauvinists.

When Mary arrived at the tomb, she saw that the stone was rolled away. How? Who moved the stone? The women could not have moved it. It took many strong men to move it. Neither the Jews nor the Romans would have moved it, because they both wanted Jesus to stay very, very dead. It was guarded by armed Roman soldiers, so the disciples could not have done it. And if they did, then they deliberately lied about the Resurrection; so, if they knew it was a lie, why would they all let themselves be arrested and imprisoned and tortured and martyred for this lie? Martyrdom doesn't prove truth, but it certainly proves sincerity.

Mary didn't go into the tomb and see the grave clothes neatly folded away, but she assumed that someone had stolen the body. She couldn't believe Jesus had risen either, until he appeared to her and addressed her by name.

Mary tells Peter and John, and they don't just go to the tomb—they run. As fast as they can. And John, who is younger, gets there first, but he doesn't go in. Why? He lets Peter go in first because Peter was the first, the head of the Apostles. Jesus made him that and called him the rock on which he would build his Church (Matt. 16:18).

What Peter and John see is not just an empty tomb but the grave clothes, both the shroud that wrapped the body and the face cloth, neatly folded away. Jesus forgets no detail! Remember, he was the one who had to remind the family of the little girl he brought back from the dead to give her something to eat! Everyone else was too stunned to think. He was not.

We have both of these linen cloths today: the Shroud at Turin, and the sudarium, the face cloth, at Manoppello in Italy; they have both withstood sober, secular, scientific analysis. They are genuine. The outline of Christ's body and face is on them, produced by a light energy that no scientist can identify or debunk.

John says "he saw and believed." He hadn't believed until he saw. He sees himself as not much better than Doubting Thomas, who also said, in effect, "Seeing is believing."

When Thomas believed, even though he had to see first, Jesus then responded, "Blessed are those who have not seen and have believed" (John 20:29). That's us. Jesus is pronouncing a blessing on our faith. Accept that blessing. Your faith was both your free choice and a gift of God, the work of the Holy Spirit.

Like Peter and John, we understand only after we believe. Faith is an understanding, a spiritual seeing. It is not a leap in the dark. It is a leap in the light.

SECOND SUNDAY OF EASTER
(OR OF DIVINE MERCY)

FIRST READING

<small>ACTS 4:32–35</small> ─────────────────────────

The community of believers was of one heart and mind, and no one claimed that any of his possessions was his own, but they had everything in common. With great power the apostles bore witness to the resurrection of the Lord Jesus, and great favor was accorded them all. There was no needy person among them, for those who owned property or houses would sell them, bring the proceeds of the sale, and put them at the feet of the apostles, and they were distributed to each according to need.

───

This community of property that was practiced in the early Church was not communism but communalism. It was not communism for at least ten reasons.

First, it was free and voluntary, not imposed by force. Communism abolishes freedom. The psychological origin of communism is not "caring and sharing" but greed, fear, and envy: on the part of the party, it is greed for power, and on the part of the poor, it is the fear of poverty and envy of the rich. The psychological origin of community of property in the early Church was love and trust, not fear.

Love always appeals to the other person's freedom, free choice, free will. Communism does not believe in free will, or in love, either in theory or in practice. It believes, in the words of Machiavelli, that "it is better to be feared than to be loved, because others will love you when *they* will, but they will fear you when *you* will." That's why Machiavelli was popularly called "the son of the devil": because that is the philosophy of the devil. God's philosophy is the opposite, that it is better to be loved than to be feared, and for the very same reason: because others' love must be given freely, not by force and fear; and that love is the greatest gift in the world, the most valuable and most happifying gift you can ever receive. Who, after all, is happier: the slave owner who appeals to force and fear or the romantic lover who appeals to love and freedom?

The communal ownership of property in the early Church was not communism for a second reason, one that flows from the first reason, which was its freedom: it was an option. It was not demanded or expected of everyone. It was a choice. You didn't have to give up your private property to become a Christian, although you could if you chose to. That choice remains in the Church today: there are many clerical and lay orders in the Church where members take vows of poverty, usually joined to vows of chastity and obedience, and there are also unofficial private communities, usually called "houses," where individuals and families voluntarily choose to do the same sharing of all property, like a large extended family.

Third, communism is a political system. What the early Church did was not political. It was not done by the state. There was a true "separation of church and state." That idea was not invented by America.

Fourth, communism is based on a philosophy of human nature that says that class conflict between the "haves" and the "have nots," between rich and poor, and the oppression of the poor by the rich are the single, simple, universal essence of all human history; that until communism takes power, there can be no cooperation or community, no common good. Communism assumes a view of human nature and human history as totally selfish and egotistic.

Fifth, communism is officially and explicitly materialist. In its philosophy, there is no such thing as a spiritual soul. The soul is nothing but the biological life of the body. Thought is nothing but brain chemistry. Man is nothing but the animal with the most highly evolved brain.

And therefore, there is no life after death. That is why communism is totalitarian: the state is bigger than any individual and lasts much longer, and therefore it is much more important and individuals can be sacrificed to it. The strongest dam against totalitarian politics is the religious belief in the immortality of the individual soul.

Sixth, since communism is materialist, it has to be atheist. If there is no human spirit, there is no divine spirit either. Karl Marx went so far as to say that atheism was even more nonnegotiable than the abolition of private property, which is usually thought to be the essence of communism.

Seventh, communism claims to change human nature itself by abolishing private property and thus abolishing the difference between rich and poor. Why does this change human nature itself? Because since communism is materialist, all value is materialistic: everything in life depends on the power to control material property and the money that can buy it. Economics determines everything for communism.

Since communist materialism teaches that individuals are not free but are like very complex machines, not free and self-determined by their own thoughts and choices but totally determined from without by their economic system, if the economic system changes, so does human nature. Communism and Christ both claim to change human nature itself, but Christ claims to do it by God's grace and our free choice to receive it, by faith; communism claims to do it by economics and politics.

Eighth, communism in theory calls for the abolition of the family, though all communist regimes in history so far have had to compromise on that.

Ninth, Marx's communism explicitly requires violent revolution and the elimination of all political opponents by force.

Tenth, communism has been proved by facts, by real events, to be history's most total and disastrous failure. It has never worked, either economically or in terms of human happiness. And it has caused more murders, more deaths, more genocide, and more human suffering than any other public movement or philosophy in the entire history of the world.

The communalism of property that began in the early Church, on the other hand, has worked very well in many happy religious orders and in some communities like the Bruderhof among Protestants and some charismatic communities among Catholics.

On the other hand, the one principle of communism that is profoundly *true* is the principle that successful communities in the early Church and the Church today still practice: "From each according to his ability to each according to his need."

That is the principle behind graduated income taxes and using some of the money that the rich have but do not need to care for the poor, who need but do not have. This is done voluntarily by many private organizations such as the Catholic Church and the Salvation Army, and it is also done involuntarily by the government taxing the rich to pay for services to the poor. The principle of Catholic social ethics that justifies that practice is that the common good takes precedence over the private good, that the private good exists as a means to the end of the common good; that the good of the many, or of the whole, of society is prior to the good of the one, or of the part.

That "communitarian" principle of the common good, which in one way resembles communism, is balanced by another social and political principle, which is the exact opposite of communism—namely, the principle of subsidiarity, which says that the larger, more public, and more official organization or branch of government should not do what the smaller, more private, and more unofficial group or branch or individuals can do. The nation should do for the cities and states only what the cities and states cannot do as well for themselves (for instance, interstate highways, the post office, the internet, the army, and laws defending basic human rights). The same holds for the relationship between nations and states, states and counties, counties and towns, towns and neighborhoods, neighborhoods and families, and families and individuals.

The strongest obstacle to communism and to all other forms of totalitarian politics is the fact that all individual persons are created in God's image as immortal and eternal and intrinsically valuable, loved by God for their own sakes, while all nations and governments and organizations are mortal and temporal and are only means to the end of the good of persons and personal relationships. For when all nations and political parties are dead, every one of us will still be young.

God loves all that is good in America, and so should we. But he loves Americans more, and so should we. And he loves America *because* he loves Americans, not vice versa. And so should we.

Christianity, like Judaism and Islam, has always strongly taught the responsibility of caring for the poor, not as an extra, an option, but as essential to religion. The social Gospel, or social ethics, is part of the whole Gospel. It is not the whole of it, but it is a necessary part of it. Thus, the communalism of the early Church was not something new or extrinsic or added from outside but a growth from within, from the heart of the Gospel, which is Jesus himself, who said that "whatever you did for one of these least brothers of mine, you did for me" (Matt. 25:40). Christianity loves and empowers the poor; communism enslaves them and manipulates them.

RESPONSORIAL PSALM
PSALM 118:2–4, 13–15, 22–24

R. (1) **Give thanks to the Lord for he is good, his love is everlasting.**

Let the house of Israel say,
    "His mercy endures forever."
Let the house of Aaron say,
    "His mercy endures forever."
Let those who fear the LORD say,
    "His mercy endures forever."

I was hard pressed and was falling,
    but the LORD helped me.
My strength and my courage is the LORD,
    and he has been my savior.

The joyful shout of victory
in the tents of the just:

The stone which the builders rejected
has become the cornerstone.
By the LORD has this been done;
it is wonderful in our eyes.
This is the day the LORD has made;
let us be glad and rejoice in it.

The more familiar we are with the Old Testament, the better we understand the New. And the more familiar we are with the New Testament, the better we understand the Old. Today's Psalm verses are a good example of that.

The Psalms have many dimensions, many levels, and the deepest and most important one is Christ. When we read the Psalms in the light of Christ, we see their deepest and most ultimate mystery. Let's look at this one as an example.

It's very right to do this because the very same divine person, the Logos, the Word of God, the Mind of God, the Son of God, the Self-Expression of the God who inspired the Old Testament, is the one at the center of the New. Jesus is the Mind of God who inspired the Psalms. That's why it's not wrong to look for him there.

Let's begin with the first verse: "Let the house of Israel say: 'His mercy endures forever.'" Why should Israel say that? David did not endure forever. He died. The nation of Israel did not endure forever. It ceased to exist during the Babylonian exile, and for 1878 years between AD 70, when Rome destroyed Jerusalem, and 1948, when Britain and the United Nations restored it. What is this "mercy of God" that "endures forever" without ever ceasing? Only God endures forever, so God's mercy must be God himself. But mercy is not just God in himself, eternally, but also God to us, here in time. Jesus is both God in himself and God's mercy to us here in time. God's mercy is not just an abstract idea or feeling or attribute of God: it is a concrete person, Jesus, the Son of God incarnate with us in time. Jesus concretizes God's mercy, focuses God's mercy, incarnates God's mercy.

The Psalmist then goes on to confess that "I was hard pressed and was falling, but the LORD helped me. . . . He has been my savior." When he wrote these words, the Psalmist probably had in mind the many military victories God had given to him and to Israel in Old Testament times. But the God who inspired these words had deeper meanings in mind. "Falling" in battle to human enemies is not the worst kind of falling or failing; falling in spiritual battle to our spiritual enemies, the evil spirits who seek to destroy our souls, is the infinitely more serious fall. God is our Savior because he rescues us from eternal death, from spiritual death, from the death of our souls, not just from temporal, physical death. The human name of that Savior is Jesus. The name "Jesus" literally means "Savior," or "God saves."

So when David the Psalmist then praises "the joyful shout of victory in the tents of the just," he was probably thinking of a celebration on the physical battlefield in a war; but the God who inspired these words is thinking of a far greater celebration of a far greater victory, Christ's victory over Satan and sin and death and hell, the victory we celebrate every Easter.

Israel rejoices "in the tents of the just." Our "tents" are not canvas anymore; they are cathedrals. We are "just" not because we have succeeded in obeying God's law perfectly but because Christ has done that for us, has justified us and reconciled us to God.

And then comes the line that most obviously applies to Jesus: "The stone which the builders rejected has become the cornerstone."

The cornerstone is the stone that holds the whole building together. Christ holds together the whole Church, all "the people of God," all the saved, all God's family. And this cornerstone was rejected by the builders of Israel. "He came to what was his own, but his own people did not accept him" (John 1:11). They crucified him. We all did: the Jews, the Romans, the Greeks, the Americans. Our sins did.

The sign on the cross that read "Jesus the Nazorean, the King of the Jews" was written in all three languages of the time and place, Hebrew, Latin, and Greek. That's a double irony: first, he was rejected and crucified by the very ones he designed and loved and came to save, and second, that very rejection was part of God's plan of our salvation. That's what the Psalmist says next: "By the LORD has this been done; it is wonderful in our eyes." God used the worst evil in the world, the deliberate torture and murder of God incarnate, to save us, so that we call the feast day that commemorates this atrocity "*Good Friday*." God brings good out of evil. What he did on Good Friday in a big and obvious and public way, he does again and again in smaller and more hidden ways our lives. Not all things are good, but he makes "all things work for good" to us who love him and trust him (Rom. 8:28). As the poet Edwin Markham wrote,

> He drew a circle that shut me out—
> Heretic, rebel, a thing to flout.
> But Love and I had the will to win:
> We drew a circle that took him in!

Who says that? God says that.

Finally, when David the Psalmist rejoices, saying, "This is the day the LORD has made; let us be glad and rejoice in it," he is talking about the sabbath day; but the Christian sabbath, Sunday, is holy because of what happened on Easter Sunday: Jesus' Resurrection. That event, that reality, that triumph over the forces of evil, is the "day" the Lord has made, and that's what the literal twenty-four-hour day of Sunday symbolizes and expresses. Its purpose is joy: "Let us be glad and rejoice in it." We do not work on the sabbath, not because we have been forbidden, but because we have been freed. We are freed from our work because God has done and completed *his* work when he said, on the cross, "It is finished" (John 19:30), and then rose in triumph. Sunday is for rejoicing in the Son-light, the light of the Son of God.

SECOND READING
I JOHN 5:1–6 _____

Beloved: Everyone who believes that Jesus is the Christ is begotten by God, and everyone who loves the Father loves also the one begotten by him. In this way we know that we love the children of God when we love God and obey his commandments. For the love of God is this, that we keep his commandments. And his commandments are not burdensome, for whoever is begotten by God conquers the world. And the victory that conquers the world is our faith. Who indeed is the victor over the world but the one who believes that Jesus is the Son of God?

This is the one who came through water and blood, Jesus Christ, not by water alone, but by water and blood. The Spirit is the one that testifies, and the Spirit is truth.

_____

St. John makes some connections in this passage that are at the very heart and center of our religion.

First, John says: "Everyone who believes that Jesus is the Christ [that is, the Messiah, the promised one, the object of God's promise and of our hope] is begotten by God." To be begotten by God is, as Jesus said to Nicodemus, to get a new kind of life, to be "born again" into eternal life, supernatural life; born not of the flesh by biological sexual intercourse but born "by water and the Spirit" by Baptism and the Holy Spirit, God himself. It's a cause-effect relation: to *believe* in Jesus is to *receive* him and his supernatural life. When, by faith and Baptism, you say yes to God, God sends his Holy Spirit to do in your soul what he did in Mary's body at the Annunciation: he spiritually impregnates you with divine, supernatural, eternal life. When we let him in, he really comes in.

Second, John says that "everyone who loves the Father loves also the one begotten by him"—that is, Christ the Son. Why? Because Christ is all that the

297

Father is, so if we truly love all that the Father is—infinite love, truth, goodness, and beauty—we will love Christ because that is what he is too. You cannot love God and not love God's Son, who is the perfect copy of him, any more than you can love a great work of art and not love the perfect copy of that art.

Third, John says that "in this way we know that we love the children of God when we love God and obey his commandments." Do I really love God? If you love God's children, you do. Why? To love God's human children *is* to love God, because loving God means obeying his will, his commandments; and his commandment is exactly that: to love his children, to love each other.

Fourth, John says that "the love of God is this, that we keep his commandments." Love is not a feeling but a free choice, a deed. And since God's commandment is to love our neighbor, God is saying to us here, "Just as to love my kids is to love me, so to love me is to love my kids." It's two sides of the same coin. Love of God and love of neighbor are not two loves but one love, as a coin is one coin.

Then, John makes the amazing claim that this love "conquers the world." Three world-famous people have claimed to conquer the world. Alexander the Great conquered the known world with military force. But he died unhappy because, having conquered the world, he had no more worlds to conquer. Buddha also claimed to conquer the world, not militarily but by a mystical experience that he called Nirvana, which claimed to perceive that the exterior world of matter and the inner world of our souls were both illusions, dreams from which Buddha woke up. Jesus also conquered the world—not the material world of war, or the world of bad dreams, but the fallen world-order of sin and separation from God. Alexander conquered the world by force, by killing, by creating suffering and death in his military enemies. Buddha conquered the world by killing the so-called dream of a real external and internal world, and thus, he said, his Nirvana conquered sufferings, all of which were in the dreams that he claimed to wake up from. Jesus conquered the world not by killing but by being killed, and not by avoiding suffering but by suffering and dying out of love for us.

Military might is the way to conquer the world with Alexander the Great. Becoming a Buddhist and waking up from the dream of a real world and a real soul is the way to conquer the world with Buddha. How do we conquer the world with Christ? John says, "The victory that conquers the world is our faith." Faith conquers even death because faith lets in to our souls the one who is stronger than death, the one who promised us, "Behold, I am with you always, until the end of the age" (Matt. 28:20).

GOSPEL
John 20:19–31 _____

On the evening of that first day of the week, when the doors were locked, where the disciples were, for fear of the Jews, Jesus came and stood in their midst and said to them, "Peace be with you." When he had said this, he showed them his hands and his side. The disciples rejoiced when they saw the Lord. Jesus said to them again, "Peace be with you. As the Father has sent me, so I send you." And when he had said this, he breathed on them and said to them, "Receive the Holy Spirit. Whose sins you forgive are forgiven them, and whose sins you retain are retained."

Thomas, called Didymus, one of the Twelve, was not with them when Jesus came. So the other disciples said to him, "We have seen the Lord." But he said to them, "Unless I see the mark of the nails in his hands and put my finger into the nailmarks and put my hand into his side, I will not believe."

Now a week later his disciples were again inside and Thomas was with them. Jesus came, although the doors were locked, and stood in their midst and said, "Peace be with you." Then he said to Thomas, "Put your finger here and see my hands, and bring your hand and put it into my side, and do not be unbelieving, but believe." Thomas answered and said to him, "My Lord and my God!" Jesus said to him, "Have you come to believe because you have seen me? Blessed are those who have not seen and have believed."

Now Jesus did many other signs in the presence of his disciples that are not written in this book. But these are written that you may come to believe that Jesus is the Christ, the Son of God, and that through this belief you may have life in his name.

Reflection 1: on St. Thomas the Apostle

We call him "Doubting Thomas," but he was an Apostle and a saint. Jesus chose him for a reason. Let's see what we can learn from him.

The other three Gospels only mention his name as one of the Twelve, but John gives us three more bits of information about him: the story in today's Gospel, about Thomas' refusal to believe until he had seen the risen Jesus' wounds, and two other events.

One of these is when Jesus heard that his friend Lazarus was ill in Bethany, near Jerusalem, where the Jews were plotting to kill him. He stayed away for two days, because he knew he would raise Lazarus from the dead when he came. And when he said, "Lazarus has died. And I am glad for you that I was not there, that you may believe. Let us go to him," Thomas replied, "Let us also go to die with him" (John 11:14–16). That response shows three things, all about death: his pessimism about Jesus being able to escape the death threats from his enemies, his doubt that Jesus could raise Lazarus from the dead, and his courage in being ready to die with Jesus.

On another occasion, when Jesus was preparing his Apostles for his death, he said, "If I go and prepare a place for you, I will come back again and take you to myself, so that where I am you also may be. Where I am going you know the way." Thomas questioned him: "Master, we do not know where you are going; how can we know the way?" And Jesus replied, "I am the way" (John 14:2–6). This also shows three things about Thomas: again his doubts, and his honest confession of his ignorance, and his questioning demand to know.

In today's Gospel, we again see his resolve to doubt—like a scientist, who demands concrete data, empirical evidence, before he will believe any truth-claim, however attractive. But Jesus on all three occasions answered Thomas by turning him toward the ultimate datum, the ultimate fact: toward Jesus himself.

The two most important points here for us, I think, come from Jesus' treatment of Thomas, not Thomas' treatment of Jesus. The first point is very simple and obvious. The second is profound and elusive.

The first point is that Jesus came down to Thomas' level. Jesus knew, and we should also know, that some people are just temperamentally pessimistic and skeptical. They see the negative possibilities very clearly, even though they often ignore the positive ones. They see the half of the glass of water that is empty where others see the half that is full. We need both kinds of people because both halves of the glass are real. These pessimistic people are needed, and valuable. God invented them.

Pessimism is not a sin. Temperamental pessimism is largely a psychological trait that they have received in their emotional DNA rather than something they have freely chosen. God only knows how much free choice is mingled in whatever instinctive and emotional tendencies we have in ourselves, and we should be far more reluctant than we usually are to judge people, as distinct from actions.

We are all disabled, in different ways; we all have special needs. And when we find someone with special needs in the faith department, like Thomas, someone who finds it temperamentally hard to believe and trust, our first instinct should be to do what Jesus did: to understand his needs and to supply them as best we can. That includes coming down to their level, as it were. It was harder for Thomas to believe than it was for the other Apostles, so Jesus made it easier for him. When we meet someone like Thomas, we, too, should not make it harder for them to believe, but easier; and the first step in doing that is empathy, not judgment; listening, not preaching. Jesus respected Thomas' skepticism, even though he said that those who had not seen and yet believed were blessed.

Now comes the second and less obvious point. "Doubting Thomas" would not believe unless he had enough reason, enough evidence. Let's look at the nature of the evidence that Jesus gave him. Thomas would not accept the secondhand evidence from the other Apostles, so Jesus gave him what he needed: firsthand evidence. Thomas doubted the other Apostles, doubted their faith, their belief that Jesus had resurrected. Belief, like reason, is in the mind. So instead of giving Thomas something in the mind, some argument, some reason; instead of sending mental soldiers out from his mind to defeat the mental soldiers that were in Thomas' mind, Jesus instead showed him reality, showed himself, not just a better idea or a clearer idea or the logical proof of the idea.

Many people who support abortion are not moved by even the best reasons and arguments that prove that an unborn human baby is a human being and that abortion is murder. But they are often moved when they actually see an unborn baby on ultrasound, or see the steps in the growth and development of the fetus, or, most of all, actually see an abortion and its results. That's why the media in this supposedly "free" country will show any operation on TV except the one that is performed more often than any other—an abortion. That's why the Nazis took great care to cover up their Holocaust. Once you approve murder, you have to approve the lies to cover it up. Let's not be naïve. If your conscience does not fear to kill, why would it fear to lie? If you don't draw back from murder, why would you draw back from the lies that cover up the murder? If you can't be trusted to respect life, why should anyone trust you to respect truth?

The principle that underlies Jesus' response to "Doubting Thomas" is that truth exists first in reality, in facts, and only secondarily in minds, which are like mirrors that reflect facts. But mirrors can deceive. Mirrors can be cracked, or dirty, or foggy. Ideas and words are like mirrors. They can lie. Facts do not lie. Facts speak louder than words. You can always argue with abstract ideas and words but not with concrete realities. That's why you can't argue with the deep happiness of a saint.

What Jesus did with Thomas was the same thing Jesus did with Martha when he was testing her faith after Lazarus had died. Martha said, "I know he will rise, in the resurrection on the last day," and Jesus said, "*I am* the resurrection and the life" (John 11:24–25). Jesus turned Martha from the abstract general idea to the concrete particular reality of himself.

Similarly, when Jesus answered Thomas' question about where Jesus was going and the way, or the road map, to get there, he said "*I am* the way." Jesus gave Thomas something much better than a road map: he gave Thomas the road itself; and that road, the road to heaven, was not an "it" but a "he."

When Christ said to St. Thomas Aquinas, shortly before Thomas' death, "You have written very well about me, Thomas; what will you have as your reward?" Thomas answered, "Only yourself, Lord." The absolutely best possible answer.

That's also why Job was satisfied with God's answer to the great riddle of why the righteous suffer. Job asked a hundred good questions, in thousands of words, but God gave him not just words but himself. Thus, Job replied, "I had heard of you by word of mouth, but now my eye has seen you" (Job 42:5). And that totally satisfied him, as it will satisfy us in heaven.

He also said not only "I am the way" but also "I am the truth." Thomas was a philosopher, a truth-seeker, and Jesus said to him not just "I *teach* the truth" but "I *am* the truth." Jesus is the eternal Logos, the Mind of God, become a human being in time.

Jesus is eliciting Thomas' faith here—not just in certain truths but in *him*. For although faith involves beliefs, its primary object is not beliefs about Christ but Christ himself; not an idea but a divine person. We are saved by knowing *Jesus*, not by knowing many truths *about* him. The devil knows many truths about Jesus, but that does not save him. You don't get to heaven by passing a theology test.

How do we actually meet this person, then, if not just by thinking correct thoughts about him? In two ways, both of them more concrete than thinking: by sight or by faith. Thomas demanded sight. "Seeing is believing" was his motto. He said, "I won't believe Jesus is alive until I see him with my own eyes." So what did Jesus do? Jesus came down to Thomas' level and showed himself to Thomas' eyes.

Actually, what Jesus did for Thomas was no more than what he had done for the other Apostles, who also did not believe until they saw him a week earlier. They had the same need, the same doubt; they just got their need met earlier. But when they told Thomas what they had seen, he did not believe *them*. There was another link in the chain for Thomas: the other Apostles, who saw Jesus first. Thomas had a greater need than they did because, unlike Thomas, they did not need faith in the other links of the chain; they saw Jesus with their own eyes.

Thomas was not doubting God so much as he was doubting man; and that is not a totally bad thing, for man is not infallible; only God is. We call him "Doubting Thomas" not because he doubted *Jesus* any more than the other Apostles did but because he doubted *them*; he doubted their testimony, their witness. He did not believe the Church. The Church is most basically the chain of witnesses to Christ and his Resurrection.

There are two ways of going beyond ideas and thoughts and beliefs to realities. One is seeing for yourself. All of the Apostles, like Thomas, needed to see Jesus to believe in his Resurrection. The other way, which Jesus says is even more blessed than seeing, is faith. He said to Thomas, "Have you come to believe because you have seen me? Blessed are those who have not seen and have believed."

He is speaking of this life, of course, because in the next life we will be much more blessed in our seeing God face to face, in the "beatific vision," than we are in this life either by seeing Jesus face to face in his human Incarnation, as the Apostles did, *or* in believing even though we do not see.

Faith is for us today the *only* way, because we can no longer see Jesus face to face with our physical eyes, as the Apostles did, and we do not yet see him in his divinity face to face as we will in heaven. But that does not make the Apostles more privileged; it makes *us* more privileged, more blessed, according to the very words of Jesus himself. When he said to Thomas, "Blessed are those who have not seen and have believed," he was thinking of us, each one of us, by name.

When we look at the Eucharistic Host, whether with our physical eyes or with a physical microscope, which only magnifies what we see with our eyes, or test it with scientific chemical analysis, it looks no different from ordinary bread and wine. But when we open the eyes of our faith, it's like x-ray vision: we see Jesus hiding behind the appearances as an x-ray sees the bones that are hiding behind the flesh.

Miracles are visible to the visible seeing of the physical eyes. Faith is an invisible seeing. Jesus still performs some miracles today, but most of us do not see these with our own eyes. But we see Jesus, we really do see Jesus, with the eyes of faith. Faith is a seeing, not just a feeling. That's what the Letter to the Hebrews says: "Yet at present we do not see 'all things subject to him,' but we do see Jesus" (Heb. 2:8–9). We do not yet see the miracle of resurrected bodies, or a renewed world, with our eyes; we do not yet see Jesus coming on the clouds at the end of time. But we even now see Jesus, in a real way, by our faith.

Faith is not based on feeling but on fact. We believe because we have the eyewitness testimony of the Apostles and of Jesus' other disciples who saw him, and of the more than five hundred people who saw him after the Resurrection, whom St. Paul writes about and appeals to and invites his readers to meet when he is writing to the skeptical Corinthians (1 Cor. 15:6). They and the Apostles were the beginning of the two-thousand-year-long chain of witnesses that constitute the Church, which includes myriads of martyrs, saints, and sages, and at the center of which are the Apostles and their ordained successors, who are the bishops of the one, holy, catholic, and apostolic Church. Like the Resurrection to which it witnesses, the Church is visible and not just invisible; objective and not just subjective; concrete, not just abstract; material, not just spiritual; a historical fact, not some timeless abstract *idea*, however exalted. The Church is as historical and concrete and visible and material as the Resurrection, because it is the chain of witnesses to the Resurrection.

But that was Thomas' obstacle: the Church, the links in the chain that connected him to Christ. He wanted to skip the chain of witnesses and see the resurrected Christ with his own eyes. The Church then consisted mainly of these ten men, who had seen Jesus resurrected, and Thomas would not believe their witness. They were to him the weak link in the chain. After all, they were sinful, selfish, stupid, shallow, fallible human beings like all the rest of us, including priests and bishops and popes and even saints.

So what did God do about that? He did not just sit there and wait for Thomas to change his mind; he acted. He came to Thomas. He gave Thomas what he needed, to elicit his faith. God will always do that. He will not always give us what we want, but he will always give us what we need; and we all need faith, and therefore God will give the gift of faith to anyone who is honest and open and sincere and who asks for it.

To ask is already to believe; thus the paradoxical prayer "I do believe, help my unbelief!" (Mark 9:24). Of course, God will do it in his time and in his way, not in ours, because he's a lover, not an airplane. He doesn't publish schedules or routes for his services. He's not predictable, but he's trustable.

So if you know anyone who says they "simply can't believe"; if they tell you they just don't have the gift of faith that you have, tell them to ask God for the gift of faith, and tell them that if they do that honestly and sincerely, they will get it, because Jesus promised that. He said, "Seek and you will find. . . . The one who seeks, finds" (Matt. 7:7–8). In fact, the very asking God for the gift of faith is already to have some faith and trust in God, or at least hope in God, in the God you ask and pray to. Even if you are an agnostic and don't even know whether God exists, if you at least hope that he does, you can pray to him, honestly, and say, "I don't know that you exist, but I don't know for sure that you don't exist either, so if you do, please get through to me."

And if you pray to God, you don't pray to a liar, any more than you ask for love from a murderer or ask for gifts from a Scrooge. And you don't ask for the supernatural gift of faith from a mere natural human being. No one else can give you the gift of faith; only God can.

Faith is not a feeling, or a wish, or a desire, or a myth, or a fantasy. It's not just something inside of you: it's *between* you and another person. It's trust. Secular faith is trusting other human beings. It's the basis for all stable societies. You trust your money to the First National Bank & *Trust* Company. And you can trust your soul to the First Supernatural Bank & Trust Company.

Religious faith is saying yes to God whenever God tells us anything, because God can never deceive or be deceived. And how does God tell us anything? Through Christ and the Church he instituted, which is the chain of witnesses to the Resurrection.

Thomas would not believe the witness of the Church, the other Apostles. So Jesus did something special for him. He keeps doing that to other "Doubting Thomases" today, in ways that are more invisible and mysterious.

Thomas was blessed because he saw the resurrected Jesus with his own eyes. But we are just as blessed as Thomas, even though we don't see Jesus as Thomas did. So don't envy the Apostles who saw Jesus with their eyes, the eyes in their bodies. You have eyes too, in your soul. Faith is a set of eyes, and when those eyes are turned to God, they see God's light, God's revelation. The only honest reason for believing that something as astonishing as the Incarnation and the Resurrection is true is that God said so. "God said it; I believe it; that settles it"—that is not fundamentalist irrationalism but totally reasonable. It's what Thomas responded to Jesus when he said, "My Lord and my God."

And that's the perfect thing for each of us to say and mean with all our heart when we receive that same Lord and God invisibly but truly and really in Holy Communion.

Reflection 2: on St. John's summary of his Gospel (John 20:31)

Many learned scholars have written many articles and books on the question of why John wrote his Gospel, of what was in his mind and in his world that motivated him. One theory was that he was writing to reconcile the other three Gospels, since his was the last, or just to supplement them with the missing parts. Another was that he was writing against some fake Gospels, many of which were circulating in the early Church. For instance, the Gospel of Thomas was probably written by Gnostics, a heretical sect that believed Jesus was a pure spirit, that the body was evil, and that Jesus saved us by giving us his mind, not his body; that he was a philosopher and a mystic who taught a higher, hidden, mystical kind of knowledge. Still another theory was that John himself was a kind of Gnostic. The fact that there is so much controversy among scholars about this question, and the fact that there are so many books and articles that claim to answer it in so many different ways, is truly amazing, and a testimony to how arrogant and how stunningly stupid professional scholarly theologians can be, because John himself tells us, in his own words, as clearly and as simply as anyone ever has done, exactly why he wrote this Gospel. It's in its last verse, which is the last verse of today's Gospel reading. (It's the last verse of chapter 20, and chapter 21 was probably added by John's disciples, because it speaks of John as someone else when it says that "we know that his testimony is true" [v. 24]). Here's the verse:

> Now Jesus did many other signs in the presence of his disciples that are not written in this book. But these are written that you may come to believe that Jesus is the Christ, the Son of God, and that through this belief you may have life in his name.

So after John clearly tells readers the exact reason why he wrote the book, what do scholars do nineteen centuries later? They write thousands of books explaining why John really wrote the book! Of course, they must know better than John does what was in John's mind when he wrote! After all, they had an advantage over John: John only went to heaven, but they went to Harvard.

Let's do two radical and unfashionable things: let's first ignore the scholars and then listen to the author.

There are seven important words in this sentence: "Jesus," "Christ," "Son," "God," "belief," "life," and "name." There is no secret to what these words mean.

"Jesus" is the personal name that God's angel told Joseph to give Mary's son.

It means "Savior," or "one who saves," or "God saves." The angel said, "You are to name him Jesus, because he will save his people from their sins" (Matt. 1:21). The angel did not say that Jesus would be the savior because he would save us from unenlightened political opinions, or inefficient anti-poverty programs, or psychological confusion, or failure to adjust to society, or lack of self-esteem, or being misunderstood by others, or lack of diversity or dialogue or inclusion or tolerance, or from discomfort or suffering, or even from martyrdom. Jesus is the Savior because he saves us from our *sins*.

Sin is not merely doing bad things. Sin is separation from God, divorce from God. The result of sin is death, eternal death, because God is the source of all life. St. Paul writes, "The wages of sin is death, but the gift of God is eternal life in Christ Jesus our Lord" (Rom. 6:23).

Think of an electrical appliance. When it's plugged in, it works; it lives. When the plug is pulled, it dies. When it's plugged back in, it lives again. We are like that appliance; and eternal life, divine life, supernatural life, is the electricity; and God is the dynamo that is the source of it. When we sinned, we unplugged ourselves from God—both collectively, as a race, in Adam, the literal father of all humans, and individually, in our own lives and our own free choices to sin. Jesus plugs us back in.

But just as our unplugging was our own free choice, the re-plugging must also be our own free choice. We can't do it without Jesus, but Jesus won't do it without our consent, our choice, which is what faith in him is.

"Sin" means three things, or has three dimensions. First, sins are freely chosen human acts of disobedience to God's will, as known through God's law, which is revealed both supernaturally in Scripture, especially in the Ten Commandments, and naturally, by conscience, which is our natural knowledge of the "natural moral law," the law of human nature. Second, sin is the moral character, or set of habits, that these acts create, and from which, in turn, more acts flow, so that these acts become habits. The first meaning of sin is what we do, the second meaning is what we are. The third meaning is our broken relationship with God.

Salvation from sin addresses all three of those dimensions. It first restores our relationship with God. This is called "justification." It then gradually improves both our character and our actions, until we become the holy and happy saints God designed us to be. That is "sanctification."

For most of us, that process is completed only in purgatory. But Jesus is called our "Savior" not just because he saves us from the *consequences* of our sins, our eternal punishment, but also because he saves us from sin itself. He saves us from the evil in what we do, from the evil in what we are, and from the evil in our relationship with God. He reconciles us to ourselves and to God.

The next important word in this last verse from St. John is "Christ." That's not his name but his title. It means "Messiah," or "anointed one," or "divinely promised one." There are literally hundreds of prophecies about the Messiah in the Jewish Scriptures, what we Christians call the Old Testament, and Jesus fulfilled them all.

While the name "Jesus" ("Savior") is addressed to the whole world, since the whole world needs to be saved from sin, the word "Christ" ("Messiah") is addressed especially to Jews, and to their special prophecies, since Jesus came to them and from them. They were chosen by God, not for their own sake but for the sake of the world, to be his collective prophet to the world. Jesus is the whole point of Judaism. He is to Judaism what the point of an arrow is to an arrow. His mother Mary, who inherits all of Judaism both biologically and spiritually, is the shaft of the arrow, his Father in heaven is the archer, and we are the target.

John says he wrote the Gospel to help readers to "believe" in Jesus. That word, "belief," or "faith," means two things: to believe in the truth about him and to believe in *him*, to trust him personally. Faith has two objects: truth about Christ and Christ himself. Obviously, the first of these two things is relative to the second. If a firefighter comes to save you from a burning building, you need to believe two things: truths about the firefighter and the firefighter himself. You need to believe that he is a firefighter, not an imposter, and that he knows what he is doing and that if you do what he tells you to do—for instance, jump out of a fourth-story window into his safety net—you will be saved. But you believe what he *says* only because you believe what he *is*. You trust him.

What does John say we should believe about Jesus? Two things especially: that he is the Christ, the promised Messiah, and that he is the Son of God.

What does the phrase "Son of God" mean? It is an analogy to natural, biological, physical sonship and fatherhood. Of course, God is not a material, biological being, and he does not have a wife, and he does not father a son by sexual intercourse. Spiritual sonship is an analogy to biological sonship.

(By the way, like all premodern writings, the Bible uses "father," "son," and "he" not exclusively but inclusively, to include rather than exclude "mother," "daughter," and "she" in their meaning. That is the clear and obvious meaning, whatever the historical situation that produced this use of masculine words for things that can be equally masculine or feminine. The meaning does not depend on the motive, which may or may not have included a deep unconscious prejudice against women.)

The two most essential things about a father and a son are that they are two different persons and that they have the same essential nature. If they are biological persons, they are of the same species; if they are divine persons, they have the same divine nature. So "Son of God" means "a distinct person but of the very same nature as God the Father, equally divine: eternal, perfect, all-good, all-wise, and all-powerful." The son of an ape is an ape, and the son of a man is a man, and the son of a Martian is a Martian, and the son of God is God.

If Jesus is only human and not divine, only man and not God, he cannot bridge the gap between us and God; he cannot reconcile us to God. He can bridge the gap, the abyss, the separation, between us and God only if he stands on both sides of the abyss, like a bridge.

Here is another way of seeing the same point, that in order to be our Savior, Jesus has to be divine as well as human. Nothing can give what it does not have. The sun gives us energy only because it has energy to give. Dogs give dog life to their puppies only because they have dog life to give. Wise teachers give wisdom only because they have wisdom to give. Each living thing can give only the kind of life it has. Our natural life is mortal. Death ends it. Jesus cannot give us a share in the eternal life of God if he is only human. Only God can give divine life, eternal life, supernatural life.

Now let's bring our words together. It's faith in Jesus as the promised Messiah and the Son of God that gives us eternal life, "in his name," which means "by his authority, by his real presence and power." When a policeman arrests you, he does so in the name of the state. When a bank cashier gives you a large amount of money because you present the check your father has written to you, you get that money only because your father's name is on the check. It is by his authority that you get it. The same is true of eternal life: we get it "in Jesus' name," that is, by his personal authority, which means both the right and the might. So the result, the payoff, of this faith is "life in his name."

The last thing we need to understand is the *relationship* between this faith and this eternal life, the relationship between the cause and the effect. Why does God require faith on our part before he gives us eternal life? Is it a legal contract, a kind of deal that he invented, a "quid pro quo," a "you do this for me and then I will do this for you"? No, it's not a deal that God makes that he could have made differently. It's not like "I will reward you with wages if you do this work for my company," or "I will share my house with you if you pay me rent." It's more like "If you jump into my arms, I will catch you." To use the favorite image of the saints and mystics, it's like sex. It's like "If you have sex, you will get pregnant." That's God's Good News, God's Gospel, God's offer: "If you believe me, if you trust me, if you choose me, if you let me, I will impregnate your soul with my eternal life."

God requires our free consent because he is a gentleman, not a bully. He respects our free will to the end. That is the only reason there is a hell as well as a heaven. He knocks at the door of our soul, but we have to freely choose to open the door and let him in. He will not knock it down. The lock is on the inside. And faith is the key that turns the lock.

We all seek happiness. There are only two roads to that end: God's way or our way. Jesus is God's way to happiness and heaven; sin and selfishness are our way to hell. There is a famous song lyric that everyone sings as they enter hell and no one sings as they enter heaven. It's "I did it my way." Sin, death, and hell are the three greatest enemies of happiness. Jesus saves us from all three. That's the Good News of the Gospel.

It's really very simple and obvious, like the sea, and like the sun. It's also very deep and mysterious, like the sea, and like the sun. Like Jesus. It *is* Jesus.

THIRD SUNDAY OF EASTER

FIRST READING

ACTS 3:13–15, 17–19 _____

Peter said to the people: "The God of Abraham, the God of Isaac, and the God of Jacob, the God of our fathers, has glorified his servant Jesus, whom you handed over and denied in Pilate's presence when he had decided to release him. You denied the Holy and Righteous One and asked that a murderer be released to you. The author of life you put to death, but God raised him from the dead; of this we are witnesses. Now I know, brothers, that you acted out of ignorance, just as your leaders did; but God has thus brought to fulfillment what he had announced beforehand through the mouth of all the prophets, that his Christ would suffer. Repent, therefore, and be converted, that your sins may be wiped away."

_____

Today's first reading is from the first sermon of the first pope, St. Peter. It contains a pattern that we find repeated in sermons, homilies, exhortations, creeds, and papal encyclicals ever after. It has two parts: the objective facts and our subjective, personal response.

The first part, the objective part, consists of three essential facts: the truth about God, the truth about Christ, and the truth about ourselves.

First, it begins at the beginning, with God himself: "the God of Abraham, the God of Isaac, and the God of Jacob, the God of our fathers." This is the eternal fact.

Next, it asserts the historical fact, what God has done in history: that he "has glorified his servant Jesus . . . [and] raised him from the dead; of this we are witnesses." Christian preaching is witnessing to the facts, telling the truth.

So it begins with the two greatest objective facts of God the Father and God the Son, God unincarnate and God incarnate.

The next fact it asserts is human sin—in fact, the most sinful deed in history, what we did to God when he became incarnate: we murdered him. Our sins killed him. He died at our hands, and he died for our sins. As Peter put it, "The author of life you put to death." So we have these three basic facts, two about the good news of God and one about the bad news of sin.

What happens when these facts come together? A cross. A conflict. And who wins? God wins, by apparently losing. That's the next fact: that "God has thus brought to fulfillment what he had announced beforehand through the mouth of all the prophets, that his Christ would suffer." The bad news, our sins, which killed Christ, was used by God as part of the Good News, our salvation from sin by Christ's sufferings. God did the impossible. He did not declare evil to be good; that's not possible. But he used our evil and brought his great good out of it; in fact, he used the worst evil ever, our deicide, to bring about the best good ever, our salvation. What incredible grace!

If those are the objective facts, what's the subjective response to them? What's the practical bottom line? How does the rubber meet the road? What's the upshot, the practical conclusion? It is that we can receive this incredible gift, this grace of salvation and sanctification, if only we do two things: the negative thing of repenting of our sins and the positive thing of converting, believing, accepting God's salvation by faith, turning back to God. That's what "conversion" literally means: "turning back," turning back to the God of infinite grace and costly love, so that "your sins may be wiped away," in St. Peter's words.

This piece of good news for us personally, this offer, this appeal to our free choice to repent and convert and receive our salvation, is dependent on the first point, the objective facts, the truth. Our personal, subjective act of repentance and conversion is not just a kind of psychological technology, a thing we do with ourselves; it's our *response* to three great objective truths, three infinitely important facts: first, that God is God; second, that Jesus is the

Son of God who became man, suffered, died, and rose for our salvation; and third, that it was our sins that made that necessary, our disease that called for God's cure. If any one of these three objective facts is denied, our subjective, personal repentance and conversion make no sense. *Our* faith depends on the truth of *the* faith.

That's why dogmas and creeds and theology are necessary. They are like x-rays: without them, the operation cannot succeed. They are like road maps: without them, the traveler is lost. They are like light: without it, we cannot deal with the real things in the world.

Faith has these two dimensions, and both are absolutely necessary: the subjective and the objective, the personal and the impersonal.

We personally believe in Christ as a person; we love him and we trust him. But we also believe objective truths about him: that he is totally divine, that he is also totally human, that he lived and died and rose to save us from sin and death and hell.

Both the subjective half and the objective half are necessary. If we only believe objective truths about him but do not personally believe *him*, trust him, hope in him, love him, we are no better than the devil, who is also intelligent enough to know these facts about him but does not believe or trust *him* or put his hope or love in *him*. The objective dimension of our faith without the subjective, personal dimension is not enough. But neither is the subjective without the objective. If we personally love him and trust him but deny that he is divine, then he is no longer our Savior, because no mere man, however holy and wise, can save us from our sins and open heaven for us. Only God can do that. And if we love him personally but deny that he is human, then again he cannot be the Savior of our humanity. If he is not both God and man, he cannot bridge the gap between God and man.

And if we deny the objective fact that we are sinners, that we need a new heart, a heart transplant operation, then we will not get that new heart, because God requires consent to his holy heart surgery, because God is love, and love always appeals to freedom, to free choice, not power or compulsion.

So both the objective truth and our subjective response to it are necessary for our salvation.

That's why our religion never separates these two things and never pits one against the other, as our critics usually do. On the one hand, we are told that we believers are only subjective mythmakers and dreamers and that we ignore objective facts and history and science. But our whole religion is based on the objective facts of God's reality and the history of Christ's life and death and Resurrection and the science of theology, which is a rational, intellectual enterprise, like the other sciences, but with different subject matter.

On the other hand, we are told that we are builders of impersonal systems of ideas, in our creeds and our theology, and builders of institutions of power, in our churches, and that we ignore human feelings and human loves and human needs. But our whole religion is based on God's dealing with our sinful, selfish human psyches and loves and desires. It is all about God's heart and ours, God's love and ours.

To love is to meet the beloved's deepest need. What do we need most? We need love, but we need *true* love. We need truth, but the greatest truth is that God is love, that the greatest thing is love.

Let us never, never compromise either of these two things: truth or love; objective truth or subjective, personal love. Our love is wholly based on the truth, the truth about God and man and Christ. And all the truths of our faith are based on the fact that God is love.

The truth that "God is love" does not mean that "love is God," that our love is God, but that God is love, true love. If you want to know what true love is, look at God: look at God's love for you; look at a crucifix. My prayer for you is that *that* should be the last thing in this world that you see, and grasp, and hope in as you die.

RESPONSORIAL PSALM

PSALM 4:2, 4, 7–8, 9 _____

R. (7a) **Lord, let your face shine on us.**

When I call, answer me, O my just God,
    you who relieve me when I am in distress;
    have pity on me, and hear my prayer!

Know that the LORD does wonders for his faithful one;
    the LORD will hear me when I call upon him.

O LORD, let the light of your countenance shine upon us!
    You put gladness into my heart.

As soon as I lie down, I fall peacefully asleep,
    for you alone, O LORD,
    bring security to my dwelling.

_____

The Psalmist prays, "As soon as I lie down, I fall peacefully asleep, for you alone, O LORD, bring security to my dwelling."

We all need security systems, whether we are rich or poor. The richer you are, the more worries you have and the more security systems you need. We all need at least locks on our doors and windows, because there are a small but real number of warped and wicked people in the world who would rob us or even kill us if they could. And when we are asleep, we are the most vulnerable; so we lock our doors especially at night. In today's Psalm verse, the Psalmist says that God is his spiritual security system.

That does not mean that he does not lock his doors. It means that in addition to locking the doors of his house to his enemies when he sleeps, he also locks the doors to the enemies of his soul and unlocks the doors of his soul to God. He does this because he knows God; he knows that God is his friend, not his enemy, and he wants God to rule over his whole life. He knows that God is not stupid or wicked or weak but infinitely wise and good and powerful. He may not *feel* this all the time, but he knows it all the time. That's what gives him security.

When he says, "As soon as I lie down, I fall peacefully asleep," he may or may not mean this literally. David the Psalmist was a king, a busy and responsible king, with many enemies, so David might have been bothered with all sorts of worries, small or great, real or unreal, as he lay down to sleep. He might even have had sleep apnea. But that does not mean that he does not have faith. Faith is rooted in fact, not in feeling. He knows and believes what he prays, that "you alone, O Lord, bring security to my dwelling." So even if he does not feel what he knows, he knows what he knows: he knows who God is, and what God does, and that what God lets happen is part of God's providence, part of God's wise and good will for him, part of God's love for him; that God takes care of him in every detail and therefore also allows the worries and the sleeplessness that David, like all of us, naturally has.

That's true even of doubts. We all have doubts. Faith and doubt do not totally exclude each other. Believers are always tempted by doubts, and doubters are always tempted by faith, by the temptation to believe. Life is spiritual warfare; you have to fight, either to keep going or to stop, either to stay or to change. If the devil is always there to tempt you, he always casts a vote against you, and if God is always there to help you, he always casts a vote for you. You have free will; you always cast the deciding vote.

That does not mean that if you vote for God the temptations stop, but it means that you know that God will win this election.

The fact that you know it does not mean that you also necessarily feel it. So what? It's still true. We all worry too much about our feelings. Give up that battle. Exit that battlefield. Let God take care of your feelings, and your worries.

Trust him. He said, "Come to me, all you who labor and are burdened, and

I will give you rest" (Matt. 11:28). When you come to him and let him carry you, you don't need to keep carrying all those burdens on your own shoulders. Imagine a man carrying a big, heavy pig. A farmer with a horse-drawn cart stops and says, "That pig is too heavy for you to carry. Here, climb onto my cart and I will drive you into town." The man obeys but keeps the pig on his shoulders. That's us. That's how stupid we are.

So what mental operation should we perform on ourselves to stop being so stupid? What little psychological trick should we play on ourselves? How do we get out of this spiderweb? Don't try. You *know* that God is real, and God is there, and God is in fact carrying the whole load, including yourself, whether you're still carrying the pig or whether you've put the pig down in his cart. God is not a feeling; God is a fact. And if you believe that fact, that's all you need. Whatever feelings you have, after you decide that you do really believe that fact of God's love and God's providence, all those feelings are now part of that fact! They are being allowed by God, the God of total wisdom and love and power, and therefore they are for your good, and therefore you can stop worrying about them. The enemy will never penetrate God's security system around your inmost soul, no matter how much you worry. He will not allow the enemy into your soul, into your spiritual house, no matter how much you hear the enemy making scary noises outside your windows. Just trust the manager of your life's security system.

And if you only stop worrying about what to do to go to sleep, you will be able to go to sleep. Going to sleep is a lot like dying. Letting yourself go, letting yourself go to sleep, giving up the conscious knowledge and control of your body, is a kind of faith. It is a good preparation for dying. Jesus taught us how to die. His very last words were "Father, into your hands I commend my spirit" (Luke 23:46). They should be our last words too. And we should practice them every night.

SECOND READING

1 JOHN 2:1–5A _____

My children, I am writing this to you so that you may not commit sin. But if anyone does sin, we have an Advocate with the Father, Jesus Christ the righteous one. He is expiation for our sins, and not for our sins only but for those of the whole world. The way we may be sure that we know him is to keep his commandments. Those who say, "I know him," but do not keep his commandments are liars, and the truth is not in them. But whoever keeps his word, the love of God is truly perfected in him.

_____

The New Testament was written in Greek. The Greek language has more distinctions in it, more choices of words, more exact words, especially for basic concepts like "knowing" and "loving" and "good" and "evil," than any other language in history. One of those distinctions is important for us to understand if we want to understand our epistle for today, the first epistle of the Apostle John.

It is the distinction between an act that is a one-time thing, like "I swallowed the pill" or "he kissed me," and an act that is repeated and habitual, like "he takes drugs" or "she fixes transmissions" or "they love their kids." (The technical term in Greek grammar for the one-time meaning is the aorist tense; the technical term for the ongoing, habitual meaning present tense or imperfect tense.)

We are all born with the habit of habitual sin, habitual selfishness. That's what "original sin" means: not our first actual sin, or Adam's first actual sin, but the sinful habits that we are born with, our addiction to sin and selfishness. We are all sinaholics. When we believe and are baptized, we get Christ's gift of a real but finite share in his own divine life in our soul; and that gives us another, contrary habit, the habit of faith and hope and love, and that is now our deeper identity. But we still act out of our old sinful habits sometimes; we still sin, again and again. That's why we need the sacrament of Confession. But that's not the self we want to be; that's the self we don't want to be. That's why we repent. Acts of sinning, and also acts of repenting, are one-time things for us: not that they happen only once, but that after they happen, we change; we repent.

And then, when John says that "the way we may be sure that we know him is to keep his commandments" and that "those who say, 'I know him,' but do not keep his commandments are liars," "keep" is in the habitual sense again. John is not saying that we have to be perfect and never disobey his commandments in order to truly know him.

Then John ends this passage by saying that "whoever keeps his word, the love of God is truly perfected in him." Again, "keeps" is in the habitual tense. We don't have to be sinless to have the love of God in us.

God is not a perfectionist. He does not wait until we are perfect to love us. He truly loves his seriously stupid, selfish, shallow, silly children. He will make us perfect, eventually, in heaven, but meanwhile he loves every stumbling step we take in his direction. He is very easy to please, even though he is very hard to completely satisfy—because that's what love is like, as every good human parent knows.

There is another distinction here in today's epistle that works in Greek but not in English. John says if we keep his commandments, we "know" him. The word for "know" here is not the word for knowing an idea or a fact but for knowing a person. English does not have that distinction between two kinds of knowing, but many other languages do. In German, for example, the word for knowing a fact is *wissen*, and *Wissenschaft* means "scientific knowledge." The word for knowing a person is *kennen*. It's the difference between knowing by an impersonal description and knowing by personal acquaintance, by some degree of intimacy. German also has two pronouns for the word "you." *Sie* is the polite, impersonal "you," and *du* is the familiar, intimate "you." There's a phrase in German that means "they say *du* to one another," which means they know each other as friends. A similar distinction exists in French: *savoir* means expertise, or "knowing facts," and *connaître* means knowing other persons, by experience, by empathy, by sharing the same human nature and the same kind of human life.

What saves us is not knowing facts about Jesus but knowing Jesus. When God takes us into heaven, he will not say, "Congratulations, you passed your theology test." He will say, "I know you. You're one of my children. You know me; I'm your Father."

That distinction is the point St. James is making when he writes, "You believe that God is one. You do well. Even the demons believe that and tremble" (James 2:19). The object of our faith is God himself, not only true ideas about God. We have faith in *him*, not in our ideas about him. We don't have faith in our faith; we have faith in him, in his love and mercy, in him personally. Justice is impersonal; love is personal. Justice is good, and necessary, but love is greater than justice. God is more than perfect justice. God is perfect love.

GOSPEL
LUKE 24:35–48

The two disciples recounted what had taken place on the way, and how Jesus was made known to them in the breaking of bread.

While they were still speaking about this, he stood in their midst and said to them, "Peace be with you." But they were startled and terrified and thought that they were seeing a ghost. Then he said to them, "Why are you troubled? And why do questions arise in your hearts? Look at my hands and my feet, that it is I myself. Touch me and see, because a ghost does not have flesh and bones as you can see I have." And as he said this, he showed them his hands and his feet. While they were still incredulous for joy and were amazed, he asked them, "Have you anything here to eat?" They gave him a piece of baked fish; he took it and ate it in front of them.

He said to them, "These are my words that I spoke to you while I was still with you, that everything written about me in the law of Moses and in the prophets and psalms must be fulfilled." Then he opened their minds to understand the Scriptures. And he said to them, "Thus it is written that the Christ would suffer and rise from the dead on the third day and that repentance, for the forgiveness of sins, would be preached in his name to all the nations, beginning from Jerusalem. You are witnesses of these things."

Notice how surprisingly physical many things are in the Gospel. We expect something as abstract as an ideology, and God gives us something as concrete as a sidewalk.

God assumes a physical human nature in the Incarnation. Jesus is born out of a woman's body. He performs physical miracles. He dies physically. He resurrects physically. And he appears to his disciples physically after his Resurrection.

The first thing today's Gospel passage mentions is that the two disciples who met him on the road to Emmaus after his Resurrection did not recognize him until he celebrated the Eucharist with them. They narrated how Jesus "was made known to them *in the breaking of the bread.*"

Then, when he appeared to the eleven, they thought he was a ghost, not a physical body. He said: "Look at my hands and my feet, that it is I myself. Touch me and see, because a ghost does not have flesh and bones as you can see I have." And as he said this, he showed them his hands and his feet. He did for them the very same thing he did with "Doubting Thomas." It was very, very literal.

Then, to prove he was not a ghost, he ate some food in front of them. It was very literal. The writer even tells us exactly what kind of food it was: a piece of baked fish. They noticed that one piece of baked fish was missing when Jesus left them. That proved it was not a vision, a dream, or a hallucination but a literal reality.

Jesus commissions his Apostles to be his witnesses, to preach the Good News: the very literal, very physical, very concrete fact that Jesus rose from the dead. And we will rise too. The words in the Apostles' Creed are very literal and very concrete: the Greek words translated as "the resurrection of the dead" are *anastasis nekron*, which means "the standing-up of the dead body."

If God can create the universe out of nothing, he can certainly make a living man out of a dead man.

And what he does to our bodies, he also does to our souls. He is the author of the life of both our bodies and our souls, and he is also the author of the new life, the supernatural life, the eternal life, of both our bodies and our souls. Heaven will not turn us into ghosts. We will have human bodies in heaven, and so will Jesus. We will see him with our own eyes, as his Apostles did. We will not turn into angels or ghosts. Our humanness will not be lost but perfected.

Our new, resurrected bodies will have more powers, not fewer powers, than these present bodies have. They will be like Christ's resurrected body. He could eat, but he didn't have to eat. He would not starve. He could walk and talk and be touched, but he could also walk through walls and move from one place to another just by willing to do so.

It's good that we do not have those powers yet. We are fools who abuse even the limited powers we have. When our souls become perfect, our bodies will become perfect too. Until then, God cannot trust us with supernatural powers like the ones Christ's resurrected body had. We are like little children who can barely ride ponies; we need to grow before we can ride stallions.

What we will be after death, what kind of bodies we will have, we do not fully comprehend, any more than an unborn baby can comprehend what life in the world outside the womb will be like. We have hints of it in Christ's Resurrection appearances and in other places in Scripture, especially the fifteenth chapter of St. Paul's First Letter to the Corinthians. But though we do not have clear answers to our questions about it, we have an infallible guarantee from God that we will rise, with our Lord, and be like him. As for the details, the best answer to our questions comes from Scripture. Here are St. Paul's words: "What eye has not seen, and ear has not heard, and what has not entered the human heart, what God has prepared for those who love him" (1 Cor. 2:9).

Until then, "we walk by faith, not by sight" (2 Cor. 5:7). To the skeptic who argues, "Seeing is believing, and I don't see, so I don't believe," we reply, "You have it backward. Believing is seeing. If you believe, you will see. If you trust God, you will see for yourself what wonderful things he has in store for you."

FOURTH SUNDAY OF EASTER

FIRST READING
Acts 4:8–12 _____

Peter, filled with the Holy Spirit, said: "Leaders of the people and elders: If we are being examined today about a good deed done to a cripple, namely, by what means he was saved, then all of you and all the people of Israel should know that it was in the name of Jesus Christ the Nazorean whom you crucified, whom God raised from the dead; in his name this man stands before you healed. He is *the stone rejected by you, the builders, which has become the cornerstone.* There is no salvation through anyone else, nor is there any other name under heaven given to the human race by which we are to be saved."

_____

In today's reading from the Acts of the Apostles, Peter has just miraculously healed a lifelong cripple by the authority of Christ, who had risen from the dead and who remains risen and active in the world through his Apostles even after he ascended back to heaven. In his preaching, Peter is responding to the fear and hostility on the part of the religious and political rulers against the Apostles, whom they saw as dangerous, threatening, radical revolutionaries. He does not apologize or compromise or mollify or pacify them. He does the opposite.

He does four things. First, he redirects their focus, the focus and target of their fears and hostility, and the real reason for the commotion and the conflict, from himself and the other Apostles to Christ. He says that "it was in the name of Jesus Christ the Nazorean whom you crucified, whom God raised from the dead; in his name this man stands before you healed." In hating Christ's faithful Apostles, they were hating Christ, and in hating Christ, they were hating God, the God they claimed to believe in. Christ himself had said that "whoever listens to you listens to me. Whoever rejects you rejects me. And whoever rejects me rejects the one who sent me" (Luke 10:16).

The second thing Peter did was speak the hard truth to them that it was they who had crucified Jesus. He speaks the uncomfortable truth that they need to repent and be forgiven, but he does not speak the comfortable lie "There's nothing to forgive." There is! Peter speaks the truth, the whole truth, and nothing but the truth, no matter how dangerous or inconvenient it is.

Throughout the whole Bible, God does the same to us in reminding us of our own sins. We all crucified Christ, not just the Jews, or the pagan Romans. Peter was here blaming himself as well as his enemies, because he could not forget how at Jesus' trial he had three times denied him; Jesus' response was simply to turn and look at Peter, and Peter "went out and began to weep bitterly" (Luke 22:62). If we do not do the same, if we do not also weep for our sins, we are not listening to God, who speaks to us through our own conscience, and through Peter and all his successors.

The third thing Peter does is connect Christ with the Jews' own prophetic Scriptures in quoting the Psalm verse: "He is *the stone rejected by you, the builders, which has become the cornerstone.*" Jesus' own beloved and chosen people rejected him, hated and feared him, and made the Romans crucify him; and the supreme irony of this was that the one they crucified—the one we crucified, the one our sins crucified—was the cornerstone of the whole building that God was building, God's kingdom, the work of our salvation. God used this greatest of all evils for the greatest of all goods. God's mysterious, loving plan and providence was behind all this, not just the Jews or the Romans or the rest of us.

The fourth thing Peter does is tell them the whole truth about who Jesus is: not just one of many prophets, and not just an option, but the one and only Savior. He says, "There is no salvation through anyone else, nor is there any other name under heaven given to the human race by which we are to be saved." Jesus is not just a great prophet or philosopher or moralist or guru; Jesus is God become man; Jesus is the one and only Lord.

Those three words, "Jesus is Lord," were the first and shortest of all the many Christian creeds. St. Paul repeats the formula twice in his epistles. The Greek word translated "Lord" here, *kyrios*, was the same word used by Jews and Christians to refer to the one true God. That three-word creed, that "Jesus is Lord," is the hard, bright, clear line in the sand that separates all Christians from all non-Christians. Believing that makes you a Christian; not believing that makes you not a Christian. Jesus is divine; Jesus is God become man to be our Savior. He is not one of many saviors, because only God can save us, and God is not one of many gods.

Peter did not yet fully understand the mystery of the Trinity at this point in history, of course. For that matter, neither do we. But he remembered that Jesus said, "The Father and I are one" (John 10:30), and he understood that therefore it is impossible to relativize Jesus. He is the one and only begotten Son of God and is equal to the Father. He is not one of many. He is the absolute good and the ultimate truth.

And therefore, it is Jesus who is hated and feared and rejected and silenced when the Apostles of Jesus, the Church of Jesus, the continued work of Jesus in the world, is hated and feared and rejected and silenced. That happened here in today's reading, and it has happened over and over again throughout history, and it continues to happen today, not only in places where Christians are overtly hated and killed in countries far away, but also here in our own culture, in much of our once-Christian, ex-Christian, re-paganized culture, and its educators and its media.

Christophobia, the fear of Christ, is the deepest motive behind the world's fear and hate of the truth that Christ's Church continues to preach: the "intolerant" and "divisive" claim that Jesus alone is God, that Jesus alone is the Savior from sin, that we are all sinners in need of salvation; and that we cannot have two Gods, two Lords, two Saviors; that we cannot be faithful to both the sacraments of Christ and also the sacraments of the Antichrist, the sacraments of the anti-Christian "sexual revolution," the very fashionable sacraments of pornography, fornication, divorce, contraception, abortion, same-sex "marriage," and transgenderism. We cannot do that any more than we can be faithful to two spouses. We cannot reconcile light and darkness.

Throughout Western civilization today, the civilization that used to be called Christian civilization or Christendom, for every convert who enters the Church, ten Catholics leave it. Ex-Catholics are the second largest religious group in America, next to Catholics. Soon they will be the largest. And the main reason is that they want to partake in those seven sacraments of the sexual revolution.

These are hard words to hear, but they have to be spoken and heard because they are true. We prefer not to hear hard words, only soft and comforting words. We prefer the Church of Cheap Grace to the Church of the Costly Cross. We prefer the Church of Comfortable Compromises to the Church of Christ Crucified. Everybody loves cheap grace. Everybody loves the Church that's defined as "Here comes everybody." But the Church of everybody and everything really means the Church of nobody and nothing. The Church that embraces everything and wants to be loved by everybody eventually becomes the Church that embraces nothing and is loved by nobody. The reason ten people leave the Church for every one who enters it is the same reason why no business succeeds when its advertisements say that their product is equal to every other one.

Peter did not expect everyone in his audience to smile and love him and agree. He expected to be murdered and martyred for what he said. And he was, eventually. So were all the other Apostles, except John. That courage, and that willingness to be hated by the world, changed the world and saved the world. Our cowardice is losing it.

But cowards and compromisers can become courageous witnesses, truth-tellers, and martyrs. Peter did exactly that. And so can every single one of us. Every person who is reading this, every person who has a comfortable butt to sit on, is called by God to become a saint and an apostle, a warrior of love and truth, which are our only two weapons in this great spiritual war of Christ versus Antichrist. At stake in this war is not just America or Western civilization, which are of real but relative value, but human persons, each of whom is eternal and immortal and of absolute value. St. Thomas Aquinas says that the first thing that love and charity to our neighbor demands of us is to lead them to the truth.

RESPONSORIAL PSALM
Psalm 118:1, 8–9, 21–23, 26, 28, 29 _____

R. (22) **The stone rejected by the builders has become the cornerstone.**
or: R. **Alleluia.**

Give thanks to the Lord, for he is good,
    for his mercy endures forever.
It is better to take refuge in the Lord
    than to trust in man.
It is better to take refuge in the Lord
    than to trust in princes.

I will give thanks to you, for you have answered me
    and have been my savior.
The stone which the builders rejected
    has become the cornerstone.
By the Lord has this been done;
    it is wonderful in our eyes.

Blessed is he who comes in the name of the Lord;
    we bless you from the house of the Lord.
I will give thanks to you, for you have answered me
    and have been my savior.
Give thanks to the Lord, for he is good;
    for his kindness endures forever.

Today's Psalm verse is a sample of the Psalm, skipping around in it like a flat stone skipping on the surface of water. This selection of separated verses from the Psalm has no obvious single focus and no surprises except for the verse that Peter quoted in our passage from Acts. The point of that verse was the supreme irony (almost, one might say, God's supreme joke) that "the stone which the builders rejected has become the cornerstone." What that meant was that the thing that seemed to be the devil's supreme triumph, the death of Christ, was in fact the devil's supreme defeat, for that death was not an accident but a plan, and not a loss but a gift, the gift of eternal life through the body and blood of God incarnate, for all who accept it, all who believe in him.

In Mel Gibson's movie *The Passion of the Christ*, a horrible groan is heard coming from the depths of the ground at the moment Christ dies. That's the voice of the devil, suddenly realizing that God had tricked him; that the devil's carefully planned triumph over Christ, through manipulating his agents Judas Iscariot and Pontius Pilate and King Herod and the Sanhedrin and the corrupt high priest and the cruel Romans—that this careful and elaborate plan of Satan's was really part of God's plan to save the world and to rescue sinners from the power of Satan. It is the greatest irony, the greatest paradox, the greatest joke in the history of the world. It is also the most serious and terrible. (We laugh the most deeply at the most deep and serious things: religion, sex, and politics—in other words, ourselves.)

"By the Lord has this been done; it is wonderful in our eyes." "Wonderful" means not just "good" or "very good" but "full of wonder and surprise." If we are ever tempted to be bored at God and to expect no great wonders and surprises, remember this verse.

Everything God does is wonderful, amazing, surprising, not obvious. He creates the universe out of nothing. He creates man in his own image. He does not abandon man after he falls through his own fault but tenderly and patiently educates him, through prophets and miracles. He teaches us not only the easy way but also the hard way, through our own sins and their inevitable consequences, that they never deliver the happiness they promise. He chooses as his chosen people one of the least likely peoples in the world. He becomes one of these people. And, to top it all off, he saves them precisely by not being saved from crucifixion. "He saved others; he cannot save himself," they jeered at him as he hung there dying (Matt. 27:42). They did not know how ironically true that was. That was precisely how he did save others; by not saving himself but giving himself up.

And now the surprising meaning of our lives is to be like him, to do the same kind of thing, to give our hearts away, to die to our natural egotism, and to discover by experience the surprising truth that that is the only path to life even in this world. Everything in this story is a surprise and a paradox.

God always surprises us. He is never predictable. He is always faithful to his promises, but the forms his faithfulness takes are always better than we expect. There is a Greek word *thaumazein*, which means "to wonder" or "to be amazed and astonished," which is used to describe the reactions everyone had to Jesus—both his friends and his enemies, both those who came to believe in him and worship him and those who came to hate and fear him, and also the agnostics who did not know which group to join but went away saying "never before has anyone spoken like this one" (John 7:46). Jesus is the only human being who ever lived who never bored anybody who ever met him.

That's why heaven will not be boring. Because heaven is relative to God, not God to heaven, and the most perfect and complete knowledge of God that we have is in Jesus Christ, the God-man. All our pictures of heaven, all our movies and stories about heaven, all our imaginations about heaven are boring, because heaven infinitely exceeds them and us. "What eye has not seen, and ear has not heard, and what has not entered the human heart, what God has prepared for those who love him" (1 Cor. 2:9). Throughout history, God has always surprised us. Our present lives are full of surprises from God. "If you want to give God a good laugh, tell him your plans." And our future in heaven will be even more full of divine surprises and unexpected joys, forever.

SECOND READING

1 JOHN 3:1–2 _____

Beloved: See what love the Father has bestowed on us that we may be called the children of God. Yet so we are. The reason the world does not know us is that it did not know him. Beloved, we are God's children now; what we shall be has not yet been revealed. We do know that when it is revealed we shall be like him, for we shall see him as he is.

Look at the first word St. John uses in today's epistle. He writes, "See what love the Father has bestowed on us!" Look! Look at that! Linger on that. Be amazed by that. Don't take it for granted. It's astonishing. God, the one true God, the eternal, immortal, omnipotent, omniscient, absolutely perfect God, who needs us as much as we need viruses, loved us so much that he sent his infinitely precious Son to die for us so that we could be saved, adopted into God's family forever, given a share in God's own eternal life, become his children, become something as different from what we are now, as much better than what we are now, as what we are now is better than a mangy, mud-matted mad dog with fleas and rabies.

He didn't just *call* us his children; he really made us his children: "See what love the Father has bestowed on us that we may be called the children of God. *Yet so we are!*" It's not a dream; it's not an abstraction; it's not an ideal; it's not a set of principles; it's not a lifestyle; it's a life, as real as the life of your body and mind, not something as abstract as an abstraction but something as concrete as concrete, though it's invisible.

But that life is hidden behind what is visible, what we can see in each other, as Christ's divinity was hidden behind his humanity and as both his divinity and his humanity are hidden behind the sensory appearances of the Eucharist. Only the eyes of faith see it. That's why, as John says, "the reason the world does not know us is that it did not know him."

That new life, that seed of divine life, is in us now, through our faith and Baptism. "Beloved, we are God's children now." But "what we shall be has not yet been revealed." If we saw our future selves in heaven in all their sinless glory and ecstatic joy, we would probably be tempted to bow down and worship them as gods and goddesses.

The myths and fairy tales are full of this theme of transformation into a higher form of life, probably based on observation of tadpoles turning into frogs and caterpillars into butterflies. These human myths and fairy tales come from the human heart and its innate longing for transformation into not just a better life but a higher *kind* of life: stories like Beauty and the Beast, or the beautiful princess kissing a frog and turning it into a prince, or Pinocchio changing from a wooden puppet to a real boy.

But God's truth is even stranger and more wonderful than our fictions. We cannot imagine what we will be in heaven. John tells us, "What we shall be has not yet been revealed. We do know that when it is revealed we shall be like him," like Jesus after the Resurrection; that we "shall be like him" and that "we shall see him as he is," that is, in all his glory. We shall see God face to face; we shall know the eternal source of all truth and goodness and beauty not as abstractions but as our own Father.

Christ came down to share our humanity so that he could bring us up to share his own divinity. We could not in our present sinful condition see God face to face and live. God changed that, because he gave us Jesus Christ as the human face of God. If we saw God face to face without Christ our Mediator, we would be consumed like fleas in a volcano.

The difference between any finite number and infinity is not a finite difference; it is an infinite difference. The gap between the infinite God and the finite creature is itself infinite. Jesus Christ is the bridge that bridges that gap. The gap is not only our finitude but also our sin. But Jesus is the "bridge over troubled waters" that overcomes even that separation, that divorce between us and God. In him alone we can do the thing John tells us to do in today's reading, to "*see* what love the Father has bestowed on us." Here is my fondest wish and dearest prayer for every one of you: when you are dying, may the last thing you see on earth be the face of God's love on a crucifix.

GOSPEL
JOHN 10:11–18 _____

Jesus said: "I am the good shepherd. A good shepherd lays down his life for the sheep. A hired man, who is not a shepherd and whose sheep are not his own, sees a wolf coming and leaves the sheep and runs away, and the wolf catches and scatters them. This is because he works for pay and has no concern for the sheep. I am the good shepherd, and I know mine and mine know me, just as the Father knows me and I know the Father; and I will lay down my life for the sheep. I have other sheep that do not belong to this fold. These also I must lead, and they will hear my voice, and there will be one flock, one shepherd. This is why the Father loves me, because I lay down my life in order to take it up again. No one takes it from me, but I lay it down on my own. I have power to lay it down, and power to take it up again. This command I have received from my Father."

_____

When Jesus teaches us, he uses many analogies, or images, or symbols, or figures of speech, because he knows that the most effective way for us to understand and remember invisible spiritual truths is by visible and physical images or likenesses of them. Concrete images stick in our imagination much better than abstract ideas stick in our intellect. Some of these are parables, which are stories. One definition of a parable is "an earthly story with a heavenly meaning." Some others are not parables or stories but just images, analogies, comparisons between visible natural realities and invisible supernatural realities. For instance, in today's Gospel Jesus uses the analogy of a shepherd. He calls himself a good shepherd.

It's an analogy, or a metaphor. Jesus is not literally a shepherd. He was literally a carpenter, an apprentice to his father Joseph; and then, later, a traveling rabbi and a miraculous healer. But his literal miracles and his nonliteral images and parables were both teaching devices. In the Gospels, the Greek word translated "miracle" is *semeion*, which means "sign." The miracles were signs that were meant to be looked-along rather than just looked-at. That's the whole purpose of a sign. When we see a road sign that has an arrow pointing left and on it the words "New York City, 25 miles," we do not say, "Oh, look at that: a big green piece of metal with an arrow and large white letters on it." We say instead, "New York City is twenty-five miles in that direction."

So, for instance, when Jesus heals a blind man, that is not just a literally real event, a healing of literal, physical blindness, but it is also a sign that the author of this healing of our physical blindness can also heal our spiritual blindness, our lack of faith and trust. Jesus' miracles are signs that point to his identity and his mission. When Jesus miraculously heals our physical diseases, that is a sign that he also has the power to heal our spiritual diseases.

The sign in today's Gospel is not a miracle or a parable but simply an image: Jesus is "the good shepherd." Jesus is telling us who he is and what his "job description" is by this image, this metaphor. It means at least seven things.

First, if "good" means "unselfish and altruistic rather than selfish and egotistic," a good shepherd is one whose first purpose is not to make money for himself but to care for the sheep. The hired shepherd works for money; the good shepherd works for the sheep.

The fact that these others are sheep rather than human beings is not the point. The point is not about literal shepherds and literal sheep; the point is not that a good shepherd would put the life of animals above the life of a human being in value. For human beings are created in the image of God and have immortal souls; animals do not. Nor is Jesus' point that we are like sheep, which are very stupid and stubborn animals. The point is not about the sheep but about the shepherd and his relationship to us: that he cares for us as a good shepherd cares for his sheep; and that our shepherd, our caretaker, is not just a human being but almighty God.

Second, he is *such* a good shepherd that he will do what no mere human shepherd would do: he will lay down his very life for us, his sheep, on the cross and feed us with it in the Eucharist. Because we are not his animals but his children, created in his image.

No one expects a mere man to give up his life for the life of mere animals. But the divine Son of God did something even more remarkable: the Creator gave up his life for us creatures. He is even more superior to us than we are to sheep; yet he died for us. He is not just a good shepherd but a super-good shepherd, a supernaturally good shepherd.

Third, he does not fear the wolves and run away, as the hired shepherds do, but stays and fights the wolves off to save the sheep. In Jesus' analogy, if we are the sheep, the wolves are our enemies. Who are our enemies? Scripture tells us: "For our struggle is not with flesh and blood but with the principalities, with the powers, with the world rulers of this present darkness" (Eph. 6:12). Our enemies are evil spirits and their temptations, and our own sins when we succumb to them. Jesus saves us, his sheep, from those wolves. They are quite real, and very powerful, and without our good shepherd's protection they would tear us apart.

Fourth, Jesus says that this good shepherd "knows" his sheep; in fact, he knows each one intimately and personally, by name: "The sheep hear his voice, as he calls his own sheep *by name* and leads them out" (John 10:3).

Notice also that he *leads* them rather than pushes them. A sheepdog pushes the sheep, threatens them, comes at them from behind to scare them into moving in the opposite direction. Some shepherds work like their dogs: they harry the sheep from behind. But the good shepherd leads them from ahead, because the good shepherd is loved and trusted by his sheep, so the sheep follow him wherever he goes. He leads by love, not fear.

Machiavelli famously said that "it is better to be feared than to be loved, because others will love you when *they* will, but they will fear you when *you* will." Fear works by force, while love works by freedom. Machiavelli's way is the way of Satan; Christ's way is the way of God. Machiavelli was right only about battlefields, not about anything else in life.

Fifth, Jesus adds the point that there are other sheep that do not belong to this sheepfold—that is, Israel, God's chosen people; and they, too, are his. They, too, will hear his voice and recognize it and follow him and be one with him and therefore, in their union with him, they will be one also with all the other sheep: "and there will be one flock, one shepherd." This will be perfectly true in heaven, where there will not be thirty thousand different Christian denominations; but it is true even in this life and this era because despite all the serious and sad divisions among the thirty thousand sheepfolds, there is only one Shepherd. What all Christians have in common is far greater than all the serious things that divide them: as St. Paul put it, "One Lord, one faith, one baptism; one God and Father of all" (Eph. 4:5–6).

Sixth, Jesus tells us how to understand his forthcoming Crucifixion and death when he says, "I lay down my life in order to take it up again. No one takes it from me, but I lay it down on my own. I have power to lay it down, and power to take it up again." Jesus' Passion was not *passive*; it was not an accident that "happened" to him but an act, a proactive act, a deliberate gift. It was his purpose in coming into the world. He was the only man who came into the world deliberately to die. He who had the power to resurrect after his death also had the power to escape death in the first place. But he died because he wanted to give us the gift of his life, his body and blood, for our salvation; the shepherd wanted to give himself to the sheep. That's what love does: it gives not just the many *things* the lover has or does but the lover himself. A well-programmed and powerful robot could give us many things, but only a person can give us himself because only a person has a self. That's what the essence of love is: the gift of one's self.

Finally, Jesus' ultimate motive for doing this was his love and obedience to his Father: "This is why the Father loves me, because I lay down my life. . . . This command I have received from my Father." Love and obedience go together. Some people obey God without loving him, obeying out of fear instead of love; but no one loves him without obeying him. As Jesus says, "If you love me, you will keep my commandments" (John 14:15).

And, he says, "This is my commandment: love one another" (John 15:12).

339

The commandment Jesus received from his Father, the commandment to give himself to us, is the same commandment that he gives to us: to give ourselves to our neighbors. We can love our neighbors without loving him, but we cannot love him without loving our neighbors. Our neighbors will not always lead us to him, but he will always lead us to them.

That love is the whole essence of everything in the Christian life. It is very simple to understand and very hard to live perfectly, even though the more we live it, the more joy we find even in this life. The saints are the happiest people in the world.

The most famous passage in the Bible about the good shepherd Jesus talks about in today's Gospel is of course the twenty-third Psalm, "The Lord is my shepherd," which is everybody's favorite. It was probably Jesus' favorite too. That's why he elaborated on it in today's Gospel.

I have a little piece of homework for you. When you get home from Mass, please pray the twenty-third Psalm sometime today, slowly and thoughtfully, in the presence of God. God wants to tell you something. The cell phone in your soul is ringing with a message from your Father. Listen to him. He has a gift for you: it is the secret of joy.

FIFTH SUNDAY OF EASTER

FIRST READING

ACTS 9:26–31 _____

When Saul arrived in Jerusalem he tried to join the disciples, but they were all afraid of him, not believing that he was a disciple. Then Barnabas took charge of him and brought him to the apostles, and he reported to them how he had seen the Lord, and that he had spoken to him, and how in Damascus he had spoken out boldly in the name of Jesus. He moved about freely with them in Jerusalem, and spoke out boldly in the name of the Lord. He also spoke and debated with the Hellenists, but they tried to kill him. And when the brothers learned of this, they took him down to Caesarea and sent him on his way to Tarsus.

The church throughout all Judea, Galilee, and Samaria was at peace. It was being built up and walked in the fear of the Lord, and with the consolation of the Holy Spirit it grew in numbers.

_____

Saul was like a racing car moving a hundred miles an hour in the wrong direction, and God did not slow him down but turned him around 180 degrees in a great spiritual U-turn. When God converts a passionate anti-Christian, he becomes a passionate Christian. Saul had passionately persecuted Christians, who he believed were blasphemous heretics for worshiping Jesus, and he even assisted at the stoning of St. Stephen, the first Christian martyr. Now, Saul is about to redirect his passion and become the greatest Christian missionary of all time and also a martyr himself, after God knocked him off his high horse on the road to Damascus by a voice from heaven that identified itself as "Jesus, whom you are persecuting" (Acts 9:5). Saul was doubly astonished at this: first, that the voice of God was the voice of Jesus, and secondly, that in persecuting Christians he was persecuting Jesus, for they were his Body. Saul thought he knew exactly who God was and exactly who Jesus was and exactly who these Christians were, and he was totally wrong on all three counts.

Once Saul became Paul and started preaching for Jesus instead of against him, he became the hunted one rather than one of the hunters. His enemies now tried to kill him. The war between Christ and Antichrist is real, and perpetual. Christians have been hated and feared and persecuted and killed in various parts of the world for two thousand years, and continue to be, wherever the faith is alive and strong and growing—in communist countries, in Islamic countries, and even, recently, in India.

But not here. Satan doesn't need to inspire violence against Christians in Europe or America because the faith is not growing here but rapidly diminishing. Soon there will be more practicing Muslims than practicing Christians in Western Europe, where ten times more Catholics leave the Church each year than enter it. Here, it's only six to one. But elsewhere in the world, the Church is growing, not in spite of its persecutions but because of them. There have been more martyrs in the past century than in all nineteen centuries before it.

When Luke, the author of the Acts of the Apostles, writes that there was peace for a while in the Church in Israel, he mentioned that because it was unusual. Of course, we should be thankful for peace wherever we have it, but we should not take it for granted. And we should not *seek* peace with the world, the flesh, and the devil, only with neighbors, self, and God. Whether the society we live in hates and fears us or whether it just tolerates us or whether it loves and respects us, in all three circumstances we are all called to be witnesses, evangelists, missionaries; to be distinctive and challenging to the world by our lives.

Politics is the art of compromise, indeed, but there is no compromise or neutrality in the spiritual war that St. Paul found himself in, which is the same war every Christian must fight, whether in great ways, like St. Paul, or in small ways, like most of us. Everything counts. When we pick up a piece of trash, that is part of the spiritual war, for we are called to do all things for him, not just big things. St. Teresa of Kolkata loved to say, "Do small things with great love." St.

Paul wrote, "Whether you eat or drink, or whatever you do, do everything for the glory of God" (1 Cor. 10:31). God is not a *part* of our lives because God is not a *part* of anything. God is the one ultimate origin and the one ultimate end of *all* of our lives and of everything in our lives. If that's not your God, then your God is too small.

RESPONSORIAL PSALM

PSALM 22:26–27, 28, 30, 31–32 _____

R. (26a) **I will praise you, Lord, in the assembly of your people.**
or: R. **Alleluia.**

I will fulfill my vows before those who fear the LORD.
    The lowly shall eat their fill;
they who seek the LORD shall praise him:
    "May your hearts live forever!"

All the ends of the earth
    shall remember and turn to the LORD;
all the families of the nations
    shall bow down before him.

To him alone shall bow down
    all who sleep in the earth;
before him shall bend
    all who go down into the dust.

And to him my soul shall live;
    my descendants shall serve him.
Let the coming generation be told of the LORD
    that they may proclaim to a people yet to be born

the justice he has shown.

The Psalmist says, "They who seek the LORD shall praise him." Why? Because all who seek him shall find him, and all who find him shall praise him; therefore, all who seek him shall praise him.

All who seek him shall find him because Christ clearly and deliberately promised us exactly that. Pascal said there are only three kinds of people. First, there are those who have sought God and have found him, and these people are both wise and happy: wise because they have sought God and happy because they have found him. Second, there are those who are seeking God with an honest and open heart but have not yet found him. These people are wise but not yet happy: wise because they are seeking God but not yet fully happy because they have not found him. The third kind of people are those who neither seek God nor find him; and these are both unwise and unhappy: unwise because they do not seek God and unhappy because they do not find him.

Notice that there is no such thing as a fourth class of people, those who do not seek God yet find him. God does not rebuff anyone who seeks him, but he does rebuff those who do not seek him. He does not force himself on us. He respects the power of free choice that he gave us in creating us.

So all who seek God will eventually find him: sometimes quickly, sometimes not; sometimes easily, sometimes not; sometimes clearly, sometimes not; sometimes before death, sometimes not.

And all who find God will praise him, because God is all-good and all-wise and all-loving and all-powerful and worthy of all praise. To know God is to know the source of joy, the reason for joy, the cause of our joy. To know him is to praise him. So if you don't praise him, you don't really know him.

So the links in this chain are unbreakable: if you seek him, you will find him, and if you find him, you will praise him; therefore, if you seek him, you will praise him.

All three of these things, seeking and finding and praising, are not mere feelings or emotions. Seeking is not a feeling: it's a choice. You choose to be honest and seek the truth—or you don't. And praise is also not a feeling, though feelings usually motivate it and accompany it. You don't need to feel praise of something in order to praise it. We all praise medicines and money and hard work and common sense without feeling sweet, passionate feelings like romantic love for these things. What we should seek and what we should praise is God, not our feelings about God. What we should have faith in is God: we should have faith in God, not faith in faith; trust in God, not trust in trust; joy in God, not joy in joy; praise of God, not praise of praise; celebration of God, not celebration of ourselves or of our own celebration.

God is who he is no matter what you feel or don't feel. He is not a figment of our feelings or of our faith or of our imagination. He is as real as a rock.

SECOND READING
1 JOHN 3:18–24 _____

Children, let us love not in word or speech but in deed and truth. Now this is how we shall know that we belong to the truth and reassure our hearts before him in whatever our hearts condemn, for God is greater than our hearts and knows everything. Beloved, if our hearts do not condemn us, we have confidence in God and receive from him whatever we ask, because we keep his commandments and do what pleases him. And his commandment is this: we should believe in the name of his Son, Jesus Christ, and love one another just as he commanded us. Those who keep his commandments remain in him, and he in them, and the way we know that he remains in us is from the Spirit he gave us.

We all know that love is the greatest thing in the world, but we don't all know what love is. Some think that love is a promise, a hope, an ideal, an idea, a concept, a word. St. John says, "Let us love not in word or speech but in deed and truth."

Love is a truth, a true thing, a real thing, as real as raspberries. Love and truth always go together, for two reasons: first, if love is not true love, it's not love at all; and second, if truth is not loved, it will never be known.

Our hearts and minds are fickle and fallible and foolish. We must judge our hearts—that is, our feelings and emotions and impressions and imaginations. They are not infallible. God is. So instead of judging God with our hearts, we must let God judge our hearts. He knows our hearts better than we do.

In today's epistle, St. John writes, "Now this is how we shall know that we belong to the truth and reassure our hearts before him in *whatever* our hearts condemn [a clearer translation, I think, was the older one: "*whenever* our hearts condemn *us*"], for God is greater than our hearts and knows everything."

There are two ways our hearts can deceive us. We can think or feel that we are far from God, displeasing to God, when we are actually close to him and pleasing to him. We can despair of our relationship to God. Our conscience can be too sensitive, too pessimistic. Or the opposite: we can be proud and arrogant and presumptuous, with a conscience that is too optimistic and not sensitive enough. In both cases, God knows us accurately even if we do not know ourselves accurately, and that's what matters most. Of course, what we think about God is important, but what God thinks about us is infinitely more important.

But how can we know where we stand with God? By his word, his revelation, by what his Son Jesus Christ told us and what the Church Christ established to teach in his name and with his authority tells us, and by what the Bible that was authored and canonized by that Church as God's Word tells us.

And there is also a second way, especially effective for those with a conscience that is either too easy or too hard, too optimistic or too pessimistic, too loose or too strict. It is our deeds, rather than our words or our thoughts or our feelings. Obviously, there is a little good in the worst of us and a little bad in the best of us, but if we are living in continued, deliberate obedience

346

to him and his will and his commandments, we are pleasing to him; and if we are living in continued, deliberate disobedience to his commandments, we are not. And his commandments are very clear. They are as easy to understand as they are hard to perfectly obey.

That's why we have the sacrament of Penance, or Confession: for those who are trying to live in obedience but who repeatedly fail. That's where most of us are. We examine our consciences honestly and we discover two things: that we do believe in God and in his commandments, and that our faith and obedience are very weak and imperfect. So St. John says to us, if our hearts condemn us, "God is greater than our hearts and knows everything." This is the God who assures us, with infallible divine authority, in the sacrament of Confession, that if we have sincerely repented of our sins, we are forgiven; we are accepted; we are clean; we are reconciled to God. If we believe that, a great burden of guilt is lifted from our hearts.

And even if we do not feel that burden of guilt lifted, we can be sure that it has been lifted. Guilt is not a feeling. Guilt is a fact, a fact about our relationship with God. And when God assures us that we are forgiven and reconciled to him, we can know that we are forgiven, no matter how we feel; and when God tells us that we are not reconciled to him, that we are living in sin and need to repent and turn around and come home to our heavenly Father, we can know that is also true, and we can freely choose to act on that knowledge.

There are three rungs of the ladder to God, three states our soul can be in: we can be in sin and not repentant; we can be in sin and repentant but not yet confessing and being forgiven; or we can confess and be forgiven. God invites all on the first rung to make a step up to the second rung, and all on the second rung to make a step up to the third. One of the things priests do for us in the sacrament of Confession is help us to honestly judge where we are on that ladder, to judge our own hearts and lives, and to act on that judgment. For actions are more important than either words or thoughts or feelings. "Actions speak louder than words." That's St. John's first principle in today's epistle: "Children, let us love not in word or speech but in deed and truth."

GOSPEL

Jesus said to his disciples: "I am the true vine, and my Father is the vine grower. He takes away every branch in me that does not bear fruit, and every one that does he prunes so that it bears more fruit. You are already pruned because of the word that I spoke to you. Remain in me, as I remain in you. Just as a branch cannot bear fruit on its own unless it remains on the vine, so neither can you unless you remain in me. I am the vine, you are the branches. Whoever remains in me and I in him will bear much fruit, because without me you can do nothing. Anyone who does not remain in me will be thrown out like a branch and wither; people will gather them and throw them into a fire and they will be burned. If you remain in me and my words remain in you, ask for whatever you want and it will be done for you. By this is my Father glorified, that you bear much fruit and become my disciples."

Three points: a preliminary point about the word "remain," the main point about us being branches and Christ the vine, and the practical conclusion that follows from this principle about there being two givers in every gift, Christ and Christians, who are his branches.

☙

First, a beautiful old word is lost in the new translation. Eight times, Jesus says, "Remain in me." But the word he uses, *meno*, means more than just "remain." "Remain" is negative. It means "don't go away." But the Greek word *meno* is positive. It means "live," as you live in a home. The old-fashioned English word for it is "abide," and that is how it was translated in the past. People don't use it much anymore, except in the South, and that's why the new translation doesn't use it. But we still understand it, so I think we should use it here because it's more accurate and richer than "remain."

When a branch is broken off a vine or a bush or a tree, it does not "remain" in the place it used to be in. But more importantly, it no longer gets sap, and thus life, from the tree. It dies. It loses its life. That's the richer and more positive meaning Jesus is making here with this analogy of the vine and the branches. The very same life flows through the vine and all the branches, and that is the supernatural life, the eternal life, the divine life, of Christ. We get that life through faith and Baptism. It is the most precious thing in the world. It is the only thing in the world that is stronger than death.

The life is the life of love, *agape* love, unselfish love, genuine love; for "God is love." To live in God is to live in love. It is much more than a feeling. It is a reality, like the sap in a tree or the blood in a body or the life in a vine and its branches.

※

The main point of Jesus' sermon about the vine and the branches is absolutely astonishing. We are not just his admirers, his students, his disciples. We are not just his workers, his employees, his laborers. We are not just his people, his associates, his friends. We are his organs, his feet and hands, his body parts! That hairy ball between your shoulders and your body make up one natural organism, head and body. Christ the Head and we his Body make up one supernatural organism, one complete Christ.

Notice that Jesus does not say, "I am the stem, you are the branches." Although the branches are dependent on the stem, they are not part of the stem. But the branches and the stem are both parts of the vine, the whole vine. The point is that we are not just *dependent on* him: we are *parts of* him, "members," St. Paul says: members of his Body, not members of his club but organs in his Body. The Church is an organism, not an organization. It is the whole Christ, Head and Body (see 1 Cor. 12:12–13; Eph. 4:15–16). The same point is made by the image of the head and the body as is made by the image of the vine and the branches. The head is not the CEO or the boss of the body but the head of the body, the chief organ, a part of the whole, as the husband is the "head" of the wife, not the boss. They are no longer two but one flesh, one body. Similarly, we are "in-corporated" into Christ. The word *corpus*, meaning "body," is the center of the word "incorporated." We are put into Christ's Body, not just into an external relationship with him. We are married to him, and just as husband and wife become "one flesh," one body, we become one spirit, one mystical person, with Christ.

That is the highest and profoundest reason why we are holy and why we must respect each other: because, as he himself said to us, "Whatever you did for one of these least brothers of mine, you did for me" (Matt. 25:40). When you kiss or slap my face, you don't just kiss or slap my *face*: you kiss or slap *me*. When you shoot a bullet into my torso or when you hug my torso, you shoot *me* or hug *me*. And when we love or hate any part of Christ's Body—we love or hate Christ. We don't just love or hate Tom or Dick or Harry or Mary or Martha or Maud—we do it to Jesus Christ. What we do to his members, his body parts, we do to him.

Complain all you want to about "organized religion." The Church of Christ is not "organized religion" for two reasons. One is because it's more like disorganized religion than organized religion. It's more like a Noah's ark, a zoo full of quarreling and pooping animals than it is like a perfect, clean, "gated community." The second reason the Church is not "organized religion" is because it's not a merely human organization; it's a supernatural organism. It has two natures, like Christ. It looks like a merely human organization, like a club or a state or a business; but that's its disguise. Christ wears many disguises. He hides both his divine nature and his human nature behind the appearances of bread and wine in the Eucharist. He is very tricky and very clever and much, much more than he seems to be.

Whatever the vine does, the branches also do. The branches live by the same life as the vine. Without the vine, the branches can do nothing. Break a branch off the vine and it dies. Thus, Christ says, "Without me you can do nothing."

⇛

The practical consequence of that changes everything. When a Christian does any good work, there are always two workers, two actors, one human and one divine. That's the main way God shows his love for us: by the love of other people to us.

When we say grace before meals, we thank both God the Creator *and* all the human intermediaries he uses to give us our food: the farmers, the truckers, the food business people, and the cooks. Similarly, when anyone gives us a gift, whether it's a present or a sacrifice or just a kind word, we should thank both them *and* the Christ whose Body they are.

SIXTH SUNDAY OF EASTER

FIRST READING
ACTS 10:25–26, 34–35, 44–48 _____

When Peter entered, Cornelius met him and, falling at his feet, paid him homage. Peter, however, raised him up, saying, "Get up. I myself am also a human being."

Then Peter proceeded to speak and said, "In truth, I see that God shows no partiality. Rather, in every nation whoever fears him and acts uprightly is acceptable to him."

While Peter was still speaking these things, the Holy Spirit fell upon all who were listening to the word. The circumcised believers who had accompanied Peter were astounded that the gift of the Holy Spirit should have been poured out on the Gentiles also, for they could hear them speaking in tongues and glorifying God. Then Peter responded, "Can anyone withhold the water for baptizing these people, who have received the Holy Spirit even as we have?" He ordered them to be baptized in the name of Jesus Christ.

We need some essential historical background to understand today's reading from Acts. Jews were forbidden to enter the houses of pagans—Romans and other Gentiles—because they were worshipers of false gods and idols. The early Christians were almost all Jews who had accepted Jesus as the Messiah, but they were not yet clear that this new revelation of the true God was for the whole world and that the confinement of the revelation of the true God to the Jews as God's chosen people was only temporary; that the Jews were chosen not just for themselves but to be God's collective prophet to the whole world. God had revealed this to Peter in a vision of an enormous sheet held at its four corners by the hand of heaven and let down to earth, full of clean and unclean

352

animals together. Then, immediately afterward, God brought messengers from the Roman soldier Cornelius to Peter to ask Peter to come to his house to teach him about Jesus. The fact that Peter overstepped the Jewish law to enter a pagan house surprised everyone; and they were even more surprised when they saw the Holy Spirit descend on the pagans as well as the Jewish Christians who were in Cornelius' house with Peter, in another little Pentecost, complete with the charismatic gift of tongues.

The point that so shocked Peter's audience of both Jews and Gentiles— namely that a new era had begun, in which God's unique revelation to his chosen people the Jews had accomplished its highest purpose in Christ and was now about to be given to the whole world—this point does not shock *us* at all, as it shocked *them*. In fact, it seems obvious to us that the God who created all mankind in his image had from the beginning a love and providential care for all of his children, not just some; that, as Peter put it, "God shows no partiality."

What surprises us is that this revelation was so long in coming. That is what needs explanation in our mind. Why didn't God reveal himself to the whole world in Old Testament times as well as in New Testament times? Why did he confine himself to the Jews for the two thousand years between Abraham and Christ?

At least a good part of the answer is that that was not a change of plans on God's part, but part of God's wise, providential plan from the beginning. God does not change; we do. We are like the ball of a pendulum that swings from a hinge that is fixed and changeless, like God. The arm of the pendulum is religion, which means literally "a binding relationship"—the relationship between the unchanging God and changing mankind. In order for the unchanging God to relate to changing mankind, the relationship itself has to change.

In earlier, more primitive times, the truth and goodness of God had to be taught in a very concrete and particular way, like planting a seed in one particular tiny hole in the ground, so that later it could spread and grow over the whole area. From the beginning, God loved all mankind universally, but universal truths, for us, can be learned only through particular realities. Thus, the Incarnation of God as this particular man Jesus was universal, not just for Jews, or for males, or for adults, or for Middle Eastern peoples, but for all. But for the sake of all people everywhere, God had to start with some people somewhere.

Christianity is still as concrete and particular as Judaism even while it is also as universal as universalism. Christ is this one concrete, particular person, not merely a symbol for all persons. Yet he came for all.

The Jews of Peter's day were reluctant to embrace the universality of Christ because they knew so very well the particularity of God: that God was distinctive and unique and unlike all the other gods of all the other peoples of the world. We today are in the opposite position: we are so strong on the universal, on human equality, and on God showing no partiality that we downplay the particular. In fact, scholars often use the term "the scandal of particularity" for both Judaism and Christianity. It seems a scandal because in pre-Christian times, one people alone knew the true God: Jews, not Gentiles; and during Jesus' lifetime, one man alone was the Messiah, the Savior, and the incarnate Son of God: Jesus, not Buddha or Socrates or Confucius or anyone else. And after Jesus' Ascension, there is only one concrete, particular, visible Church that was established by this concrete, particular, visible Savior and given the authority to teach in his name. That is our "scandal of particularity." But this very particular truth of Christianity that is *from* this one particular source is *for*, universally, all persons.

We, too, must be both particular and also universal. We must be both discriminating and nondiscriminating. We must judge and discriminate between ideas but not between persons. All persons are equal in value, but not all ideas are.

In the past, many of our ancestors made the mistake of being just as discriminating to people as they were to ideas, hating heretics as well as hating heresies. We often make the opposite mistake of loving heresies as well as loving heretics, loving all ideas as well as all people. Our ancestors tended to judge and reject Protestants as well as Protestantism, atheists as well as atheism. They all too often hated sinners because they hated sins, but we all too often love sins because we love sinners. The very concept of sin, and certainly the concept of heresy, has become unpopular and "judgmental."

But God is wiser than both of these human errors. We tend to see always just half the truth while God sees all of it, both sides of it, when it is paradoxical, as it often is.

So what do you think: do we need to learn from God how to be religiously correct, or does he have to learn from us how to be politically correct?

We cannot neglect either truth or love, either the objective or the subjective, either the impersonal or the personal, either the sin or the sinner, the heresy or the heretic, the subject or the student. Good teachers must love both their subjects and their students, both objective truth and subjective persons. That's how Christianity conquered the world, by a total and uncompromising devotion to both truth and love, because God is truth and God is love. And that's the only way we can do it again.

RESPONSORIAL PSALM

PSALM 98:1, 2–3, 3–4 _____

R. (cf. 2b) **The Lord has revealed to the nations his saving power.**
or: R. **Alleluia.**

Sing to the LORD a new song,
    for he has done wondrous deeds;
His right hand has won victory for him,
    his holy arm.

The LORD has made his salvation known:
    in the sight of the nations he has revealed his justice.
He has remembered his kindness and his faithfulness
    toward the house of Israel.

All the ends of the earth have seen
   the salvation by our God.
Sing joyfully to the LORD, all you lands;
   break into song; sing praise.

The Psalmist writes: "Sing to the LORD a new song, for he has done wondrous deeds." What God has done is indeed wondrous. He created the entire universe out of nothing. He created mankind in his own image, with reason and free will. He performed many mighty miracles for us and sent prophets to us. Above all, he sent his own divine Son to us to become a man without ceasing to be God, to live a perfect life and die a perfect death to save us from our own sins, and to conquer death and resurrect and ascend to heaven and to come again in the future to establish a new creation of unimaginable beauty and goodness and joy. This is not just a series of great *truths*: it is a series of great *deeds*, great events; it is good *news*—in fact, the best news ever, the greatest deeds ever done, the greatest story ever told.

So how do we react to these deeds?

The answer to that question tells us nothing about the deeds, but everything about ourselves. If we react to a war or a pandemic with joy, or if we react to the end of a war or a pandemic with sorrow, we are morally insane. But no matter how we change, the truth does not change; when we become morally insane, the wars and diseases do not become less evil, and the peace and healing do not become less good. If we react to bad news with the same flat-line reaction as we react to good news, we are spiritually dead. If we react to our little molehills of good news with more passion than we react to the Gospel's massive mountains of good news, if we care more about our favorite sports team winning a championship than we care about God saving us from hell and giving us a living ticket to heaven, what does that prove? It proves that we are sinful and selfish but stunningly stupid, spectacularly shallow, supernaturally silly.

A great saint like King David the Psalmist is not stupid, shallow, or silly. So how does he react to the incredible good news that the all-powerful, all-wise, all-holy God of the whole universe loves him and cares for him and does the most remarkable series of deeds for him?

He sings. And he calls on us to sing too.

God's Word does not invite us to perform, only to sing. It does not tell us "Sing perfectly," or "Sing operatically," or even "Sing on key," but simply "Sing!" It invites us to "make a joyful noise unto the LORD" (Ps. 100:1 KJV). If you have a mouth, you can do that. God gave you a mouth not only to eat and not only to speak but also to sing.

If you're embarrassed at the sound of your own voice, that's no excuse, because more than half the people who go to church feel the same way you do. God can listen to his angels anytime he wants to, and they can sing better than any of us can, so he does not need our musical perfection; but there is one thing he does dearly want, and it is the one thing he cannot give to himself or do all by himself: he wants the freely chosen love of our hearts. Singing is an expression of that love.

Why don't Catholics sing? Is it because many of our new hymns are embarrassingly stupid and sappy? Sometimes, yes. Is it because so many of our ancestors were Irish, who, when the English owned Ireland and persecuted Catholics, were often killed when they were heard singing Catholic hymns? Perhaps that is part of the tradition of keeping quiet. Or is it because many of our ancestors were Italian, who were used to listening to great opera singers perform their church music instead of singing themselves? Perhaps. Perhaps there are these reasons, these excuses. But perhaps the real reason is that we just don't appreciate and don't really value the greatest thing in the world: God and God's incredible deeds of goodness and grace and glory for us. Perhaps it has all become so familiar that we just take it for granted. If so, that must be remedied. The remedy is simple: sing, for God's sake. I am not taking God's name in vain; I mean it literally: sing *for God's sake*, not for your own sake or your neighbor's sake but for God's sake. Doesn't God deserve more cheers than your favorite sports team?

Or perhaps the reason we don't sing—and this is a darker suspicion still—perhaps it's because we really don't believe what we're supposed to be singing. Perhaps we think we come to church as we come to a movie theater: to be entertained by a religious movie, a pleasant fiction, a few moments of escape from real life, rather than the heart and center of real life.

Or perhaps, worst of all, by our silence we are saying to God the famous line Rhett Butler says to Scarlett O'Hara in the classic movie *Gone With the Wind*: "Frankly, my dear, I don't give a damn."

I don't know your reasons. Examine your own hearts and consciences. Pray about it.

If you want to see what obeying David's command to "make a joyful noise unto the Lord" sounds like, if you want some encouragement and example, visit a Pentecostal church sometime. Or visit a contemplative monastery, for instance, the Carmelites or the Benedictines, and listen to them chant. It's the same faith and love and passion, in a very different style. God does not care about the style; he cares about the love. God speaks to us both in thunder and in whispers, and we can speak to him in both ways too. Singing is a form of praying. St. Augustine said, "He who sings, prays twice." Do you have trouble praying, trouble concentrating? Hymns help, if you sing them as prayers, if you sing them into the ears of God, not into the ears of the rest of the congregation. After all, we come together to celebrate God, not to celebrate ourselves.

SECOND READING

1 JOHN 4:7–10 _____

Beloved, let us love one another, because love is of God; everyone who loves is begotten by God and knows God. Whoever is without love does not know God, for God is love. In this way the love of God was revealed to us: God sent his only Son into the world so that we might have life through him. In this is love: not that we have loved God, but that he loved us and sent his Son as expiation for our sins.

Today's reading from St. John's first letter is a short but packed summary of the essentials of Christianity. It connects what we might call vertical love and horizontal love together, like the two bars of the cross, and at the very center of it stands Christ. Christ stands at the very center of everything, even the Trinity.

We fallen fools have the most unfortunate tendency to separate and even to contrast those two dimensions of our faith, the vertical and the horizontal, the divine and the human, the supernatural and the natural, and the two great commandments, which command the two greatest things in the world, the love of God and the love of neighbor, the vertical and the horizontal bars of the cross. Some so-called progressive or liberal Christians ignore or downplay or even deny the vertical, supernatural dimension of their faith (and that is not really "progressive" at all but regressive); and some so-called conservative or traditional Christians tend to ignore or downplay or even deny the horizontal, natural, human and social dimension of their faith (and that is not really traditional at all but contrary to the tradition). But it's one and the same faith and one and the same Christ, who is both fully divine and fully human and who demands the love of both God and man, both theological love and social love.

Two *dimensions* of a thing are not two *things*. We can distinguish the height and width of any shape as its two dimensions, but neither can exist without the other. We can distinguish the words and the meaning of a book, or the sounds and the beauty of a piece of music, but neither can exist without the other.

For us to *distinguish* two different dimensions of a single thing in our mind is good, and necessary; but that is very different from *separating* them into two different things. To separate your body and your soul in your mind is to think of your body as a machine or an animal and your soul as a ghost or an angel. To separate them in reality is what killing means. To separate the words and meaning of a book in your mind, and to think of them as two independently existing *things*, is a mistake. We can have meanings without words, but we cannot have words without meaning. Christ's divine nature and his human nature are not two things, two entities, two realities, or two persons, but the two natures of one and the same reality, one and the same person. The same is true of our body and our soul. A human body without a human soul is not a human being; it is a corpse. A human soul without a body is not a human being; it is a spirit, a ghost. For us to not just *distinguish* but to *separate* body and soul in our thinking is to create the artificial problem of "the ghost in the machine," the problem of how the ghost, the spirit, that lives in the machine, the body, can push the buttons of the machine if it has no physical fingers. Our bodies are not haunted houses. They are sacramental.

Separating body and soul in reality is even worse than separating them in thought. It is the definition of murder. The same is true of our faith: we kill it if we separate the vertical and the horizontal dimensions, the divine and the human. We know nothing of a Christ who is merely divine or merely human, or of a faith that is merely supernatural or merely natural.

❧

The essence of both dimensions of our faith is love, or charity.

The very essence of the theological or supernatural dimension is love. Scripture says that God is just, but not that God is justice itself, that his essence is justice. Scripture says that God is all-knowing, but not that God is knowledge itself. But it does say that God *is* love. Justice is necessary, and knowledge is necessary, but love is the source of both because if we do not love justice, we will not do it, and if we do not love the truth, we will not find it.

The essence of the social, human, horizontal dimension of our faith is also love. Social justice is very important indeed, but it is not the essence of the horizontal bar, much less of the whole of Christianity; social love and friendship is. Both the great pagan philosopher Aristotle and the great Christian theologian Augustine said that it is friendship that holds together a community more truly and securely than justice does. You can see this in history. Look at the situation in the Holy Land today. Both Israelis and Palestinians rightfully complain about injustice and demand justice, and the result is that there is a constant tension and threat of violence. Friendship transcends justice because justice does not forgive, but friendship does. For friendship is a form of love. When lovers start demanding justice from each other, they are starting to be no longer lovers, and when friends start demanding justice, they are starting to be no longer friends.

Neither of these two dimensions of love, neither bar of the cross, the vertical or the horizontal, can exist without the other. The vertical cannot exist without the horizontal because, as St. John writes, "If anyone says, 'I love God,' but hates his brother, he is a liar" (1 John 4:20). And on the other hand, the horizontal cannot exist without the vertical because, as St. John also says, "Everyone who loves is begotten by God," which means that authentic love of neighbor always comes from God's inspiration even when it is done by an unbeliever. Even when God remains anonymous, God remains God. The two dimensions are necessarily connected, because the vertical dimension, the divine dimension, is always the cause and source of the horizontal one, the human one.

❧

Nearly everyone knows that love is the most important thing in the world; that in the last analysis, love is the meaning of life. The last words every dying person wants to say and to hear are the words "I love you." But what is love? What is true love? What does John mean, what does Scripture mean, what does God mean, by the word "love"?

There is nothing our culture is more confused about than the meaning of love. And there is no confusion that is more important and more harmful than confusion about love, because love is the greatest thing in the world, the highest value in life; in fact, the very essential nature of God. "God is love." But what kind of love?

There are four words for "love" in Greek: *eros, storge, philia,* and *agape.*

Eros means "desire." Our sex-obsessed society reduces that to sexual desire, but the word means more than that: it includes desire for food, drink, beauty, pleasure, power, health, wealth, victory—whatever appears desirable to us, whether it really is or not, whether it is morally good, evil, or neutral.

Storge means "liking" or "spontaneous, natural affection," the kind of love we have for familiar and comfortable things: our own home and family and even clothes and food and furniture. We have *storge* for kittens and puppies and babies but not for scorpions and sharks and lawyers.

Philia means "friendship." It's the highest merely human kind of love: respect and goodwill toward another person and delight in their company.

Finally, *agape* in most Greek literature before Christianity means simply "some kind of love." It was a generic term without any sharp, specific meaning or concrete content. The ancient Greeks loved clarity and loved to define and distinguish concepts, so the vague, generic word *agape* was not used much in pre-Christian Greek. But the writers of the New Testament gave this word a new, specific, concrete meaning when they used it to describe the love of God that was revealed in Christ. It means self-forgetful love, self-giving love, the gift of your very self to another person, the will to the best good of the other, even if it means self-sacrifice, and even to the point of martyrdom if necessary.

Agape is the word for "love" that John uses when he writes that "God is love" and "Love is of God" and "Whoever loves is begotten by God." That's not true of the three natural loves, only of *agape*, because the origin of this love is supernatural: it is in God; in fact, it is God's very nature.

Agape begins in eternity, in the eternal nature of God. The three divine persons of the Trinity eternally love each other and freely and totally give themselves to each other. "God is love" means that God is that whole reciprocating family of total and perfect and eternal self-giving. And when God created us in his own image, he created us as capable of that love. That's why he gave us the two powers animals do not have: reason, or understanding, and free will; that is, the power to know and understand the truth and the power to will and choose the good.

When Jesus came into the world, he revealed that *agape* love. He incarnated it. He was love incarnate, *agape* incarnate. Christians did not begin with the abstract idea or ideal of *agape* and then see Jesus and judge him as the perfect example of it. It was the other way around. They first met Jesus, they met *agape* in person, concretely, and only then did they develop the concept of it, the idea of it, the ideal of it. They learned it from their experience of it in Jesus, most completely in his martyrdom, his Crucifixion, his giving us his very life, his literal body and blood, for our salvation. Thus, John wrote, in John 3:16, the most famous verse in the Bible, "God *so* loved the world that he gave his only Son, so that everyone who believes in him might not perish but might have eternal life."

How do we know that "God is love"? That's an extremely important question. And the answer is: Not by our clever philosophizing or theologizing; not by our own thinking. It's not a theory, it's a fact. The fact has a name. His name is Jesus. We know this fact because we know the person who *is* that fact. We don't learn the fact from the idea; we learned the idea from the fact. The fact is Jesus.

℘

John says that "God is love," but he does *not* say that "Love is God." The difference is not some clever trick of language; the difference is terribly important. "Love is God" is our most popular heresy; "God is love" is our profoundest wisdom.

To understand this, we have to understand a very basic principle of language. A sentence is in one way like a mathematical equation in that it has two parts, a subject and a predicate. But a sentence is not a mathematical equation because it's not reversible. "Two plus two is four" is reversible. "Two plus two is four" and "four is two plus two" mean exactly the same thing. But "A cloud is white" does not mean the same as "White is a cloud." White is not a cloud; it's a color. "Is" does not mean "equals" in an ordinary sentence, only in a mathematical equation.

An ordinary sentence has a subject and a predicate. The subject is what you're talking about; the predicate is what you say about it. The subject is your title; the predicate is your speech. The subject is something you and the other person already understand, and the predicate is something new that you want to tell the other person about the subject. So when I say, "Clouds are made of water vapor," I assume you already know what clouds are, and I tell you something else, something new, something you may not have known before: that they're made of water vapor.

So when we say, "God is love," we're saying that the God we already know, the God who created the world, the God who revealed himself in the Bible, is love; is made of love, so to speak; is eternal and essential love. That's new and startling information. Many people just can't believe that. The God who is perfect and has no needs and does not need to love anyone or anything is pure self-giving love. He doesn't *have* to love us, yet he does. He startles us, he amazes us, by what he does in loving us so much that he sacrifices himself for our salvation. So to say that "God is love" is to say that if we *really* knew the true God that we think we know, we'd know that God is love.

That's why John says, "Whoever is without love [*agape*] does not know God." If you know everything else about God but not *agape*, if you know God is perfect and eternal and all-powerful and all-wise and all-just and all-holy but do not know that he is *agape*, if you do not know *agape*, then you do not know the true God. Because that's who God is; that's his very essence; that's the heart of his personality. God is not just someone who happens to have some *agape* now and then; God *is agape*, totally and perfectly and eternally.

Okay, so that's what we mean when we say, "God is love." But when we say, "Love is God," we mean something very different from that. We mean that the love we already know, which is presumably human love, natural love, either *eros* or *storge* or *philia*, either erotic love or affection love or friendship love—that this love we already know is really God, is the highest thing, the greatest reality. Look no further; this is God. Worship it. That's all there is; there is nothing more, nothing greater. In other words, when we say, "Love is God," we are making an idol, a false God, of ordinary human love.

Our favorite idol is usually some form of merely human love. Human love is the second greatest thing in the world, but it's not God. We idolize great things, not little things. No one worships paper clips or grains of sand or worms. But we do worship theological orthodoxy, social justice, freedom, peace, moral purity, mystical experience, romantic love, or religion itself, all of which are very good things—but they are not God himself. We make idols of second things, things that are great but not the very greatest. The three human loves are great things, but *agape* is greater.

The distinction between "God is love" and "love is God" may sound like a clever scholarly lesson in linguistics or philosophy, but it's the difference between profound truth and profound error. Look at what the Bible is saying. Read it carefully. John does not say "love *is* God" but "love is *of* God." Love is to God what light is to the sun. The sun is made of light, and light comes from the sun, but you can't reduce the sun to light; the sun is not just light: it's the source of light. You can't reduce a singer to a song, or a sinner to a sin.

So even if we use the word *agape* instead of *eros* or *storge* or *philia* and say, "*Agape* is God," we are not saying what is true because we are saying that this abstract ideal, this value, this virtue, is the thing that we are to adore and worship, not God as a person. That's like loving your spouse's good qualities and virtues instead of loving your spouse, or loving your parents' career instead of loving your parents, or loving your children's intelligence and potentialities instead of loving your children.

Alas, that's what too many of us do. We worship a value instead of a person. We worship what God stands for instead of God. But you can't pray to a value. You can't be saved by a value. You can love a value, but a value can't love you. Values don't act; persons do.

So it's true that God is love, but it's not true that love is God.

✑

John says that if we live in *agape* love, this means we have been "begotten" of God, born of God, "born again," to use Jesus' term, born by water and the Spirit, not just by the flesh; that is, we get a new nature, a new *life*, not just a new life*style* but a new *reality*, a share in God's own supernatural life, a life that is stronger than death, a life that can endure the light of heaven. We received this life by Baptism from the Holy Spirit. We became God's children—in fact, not just by a legal fiction. We became branches of Christ the vine. The same divine life that Christ has eternally by nature, we got in time by God's grace and our free choice to believe and receive it.

☙

The first initiative is always God's. Our job is to respond to him. He proposes spiritual marriage to us, and we accept or reject his proposal. The roles cannot be reversed. In human society, roles can be reversed; for instance, a woman could propose marriage to a man rather than the traditional role where the man proposes to the woman. Whether that role reversal *should* happen or not is not the point; the point is that it *could* happen. But the roles cannot be reversed with God. God is Romeo; we are Juliet. We do not invite him to elope with us; he invites us to elope with him. To use a natural biological analogy, in the spiritual marriage, God is always "he" because he makes our souls pregnant with his divine life; we do not do that to him. He is our Father. He created us in his image; we did not create him in our image. That's atheism.

☙

Our response is free, our choice is free, our faith is free, our acceptance of that new birth is free—unlike our first, natural birth, where we had no say in the matter. But even though our response is free, God's grace always comes first. He moves us to move toward him. He seeks us long before we had even a thought of seeking him. Even our motivation to seek God, even the first prompting of our conscience to repent and accept God's forgiveness, is inspired by the Holy Spirit. Even our faith, our response to God's gift of himself, is itself a gift of God.

But it is also free, because God's grace does not take away our freedom. It created our free will in the first place, and it perfects our free will. God uses our free will, not his force, to save us. That's why our good works, our works of love, our free choices to love, are a necessary part of our salvation in addition to our faith. Thus, John does not say merely that "whoever remains in faith remains in God" but "whoever remains in *love* remains in God" (1 John 4:16). Faith is the root, but love is the fruit.

GOSPEL
JOHN 15:9–17 _____

Jesus said to his disciples: "As the Father loves me, so I also love you. Remain in my love. If you keep my commandments, you will remain in my love, just as I have kept my Father's commandments and remain in his love.

"I have told you this so that my joy may be in you and your joy might be complete. This is my commandment: love one another as I love you. No one has greater love than this, to lay down one's life for one's friends. You are my friends if you do what I command you. I no longer call you slaves, because a slave does not know what his master is doing. I have called you friends, because I have told you everything I have heard from my Father. It was not you who chose me, but I who chose you and appointed you to go and bear fruit that will remain, so that whatever you ask the Father in my name he may give you. This I command you: love one another."

In the nine short verses in today's Gospel, we find Jesus using the word "commandment" five times and the word "love" nine times, the word *agape*, which means not just any kind of love but his kind, God's kind, self-giving love, the total gift of the self to another.

Our spontaneous reactions to those two words, "commandment" and "love," are very different, and therefore we are surprised at Jesus' juxtaposition of the two of them together. Our reaction to the word "love" is very positive, and our spontaneous reaction to the word "commandment" or "command" is somewhat negative, or at least suspicious. We feel happy when we think of love, and we feel unhappy when we think of commandments. We think of love as free and commandments as constrained. We think of love as joyful and commandments as joyless. We think of love as delicious food and commandments as bitter medicine. We think of love as something that expands us and commandments as something that contracts us and limits us. We think of love as expressing our will and commandments as thwarting our will.

That's how *we* think about these two things, but clearly that is not how Jesus thinks about these two things.

So if Jesus connects these two concepts so very closely while we separate and contrast them, we are not really in line with his mind. So who do you think should teach and who should learn? Shall we give Jesus lessons in love, or should he give us those lessons?

Okay then, let's try to listen to his teaching. Let's open our baby mouths so that we can eat the good food that Mother Church gives us, the mother that Jesus gave us. The analogy with baby and mommy is weak not because we are closer to the mind of Christ than a baby is to the mind of its mother but because we are farther away from it. Mommy's mind is as far above baby's mind as an eagle is above a worm, but Christ's mind is as far above our mind as the sun is above an eagle.

Jesus is telling us something about love, and we love that because we all love love. But what is love?

It's the first and greatest commandment: to love God with all our heart, all our soul, all our mind, and all our strength, and our neighbor as ourselves. But what is it to love?

There are four words for "love" in New Testament Greek: *agape*, which means the gift of yourself to another; *philia*, which means friendship, the respect and admiration between two people; *eros*, which means "desire," especially "passionate desire" and "romantic desire"; and *storge*, which means "spontaneous, natural affection."

Jesus uses both *agape* and *philia* here, both self-giving and "friends," but not *eros* or *storge*. So the love he's talking about, which is the love between us and him and which he says also exists between him and his Father, is not *eros*, not erotic love, not romantic love, not a passionate desire. Nor is it *storge*, which is a spontaneous natural affection for familiar old things that make us comfortable, like old furniture, informal clothing, or puppies. It's *agape* and *philia*. *Agape* is self-giving and *philia* is friendship.

The love God has for us is *agape* or self-giving love, because God gives himself wholly to us, first of all in creating us, because that was wholly for our benefit, not his. And also in suffering and dying for us, which was also wholly for our benefit, not his.

And since we are created in God's image, our love must image his love. There is no other source of the essential nature of our love than the essential nature of its Creator. As inventions come from an inventor, and as art comes from an artist, love comes from God, the lover, the first lover.

God's love for us is also *philia*, or friendship, because God, incredibly, wanted to be friends with us. Friends share things in common, so God shared all of our humanity so that we could share a finite but real part of his divinity, his divine life. Obviously, we finite creatures can share his infinite divinity only in a very finite and limited and partial way, while he can share our humanity totally and completely, but both are real sharings. It's astonishing that God wants to be friends with us, that God really enjoys our company. It's like a human being enjoying the company of an insect and making friends with it.

That's the love Jesus is talking about: *agape* and *philia*, self-giving and friendship. But does Jesus identify this love with obedience to his commandments?

We can see the answer to that question when we ask another question about love: What is the concrete proof of love? What is the true test of love?

How do we identify it? What is its essential expression? The answer is obedience to the will of the beloved. "Your will be done" is both the essential word of love and the essential word of obedience.

So to love God is to obey his will, which is expressed in his commandments. Jesus says, "If you love me, you will keep my commandments" (John 14:15).

Jesus' commandments are God's commandments because Jesus is God the Son. So to love Jesus is to love God, and to obey Jesus' commandments is to obey God's commandments.

And what is Jesus' commandment? It is to love one another.

So the definition of loving God is obeying him, and the definition of obeying him is loving him (and loving each other).

So Jesus defines love as obedience, and obedience as love. The two are not only not in contrast to each other, they *are* each other. To love is to obey, and to obey is to love.

Why are we startled and confused by this? Because we think of love only horizontally, between ourselves and other imperfect human beings; but Jesus is thinking of love first of all vertically, between ourselves and God. And on a merely human level, we are not totally wrong. We think, quite reasonably, that we can still love someone even when we don't obey them. Surely, we love an addict even when we don't obey his desire for his own self-destruction through his drug. And we also think, again quite reasonably, that we can obey even when we don't love. Surely, a slave's or a prisoner's motive for obeying is not love but fear.

We are right when it comes to our relationships with other human beings, but we are not right when it comes to our relationship with God. For God is never anything like a drug addict to be pitied or a slave master or an enemy to be feared. The "fear of the Lord" that the Bible calls "the beginning of wisdom" (Prov. 9:10) is filial fear, not servile fear: the fear that the good child has of disappointing a loved and loving Father, not the fear that the slave has of receiving harm from a loveless and unloved tyrant.

But even when it comes to our relationship with God rather than with other human beings, we don't usually see love and obedience to God's commandments as identical. We think we can love God even when we do not obey him, and we think we can obey him even when we do not love him. But Jesus does not think this way. Why? Let's see how Jesus connects them, why he sees love and obedience to commandments as one thing, not two things.

It involves two changes in our thinking. One change is about how we think about love, and the other change is how we think about obedience. First, we have to change our concept of love from a *feeling* to a *choice*, a choice to obey, a choice of the will. Second, we have to change our concept of the motive for our obedience to his commandments from a kind of reluctant *duty*, like a soldier obeying orders to clean the latrines, to a kind of eager *hope*, like a doctor in a life-saving operation on the body of a patient that he loves. Those two changes bring obedience and love together.

Jesus gives us three reasons for this equation of love and obedience.

The first reason goes back to the eternal and unchangeable nature of ultimate reality, the nature of God, the Trinity, Jesus' relationship with his Father.

The second reason is the relationship of this obedience to the thing we all want most deeply—namely, joy.

The third reason is its relationship to friendship and its difference from slavery.

℘

The first reason love requires obedience is rooted in the nature of God, the eternal life of God within the Trinity. Jesus says, "If you keep my commandments, you will remain in my love, *just as I have kept my Father's commandments and remain in his love.*" That is the eternal, unchangeable, unavoidable model and standard for our love: *"As the Father loves me, so I also love you."*

The Father's *love* for his Son is expressed in his *will* toward his Son, and his *will* toward his Son is expressed in his *commandments* to his Son. Love is essentially an act of the will, and the will is expressed in commandments. The loving commander gives his commandments out of love, the love for the best

371

good of the other, who is being commanded. And the one who is being commanded obeys those commandments because of his love of the commander and his faith and trust in the commander.

The same pattern that defines the relation between God the Father and God the Son must exist also between us and Christ: his love toward us is expressed in his will for us, and his will for us is expressed in his commandments to us. And our love for him is expressed in the same way as his love for his Father: in obedience to his will, as expressed in his commandments.

Love, will, and obedience—the three always go together. Love is essentially an act of the will, not a feeling; and the act of the will is to choose, either to obey or to disobey. The will does not generate its own values, its own morality, its own laws. It responds to a higher will, either by obedience or disobedience, either by conflict or by peace that comes from surrender and submission. That surrender or submission to God is the heart of all true religion. "Thy will be done" is the essential prayer in all prayers.

Jesus is not saying here that if we stop obeying his commandments he will stop loving us, but he is saying that if we stop obeying his commandments we will stop remaining, or abiding, or living, in his love. The sun will not stop shining if we close our eyes, but we will no longer see it and live in its light.

※

The second reason Jesus shows us for identifying love with obedience is that this is the secret of joy. He says, "I have told you this [about love] *so that my joy may be in you* and [thus] your joy might be complete."

Notice that he does not say simply "so that *joy* may be in you" but "so that *my* joy may be in you." His joy is the greatest joy, the most joyful joy, the most complete joy. We get joy from many things in this world, but the joy we get from him exceeds all other joys in this world as much as he exceeds all other things in the world.

And what is "his" joy? It is the joy that he gets from the love between himself and his Father. And how is that love expressed? By his Father's commandments and by his own obedience to them.

Jesus is saying that that same pattern must characterize our love. The greatest joy there is is in the Trinity; and that joy comes from love and obedience. The more we participate in that joy, the greater is our joy. Everyone wants joy, but not everyone knows how to get it; not everyone knows the secret of joy. Jesus here tells us the secret of joy.

Joy is deeper than happiness, just as happiness is deeper than pleasure. Pleasure is on the surface. It is dependent on the world outside of us. It is external. And, therefore, it is fleeting and not guaranteed. We get pleasure, we are pleased, when we get what we want from the outside world; but that world is uncertain and unreliable; it keeps changing. Happiness is more long lasting because it is more internal. It is contentment, or peace of mind. But even happiness can get boring. Joy is never boring. It's a gift, a surprise, a delight.

Jesus here tells us the surprising secret of joy: to obey the will of God, and the law of God, and the commandments of God, is our supreme joy.

We are surprised by this, as we are surprised by the Psalmist when he keeps saying how much joy God's law brings to him. The Psalmist says that there is more joy in obedience to God's law than there is in gold and silver and delicious food and drink. That surprises us. Why? Let's think about it.

We think of a law as something that limits us and confines us, that thwarts our will. But the Bible and the saints don't see God's law, God's commandments, in that way at all. They "enjoy" the divine law. Why? Because they love it. Why do they love it? Because it is their connection with the God they love. They love him and trust him because they know that he loves them, and they know that his will for them is always for their best good, for their deepest joy.

If you don't love and trust the lawmaker, you don't love his laws. But if you do, you do. It's that simple. To do God's will, and to know that we are doing God's will, gives us deep joy—but only if we *love* God and therefore *love* God's will and therefore love God's law and commandments. Love changes everything.

Imagine you have a cruel boss, and he wants a certain expensive wine, and because there's no car available he orders you to run to the liquor store as fast as you can to get there before the store closes, and he threatens to fire you if you don't make it. There's no joy in that running. But suppose you just found out that your beloved loves that same wine. You decide to be the knight in shining armor and run to the store to get it. There's joy in that running. The very same running.

Here's another example of the same principle. There's a rhyme that goes "One foot up and one foot down, that's the way to London town." But suppose you are putting one foot up and one foot down in marching to London town to be executed at Tower Hill. The walk has no joy in it. Now change the narrative and suppose you are marching to London town to be crowned king. The very same walk is full of joy.

There are two ways to walk through life. The first is in God's will and God's law and God's commandments because you love him and believe in him and trust him and hope in him. Your philosophy is "Thy will be done," not as your defeat but as your victory; you will not be reluctant but eager. The other way to walk through life is with the philosophy "*My* will be done." That just doesn't work. Mick Jagger tells you why in his most famous line: "You can't always get what you want." But you *can* always get what God wants.

There's an old hymn that goes: "God's way is the best way." That's the song the saints sing as they go marching in to heaven. There's a more popular song that goes: "I did it my way." That's the song everybody sings as they go marching in to hell. Now you tell me: where is the joy?

❧

The third reason Jesus gives for connecting love and obedience is *friendship*. He says: "No one has greater love than this, to lay down one's life for one's friends. You are my friends if you do what I command you. I no longer call you slaves, because a slave does not know what his master is doing. I have called you friends, because I have told you everything I have heard from my Father."

Like love and trust, friendship changes the experience of obedience by changing its context—from slavery, which is never freely chosen, to friendship, which is always freely chosen. No one wants to be a slave, and the slave doesn't want to obey his master, but he has to. But everyone wants friends, and friends love to obey each other's requests and fulfill their desires and needs because they want to, because friendship always involves free will, freely chosen love and trust.

It's amazing that Jesus calls us his friends. Friends share everything, and Jesus says he has shared everything he gets from his Father with us. That includes his wisdom and his love and even his own life, which he gives up for us. That the mighty God, the eternally perfect God, who does not need us, who needs nothing, should choose to come down to our level and call us his friends—that is more amazing than a lion making friends with a mouse.

True friends, like true lovers, want only to give each other good things. They never want to take advantage of each other. Thus, Jesus explains why he instituted this amazing friendship with us by telling us his goal for us, what he wants for us, how we will benefit from it; and the answer is as amazing as the friendship itself. It is that everything we ask for in faith, in his name, God will give us. He says, "Whatever you ask the Father in my name he will give you" (John 16:23).

But that doesn't seem to be true. We can't win the lottery just by claiming this promise. What does Jesus mean by it, then?

We have to look at the context that surrounds this promise. That context is the relationship with God that Jesus is talking about here, a relationship of trust, of faith and hope and love. If we are in that context, if we love God and therefore love his will, we will always get what we most deeply want because we will most deeply want his will above all things. That's the context that explains Jesus' apparently unbelievable promise that "whatever you ask the Father in my name he will give you." Jesus isn't telling us that we can use prayer to win the lottery. He's telling us that if we obey his commandment to love, if we live in his love, in that kind of love, *agape*, then we will always get what we ask God for because we will ask God only for what God wants.

In other words, we will no longer live out Mick Jagger's line "You can't always get what you want" because what we want is for God's perfect will to be done, and that always *will* be done, and it will be done in God's time and way rather than ours, which is what we want the most. "Thy will be done" is the prayer that is always answered.

We don't pray to change God's will, to conform it to ours; we pray to change our will, to conform it to his. The context is the relationship between two friends, not the relationship between a consumer and a vending machine.

We don't know whether God's will is for us to win the lottery, so we can't use Jesus' promise to win the lottery. But we do know that God's will is for us to be holy and happy, so we can use Jesus' promise to ask for holiness, which is the key to happiness, and we can know with absolute certainty that God will give us that thing that we ask for, in his own time and in his own way. When our wills are in line with God's will, when our hearts are in line with his heart, as Jesus' Sacred Heart is, then our holiness and our happiness will follow as inevitably as a shadow. That's his solemn promise. The promise does not include a timetable or a schedule because God is a lover, not an airline.

SOLEMNITY OF THE ASCENSION
OF THE LORD

FIRST READING

ACTS 1:1–11 _____

In the first book, Theophilus, I dealt with all that Jesus did and taught until the day he was taken up, after giving instructions through the Holy Spirit to the apostles whom he had chosen. He presented himself alive to them by many proofs after he had suffered, appearing to them during forty days and speaking about the kingdom of God. While meeting with them, he enjoined them not to depart from Jerusalem, but to wait for "the promise of the Father about which you have heard me speak; for John baptized with water, but in a few days you will be baptized with the Holy Spirit."

When they had gathered together they asked him, "Lord, are you at this time going to restore the kingdom to Israel?" He answered them, "It is not for you to know the times or seasons that the Father has established by his own authority. But you will receive power when the Holy Spirit comes upon you, and you will be my witnesses in Jerusalem, throughout Judea and Samaria, and to the ends of the earth." When he had said this, as they were looking on, he was lifted up, and a cloud took him from their sight. While they were looking intently at the sky as he was going, suddenly two men dressed in white garments stood beside them. They said, "Men of Galilee, why are you standing there looking at the sky? This Jesus who has been taken up from you into heaven will return in the same way as you have seen him going into heaven."

This beginning of the Acts of the Apostles, which is St. Luke's sequel to his Gospel, is rich with basic themes. Here are four of them.

377

First, the centrality of Jesus' Resurrection. Luke begins by referring to his Gospel, which he wrote for a man named Theophilus, evidently a convert to Christianity, and he writes: "In the first book, Theophilus, I dealt with all that Jesus did and taught until the day he was taken up [to heaven by the Ascension], after giving instructions through the Holy Spirit to the apostles whom he had chosen. He presented himself alive to them by many proofs after he had suffered, appearing to them during forty days."

Was the Resurrection a hallucination? No hallucination in history has ever lasted forty days and been the same detailed hallucination for twelve different people. And if the story of Jesus' Resurrection were a deliberate lie rather than an honest hallucination, why did the Apostles all suffer and die for this lie when they were martyred? St. Paul, in one of his letters, mentions that there were over five hundred people who were still alive at that time who had seen Jesus after his Resurrection, inviting his readers to check the evidence, the hundreds of eyewitnesses.

Here's a second point. The Apostles in this passage asked Jesus one of the dumbest questions in history. After a forty-day course on the theme Jesus kept preaching about to them for three years, the "kingdom of heaven," and after seeing him die and rise again, you'd think they'd get the main point of all his preaching right, but they didn't. Like most of the Jews, they thought the kingdom of heaven that was going to be established by the Messiah was a political kingdom. Now imagine you were one of the Apostles, and Jesus kept correcting that mistake for three years, and then again for forty days, and then at the end of this course Jesus gave you a simple, short exam on the topic of the kingdom of heaven, with just one question, a true or false question: "True or false? The kingdom of heaven is a political kingdom." Do you think you could pass that test? Well, they didn't. Look at the question they asked: "When they had gathered together they asked him, 'Lord, are you at this time going to restore the kingdom to Israel?'" In other words, "Now that all this supernatural stuff is over, are we finally getting down to the bottom line of kicking out those awful Romans and reestablishing the political success of the old kingdom under David and Solomon for the nation of Israel?"

Our idolatries and obsessions die very hard and very slowly. And things have not changed much in the last two thousand years, have they? Most Catholics today are more passionate about their politics than about their religion. They've politicized their religion and religionized their politics. They worship either the donkey or the elephant, and the devil doesn't care which one it is as long as it's not the Lamb.

A third surprising thing in this text is that Jesus tells them not to go out into all the world and preach the Gospel until the Holy Spirit comes upon them at Pentecost, and only then will they be his witnesses, first in Jerusalem, and then, outside Israel, in Samaria, and finally to the ends of the earth. They are not ready yet to be his witnesses. (By the way, the word translated "witnesses" means "eyewitnesses" to things literally seen, and the same word also means "martyrs.")

Why did Jesus say that? Why weren't they ready? What did they lack? They lacked the power, the fuel. The Holy Spirit was to be the fuel in their gas tank, the energy in their wires, their power source. This Gospel was going to change the world, and they were not going to be able to do that on their own.

Back in Matthew's Gospel, Jesus told them, "When they hand you over, do not worry about how you are to speak or what you are to say. You will be given at that moment what you are to say. For it will not be you who speak but the Spirit of your Father speaking through you" (Matt. 10:19–20).

When St. Paul visited the church in Ephesus, he asked them, "Did you receive the Holy Spirit when you became believers?" and they said, "We have never even heard that there is a Holy Spirit" (Acts 19:2). Why did Paul ask that question? He must have noticed something missing: the power source, the electricity, the fire. Maybe they, too, had transferred it to politics.

The fourth thing to notice in this passage is that when Jesus ascended into heaven on a cloud, the Apostles kept staring up into the sky after he had disappeared from sight, and the two angels who appeared corrected their focus. They said, "Men of Galilee, why are you standing there looking at the sky?" Their business was not to follow Jesus to heaven yet, but to preach and live the Gospel on this earth.

These two angels were perhaps the same two angels who appeared to the two women on Easter morning at Jesus' empty tomb, asking them, "Why do you seek the living one among the dead?" (Luke 24:5). Jesus is not there anymore. Everybody else's tomb is full, but Jesus' tomb is empty. He is risen. And now he's risen further into heaven and left us with his Holy Spirit to inspire us to do his work, and with his Body hidden in the Eucharist and in his Mystical Body, the Church.

We know our Lord's two great commandments, and now it's time to get on with doing them. Will he find us doing them when he comes to take us home? Because he will come again, at the end of time, to judge the whole world, and, for each of us, at the end of our time, at our death. So let's work and love while the light lasts.

SECOND READING

EPHESIANS 1:17–23
(OR EPHESIANS 4:1-13) _____

Brothers and sisters: May the God of our Lord Jesus Christ, the Father of glory, give you a Spirit of wisdom and revelation resulting in knowledge of him. May the eyes of your hearts be enlightened, that you may know what is the hope that belongs to his call, what are the riches of glory in his inheritance among the holy ones, and what is the surpassing greatness of his power for us who believe, in accord with the exercise of his great might, which he worked in Christ, raising him from the dead and seating him at his right hand in the heavens, far above every principality, authority, power, and dominion, and every name that is named not only in this age but also in the one to come. And he put all things beneath his feet and gave him as head over all things to the church, which is his body, the fullness of the one who fills all things in every way.

Today's passage from St. Paul's Epistle to the Ephesians uses exalted language because it is about our exalted destiny as a result of Christ's exaltation in his Ascension. Like a victorious warrior, Christ returned home to heaven with booty, with captives whom he rescued from his enemies and ours, which are the evil spirits who hate us. We are that booty; we are those captives.

This is the vision that St. Paul has and prays we have too. Thus, he prays, "May the God of our Lord Jesus Christ, the Father of glory, give you a Spirit of wisdom and revelation resulting in knowledge of him." Of whom? Of our Savior, our Redeemer, our rescuer from slavery to sin and its consequence, eternal death. "For the wages of sin is death, but the gift of God is eternal life in Christ Jesus our Lord" (Rom. 6:23).

This wisdom and knowledge is not just knowledge of facts but the knowledge of a person, of Jesus Christ himself. Thus, this knowledge is lodged not first of all in the head but in the heart. So he prays, "May the eyes of your hearts be enlightened." The heart has an eye in it! Love sees.

Enlightened to what? Not just to our past slavery or our present freedom but also to our future glory, our hope, our destiny, our inheritance: "That you may know what is the hope that belongs to his call, what are the riches of glory in his inheritance among the holy ones." We sinners are to be raised up to mingle with the saints, "the holy ones," in heavenly glory. ("Glory" is a word we almost never hear in our secularized society. Yet it is a need of the deep part of the human heart.)

God alone can do this because he alone is omnipotent. Thus, St. Paul extols "the surpassing greatness of his power for us who believe, in accord with the exercise of his great might, which he worked in Christ, raising him from the dead and seating him at his right hand in the heavens, far above every principality, authority, power, and dominion, and every name that is named, not only in this age but also in the one to come. And he put all things beneath his feet."

It is good for us to meditate lovingly and lingeringly on each of the divine attributes, including God's power, which is literally limited by nothing. This God, who loves us, has unlimited power to do what that love demands for us, which is everything! This same St. Paul therefore says, in another epistle, that "all things work for good for those who love God, who are called according to his purpose" (Rom. 8:28). All things, including bad things, including sufferings. St. Paul has a right to say this: read the list of some of his sufferings in 2 Corinthians 11:24–29.

Where is this power? In the Body of Christ, which is the Church: "He put all things beneath his feet and gave him as head over all things to the church, which is his body, the fullness of the one who fills all things in every way." The Church is the fullness of power, wisdom, and goodness not merely because there are holy humans in it but because Christ is in it. That is why she is the "Holy Catholic Church": because she is the very Body of Christ, who is not only all-holy but also all-powerful, and who said just before his Ascension, "All power in heaven and on earth has been given to me" (Matt. 28:18).

Did you hear that? All authority. Christ our Lord and Savior, our friend and lover, is the supreme, all-powerful ruler of everything in the universe. Nothing can conquer him, and he has conquered everything.

If this vision becomes ours, we will shine with glory and march with confidence even into the valley of the shadow of death, fearing no evil because our shepherd, the ruler of our lives, is the one who has conquered sin and death and hell. We are held in his hand, and he will never let us slip through his fingers, because we are his fingers, his "members," the organs of his body (see 1 Cor. 12:12–27).

GOSPEL
MARK 16:15–20 _____

Jesus said to his disciples: "Go into the whole world and proclaim the gospel to every creature. Whoever believes and is baptized will be saved; whoever does not believe will be condemned. These signs will accompany those who believe: in my name they will drive out demons, they will speak new languages. They will pick up serpents with their hands, and if they drink any deadly thing, it will not harm them. They will lay hands on the sick, and they will recover."

So then the Lord Jesus, after he spoke to them, was taken up into heaven and took his seat at the right hand of God. But they went forth and preached everywhere, while the Lord worked with them and confirmed the word through accompanying signs.

_____

The Church's first and foundational task, underlying all the others, is defined here from the mouth of Christ himself. It is "evangelization," the proclamation of the Gospel, the "Good News." This is not one of the already well-known, timeless truths like "God exists and we ought to love each other" but is one of the utterly unforeseen and surprising historical facts about Jesus, the Lamb of God who takes away the sins of the world by dying and rising. That God has a Son; that he became a man; that he performed miracles, including raising the dead; that he was crucified; that he rose again; that he ascended into heaven; and that he will come again to judge the world at the end of time—not one of these seven facts is less than startling.

"Whoever believes and is baptized will be saved; whoever does not believe will be condemned." Christ repeats here, at the end of his earthly ministry, what he had often said: that our relationship to him determines our eternal salvation or condemnation. Salvation comes through faith and Baptism (which are almost always mentioned together in Scripture). Faith determines salvation because faith is more than an intellectual opinion (our opinions can't save us) or a feeling of assurance (feelings can't save us); it is a free choice, a personal "yes" to God's offer of spiritual marriage and a share in his eternal life.

The subjective dimension of faith is not sharply defined. We are not told where the definition and demarcation of faith is in the psyche—that is, how conscious and explicit it has to be; so we can and should hope that many who do not define themselves as Christians can be saved. But we are told very clearly the objective dimension of faith: it is Christ himself. He was very clear about that: "No one comes to the Father except through me" (John 14:6). We do not know how many will be saved, but we know how many Saviors there are: one.

In this passage Christ then predicts some of the miracles that believers will see, but he does not say how many believers will see how many of them. All of these visible miracles have in fact appeared many times in Christian history. But they are only "signs" of the essential miracle, which is God's invasion of our world and our life in Christ and the conversion of the heart in accepting God's gift of supernatural life.

Christ mentions Baptism as well as faith as a requirement for salvation, but the Church recognizes three kinds of Baptism: ordinary water Baptism, the "Baptism of blood" (martyrdom), and "the Baptism of desire" (i.e., the free human will's fundamental yes to God and his will). This desire may be implicit, if knowledge of the Gospel is missing, but it must be really there, in the heart, whose movements God alone sees infallibly.

Mark's Gospel is by far the shortest, and Christ's Ascension is described here in very few words. But its consequences have changed everything both in heaven and on earth. Because of what Christ has done, heaven's door is now open to mankind on earth, and earth is open to heaven's Gospel, which is described as both "the word" and "accompanying signs," that is, miracles.

The word "angel" means literally "one who delivers a message or tells the news." Some people believe the strange idea that in heaven we will literally become angels. That is not true, of course—the Creed assures us of "the resurrection of the body," and angels are pure spirits, without bodies. But since our essential task on earth as Catholic Christians is to tell the Good News of

Jesus, that means we are to become "angels," that is, messengers, announcers of the Good News of God by both word and deed.

SEVENTH SUNDAY OF EASTER

FIRST READING
Acts 1:15–17, 20a, 20c–26 _____

Peter stood up in the midst of the brothers—there was a group of about one hundred and twenty persons in the one place. He said, "My brothers, the Scripture had to be fulfilled which the Holy Spirit spoke beforehand through the mouth of David, concerning Judas, who was the guide for those who arrested Jesus. He was numbered among us and was allotted a share in this ministry.

"For it is written in the Book of Psalms: *May another take his office.*

"Therefore, it is necessary that one of the men who accompanied us the whole time the Lord Jesus came and went among us, beginning from the baptism of John until the day on which he was taken up from us, become with us a witness to his resurrection." So they proposed two, Judas called Barsabbas, who was also known as Justus, and Matthias. Then they prayed, "You, Lord, who know the hearts of all, show which one of these two you have chosen to take the place in this apostolic ministry from which Judas turned away to go to his own place." Then they gave lots to them, and the lot fell upon Matthias, and he was counted with the eleven apostles.

One of the four marks of the true Church mentioned in the Creed is "apostolic." We say, "I believe in one, holy, catholic, and apostolic Church." We are connected to the historical Christ two thousand years ago through the Apostles Christ appointed and the successors they ordained (i.e., the bishops). Christ said to his Apostles, "Whoever listens to you listens to me" (Luke 10:16). The Apostles spoke with Christ's authority, and their ordained successors have carried on this authority to all future generations. The number of bishops and the way they were appointed changed down through history. Here, in the earliest Church, it was by casting lots. Today, it is appointment by the pope, or by the pope consulting other bishops. At times it was by appointment by the emperor. But even though the mechanism changed, "apostolic succession" has always remained our unchanging visible connection with the historical Christ, his teaching, and his authority.

Not all bishops are good. One of the Twelve was Judas Iscariot, the first bishop who accepted a government grant and the first bishop to commit suicide. The qualification to be Judas' successor as one of the Twelve was spelled out here: he had to have accompanied the others during the three years of Jesus' public ministry, beginning with Jesus' baptism by John the Baptist and ending with Jesus' Ascension. He also had to be an eyewitness of the resurrected Christ. The Church is essentially the chain of witnesses to the historical Christ, especially his Resurrection. Thus, St. Paul writes, "If Christ has not been raised, then empty is our preaching; empty, too, your faith. . . . you are still in your sins. Then those who have fallen asleep in Christ have perished. If for this life only we have hoped in Christ, we are the most pitiable people of all. But now Christ has been raised from the dead, the firstfruits of those who have fallen asleep" (1 Cor 15:14, 17–20). Christianity is based on a fact, not a fable or a fiction; a truth, not a theory.

RESPONSORIAL PSALM

Psalm 103:1–2, 11–12, 19–20 _____

R. (19a) **The Lord has set his throne in heaven.**
or: R. **Alleluia.**

Bless the LORD, O my soul;
    and all my being, bless his holy name.
Bless the LORD, O my soul,
    and forget not all his benefits.

For as the heavens are high above the earth,
　so surpassing is his kindness toward those who fear him.
As far as the east is from the west,
　so far has he put our transgressions from us.

The LORD has established his throne in heaven,
　and his kingdom rules over all.
Bless the LORD, all you his angels,
　you mighty in strength, who do his bidding.

In this Psalm, David the Psalmist commands his soul and all his being to bless the Lord. What does this mean? How can we command our own soul? Our souls are often sleepy and sloppy, and they need to be roused. Who does this rousing? We do, for David calls it "*my* soul" and "all *my* being." We can command our soul, as we can command our body, because we *have* a soul and a body. What, then, is doing the commanding? Scripture calls it the "heart," which means not the feelings or emotions but the very center of the soul and the source of its life, as the physical heart is the center of the body and the source of its life through its blood. David's heart or will commands the rest of him—his whole soul and in fact his whole being—as a captain commands a ship. The free choice of the will commands all the powers of the soul to act: the mind, the desires, and the emotions. Our will should be absolutely and nonnegotiably set on God, fixed on God, given to God, even when our minds, desires, and emotions are not, so that we can thus wake up our own sleepy, sloppy souls.

One reason for this rousing the soul to bless and thank God is God's total mercy, which is not merely "great" but "higher than the heavens," and which has taken our sins not merely a short distance away but farther away from us than the east is from the west. How far is that? East is farther from west than New York is from San Francisco. It is infinite. The Lamb of God has actually taken away the sins of the world. We cannot do this, and we have not done this; only God can do it, and only God has done it. Our only sane response is total and eternal gratitude.

This Lord of mercy and goodness is also the Lord of power and authority: "His kingdom rules over all." Goodness and power, right and might, are never completely joined in our world. Those in power always lack some goodness, and those who are good always lack some power. How awful if goodness and power were not joined in the Creator and Ruler of the world! But they are.

SECOND READING
1 JOHN 4:11–16 _____

Beloved, if God so loved us, we also must love one another. No one has ever seen God. Yet, if we love one another, God remains in us, and his love is brought to perfection in us.

This is how we know that we remain in him and he in us, that he has given us of his Spirit. Moreover, we have seen and testify that the Father sent his Son as savior of the world. Whoever acknowledges that Jesus is the Son of God, God remains in him and he in God. We have come to know and to believe in the love God has for us.

God is love, and whoever remains in love remains in God and God in him.

_____

This is one of the most beautiful, most profound, and most beloved passages in Scripture. We could probe into it endlessly, like the depths of the sea. This letter was written by St. John the Apostle, who in his Gospel calls himself "the disciple whom Jesus loved." (That is our identity too, and our passport to heaven!) John tells us both that God not only loves us, as God loved him, but that "God *is* love" (*agape*, total self-giving). God is not just someone who loves; God is complete love itself. And that implies (1) a lover, (2) a beloved, and (3) the act of loving or the relationship of loving. That is why God is a Trinity. And John tells us that this love, the love that God is—this *agape*, this total self-giving—is "in" us and we are "in" it. To remain "in" God, to abide "in" God, to live "in" God, is to remain and abide and live "in" that love. If we remain "in" that love, we remain "in" God, and if we do not remain "in" that love, we do not remain "in" God. The only way to be "in" God is to be "in" *agape*.

It is supernatural. And it is immortal. It is the love that is stronger than death. It is the very life of God, and God shares it with us, as the sun shares its light and heat with the earth.

He also tells us that to remain "in" that love is to remain "in" God, because God is the source of all of that love, and it makes its home "in" us if we make our home "in" it—that is, if we choose it, if we accept it, if we believe it.

So many "ins." What does that little word mean?

It is nearly indefinable. It is not spatial, like a dog "in" a cage or a block "in" a neighborhood, for neither God nor his *agape* love is "in" space in the sense of being limited by space or extended in space at all. God and his love are not made of atoms. Yet God makes himself present "in" or to all places. He is not absent.

And it is not that God or his love are a *part* of us, as a thought is a part of our mind, or as our mind is a part of our soul, or as our desires are a part of our personality. For God is not a part of any greater spiritual whole, any more than he is a part of a greater physical whole. The whole is greater than the part, and there is nothing greater than God.

Perhaps the best word to explain "in" is "presence." God is present "in" us without being confined by us. He acts in us and works in us, as sunlight acts and works in Earth's atmosphere to fill it with its light and heat. But just as the sun is much more than its light and heat that it sends to earth, God is much more than his works in us. He is transcendent as well as immanent (i.e., present).

What are his works in us? They are to know us totally and to love us totally, and to gradually transform us into holy and happy saints who will be able to endure and enjoy the presence of God himself face to face in heaven forever, without any sin, pain, fear, doubt, or boredom.

How do we become saints? How do we live "in" love? By living "in" God. Only God can make us saints. We can't do it ourselves. And how do we live "in" God? By living "in" love. The only way to become lovelike is to become Godlike, and the only way to become Godlike is to become lovelike.

"God is love" is probably the single most popular sentence in the Bible. But beware: "God is love" does not mean the same thing as "love is God." When we say that A is B, we assume our hearers already know A and then we go on to tell them something new about it: that it is B. So when we say that "God is love," we say that God, the God whom we already know by faith, is, in his own eternal and essential nature, absolute love, total love, nothing but love. And that is new and startling. That is the best of good news.

To say that "love is God," on the other hand, is to say that the love we already know by human experience is God himself, the Creator of the world, a person, our Savior, the highest and greatest being. That is not true. That is idolatry. Our little sparks of the fire of *agape* are finite; God is infinite. Do not adore anything or anyone but the one true God.

We adore him both as he is in heaven, transcendent to the whole creation, and as really present in the souls of his children, yourself and your Christian neighbor. Next to the Eucharist itself, your neighbor is the holiest thing in the universe, because God lives there. The same God who is really present "in" the Eucharist "in" the tabernacles on the altars of our Catholic churches is also present "in" your neighbor's soul, and even "in" your own, however obscured by our sins and imperfections. Seeing that, seeing Christ in all human persons, is what makes a saint. That was Mother Teresa's un-secret secret. Let us keep reminding ourselves of it, and we will gradually become more and more what she became.

GOSPEL

JOHN 17:11B–19 _____

Lifting up his eyes to heaven, Jesus prayed, saying: "Holy Father, keep them in your name that you have given me, so that they may be one just as we are one. When I was with them I protected them in your name that you gave me, and I guarded them, and none of them was lost except the son of destruction, in order that the Scripture might be fulfilled. But now I am coming to you. I speak this in the world so that they may share my joy completely. I gave them your word, and the world hated them, because they do not belong to the world any more than I belong to the world. I do not ask that you take them out of the world but that you keep them from the evil one. They do not belong to the world any more than I belong to the world. Consecrate them in your truth. Your word is truth. As you sent me into the world, so I sent them into the world. And I consecrate myself for them, so that they also may be consecrated in truth."

What is the one thing Jesus always does before he does anything important, such as institute the Eucharist, choose his twelve Apostles, or undertake the deed he came to earth for in the first place, to die on the cross for our salvation? He prays.

So here, at the end of the Last Supper, he lifts up his eyes to heaven and prays. The eyes are the expression and symbol of the mind, and Christ's mind, commanded by his will, is now turned wholly to his Father. He is practicing what we need to practice, "the practice of the presence of God," which is the essence of prayer.

Prayer is an act of the mind's attention, but it is commanded by the will. What matters most in the eyes of God is not the quality of that mental attention. It may be confused and distracted and beaten down by agony. Its faith and hope and charity may be fragile and stretched to its breaking point. What matters most is that the will chooses it, commands it, prays, no matter how "bad" the prayer is. That we pray is more important than how we pray. The most important law of prayer is "just do it."

This "high priestly prayer" of Jesus in the seventeenth chapter of John's Gospel is the closest look mankind has ever been given of the inner life of the Trinity, the intimate personal relationship between the Son and the Father. Jesus here reveals to us his and his Father's deepest heart and desire, which is that we may be saved and share their divine joy. This is what Christ wanted the most to reveal to us; he says, "I speak this in the world so that they may share my joy completely."

That is what *agape* is: to will the greatest good of the beloved. And the greatest good is God's own divine joy. That will is the one simple motive behind absolutely everything God does for us, including allowing the evils that happen to us! For he works all things, even evil things (like the Crucifixion!), together for our greatest good. God is love and nothing but love. He is totally simple.

"The world," that is, fallen humanity and human culture, is under the sway of "the evil one" (the devil), who is the enemy of this divine love, and therefore it fears, hates, tempts, and persecutes the saints. Christ says, "The world hated them, because they do not belong to the world any more than I belong to the world." But "what profit is there for one to gain the whole world and forfeit his life?" (Mark 8:36). We should be wise enough to say, "You can take this whole world; just give me Jesus."

That is what "consecration" means: the total unification of will and desire and love. When the voice of Christ spoke to St. Thomas Aquinas from the crucifix after he had completed his treatise on the Eucharist, and said, "You have written well of me, Thomas. What will you have as your reward?" Thomas answered in three words: "Only yourself, Lord." One of Jesus' beatitudes is "Blessed are the clean of heart, for they will see God" (Matt. 5:8). To quote the title of one of Kierkegaard's great books, "Purity of heart is to will one thing." It is the first and greatest commandment: to love the Lord God with all the heart, mind, soul, and strength. You cannot become a saint without becoming whole, without becoming one. You cannot become one great person without one great love. Saints are fanatics about the one and only thing it is right to be a fanatic about: everything. If God is not everything, he is not God. If God is not everything, he is nothing.

God is a fanatic about love (*agape*). God is totally unified. He is love and nothing but love. So for us to be wholly "consecrated" to God is for us to be similarly unified within ourselves.

The Trinity is the highest, most unified unity, because love is more single and unified than the number one in arithmetic. God is one not merely in number (there is only one God) but also in will. Love is a stronger glue than arithmetic. When you love someone totally, you are far less threatened by your own sufferings and death than by that of your beloved. That shows that your personal, willed unity with your beloved is greater than your impersonal, factual unity with yourself. That is a remote image of the love in the Trinity.

Of course, that love is far from easy for us fallen, foolish, fearful sinners. That's why for most of us there is a purgatory. And that's why we will willingly embrace the purifying fires of purgatory, painful though they are: because we will know they are bringing us closer to this God who is supreme joy. That's what God put us on earth for: to begin to learn how to do that, to willingly let ourselves be "consecrated" by Jesus, who was sent by the Father to do just that to us, and who sends his Spirit into us to do just that, and who sends us into the world to share that secret with the world. That is the whole purpose of the Church. The Church is a saint-making machine. Its parts are not made of metal or computer chips; they are made of human bodies and souls.

PENTECOST SUNDAY: MASS DURING THE DAY

FIRST READING

ACTS 2:1–11 _____

When the time for Pentecost was fulfilled, they were all in one place together. And suddenly there came from the sky a noise like a strong driving wind, and it filled the entire house in which they were. Then there appeared to them tongues as of fire, which parted and came to rest on each one of them. And they were all filled with the Holy Spirit and began to speak in different tongues, as the Spirit enabled them to proclaim.

Now there were devout Jews from every nation under heaven staying in Jerusalem. At this sound, they gathered in a large crowd, but they were confused because each one heard them speaking in his own language. They were astounded, and in amazement they asked, "Are not all these people who are speaking Galileans? Then how does each of us hear them in his native language? We are Parthians, Medes, and Elamites, inhabitants of Mesopotamia, Judea and Cappadocia, Pontus and Asia, Phrygia and Pamphylia, Egypt and the districts of Libya near Cyrene, as well as travelers from Rome, both Jews and converts to Judaism, Cretans and Arabs, yet we hear them speaking in our own tongues of the mighty acts of God."

_____

Why did the fire at Pentecost take the shape of tongues? And why did it appear on their heads? Because it gave the Apostles the power to speak not their own minds but the mind of God, and not with their own tongues but with tongues—that is, languages—that they had never learned from human beings. This was a miracle from heaven.

In pagan Greek mythology, Prometheus stole heavenly fire to give it to mankind, and Zeus was so angry at this act of charity to man that he chained Prometheus to a rock. But in Christianity, God is not jealousy but love, and he himself gives us the fire from heaven, the Holy Spirit, who is the very life of God himself.

John the Baptist had prophesied this when he said, "I am baptizing you with water, for repentance, but the one who is coming after me is mightier than I. I am not worthy to carry his sandals. He will baptize you with the Holy Spirit and fire" (Matt. 3:11).

This is a fire that does not destroy. It is the fire Moses saw in the burning bush that was on fire but not consumed (Exod. 3:2–3). But the author of the Letter to the Hebrews wrote, "Our God is a consuming fire" (Heb. 12:29). Why is this not a contradiction? Because this fire consumes nothing good (as in Exod. 3:2) but everything evil (as in Heb. 12:29). This is a fire that burns less and less the nearer you get to it and that burns more and more the farther you distance yourself from it. It is the fire that is the Holy Spirit of God, who is the very love between the Father and the Son that is the very life of God himself.

Pentecost's miracle, where everyone understands each other's tongues, reverses the babble of the Tower of Babel, where language was confused. Mankind in its pride had built a great tower to storm heaven itself, saying, "Let us build ourselves a city and a tower with its top in the sky, and so make a name for ourselves" (Gen. 11:4). But the foundation of that tower was only human pride and human cleverness, and that tower collapsed when language itself collapsed into many languages so that they could no longer understand each other. Pentecost reversed that confusion of languages and restored unity to humanity, as a foretaste of heaven, where we will all understand each other and speak the same language.

What language will that be? I think the closest approximation to it on earth is music, the universal language. There is an old Jewish and Christian story that God created the world by singing it into existence. Both C.S. Lewis, in his *Chronicles of Narnia*, and J.R.R. Tolkien, in his *Silmarillion*, used that tradition in their stories of the creation.

Pentecost "worked" because it did not proudly try to rise from earth to heaven, like the Tower of Babel, but humbly descended from heaven to earth, like Christ—the Christ who said, "Amen, amen, I say to you, unless a grain of wheat falls to the ground and dies, it remains just a grain of wheat; but if it dies, it produces much fruit. Whoever loves his life [that is, greedily grasps his life] loses it, and whoever hates his life in this world [that is, gives it up, gives it away in love] will preserve it for eternal life" (John 12:24–25).

Mary understood that that was the way God worked when in her "Magnificat" she said, "He has shown the strength of his arm, and has scattered the proud in their conceit. He has cast down the mighty from their thrones and has lifted up the lowly. He has filled the hungry with good things, and the rich he has sent away empty" (Luke 1:51–53). As Christ said, "Whoever exalts himself will be humbled; but whoever humbles himself will be exalted" (Matt. 23:12). Love gives itself away and thus saves itself. It dies and resurrects. Nothing that has not given itself away and died to itself will be resurrected.

C.S. Lewis, who had thousands of books and loved them deeply, was once asked whether he thought he would have his books in heaven, and he answered, "Probably only the ones I gave away on earth." We don't know whether or not that applies to books, but we do know that that applies to life. Give your life to God and others, and you will save it eternally. Hug it to yourself, and you will lose it eternally.

At Pentecost, God gave himself away to mankind a second time. He had given mankind his Son; now he gave us his Spirit. Living in the Holy Spirit means living in what the Holy Spirit is, which is the life of self-donation, making a gift of yourself. And that life is not dull and dead like ashes but glorious and alive like fire. It's also catching; we "catch fire" from those who give that kind of love to us, and then we pass it on to others, like a good infection.

SECOND READING

1 Corinthians 12:3b–7, 12–13

(or Galatians 5:16-25) _____

Brothers and sisters: No one can say, "Jesus is Lord," except by the Holy Spirit.

There are different kinds of spiritual gifts but the same Spirit; there are different forms of service but the same Lord; there are different workings but the same God who produces all of them in everyone. To each individual the manifestation of the Spirit is given for some benefit.

As a body is one though it has many parts, and all the parts of the body, though many, are one body, so also Christ. For in one Spirit we were all baptized into one body, whether Jews or Greeks, slaves or free persons, and we were all given to drink of one Spirit.

When St. Paul writes, "No one can say, 'Jesus is Lord,' except by the Holy Spirit," he is referring to what is probably the first and shortest of all the Christian creeds, the three-word formula "Jesus is Lord." Christians, like Jews, never gave the name "Lord" to Caesar or any other earthly Lord; that's why Caesar persecuted both Christians and Jews. God alone is their Lord.

The purpose of a creed is to clearly define what we believe. This three-word creed "Jesus is Lord" draws a very clear line between Christians and non-Christians, for to affirm that Jesus is Lord, is divine, is God incarnate, as he claimed to be, is to affirm the very essence of Christianity. All who believe that are Christians, and all who do not believe that are not.

In today's epistle, St. Paul tells us that when a Christian believes and confesses this—that Christ is divine, is one with the Father, as he himself clearly claimed—then it is the Holy Spirit that inspires this confession. When Jesus asked his Apostles, "Who do you say that I am?" Simon Peter replied, "You are the Christ, the Son of the living God." And Jesus answered him, "Blessed are you, Simon son of Jonah. For flesh and blood has not revealed this to you, but my heavenly Father" (Matt. 16:15–17). It was the Spirit of God who enlightened St. Peter, and it is the same Spirit who enlightens every Christian to believe and confess the truth of who Jesus is: that he is indeed the Lord.

In the true story behind the book and movie *The Exorcist*, the evil spirit who possessed the child bragged that the one word this child would never utter was the word "Lord." He was wrong. And when that word, that confession, came from his lips, the evil spirit was conquered and exorcised.

The Holy Spirit is to the Church what the soul is to the body. As the single soul, the single life-force, gives life to each of the many cells and organs and systems in the body, the one Spirit gives life to all the different spiritual gifts and services in the Church: to clergy and laity, to preaching and teaching and service and administration, to each of the sacraments, to both secular and religious life.

The slogan of the Three Musketeers, "All for one and one for all," applies to the Church too. The common good is for each individual good, and each individual good is for the common good. As St. Paul says, "To each individual the manifestation of the Spirit is given for some benefit. As a body is one though it has many parts, and all the parts of the body, though many, are one body, so also Christ."

The Body of Christ, the Church, is not just an organization: it is an organism. An organism has both more unity and more diversity than a machine. Two wheels or two pistons in a car are not very different from each other, but two organs in the body are. They are also more unified than two wheels or two pistons because they are unified by the same life or soul or spirit.

Christ's Church is not monolithic but full of diversity; it sings in harmony; it plays a symphony. The Spirit who inspires one Catholic to run for political office inspires another to enter a monastery. The same Spirit who inspires a theologian to write a book inspires a chef to cook for a homeless shelter. Unity and diversity do not oppose each other, except through tyrants and totalitarians. And Christ is not our tyrant but our lover and our Savior. Because he is our Creator and designer, because he alone knows us through and through, we each find in his mind the secret of our identity; and because he is our lover and Savior, because he alone can fill our restless heart, we each find in his will the secret of our peace and joy.

GOSPEL
John 20:19–23
(or John 15:26-27; 16:12-15) _____

On the evening of that first day of the week, when the doors were locked, where the disciples were, for fear of the Jews, Jesus came and stood in their midst and said to them, "Peace be with you." When he had said this, he showed them his hands and his side. The disciples rejoiced when they saw the Lord. Jesus said to them again, "Peace be with you. As the Father has sent me, so I send you." And when he had said this, he breathed on them and said to them, "Receive the Holy Spirit. Whose sins you forgive are forgiven them, and whose sins you retain are retained."

In today's Gospel, Jesus gives his Apostles, and therefore his Church, and therefore us, three gifts.

First, and most importantly, his presence: "When the doors were locked, where the disciples were, for fear of the Jews, Jesus came and stood in their midst." There is no gift better than yourself, your presence. Solving your problem can usually be done by strangers, if they are competent experts, but no stranger can give you the gift you want most from the one you love most: simply their presence, simply the words "Here I am. I am here for you." That applies especially to what you can do for the sick and the dying. During the COVID-19 pandemic and the "social distancing" that it made necessary, the complaint that was the most painful and the most often heard was not that people were dying but that they were dying alone.

The disciples were cowering in fear behind locked doors because they thought, quite naturally, that those who had succeeded in killing Jesus would now come after them too. But Christ came through their locked doors, and he also comes through ours. For it's not just keys but fear that locks our doors, especially the fear that God does not wholly love us and understand us and our weaknesses; that we cannot trust him completely. And pride, and the refusal to admit that we are in the wrong. But faith and love cast out fear. Even weak faith and love let him in. Open the door to him one inch, and he will come in a mile.

In the famous painting of Jesus outside a door, holding a lantern, there is no knob on the door. The knob is on the inside. It opens only from within.

Jesus no longer stands before us in his human body as he stood before the eleven Apostles, but he is still with us in at least four ways.

He is present in the Eucharist, in his full divinity and humanity. And, within his humanity, both in his human soul and his human body. And, in his body, both in the flesh and in the blood, which were separated in death.

He also is still before us in our souls. He is present there spiritually rather than materially, but he is really present, and present actively. He keeps doing things to us if we let him. He is as really present in our souls as the Eucharist is really present in our bodies for about fifteen minutes after we receive Holy Communion.

And since he is present in every Christian soul, he is present to you in your Christian neighbor. Mother Teresa famously said she sees Jesus everywhere, especially in the "distressing disguise" of the poor.

Finally, he is present in his Holy Spirit, whom he sent at Pentecost. It's his Spirit, after all, not a stranger's: his and his Father's. The Holy Spirit is the eternal love between the Father and the Son—the love that is so real that it is not just a force but a person. That love lives in us and we in him.

So the first and most important gift Jesus gives us is simply himself. All his other gifts depend on that one.

A second gift is his peace. Twice he pronounced these words to his Apostles: "Peace be with you." That was not just a wish or even a prayer but a word of command that accomplished what it signified, like a sacrament. It was like God saying, "Let there be light," and there was light (Gen. 1:3).

Jesus does not just give us peace; Jesus is our peace. It is a peace the world cannot give: a peace with God, not with the devil; and with ourselves, not with our false selves, our masks and evasions and hidings; and with our neighbors, all of them, not just the easy ones. It is a peace that accepts poverty, chastity, and obedience, and therefore it is also a war against greed and lust and pride. We live in a war between those two kinds of peace, the peace of Christ and the peace of the Antichrist. So Christ gives us two gifts: the gift of his peace and the gift of war against peace with the world, the flesh, and the devil, with greed and lust and pride.

A third gift Christ gives is the Holy Spirit. The word for "spirit" in both Hebrew and Greek is the same word that also means "breath" or "breath of life." So Jesus gives his Apostles this gift sacramentally by breathing on them. God usually gives us spiritual gifts through material means, which are sacramental signs.

And one of the first powers of the Spirit is the authority to forgive sins.

"Authority" means both the right and the power. He had promised earlier that he would give this gift to his Apostles when he said, "Whose sins you forgive are forgiven them, and whose sins you retain are retained" (John 20:23). It is the power of binding and loosing.

We don't have to wonder and worry about whether our sins are really forgiven if we are Catholics because our priests have the real power to authoritatively administer Christ's forgiveness in the sacrament of Confession. The authority is from Christ—that's why it is absolute and guaranteed. It's Christ's own power to forgive that we receive in that sacrament, just as it's Christ's own Body that we receive in the Eucharist. It's not just a symbol, or a word, or an assurance; it's a reality.

Forgiveness is not just a subjective attitude but an objective reality, like forgiving a debt. Christ paid the debt on the cross, and that means we don't pay it. We are free. He has untied the knots that bind our souls. They are just as real as the knots in a rope that tie you to a chair. He really sets you free. You walk into that confessional box full of spiritual dirt and you walk out clean. It's like a shower. It really works because he really works; he does his job. That's his job description. That's what he came to earth for: to take away your sins; he is "the Lamb of God, who takes away the sin of the world" (John 1:29). In today's Gospel, Jesus gives that power to forgive sins to his Apostles and to their successors, the priests and bishops they ordained, in an unbroken chain that will last until the end of time.

Christ left the Church seven sacraments that have the power to give us his grace for different aspects of our life, for different rooms in our house. Baptism is like a bed, a birthing room. Confirmation is like a gym, a workout room. Confession is like a bathroom, a washroom. The Eucharist is like a dining room, a banquet. Both marriage and priestly ordination are like the entry room. And Viaticum, or "Last Rites," is like the bed again, our death bed, to give us strength for the final journey. As St. Paul wrote, "My God will fully supply whatever you need, in accord with his glorious riches in Christ Jesus" (Phil. 4:19).

ORDINARY TIME

SECOND SUNDAY IN ORDINARY TIME

FIRST READING

1 Samuel 3:3b–10, 19 _____

Samuel was sleeping in the temple of the Lord where the ark of God was. The Lord called to Samuel, who answered, "Here I am." Samuel ran to Eli and said, "Here I am. You called me." "I did not call you," Eli said. "Go back to sleep." So he went back to sleep. Again the Lord called Samuel, who rose and went to Eli. "Here I am," he said. "You called me." But Eli answered, "I did not call you, my son. Go back to sleep."

At that time Samuel was not familiar with the Lord, because the Lord had not revealed anything to him as yet. The Lord called Samuel again, for the third time. Getting up and going to Eli, he said, "Here I am. You called me." Then Eli understood that the Lord was calling the youth. So he said to Samuel, "Go to sleep, and if you are called, reply, Speak, Lord, for your servant is listening." When Samuel went to sleep in his place, the Lord came and revealed his presence, calling out as before, "Samuel, Samuel!" Samuel answered, "Speak, for your servant is listening."

Samuel grew up, and the Lord was with him, not permitting any word of his to be without effect.

_____

Today's reading from the Old Testament book of Samuel is about a miracle, a miraculous, supernatural intervention by God into the life of the young Samuel. God spoke audible words to him in the middle of the night, words that he literally heard with his ears. Since that does not ever happen to most of us, we probably wonder how this story is relevant to us. Is it merely a story about a hero and a saint who we admire from a distance, like watching a sports hero or a mountain climber doing something we could never do ourselves?

Even if that were its only purpose, that would justify its being in the Bible and being in our souls, because admiring heroes, looking up to our superiors, is a very good thing and very neglected in our culture. The very word "superiors," and even the word "heroes," is seldom used by our culture without irony, without a kind of sneer. But of course, we all have superiors. If you don't think St. Teresa of Kolkata, or Pope St. John Paul II, or St. Francis of Assisi, is spiritually superior to you, you are worse than an arrogant fool; you are morally insane.

But the point of today's story from Samuel is more than that. It applies not only to a few heroes but to all of us. For God speaks to all of us, even though he very rarely speaks by miracles. How? How does God speak to us?

That question has an answer, but the answer is not easy or obvious. Even when God speaks miraculously, what we are supposed to do about it is not easy or obvious, and we can make mistakes about it. As Samuel did. God spoke to Samuel miraculously, and Samuel had to learn how to listen and respond, even to the miracle. Three times he mistook the voice of God for the voice of Eli the priest. So if even a saint like Samuel could make three mistakes about a miraculous word from God, we certainly can make many more mistakes about non-miraculous words from God. So the question is: How and where and when can we, in a non-miraculous and everyday way, hear the voice of God, the will of God, of the same God that Samuel heard in a miraculous way?

There are many answers to that question. In fact, there are at least seven.

The first and most complete answer is: in Jesus Christ, in the words of Christ in the Gospels. Jesus is the primary miracle, and he is the whole revelation of God. St. Paul says in Colossians that "in him all the fullness was pleased to dwell" (Col. 1:19). And we know him, and his words, by the Gospels. We all received that miracle, the greatest of all miracles.

The second answer is that we not only *hear* the *words* of God ("words" in the plural) but we actually become personally *united with* the *Word* of God ("Word" in the singular)—that is, Jesus Christ, the Son of God. We actually

407

become united with him in our souls and even in our bodies in Holy Communion, in receiving him, all of him, Body and Blood, Soul and Divinity, in the Eucharist.

The third answer is that we hear the voice of God, the word of God, and the will of God in what we are told authoritatively by the Church that Jesus instituted and gave us as the living interpreter of his words. He said to his Apostles, "Whoever listens to you listens to me" (Luke 10:16). And he who hears Jesus, hears God.

The fourth answer is that we hear the voice of God in nature, in everything he created. We can find God in all things because he is the Creator and Designer of all things. Lying on your back and looking at clouds can be a form of prayer. Listening to rain, listening to thunder, listening to the mewing of kittens, is listening to something God gave us, so it is in fact listening to God's voice, however indirectly. Nature did not just happen by chance. It was designed by God, not for itself or for him but for us. Nature is a playpen full of toys for us spiritual babies to play with and love and learn from. On a higher level, nature is a great cathedral for us to wonder at and for us to worship in. We worship the Creator, not the creature, but the Creator is the Creator *of all these creatures*.

The fifth answer is: we can hear the voice of God in all the events in our lives, because everything in our lives is part of God's providence, part of the story he is writing. He is all-wise, so he knows exactly what we most need, and he is all-good, so he wants nothing but our best good, and he is all-powerful, so he can do anything; he can use anything and all things, even evils, for the ultimate end of our best good, our deepest joy. We cannot usually see this with the eyes of our bodies or even with the eyes of our human reason, especially in the things that cause us pain, but only with the eyes of faith and trust in his promises. So we can find God in all things, and trust him in all things and worship him in all things, because he has promised us that he works in all things; in fact, that he works all things together for good for all who love him. And God cannot lie; he cannot renege on a promise. As the great old hymn says,

God moves in a mysterious way
His wonders to perform.
He plants his footsteps
In the sea and rides upon the storm. . . .

Ye fearful saints, fresh courage take;
The clouds ye so much dread
Are big with mercy and will break
In blessings on your head.

Judge not the Lord by feeble sense,
But trust him for his grace;
Behind a frowning providence
He hides a smiling face.

His purposes will ripen fast,
Unfolding every hour;
The bud may have a bitter taste,
But sweet will be the flower.

Blind unbelief is sure to err
And scan his work in vain;
God is his own interpreter,
And he will make it plain.

The sixth answer is that we hear God's voice in our conscience. Conscience is God's inner prophet to all of us, the prophet in our souls. We must honestly inform our conscience, of course; it is not infallible; it is not God. But it is God's prophet, and it has moral authority, and it is therefore always morally wrong to deliberately disobey your conscience and always right to obey it. And when we do obey it, when we perform the works that God commands us to perform through that voice of conscience, we hear God's voice of approval in our conscience; just as when we disobey that voice, we hear God's voice of disapproval, which is called guilt. Guilt is like pain; its function is to be like a smoke alarm to wake us up.

The seventh answer is that we can hear the voice of God in prayer. When we pray, how much of our prayer time is listening and how much is talking? We need both, but we especially need to listen, because God is much wiser than we are. When you talk to a student, or a child, you do most of the talking because you know much more. When you talk to an equal, you do an equal amount of talking and listening. When you talk to someone much wiser than you, you mostly listen. So why don't we spend much time listening to God when we pray? Because we are fools. Or because we are lazy. It takes much more effort to listen than to talk. It's harder to be silent than to speak. But it's much more important when our conversation partner is God.

So next time we pray, let's reserve at least half of our prayer time for listening, in silence and with an open mind and an open heart. Let's speak those wonderful and powerful words that Eli taught Samuel: "Speak, LORD, for your servant is listening." Those were like the words that Mary spoke to God's angel, the words that allowed God to send his Son into her womb and her world; they were the words that saved the world by bringing Christ down. The angel did not force her but proposed to her, like an old-fashioned marriage proposal. What he proposed was the Incarnation. And Mary said yes. Her first word was the word *fiat*, which means "Let it be done." She said: "I am the handmaid of the Lord. May it be done to me according to your word" (Luke 1:38). That word, *fiat*, was the first word ever spoken in history, the first word ever spoken in time, for it was the word God spoke to create the world: *Fiat lux*; "Let there be light." That was God's first word to us, and it should be our first word to God too.

And when we speak it, we have to mean it, with our whole heart. We have to be open, willing, ready for anything God wants to give us. We have to say "Thy will be done" without reservation. And if we really do mean it, then the next thing we will do is listen, in silence, because that is what his will is. We will probably not hear literal words, as Samuel did, and we will only sometimes get a clear and strong intuition of what God wants to teach us, but the very act of being open to God in our will and our mind is the thing God wants most; it is valuable in itself, even if nothing else comes of it. God is a great psychologist; even when he seems to us to be silent, he is working on our subconscious mind, the part of us that we are not aware of. He transforms us, he really does things to us, every time we pray, even if we do not feel it.

If we really believed that, we would be content with the silence and not obsessively fill it up with our own words. When we say, "Speak, Lord, for I am your servant and I am listening," and then immediately fill up the silence with our own words, that means we didn't really mean what we said, because when we're doing the talking, we're not doing the listening. Actions speak louder than words, so those words "Speak, Lord, for your servant is listening" have to be not just words but an act, an action, a choice, a deed. We have to actually open the eyes of our heart and our will to God at that moment. We have to actually shut up. Only when Job stopped speaking, after about thirty chapters, did God start speaking. Only when Job shut up did God show up.

And if we do that, if we do what Samuel did and what Mary did, what will happen next? We don't know in the short run, but we do know in the long run. We don't know in the short run because God is patient and does not usually give us instant responses. He's preparing for us a great gourmet dinner with twelve courses, not a cheap, instant, fast-food hamburger. Since he is patient, we have to try to be patient. And that's hard. We are naturally impatient. Fortunately, God is so patient that he is even patient with our impatience. So keep trying.

And in the long run, gradually, that silence and darkness will bring the dawn and the light and the sunrise. We have to keep at it. Keep praying, many times every day, at least for a few minutes. Even when nothing seems to happen, something always really happens, because what happens is that we have changed the direction of our soul; we have stopped running in all directions and have steered our soul straight forward toward the Lord. If we have said, and meant, that prayer—"Speak, Lord, for your servant is listening. Command me, Lord, for with all my heart I want to obey your will, which I trust completely"—then the mere fact of just having prayed that prayer is sufficient even if we apparently get no answer to it at all. Just resting in God's will is our greatest peace and deepest joy, and that peace and joy can really be there even when we don't feel it.

RESPONSORIAL PSALM
PSALM 40:2, 4, 7–8, 8–9, 10 ⸺

R. (8a and 9a) **Here am I, Lord; I come to do your will.**

I have waited, waited for the LORD,
 and he stooped toward me and heard my cry.
And he put a new song into my mouth,
 a hymn to our God.

Sacrifice or offering you wished not,
 but ears open to obedience you gave me.
Holocausts or sin-offerings you sought not;
 then said I, "Behold I come."

"In the written scroll it is prescribed for me,
to do your will, O my God, is my delight,
 and your law is within my heart!"

I announced your justice in the vast assembly;
 I did not restrain my lips, as you, O LORD, know.

What is the unifying theme in the different verses of today's Psalm? I think it is the question "What does God want from us?"

If this question is uppermost in your mind, your mind is ready to align itself with God's; if not, not. In other words, if you really ask that question, if you really want to know, then you will get God's answer to it; if not, not.

So what does God want from us? What is his will for us? What is his policy, his method, his strategy, his plan for us? How does he nourish the relationship between us? Some parts of the answer are what we do, and some parts of the answer are what he does. The Psalmist mentions seven things.

The first thing we can do is wait. "I have waited, waited for the LORD." The Psalmist says it twice because waiting always feels too long and tries our patience. But we must never, never, never, never, never give up. Because God will always respond.

The second thing the Psalmist tells us is what God does in response to our waiting for him: he "heard my cry." Waiting is a "cry," a cry from the heart. Waiting is an active, passionate, and painful thing, not a passive, easy, comfortable thing. If we wait for God in this way, he will always hear us and answer us. And in answering us, the Psalmist says, he "*stooped* toward me," as a tall adult stoops to talk to a tiny child. He humbled himself. He came down to our level, since we cannot raise ourselves up to his level by ourselves.

The third point is in an unusual word that the Psalmist uses. He says that God gave him "*ears* open to obedience." God heard us with the ears of his divine heart, and his response was to give us more power to hear him with the ears of our human heart. God's ear heard us, and his response was to enlarge our ears.

How do we hear God? In the events of our lives; in Scripture; in prayer, when we stop talking and start listening; in conscience; and above all in the Gospel, in Christ's life and death and Resurrection. We do the same thing in all these hearings: we simply open the ears of our souls and pay attention.

The fourth point is that God gave us "ears open to *obedience*"—not just to hearing but to obeying, not just to thought but to action, not just to filling our minds with more knowledge but filling our lives with more giving of ourselves.

413

In Scripture, the most usual meaning of the word "faith" is not just "belief" but "fidelity," which is expressed in acts of obedience.

Fifth, God's gift is not only new ears but also a new *tongue*: "He put a new song into my mouth." God gives us joy, and a *new* joy, a new song. He always surprises us. The faithful are not surprised that God keeps his promises, but the *way* God does that always surprises us. No one expected a Messiah like Christ: not his friends, not his enemies, not even the devil.

Sixth, the Psalmist says that what God wanted was not first of all the material sacrifices that he himself commanded in the Old Testament, lambs and rams and bulls and vegetable offerings. These were only symbols and expressions of the gift all lovers want: not jewelry or flowers or even bodies but hearts, selves, the gift of the self, which is what love is.

God actually wants your heart. He longs for it. He is happy every time you make every act of love, every time you give a bit of your heart to him or to your neighbor. He cares about that; he is not indifferent to it. It makes an enormous difference to him, because he really loves you; he really cares. How big a difference? Look at a crucifix. He showed you how much he cares by dying on the cross for you.

Now comes the seventh and final answer to how God strengthens the relationship between us and him. We're all selfish and sinful and not very good at that gift of self that God wants above all. But Christ is good at that. Thus, what God does finally, and definitively, is to give us Christ, his own divine Son, who is the song and the offering and the obedience. For us, it is a struggle to say with all our heart and soul, "Thy will be done," but not for Christ. "I come to do your will" (Heb. 10:7)—that is the essence of Christ's will; that is why Christ came; that is the whole meaning of Christ's life; and that is why Christ gave himself as a sacrifice in our place. He came to do that because that was God's will. Jesus gave himself for us because he first gave himself to the will of his Father. We must not think of the Father as cold and distant, as less passionately loving to us than Christ the Son. For Christ the Son is the total, complete, and perfect revelation of the Father. When St. Philip asked him,

"Show us the Father, and that will be enough for us," Jesus replied, "Have I been with you for so long a time and you still do not know me, Philip? Whoever has seen me has seen the Father" (John 14:8–9). "God so loved the world that he gave his only Son, so that everyone who believes in him might not perish but might have eternal life" (John 3:16).

And that everlasting life, that salvation that God gave us in giving us Christ his Son, is not just salvation from hell, from the punishment for our sins, but also salvation from sin, from sinning. We now can become saints. We cannot be instantly perfect, as he is, but we can be on the road to it; we can grow toward it. And since we cannot yet love God with our whole heart and soul and mind and strength, he helps us by giving us himself in the sacraments, so that he is in us and we are in him in each stage of life and in all our struggles. As St. Paul wrote, "Yet I live, no longer I, but Christ lives in me" (Gal. 2:20). He is *with* us. His name, "Emmanuel," means literally "God with us."

Of course, we still sin. We still need patience. We still wait, and then wait some more, for the fullness of our salvation and redemption and sanctification. Our lives may seem as imperfect and as messy and as full of struggles as before Christ came to us. But they are different, and the difference is not just in one area of life that we call "religion." He said, "Behold, I make *all* things new" (Rev. 21:5). Everything is different now, because now it is Christ within us who is sharing all those struggles and imperfections with us; and that changes everything. It's like the difference between not being married and being married. Before you got married, you worked and played and you did many things, both good and bad; and now that you are married, you still work and play and do many things, both good and bad; but everything is different because now you do it as a married man or woman. The things you did alone, you now do together. Spiritual marriage to Christ is like that. You are never alone.

SECOND READING

1 Corinthians 6:13c–15a, 17–20 _____

Brothers and sisters: The body is not for immorality, but for the Lord, and the Lord is for the body; God raised the Lord and will also raise us by his power.

Do you not know that your bodies are members of Christ? But whoever is joined to the Lord becomes one Spirit with him. Avoid immorality. Every other sin a person commits is outside the body, but the immoral person sins against his own body. Do you not know that your body is a temple of the Holy Spirit within you, whom you have from God, and that you are not your own? For you have been purchased at a price. Therefore glorify God in your body.

The Greek word St. Paul uses that our modern translations render as "immorality" is *porneia*, from which we get our word "pornography." It does not mean just a general or generic "immorality" or moral evil. That is simply not an accurate translation. It means "sexual immorality."

The modern translation of *porneia* as "immorality" instead of "sexual immorality" reflects the modern reduction of morality to sexual morality, which is a ridiculous mistake, as ridiculous as reducing morality to economic morality or military morality or ecological morality. There are, after all, nine other Commandments.

Today in our sex-obsessed culture, we tend to use the word "ethics" for every *other* moral issue and use "morality" for only sexual issues, thus implying that sexual morality is different: that it is personal and subjective and not subject to other moral laws like truth and honesty and fidelity and promise-keeping and justice. We make an exception to all the universal moral laws for sexual matters.

Nowhere else do we believe that morality is individual and subjective and there are no universal objective rules. We do *not* wink at insider stock trading, or racism, or bullying, or environmental pollution, or nuclear threats, or even smoking! We do *not* believe it is okay to lie to and cheat each other or to renege on our promises in any other areas, but we do say it is okay to do that on our sexual promise to be faithful to our spouse. When we get married, we promise to be faithful "till death do us part," and when we divorce, we show the world how seriously we meant that promise. If the most important person in our life can't trust us to keep our most serious promise, why should anyone else trust us to keep any other promise? Or, when we got married, did we promise something else? Did we promise to be faithful "only till I find somebody I like better than you"? If that's all we meant, we never really got married in the first place. And we lied when we spoke our wedding vows.

We do not believe that it is ethically or morally permissible to do what history proves will more securely and certainly destroy our society than anything else—namely, to ruin society's most important foundation, the stable and faithful family; but that is what divorce does, and we okay it because it's about marriage and marriage is about sex. Our sexual autonomy and sexual freedom trump everything else.

Here's another popular modern example of *porneia*. We do not believe it is ethically or morally permissible to murder innocent human beings simply because we find them inconvenient to us, especially if they are vulnerable and defenseless; but we do say it is okay to do that to our own unborn children. Why? Because abortion is backup contraception, and contraception is our demand to have sex without having children.

Neither St. Paul, nor his Jewish culture, nor his Christian culture, nor the Church, for two thousand years, nor other religions of the world, nor any great sage or saint or prophet, ever believed that sexual freedom trumps all other moral laws. Our society is the first in history to believe that. We have never been very good about *obeying* the moral laws about sex, but we have at least *believed* in them—until now. That's why we speak of "the sexual revolution." It is a revolution that is far more life-changing and society-changing and future-changing than any political revolution, because it is about sex, and sex is the origin of life (or was, at least, until contraception was invented, which is the foundation for the whole sexual revolution).

By the way, most people do not know the historical fact that for the first nineteen Christian centuries, not a single Christian and not a single Christian church or denomination ever permitted contraception, until the Church of England did in 1930, and subsequently every Christian church and denomination in the world has changed its 1,900-year stand on contraception, and also on divorce, except one: the Catholic Church.

That fact is the main reason why the secular media all hate and fear and despise the Catholic Church: not for its theology or the rest of its morality but just because we alone still stand against the tsunami of *porneia*. We alone refuse to worship the new Caesar, the new god.

Either the Bible speaks the truth or it lies when it says that your body is holy, that it is the temple of the Holy Spirit. Either St. Paul or Sigmund Freud is mistaken. Either the Bible or *Playboy* magazine does not understand sex. Either the saints or the secular media are really stupid. Either God or Hollywood has this all wrong. I wonder which it is. Which of the two ought to be teaching and correcting the other? Should we try to get God to repent and conform to our secular anti-Catholic times, or should we repent and try to conform to eternity? Gee, that's a tough one to figure out, isn't it?

The world tells big lies about the Church in this area above all. The Church's view of sexuality is *not* that it is "dirty." That's the world's view! It thinks it's so much fun because it's forbidden, because it's "dirty," and it thinks the Church forbids it because it's so much fun. But it's not the Church that's "obsessed" with sex; the world is. The Church has even greater things to think about, infinite things, like God and heaven and eternal joy; but the world does not; that's why the world is obsessed with sex. It's all they've got left.

The Church's view of sex is that sex is far greater than the world thinks it is. It's not only good, it's holy. God invented it, and even commanded it. The very first commandment God gave to us in the Garden of Eden was to "be fruitful and multiply," and I don't think he meant to grow oranges and memorize the multiplication table. God designed sex, and life, and the connection between the two.

Pope St. John Paul II called our modern Western culture a "culture of death" because if we don't love human life, new human life, other human lives, if we look on new human lives as "problems" or "issues" rather than infinitely valuable images of God destined for eternity, then we will abort these "problems"; we will choose death, not life, for those persons that we label "problems." They are threats to our autonomy and to our planning and to our income. We want to play God; we don't want other lives to exist if we didn't plan them.

If that's what we think, then we are missing out on life's greatest joy. Family and children give us life's greatest joys as well as life's greatest inconveniences, because they give us life's greatest loves. The nature of love is really what the sexual revolution is about. It's about the meaning of love, and the confusion between love and lust, and the separation between love and life, love and procreation. Our culture wants to separate sex from procreation for two reasons: because it reduces love to sex, and because it doesn't love life. But God thinks otherwise about those two things. God doesn't reduce love to sex, and God doesn't want to separate sex from procreation, because God does love life, and he also loves sex. It's his invention.

That's the elephant in the living room. That's the big picture that we forget. It's usually the big picture, not the details, that we forget. There are important and legitimate details about sex, like responsible family planning, for instance, which is reasonable and right, and there are good and natural and happy ways to do it in Natural Family Planning. But it's the big picture that we forget: the nature of love and the love of life. And because God is love and God is life, God is always in the big picture.

Part of God's business could rightly be called "planned parenthood," because God planned it. God planned parenthood; God invented parenthood. The Church deserves that name, not the organization that murders parenthood by murdering the children parenthood produces. Abortion is not planned parenthood; it's planned un-parenthood. If you want to be a parent, you don't go to Planned Parenthood. You go there if you *don't* want to be a parent, even though you already are, because you have already procreated a son or a daughter, but you hate being a parent and will do anything to alter it, even killing your own son or daughter. That is what abortion does, literally. We have to be literal here and inevitably offend many people, because polite euphemisms are lies and coverups. Unborn babies are human beings, persons, not "problems" or "issues" or "clumps of cells." They do not suddenly change from "its" to "hes" or "shes"; they do not suddenly become human persons, when the two blades of the obstetrician's scissors meet in cutting the umbilical cord.

Abortion is the central sacrament of the sexual revolution. Listen carefully to the words that express the central motive for abortion, the central reason for abortion, the central justification for abortion. Listen carefully to the four words a mother most often speaks to justify destroying her son's or daughter's life by abortion: "This is *my* body." Those are the exact same words that are spoken by a Catholic priest—or rather, by Christ himself, using the mouth of the priest—to give supernatural life, to bring the life of God incarnate into the Eucharist and into the bodies and souls of all who receive it.

One of those two people is lying when they speak those words, "This is my body." I wonder which one it is.

Jesus said, "Whatever you did for one of these least brothers of mine, you did for me" (Matt. 25:40). All human beings, without exception, born or unborn, are our sisters and brothers, because God is our one Father. Cain justified the murder of his brother Abel with these words: "Am I my brother's keeper?" (Gen. 4:9). Cain's answer to his own question was no. God's answer was yes. I wonder which one spoke the truth? Do we have the courage and honesty to ask that question?

(Personal postscript to priests: I am fairly certain that many people will hate you if you give this as a homily. And I am even more certain that God will love you. See Isa. 49:15.)

GOSPEL
JOHN 1:35–42 _____

John was standing with two of his disciples, and as he watched Jesus walk by, he said, "Behold, the Lamb of God." The two disciples heard what he said and followed Jesus. Jesus turned and saw them following him and said to them, "What are you looking for?" They said to him, "Rabbi"—which translated means Teacher—, "where are you staying?" He said to them, "Come, and you will see." So they went and saw where Jesus was staying, and they stayed with him that day. It was about four in the afternoon. Andrew, the brother of Simon Peter, was one of the two who heard John and followed Jesus. He first found his own brother Simon and told him, "We have found the Messiah"—which is translated Christ—. Then he brought him to Jesus. Jesus looked at him and said, "You are Simon the son of John; you will be called Cephas"—which is translated Peter.

_____

Today's Gospel reading, about Jesus' first few disciples choosing to follow him, is quite clear. But there are three points in it that we may overlook, but which are so important for us all that they can change our lives.

The first point is that most of the disciples don't simply come to Jesus on their own; they are led by others. Andrew brought his brother Peter to Jesus; and John the Baptist brought many to Jesus by identifying Jesus, not himself, as "the Lamb of God" and as the promised Messiah. Because they trusted John, they trusted Jesus, for John pointed to Jesus. They followed his pointing finger because they trusted it; they trusted his *words* because they trusted *him*.

That's the way the Church grows. No one ever became a Catholic without the help of other Catholics who got there before them, both the living and the dead. The most important of these are called parents. There is abundant scientific research that shows that by far the single most effective predictor of children's continued faith and fidelity to the Church is the presence of a father who goes to church regularly.

Jesus' last words to us were his commandment to go out and preach the Good News to the whole world. He didn't limit that to preachers. We don't all need to be like John the Baptist in going out into the wilderness and living a monastic and ascetic lifestyle, but we all need to be like John the Baptist in leading others to Christ. That's the mission of every Christian. There are many kinds of Christians, and there are many tasks that are specific to some Christians but not others, like John the Baptist's; but to be any kind of Christian at all is necessarily to be a missionary. A missionary is simply one on a mission, and we are all given the same mission by Christ, to preach the Gospel, using words when necessary.

"Oh, good," we think when we hear that. "Then I don't have to use words. That makes things easier and less embarrassing." No, your mission is not easier but harder than just using words. It's using deeds. Your essential mission is becoming more and more like the saints. If we become trustable people, others will trust us when we speak, and then they will learn that we are not the source of our own trustable qualities, but Jesus is. In one of his epistles, St. Paul says to the ordinary Christians he is writing to that "you are our letter, written on our hearts, known and read by all" (2 Cor. 3:2).

We are books. People read us. We are pointing fingers. Do we point to ourselves or to our Lord? The pointing doesn't have to be done in words, and often shouldn't be, but it always has to be done in deeds of love and honesty and caring. G.K. Chesterton wrote that there is only one really strong argument against Christianity: Christians. He would also say that there is only one really strong argument *for* Christianity: Christians—joyful Christians, loving Christians, honest Christians, trustable Christians.

It's a tremendous responsibility that we have, and it's one we cannot escape. Everything we say and do answers the world's question "What does a Christian look like?" And that's an unanswerable argument because it's a fact, and you can't argue with facts. That's why the saints conquered the sinners, that's how the martyrs conquered the lions, and that's how Christians conquered the pagan world. And that's the most fundamental reason why Christians are losing the world and diminishing today in our culture—that is, in Europe and North America—while they are expanding in many other cultures around the world, especially where they are poor and persecuted.

◑◐

In the very first words of Jesus recorded by John, we find the second important point we might miss in today's Gospel. John's disciples come to Jesus, and Jesus asks them a question: "What are you looking for?" In other words, What do you want? What are you looking for in coming to me? We seek him; we quest for him; we question him; and his answer is to question us, to question our heart, our love, our motive.

Whenever God shows up in the Bible, he reverses the relationship that people expect: they expect him to give them answers, but he gives them questions instead, and *they* have to give the answers. They do that by their choices. Life is a test, a true-false test, or a multiple-choice test between good and evil. We don't give God the test; he gives us the test. And we respond. That's what's meant by responsibility: literally, *response*-ability, the ability to respond.

The question Jesus asks his prospective disciples is "What are you looking for?" In other words, he's testing their hearts, not just their heads. He's asking what they love. Do they love what he is, or something else? Are they looking for a political leader who will help them with their political agenda, whatever it is, either rebellion and revolution against the Roman Empire or collaboration with it and profit from it? If so, they shouldn't come to him, because that's not what he is. Do they love comfort and convenience and ease and wealth and worldly success and power? If so, they shouldn't come to him, because if they do, they will find the opposite: discomfort and inconvenience and hard challenges and even persecution. And they won't get rich. None of Jesus' saints ever made a million dollars building a Jesus theme park or a Jesus megachurch with rock bands and gold costumes. Most of the saints were poor, and the ones who were rich gave away most of their riches.

But if what they are looking for is God, and what God is, which is total truth and total love, total honesty and total self-giving; if they are ready to give rather than to get, if they are looking to give themselves away to the God who is greater than they are rather than get for themselves some advantage, some improvement, some perks; if they want to belong to God and live for God and become more like God and conform to God and his will rather than having God conform to them and their will—if that's what they want, if that's where their heart is, why, then, he is their man. But if not, he's not.

Or, if they are halfway in between these two states of soul, as many of us are; if half of them wants to give and half wants to get; if half wants to say to God, "Thy will be done," and the other half wants to say, "My will be done"; and if they want to grow the half that says to God, "Thy will be done," and shrink the half that says, "No, *my* will be done, my sinful and selfish and stupid will"—if that's what they want, then they should also become his disciples, because he will teach them how to grow one half of their heart and how to shrink the other half.

Becoming a Christian is a lot like getting married and like becoming a parent. Do it only if you want your whole life turned inside out, if you want it to center on the good of your spouse, not on yourself, and on the good of those little, vulnerable, needy people who are your children, instead of centering your life on your own good. If that's what you want, you will get it, and you will certainly get life's greatest joys and deepest satisfactions, and also life's greatest sorrows and sufferings. You will get both crosses and resurrections. But they won't be just yours. They will be *his* too, because you will be his and he will be yours. That's the business he's in. (You can enroll in that business in the single life too, by the way.)

ↄ

The third remarkable thing in today's Gospel is what Jesus says to Simon. He changes his name to Peter. This was one of the many different ways Jesus claimed divinity. For in Judaism, only God can change your name. No Orthodox Jew, to this day, is allowed to change his name. In Judaism, as in most ancient cultures, names are not just man-made labels. Names are sacred, because your name signifies your identity and your destiny, and only God can give you that. God changed Abram's name to Abraham, Sarai's name to Sarah, and Jacob's name to Israel; and in doing so gave them a new meaning, a new reality, a new identity and destiny. This is what Jesus now does to Simon, changing his name to Peter, which means "rock."

It was almost a joke, because if you follow everything that's written about Peter in the four Gospels, you see that Peter is not at all rocky but sandy; he's always putting his foot in his mouth and saying the wrong thing. Jesus deliberately chose this "sandy" man to become the rock on which he promised he would build his Church. On the beach, many centuries of waves turn rock into sand, but Jesus turns sand into rock. This "Rock" was made, not born. Peter was made a rock by God, not by man; he was *re*-made by God. He was not born as Rocky; he was "born again" as Rocky. You see that "Rocky" in the Acts of the Apostles, when he is clearly the one in charge and in authority in the early Church. So today's Gospel is really the earliest beginning of the Church.

Peter became the first bishop of Rome, the capital of the world; and like the other Apostles, he ordained successors, as Jesus had commanded them to. This line of apostolic succession has remained intact for two thousand years. The bishop of Rome, from the beginning, was always the court of last resort in the Church, where this formula emerged: "Rome has spoken, the case is closed." We call them "popes" today; the name has changed but not the reality, and not the Christ-given authority.

There have been many ineffective popes, some stupid popes, and even a few spectacularly wicked popes in the history of the Church, especially around the time of the Protestant Reformation; but not one of them ever changed or contradicted the public, authoritative, official teachings of his predecessors on faith and morals, even if some of the wicked popes may not have even believed them, cared about them, or practiced them. That is literally a miracle. From the time of St. Peter and the Apostles, the Church has never once changed, repudiated, denied, gone back on, or contradicted what she has always officially taught, and she never will, because of the promise Jesus made to Peter in the Gospel: "Upon this rock I will build my church, and the gates of the netherworld shall not prevail against it" (Matt. 16:18). No other institution on earth has ever been able to make that claim. No other institution can make that claim of total consistency of teaching for two thousand years.

The teachings of the Church—the one visible Church that Christ created and gave his divine authority to—are not just the teachings of the Church but the teachings of Christ; that is why they are binding for all places and times, universally. That's the literal meaning of the word "catholic"; it means "universal," that is, for all places and all times and all people.

That is why we are Catholics: because we are Christians. Our fidelity to the Church that Christ founded, and to her popes, beginning with Peter, is grounded in our fidelity to Christ. It is made necessary by our fidelity to Christ. Imagine the Church as an orange. Christ is not the juice we squeeze out of the orange; Christ is the farmer who planted the orange tree. Christ made the Church; the Church didn't make Christ. Christ made Simon into Peter; Peter didn't make Jesus into Christ.

THIRD SUNDAY IN ORDINARY TIME

FIRST READING
JONAH 3:1–5, 10 _____

The word of the LORD came to Jonah, saying: "Set out for the great city of Nineveh, and announce to it the message that I will tell you." So Jonah made ready and went to Nineveh, according to the LORD's bidding. Now Nineveh was an enormously large city; it took three days to go through it. Jonah began his journey through the city, and had gone but a single day's walk announcing, "Forty days more and Nineveh shall be destroyed," when the people of Nineveh believed God; they proclaimed a fast and all of them, great and small, put on sackcloth.

When God saw by their actions how they turned from their evil way, he repented of the evil that he had threatened to do to them; he did not carry it out.

_____

Jonah was history's most successful prophet. No one else ever converted a whole large city so suddenly and so completely.

We do not know whether the story of Jonah is meant to be literal history or a parable, a fiction; but in either case its messages are true, for all of us. And its four main messages are the following: first, that we are all citizens of a sinful city, whether it is called Nineveh or New York or simply fallen mankind; second, that God requires repentance and conversion and change of life; third, that God calls and authorizes and sends prophets to speak the truth to us with his own divine authority; and fourth, that if we do repent, his threats will change into promises and his punishments into blessings.

These four points are well known and not controversial among believers. What is puzzling and needs explanation is the author's use of one word in the story: the word "repent." It is not used of the citizens of Nineveh, though it is certainly implied. The author simply describes their visible actions; he says only that they fasted and turned from their evil way, but these external actions clearly are caused by inner repentance and conversion. What is puzzling, then? That the word "repent" is used of God. The writer says, "When God saw by their actions how they turned from their evil way, he repented of the evil that he had threatened to do to them; he did not carry it out." That seems to mean that God changed his mind, and therefore *that God changes*, that God is not the unchanging God that the rest of the Bible says he is. And it also seems to mean that *we* can change *God*, that we can change his mind. It even seems to mean that God can admit that he had been wrong about us, about Nineveh.

These three ideas—that God changes, that we can change God, and that God can be wrong—are all clearly labeled as heresies, as falsehoods about God, by the Church, by all the saints, and by the rest of the Bible. So this passage in the Bible cannot really teach these three heresies that it may seem to teach.

How, then, should we interpret these words, especially the word "repent" when it is ascribed to God?

Let's use an analogy. Suppose your diet included a lot of sugar, and you got diabetes, and you kept eating sugary foods. You would get sicker and sicker, of course, and you might say that your body was punishing you, was angry with you, and was even threatening you with death if you kept eating more sugar. Suppose then that your doctor, like a prophet, told you that you would die if you didn't change your diet, so you repented and changed your diet, from sugary foods to sugarless foods. The result would be that your body now rewarded you in not making you sicker but healthier. You might say that your body changed its mind and repented of the harm it was threatening to do to you, that it became your friend instead of your enemy.

That analogy is not perfect, because your body really did change, and God does not change. So let's use another analogy that's a little better than the first one. Let's say you go out into the summer sun without sunblock and stay out all day, and you come back with a really painful and really harmful sunburn. You might say the sun was punishing you. And in a sense it was: it was punishing you for being in the wrong relationship to it. In fact, the sun did not change at all; only you changed. But you might express that change by saying that the sun had become your enemy. And that was true, but it did not mean that the sun had changed, only that you had, and that therefore your relationship to the unchanging sun had changed.

God is always perfect: perfectly just and perfectly merciful, perfectly punishing sinners who do not repent and perfectly forgiving sinners who do repent. There is no change in God, and no contradiction between justice and mercy in God. But there is change in us, and therefore also in our relationship to God. When that change is a sin, it moves us farther away from God, and when that change is repentance and conversion, it moves us back to God, closer to God. When we receive the sacrament of Confession, we are radically changed, but God is not. What St. Paul calls "the old man" walks into that sacrament, and what he calls "the new man" walks out. Adam walks in, and Jesus walks out. Eve walks in, and Mary walks out. A dirty soul walks in, and a clean soul walks out. That is a change, and a truly tremendous change. But it does not change God; it lets God change us.

So the word "repent" ascribed to God in this passage from Jonah, and in some other, similar passages in Scripture, is true—everything the Word of God teaches us is true—but it is not literal. God does not literally repent and change any more than the sun changes.

How do we know that? How do we know what passages to interpret literally and what passages to interpret nonliterally? By the rest of the Bible and by the uniform, unchanging, official teaching of the Church that Christ established for us. If a literal interpretation contradicts the clear and uniform teaching of the rest of the Bible and the Church, then a nonliteral interpretation is called for.

For instance, when Genesis says that God walked with Adam and Eve in the Garden of Eden in the cool of the day (Gen. 3:8), that should be interpreted symbolically rather than literally because the Bible clearly teaches that God is a spirit and did not take a human body until the Incarnation. So it is a physical *analogy* for the spiritual state of Adam's and Eve's souls rather than a literal fact about their bodies. It describes their intimate and joyful relationship with God. It's not meant to describe the literal nature of God as if he had a human body long before the Incarnation. So questions like "Was God male or female?" or "Did God have white skin or black?" are simply wrong questions, based on a misunderstanding.

We could call this nonliteral meaning figurative or allegorical or symbolic or analogical or metaphorical. Nonliteral language does not mean false language. When we say, "I see your point now," or, "that idea never entered my mind before," we can still be telling the truth, but we don't mean the literal truth of seeing a physical point or entering a physical room. We often make mistakes in interpreting God's Word, but God's Word does not make mistakes in interpreting us.

The literal truth about God is that God does not really change, but our relationship with him does change, and needs to change, again and again, by our repeated repentances and conversions, or turn-arounds (which is what the word "conversion" literally means). That's why we have the sacrament of Confession. We do not change God, but he really changes us.

RESPONSORIAL PSALM
PSALM 25:4–5, 6–7, 8–9 _____

R. (4a) **Teach me your ways, O Lord.**

Your ways, O LORD, make known to me;
   teach me your paths,
Guide me in your truth and teach me,
   for you are God my savior.

Remember that your compassion, O LORD,
   and your love are from of old.

In your kindness remember me,
    because of your goodness, O Lord.

Good and upright is the Lord;
    thus he shows sinners the way.
He guides the humble to justice
    and teaches the humble his way.

Today's Psalm speaks of God's "ways" and asks God to teach us his "paths." What do those words mean? Jesus says, "I am the way" (John 14:6). What does he mean? Instead of just sitting back passively and feeling bored because we've heard all this so many times before that it all has become a cliché that says nothing to us, let's dare to think about the actual words in this Psalm, especially the word "way." What are God's "ways"?

It means God's character, God's style, God's personality, God's nature, as manifested in the ways God acts, the ways God does things. God has a character, a personality. He is not everything in general and nothing in particular. He is infinite, but infinite in each of his very definite and definable attributes: he is infinitely wise, not foolish; infinitely powerful, not weak; infinitely good, not evil; infinitely alive, not dead, and so forth. We can make his acquaintance, we can get to know him, we can have a personal relationship with him, because he has a distinctive personality, just as we can get to know each other. He is not "everything." "Everything" has no personality. He is not "being in general." You can't get to know or make the acquaintance of "being in general."

The Psalmist mentions seven words, seven nouns that describe that "way" of God: "truth," "compassion," "love," "kindness," "goodness," "upright," and "justice." So if our personality is like God's, and if therefore our way of living and acting is like God's, then we will have truth in our mind, uprightness in our will, love in our heart, goodness in our intentions, compassion in our emotions, justice in our actions, and kindness in our style. God's "way" is complete; it's in all the dimensions of our life.

The Psalmist then uses five words, five verbs, to describe the relationship he prays for: that God may "teach" or "make known" to him his ways, that God may "guide" him, that God may "remember" him, that God may "save" him, and that God may "show" him. Let's examine what these familiar words mean.

God *remembers* us because he never forgets us. He forgets nothing; he knows everything, and he does not change.

He *teaches* us by revealing his ways, by *showing* us, not just by telling us—that is, by showing us his saints, and above all his Son.

He *guides* us in our choices and our actions by his law, his commandments, which is our road map through life.

And he *saves* us from our three worst enemies, sin and death and hell, by coming among us to live and die and resurrect for us.

The Psalmist then, finally, uses two words to describe us, who are the objects of God's teaching and making known and guiding and remembering and saving and showing. They are "sinners" and "the humble."

If we do not know and admit that we are sinners—that is, if we are not humble—we will not receive any of these "ways" of God. Humility and confession and repentance of sin is the first and most nonnegotiable requirement for getting to know God. All the saints, without exception, say that. We must begin not with "I'm smart" but with "I'm stupid"; not with "I was right" but with "I was wrong"; not with an "Aha!" but with an "Oops!" And not with speaking but with listening; not with noise but with silence. God speaks in amazingly diverse ways, but we'll never hear him if we never shut up.

What are those "amazingly diverse ways" of learning God's "ways"? How do we humble sinners receive that teaching, guiding, remembering, saving, and showing from the God whose "way" is truth, compassion, love, kindness, goodness, uprightness, and justice? Where do we find God and his unique personality? In the beauty and intelligence manifested in the universe he created, and in the providential events of our lives, and in his prophets, and in the writings of Scripture, and in the teachings of the Church, and in her creeds, and in our own conscience and its awareness of the natural moral law, and in our prayer life, and in the lives of the saints, and above all in Christ, who is known in the Gospels and received in the sacraments.

That's ten ways, ten ways we find God and ten ways he finds us. That's not a snack; that's a banquet. So let's nibble more and more at this magnificent banquet table. It's not too little: it's too much for us to appreciate.

SECOND READING
1 Corinthians 7:29–31 _____

I tell you, brothers and sisters, the time is running out. From now on, let those having wives act as not having them, those weeping as not weeping, those rejoicing as not rejoicing, those buying as not owning, those using the world as not using it fully. For the world in its present form is passing away.

What does St. Paul mean by his strange words in today's reading? The first and last lines are clear: "the time is running out" and "the world in its present form is passing away." That means two things: that we will not last forever in this world and that this world will not last forever, that everything in the created universe is mortal and will die, especially us. Even if we are not alive at the end of *the* world when *it* dies, we will be there at the end of *our* world when *we* die. In other words, St. Paul could have invented the bumper sticker recently seen on a Catholic college campus: "Study for your finals; read your Bible."

But what does St. Paul mean by his five paradoxes in the middle? He says that, because time is running out, because the world in its present form is passing away and therefore so are we, if we have wives, we should act as not having them (and of course this equally means wives should so regard their husbands, but Paul is writing as a man, not as a woman); and if we weep, we should act as if we are not weeping; and if we rejoice, we should act as if we are not rejoicing; and if we buy and own things, we should act as if we are not owning them; and if we use the world and the things of this world, we should act as if we do not do that—what does he mean? Are we to be pretenders and liars?

Perhaps a simpler and clearer translation might be the RSV: "Let those who have wives live as though they had none, and those who mourn as though they were not mourning, and those who rejoice as though they were not rejoicing, and those who buy as though they had no goods, and those who deal with the world as though they had no dealings with it."

St. Paul is not saying we should simply stop all marriages, all weeping, all rejoicing, all buying, and all dealings with the world. He is saying we should do these things as if we were not doing them, with a kind of detachment, remembering that they, like us, are all dying, and that in the new world, in the resurrection, they will not be part of our eternal lives; they will be replaced by something far better. We will rejoice there, but not over worldly things like money and worldly pleasures and powers and promotions. In heaven, we will not weep at all; or if we do, God will wipe away every tear from our eyes. We will not need to buy or sell or own any private property because everything will be free. We will not marry because we will not procreate more children in heaven. (Children are the forgotten reason, the primary reason, for the importance of monogamy and fidelity on earth.) The most important and fundamental of all human relationships on earth—namely, marriage—will not be in heaven, or will be radically changed in heaven. So will the four other aspects of human life: sorrows, joys, property, and even earthly justice and injustice in dealings with the world.

So St. Paul is simply saying that all these things are only temporary and mortal, so we should not set our very deepest hearts on them. We may love them but not worship them. They are not our gods. We should be detached from them even as we are rightly involved in them. Of course, we must still marry and weep and rejoice and buy and deal, but that is no longer our deepest identity and our greatest good and hope and meaning. God is. This world is precious and beautiful and good and God-created, but it is not our ultimate goal and meaning and home and resting place. Neither life above the ground nor underground in the cemetery is our final resting place. Heaven is. This world is only heaven's womb.

That does not mean this world and its marriages and joys and sorrows and possessions and dealings are worthless and meaningless. It means that they are like rainbows or fireflies: beautiful but short-lived. They are like our pets. They are precious, and we are to love them and care for them, of course, but they will die and we will live on, and our eternal life is not totally bound by them, defined by them, or relative to them.

And that is true even of other people, even our best friends and even our families. We must love them, of course, but not worship them, not treat them as our God. We are defined by God, relative to God. God's first commandment to us, the one Jesus calls "the greatest and the first commandment" (Matt. 22:38), is to adore God alone, nothing else, no idol, no created thing, however good and precious.

If we get that first commandment wrong, we will get the second great commandment wrong too, the commandment that tells us to love our neighbor as ourselves. If we forget the first great commandment and worship our stuff, or our life in this world, or even our neighbor, who is only God's image-bearing child, not God—if we treat any of them as God, we will put divine burdens on human shoulders and those shoulders will break, and it is not right to do that to them any more than it is right to not do that to God. Use things, love people, and worship God. Don't use God, love things, or worship people.

Adoring God alone actually frees us to love the mortal things in our lives more, not less; because only when we put first things first can we do justice to second things. But when we put second things first and first things second, we not only lose the first things, but we also spoil the second things by making them into gods. They become addictions.

Detachment—the detachment from our can't-let-go grasping of the mortal things of this world, even the best of them, namely marriage and family; the detachment that St. Paul teaches us in today's epistle—is the only way to freely enjoy these worldly things, especially the best of them.

There are two reasons for this, one positive and one negative. (They are really only the two dimensions of one and the same reason.) The first reason, the positive reason, is the principle of first and second things that I just mentioned. The only way to truly appreciate second things is to put them second to first things. The only way to enjoy mortal goods is to realize they are mortal. The best way to appreciate life is to realize that you will die.

The second reason, the negative reason, is that the alternative to detachment is addiction, and addiction never brings joy, only misery. All idols break.

This is probably why ghosts haunt houses: they were so addicted to their place on earth that they could not go to heaven yet. They are working out their painful purgatory, gradually learning detachment the hard way—that is, by experience.

We can only do justice to the second great commandment, to love our neighbor as we love ourselves, if we first do justice to the first great commandment, to love God *not* as we love ourselves but with our whole heart and soul and mind and strength. If we love ourselves with our whole heart and soul and mind and strength, we are treating ourselves as God!

Social justice is a very important second thing, but it is not the first thing, and we cannot do justice to justice unless we love love more than justice, and we cannot do justice to either social justice or human love if we idolize them, or anything else—if we treat them as our God.

Muslims wisely and devoutly repeat five times every day "La ilaha illa Allah," "Only God is God." That's our Lesson One too. There are many more lessons than this Lesson One; and some of those further lessons, especially about Christ and his forgiving love, are not fully understood by our beloved brothers the Muslims, who are also God's precious children. But if we don't learn Lesson One, we make a worse mistake than the Muslims make because then we have a big building without a foundation, even if they have the foundation without much of a building.

So let us certainly love and enjoy our God-given blessings in this world, and above all our spouses; but let us not worship and adore them as our god. Because if we do, if we make them our God, we will find one day that Nietzsche was right when he said that God is dead.

GOSPEL
MARK 1:14–20 _____

After John had been arrested, Jesus came to Galilee proclaiming the Gospel of God: "This is the time of fulfillment. The kingdom of God is at hand. Repent, and believe in the gospel."

As he passed by the Sea of Galilee, he saw Simon and his brother Andrew casting their nets into the sea; they were fishermen. Jesus said to them, "Come after me, and I will make you fishers of men." Then they abandoned their nets and followed him. He walked along a little farther and saw James, the son of Zebedee, and his brother John. They too were in a boat mending their nets. Then he called them. So they left their father Zebedee in the boat along with the hired men and followed him.

_____

We see in today's Gospel the same principle we see in today's epistle, where St. Paul said we are to look on our most precious things in this mortal world—our spouses, our temporal joys and sorrows, our property, and our jobs—as if they were already gone, because some day they will be; because this whole world is destined to die, and our share in it is destined to die very soon, sometime in the next hundred years or so. If we make these things our God, if we treat them as our ultimate end and good and hope and happiness, we will be terribly disappointed when we lose them, which we will inevitably do when they die or when we die. So when God commands us to give up any of these earthly goods of ours for his sake, we are wise to do it.

And that is what Jesus' first four disciples did when he asked them to. They were all fishermen (Peter and Andrew, James and John) and they were all brothers, and all of Jesus' disciples are called to be fishermen and brothers: fishers of men, of souls, not of fish, and also brothers, under our one Father, God. When Jesus called them away from their job and their father Zebedee, they followed him immediately, without even picking up their nets.

That's what it means for us, too, to follow Jesus as our Lord, our Savior, and our God: our Lord to obey totally, our Savior to put all our hope in, and our God to adore alone. He is our only absolutely absolute absolute in this relative world, the only eternal thing in this temporal and mortal world.

If that's not true, the whole faith is a lie. And if it is true, then when these four disciples left everything in their life to follow Jesus, they were not being foolish; they were being realistic—that is, they were living in reality, living in the real world, the world in which only this man is God, only this man is "the way and the truth and the life," our ultimate good and end, our whole hope and home and happiness and holiness.

So let's resolve to be like those four fishermen. Let's love the things and persons in this world as we should; not less than we should and not more than we should; as precious but mortal, as goods but not gods, as images of God but not idols. Let's not be like those ghosts that can't leave their houses. Let's remember that the words of the old Southern Gospel song are literally true, that "This world is not my home, I'm just a-passing through." That's not dreamy idealism, that's utter realism. Let's live in reality instead of living in our fantasies.

What is reality? That the whole world is the *Titanic* and that Jesus is our lifeboat.

This vision is not just about the future, about death. It is also about the present. For like the four fishermen who abandoned their nets "immediately" when Christ called them (Mark 1:18 NRSV-CE), we are called on to die to whatever we are doing at the moment Christ calls us to stop doing it or to do something else.

This "immediately" is important. It is a word that St. Mark uses constantly, over and over again, in his Gospel. The reason it is important is not that we never get second chances. We do, repeatedly, though not forever. (There are no second chances after death.) But the reason the "immediately" is important is that that word signifies the present time, and the present time is the only time that is real. The past is no longer real; it is dead; and the future is not yet real; it is unborn.

If the whole meaning of life is our relationship to our Creator and Redeemer, it is important to know when that relationship can happen, or be changed and improved. And the answer is: not in the past or in the future but only in the present. We cannot rely on what we used to do or on what we plan to do, that cannot take the place of what we must do now. As St. Paul says in one of his letters, "Now is a very acceptable time; behold, now is the day of salvation" (2 Cor. 6:2).

So if you have never definitively and irrevocably given your whole self and your whole life to Christ your Lord and Savior and only hope, do it now. Now, before you think one more thought, before I say one more word. The heart of all true religion is what the Muslims call "islam," which is a word that means total and absolute surrender to the one true God.

We will have to repeat that act of total surrender thousands of times, but if we do not do it the first time, we will never be able to repeat it.

So please don't be satisfied with giving God large chunks of your life, those chunks that you define as religious. Give him all of it. It is foolish, it is really impossible, to try to bargain with God, to try to give him an important *part* of your life but to keep back a little bit of it for yourself alone; to say "Thy will be done" about most things but to say "My will be done" about other things. That will always produce endless struggle and frustration and a divided heart. The only way to be free from that struggle is to give him everything. Say, and mean, "Thy will be done," "Thy perfectly loving will, thy perfectly wise will, thy perfectly perfect will, be done to me and in me and by me and through me in every single part of my life."

And make no exceptions for your sex life or your financial life or your thought life. God is the creator and designer and friend of your sex life and of your financial life and your thought life. He is not your enemy.

We all cherish freedom from our enemies, but God is not our enemy but our friend. We cherish freedom from all evils, but God is not ever any kind of evil; he is our greatest good. We cherish freedom from tyranny, but God is not a tyrant but our Father. We cherish freedom from force, but God is not a Force but a person. We cherish freedom from fear, but God is not to be feared with slavish fear but to be loved. The fear of the Lord is only the beginning of wisdom; the end is love, a love that includes total trust and faith and hope in God no matter what, because there is no limit to his power, or of his wisdom, or of his goodness, his love for you personally. He designed your personal genetic code. He gave up his body and blood on the cross and in the Eucharist for you—for you personally, not for "humanity" in the abstract. He wants the love of your heart, your unique and irreplaceable self. If you truly love someone, the one thing you most want from them is love in return.

Lovers don't want freedom from each other. They want *union* with each other, and God wants union of heart and will and mind with you. Lovers want freedom only from whatever is an enemy of their love. The only enemy of our love of God is sin, and the central sin is selfishness, self-worship. Don't worship yourself or your freedom or your autonomy; worship God. He is the source of every true good, and freedom is a good, therefore God is the source of your true freedom. He will not diminish it, he will enhance and perfect it.

So if and when he calls you to leave your fishing nets, leave them for him. And if he calls you to work your nets, work them for him.

FOURTH SUNDAY IN ORDINARY TIME

FIRST READING
Deuteronomy 18:15–20 _____

Moses spoke to all the people, saying: "A prophet like me will the Lord, your God, raise up for you from among your own kin; to him you shall listen. This is exactly what you requested of the Lord, your God, at Horeb on the day of the assembly, when you said, 'Let us not again hear the voice of the Lord, our God, nor see this great fire any more, lest we die.' And the Lord said to me, 'This was well said. I will raise up for them a prophet like you from among their kin, and will put my words into his mouth; he shall tell them all that I command him. Whoever will not listen to my words which he speaks in my name, I myself will make him answer for it. But if a prophet presumes to speak in my name an oracle that I have not commanded him to speak, or speaks in the name of other gods, he shall die.'"

_____

Two of the most prominent teachings in the Old Testament are, first, that "the beginning of wisdom is fear of the Lord" (Prov. 9:10) and, second, God himself says that "you cannot see my face, for no one can see me and live" (Exod. 33:20). Moses, who received the Ten Commandments from God himself on Mount Sinai, was the only exception to that. The typically modern impulse to see God as nice, as comfortable, as chummy, is as radically out of line with reality as a butterfly thinking it can live in a volcano. The Jews knew God well enough to pray, after they heard the voice of God speaking, "Let us not again hear the voice of the Lord, our God, nor see this great fire any more, lest we die." And God approved their fear. He said, "This was well said."

Moses was the only man who ever saw God's face and lived. He was the

441

mediator between God and his people. Even this did not take away the fear: they were even terrified by the light that came from Moses' face when Moses came down from the mountain from his meeting with God. And God's response to their wise and prudent fear was to promise them another mediator, another prophet like Moses, a human being, from among their kin, whose words would be God's words. This prophet's human name was not named here, but his divine name was implied by these words spoken by God: "I will put my words into his mouth." His divine name is the Word of God. His human name would be Jesus.

How serious, in God's eyes, is the sin of claiming divine authority when you do not have it? Of claiming to be a divinely authorized prophet, a mouthpiece, of the true God when you are not? That is so serious that God instituted the ultimate punishment for that sin: death. "If a prophet presumes to speak in my name an oracle I have not commanded him, or speaks in the name of other gods, he shall die."

Jesus claims to be that mediator and that divine authority. If that claim is false, no one ever deserved to be crucified more than Jesus did. Jesus claimed to be more than a merely human prophet; he claimed to be divine. He claimed more than any other sane man in human history ever claimed. And if that is not true, then Jesus is the most blasphemous liar in the history of the world.

The Catholic Church claims to be the one true Church, the one divinely authorized prophet from God. If that is not true, then the Catholic Church is the most blasphemous false prophet among all the churches and denominations in the world, and it deserves the death penalty, it deserves to be annihilated, according to God's own words in Scripture.

So we cannot be just nice and polite and tolerant and indifferent to the Church, as if it's just a religious version of a social club, any more than we can be just nice and polite and tolerant and indifferent to Christ, as if he's just a sickeningly sweet nice guy like Ned Flanders on *The Simpsons*.

In a similar way, we cannot take that attitude toward the Eucharist, because the Eucharist, after the consecration, is Christ himself, hiding behind the appearances of bread and wine. If not Christ, it is the Antichrist; it is the work of the devil; it is idolatry.

At the Mass, Christ uses the lips and tongue of his consecrated priest to speak the words that actually bring about what they say, "This is my Body" and "This is my Blood"; and we worship and adore as our God what looks like a little round piece of bread and a cup of wine. If it is only what it looks like, if it's really only bread and wine, then we are the world's worst idolaters; we are bowing down to bread and worshiping wine. But if it is what Jesus said it is, if it is really his Body and Blood, then we Catholics are the world's most fortunate persons, for God has allowed us the incredible privilege of taking the whole Christ, God and man, divinity and humanity, body and soul, into our body and soul, uniting all of us with all of him.

RESPONSORIAL PSALM
PSALM 95:1–2, 6–7, 7–9 ⸻⸻⸻⸻⸻⸻

R. (8) **If today you hear his voice, harden not your hearts.**

Come, let us sing joyfully to the LORD;
    let us acclaim the rock of our salvation.
Let us come into his presence with thanksgiving;
    let us joyfully sing psalms to him.

Come, let us bow down in worship;
    let us kneel before the LORD who made us.
For he is our God,
    and we are the people he shepherds, the flock he guides.

Oh, that today you would hear his voice:
    "Harden not your hearts as at Meribah,
    as in the day of Massah in the desert,

Where your fathers tempted me;
   they tested me though they had seen my works."

The heart of human life is religion, which means relationship with God. At the heart of our religion is the Mass. At the heart of the Mass is the consecration of the bread and wine that transubstantiates them into the real presence of Christ, Body and Blood, Soul and Divinity. When we come into this presence, the real presence of the real God, what is our attitude? How do we respond to the Real Presence?

There are two possibilities, and these are contrasted in today's Psalm verses. The first is thanksgiving: "Let us come into his presence with thanksgiving; let us joyfully sing Psalms to him. Come, let us bow down in worship; let us kneel before the LORD who made us. For he is our God, and we are the people he shepherds." The very word "Eucharist" means literally "good gift"; and when we are given a good gift, our only fitting response is thanksgiving. The gift here is the Giver himself, giving himself to us in the most total, most concrete, and most intimate way possible: both his divinity and his humanity, and, within that humanity, both his human soul and his body, and, within his body, both his flesh and his blood.

The other possible reaction to this amazing gift is also mentioned in this same Psalm passage: it is to harden our hearts and to test God, as if we were the teachers and God was our student taking our test and we were correcting his answers. We do that when we refuse to believe in him and trust him unless he does what we expect him to do and says what we expect him to say and wills what we expect him to will. We do that when we judge the amazing and stunning things he did do and say to be unbelievable, and we cut it down to size, so to speak, to fit it into our minds and our expectations.

One way of doing that is to say that Christ's Real Presence in the Eucharist is a beautiful holy symbol but not literally true, as Christ clearly said and as the Church for two thousand years has always clearly said it is. That is an example of what the Psalmist is talking about: to harden our own hearts and minds and try to soften God's; to correct God's Word and God's words and ideas by ours rather than vice versa; to edit God's mail instead of delivering it intact; to claim to teach our divine Teacher instead of studying under him as his students. And now comes the shock: according to the polls, that is the attitude the majority of people in America who call themselves Catholics have toward this most holy and sublime mystery in the universe, the Eucharist.

Please do not be one of these stupendously shallow and stupid souls. Please give God the credit for knowing exactly what he is doing and for meaning exactly what he is saying. And please learn the meaning of the word "humility." God is the only "know-it-all," and you're not God. Sorry to have to tell you that shocking news.

And if you feel hurt by this and you sincerely believe that it is I, not you, who manifest this arrogant lack of humility, then please come to me and confront me and correct me, because that is the very last thing in this world I ever want to do; and I promise that I shall listen to you attentively and sincerely and be grateful to you for your honesty.

SECOND READING

1 Corinthians 7:32–35 _____

Brothers and sisters: I should like you to be free of anxieties. An unmarried man is anxious about the things of the Lord, how he may please the Lord. But a married man is anxious about the things of the world, how he may please his wife, and he is divided. An unmarried woman or a virgin is anxious about the things of the Lord, so that she may be holy in both body and spirit. A married woman, on the other hand, is anxious about the things of the world, how she may please her husband. I am telling you this for your own benefit, not to impose a restraint upon you, but for the sake of propriety and adherence to the Lord without distraction.

How things have changed since the days of St. Paul! Today it is almost exactly the opposite from what it was when Paul wrote these words: "An unmarried man is anxious about the things of the Lord, how he may please the Lord. But a married man is anxious about the things of the world, how he may please his wife, and he is divided." Today, it is *un*married men who are the most worldly, the most irreligious, the most violent, the most murderous, the most drug-addicted, the most incarcerated, the most anti-God, anti-Christ, anti-Church, anti-religious, anti-moral, selfish, self-indulgent, unfaithful, uncommitted, and irresponsible class of people in the world, and it is married men who are the opposite of all these things.

Race and gender and economic class does not divide us into those two categories at all, but marriage does. Marriage and childbearing are the world's most effective teachers of sanity, morality, unselfishness, responsibility, and fidelity. And deep happiness. Because they teach the most important lesson in life: that the only way to be happy is to stop thinking of your own happiness first and other people's second. The only way to get is to give; the only way to live is to die to your self-centeredness. And the best way to learn to do that is the way God invented for the majority of the human race—namely, marriage and family. God's greatest gift to humanity, next to Jesus Christ himself, is a spouse and children to give your heart and your life to.

We have a vocations crisis today, but the vocations crisis is in the world more than in the Church. The Church can get along with only a few good priests, but the world cannot get along with only a few good mothers and fathers. The Church is not collapsing, and never will, but the family is collapsing, and all of society is collapsing with it. All the happiest civilizations in history have been family friendly.

Our changing situation does not make St. Paul's principles untrue. Just the opposite. For what St. Paul says about the value of remaining unmarried, so as to give all of your life to God in the most complete and concrete way, is still a valid reason for celibacy among the clergy, and for vocations to the celibate religious life, for being a nun or a monk or a religious brother.

This is not because marriage and childbearing are not good and honorable.

In fact they are more than that: they are essential to living a complete human life. Celibacy is not an escape from them but another form of them.

To see that, let's begin with the fundamental reason and purpose God had for inventing marriage and the family. It wasn't just to propagate the race biologically, for animals do that without the institution of marriage and the family. And God could have multiplied the human race the same way he multiplied angels: simply by creating more individuals one by one. But God designed marriage and the family as the primary way to accomplish the central purpose of every human life: to wean us away from our natural childish selfishness and into the life of self-giving which is the essence of sanctity.

So the vocation of celibacy is not an alternative to marriage and family. It is another kind of marriage—being married to the Church—that's why priests must be men, because the Church is a woman, our Mother, not our Father. God is our Father, and not our Mother.

And priestly celibacy is also another kind of family and children—a family of many spiritual children, many more of them than one could ever have physically. The same goal and the same principle applies to both vocations, lay and clerical: that our natural tendency to selfishness must be broken, like the Eucharist, to be given to others.

And the same is true of the third vocation, the vocation to the single life of service. There is no fourth vocation to the single life of self-indulgence, any more than there is a vocation to the married life of self-indulgence or the clerical life of self-indulgence. We all have one of three vocations; we are all called to a life of service and self-giving, whether in the married life, the religious life, or the single life.

And that remains true not because our culture designed it but because God designed it. So it was true when we lived in a premodern culture of wisdom and piety to God, family, and ancestors, a society that began by accepting duties; and it remains true today in our modern culture of foolishness and impiety and self-indulgence and demands rather than duties, a society that begins by insisting on "rights."

Our society is not our God. The *New York Times* and the *Wall Street Journal* are not our Scriptures. Harvard University is not our Magisterium. And Hollywood's stars are not our angels or our saints. We can do a heaven-of-a-lot better than that.

GOSPEL
MARK 1:21–28 _____

Then they came to Capernaum, and on the sabbath Jesus entered the synagogue and taught. The people were astonished at his teaching, for he taught them as one having authority and not as the scribes. In their synagogue was a man with an unclean spirit; he cried out, "What have you to do with us, Jesus of Nazareth? Have you come to destroy us? I know who you are—the Holy One of God!" Jesus rebuked him and said, "Quiet! Come out of him!" The unclean spirit convulsed him and with a loud cry came out of him. All were amazed and asked one another, "What is this? A new teaching with authority. He commands even the unclean spirits and they obey him." His fame spread everywhere throughout the whole region of Galilee.

Jesus was an exorcist. He freed many people from evil spirits, demons, devils, fallen angels. That's literal fact, not symbolism or mythology or fantasy. God is pure spirit, and he created angels, who were also pure spirits, and he gave them free will, and some of them chose evil rather than good, and these are evil spirits. They hate us and want to ruin our souls and our lives. They have three levels of power over us: temptation, oppression, and possession. All of us are tempted by them, and when we sin we lose our innocence; some of us are deeply oppressed by them, and we lose our joy; and a very few are possessed by them, and they lose their freedom. Jesus freed many people from demonic oppression and demonic possession. Freeing from demonic possession is called exorcism.

Today every diocese in the Church has an exorcist. Jesus, in the Gospels, explicitly said that one of the things his Church would do, in continuing his work in this world in every age until the end of time, would be to exorcise demons (Mark 16:17).

Cases of demonic possession are very rare but very real. Mistakes are easy to make about this, confusing merely human, natural psychological disturbances with supernatural demonic possession. The Church is very careful to rule out purely natural causes, psychological causes, before she calls on exorcists.

Those who saw Christ's exorcisms were astounded because they knew that no merely human being has power to control demons, any more than our pets have the power to control us. Today, as in Christ's day, only Christ can exorcise demons. Christ's exorcisms were evidence of his divinity. The same Christ who worked through his biological human body in first-century Israel continues to work through his Mystical Body the Church and her exorcists today.

Although we cannot by our own power conquer demonic *possession*, we can always conquer demons' *temptations*. The Bible says that "No trial has come to you but what is human. God is faithful and will not let you be tried beyond your strength; but with the trial he will also provide a way out, so that you may be able to bear it" (1 Cor. 10:13). Notice it does not say God will make it *easy* to resist temptation, only possible. If it was *impossible* to resist temptation, we would not be responsible for yielding to it. Temptation always appeals to some degree of free choice, not sheer force. If a murderer, by sheer force, put a gun in your hand and forced your finger to pull the trigger, you would not be responsible for the murder.

Temptations are common and do not remove free will; demonic posses- sion is very rare and does remove free will, for a while. The middle category, demonic oppression, is less clear: it's somewhere between resistible and irre- sistible, and somewhere between very common and very rare. Not all lines between natural and supernatural evils are clearly drawn, and neither are all lines between natural and supernatural goods. We sometimes don't know whether that surprisingly sudden remission of a malignancy was a supernatural miracle or just divine providence using natural forces. There are gray areas as well as blacks and whites; fogs as well as darkness and light. But demon possession is clearly darkness, and Jesus is clearly light. And when the two meet, darkness has absolutely no chance.

If Jesus can easily and infallibly defeat even demons, he can certainly defeat all our lesser, foggier pieces of darkness. His power, his love, and his wisdom are infinite. Don't give him 99 percent of your trust; give him 100 percent. That's the practical, bottom-line takeaway from today's Gospel for all of us.

FIFTH SUNDAY IN ORDINARY TIME

FIRST READING
Job 7:1–4, 6–7 _____

Job spoke, saying:
Is not man's life on earth a drudgery?
   Are not his days those of hirelings?
He is a slave who longs for the shade,
   a hireling who waits for his wages.
So I have been assigned months of misery,
   and troubled nights have been allotted to me.
If in bed I say, "When shall I arise?"
   then the night drags on;
   I am filled with restlessness until the dawn.
My days are swifter than a weaver's shuttle;
   they come to an end without hope.
Remember that my life is like the wind;
   I shall not see happiness again.

_____

The question of how we should interpret any passage of Scripture is most basically the question of what God wants to teach us in it, what God wants us to learn from it, what the Holy Spirit is telling the Church, and therefore each of us, in inspiring this passage. For nothing in Scripture is accidental, and nothing is for a few people only; everything is deliberately intended by God for all of us.

The first thing we can learn from this passage is empathy and sympathy for Job, and for others today who, like Job, are suffering terribly and do not understand why God is allowing it. In other words, our first response to the classic "problem of evil"—Why does God allow bad things to happen to good people, sometimes even very bad things to very good people?—should be not a philosophical explanation but a personal empathy. That gets us inside the problem rather than outside it. We need objective truth about the problem of evil, but we also need subjective compassion and love and sympathy. Head and heart both have their work to do.

Job's three friends argue that since God is just, Job must deserve his sufferings. They are right about God but wrong about Job, and God, at the end of the book, is angry at them for not beginning with human sympathy for Job. They have logical heads, but they lack loving and sympathetic hearts.

We know from God's own words about Job that he is not suffering because he deserves it; he is a saint. So Job's three friends, all of whom try to defend God's justice by arguing that Job must be a great sinner and must deserve all that suffering, are wrong.

It's true that God is just, but it's also true that God's justice is mysterious, that God works out his justice in mysterious ways. He allows evils, even great evils, to happen to those whom he loves only because he brings even greater goods out of them in the end. He works out all things, even very bad things, for the eventual greatest good of all who love him and trust him. That's the plotline of God's divine providence.

But even this answer, which we find in the Old Testament as well as the New, is not the deepest answer to the problem of evil. Christ is. Though Christ is even more righteous than Job, he suffers even more than Job. In Christ, the very worst things happen to the very best person. Christ reveals the deepest answer to the problem of evil, and it is a very different answer than either the justice answer of Job's three friends or even the mysterious divine providence answer of the rest of the Bible.

Christ is the ultimate answer to Job; Job suffers not only because God, in his infinite wisdom and love, sees that it will bring him more joy in the end, but also because Job is a Christ figure; Job's sufferings are part of the sufferings of Christ because Job, as a righteous man, is part of the Body of Christ.

One more thing we can learn from this passage is a simple truth about human life on earth that applies to every single person who has ever lived: that this life is indeed full of misery as well as joy, that "this world is not enough."

Let's look at the details of Job's complaint.

First, he says that life seems like drudgery, like slavery, like working for money instead of for the job itself. "Is not man's life on earth a drudgery? Are not his days those of hirelings? He is a slave who longs for the shade, a hireling who waits for his wages."

This is a real complaint, and we all feel it at times, and it gives us a very practical piece of wisdom about choosing a career. We should never choose a career just for its wages, if we do not love it, if we don't think it is worth doing even if we don't get paid for it, if we would never do it for free, for its own sake. Of course, we all need money, but we need meaning even more. A well-paid slave is not as happy as a poor artist doing work he loves.

And once we have chosen a career, or even a temporary job, even if we think it is worth doing, there will always be moments when it feels to us more like slavery than like love, as life felt to Job. And at those times, we must remember our reasons for our choice to do this job in the first place, and recapture that motivation, that purpose, that good end.

And what we should do about our job is also what we should do about life itself.

Job's second complaint is about time. During the day he longs for sleep, and during the night he longs for the day. But his days, in turn, are days of drudgery and misery, and he longs for rest and sleep. That restlessness, though painful, can be instructive, and even good: it is Augustine's famous restless heart, which is bound to be restless until it rests in God. This world is not enough, and it is not meant to be enough. It is meant to give us only appetizers of meaning and happiness, not the main course. We are meant to find in it something between meaningless and our ultimate meaning. In heaven, in eternity, we will not find our meaning in being a good car salesman or a good nurse or a good environmental scientist or a good firefighter, because there will be no need for those things in heaven: no cars, diseases, pollution, or fires. We must find meaning in our work here, but we should not idolize it and say, "That's it; that's all; that's enough." We *should* complain that it's not enough; we *should* be restless until we rest in God. Our ultimate happiness is not in time, whether in work or rest, whether day or night, but in God, in eternity. He's not one among many good options; he's the source of all good.

A third thing Job complains about, after drudgery and time, is death. Like the words of the old song "Ol' Man River," Job says he is tired of living but also scared of dying because he is not confident of the next life. At this point in history, well over three thousand years ago, God had not yet clearly revealed the resurrection and the next life. Job complains that his days are few and pass quickly: "My days are swifter than a weaver's shuttle; they come to an end without hope. . . . My life is like the wind; I shall not see happiness again."

Hope is one of the three greatest things in the world, along with faith and love. In Dante's *Inferno*, the sign on the gate to hell reads: "Abandon all hope, ye who enter here." But no one can hope to keep the good things of this life forever. Everything in this universe is guaranteed to end in death, even the galaxies. That is the single most certain fact about life. Even taxes are escapable sometimes, but never death. If there is no life after death, then our complaints that this world is not enough and that our hearts are restless are meaningless, and we long for something that simply does not exist. And how could that be? Every other need can be met, at least for a time; every other hunger has a food. But the need and the hunger for a life that is stronger than death, a life that conquers death rather than being conquered by it, is a need in every human life, and a hunger in every human heart. If it all ends forever when we die, then even the most glorious and happy and meaningful life is hopeless, in the end.

In the book of Job, we find Job expressing his complaints, but we also find him expressing his faith and hope, as when he said, "I know that my Vindicator lives, and that he will at last stand forth upon the dust; Whom I myself shall see" (Job 19:25–26). That faith and hope are what keep Job going even through his terrible sufferings. And that's what must keep us going too. Of course, Job did not know about Christ and the Resurrection; he did not fully understand his own words here. The Holy Spirit inspired them for us more than for Job. But we do understand those words, and it's faith and hope that enable us to say yes to life even when our life, like Job's, has so many nos in it: because we hope in God, not in ourselves or the things of this world; because we know the God whose love is stronger than death.

Finally, there's a lesson in Job's complaints. God approves of them. It is not a sin to complain. Job is a saint, and saints complain. In fact, if we do *not* complain about evil, about physical evil, or suffering, and emotional evil, or depression, as well as moral evil, or sin; if we simply passively sit back and say, "Oh, well, whatever will be, will be; I can't do anything about it, so I may as well not add to my sufferings by complaining; I shall be a Stoic and suppress my natural human emotions"—if we say that, there is something missing in us, something very good and very natural. God does not want us to be doormats or dishrags. He respects our Job-like complaints if they come from our restless heart that he himself designed not to rest until it rests in him.

Job's three friends never said anything like this. Everything they said about God was right and proper. Yet when God showed up at the end, his judgment on their words was disapproving, and his judgment on Job's words was approving. He said, "You have not spoken rightly concerning me, as has my servant Job" (Job 42:7). Why?

Because Job was honest, and they were dishonest? Perhaps. Job was certainly honest, but there is nothing to suggest that they were dishonest.

Because Job's theology was right and theirs was wrong? No, because they said about God only what the rest of the Bible says about God, while it was Job who questioned God. He did not deny God, but he did question God. Jesus never once told his disciples, "Don't ask so many questions!"

I think the only answer to why God loved Job's words and Job's attitude more than those of the three friends was because they only preached, but Job prayed. They spoke only *about* God, as if he were absent, while Job spoke *to* God, in prayer. Job lived in the real world, the world where God is always present, never absent; the three friends did not. Job "practiced the presence of God." That is the first step in prayer, and prayer is the first step in attaining the whole meaning of life, which is to become a saint.

RESPONSORIAL PSALM
PSALM 147:1–2, 3–4, 5–6 _____

R. (cf. 3a) **Praise the Lord, who heals the brokenhearted.**
or: R. **Alleluia.**

Praise the LORD, for he is good;
    sing praise to our God, for he is gracious;
    it is fitting to praise him.
The LORD rebuilds Jerusalem;
    the dispersed of Israel he gathers.

He heals the brokenhearted
    and binds up their wounds.
He tells the number of the stars;
    he calls each by name.

Great is our Lord and mighty in power;
    to his wisdom there is no limit.
The LORD sustains the lowly;
    the wicked he casts to the ground.

_____

Today's Psalm verses seem to say nothing new, nothing remarkable, nothing surprising. Yet everything they say is new and remarkable and surprising. Let's take the time to use this as an example of how to read and meditate on Scripture.

    It begins: "Praise the LORD, for he is good." "Well, of course," we think. No, it is not at all an "of course." Pagans and polytheists do not praise their gods; they fear them. If they reverence them, it is not a joy; if they praise them, they do not "*sing* praise to our God." What does our pagan culture sing about? Where is its joy? Where is its heart? Where is its love? It is in shallow pleasure, not deep and lasting joy; in lust, not love; in recreational sex, not marriage and family; in selfishness, not in sanctity; in the worship of the self, not the worship of God.

The Psalmist's confession that God is good is far from obvious. In fact, it takes a great act of faith to believe that. The world is full of evils, physical and emotional and moral, sufferings and sadnesses and sins. Believers are few, and unbelievers are many. We've made great progress in science and technology, but almost nowhere else: certainly not in happiness or social harmony or holiness. We are commanded to pray "Thy kingdom come, thy will be done, on earth as it is in heaven," but that is apparently not happening. To sing praise to God takes deliberate effort. It is not obvious or automatic. It's not easy to sing the hymn

This is my Father's world:
O let me ne'er forget
That though the wrong seems oft so strong,
God is the ruler yet.

We need to keep instructing and correcting our own souls and reminding them that, in the words of another great old hymn,

Ye fearful saints, fresh courage take;
The clouds ye so much dread
Are big with mercy, and shall break
In blessings on your head.

We praise God most of all for the fact that he is more than just good, and perfect, and righteous, and just; he is "gracious." Grace goes far beyond justice. Grace does not mean giving good things to those who deserve them—that's justice—but to those who do not. Even if it is obvious to the reason that God must be perfect and therefore always just, it is not at all obvious that God freely chooses to go beyond justice into grace and mercy and forgiveness; that he casts his pearls of grace before us swine. He has to be just, but he does not have to go way beyond justice; that is his free choice.

How far does he go with this apparently irrational and even crazy love for us? To answer that question, just look at a crucifix and remember the words "My God, my God, why have you forsaken me?" That self-sacrificial love was so far from obvious that no one in the whole world expected it.

But what does God do about history's repeated victories by the bad guys over the good guys? What about the ongoing defeats of God's own chosen people, both before the coming of Christ and after? The Jews are persecuted, hated, and oppressed by everybody. In AD 70, the temple was destroyed, and with it the worship that God commanded; the whole holy city of Jerusalem was destroyed, and God's people exiled again, this time not just for seventy years in Babylon but for 1878 years, all over the world, from AD 70 until 1948, when they got their own country back again. And Christians, too, are persecuted and martyred in every century—in fact, far more today than ever before—and God's Church is reviled, hated, and feared by the world (unless the Church compromises itself, because that's the only way to win the world's love). What does God do about that?

The Psalmist's answer to this question is that "the Lord rebuilds Jerusalem; the dispersed of Israel he gathers." The faith, like Christ, is murdered, and then it rises from the dead. After defeat, victory; after death, life; after scattering, gathering. And just as the body Christ had after his death and Resurrection was more glorious than the one he had before, so with the Church: after its times of persecution and defeat, after its martyrdoms and crucifixions, it always resurrects to greater glory, not less. Christ promised that the gates of hell will not be able to prevail against his Church. He told us, "In the world you will have trouble, but take courage, I have conquered the world" (John 16:33). That

458

is not obvious or commonsensical; that is dramatic and shocking. This Psalm is just the opposite of a platitude or a cliché: it is almost unbelievable good news.

But why does God allow heartbreaking things to happen to us first? If he is pure love and wills our highest joy, why does he allow so many tears? The Psalmist prophetically affirms the answer: because "he heals the broken-hearted and binds up their wounds." It's all part of God's plan. The heart that was broken and is now healed is a heart with more joy, as well as more love and wisdom, than the heart that was not broken. Those who were wounded and then healed are stronger and have a deeper joy than those who were not wounded and were not healed. If we did not die, we could not be resurrected; and those who have died and have resurrected are in far greater glory and joy than those who have not died.

God alone has the power to do that, to resurrect the dead, to bring back a greater joy and glory than all that we have lost. And God alone has the wisdom to know how to do that, and when; we do not; that's why we need faith: because *we're not God.* To many people that's shocking news. Stop the presses! Call out the reporters. But our newspapers will never print that news.

How much does God's wisdom transcend ours? The Psalmist says, "He tells the number of the stars; he calls each by name." There are trillions of stars, far more than there are grains of sand on all the beaches of the world. God knows every one. In fact, God knows every atom and subatomic particle in the universe. Is it conceivable that he does not know and love you in every little detail of your life?

Who is God? The Psalmist's answer: "Great is our Lord and mighty in power; to his wisdom there is no limit." What does he do? The Psalmist's answer: "The Lord sustains the lowly; the wicked he casts to the ground."

God does that down-casting of the wicked as well as that sustaining of the lowly, the humble, out of his love, for he knows that the wicked can be changed into the lowly only by being cast to the ground. We all need some down-casting as well as some uprising because we are all partly righteous and partly wicked. The good shepherd knows his sheep. Sheep are very stupid and stubborn and need to learn many things the hard way. But God is very patient and very wise and dearly loves his foolish children. And so must we.

SECOND READING
1 Corinthians 9:16–19, 22–23 _____

Brothers and sisters: If I preach the gospel, this is no reason for me to boast, for an obligation has been imposed on me, and woe to me if I do not preach it! If I do so willingly, I have a recompense, but if unwillingly, then I have been entrusted with a stewardship. What then is my recompense? That, when I preach, I offer the gospel free of charge so as not to make full use of my right in the gospel.

Although I am free in regard to all, I have made myself a slave to all so as to win over as many as possible. To the weak I became weak, to win over the weak. I have become all things to all, to save at least some. All this I do for the sake of the gospel, so that I too may have a share in it.

St. Paul, in today's epistle, reveals one of the most important methods of preaching the Gospel, the method that Jesus himself used and the method that the early Church used to successfully convert the world. He says that he has freely made himself a slave to all; he has become all things to all. To the weak he became weak.

What does that mean? It certainly does not mean pretense, pretending you are something you're not—for instance, pretending you are weak or poor when you aren't. It means actually becoming all things to all people, sharing their life so that they may share the life of Christ, divesting yourself of all your privileges except one: you know the Gospel; you know Jesus Christ; you know the meaning of life.

People are naturally suspicious of preachers. They rightly suspect that the preacher is out to convert them, and they think that this means stealing sheep from other sheepfolds to populate the preacher's sheepfold, whatever it may be. "What's in it for him?" is their natural question. Well, St. Paul answered that question by saying that nothing was in it for him. He shared whatever weakness, whatever poverty, whatever lack of perks his congregation had. He gave up everything for the Gospel, for the truth, for the joy of knowing Christ, which he wanted to share. He says elsewhere in one of his epistles (Phil. 3:8) that all his perks—a Pharisee of the Pharisees; as to the Law blameless; educated at the feet of Gamaliel, the greatest rabbi of the century, the man the Jews called "the light of Israel"; a Roman citizen (a rare and precious privilege for a Jew)—Paul said that all these perks and privileges, compared with knowing Jesus Christ, were *skubala*. It's a Greek word, and it means waste matter, refuse, especially from the anal parts of animals such as bulls. Yes, it's the Greek s-word. Paul is deliberately using it for shock value. Compared with Christ, the whole world is a pile of that. And it's nothing to Paul to flush all that down the toilet if only he can gain Christ, who is the source of all goodness and beauty and joy and happiness because Christ is God, and God is not only all goodness and truth and beauty but also all joy and all love, and he loves us so much that all he wants is to share his joy with us, and he will do *anything* to attain that end, even give up his life, his body and blood, his everything, for us. Paul is just doing what Jesus did: becoming poor for the sake of the poor, as God became human for the sake of us humans.

That's the true test of love. If you really love someone, you will share their life and their time. You live for them, not they for you. Your free choice is to give up your freedom and make yourself their servant, because that's what God did for you. (By the way, that's the definition of marrying and having children too.) It's that simple.

And that's the love that won the world, the love of the saints. It's not that the saints were simply super social workers, or that they were televangelists who wanted bigger and bigger audiences and bigger financial contributions. They were not just super social workers because what they shared was not just food and services and political power and rights but God, God incarnate, God as our Savior. And they were not just sheep-stealing preachers because what they wanted was to enlarge God's sheepfold, not their own.

That's one of the reasons the Church mandates simplicity of life and celibacy for her priests: so that there are no earthly perks to becoming a priest. They have to give up worldly riches and even the most precious natural thing in the world—namely, private families, their own wives and children. Instead, their job is to preach Christ, to administer his sacraments, to give others Christ himself, in word and sacrament. To give, not to get.

Religious brothers and sisters do the same thing. Poverty, chastity, and obedience are their three vows. They give up money, sex, and power so that temptations to greed, lust, and pride ought not motivate them. They become poor in these three natural human goods because they know there is something infinitely better.

You can't argue with that. You can argue with their words, but you can't argue with their lives, with their gifts of themselves. And all Christians are called on to do that, in different ways: to give themselves away to others because Christ has given himself away to them, and they know from experience that that is the secret of joy.

It sounds impossible: how could joy come from poverty, even if it's voluntary, and even if it is poverty of spirit, not necessarily poverty of wealth—that is, detachment from greed rather than literally giving away all your money and property? But how can even this spiritual poverty be joyful? Especially if it's literal poverty? Why are priests and monks and nuns so happy? Why do they live longer than most people? (Literally true; check with your life insurance company.)

Don't romanticize literal poverty; most poor people are not happy. And we are called on to help them become less poor, not more. So how could anyone be happier when they are poor? How could anyone voluntarily choose to become poor, as St. Paul did, and as Mother Teresa did, and as thousands like her did?

To answer that question, just visit Mother Teresa's Missionaries of Charity, or some contemplative Carmelite nuns, and you will see the happiest, most joyful people you will ever see in this world. They are also the poorest. You can't argue with facts. Saints are facts.

Most of us are not called by God to be priests or to join a religious order. But priests and religious, those who take voluntary vows of poverty and chastity and obedience, are not meant to be weirdos to stare at but models to learn from and follow. Even if we have wealth and families and freedom, we are not to have greed and lust and pride but our own proper versions of poverty and chastity and obedience. We are all to be poor in spirit, detached from riches. Those who take vows are meant to remind us that we are all called by God to give ourselves away to him and to our neighbors.

For most of us, that means our families first of all. If Mother Teresa had been called to marry and have children, and if you were one of her family, do you think you would be a happier and better person than you are now? Of course you would. So stop dreaming and make that kind of a family for yourself. Stop putting her and the other saints on pedestals far away and up high in the clouds. Listen to them. Listen to them all say the same thing; listen to them all preach the Gospel, the Good News about the meaning of life and the secret of joy.

It's a scientific fact, statistically, that priests and religious live longer than any other group. They also die happier, just as they have lived happier, for the very simple reason that they have sought not their own happiness but something higher. Others fall into depression and addiction to sex or drugs for hundreds of different reasons, but when priests and religious do that, it's always for one reason only: because they have lost their faith and hope and love of Jesus Christ. Their very failures and falls, into depression, alcoholism, and pedophilia, abusing and using others, horrible as that is, proclaim the success of what they fall *from*—namely, a life given wholly to Jesus Christ as Lord, Lover, Savior, Joy-giver, and Saint-maker. The depth of the valley is measured by the height of the mountain.

GOSPEL
MARK 1:29–39 _____

On leaving the synagogue Jesus entered the house of Simon and Andrew with

James and John. Simon's mother-in-law lay sick with a fever. They immediately told him about her. He approached, grasped her hand, and helped her up. Then the fever left her and she waited on them.

When it was evening, after sunset, they brought to him all who were ill or possessed by demons. The whole town was gathered at the door. He cured many who were sick with various diseases, and he drove out many demons, not permitting them to speak because they knew him.

Rising very early before dawn, he left and went off to a deserted place, where he prayed. Simon and those who were with him pursued him and on finding him said, "Everyone is looking for you." He told them, "Let us go on to the nearby villages that I may preach there also. For this purpose have I come." So he went into their synagogues, preaching and driving out demons throughout the whole of Galilee.

Today's Gospel shows us the three things Jesus did during the three years of his public ministry: he preached, he healed the sick, and he drove out demons.

These three things are so closely connected that they are really three aspects of one and the same thing.

Preaching the Gospel is a form of healing the sick because even more important than the healing of the body is the healing of our souls, and this healing must happen first of all by healing that power of the soul that is called the mind—that is, by preaching the truth, which is the food of the mind.

Preaching the Gospel is also a form of driving out demons because there is nothing that demons hate and fear more than the truth of the Gospel, the Good News about Christ, the only one strong enough to conquer demons.

Healing the sick is also a form of preaching because the most effective preaching is acting ("actions speak louder than words") and because matter and the body are always expressions of spirit and the soul. Your mind can resist the words of preaching that try to heal your soul, but your body cannot resist the healings given to it, whether these are natural or supernatural healings.

Healing the sick is also a form of driving out demons because demons hate and envy all of our lives, including our bodies and their health. Natural illness is not directly a work of demons, of course, but demons love our illnesses and hate our healings. Body and soul are allies, not enemies, in our spiritual warfare.

Driving out demons is also a form of preaching because, as Jesus says, "If it is by the finger of God that I drive out demons, then the kingdom of God has come upon you" (Luke 11:20). No mere man can drive out demons; exorcism proves the divine reality and power of Christ more powerfully than almost anything else does.

Driving out demons is also a form of healing the sick because the worst sicknesses are soul sicknesses. Evil spirits do to our souls what deadly viruses do to our bodies. Jesus is "the great physician," the healer of souls, even souls infected with demons. Demon *possession* is very rare; demonic *oppression* is somewhat more common; but demonic *temptation* is universal, even among the saints. Even Christ was tempted by the devil. When we are tempted, we should remember that the tempter is the very same spirit that would like to possess us—but Christ overpowers him and prevents him.

So these three things—preaching, healing, and exorcising—are three dimensions of one and the same thing: Christ's work of healing minds, bodies, and souls.

Preaching the Gospel restores health to our mind. That health of mind is called truth. Its natural physical symbol is light. It is seen not by the eyes of the body but by the eyes of faith.

Healing the sick restores health to our bodies. That health of body is called life. It is also hope, because "while there's life, there's hope."

Driving out demons restores health to our spiritual souls. That health of soul is called salvation, or eternal life. It is the very life of God, who is love, or charity.

So the work of Christ is light, life, and love. Those are the three things God is. God is the source of all light, all life, and all true love.

Light—the light of truth—is the object of the virtue called faith. Faith is not a feeling. Faith is a knowing.

Life is the object of hope. Hope is not a feeling. Hope is a knowing, knowing God will fulfill his promises.

Love, or charity, is also not a feeling but a knowing. We know God best by charity. Saints, who love God most, know him best. The same is true with each other: the only way to truly know each other is through charity.

So preaching, healing, and exorcism instill or restore faith, hope, and charity, respectively, and these three things, faith, hope, and charity, are the three greatest things in the world. They are the three aspects of our connection with God, our glue to God, our umbilical cord to God's life. They are called the three "theological virtues" or God-oriented virtues, because their source is God and their object is God.

Our only connection with God is Christ. He himself tells us that: "No one comes to the Father except through me" (John 14:6). Much of the time, Christ works anonymously, in the souls of those who are not even thinking about him or even believing in him, at least not yet. So if Christ is our only connection to God, and if faith and hope and charity are our connection to God, then wherever we see faith, hope, or charity, we see the work of Christ, the real presence and power of Christ, even when the one who believes and hopes and loves does not know that this is Christ.

So let us be "liberal"-minded enough to recognize and praise these virtues in those persons who are, in lesser or greater degree, outside the Church, the visible Body of Christ. And let us also be "conservative" enough to see these virtues not as something outside the work of Christ but as part of it. Wherever truth is preached, wherever healings are administered to bodies or souls, and wherever anyone is delivered from the work of spiritual evil, it is Christ who is there doing it.

SIXTH SUNDAY IN ORDINARY TIME

FIRST READING
LEVITICUS 13:1–2, 44–46 _____

The LORD said to Moses and Aaron, "If someone has on his skin a scab or pustule or blotch which appears to be the sore of leprosy, he shall be brought to Aaron, the priest, or to one of the priests among his descendants. If the man is leprous and unclean, the priest shall declare him unclean by reason of the sore on his head.

"The one who bears the sore of leprosy shall keep his garments rent and his head bare, and shall muffle his beard; he shall cry out, 'Unclean, unclean.' As long as the sore is on him he shall declare himself unclean, since he is in fact unclean. He shall dwell apart, making his abode outside the camp."

_____

There are two levels of meaning in this law from God about leprosy. The first is simply wise and charitable medical practice: an examination of the facts by the experts, who were at that time the priests; full disclosure of the facts ("He shall declare himself unclean *since he is in fact unclean*"); and a quarantine for the sake of the others, so that the disease would not spread. There was a similar reason for the law prohibiting the eating of non-kosher foods like shellfish, pork, and horsemeat: it was medically dangerous at that time.

There is also a spiritual level to this law, which is symbolic, matter symbolizing spirit, bodies symbolizing souls. The diseases of the body, of which leprosy was the most terrible at that time, symbolize the diseases of the soul, and the treatment of bodily diseases symbolizes the treatment of spiritual diseases.

That is the structure and strategy of all symbolism: we use visible things to express invisible things, as when we say, "I see your point," even though we see no colors, shapes, or sizes, or when we say, "The thought just entered my mind," even though it does not move through a door into a room, or when we say God is "higher" than us even though he is not literally on a mountain or in the sky any more than he is on the ground.

Let's explore some of the aspects of that symbolism here. Leprosy does to the body something like what sin does to the soul, and God's treatment of leprosy is like his treatment of sin.

What leprosy does to the body is not kill it immediately but disfigure it. The body is still alive, and life is a good. The only place for evil to exist is in things, and all things are good because all things were created by the good God. Evil is not a thing but a lack of the right order in a thing, like illness in a body, or blindness in the eyes. God created all things and called them good, but the life of one thing, like a virus, or a cancer, or leprosy, can be harmful to the life of another thing, like a human body.

The fact that evil is a lack, not a thing, means that evil cannot win in the end. Evil cannot totally and finally overcome good because it is dependent on good; it exists only in something good. It needs the good as the only place it can live in; it is a parasite on good. If the parasite kills its host, it dies too.

Leprosy is a very ugly disease. It disfigures the most human part of our body, the most beautiful part of our body, the most holy part of our body—namely, the face. Sin does that to the soul. It disfigures not the soul's feet or hands or stomach or shoulders or legs but the soul's face, the eyes of understanding and love. Demons always attack the holiest things: saints, and reverence for Christ's Real Presence in the Eucharist, and women's wombs and our power of procreation. They attack our virtues, turning courage into pride and humility into despair and depression. Nothing is holy to them, and they want to make us like themselves, cynics who sneer at holy things. They use beauty to tempt us to ugliness, as a fisherman uses an attractive, wiggly worm to bait the ugly sharp hook to catch the stupid fish. If sin didn't look like fun, we'd all be saints. That's why discernment, and standards of judgment, and principles, and moral laws, are absolutely necessary, and why the devil wants to destroy them by calling them "moralism" and "judgmentalism" and "prejudices" and mere "opinions," and *my* values" or *your* values" instead of the real values, true values.

God deals with our sins, even today, in the same threefold way he dealt with leprosy in Old Testament times. First, get the facts. Get the truth. Shine the light of your conscience on your behavior. Admit the truth. You are a spiritual leper, a sinner. Second, *tell* the truth. Go to Confession. Go to a priest the way you would go to a doctor for leprosy. Third, for treatment, do penance: go into quarantine. Avoid the near occasions of sin. Change your life. You know you have the disease; act accordingly. Leave your previous lifestyle. Don't just go back to the human family unchanged to spread your leprosy. Cut off the part of your life that leads you into sin. It's not a body part, but if it were, it would profit you to amputate it, for as Christ said, "it is better for you to lose one of your members than to have your whole body thrown into Gehenna" (Matt. 5:29). That applies to everything from subtle spiritual sins like pride to obvious sins like pornography.

Leprosy is one of the ugliest diseases that ever existed. But sin is much uglier than leprosy, because souls are much more beautiful than bodies. The most beautiful thing we ever see in this life is the soul of a deeply committed saint, and the ugliest thing we ever see in this life is the soul of a deeply compromised sinner. Leprosy in the body reminds us of what sin looks like in the soul.

Sometimes, bodies reveal souls not to the outer eyes but only to the inner eyes, the eyes of faith and hope and love. Mother Teresa's face was full of wrinkles, and her life was full of sorrows, but if you looked into her face instead of just at it, you would see beyond the wrinkles to the twinkles, the deep happiness in her eyes.

If you had been there when Christ was crucified, and if you looked only with your outer eyes, you would probably have heard laughs and seen smiles on the clean and noble faces of the sneering, sadistic Roman soldiers who crucified Christ, and you would have heard no laughter and seen no smiles, but only agony and blood, on Christ's face. Yet if you looked with your inner eyes, the eyes of faith and hope and love, you would have seen in those respectable, clean, and powerful murderers something very ugly—a hate inspired by the devil—and you would have seen in the crucified Christ something incredibly beautiful: the love of God.

That was the most beautiful thing we have ever seen on earth; that's why we call that blood, the blood that disfigured his face and his body, the blood that he shed for our salvation, "the *Precious* Blood"; and that's why we call his whipped and broken body "sacred," and that's why we call the day of his terrible death "*Good* Friday."

Why? Because he took our leprosy out of us and onto himself. On the cross, God effected the great exchange that was our healing. St. Paul put it this way: "For our sake he made him to be sin who did not know sin, so that we might become the righteousness of God in him" (2 Cor. 5:21). Isaiah prophesied that exchange when he wrote of the Messiah: "By his stripes we were healed" (Isa. 53:5). Like Sydney Carton, the hero in Charles Dickens' great novel *A Tale of Two Cities*, Christ came into our prison to exchange places with us. He took upon himself the death sentence that we deserved, and he set us free.

That's the incredibly Good News of the Gospel. Anyone who says it's just "too good to be true" is a sad and pitiful pessimist, but at least they understand how amazing it is. Anyone who says it's just nice comforting platitudes and clichés is a fool who is far more hopeless and pitiful than the pessimist.

RESPONSORIAL PSALM
PSALM 32:1–2, 5, 11 _____

R. (7) **I turn to you, Lord, in time of trouble, and you fill me with the joy of salvation.**

Blessed is he whose fault is taken away,
    whose sin is covered.
Blessed the man to whom the LORD imputes not guilt,
    in whose spirit there is no guile.

Then I acknowledged my sin to you,
   my guilt I covered not.
I said, "I confess my faults to the LORD,"
   and you took away the guilt of my sin.

Be glad in the LORD and rejoice, you just;
   exult, all you upright of heart.

One of the conflicts of the Reformation, between Catholics and Protestants, is about justification: what does it mean that Christ justifies us, saves us, redeems us from sin? One of the aspects of that controversy concerned the Mass: does it really do anything other than remember or commemorate Christ's death? Is Christ really present there and really active, offering himself to the Father for our sins?

The answer to that question was very clear: for Catholics the answer was yes, and for Protestants the answer was no. Catholics believe that Christ is really, truly, literally present in the Eucharist, and Protestants don't. Even for those Protestants who do (Anglo-Catholics, or Anglicans, and also most Lutherans), they don't have that Real Presence even though they believe in it, because they broke apostolic succession, so they don't have a validly ordained priesthood, so their priests do not have the divinely given authority to be the instruments of transubstantiation, the changing of the very essence of the bread and wine into the Body and Blood of Christ. (The fact that they don't have the Real Presence in their Eucharist does not mean that God doesn't give them great graces too; God is always more gracious and more generous than we think, and, as our *Catechism* says, God "is not bound by his sacraments.")

But another aspect of the controversy about justification, or salvation, was whether God saved us by merely legally canceling our debt, by overlooking our sins if we only had faith, or by really, substantially changing our nature by giving us a share in his own supernatural divine life, so that our sanctification, our being made saintly and holy by our works, the works of love, was also part of our justification, or salvation.

According to Luther and Calvin, justification only "covered" our sins, so that even though we remained sinners, and guilty, God overlooked our sins and did not "impute" guilt to us even though we really had it. In one of his typically memorable and crude images, Luther is said to have called the saved sinner "a pile of [human] dung covered by [divine] snow." Catholics, on the other hand, taught that God not only legally revoked our punishment but also ontologically changed us; that our new life was not only "imputed" legally to us but also really "imparted" to us; that Christ saved us from our sins as well as from their punishment, by the gradual process of our sanctification, our cooperation with his grace in doing good works, the works of love.

This Psalm resolves the controversy by deliberately joining these two things. It teaches the Catholic position, which is almost always a both/and rather than an either/or. This "both/and" is in the first verse, where the Psalmist says we are blessed both because our sin is "covered"—that is, hidden—and also because our fault is really "taken away." It does not say merely that our *punishment* is taken away but that our fault, our sin, is taken away.

In the second verse, the Psalmist makes the same two points. First, he says, "Blessed the man to whom the LORD *imputes* not guilt"—that is, removes the legal penalty for sin. But then, immediately following, he also says, "In whose spirit there is no guile"; that is, God changes man's soul or spirit and removes the guile, the lying, the darkness, rather than just not imputing it to him (i.e., revoking his punishment).

This is why the New Testament makes both the Protestant point and the Catholic point: it says both that we are saved by faith in Christ's work rather than by our own good works in obedience to God's law (St. Paul says that in Romans) and also that we are not saved by faith *alone* but by faith *and* good works (St. James says that)—that is, by our own good works that spring from our faith as flowers spring from roots.

Taken as a whole, the Bible teaches that our life in Christ has three parts.

The root is faith, faith in him and what he has done for us to save us. The stem is hope, hope in his continuing and eventually completed work in making us saints in heaven (which for most of us will require some time in purgatory to purge our remaining sinful habits). The flower or fruit is love, the works of love, which come from the very same divine life in us that began in the roots and grew in the stem.

The Catholic view is a both/and rather than an either/or. We are saved by Christ *and* by our own faith and hope and love for him; and we are saved both legally *and* ontologically, saved both from the punishment for our sins *and* from sin itself. We are both justified and sanctified, and we are saved both by faith and by works, by our faith and by our love, not by either of the two alone.

These same two aspects of salvation are mentioned in the last two verses. The Psalmist first praises God for taking away "the guilt of my sin," that is, my legal status, my just punishment; and then he also says to "rejoice, you just" (that is, you who really are just, not just legally justified) and "exult, all you upright of heart" (that is, whose hearts really have uprightness or righteousness or holiness in them).

Of course, this real justice or uprightness or holiness is gradual, not sudden or perfect. But it is really there. To be saved is not just to go to heaven: it is to be increasingly able to endure and enjoy heaven, to gradually become a heavenly kind of person. If your salvation does not change your character, it did not really "take." "Faith without works is dead," says St. James (James 2:26). A seed that does not produce any flowers or fruit is not a real, living seed. It's dead.

You can't have a living seed without it producing living fruit; and you can't have living fruit unless you have a living seed. Good works without faith are as dead as faith without good works, because it's the very same thing, the very life of God, that comes into our souls by faith and Baptism and comes out of them by a life of good works—that is, the works of genuine love.

But one other thing is necessary for salvation, in addition to this positive thing that is faith and hope and love. That is repentance and confession. Thus, the Psalmist says, "I acknowledged my sin to you, my guilt I covered not."

(By the way, if it is disastrously wrong for us to cover over our sins, why did Luther teach that it was right for God to do exactly that same thing, to just cover our sins, to leave us as piles of dung but interpose snow between that dung and his eyes so that he did not acknowledge it? That was a ridiculous error that even many Protestants reject.)

When two chemical elements join to form a compound, the compound works to do things that neither of the two elements can do alone. Neither hydrogen nor oxygen can do what water can do—namely, to nourish all living things. Repentance is one of the two elements of the compound, and faith is the other—faith and the hope and the love that are part of it or come from it as a stem and a flower come from a root or a seed. Repentance is the negative element, and faith and love are the positive element. Our repentance unglues us from our sins, and our faith and love glue us to God. We need both.

We can't add faith without repentance any more than you can turn toward the north without turning away from the south. Sin and holiness are opposites, like darkness and light. Salvation is not like a layer of icing that you just add to the cake; it's like throwing out the rotten cake (that's repentance) before you eat the good one (that's faith and love). It's like changing sides in a war. You can't fight on God's side and on the devil's side at the same time. As Jesus says, "No one can serve two masters" (Matt. 6:24). You have to divorce the devil before you can marry God. That's why God gave us the sacrament of Confession as well as the sacrament of Communion. Confession is like a bathroom, and Communion is like a dining room. You wash the dirt off before you eat.

SECOND READING

1 Corinthians 10:31–11:1 _____

Brothers and sisters: Whether you eat or drink, or whatever you do, do everything for the glory of God. Avoid giving offense, whether to the Jews or Greeks or the church of God, just as I try to please everyone in every way, not seeking my own benefit but that of the many, that they may be saved. Be imitators of me, as I am of Christ.

St. Paul says, "I try to please everyone in every way," but he also said, just a few lines before, that "you cannot partake of the table of the Lord and of the table of demons" (v. 21). He *tries* to please everyone, but he knows he will not please the enemies of Christ; in fact, he knows that he will provoke them to hate and fear him. So St. Paul is not telling us to just be nice and go along with everything, even lies and sins.

What is he saying, then? He is saying that we should "avoid giving offense" *when we can.* "When in Rome, do as the Romans do," in everything but sin. Eat their food, speak their language, respect and learn their traditions. Don't insist on your own way and your own benefit. Be indifferent and flexible in whatever is morally and religiously indifferent. But don't compromise one inch on God, on Christ, on truth, and on love. Be flexible and indifferent and liberal and open-minded and relative with everything that is relative, but be absolute about what is absolute. If you worship the one true God, you don't need to worship anything else; you don't need to absolutize anything relative. If you don't believe in this God, you will always find yourself worshiping some idol, absolutizing something relative, and that's usually, in our day, something political, or else something sexual. Everybody has some absolute, something that is first in their life. It's either the real God or an unreal god, an idol.

St. Paul says, "Be imitators of me, *as I am of Christ.*" Was Christ a nonconfrontational, noncontentious, noncontroversial, compromising wimp? No, he was a truth-speaker, but always in love. If we want to imitate the saints, who imitate Christ, we must be ready to compromise many things that we wrongly grasp onto and absolutize, and we must also be ready to be utterly uncompromising about the two things that are absolute—namely, truth and love.

All right, now that that possible misunderstanding is out of the way, let's look at the positive point, the main point, the famous point in this passage, which is nothing less than St. Paul's answer to the most important question we can possibly ask: What is the meaning of life? What is it all about? What is our end, our purpose, our job here on this earth? Why were we born; why are we living? Why do we do all that we do?

And the answer is this: "Whether you eat or drink, or whatever you do, do everything for the glory of God." (So that's true of eating ordinary bread and also of eating the Eucharist.)

We know who God is (I hope!), but perhaps we don't know what "the glory of God" is, because we hardly ever think about "glory." So let's look at that.

"For the greater glory of God" was one of the favorite quotations of St. Ignatius of Loyola, the founder of the Jesuits. It is the heart of Jesuit spirituality: that there is no such thing as a secular department of life that is not sacred; that God is to be found everywhere and to be loved and served and adored everywhere. And glorified. But what is glory?

St. Irenaeus says, in another famous quotation, "The glory of God is man fully alive." By "man," of course, he meant males and females equally; but what did he mean by "man fully alive"? Simply someone who was feeling lively? No, that is just a feeling. Simply someone who has biological life, who is somewhere between conception and death? No, it is far more than that, more precious than that. It is man fully alive with God's life, supernatural life—not just an *imitation* of God's life but God's life itself, the life that is stronger than death, the life we are not born with but receive by faith and Baptism.

As Jesus said to Nicodemus, "What is born of flesh is flesh and what is born of spirit is spirit" (John 3:6). "Flesh" means mortal life, natural life, for both body and soul; "spirit" means not just the *human* spirit or soul—everyone has that—but the Holy Spirit, the Spirit of God. We don't get to heaven by being born but by being "born again" (to use Jesus' own analogy). Our father on earth can give us only the life of the flesh, mortal life, natural life; our Father in heaven alone can give us the life of the Spirit, immortal life, supernatural life.

If we are baptized and in the state of grace—that is, not in the state of unrepented mortal sin—we are alive with this supernatural life, but not yet "*fully* alive." Saints are more fully alive with it. We all have some of the glory of God, but saints have the most of it.

But what is the glory of God? Glory means beauty and splendor, radiating like light. It is a kind of spiritual light. We can see the glory of God in the face of a saint like Mother Teresa; we can see the love, of both God and man, the holiness, and the happiness in her eyes. We can see it in the face of Pope St. John Paul II too.

What is "the glory of God in a man fully alive"? C.S. Lewis tells us, at the end of a golden sermon entitled "The Weight of Glory":

> The load, or weight, or burden of my neighbor's glory should be laid on my back, a load so heavy that only humility can carry it, and the backs of the proud will be broken. It is a serious thing to live in a society of possible gods and goddesses, to remember that the dullest and most uninteresting person you can talk to may one day be a creature which, if you saw it now, you would be strongly tempted to worship, or else a horror and a corruption such as you now meet, if at all, only in a nightmare. All day long we are, in some degree, helping each other to one or other of these destinations. . . . There are no *ordinary* people. You have never talked to a mere mortal. Nations, cultures, arts, civilizations—these are mortal, and their life is to ours as the life of a gnat. But it is immortals whom we joke with, work with, marry, snub, and exploit—immortal horrors or everlasting splendors. . . . Next to the Blessed Sacrament itself, your neighbor is the holiest object presented to your senses. If he is your Christian neighbor, he is holy in almost the same way, for in him also Christ *vere latitat . . .* is truly hidden.

In fact, we can add that he is so actively present there in the Blessed Sacrament that he is not just passively *hidden*, like dust under a rug, but dynamically and actively *hiding*, like a child playing hide-and-seek. He is wearing a costume made of bread and wine. The heart's x-ray eye of faith pierces the costume, sees who is wearing it, and melts in tears of wonder, love, and adoration.

GOSPEL
MARK 1:40–45 _____

A leper came to Jesus and kneeling down begged him and said, "If you wish, you can make me clean." Moved with pity, he stretched out his hand, touched him, and said to him, "I do will it. Be made clean." The leprosy left him immediately, and he was made clean. Then, warning him sternly, he dismissed him at once.

He said to him, "See that you tell no one anything, but go, show yourself to the priest and offer for your cleansing what Moses prescribed; that will be proof for them."

The man went away and began to publicize the whole matter. He spread the report abroad so that it was impossible for Jesus to enter a town openly. He remained outside in deserted places, and people kept coming to him from everywhere.

_____

Today's Old Testament reading from Leviticus tells how God, through Moses, instituted rules about leprosy. Today's Gospel passage is about Jesus and a leper playing by those rules, so to speak.

The story shows three things about Jesus: his power, his pity, and his purpose.

The story shows the leper's faith in Jesus' *power* when the leper says, "If you wish, you can make me clean." God has the power to do anything, including many more miracles than he does; but he does not wish or will to do any more than he does, or any fewer than he does. So the leper expresses his faith that Jesus has the power, but he can only hope that he has the will, the free choice.

When Jesus heals him, he does it by a word of command to the leper's body: "Be made clean." The word "be" is the same word he spoke when he created the universe. He commanded light, and water, and earth, and plants, and animals, and mankind, to "*be*!" And the leper's body obeyed and was instantly filled with health, just as the void that God filled at creation obeyed and was filled with creatures: first light, then water, then life. It reminds us of how Christ stilled the storm on the Sea of Galilee: he simply said, "Quiet! Be still!" and the wind and the waves instantly obeyed him, sitting still like an obedient puppy (Mark 4:39). It's as if all Jesus had to do was say, "Down, boy!" The whole universe is just a good doggie to Jesus.

The fact that our Lord has unlimited power, the power to do anything— the fact that "with God all things are possible"—is part of our answer to the so-called problem of evil. God has the power to destroy all evils immediately and forever; so the fact that he chooses not to is not due to power that his creation has over him, or any lack of power he has over it. There is only one thing that could motivate his choices to allow evils rather than miraculously remove them: his wisdom to see that it is better for us in the long run that we suffer some evils and then be delivered from them; that that is better than our experiencing neither the suffering nor the deliverance.

In other words, it necessarily follows from God's infinite wisdom and love and power that Romans 8:28 is always true: that even though not all things are good, yet "all things work for good for those who love God." Of course, we cannot see that, because we are not God, and we cannot see the future joy that will be much greater in both quality and quantity because of our present sufferings. But we can know two things: that we are not God, and that we can trust God; that God always knows exactly what he is doing, and he never lacks either wisdom or love or power.

Christ has omnipotence because he is perfect God, but he also has *pity* because he is perfect man. Pity or compassion is an aspect of human love (though not all of it). It is an emotion, but it is a distinctively human emotion, a spiritual emotion, not just an animal emotion, and it is an essential part of holiness or sanctity or moral goodness. A pitiless person is a moral monster. Sadism and cruelty and the lack of pity are very great moral faults.

We are not responsible for our animal emotions, but we are responsible for our human emotions, our spiritual emotions, because they flow from our moral character, which includes our moral or immoral habits, which have been constructed by many repeated free choices. So even though an act motivated by the emotion of pity may be instinctive and not consciously and deliberately chosen by an act of free will at the time, yet it is praiseworthy, because it comes not merely from our animal instincts but from our human, moral instincts and habits that were formed by many free choices in the past.

Pity, or kindness, or compassion, is not the whole of morality, but it is an essential part of it. It is not even the whole of love—sometimes the other person needs tough love rather than tender love—but it is an essential part of it. Our souls need both toughness and tenderness, as our bodies need both hard bone and soft skin.

The leper is healed because Christ has the power, and the pity, and the purpose. He has perfect divine power over all evils. He has perfect divine *and* human love, including pity for us who suffer. And he has the perfect divine *purpose* and wisdom to see the greatest good, the best end, and the best timing, like a novelist writing a perfect story or a chess player playing a perfect game or a sculptor sculpting a perfect statue.

That's the literal meaning of the story. There is also an allegorical or symbolic meaning in that leprosy symbolizes sin. The body is a symbol and sign and expression of the soul (that's why we smile when we're happy and frown when we're unhappy), so bodily diseases are natural symbols of spiritual diseases, or sins, as bodily health is a natural symbol of spiritual health. Righteousness, or holiness, or saintliness is to the soul what perfect health is to the body.

Of course, that does not mean that ugly bodies always go with ugly souls, or that sufferings like leprosy are deserved. Jesus' body on the cross was certainly far from beautiful, and great sufferings often happen to great saints.

The body-soul symbolism and analogy is natural because God created bodies to show forth spirit, to make spirit visible. Our bodies are not machines that we manipulate; they are aspects or dimensions of our very selves. That's why after these bodies die, we will get new resurrected bodies, as Jesus did on Easter Sunday, so that we can be completely human, so that the goodness and glory and joy and love in our souls can expand and shine out in the goodness of our bodies, like sunlight from the sun.

Jesus heals bodies for two reasons, not just one. One is his human love and pity. The other is to symbolize and show us what he does to souls. As the Psalmist says, "He pardons all your iniquities, he heals all your ills" (Ps. 103:3). Sin is our spiritual disease. Jesus heals our physical blindness to show us his power over our spiritual blindness. He heals cripples who cannot walk to show us that we are all crippled by our sins, and he alone can make us walk upright again. Unbelievers say, "Religion is a crutch," and sneer. They are very right when they say that religion is a crutch, but they are very wrong when they sneer at us who admit that we are spiritual cripples. Religion *is* a crutch, and God gave it to us because he pities us because we are cripples. If you are so proud that you think you are the exception, that makes you the worst cripple of all. All the wise know they are fools; only fools think they are wise. All the saints know they are sinners; only sinners think they are saints.

The practical bottom line for us in this story about Jesus healing the leper is obvious and easy to see. It is that we must go to Jesus with hope and humility, begging for all our needs, physical and spiritual, and trust him that he has the power and the pity and the purpose; that the only reason he does not give us every good thing instantly and miraculously is not that he lacks power or pity or purpose, but that he is wiser than we are and knows what is best for us in the long run. Because the long run, for all of us, is eternity.

SEVENTH SUNDAY IN ORDINARY TIME

FIRST READING

ISAIAH 43:18–19, 21–22, 24B–25 _____

Thus says the LORD:
Remember not the events of the past,
   the things of long ago consider not;
see, I am doing something new!
   Now it springs forth, do you not perceive it?
In the desert I make a way,
   in the wasteland, rivers.
The people I formed for myself,
   that they might announce my praise.
Yet you did not call upon me, O Jacob,
   for you grew weary of me, O Israel.
You burdened me with your sins,
   and wearied me with your crimes.
It is I, I, who wipe out,
   for my own sake, your offenses;
   your sins I remember no more.

_____

God always surprises us. He always does something new to us. He is not predictable, like a machine. In today's reading from Isaiah, he announces that he will do the greatest new thing, the newest new thing of all: he will deal with the greatest of all human problems, the problem of sin. And the way he will do this will be the most radical thing, the most surprising thing, the most apparently impossible thing that ever happened. To save man from his sins and from the spiritual death, the eternal death, that is the result of sin, God would be born as a man. That seems impossible! How could the eternal God have a beginning in time? Who ever thought of such a thing! And God would suffer and die for us. Impossible! How could God die? And why would God do this? For sinful, rebellious, ungrateful man. Incredible! What kind of love is this? And then this God-man would rise from the dead and pour his eternal life into us by faith and Baptism and Holy Communion so that we, too, could conquer death. Astonishing! Who could possibly dream such a thing? No man. Only God. The Christian story is not a story any human being could ever have invented. That's why Jesus is the only person in history it is impossible to write convincing fiction about. All our Jesus novels and Jesus movies are embarrassingly bad compared with the real thing.

God inspires his prophet Isaiah to say that compared to this great thing God would do in the future, all the wonderful and miraculous things he did in the past are almost nothing. When he says, "Remember not the events of the past"—the deliverance of the Jews from slavery in Egypt through ten miraculous plagues and the parting of the sea, and all the subsequent miracles of Jewish history—he is not saying that those events are not great. God's point here is not literally to forget these things. On the contrary, God himself instituted all the great Jewish feasts for that very purpose: to remember these things. How ungrateful and unfaithful and dishonest it would be to forget! What he is saying in these words "remember not the events of the past" is that the new thing God will do in the future in his Messiah will be infinitely greater than all the old things. Compared with the Incarnation and death and Resurrection of God to open heaven for us, the parting of the sea is trivial.

The value of any thing is always measured by comparison. The gifts of everyday divine providence are great, and miracles like God parting the Red Sea are greater, but the Incarnation is infinitely greater than all those things. Ten is a little greater than nine, and a trillion is much greater than ten, but infinity is infinitely greater than a trillion. Every other good has limits. God has no limits. That's why it's impossible to love him too much, and that's also why what he does always surprises us, and that's also why we will never be bored in heaven.

The last part of the passage from Isaiah tells of a second unbelievable thing: despite all the incredible and wonderful things God did for us, God says, "Yet you did not call upon me. . . . You grew weary of me. . . . You burdened me with your sins." And yet this unbelievably good God saves us, his unbelievably ungrateful children: he says, "It is I, I, who wipe out . . . your offenses; your sins I remember no more."

The first thing God said in this passage was that his new miracle will be so great that in comparison all his past miracles are not worth *our* remembering them; now he says that his deed of salvation is so great that all our sins, by comparison, are not worth *God* remembering them. They are like grains of sand and God is like the ocean.

RESPONSORIAL PSALM

PSALM 41:2–3, 4–5, 13–14

R. (5b) **Lord, heal my soul, for I have sinned against you.**

Blessed is the one who has regard for the lowly and the poor;
    in the day of misfortune the LORD will deliver him.
The LORD will keep and preserve him;
    and make him blessed on earth,
    and not give him over to the will of his enemies.

The LORD will help him on his sickbed,
    he will take away all his ailment when he is ill.
Once I said, "O LORD, have pity on me;
    heal me, though I have sinned against you."

But because of my integrity you sustain me
    and let me stand before you forever.
Blessed be the Lord, the God of Israel,
    from all eternity. Amen. Amen.

Here are five lessons from these few verses from our Psalm that are taught in hundreds of other passages in Scripture and are also taught hundreds of times in each person's life.

First, the Psalmist says: "Blessed is the one who has regard for the lowly and the poor; in the day of misfortune the Lord will deliver him. The Lord will keep and preserve him; and make him blessed on earth, and not give him over to the will of his enemies."

There is a connection between giving and getting, between aiding others who are poor and needy in any way and being aided by God against our own spiritual poverty, our ignorance and our sins. God gives the most to givers.

The connection is *not* a kind of contract or bargain that we make with God—if I do this for you, will you do this for me? It's a necessary connection, in the very nature of things. For if our souls are not open to give, they are also not open to receive. Until the end of the famous Charles Dickens story *A Christmas Carol*, Ebenezer Scrooge is such a tightwad that he simply cannot receive happiness from God or from his fellow men because his heart is too cold and narrow and selfish to give it to others. His openness to God to receive and his openness to his fellow man to give are one thing because he has only one heart.

It's not true that you have to choose between being a getter and being a giver. The two go together. The only way to get happiness is to give happiness. The only way to get blessings is to give blessings. We know that's true by experience. Even people who don't know God know that fact of experience, even though they don't know it's God who designed it.

There's a second universally true lesson in this verse. It says, "In the day

485

of his misfortune the LORD will deliver him." Throughout the Bible, God is a deliverer, a savior, a helper, a redeemer. He turns our misery into joy, our darkness into light. But, we naturally ask, why does God let us fall into misery and darkness in the first place? The answer is that he doesn't put us there, but he lets us fall into it even though he could have prevented it. God is the source of all good, not evil. He does not do any evil, but he allows it. Why? Because he is the source of all good, and one very good thing is deliverance from evil. If life had no downs, we would not appreciate the ups. There would be no drama of good conquering evil. There would be no stories.

Let's be clear. God does not love to see us suffer, and he certainly does not love to see us sin. But he lets us sin, because he made us with free will, because what he wants from us is love, and love has to be free. And he lets us suffer only because we need it: it's the only way we foolish sinners will learn some necessary things like courage and compassion. We can't be happy unless we're wise, and we can't be wise unless we have both tough virtues like courage and tender virtues like compassion, and we can't have either of those two virtues if we never suffer. A world of sinners who never suffered would be a world of insufferables, of spoiled brats. So it's the very same love of God that both delivers us from suffering and that lets us suffer in the first place.

But why do we have to wait so long for the deliverance? Because we're in a story, a drama, not a machine. We don't get instant, push-button answers to any of life's greatest problems. Sometimes we have to wait a long time. Sometimes we have to wait until we get to heaven.

Here is a third lesson from this short Psalm verse, one that we find throughout the Bible. The Psalmist says two things to God that we might mistakenly think contradict each other. He says: "I have sinned against you. But because of my integrity you sustain me." Sin and integrity are opposites. But all of us have some of both. There's a little good in the worst of us and a little bad in the best of us. To deny either of those two opposite halves of human nature, of your nature, is unrealistic and naïve.

There's an upside and a downside to the Psalmist's two-part diagnosis of himself as containing both sin and integrity. The upside is that God loves us even though we're sinners. We don't have to be perfect and sinless to get his grace, his deliverance. The downside is that we don't become instant saints. To confess both sides of the truth is part of our integrity—that is, our honesty.

So when the Psalmist confesses that he is a sinner, he's not in despair and he's not denying his integrity. And when he speaks of his integrity, he's not being a proud Pharisee and denying that he's a sinner. It's his very integrity that confesses his sins; it's his very honesty that confesses his dishonesties; it's his very virtue that confesses his vices. All the saints say they are sinners; only sinners think they're saints.

Integrity does not mean perfection; it means honesty. Repentance is an exercise in honesty. Going to Confession is an exercise in honesty. Humility is an essential part of honesty.

Here is another lesson, a fourth one, that is taught in this short Psalm verse and that we might miss. The Psalmist thanks God in advance for the blessings God will give him. What is the greatest of all blessings? The Psalmist says that it is to "let me stand before you forever"! To see God face to face, to be able to endure the light of perfect holiness, the "beatific vision" of God's face. If we saw that infinite beauty now, we would probably just collapse and disappear like a ghost in the sunlight.

To endure that blessing, we need a process of thickening. We need to become more real. That's why we need to grow and learn and experience—and suffer. We're not born saints; we become saints. It takes work—a lifetime of work, and, for most of us, more than a lifetime. That's why there's a purgatory, where that work is completed. The work is hard, but it is happy because it is holy. The saints say that although purgatory is more painful than earth, it's also happier: harder yet happier because holier. Our lives as adults are harder, happier, and holier than were our lives as babies; in the same way, our lives in purgatory will be harder, happier, and holier than our adult lives on earth. Happier *because* holier. No one is happier than the saints.

SECOND READING

2 Corinthians 1:18–22 _____

Brothers and sisters: As God is faithful, our word to you is not "yes" and "no." For the Son of God, Jesus Christ, who was proclaimed to you by us, Silvanus and Timothy and me, was not "yes" and "no," but "yes" has been in him. For however many are the promises of God, their Yes is in him; therefore, the Amen from us also goes through him to God for glory. But the one who gives us security with you in Christ and who anointed us is God; he has also put his seal upon us and given the Spirit in our hearts as a first installment.

Reflection 1

St. Paul uses an unusual Greek word for the Holy Spirit in today's epistle. He says that the Holy Spirit has been given to us as an *arrabona*, which means "a first installment." Imagine you were given a unique treasure—say all of the gold in the treasure chest of Blackbeard the Pirate, a thousand gold pieces worth a thousand dollars each (that's a million dollars of gold), and today you got just ten of those thousand gold pieces as a first "installment" on the rest. An *arrabona*, or installment, is a guarantee for a promise. It combines four meanings of the word "present." It is a present, or gift, actually presented to you, now, at this present moment, so it is present, not absent. It is not just a verbal promise but an actual part of the thing promised, the first installment of a gift that will be completely given to us in the future. The promise is not just a word but a fact, an actual payment of part of the promise, an "installment."

"Promise" is the word Jesus uses for the Holy Spirit (Luke 24:49). We received the first installment of that promise when we received the Holy Spirit in Baptism. That's when the seed was planted. That seed of God's own life, planted in our life, keeps growing in us (or diminishing in us, or even dying in us if we fall into mortal sin, and returning to us when we sincerely repent and confess). It is a share in the very life of God—not just the "lifestyle" of God but the life of God.

How did we get that incredible gift from God? Only through Christ. God the Father sent us the Son, and the Son sent us the Spirit.

Even before the Incarnation, God began to give us himself: he revealed himself to the Jews, his chosen people; he spoke to them through his prophets and through his Law; and he gave them his providential guidance and many miracles. But it was still from on high, from a distance.

Then, in the Incarnation, the Son of God became a man. Without losing his divinity, he added humanity. Why? To get closer. Because that's what love always seeks: greater intimacy, greater presence, greater sharing.

And then Christ, after his Ascension, sent us his Spirit, which he said would be even better for us because he can be even more intimately present with us, not just as God outside us or God beside us but as God inside us.

Reflection 2

In today's epistle, St. Paul calls the Holy Spirit our first installment in our sharing in the very life of God that is our eternal destiny, according to the first pope, St. Peter, who wrote in his second epistle that God has "bestowed on us the precious and very great promises, so that through them you may come to *share in the divine nature*" (2 Peter 1:4). We have today an "installment" of that promise in our souls.

Another word that St. Paul uses in today's epistle for that divine presence is the simple word "yes," the total "yes" of self-giving love, with nothing held back. Even when God seems to say "no" to our prayers, he is really saying "yes" because he is saying "yes" to what we truly need, what we need even more than the thing we are praying for. God sees that our needs are much greater than our wants, and he sometimes says "no" to our wants only because he always says "yes" to our needs. Of course, we don't always *see* that, but it is always possible to *believe* that, to trust him and therefore to trust his promises, and to practice (in the words of a great spiritual classic) "abandonment to divine providence."

After all, if you can't trust him, you can't trust anybody. And not trusting anybody is not a human life. In fact, not trusting anybody is the life of "no" that's the beginning of the life of hell, even in this life. Trusting God is the life of "yes" that's the beginning of the life of heaven even in this life, of which God's Holy Spirit is our first "installment," with unimaginably more wonderful things to come.

GOSPEL
MARK 2:1–12 _____

When Jesus returned to Capernaum after some days, it became known that he was at home. Many gathered together so that there was no longer room for them, not even around the door, and he preached the word to them. They came bringing to him a paralytic carried by four men. Unable to get near Jesus because of the crowd, they opened up the roof above him. After they had broken through, they let down the mat on which the paralytic was lying. When Jesus saw their faith, he said to the paralytic, "Child, your sins are forgiven." Now some of the scribes were sitting there asking themselves, "Why does this man speak that way? He is blaspheming. Who but God alone can forgive sins?" Jesus immediately knew in his mind what they were thinking to themselves, so he said, "Why are you thinking such things in your hearts? Which is easier, to say to the paralytic, 'Your sins are forgiven,' or to say, 'Rise, pick up your mat and walk?' But that you may know that the Son of Man has authority to forgive sins on earth"—he said to the paralytic, "I say to you, rise, pick up your mat, and go home." He rose, picked up his mat at once, and went away in the sight of everyone. They were all astounded and glorified God, saying, "We have never seen anything like this."

Here are a few things you may not have noticed in today's Gospel reading.

First, the paralytic apparently did not have great faith or great love, but his four friends did—so much that they carried him to Jesus on his mat and then, when they couldn't get in, took apart the roof to lower him down to where Jesus was in the middle of the crowd. The paralytic, when he was cured, just went home. Mark does not tell us that he even thanked Jesus for his miraculous healing. Jesus did this miracle not in response to the faith of the paralytic but in response to the faith of his friends. That shows the power of intercessory prayer, no matter who we pray for and no matter whether that person has faith or not. Your faith can make up for others who lack faith.

A second point: the Gospel says Jesus "saw" their faith. Faith is invisible, but it becomes visible in works, the works of love. The controversy at the center of the Protestant Reformation about salvation by faith alone or by faith plus good works was really a stupid controversy because real faith and real works, the works of real love, are not two separate things but two dimensions of one and the same thing. Real faith, true faith, saving faith, is a faith that does good works. St. James says, "Faith without works is dead" (James 2:26). He doesn't say that faith needs to add a second thing—namely, works; he says that faith without works isn't even faith, isn't alive, isn't real. The work of love *is* faith—faith made visible.

Here is a third point. When Jesus saw their faith, he did not give them what they asked for and prayed for—namely, the physical healing of their friend's paralysis. Instead, he gave the paralytic what he needed most: the forgiveness of his sins. God never gives us less than we ask for, always more. When he apparently gives us a no, he is really giving us a bigger yes than we are expecting. Mother Teresa loved to say that "God cannot be outdone in generosity."

Here is a fourth point. Jesus performed this miracle of healing not only for its own sake, for the blessing of physical health (that too, of course), but first of all for the sake of the spiritual healing from the worst paralysis, the paralysis of the spirit, the paralysis of the will, the slavery of the will, the addiction to sin.

The connection between paralysis and sin is that Jesus' miraculous healing of the paralytic's body was a proof and a sign that he was the one who could heal souls. The Greek word for "miracle" means literally "sign." Miracles are visible signs of something invisible. We are meant to look not only *at* them but *along* them to what they show. Jesus' miracles show who he is, for only God can perform literal miracles. But God is also the only one who can perform the greater spiritual miracle of forgiving sins. The Jews who called Jesus a blasphemer for claiming to forgive sins were absolutely right in believing that God alone can forgive sins; so if Jesus can't really forgive sins, he is a terribly wicked blasphemer because he is pretending to be God when he isn't. But if he really can forgive sins, and only God can forgive sins, then he is God. So to show that he can forgive sins, he performs this miracle, which only God can do.

Remember, miracles are signs of something invisible. The healing of the paralytic is visible, but both sin and forgiveness are not visible. So Jesus says to them, "Which is easier, to say to the paralytic, 'Your sins are forgiven,' or to say, 'Rise, pick up your mat and walk?'" It's a trick question. It's easier to *claim* to forgive sins because sins are invisible and you can't see whether the claim is true or not because you can't see sin or forgiveness, while if you *claim* to heal diseases miraculously and you can't, everyone will see that you are a fake. But it's harder to *really* forgive sins because you have to be God to have that authority. So to prove that he has divine authority to forgive sins, Jesus does the other thing that only God can do—namely, the miracle. Anyone who sees a miracle and still does not believe in God is a stubborn fool and not completely honest. He's not just ignorant; he's ignoring, deliberately ignoring the evidence.

Some of us have seen miracles of healing, and we may envy those people and think they have been more blessed than those of us who have not ever seen a miracle. But that is not true. Those who have not seen are not less blessed than those who have seen. Here is the proof of that, from Jesus himself. After "Doubting Thomas" believed that Jesus was really raised from the dead only because he saw him and touched him, Jesus said, "Have you come to believe because you have seen me? Blessed are those who have not seen and have believed" (John 20:29). He was talking about us in those last words.

EIGHTH SUNDAY IN ORDINARY TIME

FIRST READING
HOSEA 2:16B, 17B, 21–22_____

Thus says the LORD:
I will lead her into the desert
    and speak to her heart.
She shall respond there as in the days of her youth,
    when she came up from the land of Egypt.
I will espouse you to me forever:
    I will espouse you in right and in justice,
    in love and in mercy;
I will espouse you in fidelity,
    and you shall know the LORD.

Some of us see the desert as a vacation spot, a nice place to visit, especially if we live in a cold climate. But to the ancients, especially in the hot and dry lands of the Near East, the desert was life-threatening. It was not warm; it was hot—too hot. It was without water, which everything needs to stay alive. It had venomous beasts in it.

God used the desert as an essential part of his plan for his people. He led Israel out of Egypt and into the desert wilderness for forty years. Egypt was full of food and water, and the desert was not. But Egypt was also full of slavery, and full of false gods, idols. He had to wipe the slate clean, so to speak, before he could teach his chosen people his truth and his laws. First, he had to free them from their slavery in Egypt. And then, before he brought them into the Promised Land, he had to lead them through the desert. Their story is like the three stages of Dante's *Divine Comedy*, from hell through purgatory to heaven. The desert, or the wilderness, is the middle stage, a kind of purgatory, a purgation, a cleansing.

God also used the desert to prepare Jesus' ministry. He prepared Jesus' way through John the Baptist, who lived in the desert. Christ himself began his public ministry by a forty-day retreat in the desert, where he was tempted by the devil.

The desert is a natural image for suffering. We all have our deserts, our sufferings, our purgatories, in this life. Why does God give us that middle stage? Why doesn't he just omit the desert and lead us directly from Egypt to the Promised Land? Why does he do what he says he does in the words of Hosea the prophet in today's reading: "Thus says the LORD: I will lead her into the desert"?

The next words are God's answer to that question: to "speak to her heart."

God is love, and love not only comes from the heart of the lover but also speaks to the heart of the beloved. What does it seek? What does love want from the beloved? Love wants love. Love seeks the return of love for love. Romeo seeks Juliet, and that means that Romeo seeks Juliet's love. God is our Romeo, and God seeks above all our love—to him and to his other children, our neighbors. That's all. That's what it's all about. True love, right love, real love, untwisted love.

When God leads us into the desert of suffering, it is tempting to think that God is doing that because he *doesn't* love us, because the desert is painful. That's what Job's three friends thought: "Job is suffering, so God must be punishing Job, and Job's sufferings are so great that Job must be a terrible sinner." They were wrong. In fact, they were 180 degrees wrong. It was exactly the opposite. It was God's love, not hate, that moved God to allow Job's terrible sufferings. God himself says so in today's reading from Hosea. He says: "I will lead her into the desert and speak to her heart. . . . I will espouse you to me forever . . . in right and in justice, in love and in mercy."

This is incredible. God is saying that he wants to marry us spiritually!

This life is the engagement (that's what "espousal" means), and heaven is the consummation of the marriage.

That's hard to believe. God does not need us; why should he want to marry us? Are we so beautiful? We are indeed created in his image, with spiritual souls that can know and freely choose, but we have polluted that image, and we are full of ugliness as well as beauty. Why does God want to marry us ugly ducklings? God is Beauty, but we are beasts; why does Beauty love the beast?

Because that's what God is. God is love. There is no higher reason to explain it or justify it. God does all the things he does to us, including leading us into the desert as well as leading us out of it, for that one overriding ultimate reason: because he loves us. There's no higher reason than that. He gets nothing out of it but our joy. He just wants to see us maximally happy, because that's what love does.

We love our spouses and children and parents for many reasons; God loves us for one reason only. A man may love a woman because she's beautiful and smart, and a woman may love a man because he's strong and reliable, and parents may love their children because they're cute and funny, and children may love their parents because they're generous and wise, but they also love each other just because they belong to each other. We love our kids not because we rate them on a scale compared with other kids, but just because they're *our* kids. We love our parents not because we compare them with other parents and give them higher grades, not because they had no faults or made no bad mistakes, but because they're *ours*. When we do that, we're loving with the kind of love God is: *agape*, love of the other for the sake of the other. That love is its own reason, its own justification.

What does that have to do with the desert? God leads us there out of love, to elicit love, to speak to us heart to heart. When we suffer, when we go into "emergency" mode, we suddenly get wise. We get humble. We see our need and our dependence on God as we never did before. We pray. Our head starts to learn wisdom from our heart. God speaks to us heart to heart, not just head to head. There are some things that we simply cannot learn from books or from teaching or from thinking but only from experience, especially the experience of suffering, and of vulnerability. In the desert, where the sun bakes everything hard, we become soft—softer of heart. We yield. We give up. We say: "I need you. I trust you. I believe in you." We may have said that before, and we meant to mean it, but now we really mean it.

And when God delivers us from the desert—as he always does—we are better and wiser and more honest and humbler and holier and happier and more loving and more lovable than we were before.

This is a large and mysterious point, and perhaps it becomes clearest by analogy with a very small and silly point. Imagine Romeo and Juliet. Romeo wants to speak tender and deep words of love to Juliet, but Juliet is busy eating a big dinner, conversing with her friends about trivia, and watching silly, stupid shows on TV, all at the same time. So Romeo lures her out of the dining room, switches off the fuse so the TV stops its blasting and the lights go out so all the guests go home—and *then* Romeo can speak his words of love and Juliet can hear them.

We can't *prove* that that's God's motive in luring us into our deserts. But we can believe it. Because God himself tells us this almost unbelievable thing.

RESPONSORIAL PSALM
PSALM 103: 1–2, 3–4, 8, 10, 12–13 _____

R. (8a) **The Lord is kind and merciful.**

Bless the LORD, O my soul;
    and all my being, bless his holy name.
Bless the LORD, O my soul,
    and forget not all his benefits.

He pardons all your iniquities,
    he heals all your ills.

He redeems your life from destruction,
    he crowns you with kindness and compassion.

Merciful and gracious is the LORD,
    slow to anger and abounding in kindness.
Not according to our sins does he deal with us,
    nor does he requite us according to our crimes.

As far as the east is from the west,
    so far has he put our transgressions from us.
As a father has compassion on his children,
    so the LORD has compassion on those who fear him.

What is surprising about this familiar and deeply beloved Psalm is its audience. Who is the Psalmist speaking to? His own soul! He sees his own soul as in need of this message. He sees himself as lacking in trust, in love, in intimacy, in hope, in confidence toward God. He sees himself truly. We are all in that situation. None of us believes, hopes, loves, and trusts God nearly enough. It is impossible. Any human being, even the greatest of saints and sages, popes and mystics, can be believed in too much, hoped in too much, loved too much, and trusted too much, because we are not God; we are all flesh—that is, finite and foolish and fallen and fallible. So we need to preach to ourselves first of all, even before we preach to others. Our deep self needs to preach to our surface self. Our conscience needs to preach to our thinking. Our heart needs to speak to our head. Our faith needs to preach to our feelings. Our unconscious self needs to preach to our conscious self.

And that means that our surface self needs to hear and believe and obey our deep self; that our thinking needs to obey our conscience; that our head needs to listen to our heart; that our feelings need to follow our faith, and not vice versa.

God speaks to us primarily in the deepest, wisest part of our soul. So listening to this voice is listening to God, to his Holy Spirit inspiring us. It is God who is speaking to us even when we are hard of hearing and even when we misinterpret him. Our deafness does not silence God's voice, any more than our blindness darkens God's light. God is not at all dependent on us; we are totally dependent on him.

Because it is hard for us to hear God and hard for us not to misinterpret his voice in our hearts individually and privately, God gave all of us one public written Word, the Bible, and his one Catholic or universal Church to correct us. We don't need the Church to tell us when we're right; we need the Church to tell us when we're wrong. We do not correct God; he corrects us.

The Church is our mother. Mothers do not need babies to correct them and to teach them; babies need mothers to correct them and to teach them. When we call the Church our mother ("Mother Church"), we are calling ourselves babies. This is not an insult but a compliment, for the distance between God's mind and ours is much greater than the distance between a mother's mind and her baby's.

Picture three levels of wisdom available to us.

The lowest level is our immediate and instinctive thoughts and desires, our spontaneous self, our surface self. That's always a mixture of wisdom and folly, light and darkness.

The middle level is our deepest heart, especially our conscience, where the Holy Spirit is speaking to us. That's much, much wiser, even though God speaks there in soft, deep whispers, and our hearing is very limited and fallible.

The third level is the Bible and the "Magisterium" or teaching authority of the Church. That's like our hearing aid. We did not invent that hearing aid; God did.

Let's not be so foolish as to reduce the higher levels to the lower ones, or to exalt the lower levels to the higher ones. Let's not confuse any two of those three levels, and above all let's not turn them upside down.

SECOND READING

2 Corinthians 3:1b–6 _____

Brothers and sisters: Do we need, as some do, letters of recommendation to you or from you? You are our letter, written on our hearts, known and read by all, shown to be a letter of Christ ministered by us, written not in ink but by the Spirit of the living God, not on tablets of stone but on tablets that are hearts of flesh.

Such confidence we have through Christ toward God. Not that of ourselves we are qualified to take credit for anything as coming from us; rather, our qualification comes from God, who has indeed qualified us as ministers of a new covenant, not of letter but of spirit; for the letter brings death, but the Spirit gives life.

Today's epistle teaches two main points. Both are very important. But the first is obvious and easy while the second one is not.

The easy one is what St. Paul means by calling his disciples a book. He means that the book that the world will read to understand what Christianity is, the book that will lead the world to the truth of the Gospel most effectively and unanswerably, is not a book of theological arguments, good as those are, and not even the Bible, but *us*, us ordinary, average Christians, imperfect as we are: our lives, our actions, our integrity, our happiness and peace and joy that comes from our faith in Christ's reality, our hope in Christ's care for us, and our genuine love of Christ and of each other.

The world can resist even the most brilliant and logical theological arguments, and they can resist and dismiss the Bible as a myth and the Church as a dead dinosaur, but they can't resist the love of a saint. They can close their eyes to the light of truth and stop themselves from seeing the light, but they can't close themselves off from feeling the warmth, the warmth of love, because their skin has no eyelids; they can't cover their skin as they can close their eyes; they can't stop being touched by the love of God that a Christian mediates to them.

They can't stop their heart from beating as they can stop their eyes from seeing. When they are loved, when they are in the presence of genuine love and charity, they can't not know that. When they are enlightened by the truth, they *can* not know that; they can ignore that; they can forget that; they can fool themselves. They have a guard at the gate of their mind, like the guard who sits at the gate of a castle, and they can command that guard to stop unwelcome visitors from entering the castle of their mind. But there is no guard who can stop the water of love from seeping into the castle of their soul under the walls, undermining its walls. There is no guard who can stop the rainwater from falling from the sky. They can survive an opponent's blows, but they can't survive a lover's charity.

We are open books to other people. The most powerful argument in the world for Christianity is Christians: honest and faithful and joyful Christians. The most powerful argument in the world against Christianity is also Christians: dishonest and unfaithful and joyless Christians.

The second idea in this reading, the harder one, is the difference between the Old Covenant and the New, the Old Testament and the New, the Law and the Gospel. Both are true, and both are revelations of the same God, but the Law is "the *letter*" while the Gospel is "the *spirit*."

To call the Old Testament "the letter" and the Gospel "the spirit" does not mean that everything in the Old Testament is to be interpreted literally, or that everything in the New Testament is not. Both parts of the Bible, and in fact all of human speech, has in it both literal and symbolic passages. When it describes something we can see with our eyes and clearly understand with our minds, it is literal. When it describes something that we cannot see with our eyes, like the eternal nature of God, it is symbolic; it uses material language to mean spiritual things. For instance, "God has a strong right hand" does not mean God has five fingers; it means "God has great power." It's *true* even though it's not *literal*. We use symbolic language like this in secular matters too. "That idea never entered my mind before" does not mean that an idea actually turns a doorknob and opens a door and enters a room with four walls. "I'm on top of the world" does not mean I'm at the North Pole.

So St. Paul is not talking about how to interpret the language of the Bible here. What is he talking about? He's talking about the difference between the Law and the Gospel. The Law of God is like an x-ray that tells us the facts, the objective truth, that shows us our spiritual diseases and our needs—which is the "bad news." The Gospel is the "Good News" of God's offer to give us a free operation, to give us heart surgery, a new heart, by his Holy Spirit, who performs this operation from within our own hearts, using our own free choice as his instrument. God's Law comes to us from outside us, from God on high, from the will of God that corrects our will and condemns us because it reveals us as sinners, just as an x-ray reveals us as having heart disease, or cancer, or some other fatal disease. Thus, St. Paul says that "the letter [of the Law] brings death." But the Gospel gives us life and healing, because it gets inside us and actually changes us, transforms us, gives us a share in the divine life of God himself, gives us a new heart, a new kind of life in our soul, supernatural life, eternal life.

Think of it this way. God the Father reveals himself from above us, as our Father. Then, in the Incarnation, God the Son reveals himself from beside us, as our brother. God gets closer to us by coming down to our level without losing his own divine nature. Finally, God the Holy Spirit gets even closer to us by coming into our hearts. He is not just above us or even just beside us but within us. Because God is love, and love seeks more and more intimacy, seeks union with the beloved. Thus, the Good News of the Gospel announces our new life—eternal life, divine life—while the bad news of the Law announced our danger of death. The Law was our x-ray, and the Gospel is our operation.

And the surgeon who performs this operation has blood on his hands. It's his own blood. He's a wounded surgeon.

This surgeon's scalpel is a cross. It's like a sword—in fact, the cross is even shaped like a sword, held at the hilt by the hand of heaven and thrust down into the world, into our hearts, not to take our blood, like Dracula's teeth, but to shed his own blood, to give us his blood, his life, for our salvation. Salvation is a blood transfusion.

GOSPEL
MARK 2:18–22 _____

The disciples of John and of the Pharisees were accustomed to fast. People came to him and objected, "Why do the disciples of John and the disciples of the Pharisees fast, but your disciples do not fast?" Jesus answered them, "Can the wedding guests fast while the bridegroom is with them? As long as they have the bridegroom with them they cannot fast. But the days will come when the bridegroom is taken away from them, and then they will fast on that day. No one sews a piece of unshrunken cloth on an old cloak. If he does, its fullness pulls away, the new from the old, and the tear gets worse. Likewise, no one pours new wine into old wineskins. Otherwise, the wine will burst the skins, and both the wine and the skins are ruined. Rather, new wine is poured into fresh wineskins."

What is Jesus saying in today's Gospel about fasting? He says that his disciples do not fast yet, while he is still with them, but that when he leaves them, to die, then they will fast. Fasting is an expression of mourning and of repentance and penance. When the Bridegroom is present, we feast; we do not fast. But when the Bridegroom is taken away, when he suffers and dies, we fast.

We fast especially when we are in Lent. But we are in Lent, in a larger sense, all during this life because we are not in heaven yet but in the waiting room. We have a special time of Lent, forty days long. Why? To remind us that all of life is a Lent, a time of suffering and waiting and of repentance for sin. And we also have special feast days to remind us that all of life is a feast, a time for rejoicing.

We learn general principles best by specific examples. We learn universal truths best by concrete instances. For instance, we have special buildings, sacred buildings, churches, to remind us that all of life is sacred. We have sacred days, sabbath days, to remind us that all times are sacred. We appreciate things by contrast. But there is no contrast to universal principles. "All" means all, not just some. So we need a special concrete instance of a general principle that is contrasted with its opposite to remind us of the general principle. Universal principles are hard to remember and hard to understand because they are abstract. Concrete examples are easy to remember and easy to understand because they are concrete.

So Jesus explains that there is a time to feast and a time to fast. Ecclesiastes 3 says the same thing, and the folk song "Turn! Turn! Turn!" by The Byrds sings that passage from Ecclesiastes: "A time to be born, a time to die / A time to plant, a time to reap / A time to kill, a time to heal / A time to laugh, a time to weep." The presence of Christ, our soul's Bridegroom, justifies feasting, and the absence of Christ our Bridegroom justifies fasting.

But Christ is both present and absent. He is really present in the Eucharist, in a perfect way, and he is really present in our hearts, in our souls, in an imperfect way but a real way; and he is really present in all the events of our lives, in our sorrows as well as in our joys, because both are part of his all-wise and all-powerful and all-loving providential plan for our lives. But he is not present as fully to us as he will be in heaven, so he is also absent now, as well as present. We are only eating heaven's appetizers, not its main course, in this life. We are sad, and we are impatient, and we are bored, and we are stupid, and we are selfish and sinful—and we will be none of those things in heaven, because we will be totally and completely present with our Lord, and his love and light will fill our souls and our lives with no dark and loveless places left over.

All of life here on earth is for us a kind of Lent, which is positive as well as negative, a time of both sorrow and joy: sorrow for our past and present sins and joy for God's future complete salvation. Life and Lent are both a kind of purgatory that contains both sorrow and joy, sorrow for our sins and joy for our salvation. If our life in heaven is like a great banquet, our life on earth is like a combination of delightful appetizers and disciplined fasting. It is full of both pleasures and pains, for all of us.

We have no choice about that. It's a fact. But we have a choice about how we react to that fact. We have a choice about our attitude toward the fact that life contains both pleasures and pains and that they are inseparable. We can choose to be resentful and think we know better than God what would be best for us. Or we can reasonably trust that God knows that better than we do.

But the pains as well as the pleasures are preparation for the heavenly banquet. And the joys outweigh the sorrows even here. The Rosary has five joyful mysteries, five luminous mysteries, five sorrowful mysteries, and five glorious mysteries. That's only one out of four for sorrow and three out of four for joy and light and glory.

NINTH SUNDAY IN ORDINARY TIME

FIRST READING

Deuteronomy 5:12–15 _____

Thus says the Lord: "Take care to keep holy the sabbath day as the Lord, your God, commanded you. Six days you may labor and do all your work; but the seventh day is the sabbath of the Lord, your God. No work may be done then, whether by you, or your son or daughter, or your male or female slave, or your ox or ass or any of your beasts, or the alien who lives with you. Your male and female slave should rest as you do. For remember that you too were once a slave in Egypt, and the Lord, your God, brought you from there with his strong hand and outstretched arm. That is why the Lord, your God, has commanded you to observe the sabbath day."

_____

God invented the sabbath day and commanded us to "take care to keep holy the sabbath day." Why did he sanctify that one day? To sanctify all days. To be a reminder, not an exception. All time is holy because God invented it. God is not in time, but God invented time in inventing the universe. Time is a feature of everything in the universe, even thought, since it takes time for us to think. God is present to us in a special way in the holy sabbath time, but God is present to all times, though he is not contained by time, as we are. He has no dead past or unborn future.

The same is true of space: God invented it in inventing the universe. And he also instituted a holy place, the Promised Land; and in that holy place a holy city, Jerusalem; and in that holy city a holy building, the temple; and in that temple a holy place, and even, within the holy place, "the holy of holies," which contained the ark of the covenant, which in turn contained the two stone tablets on which God had written the Ten Commandments. Into that holiest place only the high priest was allowed to enter, and only on one day a year. God reserved sacred places to remind us that all places are sacred because God is in them, although not contained by them, as an author or an artist is in all of his work, though not contained by it.

The same is true of matter. God invented it, and therefore it is holy. And of it he made man's body, which is the most sacred material thing in the universe, the only thing that will resurrect after death to be eternal. Even if our bodies evolved, that only means that God used evolution as his instrument in making the human body.

We are made in the image of God, and that refers to the body as well as the soul. Immediately after first mentioning that fact, Genesis says "male and female." Sexuality is an aspect of the image of God in us, and that is why it is holy: because it is an image of mutual love, like the love between the persons of the Trinity. It is holy also because it is God's invention for the procreation of more of those images of God that have intrinsic and immortal and uncountable value.

So God invented three especially sacred things: in time, the sabbath; in space, the temple; and in matter, a woman's womb.

And then, he himself entered time and space and a woman's womb in the Incarnation. He who is not in time entered one particular time in history. He who is not in space entered one particular place, one land, the Holy Land. He who is not in matter entered one piece of matter, Mary's womb, as a zygote and then an embryo and then a fetus, making all zygotes and embryos and fetuses, as well as all babies and infants and children and teenagers and adults, holy.

God also entered events, events in history, and made some of them supernatural events, or miracles. Events are made of matter and move in time and happen in space. The event of the exodus of God's chosen people from Egypt and their liberation from slavery was a series of miraculous events that all Jews lovingly and faithfully remember and celebrate each year at Passover. That event is the archetype for all events, because the divine providence in that event, the divine agency behind that event, the divine will manifested in that event, shows what is true of all events: all events show forth divine providence—that is, God's power, wisdom, and goodness.

All previous history was God's preparation for the greatest event of all, what scholars sometimes call "the Christ event": namely, the event of the Incarnation, Christ's first coming—his life, Passion, Death, Resurrection, and Ascension—which is the past part of the Christ-event, and also his second coming in glory at the end of the world, which is the future part of the Christ-event.

But Christ is not just past and future; he is also present. We confess not only that Christ "rose" from the dead in the past tense, but that he "is risen," in the present, is alive and active here and now, in all the events of our lives, by divine providence, and in our hearts, by our faith and hope and charity, and in the Eucharist, by transubstantiation, where he makes himself fully and personally present, Body and Blood, Soul and Divinity, hiding behind the appearances of bread and wine.

Time, space, matter, and events—the universe is the sum total of those four things. And all four of those dimensions are holy because God is present in them. And the fullness of God's presence is Christ, who is God and man, spirit and matter, eternity and time. At the heart of every aspect of the universe is Christ. Christ is the ultimate meaning of all things. What a privilege it is for us to know the meaning of all things, not just abstractly but personally! At Mass today, many of you will eat the meaning of life. But it will not be gradually transformed into you, like ordinary food; you will be gradually transformed into him.

RESPONSORIAL PSALM
PSALM 81:3–4, 5–6, 6–8, 10–11 _____

R. (2a) **Sing with joy to God our help.**

Take up a melody, and sound the timbrel,
　　the pleasant harp and the lyre.

Blow the trumpet at the new moon,
  at the full moon, on our solemn feast.

For it is a statute in Israel,
  an ordinance of the God of Jacob,
Who made it a decree for Joseph
  when he came forth from the land of Egypt.

An unfamiliar speech I hear:
  "I relieved his shoulder of the burden;
  his hands were freed from the basket.
In distress you called, and I rescued you."

"There shall be no strange god among you
  nor shall you worship any alien god.
I, the LORD, am your God
  who led you forth from the land of Egypt."

A little detail in this Psalm can be surprising and instructive for us. It's the phrase "our solemn feast." When the Psalmist tells us to break out the music, it's the music of rejoicing and feasting, yet it's called "solemn." He says: "Take up a melody, and sound the timbrel, the pleasant harp and the lyre. Blow the trumpet at the new moon, at the full moon, on our solemn feast."

We think of funerals as "solemn" but certainly not as "rejoicing." We rejoice by eating or drinking with our friends, or by singing or making loud music that we find pleasant; we rejoice at things that are *not* solemn. So what secret does the Psalmist know that we don't, that enables him to make solemnity a rejoicing and rejoicing a solemnity?

Connected with the apparent paradox that this feast of joy and happiness is called "solemn," it is also called "a statute" and "a decree"—that is, a commandment, a law. The Psalmist frequently rejoices over God's Law. And that sounds like another paradox. Why rejoice at a law? Laws constrain and restrain us. The Jews rejoiced at God's law because it was from God, and therefore holy.

Well, yes, but "holy" sounds *solemn* but not *joyful*, just as festive music sounds joyful but not solemn. What does it mean, what does it signify, that we have largely lost this connection that the Psalmist and his audience felt between joy and solemnity? Why are our joys lacking in solemnity, and why are our solemnities lacking in joy?

The answer is clear: if our joys are lacking in solemnity and our solemnities are lacking in joy, that is because we do not know God. We may know many things *about* him, but we do not know *him*. Because if we truly knew him, we could not *stop* rejoicing. For to know him is to know love. He is absolute love as well as absolute power, and absolute mercy as well as absolute justice, and absolute redemption and forgiveness and salvation as well as absolute perfection and holiness and beauty. The knowledge of God by reason, by good philosophical reasoning, can reveal his power, his justice, his holiness, and his perfection; and that is good reason to be solemn, but not good reason for a joyful feast. Faith knows that this solemnity is a joy and a feast because faith knows his love, his mercy, and his salvation. Faith knows God best because faith knows Jesus Christ.

But the God revealed by Christ is the God of the Jews. Christianity is not a new and different religion than biblical Judaism. The God Christ reveals is the God the Psalmist knew, the God no other pagan religion knew, the God who was both solemn and joyful. Pagans were joyful about many little things; they enjoyed and rejoiced in the many things of this world; but they were *not* joyful about their gods or about the afterlife. They were solemn but without joy about that.

G.K. Chesterton says that the difference between a pagan and a Christian is that a pagan can find joy in every single thing except one: Everything; while a Christian finds joy in Everything even if he is martyred and every single thing is taken away from him. He has God, and God is Everything. A Christian sees joy where the pagan least expects it: on the face of the solemn, holy God. St. Paul calls it, in the first sentence of today's epistle, "the glory of God on the face of Jesus Christ."

That explains the strange juxtaposition of joy and suffering in today's epistle. It's simply a fact, however you may want to explain it, that the early Christians, like St. Paul, had a radically new kind of joy that the pagan world never knew before, a joy that enabled them to sing hymns and forgive their enemies even as they were being eaten by lions in the Colosseum. What was their secret? What did they know that the pagan world did not know?

They knew Jesus. That's St. Paul's answer to our question in the first sentence of today's epistle.

SECOND READING
2 CORINTHIANS 4:6–11 _____

Brothers and sisters: God who said, *Let light shine out of darkness*, has shone in our hearts to bring to light the knowledge of the glory of God on the face of Jesus Christ. But we hold this treasure in earthen vessels, that the surpassing power may be of God and not from us. We are afflicted in every way, but not constrained; perplexed, but not driven to despair; persecuted, but not abandoned; struck down, but not destroyed; always carrying about in the body the dying of Jesus, so that the life of Jesus may also be manifested in our body. For we who live are constantly being given up to death for the sake of Jesus, so that the life of Jesus may be manifested in our mortal flesh.

_____

> Brothers and sisters: God who said, Let light shine out of darkness, has shone in our hearts to bring to light the knowledge of the glory of God on the face of Jesus Christ.

But St. Paul is a realist, not a dreamer. So the next thing he says is this:

But we hold this treasure in earthen vessels, that the surpassing power may be of God and not from us.

What are those "earthen vessels"? Our mortal bodies, subject to all sorts of pains and weaknesses. St. Paul describes the perils and pains and persecutions of his life and the lives of many of the early Christians, in these strikingly paradoxical words:

We are afflicted in every way, but not constrained; perplexed, but not driven to despair; persecuted, but not abandoned; struck down, but not destroyed; always carrying about in the body the dying of Jesus, so that the life of Jesus may also be manifested in our body. For we who live are constantly being given up to death for the sake of Jesus, so that the life of Jesus may be manifested in our mortal flesh.

The life of Jesus in our souls, which we received in Baptism and which we feed and nourish in every Holy Communion, is manifested even in our mortal flesh, in our mortality, in our dying. A Christian is happier in the act of dying than any pagan can be in the act of living. That's how great Jesus is!

That joy and hope is what converted the old pagan world two thousand years ago, and it is what will convert our new pagan world again today if we let it, if we live it, if we show it.

GOSPEL
Mark 2:23–3:6
(or Mark 2:23–28)

As Jesus was passing through a field of grain on the sabbath, his disciples began to make a path while picking the heads of grain. At this the Pharisees said to him, "Look, why are they doing what is unlawful on the sabbath?" He said to them, "Have you never read what David did when he was in need and he and his companions were hungry? How he went into the house of God when Abiathar was high priest and ate the bread of offering that only the priests could lawfully eat, and shared it with his companions?" Then he said to them, "The sabbath was made for man, not man for the sabbath. That is why the Son of Man is lord even of the sabbath."

Again he entered the synagogue. There was a man there who had a withered hand. They watched him closely to see if he would cure him on the sabbath so that they might accuse him. He said to the man with the withered hand, "Come up here before us." Then he said to them, "Is it lawful to do good on the sabbath rather than to do evil, to save life rather than to destroy it?" But they remained silent. Looking around at them with anger and grieved at their hardness of heart, he said to the man, "Stretch out your hand." He stretched it out and his hand was restored. The Pharisees went out and immediately took counsel with the Herodians against him to put him to death.

"Remember to keep holy the sabbath day" (Exod. 20:8). That is one of the Ten Commandments, one of the ten most fundamental laws that God himself gave to us. In light of that fact, it seemed to the Pharisees in today's Gospel that they were being faithful and right and holy in criticizing Jesus' disciples for not obeying the letter of the law of the sabbath, and they criticized Jesus for defending them, because they counted even a casual picking of a grain stalk as work. Jesus pointed out that there were times when holy men like David were right in not obeying the letter of the law: when he and his soldiers were hungry and had no other food, and they ate the priests' food, which the law said was only for priests. The Pharisees hated Jesus himself for disobeying the "no work" law of the sabbath by doing a miraculous work of healing in the synagogue on the sabbath day.

Why were the Pharisees wrong and Jesus right?

Of course, we know he was, because he's divine and therefore infallible, and the Pharisees were not, even though they may have acted as if they were. But we need to understand what Jesus is teaching us about the sabbath here. God wants our obedience, but he also wants our understanding. He wants us to understand his law because he wants us to understand him, and he wants us to understand him because he wants above all a relationship with us where we obey not out of fear but out of love and friendship. Jesus said to his disciples, on another occasion, "You are my friends if you do what I command you. I no longer call you slaves, because a slave does not know what his master is doing. I have called you friends" (John 15:14–15).

Jesus implies here that we can have three different relationships with him: disobedience, which is the worst; or slavish, fearful obedience, which is only a little better; and best of all, free obedience out of love and trust and friendship.

The Pharisees were at stage two, and they knew Jesus was not, and they did not understand stage three, so the only way they could classify Jesus was as being in stage one, on the level below them. In fact, he was on the level above them.

This story is relevant to us today because the vast majority of nonreligious people today, and even some religious people, and perhaps even many of us, are where the Pharisees were, seeing only two options, not three. The two options were disobedience or blind obedience, infidelity or unfree fidelity.

Today people often divide everything into these two options, which they classify as "right" or "left," "conservative" or "progressive," "traditional" or "liberal." Many people who call themselves "conservatives" tend to be like the Pharisees, forgetting that "the sabbath was made for man, not man for the sabbath." They worship the law as their God; they idolize it; they don't see beyond it; they don't really understand it. And many people who call themselves "liberals" idolize freedom in the same way that people who call themselves "conservatives" idolize law. They think that to be free, to be creative, to be themselves, they have to ignore and disobey the Commandments. So-called conservatives think that man is made for the law, and so-called liberals think that man is free from the law, but neither one understands Jesus, because Jesus says that the law is for man and for his freedom. Jesus disagrees with both legalism and illegalism.

(And by the law here, Jesus implies not just that one law about the sabbath but all laws—not just human laws, which are changeable and fallible, and which obviously are not absolute, and which permit many examples of justified disobedience, but also God's laws, the laws of morality, the Ten Commandments. Sometimes, to obey the letter of the divine law is to disobey the spirit, the purpose, of the law.)

What is the purpose of laws—*any* laws, whether human or divine?

What is the purpose of the rules of baseball, for instance, which is a set of man-made laws? It is for the game, and for the players, so that they can enjoy the game. If it had no rules, it would not be enjoyable, and no one would want to play it. The laws are made for the players, not the players for the laws. The laws are the means, not the end.

The laws are like road maps through life. They exist for the traveler, not the traveler for the road maps. There are two foolish attitudes toward road maps. One is legalism, which sees them as the end, as the absolute, and sees the journey as a means to that end rather than vice versa; it is the attitude that says that the journey is for the road maps, not the road maps for the journey. That takes all the joy out of the journey. The other foolish attitude, which is just as bad as legalism, is illegalism, which is to ignore or disobey the road maps, which guarantees that you will get lost, and that also takes the joy out of the journey.

The same could be said about laws as about x-rays. They are not the end, the point, of going to the doctor; they are a means to the end of a diagnosis and a cure. But ignoring them is as bad as idolizing them. They are not the last word, but they are the first word. An examination of conscience before you go to Confession is like an x-ray; it's the bad news of your sins that comes before the good news of your forgiveness and healing. The x-ray exists for the healing, not the healing for the x-ray.

Avoiding both these foolish attitudes is Jesus' radical common sense, or rather uncommon sense, when he says that the sabbath was made for man, not man for the sabbath. God instituted the law of the sabbath for man's good, and rest, and health, and happiness. When a man is dying and needs surgery, the surgeon who truly loves man as God loves man knows that God wants him to work at this needed surgery on the sabbath. The Church refuses to be legalistic about the sabbath and turn it into a killjoy day. God designed it to be exactly the opposite: a day of feasting, not fasting; of fasting from unnecessary work, not from good and necessary work and not from enjoyment and relaxation. God is not a killjoy; God is a makejoy.

Notice that Jesus does not merely disagree with the Pharisees: he gets angry at them, because in obeying the letter of the law, they disobey its spirit, its meaning, its purpose, which is love, the love of man, of man's true good. Thus, Jesus asks, "Is it lawful to do good on the sabbath rather than to do evil?" Refusing to do that healing work and leaving that poor man in his diseased condition when you could have healed him is doing evil. God's law never wills evil or harm, only help.

There are situations where obeying the letter of the law is disobeying the spirit and intention of the law. For instance, God's law says that bearing true witness, or telling the truth, is good and bearing false witness, or lying, is evil; but suppose you are hiding Jews from the Nazis: is it good to tell the Nazis the truth and bad to lie to them, or is it the opposite? If an attempted murderer asks which way his prospective victim ran, should you tell him the truth? Here's another such situation: Is it stealing to take away a lethal weapon from a murderer if he legally owns it? Or to violently kick the gun out of someone's hands before they can commit suicide? Is it infringing on his rights?

If you say yes, then I say, Come on, man, be human, get some common sense. Be like Jesus! He's the perfection of everything human, including common sense. You can argue about how you should justify disobeying the letter of the law in these situations, whether you should call these situations exceptions to the rule because they are not really lying or stealing, or whether you say that in these situations we ought to lie or steal because not to lie or steal would be worse, or because the criminal gave up his right to truth or his right to life; but unless you are a first-class idiot like the Pharisees, you cannot doubt that if you love human beings you know very clearly what you ought to do. Do what Jesus said and did.

Pope St. John Paul II loved to quote this line: "Christ not only reveals

God to man, but he also reveals man to himself." He is perfectly divine and perfectly human.

If you obey the law only for its own sake and not out of love for the true good of persons, then you will eventually tire of that legalistic idol, and you will feel repressed and unfree and joyless, and you will eventually sink from the second level to the first, from slavish, joyless, blind obedience to disobedience, from uncreative fidelity to creative infidelity, from legalism to illegalism. One extreme often leads to the other.

Jesus invites us all to follow him to the third level, which is creative fidelity. Law exists as a means to the end of love; love does not exist as a means to the end of law. We should obey the rules because we love the game and the players. God gave us the law out of love and for our own good, our own happiness, our own joy. And God knows his children far better than they know themselves. Even earthly fathers do that; how much more our heavenly Father?

TENTH SUNDAY IN ORDINARY TIME

FIRST READING
GENESIS 3:9–15 _____

After the man, Adam, had eaten of the tree, the LORD God called to the man and asked him, "Where are you?" He answered, "I heard you in the garden; but I was afraid, because I was naked, so I hid myself." Then he asked, "Who told you that you were naked? You have eaten, then, from the tree of which I had forbidden you to eat!" The man replied, "The woman whom you put here with me—she gave me fruit from the tree, and so I ate it." The LORD God then asked the woman, "Why did you do such a thing?" The woman answered, "The serpent tricked me into it, so I ate it."

Then the LORD God said to the serpent: "Because you have done this, you shall be banned from all the animals and from all the wild creatures; on your belly shall you crawl, and dirt shall you eat all the days of your life. I will put enmity between you and the woman, and between your offspring and hers; he will strike at your head, while you strike at his heel."

_____

After Adam disobeyed God's command not to eat the forbidden fruit, God asked him a question, a question that is more profound and more terrifying than it seems. He asked Adam, "Where are you?" He did not mean "I can't see you." God sees everything. What did he mean? He meant "Now that you have removed yourself from my presence, now that you have left the relationship of faith and trust and obedience, now that you have declared your independence from me and left your home and your innocence and the garden where everything was a joy for you and where you knew where you were because I was your center—now that all that is gone, where are you? You were my planet, staying in orbit around me as your sun. Now you have left my solar system, and you are out in the darkness and coldness and emptiness of outer space; you have lost your absolute point of reference, so you no longer know where you are. You are homeless, because I am your true home, and you have left me. You are lost. There is no other hope for you, no other sun, no other God. I am not one God among many; I am the one and only one. You have lost the one source of all light and truth and meaning, the one source of all peace and happiness and joy and hope. Where are you now? You have walked through the door from a place full of light into a place full of darkness. You have walked through the door whose entrance sign says, 'Abandon all hope, you who enter here.' You have exchanged heaven for hell. And if I left you alone and did nothing to bring you back, you would have absolutely no hope, forever. For I am not one of many hopes, one of your many options for truth and goodness and joy. There is no other. It's God or nothingness. And you have chosen nothingness. That's where you are now: you are in nothingness, you are nowhere."

Adam replied to God: "I heard you in the garden; but I was afraid, because I was naked, so I hid myself."

"The beginning of wisdom is fear of the LORD," says the Bible (Prov. 9:10); but that fear, that good fear, is filial fear, not servile fear. Filial fear is the awe and wonder, the respect and adoration, of a trusting child for a wise and loving father. Servile fear is the fear of a terrified slave for a cruel and wicked slave master. The child does not want to hide from his father, but the slave does want to hide from his slave master. When Adam fell, his relationship to God changed from filial to servile. The loving Father now looked like the angry slave master. Adam, who had rejoiced in God's attention, now feared it. That's what sin is: not merely disobeying God's laws but changing the essential personal relationship with God from a joy to a threat, from filial fear to servile fear, from trust to mistrust.

God didn't change, but Adam did; and that's why it seemed to Adam that God had changed. God does not change. God is love, forever. God continued to love Adam, but God's smile now looked to Adam like a frown of anger and wrath.

All sin wants to hide from God, from the light. All sin chooses the darkness over the light. Criminals prefer the night to the day. We can't choose evil over good without at the same time choosing darkness over light. We need the darkness to hide our sin. We can't hide it from God, but we can hide it from ourselves. We can't stop God's light from shining, but we can close our eyes so we don't see it when that light hurts us, when we are ashamed to be seen.

The story in Genesis uses the image of bodily nakedness for two reasons. First, it's a physical image for our spiritual nakedness, for the fact that God sees everything in us, and when that "everything" includes sin, we no longer enjoy his look. The Psalmist begins Psalm 139 with the words "O LORD, you have probed me and you know me; you know when I sit and when I stand"—and then he goes on to accept and celebrate that fact, that God knows even his falls and sins and failures. He confesses his sins to God. He converts and turns and faces the light again, and that is his healing. That's why God gave us the sacrament of Confession: to foster our complete and total honesty. Because God can't turn off his light, his total knowledge of us, no matter what we do, so we absolutely have to get used to it, to love it, to live with it, because it is the only game in town. Its name is God, and two other names for it are Truth and Love.

The second reason the story uses the image of nakedness is literal. Adam and Eve needed no clothes to hide themselves from each other because they saw each other with the eyes of pure love, not selfish lust. We need clothing because without clothing we know that others will look on us as objects to use to gratify their own selfish desire for sexual pleasure. Lust is a sin not because it's about sex—God invented sex, after all, and invented its pleasures—but because lust is selfish sex; it's taking something God designed as beautiful and holy, as an opportunity for total self-giving, for the joy of unselfish love, and twisting that around to make it a means to the end of something purely selfish. It's no longer loving the other person as your end but using him or her as your means, your instrument, reducing him or her to an object, and making your own selfish pleasure your ultimate end. The difference between lust and love is the difference between wanting to get and wanting to give.

So what does Adam say to God? He makes excuses. He passes the buck. He blames Eve for giving him the forbidden fruit, and he blames God for giving him Eve. "The woman whom you put here with me—she gave me fruit." When God asks Eve the same question, she, too, passes the buck and blames the devil: "The serpent tricked me into it." God accepts neither excuse. We love to blame somebody or something else for our sins. If we're Marxists, we blame the capitalists. If we're Freudians, we blame our *id*, our animal nature. If we're Darwinians, we blame our fathers, who were apes. We blame society; we blame institutions; we blame our parents; we blame our spouses, our children, our culture—anybody but ourselves. We lie. Sin makes us liars.

So what does God do? Immediately he starts the process that will take all of human history to complete—namely, our rescue, our deliverance, our salvation. The Gospel begins in Genesis 3:15. That verse is called the "proto-Gospel," or the "first good news." God promises to send a Savior, the offspring of the woman who is Eve's great-great-great (etc.) granddaughter. Mary is the new Eve, and Jesus is her son, and together they defeat the devil. The seed of the woman crushes the head of the serpent, and the serpent bites the heel of the Savior, the Achilles heel, the soft, vulnerable part, the human body of Jesus, on the cross. The devil seems to win when his evil spiritual seed (Judas and Pilate and Caiaphas and Herod and the Romans) all succeed in murdering Jesus, but that's in fact how the devil loses, and how we win. That's why we call it "*Good Friday.*" The devil tricked Eve, but God tricked the devil.

All stories have three stages: a situation is set up, then upset, then reset. First, the characters are introduced, then they are challenged, then they respond. All the stories we tell reflect that essential structure of the story we are in, the story of creation, fall, and redemption.

We can interpret the details of the Genesis story literally if we choose (God certainly could have used a tree and a fruit and a garden and a snake), or we can interpret them symbolically (the garden is a symbol of the innocence God created us in, and the tree is a symbol of God's law, and the forbidden fruit is a symbol of our sin, and the snake is a symbol of the devil), but in either case the story is true, historically true, of us all. The three great historical facts are that God created mankind good, that we became evil by our own sinful choice, and that God saved us from our own sin by sending his Son to die for us. That is not symbolic; that is the literal, historical fact.

In fact, if that's not fact but only fiction, we have no hope. Because nothing else is going to save us: not the Democratic Party or the Republican Party or science or technology or money or sex or power or psychology or drugs or even good music and food and humor. They're just temporary entertainment in our comfortable deck chairs on the *Titanic*. God is our only lifeboat. In the last analysis, it's God or nothing.

RESPONSORIAL PSALM
PSALM 130:1–2, 3–4, 5–6, 7–8 _____

R. (7bc) **With the Lord there is mercy, and fullness of redemption.**

Out of the depths I cry to you, O LORD;
  Lord, hear my voice!
Let your ears be attentive
  to my voice in supplication.

If you, O LORD, mark iniquities,
  LORD, who can stand?
But with you is forgiveness,
  that you may be revered.

I trust in the LORD;
  my soul trusts in his word.
More than sentinels wait for the dawn,
  let Israel wait for the LORD.

For with the LORD is kindness
  and with him is plenteous redemption;
and he will redeem Israel
  from all their iniquities.

Today's Psalm verses are famous: "Out of the depths I cry to you, O LORD." The first words, in Latin, are *de profundis*, from which we get our word "profound." What are these profound depths or deeps out of which the Psalmist cries to God?

They are not the depths of wisdom. He is not saying to God, "God, my mind is very profoundly wise, and I come to you as a know-it-all." Only the very young think they know it all. No, these are the depths of darkness, of suffering, and of sin.

Of darkness, because we are *not* know-it-alls, we are not gods, and we do not fully understand our own lives and our own selves. We come to God in all our ignorance.

Of suffering, because to live is to suffer. We are born in the pains of childbirth, and we die in the pains of death, and between the two no life is secure from pain, either physical or mental. God gives us plenty of fun and even joy, but never security.

Of sin, because that is the deepest evil of all. Sin means separation from God, from his will, from his loving plan for our lives. We are divorced from God; we have been unfaithful to God; we have run away from God, who is the source of all truth and goodness and joy, and that is why we have darkness as well as the light of truth, and sin instead of goodness and holiness, and suffering as well as happiness.

There are different depths of darkness. Some times are darker than others, and this Psalm is most appropriate in those times. But all times have some darkness in them, so this Psalm is appropriate for all times until we get to heaven.

Some people have lives that are darker than others, and this Psalm is most appropriate for them, but it is appropriate for all of us, for all of us live in the valley of the shadow of death.

Some sins are worse than others, and this Psalm is most appropriate for those who recognize and reject and repent of deep sins, serious sins, mortal sins; but all of us are sinners, and this Psalm is appropriate for all of us.

The depths are the result of the fall, which is what our first reading was about. We may think we have not fallen very far because we measure our fall into the depths of sin and sorrow and stupidity only by the relative and small heights of the goodness and joy and wisdom that we remember in our past or that we see in other fallen fellow human beings; but measured by the innocence and wisdom and joy of our nature as God originally created it, we have fallen very, very far, incomparably far. We have not just stumbled into a ditch; we have toppled over the cliff of the Grand Canyon.

The Psalmist's first reaction to this is to speak to God about it, and to speak honestly and humbly. Honesty and humility are perhaps not the highest and greatest of all virtues, but they are the most necessary foundation and beginning of all virtues. To confess and to complain—if we do not do that, we can make no progress at all toward God. A life without complaint, a life of perfect self-satisfaction, perfect self-acceptance, is not a good life; it is the worst of all possible lives. To be separated from God by sin is bad enough, but to be satisfied in that separation is far worse. Our secular psychologists preach self-acceptance, to just accept ourselves as we are. That is their highest praise. It is in fact the most dangerous of all sins. It is called pride, and self-righteousness, and Phariseeism. Jesus said to the Pharisees: "Those who are sick go to the doctor. You deny that you are sick, so I am not your doctor. I came only for sinners. If you say you have no sin, say goodbye to me forever."

The alternative is not self-hatred or despair. It is hope. The hope for forgiveness. I hope none of you are planning to ask God for justice when you meet him at the Last Judgment, because we will all get what we ask for. If we ask for justice, we will get it; and if we ask for mercy, we will get that. And that's the difference between hell and heaven.

There are three very different pictures we can have of God. First, and most popular today, we can see God as a pop psychologist, patting us on the head for our self-esteem and being as satisfied as we are with our sinfulness and our selfishness and our stupidity. Second, at the opposite extreme, we can see God as a legalistic judge who acts like an impersonal machine, eager to give us all the punishments we deserve. Third, we can see God as our loving Father, ready with forgiveness but demanding sincere repentance.

The first God is a God of mercy without justice. The second God is a God of justice without mercy. The third God is the true God, a God of both justice and mercy.

The first God is easy to please and easy to satisfy, like a pop psychologist. The second God is hard to please and hard to satisfy, like a legalistic judge. The third God is easy to please but hard to satisfy, like a loving father. That is the God Jesus shows us, the God Jesus calls his Father and our Father. He is both loving and demanding. He wants to make us into saints, because he loves us. But the road from sin to sanctity, from stupidity to wisdom, and from sorrow to joy is long and hard, although there are great joys all along the way; and it requires frequent trips to the spiritual bathroom that we call the sacrament of Confession. But it prepares us for the delicious banquet of love in the dining room, and the Eucharist is our appetizer for that banquet. I hope you will frequently go to both of those two rooms of our Father's house.

SECOND READING
2 Corinthians 4:13–5:1 _____

Brothers and sisters: Since we have the same spirit of faith, according to what is written, *I believed, therefore I spoke,* we too believe and therefore we speak, knowing that the one who raised the Lord Jesus will raise us also with Jesus and place us with you in his presence. Everything indeed is for you, so that the grace bestowed in abundance on more and more people may cause the thanksgiving to overflow for the glory of God. Therefore, we are not discouraged; rather, although our outer self is wasting away, our inner self is being renewed day by day. For this momentary light affliction is producing for us an eternal weight of glory beyond all comparison, as we look not to what is seen but to what is unseen; for what is seen is transitory, but what is unseen is eternal. For we know that if our earthly dwelling, a tent, should be destroyed, we have a building from God, a dwelling not made with hands, eternal in heaven.

Listen to these courageous words from a man who suffered stoning, shipwreck, plots against his life, hatred, rejection by most of his former friends, exile, betrayal, injustice, imprisonment, and eventually martyrdom. He says, "We are not discouraged; rather, although our outer self is wasting away, our inner self is being renewed day by day." Our outer self is wasting away because as soon as we are born, we begin to die. But our inner self is being renewed day by day because the Holy Spirit in us is the life of our soul, and whatever has life always grows.

St. Paul calls his mile-high pile of sufferings "this momentary light affliction" because he knows that, as he goes on to say, it "is producing for us an eternal weight of glory beyond all comparison, as we look not to what is seen but to what is unseen; for what is seen is transitory, but what is unseen is eternal. For we know that if our earthly dwelling, a tent, should be destroyed, we have a building from God, a dwelling not made with hands, eternal in heaven." What is that tent? Our mortal body. What is the dwelling not made with hands from God eternal in heaven? Our resurrection body, our immortal body that God will raise as he raised Christ's body.

Why did Paul believe that? Because Christ promised it, and Christ cannot lie. It's as simple as that.

One word for all that St. Paul is writing about in today's epistle is hope. Hope is not optimism. It's not a feeling, and it's not a wish. It's a guarantee from God. It requires faith to believe it, and it requires courage to live it. But we often misunderstand courage, just as we often misunderstand hope.

Courage is also not an emotion. It's not fearlessness, or toughness, or some special quality that only a few heroes have. It's a choice, the choice to embrace and endure any obstacles and sufferings and difficulties on the road to God and heaven. Courage is required for every Christian. It is a choice. So is the opposite of courage, discourage. St. Paul says, "We are not discouraged." Discouragement, like courage, is not just a feeling that comes over us helplessly and passively. Like its opposite, courage, it is a choice: the choice not to believe, not to trust, not to hope.

We have to freely and actively choose to encourage ourselves, as well as each other. We all have the freedom to choose between encouragement and discouragement, between courage and discourage, between giving up and going on, one small step at a time, putting one foot in front of the other, climbing, or at least trying to climb, toward God and out of ourselves, despite all the obstacles both within us and outside of us.

St. Paul knew those obstacles. They are unavoidable. We cannot avoid temptations and failures and sorrows, but we can climb over them; we can conquer them, one by one, a little bit at a time. We can resist our temptations, and we can repent of our sins and moral failures, and we can embrace our sorrows and sufferings and offer them to God in faith. (Fulton Sheen loved to say: "Don't waste your sufferings. They can be the most powerful prayers.") We can keep climbing back onto the horse every time we fall off it; we can keep coming back to the road after we wander off the road or lose sight of it, again and again, never, never, never giving up. And here's the most important thing: we can all do this *not* because we are so strong but because God our Father is. God is love, and love is the strongest thing in the world. Love is stronger than death.

That's not sentimentality because that love is not the love that comes from us but the love that comes from God and comes *into* us and works through us.

GOSPEL
MARK 3:20–35 _____

Jesus came home with his disciples. Again the crowd gathered, making it impossible for them even to eat. When his relatives heard of this they set out to seize him, for they said, "He is out of his mind." The scribes who had come from Jerusalem said, "He is possessed by Beelzebul," and "By the prince of demons he drives out demons."

Summoning them, he began to speak to them in parables, "How can Satan drive out Satan? If a kingdom is divided against itself, that kingdom cannot stand. And if a house is divided against itself, that house will not be able to stand. And if Satan has risen up against himself and is divided, he cannot stand; that is the end of him. But no one can enter a strong man's house to plunder his property unless he first ties up the strong man. Then he can plunder the house. Amen, I say to you, all sins and all blasphemies that people utter will be forgiven them. But whoever blasphemes against the Holy Spirit will never have forgiveness, but is guilty of an everlasting sin." For they had said, "He has an unclean spirit."

His mother and his brothers arrived. Standing outside they sent word to him and called him. A crowd seated around him told him, "Your mother and your brothers and your sisters are outside asking for you." But he said to them in reply, "Who are my mother and my brothers?" And looking around at those seated in the circle he said, "Here are my mother and my brothers. For whoever does the will of God is my brother and sister and mother."

The people who met Jesus in the Gospels can be classified clearly into five different groups.

First, there were those who were seeking God. Those people became Jesus' disciples, for, as Jesus himself said, all who seek, find.

Second, there were those who were seeking cures and miracles. They sought Jesus not for himself but as a means to that end. They followed him only as long as he was successful and popular, but they abandoned him when he was arrested; in fact, they cried, "Crucify him!" They couldn't use him for their own purposes anymore. Some of those purposes were political. That's why

Jesus often hid himself when the people wanted to take him and make him the literal king of the Jews. They wanted to use him to kick out their Roman oppressors.

Third, there were the curiosity seekers. They didn't know what they wanted. But Jesus was at least interesting. In fact, Jesus is probably the only person who ever lived who never bored anybody. The four Gospels use the same word to describe the reaction of every one of the five groups of people who came to him. The word is *thaumazein*, which means "wonder" or "amazement."

Fourth, some of his own relatives thought he was out of his mind, far too far beyond the normal and the safe. He inspired too much passion, too much "fanaticism." He was not respectable. He was dangerous.

Fifth, some actually thought he was literally demon-possessed. That included many of the Pharisees and the priests. After all, he had claimed to be the Son of God, and if that was true, they had to worship him, and if it was false, they had to kill him for blasphemy. This last group, who hated him most, were actually quite logical and consistent. Jesus was either the best man who ever lived or the worst. If he was divine, as he claimed to be, he was better than the best of mere men. If he wasn't divine, he was the most blasphemous, sacrilegious heretic who ever lived.

Jesus answers this fifth group's very logical argument with a logical argument of his own. If he has a demon, how can he be exorcising demons? Jesus himself had given us a practical principle for discernment and judgment: "By their fruits you will know them" (Matt. 7:20). We recognize evil people by the evil things they do, and we recognize demons by the supernaturally evil things they do. Jesus healed all evils: diseases, by miraculous cures; sin, by forgiveness; and even death itself, by raising at least three people from the dead. His works and their fruits are exactly the opposite of the devil's. How can he be possessed by a demon if he is undoing all the works of the demons? Jesus says, "If a kingdom is divided against itself, that kingdom cannot stand." "Divide and conquer" is the best strategy for winning a war. "Fight against your own soldiers" is the best way to lose a war.

In response to the accusation that Jesus, the Son of God, is really possessed by Satan, that God and the devil are together in him, Jesus speaks of an "unforgivable sin." It's the only time he ever says that. All other sins are forgivable, but this one is the exception. What is the unforgivable sin? It is somehow calling God Satan; calling the works of God the works of Satan; confusing God with Satan, light with darkness, good with evil. He also calls this the blasphemy against the Holy Spirit, probably because the Holy Spirit is inside us, directly inspiring our conscience; and to sin against our own conscience, to call the good that we know is good evil, is not excusable by ignorance. One can be ignorant of who Jesus is, mistaken about who Jesus is. Before his conversion, St. Paul was mistaken about who Jesus is, drastically mistaken. But he was at least honest. He was following his conscience, terribly wrong as it was. That's why he could be converted by the light from heaven. He was blaspheming against Jesus but not against the Holy Spirit. But that's what the Pharisees and the high priests were doing: blaspheming against the Holy Spirit. It was not just an intellectual mistake: they knew Jesus was who he claimed to be, and they hated it.

One last problem we may worry about in this Gospel is that Jesus seems to insult his mother and his family when the people tell him that they are outside and want to see him and he replies: "Who are my mother and my brothers? . . . Here are my mother and my brothers. For whoever does the will of God is my brother and sister and mother."

Two things can be said in answer to that misunderstanding. First, Jesus is not disowning his family but inviting others into it. He is not making his family smaller but larger. And second, he is not implying that his mother is not holy but telling us *why* she is holy: because she is doing the will of the Father, not just because she was his biological mother. It is not just biological genetics but spiritual genetics, so to speak, that makes Mary holy. "Thy will be done" is the prayer that makes a saint. Being a saint is extraordinarily simple (that's why it's so difficult): just say a total yes to God, as Mary did.

ELEVENTH SUNDAY IN ORDINARY TIME

FIRST READING
Ezekiel 17:22–24 _____

Thus says the Lord God:
    I, too, will pluck from the crest of the cedar
        the highest branch.
    From the top a tender shoot
        I will break off and transplant
        on a high, lofty mountain.
    On the mountain height of Israel
        I will plant it.
    It shall put forth branches and bear fruit,
        and become a majestic cedar.
    Every small bird will nest under it,
        all kinds of winged birds will dwell
        in the shade of its branches
    Every tree of the field will know
        that I am the Lord.
    I bring low the high tree,
        lift high the lowly tree,
    Wither up the green tree,
        and make the dry tree bloom.
    As I, the Lord, have spoken, so will I do!

RESPONSORIAL PSALM

PSALM 92:2–3, 13–14, 15–16 _____

R. (cf. 2a) **Lord, it is good to give thanks to you.**

It is good to give thanks to the LORD,
    to sing praise to your name, Most High,
To proclaim your kindness at dawn
    and your faithfulness throughout the night.

The just one shall flourish like the palm tree,
    like a cedar of Lebanon shall he grow.
They that are planted in the house of the LORD
    shall flourish in the courts of our God.

They shall bear fruit even in old age;
    vigorous and sturdy shall they be,
Declaring how just is the LORD,
    my rock, in whom there is no wrong.

SECOND READING

2 CORINTHIANS 5:6–10 _____

Brothers and sisters: We are always courageous, although we know that while we are at home in the body we are away from the Lord, for we walk by faith, not by sight. Yet we are courageous, and we would rather leave the body and go home to the Lord. Therefore, we aspire to please him, whether we are at home or away. For we must all appear before the judgment seat of Christ, so that each may receive recompense, according to what he did in the body, whether good or evil.

GOSPEL
MARK 4:26–34_____

Jesus said to the crowds: "This is how it is with the kingdom of God; it is as if a man were to scatter seed on the land and would sleep and rise night and day and through it all the seed would sprout and grow, he knows not how. Of its own accord the land yields fruit, first the blade, then the ear, then the full grain in the ear. And when the grain is ripe, he wields the sickle at once, for the harvest has come."

He said, "To what shall we compare the kingdom of God, or what parable can we use for it? It is like a mustard seed that, when it is sown in the ground, is the smallest of all the seeds on the earth. But once it is sown, it springs up and becomes the largest of plants and puts forth large branches, so that the birds of the sky can dwell in its shade." With many such parables he spoke the word to them as they were able to understand it. Without parables he did not speak to them, but to his own disciples he explained everything in private.

Three of today's four Scripture readings are held together by the image of a growing thing, a plant, like a tree.

Images are more important than we usually think. Images are how we begin to learn nearly everything, because images are what our bodily senses give us, and our minds depend on our bodies. The mind is spiritual, not physical—it has no size or shape or color; but a blow to the body upsets it and damage to the physical brain disables it. We are both body and soul, body and spirit, body and mind. We are not pure spirits, like angels, and we are not pure bodies like computers. We are animals, rational animals, and we learn first of all from what we see.

Images are not only our primary *learning* devices, but they are also our psychologically effective *teaching* devices, for two reasons. First, images are easier to grasp than abstract ideas. Second, they are harder to forget. That's why "a picture is worth a thousand words." That's why Jesus, like all good teachers, used them.

Most of the images Jesus used were parables. Parables are extended images, images in a very short story, a tiny "slice of life." They are images—that is, analogies, likenesses, similes or metaphors, allegories or symbols. They are the first way we learn almost everything when we are young children, and in relation to God and heaven we are all very young children. And even when we are adults, the most abstract ideas are best understood and best remembered when they are illustrated by images. This is true in every field, not just religion. For instance, physics uses images like the "Big Bang" for the universe's beginnings and romantic love for electromagnetic attraction.

Images are not just clever devices we invent; they are the way nature herself teaches us. That very pronoun, "herself," is an image: the cross-cultural image of "Mother Nature." And since God invented nature, this is one of the ways *God* teaches us. One part of nature is nature outside of us, the great work of art that God designed. Another part of nature is nature within us, our own human nature, including natural reason, which God also invented and designed in us. That's why St. Thomas Aquinas says, "To scorn the dictate of reason is to scorn the teaching of God." Conscience is simply the moral aspect of reason. The medievals used to say that God wrote two books, not just one: Scripture and nature. Both are full of images.

The image of the tree, or any other plant, is central to our Scripture readings today.

ᘯ

The prophet Ezekiel says that God, in revealing himself to Israel, and through Israel to the whole world, is doing something like planting a tree. First, he plants a shoot, or a seed; then it puts forth branches; and then it bears fruit. Those are the three stages of growth. Faith is like the roots: steadfast, stable, committed. Hope is like the branches: expanding, growing, progressing. Love is the fruit, the most beautiful and edible and delicious part, the purpose of the plant. Our souls are like trees: they grow in a similar way. For one thing, they grow naturally and organically, from within, like plants, not by artificial construction, like buildings or computers. Another similarity is the three stages of growth: a mature soul, like a mature plant, has roots and branches and fruits. The root is faith, and the branches are hope, and the fruits are the works of love. A third similarity is the unity of these three stages and three virtues: it's the very same single biological life in a plant that produces the roots and the branches and the fruits, and it's the same spiritual life in a soul, the same presence of God, that produces faith and hope and charity.

❧

In the Gospel, Jesus uses the image of the growth of a seed to explain what he calls "the kingdom of God," which means God's reign as king both in our individual souls and in the Church. For the Church is not merely an organization, like a business; it is an organism, like a plant. It is alive and growing from within, since its soul or spirit is within it. That spirit is the Holy Spirit, which is the soul of the Church. The Church, ourselves, and plants all grow from within, organically, and all three have both bodies and souls or spirits.

There is a natural, organic growth both in plants and in human beings; and, within human beings, both in our bodies and in our souls; and also both in individual souls and in the Church, which also has both a body and a soul. Her body is visible; her soul is invisible. The soul of the Church, or the life of the Church, is the Holy Spirit.

In the Gospel, Jesus compares the Church to a seed. The farmer plants the seed and then, day by day, the seed grows from within, by itself, invisibly, "he knows not how." That's the difference between living things and nonliving things: living things grow not by people adding layers from outside, like stories on a skyscraper or covers on a bed, but by themselves, from inside. That's how the Church grows, and that's how our souls grow, and that's how our bodies grow, and that's how our plants grow.

Modern Western man has lost that understanding for the first time in history. We no longer speak of "unnatural acts," or even of a "natural moral law." We see ourselves as machines, which we can manipulate and redesign as we please. Very few of us work with plants or animals anymore, and very many of us live and work with machines or computers. But machines and computers cannot give us life.

Jesus also mentions three stages of growth: "first the blade, then the ear, then the full grain." He's thinking of wheat. The same point could be made by a different image: first the seed, then the branches, then the fruit. Each stage builds on the one before it.

Jesus also adds the point that the largest bush comes from the smallest seed, the mustard seed. Thus, the Church begins as the smallest spiritual organism in the world—it began with three people: Jesus, Mary, and Joseph. Like a zygote, the Church immediately expanded when Jesus gathered his disciples, but it was still tiny. But it eventually expanded to cover the earth. There are now over two billion Christians, and the Church is still growing everywhere in the world except in one place: here, in what used to be called Christendom, or Christian civilization, which is now called simply Western civilization—Europe and North America.

Two things distinguish our culture from all others today: the decline of the Church and the decline of the family. Everywhere else, Christians are multiplying in two ways: by evangelization and by procreation. Only here are Christians leaving the Church much faster than they are entering it, and only here are they having fewer and fewer children each subsequent generation. Those are the two primary signs of life, or of the absence of life, in a civilization. Having children is like planting a tree: it is an act of faith in the future. Fortunately, our future and our hope is in the Church, not in the state. Christ did not promise that the gates of hell would not prevail against any state, or any culture or civilization, but he did promise that to his Church.

სა

The Psalm for today says that this tree, this cedar of Lebanon, is planted "in the house of the LORD." That "house" refers to the Church, which of course is not merely a building. When we are baptized, we are baptized *in* a church building, but we are baptized *into* the Church, and we are baptized *by* the Church. We do not construct the Church; we enter the Church that already exists. It's like entering Noah's ark. We don't make or remake the Church; she remakes us. There is a popular hymn with a line that is profoundly wrong: "Let us build the city of God." It's God who builds that organism. We are its cells, not its soul.

The Psalm adds a dimension to the picture of the growing tree, and here it shows the difference between our life and the life of a plant. For even as our bodies get older and weaker and eventually die, our souls get stronger and holier and more full of spiritual life, as is shown by the fruits they produce in maturity, the fruits of wisdom and holiness. That's how you know a plant is alive: if it produces fruit. By their fruits you shall know them, Jesus says. In other words, faith without works is dead.

ຊຽ

Today's epistle does not explicitly use the image of the tree, but it fits into the picture that Jesus paints in his Gospel when he says, at the end of his parable, "And when the grain is ripe, he wields the sickle at once, for the harvest has come." The point of sowing is reaping. God is a farmer. Each of us is a seed, designed to grow into a mature plant and then be harvested, gathered into God's barn, which is heaven, at the right time, which is known by God alone. That's our destiny, our home. This world is just our womb, and at death we are finally born into the bigger world, God's world. If that's not true, our whole religion is a lie and a fake.

Thus, St. Paul says, in today's epistle, "We know that while we are at home in the body we are away from the Lord." We have his presence in our souls and in the Eucharist, and that is infinitely precious; but only after death will we see him face to face and be present in his heavenly home, which is *our* real home too. I assure you that if and when you enter heaven, you will say something like this: "I could never have imagined or invented this place; it is amazingly new, yet it is not alien; this place is my home. This is what I was destined for from the beginning. This is what all of my life on earth was about, what it was all for." As with farming, the planting and the caring and the feeding and the fertilizing and the watering—it is all for the reaping, the harvesting. That's not a postscript, an extra. That's the point of the whole process.

God knows when and how to do this harvesting. He's the mind behind the whole process, including all the things we don't understand about our lives—why this, and why that? His timing is always just right: we should neither delay it unnaturally, by extending life through excessive means, nor try to hasten it unnaturally, by euthanasia. God is our farmer, and we are his seeds; and the farmer who knows how and when to sow the seed also knows how and when to harvest it.

TWELFTH SUNDAY IN ORDINARY TIME

FIRST READING

Job 38:1, 8–11 _____

The Lord addressed Job out of the storm and said:
Who shut within doors the sea,
    when it burst forth from the womb;
when I made the clouds its garment
    and thick darkness its swaddling bands?
When I set limits for it
    and fastened the bar of its door,
and said: Thus far shall you come but no farther,
    and here shall your proud waves be stilled!

RESPONSORIAL PSALM

Psalm 107:23–24, 25–26, 28–29, 30–31 _____

R. (1b) **Give thanks to the Lord, his love is everlasting.**
or: R. **Alleluia.**

They who sailed the sea in ships,
    trading on the deep waters,
These saw the works of the LORD
    and his wonders in the abyss.

His command raised up a storm wind
    which tossed its waves on high.
They mounted up to heaven; they sank to the depths;

their hearts melted away in their plight.

They cried to the LORD in their distress;
    from their straits he rescued them,
He hushed the storm to a gentle breeze,
    and the billows of the sea were stilled.

They rejoiced that they were calmed,
    and he brought them to their desired haven.
Let them give thanks to the LORD for his kindness
    and his wondrous deeds to the children of men.

SECOND READING
2 CORINTHIANS 5:14–17

Brothers and sisters: The love of Christ impels us, once we have come to the conviction that one died for all; therefore, all have died. He indeed died for all, so that those who live might no longer live for themselves but for him who for their sake died and was raised.

Consequently, from now on we regard no one according to the flesh; even if we once knew Christ according to the flesh, yet now we know him so no longer. So whoever is in Christ is a new creation: the old things have passed away; behold, new things have come.

St. Paul's words in today's epistle define the truest meaning of progress, and true progressivism.

It is not a political term, first of all. Whether we progress more by increasing or decreasing taxes, or immigration, or military resources, or government interventions in health care, or gun ownership, has no necessary connection to true progressivism. For all these political things are made *by* human beings and *for* human beings, so the most important kind of progress is not in any of these *things* but in *persons*, in human beings themselves. If we ourselves progress, in our very being, and therefore our goodness, and therefore our happiness, that is the most true and real and fundamental progressivism that there could ever possibly be, since God does not change or progress, and neither do the angels, and since everything else is comparatively unimportant, even trivial, because it is beneath us; it is about mere things, which are only means, not persons, who are ends.

So what is the greatest progress we can possibly make? It is, firstly, progress from death to life, and above all from eternal death to eternal life, from being on the road to hell to being on the road to heaven, from having only natural life to having supernatural life. The theological term for that is "justification," reconciliation with God. And then, secondly, the increase of that life in our souls and our lives. The theological term for that is "sanctification," becoming more saintly, more Godlike.

And that first progress, getting supernatural life, is not a matter of gradual improvement, like health or income; it is an absolutely new thing, like birth. That's why Jesus called it being born again.

It is a change that only God the Creator can do; it is literally "a new creation." That is what St. Paul calls it in today's epistle. He says, "Whoever is in Christ is a new creation."

And if we ourselves are new creations, then everything in our lives becomes new. Thus, Jesus says, "Behold, I make *all things* new."

Whatever changes you, changes everything else in your life. When the most important person in your life dies, that changes everything for you, not just one thing. All the places you went to together change from being places of togetherness and happiness to being places of loneliness and unhappiness. The absence of your spouse or your parent or your child or your best friend is not like the absence of one face in a crowd: it is like the sky, spread out over everything. The sun seems to have gone out of the sky, and the whole sky is dark, and that makes everything in the landscape dark. Why does that happen?

Because that other person was a real part of yourself, not just outside of you but inside of you, a part of your soul, the other pair of eyes through which you looked at your world. When you lose an eye, everything looks different. It looks flat, without depth, without the perspective of the other eye. Well, your friend is your other eye. That's why everything changes when someone you love is born or dies, and when you fall in love or out of love: because the one constant in everything you experience is you, and you have changed.

Well, Christ changes us more fundamentally than any human being can ever change us. When he died on the cross and saved us, that wasn't something external, like a judge declaring us innocent. Jesus is our Savior not only because he saves us from the punishment for our sins that justice demands, but, as the angel said to St. Joseph, "You shall call him 'Jesus' (which means 'Savior') because he shall save his people *from their sins.*" He makes us a new creation. He gives us a new nature, a share in his divine nature. He gives us a new source of life, a new kind of life, the life of unselfish love that is the essential nature of God but is not the essential nature of us. We are born selfish, like all other animals. Our most basic instinct is not "Thy will be done" but "My will be done," or "I want what I want when I want it." That's the meaning of original sin. But God gives us another nature, a new nature.

It's small and invisible at first. He plants a seed in us, at Baptism, and that's like a rose among weeds; it's not just a bigger and better weed. It's a new thing, a new creation. God alone can create, and this is a new creation, so only God can do it. We cannot lift ourselves up by our own bootstraps. We are subject to the gravity of selfishness. God alone can give us wings to fly against that gravity.

We do not know whether God gives that gift of a new nature to people who do not consciously believe in Christ. If so, those people are "anonymous Christians," so to speak. How many are there? We simply don't know, and can't judge, and shouldn't try. God has not told us that. We know for sure only what he has told us.

And what he has told us is that if we are "in Christ" by faith and Baptism, we are a new creation. We are not just rational animals, evolved apes with bigger brains. We are not King Kong's kids; we are King God's kids. That's why we should act like the King's kids, not like the ape's kids. We have been made God's children. We can now call God our Father. We are part of his family. We share his very life. We have two natures, like Christ, human *and divine*. We share a tiny participation in God's very life. The Eastern Orthodox call this *theosis* or "deification."

So what's the practical relevance of this mystical theology of our deification to our lives today? It is, in St. Paul's words, "so that those who live might no longer live for themselves but for him who for their sake died and was raised." We used to live just from ourselves and for ourselves first of all. We now live from God and for God first of all.

We have a new lifestyle because we have a new life, a new nature. We didn't create that new nature ourselves. We can't live *into* that nature; God gave it to us, in Baptism. But we *can* live *out* that nature. We can live like the King's kids. We can live like what we really are: children of God the Father, brothers of God the Son, and temples of God the Holy Spirit.

We are holy. God's commandment to be holy is simply the commandment to be what we really, truly are.

That's not easy. Learning to live out our new identity, learning to live like the King's kids, takes a lifetime and probably longer for most of us. (That learning that Hindus and Buddhists hope is completed in reincarnation, which isn't real; we hope to be completed in purgatory, which is real.) So this hopeful spiritual "progressivism" is not an easy optimism.

And it's also not an easy optimism because the fact that we are holy does not make our sins better but worse. Doing something sinful in a church is worse than doing it anywhere else. And every sin we commit is committed in a church, because we are churches: we are temples of the Holy Spirit.

GOSPEL

MARK 4:35–41 _____

On that day, as evening drew on, Jesus said to his disciples: "Let us cross to the other side." Leaving the crowd, they took Jesus with them in the boat just as he was. And other boats were with him. A violent squall came up and waves were breaking over the boat, so that it was already filling up. Jesus was in the stern, asleep on a cushion. They woke him and said to him, "Teacher, do you not care that we are perishing?" He woke up, rebuked the wind, and said to the sea, "Quiet! Be still!" The wind ceased and there was great calm. Then he asked them, "Why are you terrified? Do you not yet have faith?" They were filled with great awe and said to one another, "Who then is this whom even wind and sea obey?"

_____

Reflection 1

Last Sunday, three of the four Scripture readings centered on the image of a growing plant. This Sunday, three of the four readings center on the image of a stormy sea. Both are images of human life. The life of each individual human soul, and also the life of the Church, the kingdom of God, is like a growing plant. And life with God, life under God's providential plan for us, is also like a stormy sea. Each of these images goes through three distinct phases. The plant is first planted from a small seed, then grows, then produces fruit. The sea is first calm, then stormy, then calm again.

The sea, especially the sea in a storm, with its crashing waves, has always fascinated humanity as something not just *pretty* but *sublime*, something both beautiful and fascinating, even terrifying. Like God.

We are drawn to the sea. Waterfront property is by far the most desirable and expensive property on earth. Surfers fall in love with the sea; they brave the cold, and sharks, and the danger of drowning, all for the thrill of riding its waves. It feels like riding gigantic horses, or liquid dinosaurs, or mountains that are alive and moving.

The sea is the largest thing our eyes can see on earth. Sea water is so heavy that waves move great boulders and knock down steel and concrete buildings during storms.

In today's reading from the book of Job, God finally appears to Job and answers Job's complaints and questions about why he allowed the innocent Job to suffer such terrible tragedies. And instead of explaining the details, God simply reminds Job that he, not Job, designed the world and its seas and its waves—which here symbolize the waves of tragedies and sufferings that had rolled over Job—and that he is in control of them, as we are not; that he is the one who said to the waves, "Thus far shall you come but no farther." That is exactly what God had said to Satan at the beginning of the book of Job, when God gave Satan permission to afflict Job with his sufferings but *limited* them: "thus far but no farther."

Satan, not God, is the author of evil and of death; but God is like a fisherman, and he plays Satan like a fish at the end of his fishing line. God limits Satan's incursions into our lives and limits the harms he does to us, as he limits how far the waves of the sea can destroy the land. He allows evils that we cannot understand, and which sometimes seem to us to do us no good; but they are always for our own greater good in the end. We can't see that because we are not God, and we do not see the end.

God did that when he allowed the greatest evil that ever happened, the torture and murder of his own divine Son, for the greater good of our salvation, so that we now dare to call the day when we remember this greatest of all evils "*Good* Friday." If God can do it there, he can do it everywhere. That's why St. Paul dares to tell us in Romans 8:28 that "all things work for good for those who love God." Not all things are good, but God works even bad things for good in the end, in ways we seldom see but are invited to believe.

So the next time you see some of the terrifying, threatening waves of life about to break on you and wipe you out, remember who is holding them back and using them as part of his mysterious but all-wise and all-loving plan for your life. We cannot *see* that, but we can *believe* that; and we can believe *that* because we can believe *him* and trust him. If he is all-powerful and all-wise, he controls even the waves of the sea and the waves of our lives. And if he is all-good and loving, then he does it out of his love for us, for our greatest good in the end. We must believe it because we do not usually see it, but we have three very good reasons to believe it: there is no limit to God's power, God's wisdom, and God's love. That is why there is a limit to the waves.

There are three stages to human life as a whole, and each individual life, and each particular challenge in the drama of our lives: first calm, then storm, then calm. These are the three stages of all the stories we tell because they are the three stages of the story we live: first the situation is set up, then it is upset, then it is reset. First, in act one, there is good, a good God and a good world made by the good God, and good characters in the drama, characters that are made in God's image, beloved children of the heavenly Father. Then, in act two, the situation that had been set up is upset: there is a fall; there is evil; there are storms; there are threats; there is loss; there is death. Then, eventually, in act three, after it is set up and upset, it is re-set: there is deliverance; there is salvation; there is resurrection. The storm is calmed. "This too shall pass." Only God does not pass away. In the end, evil always passes away; good does not.

Those are the three acts of the drama of the sailors in today's Psalm. First, they go down to the sea in ships when the sea is calm. Then, by God's command (note that it is God's command, not an accident!) the sea raises up a storm and the waves mount up to heaven and sink to the depths, and the sailors' hearts melt away in fear. Like the disciples in the boat in today's Gospel, they cry to God out of their fear, out of the depths of distress, and then God rescues them. He hushes the storm.

In the story in the Gospel today, Jesus speaks to the sea, and the sea obeys him. He addresses the sea exactly as we would address our dog when it acts up: "Down, Fido! Peace! Be still!" And Fido meekly obeys. It's awesome, but it's also hilariously funny.

And that is the plot of every story we tell—those three stages—because that is the plot of the story God is writing with our lives. The theological terms for the three stages of the human story as a whole are creation, fall, and redemption. Redemption starts as soon as the fall happens, so act two and act three overlap. We are in both stages now: we are still fallen, but we are beginning to be redeemed, in the process of redemption or salvation. Because we are still in act two of that story, the stormy part, we look back to the innocence and joy we had in act one, in the Garden of Eden, which was like our mother's womb. But we've lost that. And we look forward to the holiness and joy we will have in heaven, in act three, but that's not yet our possession: it's only our hope, our promise from God. Meanwhile, the present is full of sins and sufferings and storms and shipwrecks.

Science and technology have greatly decreased our physical pains today. Think of what it was like to live without anesthesia! But we have greatly increased our mental and emotional pains. We are richer than our ancestors but not happier; smarter but not wiser; stronger physically but not stronger spiritually. The waves keep coming. We have calms between the storms, but there are always more storms brewing. We will never have heaven on earth.

But when the winds blow and the waves break, our Lord comes to us walking on the water, and he says to us: "Have faith. It is I. Be not afraid. I am the Lord of the waves: both the waves of water and the waves of suffering. I hold them in my hand. They come at my command, and they will cease at my command. I promise you that I will rescue you, I will save you, because that is who I am. Trust me. Those waves appear to be dark, like death itself; but that is only what you can see from your side. From my side they are full of light—and so is death itself. The door that looks so dark on your side is white with heavenly light on the other side. And the waves that you fear in this life are like that, like little deaths. In the words of the old hymn, 'Ye struggling saints, fresh courage take; the clouds ye so much dread / Are big with mercy and shall break in blessings on your head.' Things are more than they seem. Reality is far more than appearances, more than what you can see. That little round white thing that you eat at the

Mass looks like bread, but it is not bread. It is I. That big wave in your life looks like a storm that is out of control, but it is not. It is my tender and loving plan for your life. It looks like a weapon, but it is a scalpel, and I hold it in my bleeding hand as I perform my surgery on your soul. Trust 'the wounded surgeon.' Trust me. Trust me with everything because I am the Lord of everything."

If he is not the Lord of everything, he is not the Lord of anything. So which of those two things is he for you? Everything or nothing? It is he who is asking you that question right now, not me. Don't tell me your answer; tell him. Tell him many times each day the thing he longs to hear, the simple five-word prayer he gave to St. Faustina: "Jesus, I trust in you."

Of course, you still feel fear when you see those waves. But faith is not a feeling; trust is not a feeling; it is a choice. When you choose to put your money into a bank, you entrust the bank with your money; you trust the bank to keep it safe. You do that not by your feeling but by your freedom, by your choice, by your act of depositing your money there. That's what trust is. That's why it's called the First National Bank and Trust Company. You can bank on the bank; you can trust the trust. Well, Jesus is God's First Supernatural Bank and Trust Company.

And in the middle of the storms, he is in the boat with us, the boat that is his Church, his Noah's ark—even during storms, even when the salt water of the waves mingles with the salt water of our tears. And through those tears we can laugh even as we cry; we can laugh with delight when we hear him say, "Down, Fido!" because we know that the waves will cower at his feet like puppies. He is the Lord. We know him. And we know he knows us.

Reflection 2

We can easily relate to today's Gospel because our lives are very much like the lives of sailors in a boat at sea in dangerous storms. The parts of our lives that we ourselves designed and are in control of are like a boat, safe but small; and the parts of our lives that we did not design and are not in control of are like the sea, dangerous and large. On this sea of life, storms come up frequently, and some of them raise waves large enough to sink our boat and drown us. And we never know, from day to day, when the next storm will come up, the next tragedy, the next death of a friend or betrayal of a spouse or diagnosis of a cancer.

But we are not alone. Jesus is in our boat with us. One of his names is "Emmanuel," which means "God-*with-us*." And that makes all the difference.

Yes, but Jesus seems to be asleep. The storm still rages, and he seems to be doing nothing about it. And we of little faith are terrified by these big waves. So we wake him up, by prayer (of course he's never really asleep; he just seems to be, to test our faith), and we desperately ask him for help, and we wonder, like the disciples, "Do you not care that we are perishing?" We have faith, but it is only "little faith," smaller than a grain of mustard seed.

So he answers us, in two different ways: always by his perfect divine providence and sometimes by miracles (and miracles happen more often than we usually think). He "rebuked the wind, and said to the sea, 'Quiet! Be still!'" That sounds exactly like saying "Down, Fido!" to your dog. The sea is his dog, his pet. It's tame to him, even though it's wild to us.

And the sea obeys him. Of course it does. It's his pet; it's his sea, his creation. Everything is his. Water is his; all water is. That's why he can give it the power to transmit his own divine life to us in Baptism, and why he can roll the waters back at the Red Sea to rescue his chosen people from the Egyptian army, and why he can change it to wine at the wedding feast at Cana. It's his creation, and it can be his re-creation.

The point of the story is the last words, which the disciples say after it's all over: "They were filled with great awe and said to one another: 'Who is this whom even the wind and sea obey?'"

The Gospels are like a detective story or a mystery story, centering on the identity of its main character, Jesus. In the old radio program "The Lone Ranger," the hero always wears a mask and has a secret identity, and after he catches the bad guys and saves the good guys he rides away into the sunset, and everybody asks, "Who is that masked man, anyway?" That's the question they ask about Jesus too. And the answer is that he is the only one who tames the wind and the sea and the whole universe, because he is the Son of God and the Word of God and the Mind of God who created it all in the first place. He has not just greater power than we do: he has *infinite* power. He is *"Almighty* God."

And, therefore, he conquers death itself. Water usually symbolizes death in the Bible, so Christ's conquest of water symbolizes his conquest of death. In the book of Revelation, the beast, the devil, appears out of the sea; and in the new creation "there is no more sea"—that is, no more death.

So even when Christ does not rescue us miraculously from death by curing a deadly disease that the doctors can't cure (which he still does, more often than our secular media are allowed to tell us)—even when he does not perform that miracle on this side of death, he always performs it on the other side of death. We don't all get miracles in this life, but we all get the miracle of resurrection in the next life. He is the master of everything he created, including our bodies. So he gives us new bodies even if our old ones are cremated—which, by the way, is reluctantly permitted by the Church but not recommended because it does not reverence the holiest piece of matter in the universe, the human body.

After he stills the storm, Jesus rebukes his disciples for their lack of faith. The disciples do not yet fully realize who Jesus is. They didn't fully realize that until after his Resurrection. If they had known then, in the boat, what they knew after the Resurrection, they would not have feared the storm even if it had drowned them. They would have known that even the deadliest waves, the waves that swamp our boat, only bring us to the other shore alive.

Our "beloved dead" are not dead. They are more alive than we are, because of who Jesus is. He is the one whom everything in the universe obeys, even death. Everything else in the universe obeys him necessarily and unfreely; we do it by our free choice of faith and hope and love.

THIRTEENTH SUNDAY
IN ORDINARY TIME

FIRST READING

WISDOM 1:13–15; 2:23–24_____

God did not make death,
   nor does he rejoice in the destruction of the living.
For he fashioned all things that they might have being;
   and the creatures of the world are wholesome,
and there is not a destructive drug among them
   nor any domain of the netherworld on earth,
    for justice is undying.
For God formed man to be imperishable;
   the image of his own nature he made him.
But by the envy of the devil, death entered the world,
   and they who belong to his company experience it.

"God did not make death." This is a radical, revolutionary idea. No other religion in the world, no other philosophy in the world, came up with this idea—only Judaism, and the Christianity that sprang from Judaism and worshiped the God of the Jews, the God Jesus called his Father.

Pagan polytheists, who believed in many gods, always included gods of death and darkness and destruction as well as gods of life and light and love.

Eastern mystical religions like Hinduism and Buddhism taught either that the supreme being was unknowable or even nonexistent, as in Buddhism; or that he was beyond taking sides; or that he had a dark side as well as a light side, as in Hinduism, where *Brahman* manifests himself equally in Shiva, the god of destruction, and Vishnu, the god of creation or preservation.

In secular humanism, which is the religion of modern Western civilization, God either does not exist or is "nonjudgmental," not having a will, not taking sides, not issuing commandments. If he does not exist, there is only the universe, and the universe does not take sides; it gives us life and death equally. The same is true of a God who is nonjudgmental, who does not issue strict laws and commandments, who tolerates everything, death as well as life, evil as well as good. The God of secular humanism is definitely not "pro-life."

The true God is the God of life, not of death. The "God" who is made in *our* image is a god of death as well as life, but the God who made us in *his* image is the God of life, not death. He is the Creator of all being, not the destroyer of all being. He gives life; he does not destroy it. That is why *we* must give life, not destroy it. God is not a murderer; that is why *we* must not murder. God is pro-life, not pro-choice. It is we who chose death. God did not approve that choice. God is not pro-choice. God is not neutral. God fights with us, for us, against our enemies: sin and death. Christ came to us as a warrior to *conquer* sin and death for us, by taking our place, by dying for us and rising for us.

"God did not make death." But isn't death built into the universe God created? All living things die: plants, animals, and human beings. Even nonliving things come to an end: rocks become sand after millions of years of winds and waves, and, after billions of years, even stars and galaxies die.

Yes, but human death is different than all other death. God did not make it. He made man to live forever. Death is a consequence of the fall of man, not a consequence of the creation of God. Death was the devil's invention, not God's, and our ancestors were suckered in by the devil, who invented the world's oldest profession, advertising. "See this apple? You need this apple. It's cheap. It only costs your soul." Today's passage from the book of Wisdom says, "By the envy of the devil, death entered the world."

St. Paul says that "the wages of sin is death" (Rom. 6:23). Death is the consequence of sin, not by choice but by necessity. It's not like a parent deciding to punish a child for a misdeed. It's not "If you eat that sugary cookie, you can't have ice cream" but "If you eat that sugary cookie, you will get sick to your stomach." Why is physical death the necessary consequence of sin? Because sin is spiritual death, and the physical and the spiritual are not two separate things but two dimensions of one thing—namely, ourselves. Our body follows our soul; the body is one with the soul; it is not a separate and independent thing. When our souls fell into sin, our bodies fell to the level of animals, fell from immortality to mortality, because our souls fell from God, who is the only source of immortality. Once our souls declared independence from God by our sin, by the fall, God's life no longer flowed endlessly through our souls into our bodies. Once we pulled the plug, God's electricity no longer turned on our appliances.

God did not make death. Death is our enemy, and God is not our enemy. When someone we love dies, we should not say that God took him away from us but that death took him away. But we should add that God took death away. God's actions are always pro-life. The devil invented death, and we bought the devil's product, but God saved us from it: from the spiritual death that is sin, and from the physical death that is the necessary consequence of sin, and from the eternal death that would otherwise have been its final consequence. In other words, Christ redeemed us from all three enemies, sin and death and hell.

But isn't physical death natural to us, and shouldn't we accept it as natural? No, it is not natural to man, not part of God's design. And we cannot accept it. Deep in our hearts we all want something more. We want heaven. No animal dreams of heaven. No animal has religion, or a relationship with God. Only man says to God, "Thou hast made us for thyself, and therefore our hearts are restless until they rest in thee."

But death is built into our bodies now, into our genes, into our being. Don't we just have to accept it, because we have to accept ourselves as we are? No, we don't have to accept ourselves as we are, and we shouldn't. We are also stupid, selfish, shallow sinners: should we accept that, or should we fight against it? We naturally, spontaneously, hate death. Unless we have water instead of blood in our hearts and in our veins, we must fight death, both in ourselves and in others; we must not surrender to death; and when we die, we must surrender not to death but to God, the God who alone can conquer death for us and who promises us immortal life with him forever in heaven. Let's not listen to our false prophets, our secular psychologists, and just "accept ourselves as we are." Let's have hearts; let's have hope; let's have heaven!

RESPONSORIAL PSALM
PSALM 30:2, 4, 5–6, 11, 12, 13 _____

R. (2a) **I will praise you, Lord, for you have rescued me.**

I will extol you, O LORD, for you drew me clear
    and did not let my enemies rejoice over me.
O LORD, you brought me up from the netherworld;
    you preserved me from among those
       going down into the pit.

Sing praise to the LORD, you his faithful ones,
    and give thanks to his holy name.
For his anger lasts but a moment;
    a lifetime, his good will.
At nightfall, weeping enters in,
    but with the dawn, rejoicing.

Hear, O LORD, and have pity on me;
    O LORD, be my helper.
You changed my mourning into dancing;
    O LORD, my God, forever will I give you thanks.

The Psalmist says of God that "his anger lasts but a moment; a lifetime, his good will." What does that mean? Does God sometimes get angry, and then change his mind?

No. God does not change his mind, or his love. God *is* love; he does not simply fall into and out of love. He does not have wrath or hate one day and love the next day. So what, then, is the wrath of God? It's in the Bible, after all.

The medieval mystic Julian of Norwich was disturbed by that phrase, "the wrath of God," because she knew God was love. So she asked God to please show her his wrath. And she wrote, "And God showed me his wrath, and it was terrible, but there was no wrath except on man's part." What does that mean?

When you go out into the winter wind without a coat, the wind may seem to be angry with you, and when you go out into the summer sun for hours without sunblock, and you get sunburn, you may say that the sun was angry with you. But that's what psychologists call "projection," projecting your feeling onto something or someone else. God's wrath is a projection of our wrath, our rejection of him. He does not reject us. When we sin, we change our relationship to God, but we do not change God, nor does he change his love toward us. But that love now demands repentance and confession and change on our part. His love is eternal and unchangeable, but our receiving of it changes. We can receive it either with gratitude and obedience or with resentment and rebellion. The light does not change, but our relation to it changes when we close our eyes.

A better analogy than the wind or the sun is loving parents. When we disappoint them, when we disobey them, when we run from their wisdom, we do not change their love toward us, but we do change our relationship to them. We turn *ourselves* into their enemies, and we want to escape them. But we do not turn *them* into our enemies. They do not stop loving us even if we stop loving them. But their love then has to become tough love instead of tender love; it has to discipline and teach and punish when we seriously harm ourselves—because they love us, not because they hate us, which is what shallow, stupid, selfish children sometimes think. And we all start by being that kind of child, and we gradually learn to grow out of that. Even their anger is anger at our foolishness, not at our very being. "How could you do such a stupid thing? I can't let you do that again. There have to be consequences. If you don't learn the easy way, you will have to learn the hard way, because you have to learn somehow." God hates our sins because he loves us, just as a surgeon hates and attacks the patient's cancer because he loves the patient. We, too, must hate the sin and love the sinner. The only alternatives are loving the sin along with the sinner, which is like loving the cancer along with the patient, or hating the sinner along with the sin, which is like hating the patient along with the cancer.

Of course, no human parents are infallible, and they're constantly making mistakes too, sometimes being too strict and demanding and sometimes being too permissive and taking the easy way out. And sometimes they let their emotions get the better of them for a time and really do get angry at us and not just our sins. That's only human. Anger is not always sinful. Sometimes it's necessary. A parent who never gets angry is a worthless wimp. Jesus got so angry at the greedy moneychangers in his Father's house, the temple, that he overturned their cash registers and physically threw them out. Jesus is perfect man as well as perfect God, so his perfect human nature demanded anger sometimes. (Probably those times of anger were much less frequent than in our own lives.) But Jesus also had a divine nature, and the divine nature is eternal and unchanging, and he can no more stop loving and start hating than the sun can stop shining. How those two natures, the human nature and the divine nature, coexist at the same time in the single person of Jesus is a great mystery, but they do. And we can see a little image, a very imperfect image, of that combination of unchanging love and changing anger in our relationship with our good earthly parents: their righteous and rightful anger does not contradict their love; in fact, it manifests their love. Good parents sometimes become angry, and then they become not-angry, but they don't ever become not-loving. Their anger lasts a moment, but their love lasts a lifetime.

SECOND READING

2 Corinthians 8:7, 9, 13–15 _____

Brothers and sisters: As you excel in every respect, in faith, discourse, knowledge, all earnestness, and in the love we have for you, may you excel in this gracious act also.

For you know the gracious act of our Lord Jesus Christ, that though he was rich, for your sake he became poor, so that by his poverty you might become rich. Not that others should have relief while you are burdened, but that as a matter of equality your abundance at the present time should supply their needs, so that their abundance may also supply your needs, that there may be equality. As it is written:

Whoever had much did not have more,
and whoever had little did not have less.

_____

St. Paul writes in today's epistle that "though [Jesus] was rich, for your sake he became poor, so that by his poverty you might become rich." He's not talking about money here, so what riches is he talking about? What did Jesus have that we didn't have, that he gave us by losing it himself? That's our riddle: What is being described in all four of these sentences? Jesus had it to begin with. We didn't have it to begin with. We got it because Jesus gave it to us. And he did that by losing it himself. The answer is life—his own life. He gave up his own life, his own body and blood, on the cross, so that we could share his divine life, his eternal life.

We don't have that gift to give to others, but we do have many other gifts, including money and the things money can buy, and our time, which is our life's time, so it is in a way our very life that we are to give to others. That's how we follow Jesus: by becoming givers instead of getters.

There are two different kinds of things we can give: material things, like money and time, and spiritual things, like love and beauty and knowledge and happiness. When we give away material things, they are divided, and we lose some of them, but when we give away spiritual things, we multiply them. The more money or food or time you give away, the less you have left, but the more love and knowledge and beauty and happiness you give away, the more it increases.

St. Paul is very practical, so in this passage he is talking about material things like money and the things money can buy. His principle is to aim for equality, but not necessarily mathematical equality. He says to his congregation, in effect, you are now rich and others are poor, so you should be giving to them; when you are poor and they are rich, they should be giving to you. Each of us, equally, should stand in each other's place. There will always be rich and poor. Jesus says, "The poor you will always have with you" (Matt. 26:11). Jesus does not have a plan for enforcing economic equality, so that everybody ends up with the same unchanging income. That just doesn't work. But his principle—a very practical principle of economics—is that riches are to be shared, used, given to those in need. The private good, private riches, should serve the common good.

Money is not evil, but the greed for money is. Money is good, but what it's good for is giving, doing things with it, investing in other people and their happiness, whether individually or through social structures and institutions like graduated income taxes or investments in companies that serve the common good.

Catholics have always been suspicious of both individual greed and government greed, both of individualism and collectivism. The gap between rich and poor will always be there; it can be found in every society in history; but it can be used for two good purposes: to aid the poor materially through the generosity of the rich, and to aid the rich morally by giving them opportunities for the virtue of generosity and charity to the poor.

The spiritual gift is greater than the physical gift, because the spiritual is greater than the physical. Spiritual joys are greater than physical pleasures, and spiritual pains such as despair are greater than physical pains. So the relationship between the rich and the poor is the reverse of what it seems to be: the poor give the rich a spiritual gift, or at least a spiritual opportunity, that is greater than the physical gift of money that the rich give to the poor.

Similarly, people with disabilities give to people without disabilities a greater gift, a greater opportunity for deeper joy, than the physical gifts and services that caretakers can give to those with disabilities. Every family who raises a child with Down syndrome always says that—that this so-called handicapped child, this so-called intellectually poor child, gives to them something even more precious than they can return: a joy, a happiness, a gratitude, a door out of their natural selfishness, the selfishness that always leads away from joy.

And, of course, the disabled also teach the rest of us the lesson that we find so hard to learn: that we all have disabilities, only in different ways.

We hold each other up, like the three legs of a stool. That's why God made more than just one person, and also why he made two sexes, not just one: so that each could help and be helped by the other, and so that each could look up to and learn from the other. We are equal in value, but different in nature. We are all put on earth for each other. We all have something to teach and something to learn from each other, something to give and something to receive. And that's not obvious; that's not a cliché—in fact, that's shocking because it even applies to Republicans and Democrats, conservatives and liberals. Alas, most people nowadays seem to have forgotten that.

GOSPEL
MARK 5:21–43
(OR MARK 5:21–24, 35B–43)

When Jesus had crossed again in the boat to the other side, a large crowd gathered around him, and he stayed close to the sea. One of the synagogue officials, named Jairus, came forward. Seeing him he fell at his feet and pleaded earnestly with him, saying, "My daughter is at the point of death. Please, come lay your hands on her that she may get well and live." He went off with him, and a large crowd followed him and pressed upon him.

There was a woman afflicted with hemorrhages for twelve years. She had suffered greatly at the hands of many doctors and had spent all that she had. Yet she was not helped but only grew worse. She had heard about Jesus and came up behind him in the crowd and touched his cloak. She said, "If I but touch his clothes, I shall be cured." Immediately her flow of blood dried up. She felt in her body that she was healed of her affliction. Jesus, aware at once that power had gone out from him, turned around in the crowd and asked, "Who has touched my clothes?" But his disciples said to Jesus, "You see how the crowd is pressing upon you, and yet you ask, 'Who touched me?'" And he looked around to see who had done it. The woman, realizing what had happened to her, approached in fear and trembling. She fell down before Jesus and told him the whole truth. He said to her, "Daughter, your faith has saved you. Go in peace and be cured of your affliction."

While he was still speaking, people from the synagogue official's house arrived and said, "Your daughter has died; why trouble the teacher any longer?" Disregarding the message that was reported, Jesus said to the synagogue official, "Do not be afraid; just have faith." He did not allow anyone to accompany him inside except Peter, James, and John, the brother of James. When they arrived at the house of the synagogue official, he caught sight of a commotion, people weeping and wailing loudly. So he went in and said to them, "Why this commotion and weeping? The child is not dead but asleep." And they ridiculed him. Then he put them all out. He took along the child's father and mother and those who were with him and entered the room where the child was. He took the child by the hand and said to her, "*Talitha koum*," which means, "Little girl, I say to you, arise!" The girl, a child of twelve, arose immediately and walked around. At that they were utterly astounded. He gave strict orders that no one should know this and said that she should be given something to eat.

Today's Gospel combines and intertwines two stories of Jesus performing miracles, one story being part of the other by interrupting it, thus teaching that even the things we all hate—namely, interruptions—are part of God's wise providential plan for our lives, even when they are interruptions of good and great deeds like miracles. The interruption of the woman with the hemorrhage delayed Jesus' trip to heal the little girl, Jairus' daughter, so that what was originally a miracle of healing the sick became a miracle of raising the dead.

Interruptions of our plans are part of God's providential plan, but there are no such things as interruptions of God's providential plan, just as there are no such things as accidents or chance. We should teach ourselves to say the essential prayer "Thy will be done" to those many little interruptions we so naturally resent, and even to the big ones. (The biggest interruption of all, of course, is death.)

God does not ask us to succeed in finishing and accomplishing our enterprises, only to do our duty at each present moment. Our plans and his coincide only sometimes—in fact, rarely. As one comedian said, if you want to give God a good laugh, tell him your plans.

St. Luke, the Greek convert who wrote one of the Gospels, was a doctor, and he is especially interested in Jesus' medical healings and especially sensitive to people's physical diseases, as Jesus was. St. Matthew, who was a Jew and wrote mainly to Jews, is especially interested in issues about Jesus' interpretation of Jewish laws and about Jesus' fulfillment of many Old Testament Jewish prophecies. He was also a tax collector and was especially sensitive to issues of worldly wealth and its shallowness. He is the one who gives us the whole of Jesus' Sermon on the Mount, the greatest sermon ever preached, which centers on those two subjects. St. John, who wrote later, when the Good News had already spread around the civilized Roman world, emphasized the universal and eternal dimensions of Jesus' words and deeds, and he takes a deeper, more philosophical look at Jesus. St. Mark wrote for a more practical Roman audience and emphasizes Jesus' deeds. He's constantly using the word "straightaway" or "suddenly" or "immediately." His is the shortest and simplest Gospel, for hurried, busy people.

Notice how Jesus not only heals the woman's twelve-year-long hemorrhage, but he also draws her out of the crowd and draws out of her a public confession of faith. Jesus' miracles always heal souls as well as bodies. She had such faith that she thought, "If I but touch his clothes, I shall be cured." That faith was rewarded. But notice also that faith alone is not enough. If she had touched the hem of the garment of anyone other than Jesus—St. Peter, for instance—she would not have been healed. It was not a psychosomatic, merely psychological healing. *Jesus* healed her; she did not heal herself by faith. When Jesus said, "Your faith has saved you," he implied that her faith *in him* had saved her. Imagine yourself as being in a sinking ship, and Jesus as the lifeboat. If you don't have faith in the lifeboat, you won't be saved because you won't get in it. In that sense, it is your faith that saves you. But faith in the lifeboat is not enough; the lifeboat itself is needed, and your faith has to move you to the deed of getting in the lifeboat.

When Jesus gets to Jairus' house, Jairus' daughter has already died, and everyone has given up hope because death is absolutely the end of the story, the end of life—for us. But not for God. Like the stormy sea in last week's Gospel, death obeys the voice of God like a well-trained dog and releases the little girl from the grip of its teeth. When God says "Be" to anything, it begins to be, whether that thing is matter or light or water or stars or planets or plants or animals or new human souls, which he creates for each procreated human body; and when he says "Begone" to anything, whether it is a storm or a disease or death itself, it obeys and is gone. Everything in the universe obeys the command of God, except one thing. You see that one exception every morning when you look into the mirror, and you hear about it when you listen to the news.

When Jesus came to the house where the dead girl lay, and he said that she is not dead but only sleeping, everyone laughed at him. It is never a safe thing to laugh at Jesus—not because he will get angry and take revenge on you, but because you are infallibly wrong. There are only two absolutely certain and infallible standards of truth and falsity in this world. The only infallible standard of truth is none of the words of men but the Word of God, who is Jesus Christ, whose teaching comes to us through the Church he himself established in his Apostles, to whom he gave the authority to teach in his name. And the only infallible standard of falsehood is those who laugh at him and at his Church. God always has the last laugh.

Notice, finally, how thorough and practical Jesus is. Everyone is just standing around astonished that this girl, who was clearly dead, has come back to life, and they look at Jesus with new eyes; but they forget the poor girl, who is hungry. Jesus has to remind them to give her something to eat. That's really funny, especially in the context of such an unfunny issue as death.

Jesus cares not just that we live rather than die, but he cares about every detail of our lives. Divine love knows no distinction between the sacred and the secular.

FOURTEENTH SUNDAY
IN ORDINARY TIME

FIRST READING
Ezekiel 2:2–5 _____

As the Lord spoke to me, the spirit entered into me and set me on my feet, and I heard the one who was speaking say to me: Son of man, I am sending you to the Israelites, rebels who have rebelled against me; they and their ancestors have revolted against me to this very day. Hard of face and obstinate of heart are they to whom I am sending you. But you shall say to them: Thus says the Lord God! And whether they heed or resist—for they are a rebellious house—they shall know that a prophet has been among them.

_____

Why is this tough message from the prophet Ezekiel to ancient Israel relevant to us today?

Because as all the Church Fathers, saints, popes, creeds, and catechisms tell us, Israel is God's first version of the Church. The Church of Christ, the Catholic Church, is the new Israel. So God is saying to us what God is saying through his prophets to Old Testament Israel about who he is and who we are—the two most important things for us to know, because those are the only two realities we can never, ever escape for one second, either in time or in eternity.

The bottom-line answer to the second of these two questions—who we are—is that we, the new Israel, God's chosen people throughout the world, are sinners, rebels, just like all our ancestors. We are "hard of face and obstinate of heart" because our faces reveal our hearts. We are fools, because in disobeying the wise and loving will of our heavenly Father who wants only our own good, we are rebelling not only against God but also against our own good, our own happiness, our own best interests.

And we know this by experience as well as by faith; we know that in the long run, sin always makes us unhappy and sanctity makes us happy; that selfishness makes us unhappy and unselfish love makes us happy; that trying to make God out to be what we want him to be makes us both stupid and unhappy, and that being what God wants us to be and doing what God wants us to do makes us both wise and happy—deeply happy, long-range happy, truly happy. And yet we sin. We are fools. We are idiots. We are insane.

That's the bottom line about who we are. What's the bottom line about who *God* is? It's that God is love. Our heavenly Father dearly loves his severely brain-damaged children. We are crazy sinners, but God is a crazy lover. God is crazy in the opposite way that we are. We are crazy-bad, but he is crazy-good. Our sin goes way beyond reason and justice, but so does God's love. That is our only hope: not justice but love, and not our own weak love but God's strong love that never, never, never gives up. That's why he kept sending prophets like Ezekiel to tell us both the bad news about ourselves and the good news about himself. We need both, simply because both are true.

The bad news is not wholly bad, but the good news is wholly good. We have a good side as well as a bad side, but God has no bad side. There's a little bad in the best of us, and the best of us are the most adamant about that. Saints always say they are sinners. Are they wrong? Does holiness make you stupid? Or is it sin that makes you stupid, so stupid that you no longer think about sin?

When love meets sin, it becomes mercy and forgiveness and reconciliation: not God reconciling himself to us, to our sin, but us reconciling ourselves to God, by repentance and confession. Our sin is probably at least ten times as big and as bad as we think it is, but God's mercy is at least ten trillion times as big and as good as we can imagine. But mercy and forgiveness is a gift, and a gift has to be not only freely given—which God's grace always is—but also freely accepted. That's why there is one unforgivable sin: not repenting, not confessing, not asking for forgiveness.

Many people don't think the bad news is necessary for anybody. Many people think it's not necessary for themselves, but only for others, whoever they are. Some people think that the only sin is to believe that there is such a thing as sin. They call the saints "judgmental." (They think that judging saints isn't being "judgmental" but judging sins is. So instead of hating sins and loving sinners, they love sins and hate the saintly sinners who hate sins.)

If we didn't believe the bad news, we couldn't appreciate the good news. God offers us a new heart; God offers us heart transplant surgery, but that's good news only to those who know they have heart disease. If you don't believe God's x-ray, God's diagnosis, you won't ask God for his free operation. God is the great heart surgeon, and the prophets are his x-ray technicians.

Many people today, even many who call themselves Catholics, don't believe the bad news anymore, even though all God's prophets preach it, because almost all of our modern prophets preach the opposite: that "I'm okay, you're okay"; that all we need is more self-esteem. No one has more self-esteem than the devil. I wonder how Hitler would have responded to a psychologist who told him that he needed more self-esteem. I think he would be quite happy to agree.

There is good and there is bad. There is death and there is resurrection; there is sin and there is salvation; there is disease and there is healing; there is sorrow and there is joy; there is the bad news and there is the good news. And the good news is the final news, the last news, the bottom line. But the only way to get to the good news is to start with the bad news.

RESPONSORIAL PSALM
PSALM 123:1–2, 2, 3–4 _____

R. (2cd) **Our eyes are fixed on the Lord, pleading for his mercy.**

To you I lift up my eyes
    who are enthroned in heaven —

As the eyes of servants
   are on the hands of their masters.

As the eyes of a maid
   are on the hands of her mistress,
So are our eyes on the Lord, our God,
   till he have pity on us.

Have pity on us, O Lord, have pity on us,
   for we are more than sated with contempt;
our souls are more than sated
   with the mockery of the arrogant,
   with the contempt of the proud.

(I recommend reading the epistle first, then the Psalm verse, because the Psalm verse is the epistle's last point.)

All of our readings today have to do with the mockery that the world gives to Christ and to Christians. Jesus, in today's Gospel, was mocked by his own extended family, neighbors, friends, city, and nation. In last week's Gospel, he was mocked by those who heard him say that the little girl he was about to raise from the dead was not dead but sleeping. St. Paul was mocked by his enemies. That is one of the "weaknesses" that he lists as one of his strengths in the second reading. The Psalmist prays to God to have pity on him because unbelievers mock him. That's our situation today too, in today's post-Christian culture in which, throughout Europe and America, six to ten people lose their faith in Christ and his Church for every one person who converts to it. It is a culture in which exactly half of all who are raised Catholic no longer believe, and in which, even among those who still identify as Catholics, *only seven percent* of those who as children were raised in the faith and went to church continue to practice their faith and go to Mass by the time they are adults. Our world and our media mock us as naïve losers or misunderstand us as judgmental legalists and our God as a cosmic killjoy.

The Catholic Church in America seems to be dying very rapidly. But God can raise her from the dead, because the Catholic faith itself does not die, and truth cannot die, and the risen Christ himself cannot die.

We need to humbly pray to God, like the Psalmist, to use this weakness to make us strong, and to trust God as his faithful and obedient servants, who like Mary say simply: "I am the handmaid of the Lord. May it be done to me according to your word" (Luke 1:38). Look what that did for her. Look at the strength that "weakness" gave her. She was the strongest and best human being who ever lived, and she became the Mother of God. In contrast, what happened to all the Amazon warriors and all the proud Egyptian queens like Nefertiti and Cleopatra? What became of all the great tyrants like Alexander the Great and Caesar Augustus and Nero and Hitler and Stalin? Are they strong and happy, or are they weak and miserable? Are they in the place where there is eternal strength and joy or the place where there is eternal loss and hopelessness? Who are the real winners, and who are the real losers?

SECOND READING

2 CORINTHIANS 12:7–10 _____

Brothers and sisters: That I, Paul, might not become too elated, because of the abundance of the revelations, a thorn in the flesh was given to me, an angel of Satan, to beat me, to keep me from being too elated. Three times I begged the Lord about this, that it might leave me, but he said to me, "My grace is sufficient for you, for power is made perfect in weakness." I will rather boast most gladly of my weaknesses, in order that the power of Christ may dwell with me. Therefore, I am content with weaknesses, insults, hardships, persecutions, and constraints, for the sake of Christ; for when I am weak, then I am strong.

What does St. Paul mean by the paradox in today's epistle, "When I am weak, then I am strong"?

He lists ways in which he was weak. He mentions what he calls "a thorn in the flesh." No one knows what this was, although some think it was epilepsy. It may have been his size (he was probably short, skinny, and ugly) or his voice (it may have been squeaky). He also mentions "hardships," such as shipwrecks, and "insults," and "persecutions." Once, he was stoned and left for dead. And he mentions "constraints," which came from his imprisonment. And there were also his moral weaknesses and temptations, which we all have. That's a pretty full bag of weakness. And God accomplished so much through such weaknesses that in the whole history of the world there has never been a more successful Christian missionary than St. Paul.

Paul mentions one reason God did not take away his weaknesses: to keep him from pride, which is more dangerous than any of these other things. He says God gave him his "thorn in the flesh" so that he "might not become too elated, because of the abundance of the revelations" that God gave him. The Greek word translated "elated" here means simply "proud" or "puffed up." It does not mean the feeling of great joy—there's nothing wrong with that. God gives us great joys and even a lot of innocent fun, although he never gives us settled security, or perfect contentment with this world. If we have that, we should not consider that a gift of God but a temptation from the devil.

God gave Paul weaknesses to stop him from being puffed up, to stop his tire from being overinflated. Pride looks like a strength but really is a deadly weakness. Honest humility looks like a weakness, but it really is a great strength. That's one meaning of Paul's saying "When I am weak, then I am strong." God needed a very strong missionary to convert the world, so he used a very weak man, so that the world would be converted not to St. Paul but to God.

The very weakness and suffering that St. Paul experienced made him stronger and gave him a greater joy in the end.

Archbishop Fulton Sheen used to say that there are two philosophies of life. The world says: first the feast, then the fast; first play, then work. Christianity says: first the fast, then the feast; first work, then play. If we do our hard work first and then play, both our work and our play will be better. If we play first and then work, our play will be less fun because it will be haunted by a guilty conscience and by the knowledge that we have hard work to look forward to, and our work will also be less good work because it will be hurried and worried.

Other reasons why God gave St. Paul—and every single one of us too—"weaknesses" include the privilege of a closer union with Christ, not just suffering but actually sharing in his sufferings. Christians embrace the cross only because Christ is on it. We're not masochists; we're lovers. We don't love sufferings; we endure them, because Christ is in them. St. Paul tells us to be imitators of Christ once; he tells us we are "in" Christ dozens of times. We are not just imitators of Christ; we are "in" Christ, in Christ's Mystical Body; that's why our sufferings are "in" Christ's sufferings, are parts of Christ's sufferings, are participations in Christ's sufferings, because Christ is really in his Mystical Body, his people, as our head is in our bodies. The Church is not a corporation with Christ as its CEO; it's a corpus, a Body, and Christ is its Head.

A third reason why God gives sufferings and weaknesses to his friends is shown by today's Psalm: to elicit trust in him. The Psalmist prays the humbly trusting prayer of a servant: "As the eyes of servants are on the hands of their masters. As the eyes of a maid are on the hands of her mistress, so are our eyes on the LORD, our God." That is his response to his sufferings and weaknesses and persecutions from "the mockery of the arrogant [and] the contempt of the proud."

You say that nobody is persecuting and mocking and scorning your faith today? Then you probably don't have much. Somebody once said, "If you were brought to court on the charge of being a Christian, would there be enough evidence to convict you?"

GOSPEL
MARK 6:1–6 _____

Jesus departed from there and came to his native place, accompanied by his disciples. When the sabbath came he began to teach in the synagogue, and many who heard him were astonished. They said, "Where did this man get all this? What kind of wisdom has been given him? What mighty deeds are wrought by his hands! Is he not the carpenter, the son of Mary, and the brother of James and Joses and Judas and Simon? And are not his sisters here with us?" And they took offense at him. Jesus said to them, "A prophet is not without honor except in his native place and among his own kin and in his own house." So he was not able to perform any mighty deed there, apart from curing a few sick people by laying his hands on them. He was amazed at their lack of faith.

_____

Everywhere Jesus went, he found believers, except in one town only: Nazareth, his hometown, where he grew up. Strangers flocked to him, but many of his own extended family did not believe in him. Prostitutes, murderers, and even tax collectors came to him, but the religious authorities who were authorized by God himself in the Old Testament, the leaders of God's own chosen people, rejected him, and they persuaded their oppressive enemies the Romans to torture and crucify him. Most of the priests and scholars and experts in the Law rejected him. Pagans believed in him more readily than Jews.

After performing miracles everywhere else, when Jesus came to his hometown, Mark notes that "he was not able to perform any mighty deed there." Why was he unable? Isn't Jesus divine? Can't he perform miracles? Yes, but the whole point of his miracles was not just to heal bodies but to heal souls, to elicit faith and trust and love. But faith and trust and love are free; they cannot be forced. Jesus will not force us to choose him. In fact, he *cannot* do that, because that is simply a meaningless contradiction in terms. A human act is either free and not forced, or it is forced and not free. It can't be both unforced and forced, both free and unfree.

The Greek word that means "amazement" or "astonishment" is used to describe the reaction of almost everyone who met Jesus, but it is used only once to describe the reaction of Jesus himself: in today's Gospel, he is amazed at his people's lack of faith.

It's supremely ironic. As Jesus said, "A prophet is not without honor except in his native place and among his own kin and in his own house."

The same principle is true today. The most anti-Catholic, pro-death, anti-life, pro-abortion, anti-religious freedom, anti-family politicians in Washington are almost all Catholics. Pope St. John Paul II's biographer, George Weigel, wrote that if the pope wanted to get the pro-life, pro-family social morality agenda of the Catholic Church through Congress in Washington, DC, he should get rid of every Catholic politician and replace them with either a Mormon or a Muslim.

Catholics who go to Catholic colleges leave the Church at a rate that is more than double the rate of Catholics who do not go to Catholic colleges. Archbishop Fulton Sheen said, shortly before he died, that if he had to give Catholic parents advice about their kids, he would tell them that if they wanted the surest and most effective way to get them to lose their faith, send them to a typical Catholic college.

The man who was most responsible for the greatest sin ever committed, the deliberate murder of God incarnate, the only named individual in the Bible we can be almost certain went to hell, was one of Jesus' twelve closest associates, one of the twelve Apostles, Judas Iscariot. He was the first Catholic bishop to accept a government grant.

What's going on here? Part of it is the devil's strategy. The devil is very clever. He knows that the most efficient way to win a war, whether a material war or a spiritual war, is to infiltrate, to get as close as possible to your enemy, to divide and conquer. A few spies inside the castle can do more to undermine it than a thousand warriors outside it.

Those who persecuted the Church and threw the Christians to the lions only made the Church stronger. As Tertullian wrote, "The blood of the martyrs is the seed of the Church." But when the Church becomes easy and fashionable and successful and taken for granted, she becomes lazy and bored and worldly, and her people drift away.

Part of the reason Jesus' close friends and family rejected him is the curse of familiarity. Jesus was much too familiar, much too ordinary, much too human to those who knew him for the first thirty years of his life, before he began his public ministry, for them to believe he was literally divine. It was much easier for those who didn't know him. If a total stranger claimed to be a visitor from another planet, some people would believe him, but if one of twelve family members who had lived together for thirty years claimed that, none of his family would believe him.

So how can we avoid this trap, we who have known Jesus for a while, especially we who have grown up in Catholic families, we "cradle Catholics"? Only by not relying on that familiarity. Every single Christian has to meet Jesus anew, personally, as if they had never heard of him before. They have to stand before him and be amazed at him, so that he will not have to stand before them and be amazed at their lack of faith.

The gift of faith cannot be passed on by parents to children, like genetics, like eye color. God has many children, but God has no grandchildren. The only road to faith is to stand in that terrifying, lonely, silent place of your own unique, individual, personal freedom, of your own free will, and to decide for yourself that Jesus is your Lord and your Savior. Others in the Church, especially your family and the Catholics of the past, can only give you good reasons for doing that, especially the most unanswerable reason, that of being good examples, the example of being saints, of loving and living the faith with their whole heart and soul and mind and strength; but no one else can do it for you; no one else can make *your* choice to believe. Not even God himself can do that, because God is not you.

And after you do that, please tell your children that they, too, will have to do the same thing for themselves as well as telling the same thing to their children. That's how the faith is passed on. The theological term for that is "evangelization."

Pope St. John Paul II was a big promoter of what he called "the new evangelization." He called it the new evangelization because the radically new thing is the audience. It used to be non-Catholics; now it has to be first of all Catholics. Two generations ago we sent missionaries to Africa; now they are sending missionaries to us. Why? Because they have something to give: the living, acting, life-changing Christ. That's why their seminaries and churches are overflowing and multiplying as fast as ours are dying. We have to evangelize ourselves. The Church has to evangelize herself before she can evangelize the world.

That's an enormous task. Where do you begin? Every journey, however long it is, has to begin with a first step. Where and when is that? It all starts right here, and right now. How? Pray the perfect prayer. Say to God what Mary said: "May it be done to me according to your word" (Luke 1:38). And if you mean that with all your heart, you'd better duck because he is going to take you seriously. Look what happened when he took her seriously.

When you pray that prayer, don't worry that you're not a saint or even a good pray-er. And don't ask "how?" Don't worry about methods of prayer, because as Catholics we have something much more powerful than any method or means or technique that we could ever use; we have the actual prayers—not just the words but the actual, present acts of prayer, the praying—of the greatest saint who ever lived, the Mother of God, to pray *for* us, to pray in our place, to make up for our own personal weaknesses in prayer. Methods just teach us how to do it; she actually does it for us.

Let's all ask her right now to do that for us, to pray for us, to lead us in re-committing our whole selves and our whole lives to her divine Son and our Lord, with no reservations and no exceptions and no escape clauses, a spiritual marriage without a pre-nuptial agreement, a check made out to God and signed with your own name with a blank on the line for God to write in the amount.

If you don't mean it, don't pray it. But if with all your heart and honesty you do mean it, or want to mean it, please pray it now with me: "Hail, Mary, full of grace. The Lord is with thee. Blessed art thou among women and blessed is the fruit of thy womb, Jesus. Holy Mary, Mother of God, pray for us sinners now and at the hour of our death. Amen."

FIFTEENTH SUNDAY
IN ORDINARY TIME

FIRST READING

Amos 7:12–15 _____

Amaziah, priest of Bethel, said to Amos, "Off with you, visionary, flee to the land of Judah! There earn your bread by prophesying, but never again prophesy in Bethel; for it is the king's sanctuary and a royal temple." Amos answered Amaziah, "I was no prophet, nor have I belonged to a company of prophets; I was a shepherd and a dresser of sycamores. The LORD took me from following the flock, and said to me, Go, prophesy to my people Israel."

_____

In Old Testament Israel, God established prophets as well as priests. There were false prophets as well as true prophets, and there were wicked priests as well as good priests, then as now. A true prophet was called by God to speak God's own words. His formula was "Thus says the LORD." False prophets spoke that formula too, but they lied. And then as now, false prophets were typically popular, while true prophets were rejected and often martyred; there was little profit in being a prophet.

The prophets did what no one else dared to do: they spoke truth to power. That is what Amos is doing in today's reading, and that is what Pope St. John Paul II did under both Nazi and communist tyranny as a seminarian and what he did to the evil empire of communism when he became pope, and that helped win the Cold War without shedding a drop of blood. He also did the same to the subtler tyranny of modern Western secularism, materialism, and consumerism, which have proved far more resistant to Christ's vaccines than communism has.

The prophets claimed a higher authority than kings, and therefore kings (and their lackeys among the priests) feared the prophets because they alone appealed to a higher authority.

The two authorities—kings and prophets, politics and religion—do not always have to be in conflict. Christ does not set himself up against Caesar; in fact, he commands us to give to Caesar what belongs to Caesar, including the dirty coins of our tax money with Caesar's ugly head on them. But he also commands us to give to God, not to Caesar, what belongs to God. One of the things that belong to God, not Caesar, is the bodies of God's unborn children.

Today we live in a nation with the fundamental right to religious freedom. The state is forbidden to establish or dis-establish any religion. This is the clear and simple legal meaning of what later came to be called the "separation of church and state." But that is not what many say it means today. They say it means silencing the Church's voice in the public and political sphere. This is a "big lie" because what it means, in fact, is exactly the opposite: not silencing, not censoring, not judging religious correctness by political correctness.

Politics and public law have to appeal to power, and in a democracy that means the power of the majority of the voters. Man's laws must be enforced by force. God's laws are enforced by conscience. Religion does not appeal to power but to truth and moral goodness. We worship God not because he is power but because he is truth and love. That is the ultimate reason why religion cannot bend to politics: because truth and love cannot bend to power; because might does not make right; because there is a God-made "natural moral law" above all the man-made laws, and man does not judge God; God judges man.

Christianity has some basic principles about politics, but it does not have a detailed political program, as Old Testament Israel had and as Islam has. Islam has no "separation of church and state" because Muslims believe God himself authorized detailed political public laws and structures. Christians do not.

Christians have moral principles by which to judge states, but they are not principles that come from politics; they come *to* politics. Many Christians today make politics their religion. Their God is Caesar, whichever side of the aisle he sits on; and these politicized Christians have no higher authority, no prophetic authority, to criticize their Caesar, except their own personal private preferences. If they worship either of these two Caesars, either their political party or their personal preferences, they dare not criticize either of these two Caesars by asking the question: What does my Lord say about this?

And Catholic Christians know what their Lord says about this by listening to what their Lord's authorized Church teaches in his name—about everything: immigration, the poor, abortion, marriage, the environment, business, law, education, the arts, the media, everything. If Christ is the Lord, he must be the Lord of everything. If he is not the Lord of everything, he is not the Lord of anything.

This cosmic Christocentrism, this universal Lordship of Christ, is omnipresent in the writings of St. Paul—so much so that we do not even notice it anymore, like the air we breathe. Look at today's epistle and count how many times Paul brings everything back to Christ, or, as he says in his conclusion, sums up all things in Christ, all things on earth as well as all things in heaven.

RESPONSORIAL PSALM
PSALM 85:9–10, 11–12, 13–14 _____

R. (8) **Lord, let us see your kindness, and grant us your salvation.**

I will hear what God proclaims;
> the LORD—for he proclaims peace.
Near indeed is his salvation to those who fear him,
> glory dwelling in our land.

Kindness and truth shall meet;
> justice and peace shall kiss.
Truth shall spring out of the earth,
> and justice shall look down from heaven.

The LORD himself will give his benefits;
  our land shall yield its increase.
Justice shall walk before him,
  and prepare the way of his steps.

We find three words in the first verse of Psalm 85 that are so familiar that when we hear them we are threatened with boredom and sleep, even though each one of them is like the sound of a trumpet and the refreshment of ice water on a hot summer day. The words are "peace," "salvation," and "glory."

We appreciate things only by contrast with their opposites, so we can appreciate these three things God gives us by thinking of their opposites.

The opposite of peace is war. What is war? Not according to those who design it but according to those who fight in or die in or are bereaved by it: "war is hell"—hell on earth. War is slaughter, horror, hate, and fear. War is giving and receiving death as we ought to be giving and receiving life. And the greatest war is spiritual war, as the greatest peace is spiritual peace.

The opposite of salvation is damnation. Damnation is worse than war because war is only hell on earth, but damnation is hell in hell. Whatever hell is, and however many people are in it—neither of which anybody knows—it is total, hopeless, eternal misery because it is the loss of God, the source of absolutely everything good. The one thing we do know about hell is that it is real, because our only absolutely infallible authority, Jesus Christ, God incarnate, says it is.

The opposite of glory is grayness, the favorite color of our cars and of our lives: dullness, depression, compromise, vagueness, emptiness, fogginess, and boredom. Sound familiar? Are our lives full of glory? There is one class of people who answer yes, whose lives are full of glory. They are called the saints. They are the bright stained-glass windows; we are the dull, neutral paint on the walls.

The rest of today's Psalm is one of the most practical passages in the whole

Bible because it solves one of the most pressing moral problems of our time: how to solve the problem of the division of good people, and the good things they love, into two warring camps.

Nearly everybody today classifies themselves as traditional or progressive, conservative or liberal, Republican or Democrat. Conservatives love and prize the old-fashioned, tough virtues of honesty, courage, chastity, self-control, and hard work. Liberals love and prize the virtues of freedom, forgiveness, compassion, sensitivity, mercy, and tenderness. The hard virtues versus the soft virtues. Conservatives emphasize faith and truth as the foundation of all other virtues. Liberals emphasize love as the fruit or flower of all other virtues. Conservatives emphasize law and order; liberals emphasize freedom and progress. Just to take one example: on immigration, conservatives insist on respect for the law, and liberals insist on respect for hospitality to those in need.

Both sides are absolutely right, but they do not listen to each other, so they fight. That's like a fight among body parts, a war between the bones and the skin. But the bones without the skin is a scary, skinny skeleton, and the skin without the bones is a big wet lasagna noodle.

This Psalm talks about the reconciliation of these two opposite tendencies, the tendency to prioritize the hard virtues versus the tendency to prioritize the soft virtues. "Kindness" and "peace" are two words in today's Psalm for the soft virtues, and "truth" and "justice" are two words for the hard virtues; and here is what the Psalm says about them: "Kindness and truth shall meet; justice and peace shall kiss."

Notice that the verb is in the future tense: this "shall" happen, but in the future. It's a prophecy, a prediction. How and when will the prophecy come true? All the prophecies in the Old Testament come true in the same way and at the same time and in the same person. His name is Jesus, and his title is "Christ," which means "Messiah" or "promised one" or "the fulfiller of the promises."

So the next verse of the Psalm tells us about Christ, who is the answer to the question of *how* God will reconcile these two warring sides of our politics and our history and our human nature and our human virtues: by having the hard, eternal good, the divine good, the traditional good, the conservative good, so to speak, incarnate itself in the soft, "liberal" flesh of time and history and this world. Truth and justice, which are the hard, eternal, nonnegotiable virtues, will not oppose the soft and compassionate virtues of mercy and peace anymore because they will come down to the horizontal level, the earthly level, the human level; they will be incarnated. "Truth shall spring out of the earth, and justice shall look down from heaven." Without ceasing to be heavenly, they will become earthly. God will incarnate his eternal, hard, tough, nonnegotiable truth and justice in the soft human flesh and blood of Christ, the human heart of Christ, who will incarnate love not by compromising truth and justice but by revealing it, showing it, doing it. Divine, eternal, unchangeable justice will not be just an abstract, timeless ideal but will walk the dusty roads of the Holy Land: "Justice shall walk before him, and prepare the way of his steps." Justice shall *walk*. Eternity will enter time. The divine Logos, the divine truth, the eternal Mind of God, will become human flesh. His cross reconciles truth and love, justice and mercy "horizontally," so to speak, by reconciling heaven and earth, divinity and humanity "vertically." The vertical and horizontal bars of the cross meet in him.

Thus, the three great goods that the first verse of this Psalm prophesied—peace, salvation, and glory—are all fulfilled in Christ. For the four arms of his cross reach out to both left and right, and to both heaven and earth. They reconcile the soft virtues like mercy and the hard virtues like justice, and they also reconcile eternity and time, divinity and humanity. At the center of the cross is the one who reconciles all things: Christ. As St. Paul says in today's epistle, God sums up all things in Christ.

SECOND READING
Ephesians 1:3–14
(or Ephesians 1:3–10) _____

Blessed be the God and Father of our Lord Jesus Christ, who has blessed us in

Christ with every spiritual blessing in the heavens, as he chose us in him, before the foundation of the world, to be holy and without blemish before him. In love he destined us for adoption to himself through Jesus Christ, in accord with the favor of his will, for the praise of the glory of his grace that he granted us in the beloved.

In him we have redemption by his blood, the forgiveness of transgressions, in accord with the riches of his grace that he lavished upon us. In all wisdom and insight, he has made known to us the mystery of his will in accord with his favor that he set forth in him as a plan for the fullness of times, to sum up all things in Christ, in heaven and on earth.

In him we were also chosen, destined in accord with the purpose of the One who accomplishes all things according to the intention of his will, so that we might exist for the praise of his glory, we who first hoped in Christ. In him you also, who have heard the word of truth, the gospel of your salvation, and have believed in him, were sealed with the promised holy Spirit, which is the first installment of our inheritance toward redemption as God's possession, to the praise of his glory.

Paul begins by addressing God not just as God but as the Father. That's Jesus' favorite name for God. Why is God the Father? Not first of all because he is our heavenly Father—that only became true through our faith and Baptism—but because he is eternally the Father of Christ the Son. Paul therefore addresses God this way: "Blessed be the God and Father of our Lord Jesus Christ."

The very next thing Paul says is that this blessed God has blessed us. But how? Only "in Christ." His first sentence says "Blessed be the God and Father of our Lord Jesus Christ, who has blessed us *in Christ* with every spiritual blessing."

How did we get into this fortunate spiritual position of being blessed by God? Paul's very next words tell us: "As he chose us *in him* [that is, in Christ], before the foundation of the world."

The very next point after this, which was about our first beginning in the mind of God "before the foundation of the world," is our last end and destiny. What did God choose us *for*? "To be holy and without blemish *before him*," that is, Christ.

And how did God do that? How did he put us in this position of being his own adopted children? Paul's very next words tell us: "In love he destined us for adoption to himself *through Jesus Christ*."

That was God's grace, not our deservingness. Paul's next words tell us where God's grace is to be found: "His grace that he granted us *in the beloved*," that is, in God's beloved Son, Jesus Christ.

This grace saves us, or redeems us, from sin and death and hell. So the very next thing Paul says is specifically and exactly where this redemption is to be found: "*In him* we have redemption *by his blood*, the forgiveness of transgressions."

The very next point Paul makes is how we know this, how we learned this, how we were told this divine plan: "He has made known to us the mystery of his will in accord with his favor that he set forth *in him* [there's that phrase again, for the seventh time!] as a plan for the fullness of times."

Finally, Paul sums up everything God has done for us in these words: "To sum up all things *in Christ*, in heaven and on earth." All things! No exceptions. All things on earth as well as all things in heaven; all things secular as well as all things sacred. Christ is the beginning and the end, the Alpha and Omega, of all things.

He is all things objectively and subjectively. Objectively, because if Christ is not the Lord of all things in fact, in objective truth, then he is a fake and a liar and is really the Lord of nothing. Subjectively, for us, because (as St. Augustine says) if we have him, we have everything, even if we have nothing else; and if we have everything else but not him, we have nothing; and if we have him plus everything else, we do not have a single thing more than if we have him alone. Because in him God has given us all things.

GOSPEL
MARK 6:7–13 _____

Jesus summoned the Twelve and began to send them out two by two and gave them authority over unclean spirits. He instructed them to take nothing for the journey but a walking stick—no food, no sack, no money in their belts. They were, however, to wear sandals but not a second tunic. He said to them, "Wherever you enter a house, stay there until you leave. Whatever place does not welcome you or listen to you, leave there and shake the dust off your feet in testimony against them." So they went off and preached repentance. The Twelve drove out many demons, and they anointed with oil many who were sick and cured them.

_____

How to re-convert the world? How to do what the Church did two thousand years ago? How to reverse the apostasy that has been accelerating since the sixties throughout the culture that used to be called Christendom?

Different individuals, experts, organizations, and denominations have many different answers. They are confusing and complicated and contradictory. Why don't we do something really radical and really simple instead? Why don't we listen to Jesus' answer to that question? Why don't we turn back the clock two thousand years? Turning the clock back is the most progressive thing we can do when the clock starts keeping bad time.

Seven things stand out in Jesus' instructions to his disciples on their mission.

The first is leaving home, leaving their comfort zones. Jesus sends them out, not in. That's his instruction for us, too, because it doesn't apply only to a very small group of professional missionaries, full-time missionaries who go to foreign countries or knock on doors.

We are many other things full time. We are mothers and fathers and teachers and soldiers and nurses and doctors and lawyers and salespersons and hamburger-flippers and firefighters and factory workers and computer programmers and farmers and pilots—and none of these jobs is for every Christian; but there is one job that *is* for every Christian. Whatever else we do as our full-time job, our most important full-time job is being a Christian. Being a Christian means being a missionary because being a Christian just can't help being an advertisement for what it is to be a Christian. And being a Christian missionary is a full-time job because being a Christian means being a full-time Christian.

The second thing Jesus gives his missionaries is authority: his own authority. Jesus' last words to us on earth, before his Ascension, were these: "All power in heaven and on earth has been given to me. Go, *therefore*, and make disciples of all nations" (Matt. 28:18–19). The only justification for missionary activity is the divine, infallible, absolute authority of Jesus Christ, who is not just a nice guy, or Super Social Worker, or even Superman, but God incarnate.

That authority extends even to the supernatural—to heaven and hell—and therefore even over evil spirits, who are our real enemies. Jesus explicitly mentions them here. Of course, we are not all exorcists; the Church trains those, one at least for every diocese. But we should know that our little skirmishes with evil spirits and their temptations here below are part of a far greater battle, and we should also know that in that battle we are always aided by the help of the angels and hindered by the temptations of the demons. That's not fantasy; that's reality. What we see with our eyes is only the surface of things. Reality is like the ocean. We usually see only the surface of a reality that is miles deep and dark and powerful and full of very strange creatures.

Third, Jesus tells his Apostles to leave behind their three most common security blankets: money, food, and even extra clothing. Henry David Thoreau's most quoted and most popular word, from *Walden*, is "simplify." Voluntary poverty doesn't always need to be as literal and radical as it was for Jesus' Apostles, and as it is for monks and nuns, but it does always need that *spirit* of total poverty. Jesus' first beatitude was "Blessed are the poor *in spirit*" (Matt. 5:3). That's a spirit of detachment from greed and need, a spirit of total trust in God, total reliance on God, that gives us freedom from the fear that comes from idolatry, from addiction to God's creatures, to ordinary human powers and devices, even money and food and clothing. And our technology. We're not forbidden to use it, but we *are* forbidden to rely on it, to trust in it. King David says, "Some rely on chariots, others on horses, but we on the name of the LORD our God" (Ps. 20:8). That doesn't mean we all sell our horses and burn our chariots. But it means we remember whose instruments they are. As Muslims wisely love to repeat, "Only God is God."

The fourth principle of our missionary work that Jesus mentions is to expect a lot of rejection and opposition. We are to expect rejection because we are to appeal always to free choice, not to any kind of force or fear or greed or earthly gain. We are missionaries for God the Father, who makes us an offer we can refuse, not for the Godfather, who makes you an offer you can't refuse.

Evangelizing is not a form of advertising. God invented evangelization; Satan invented advertising, in the Garden of Eden. "See this apple? You need this apple. You can afford it. The price is only one soul." Advertising is the world's oldest profession, from "the father of lies" (John 8:44).

Since Jesus' missionaries are not advertisers, they are not to worry about results, and numbers, and success. As Mother Teresa so liberatingly said, God did not put us here to be successful; he put us here to be faithful.

The fifth principle is to do what all true prophets dared to do: to preach not only the good news but also the "bad news" of sin and the need for repentance. This is done out of love; it is what St. Paul calls speaking "the truth in love" (Eph. 4:15) rather than in judgment and condemnation. Jesus said that he came into the world not to condemn the world but to save it (John 3:17), to save sinners. But that implies the condemnation of sins. It means speaking the truth—the whole truth, including the truth about sin and man's long rebellion against God that is the main line of human history.

And that includes the new form that rebellion is taking today, the rebellion against the sacredness of family and marriage and sexuality. It means telling the truth about divorce and gender and the "sexual revolution" and its cost, including the enormous holocaust of millions of our unborn children, *God's* children, who for the sake of so-called sexual freedom have been slaughtered like cattle; and the truth about the positive promotion and approval of this holocaust by so-called Catholic politicians whose king is clearly Caesar, not Christ.

Sixth, Christian missionaries should expect that miracles will happen. Miracles are not happening much in Western civilization, but they *are* happening in other parts of the world, especially where Christians are poor and persecuted, because the real Gospel is being preached there, and therefore both the angels and the demons are hard at work there: in Africa and in China and in Islamic countries and in Latin America. Where missionaries take it easy and relax, so do demons and angels; where missionaries fight, so do demons and angels.

Seventh, Christ's mission and ministry includes a medical ministry, a ministry of healing, spiritual and emotional and physical, of bodies and psyches and souls, since all human dimensions are holy to the God who made them.

Read today's short Gospel passage again and you will find all seven of these principles. They are not for some; they are for all. They are not for others; they are for you. Live them out. How? In many different ways. How can you find out what way is God's way for you? Pray. Ask your Lord that question, tell him you are his servant, and mean it, and he will answer it in your life. He's not deaf and mute. He has different jobs for different people, but he has jobs for all of us. He is an equal opportunity employer, and he hires all applicants.

All seven of these principles have been practiced by all great prophets, missionaries, and saints, starting with St. Paul, the greatest missionary of all time.

When Jesus gave us our job description—"Go, therefore, and make disciples of all nations" (Matt. 28:19)—he didn't add "if you're clergy" or "if you've been to seminary" or "if you're a theologian or a psychologist or a sociologist or a politician or an organizer or if you've taken some vague, vapid course in so-called leadership." He didn't add anything except eye contact, like the eye contact from the Uncle Sam figure in the famous World War II poster that said "Uncle Sam needs YOU!"

How to win the world? Do you want the guaranteed answer? Here it is: be a saint.

SIXTEENTH SUNDAY
IN ORDINARY TIME

FIRST READING

JEREMIAH 23:1–6 _____

Woe to the shepherds who mislead and scatter the flock of my pasture, says the LORD. Therefore, thus says the LORD, the God of Israel, against the shepherds who shepherd my people: You have scattered my sheep and driven them away. You have not cared for them, but I will take care to punish your evil deeds. I myself will gather the remnant of my flock from all the lands to which I have driven them and bring them back to their meadow; there they shall increase and multiply. I will appoint shepherds for them who will shepherd them so that they need no longer fear and tremble; and none shall be missing, says the LORD.

Behold, the days are coming, says the LORD,
    when I will raise up a righteous shoot to David;
as king he shall reign and govern wisely,
    he shall do what is just and right in the land.
In his days Judah shall be saved,
    Israel shall dwell in security.
This is the name they give him:
    "The LORD our justice."

_____

In today's Old Testament reading from the prophet Jeremiah, God warns Israel that he will punish their unfaithful priests who both mislead and scatter God's people as a wolf scatters a flock of sheep.

There have been bad shepherds as well as good ones throughout the history of the Catholic Church, just as there were throughout the history of Old Testament Israel, which was the first form of God's Church.

Jeremiah mentions two things the bad shepherds do to God's people: they mislead, and they divide. That is, they do not teach the truth, the whole truth, and nothing but the truth; and by doing so, they divide the people. Truth unites; error divides. There is one angle for standing upright but many angles for falling.

The division and disunity and polarization and mutual mistrust that we find between different groups of Catholics today is far greater than any time in living memory. That division imitates and reflects the disunity and polarization and mutual mistrust we find in our secular society. Too many Catholics see themselves as primarily "conservatives" or "progressives" and only secondarily as Catholics. They let politics determine their religion; they look at Christ through the eyes of Caesar instead of vice versa.

"Conservatism" and "liberalism" were both originally good, reasonable, and honorable words. But they can be mutually beneficial instead of mutually exclusive. If you think of yourself as a "conservative," ask yourself this question: Isn't the whole point of conservativism to preserve and conserve the tradition, the foundation, *for the sake of the building*, to preserve and conserve the roots *for the sake of progressing to the fruits*? And if you think of yourself as a "liberal" or a "progressive," ask yourself this question: Isn't that "conservative" respect for foundations and roots absolutely *necessary* for all progress in building and in fruits? Roots without fruits and fruits without roots both die. They need each other. We need each other.

That doesn't in itself solve any of the problems that divide us, but it gives us a compelling reason to listen to and learn from each other on those issues— which we are increasingly not doing.

Issues about social justice divide us, but God tells us the ultimate answer to all questions about justice in this passage from his prophet Jeremiah. The prophecy is about the coming Messiah, who for Jeremiah was in the future but who for us is in the past *and* in the continuing present. Because the Messiah has come, because God's definitive answer has been given in Christ, he himself is our standard of justice. Thus, Jeremiah says, "This is the name they give him: 'The LORD our justice.'" Perfect justice is not just a concept; it is a person.

The Hebrew word translated "justice" here means more than just deserved punishments and rewards. It means "righteousness," moral goodness in general. God is the ultimate standard of all justice, righteousness, and goodness; and Jesus is the final, complete, and definitive revelation of God; so Jesus is the answer to questions about justice, or righteousness, or goodness, whether sexual or political or economic.

Jesus, and his Church, and her Scriptures, have clearly revealed the basic principles of morality. We can disagree about how to apply those principles to different circumstances and situations, especially in areas that are full of uncertainties and changing circumstances like economics and politics; but we cannot and must not disagree about the moral principles themselves, whether those principles command respect for laws or respect for freedoms, whether they command hospitality to immigrants or to unborn babies, whether they command justice and charity about race or about sex, about human rights or about the environment, about capitalism or about capital punishment. The Church's basic moral teachings have been consistent and unified across time and place, because its *source* is not just human but divine. It's not a cafeteria for us to pick and choose from. We are not invited to choose whether we want to ignore or disobey God's clear commandment to love and respect all of our neighbors, who are his beloved children, including our neighbors with same-sex attraction, or whether we want to ignore or disobey God's clear command to respect and obey his clear sexual design in our bodies. We are not invited to choose whether to ignore God's commandment about respecting human life inside the womb or outside the womb. Those are the either-or questions the devil wants us to ask, because the devil is a warrior and knows that the most efficient tactic in battle is to divide the enemy and set him to fighting civil wars against himself.

Since, as Jeremiah says, the Lord *is* our justice, and Jesus is the Lord,

Jesus *is* our justice. So if our understanding of and fidelity to Jesus were only stronger, our understanding of and fidelity to justice would be stronger. And if our understanding and fidelity to the principles of justice were stronger, we would come closer to each other and listen to each other when we argue about our disagreements about how to apply these principles.

It's right that we are different, that we are playing different instruments in God's symphony orchestra; and it's right that we are not all playing the same notes; but we should be playing in harmony. If we all paid attention to the single baton of our single divine conductor, we *would* play in harmony, because we know that that is the point of his baton, that harmony is his will. So if we paid attention to that baton first and our own individual pieces of sheet music second, we would play a symphony rather than a cacophony. If we let Jesus remake us in his image rather than trying to remake him in our image, we will have unity because he *is* our unity, he *is* our righteousness, he *is* our justice.

Another division even more crucial and concrete than the division between conservatives and progressives is addressed in our epistle for today: the division between Jews and Christians. Read the second reading to see what St. Paul says about that, and about the unity that Jesus brought between Jews and Gentiles, the unity that is worldwide or universal or "catholic" (the word "catholic" means "universal").

RESPONSORIAL PSALM
PSALM 23:1–3, 3–4, 5, 6 ⎯⎯⎯⎯⎯⎯⎯⎯⎯⎯⎯⎯⎯⎯⎯⎯⎯⎯⎯⎯⎯⎯⎯

R. (1) **The Lord is my shepherd; there is nothing I shall want.**

The LORD is my shepherd; I shall not want.
   In verdant pastures he gives me repose;
beside restful waters he leads me;
   he refreshes my soul.

He guides me in right paths
    for his name's sake.
Even though I walk in the dark valley
    I fear no evil; for you are at my side
with your rod and your staff
    that give me courage.

You spread the table before me
    in the sight of my foes;
you anoint my head with oil;
    my cup overflows.

Only goodness and kindness follow me
    all the days of my life;
and I shall dwell in the house of the LORD
    for years to come.

The twenty-third Psalm is the single best-known and best-loved Psalm. The Psalms are the best-known and best-loved book in the Bible. The Bible is the best-known and best-loved book in the world. Therefore, the twenty-third Psalm is the best-known and best-loved passage in all the books in the world. It is certainly the best-known and best-loved passage in the English language.

Here it is in the more famous words of the King James Bible, in the language of Shakespeare, Elizabethan English:

> The LORD is my shepherd; I shall not want. He maketh me to lie down in green pastures. He leadeth me beside the still waters. He restoreth my soul. He leadeth me in the paths of righteousness for his name's sake. Yea, though I walk through the valley of the shadow of death, I will fear no evil, for thou art with me; thy rod and thy staff, they comfort me. Thou preparest a table

before me in the presence of mine enemies. Thou anointest my head with oil. My cup runneth over. Surely goodness and mercy shall follow me all the days of my life, and I will dwell in the house of the LORD for ever.

The striking thing about this Psalm is its blend of power and gentleness. The LORD, the all-powerful Lord of the universe, comes down to our level and cares for us as a good shepherd cares for his sheep. That's astonishing! That's like an elephant caring for a hamster. To put the same point in the opposite way, it is astonishing that the one who cares for us, the one who is so intimate and friendly and compassionate and close to us, is the transcendent, superhuman, eternal, infinitely perfect, all-powerful, all-wise, and all-righteous Creator of the universe!

There are thus two things that the religious Jew or Christian can say to his pagan neighbor about the difference between their two religions. He could say to his ancient pagan neighbor: "Your god may be a great and distant Lord, but mine is the loving, caring shepherd. Your god may be awesome, but mine is also intimate." He could also say to his modern pagan neighbor: "Your god may be your sweet and chummy shepherd buddy, but mine is the Lord of the universe. Your god may be intimate, but mine is also awesome."

No pagan can say, "The LORD is my shepherd." Ancient pagans can only say they have many Lords and gods, but none of them is their shepherd. Modern pagans can only say that they are vaguely "spiritual" and that their God is a nice, chummy shepherd, but not that he is the Lord. Only the worshipers of the true God can say both that their Lord is their shepherd and that their shepherd is their Lord.

SECOND READING
EPHESIANS 2:13–18 _____

Brothers and sisters: In Christ Jesus you who once were far off have become near by the blood of Christ.

For he is our peace, he who made both one and broke down the dividing wall of enmity, through his flesh, abolishing the law with its commandments and legal claims, that he might create in himself one new person in place of the two, thus establishing peace, and might reconcile both with God, in one body, through the cross, putting that enmity to death by it. He came and preached peace to you who were far off and peace to those who were near, for through him we both have access in one Spirit to the Father.

In reconciling both Jews and Gentiles with God, Jesus also reconciles them with each other. He does the same thing when he reconciles conservatives with progressives, men with women, parents with children, rich with poor, rulers with citizens, and masters with servants. The two bottom points of a triangle are separated from each other by the baseline, but they come together in a single point at the summit. They cannot achieve unity on the horizontal line, but they can do that if they both reach upward. It's the vertical dimension that allows them to do what simply cannot be done on the horizontal dimension. The horizontal dimension is the human dimension, the dimension of all material things in space and time. The vertical dimension is the divine dimension, the dimension of spiritual things. When we share material things, like money or food or time, we lose what we give away. But when we share spiritual things like knowledge and love and joy, we do not divide them but multiply them. God performs his work of unity not by destroying or diminishing diversity but by perfecting it, as the unity of all colors in white light perfects all colors yet preserves the diversity and differences between them. The unity of all shapes and sizes happens only in the mind, not in matter. It cannot be done in matter without fusing and confusing different shapes and sizes. The unity of the mind perfects the diversity of shapes and sizes rather than confusing them.

God performs that miracle of uniting people without sacrificing differences in many areas of everyday secular life. He wants to perform the same miracle in our religious life. He wants to bring us together with each other, especially Jews and Christians, by bringing both sides of the triangle into unity in him.

One concrete example of that is that Messianic Jews—that is, Jews who accept Jesus as their Messiah—always say they have become more Jewish, not less, than they were before. They are also stronger Christians than most other Christians.

Something similar happens when biblical Protestants, Evangelical Protestants, become Catholics. They always say that they now, as Catholics, love and understand the Bible more, not less, than they did as "sola scriptura" Protestants, and that they are more evangelical, not less, more Gospel-centered and more Christ-centered, not less, as Catholics than they had been as Protestants.

That's because, as Teilhard de Chardin said, "everything that rises must converge." Flannery O'Connor loved to quote that line. The higher up we get, and the closer to God we get, the closer we get to each other. The way to unity is vertical, not horizontal.

The two great commandments are the "vertical" commandment to love God with your whole heart and soul and the "horizontal" commandment to love your neighbor as yourself. Jesus put the first great commandment first because that's the foundation for the second great commandment—because the only way to perfectly love your neighbor as yourself is by loving God with your whole heart and mind and soul and strength. Your neighbor will not always send you to God, but God will always send you to your neighbor. The brotherhood of man is founded in the fatherhood of God.

GOSPEL
Mark 6:30–34 _____

The apostles gathered together with Jesus and reported all they had done and taught. He said to them, "Come away by yourselves to a deserted place and rest a while." People were coming and going in great numbers, and they had no opportunity even to eat. So they went off in the boat by themselves to a deserted place. People saw them leaving and many came to know about it. They hastened there on foot from all the towns and arrived at the place before them.

When he disembarked and saw the vast crowd, his heart was moved with pity for them, for they were like sheep without a shepherd; and he began to teach them many things.

Mark tells us how crowded Jesus' space and time was with other people's needs. He writes vividly, "People were coming and going in great numbers, and they had no opportunity even to eat." Jesus saw that he and his disciples needed rest, and so he said to them, "Come away by yourselves to a deserted place and rest a while." But when they tried to escape, they were followed. So, Mark says, "They went off in the boat by themselves to a deserted place. People saw them leaving and many came to know about it. They hastened there on foot from all the towns and arrived at the place before them."

So what did they do about this? Since they were Jesus' disciples, they did the same thing Jesus did. With Jesus, they let their hearts lead their legs. Mark writes, "When he disembarked and saw the vast crowd, his heart was moved with pity for them, for they were like sheep without a shepherd; and he began to teach them."

Jesus saw that both he and his disciples needed rest. (He did too! Remember, he was completely human in all things except sin.) But rest is a means to the end of meaningful work, not vice versa. We often think that the purpose of work is to make money so we can enjoy our rest. That's backward. Rest is needed for the sake of better work, better action, whether that action is paid or unpaid. (The most important actions in life are unpaid, like parenting.) The basic meaning of our life is an activity, whether we get paid for it in money or not and whether that activity is physical or mental. God's call to Adam was a job: to care for the garden. He also established a sabbath day for rest, but he established six days for work.

So our vacations are for better work, not our work for better vacations. That's reversing the means and the end.

Here is another example of our backward thinking about means and ends: we spontaneously think of other people's contributions to our lives through making and distributing material goods as a means to the end of our own comfort and pleasure and the enjoyment of our property. But the Church teaches that private property, although it is a right and a good, is also for the common good. And our own comforts and pleasures are to be shared with others. In fact, every single individual person is designed for self-giving and self-sharing with others. Though it is true that each individual person is an end and a value in himself and not merely a means to anyone else's end (that's why slavery is evil), it is also true that each person's vocation is to work for others. Christianity is neither individualism nor collectivism, neither capitalism nor communism, but communalism.

This unselfishness is not easy for us fallen creatures. We need to learn it, to be conditioned to it, to be socialized. We learn this lesson only in a community—most effectively in the family. It is reciprocal: parents need children and children need parents; men need women and women need men; the young need the old and the old need the young. And when both parties work for each other rather than just for themselves, both find that, despite the difficulties and the sacrifices, their mutual love makes it a joy.

The primary place God designed for most of us to learn that mutual self-giving is in marriage. In the old marriage ceremony, the priest said to the couple these words of wise advice: "Rest the security of your wedded life upon the great principle of self-sacrifice. . . . We are willing to give in proportion as we love. And when the love is perfect, the sacrifice is complete. . . . Sacrifice is usually difficult and irksome. Only love can make it easy and perfect love can make it a joy." So if you want a happy marriage, don't marry to find happiness; marry to give happiness.

God's design was that this lesson of marriage, this universal vocation of unselfish love, this experience of becoming yourself by giving yourself away, should expand outward, like circles of water rippling from a stone thrown into a pool. The ripples become increasingly large but decreasingly strong as they move away from the center, where they begin. The center is the first act of self-giving which is God's, both in creating us and in redeeming us at the price of his own life. Without that self-giving of the divine stone thrown into the center, there are no ripples of the human water.

Therefore, there is no human substitute for God. And if we want a society that is happy even on a purely human level, there is no adequate substitute for self-giving.

That work of self-giving is our fundamental vocation, whether we are preachers, teachers, healers, farmers, bankers, lawyers, hamburger flippers, construction workers, or comedians. We work for others, and others work for us. We row each other's boat.

And we do not work just for the sake of the money either, any more than we drive for the sake of the gasoline. The money is just the fuel that enables the vehicle to do its work. We work not to make money but to make love. And there are many kinds of love. Some of them are sentimental, and most of them are not.

SEVENTEENTH SUNDAY
IN ORDINARY TIME

FIRST READING

2 KINGS 4:42–44 _____

A man came from Baal-shalishah bringing to Elisha, the man of God, twenty barley loaves made from the firstfruits, and fresh grain in the ear. Elisha said, "Give it to the people to eat." But his servant objected, "How can I set this before a hundred people?" Elisha insisted, "Give it to the people to eat. For thus says the LORD, 'They shall eat and there shall be some left over.'" And when they had eaten, there was some left over, as the LORD had said.

_____

The reading from the Old Testament today is an account of a miracle, a kind of small version of the more famous miracle in which Christ performed a thousand-fold multiplication of five loaves to feed five thousand people. Here Elisha performs a five-fold multiplication of twenty loaves to feed a hundred people.

What are we to learn from this story? Obviously, that God can perform miracles, and occasionally does. Miracles are rare, and meant to be rare. But their point is not material but spiritual. They are words, communications from God, revelations from God, designed to teach us something. One of the Greek words translated "miracle" in the New Testament is *semeion*, which means "sign." Miracles are signs. Signs are teaching devices. Like pointing fingers, they call attention to something else beyond themselves, something more important than themselves. We are supposed to look along signs to the things they point to, not just sit and stare at the sign, like a dumb dog staring at the finger that's pointing to his food.

So what does this miracle teach us?

All miracles teach us at least this one truth: that there is a miracle-working God, a God who is all-powerful, a God who, since he created the universe, can change it whenever and wherever he wills. If I were an atheist, I would spend a lot of time and money and energy checking out all the miraculous claims in the world and trying to debunk every one of them, because if any of them is real, then God is real. I'd interview the scientists who checked out the Shroud of Turin and the scientists who checked out Juan Diego's miraculously preserved burlap tilma in Mexico City where Our Lady of Guadalupe appeared; and I'd watch the centuries-old, dried-up blood of St. Januarius miraculously liquefy every few years on his birthday; and I'd carefully examine the thousands of miraculous cures at Lourdes and Fatima; I'd interview the people and their doctors. Because miracles are like fingerprints: if there are supernatural fingerprints all over the world, then there are supernatural fingers.

But each miracle is also different, and in addition to the one thing that all miracles teach us—that there is a God who can do anything, that, as Jesus said, "For God all things are possible" (Matt. 19:26)—there are also different things that different miracles teach us. God did not multiply stones or stars or mountains but bread. Why?

The words "bread" and "meat" are often used generically to stand for all food and drink, just as "water," "wine," and "milk" are sometimes used generically for all drinks, and just as "man" is often used generically to stand for both male and female human beings. So when God multiplies this particular food, bread, he is showing us that he is the source of *all* of our food.

And this includes both our physical food and also our spiritual food, our truth and goodness and beauty and joy. Just as our bodies cannot live without foods like bread and meat and fruit, so our souls also cannot live without their proper food, their "soul foods" or spiritual foods, which are truth and goodness and beauty. God is our food source in both senses because he is the Creator both of our bodies and our souls. He is the source of the physical universe that provides our body's food and also the source of the spiritual universe of truth and goodness and beauty that provides our soul food.

What does it mean, then, when he miraculously multiplies bread? What are we supposed to learn from that? That he is not only the source of these foods from the beginning but also the source of the multiplication of these foods, both miraculously and non-miraculously, by being the source of the mysterious force called "life" that makes both foods grow, both body foods and soul foods. That when we hunger for more truth or virtue or joy, we should ask him, because he is the first cause of both the creation and the growth of all good things. As St. James writes, "If any of you lacks wisdom [and that means all of us!], he should ask God who gives to all generously and ungrudgingly" (James 1:5).

For instance, take the gift of joy, one of the foods of our soul. No one can live without joy. There are many true joys and many false joys, and the source of all true joys is God. God tells us through the prophet Nehemiah that "rejoicing in the LORD must be your strength" (Neh. 8:10).

Take also the spiritual food of beauty. Isaiah writes, "The LORD of hosts will be a glorious crown and a brilliant diadem for the remnant of his people" (Isa. 28:5).

Take also the spiritual food of moral goodness, virtue, righteousness. St. Paul writes, "You are in Christ Jesus, who became for us wisdom from God, as well as righteousness, sanctification, and redemption" (1 Cor. 1:30).

This is true of all true goods, for as St. James says, "*Every* perfect gift is from above, coming down from the Father" (James 1:17).

And lest we think that these spiritual things are only symbols for physical things, only pale copies and abstract copies of concrete physical things, please remember the passage in the Gospels when Jesus' disciples urge him to eat, and Jesus says, "I have food to eat of which you do not know." The disciples expect physical bread, but Jesus says, "My food is to do the will of the one who sent me." He brings them up short by telling them that it really is bread; it is bread indeed (see John 4:32–34). In other words, soul food is real food; it's the stuff we eat with our bodies that is only a symbol of that, not vice versa. God created the physical world to symbolize and teach us about the spiritual world, not vice versa.

So Jesus is our true bread; the bread we eat is only a symbol of that. The bread of life, the Eucharist, is not symbolic; bakers' bread is symbolic. For we are made in God's image; he is not made in ours. The physical miracle, like the whole physical world, points beyond itself, as physical art points to the creative mind and heart of the artist.

So just as we have sacred times and places—sabbaths and church buildings—to remind us that all times and places are sacred, so we are given miracles as gifts from God, as signs to show us and to remind us that God is the giver of all gifts, all goods, all of nature, the whole universe. God is not a local deity; he is the Creator and Lord of the universe.

RESPONSORIAL PSALM
Psalm 145:10–11, 15–16, 17–18 _____

R. (cf. 16) **The hand of the Lord feeds us; he answers all our needs.**

Let all your works give you thanks, O Lord,
    and let your faithful ones bless you.
Let them discourse of the glory of your kingdom
    and speak of your might.

The eyes of all look hopefully to you,
    and you give them their food in due season;
you open your hand
    and satisfy the desire of every living thing.

The Lord is just in all his ways
    and holy in all his works.
The Lord is near to all who call upon him,
    to all who call upon him in truth.

Anyone who has a pet cat or dog look up at them in hope and anticipation as they are filling their food dish will identify with this line from today's Psalm: "The eyes of all look hopefully to you, and you give them their food in due season; you open your hand and satisfy the desire of every living thing." God satisfies the desires of pets through people, and he satisfies the desires of people through other people: men through women, women through men, children through parents, parents through children, artists through engineers, engineers through artists, and so forth.

It's that hopeful, trusting, longing look in the eyes of your hungry dog or cat that is what God sees in your heart. It's not usually on your face, and not even in your conscious mind most of the time, but it's in your deepest heart. Your heart is hungry, and God alone can feed it, because you were designed by God for God, and for nothing less.

That's why nothing less is enough, nothing in this world is enough, to give you perfect happiness. The most famous and well-loved sentence in all of Christian literature outside the Bible is the theme of St. Augustine's *Confessions*. The whole book is a letter or prayer to God—we readers of the book are privileged to listen in—and on the very first page he says to God: "You have made us for Yourself, and our hearts are restless until they rest in You."

That's why we are restless, why we are never totally satisfied, never totally happy in this world. Imagine eating birdseed and cat food and dog food instead of people food. Not very satisfying, though it might keep you alive in a pinch. Real people food is God. The food for our souls, the only food that satisfies the deepest, most precious, and most hidden longing of our hearts, is not body food but soul food, and all the great soul foods in this life are only appetizers. In this life, everything that deeply satisfies our desire is an appetizer of heaven. It's always mixed with earthly stuff and received into very imperfect and foolish and selfish human souls (there are no other kinds of souls), and it's only a tiny, tiny appetizer; but everything good or true or beautiful in the universe, everything loving and joyful and holy in human life, is a gift of God and an appetizer of heaven.

That's why we have that look in our eyes when God feeds us with himself in the Eucharist. It's called hope. We see it in our dogs. After all, "dog" is "God" spelled backwards. God is to us what we are to our dogs.

Of course, we're not just pets to God; we are his dearest children. But God is farther above us than we are above our pets. So please don't be insulted by the analogy to dogs and cats, because the difference between us and our pets is only finite and not nearly as great as the difference between us and God, which is infinite.

Our primary soul food in this life is the Eucharist. The Eucharist is somewhat like a vitamin pill in that it does not have a physical or emotional taste or thrill, but it has the power of life; it is truly life-giving food; it gives life to our souls. The first part of the word "vitamin," the word *vita*, means "life." What our souls are to our bodies, Christ is to our souls. As the soul is the very life of the body, Christ is the very life of the soul. When the body loses its soul, it loses its life and becomes a corpse, a dead body. Souls can also die and become corpses, dead souls, souls without life. That's why repentance and confession are like emergency surgery, life-restoring operations, or blood transfusions. Because this life is truly an emergency, "a matter of life or death." And the Church is, as Pope Francis says, "a field hospital on a battlefield."

SECOND READING

Ephesians 4:1–6 _____

Brothers and sisters: I, a prisoner for the Lord, urge you to live in a manner worthy of the call you have received, with all humility and gentleness, with patience, bearing with one another through love, striving to preserve the unity of the spirit through the bond of peace: one body and one Spirit, as you were also called to the one hope of your call; one Lord, one faith, one baptism; one God and Father of all, who is over all and through all and in all.

Today's epistle speaks about unity and peace, two things that are increasingly rare in today's world and also, alas, in today's Church. They are marks or fruits of the Holy Spirit; so when they are absent, that is evidence of the absence of the Holy Spirit. As Jesus so practically said, "By their fruits you will know them" (Matt. 7:16).

How do we recover the unity, the brotherhood, the amity among different and disagreeing factions in the Church and in the world?

St. Paul's prescription is not vague platitudes but specific steps. The first is the honesty of humility. We need to remember who we are: that we are fallen, finite, fallible, foolish human beings, not gods.

The second step, which flows from the first, is gentleness. When we feel arrogant and self-righteous, we are tempted to bullying. When we are cocksure that we are totally right, it is hard to avoid at least verbal violence.

The third step is patience. Even when we are sure others are wrong, we must treat them as human beings who need to learn, gradually, not as machines that need to be fixed, suddenly.

Patience is hard—unless there is love. Patience is one of love's children. And love, goodwill, honest desire for the good of the other is our absolute duty, because it is the very essence of God, the nature of God: "God *is* love" (1 John 4:16).

Love is the primary fruit of the Holy Spirit. So he is the next thing St. Paul mentions: "Striving to preserve the unity of the spirit through the bond of peace."

The Holy Spirit is God himself, our Lord. As the Father is God above us and the Son is God beside us, the Spirit is God within us. How did we receive the Holy Spirit? First, through Baptism. And what motivated our Baptism? Our faith, or, if we were baptized as infants, the faith of our parents and the faith of the Church. So St. Paul next connects these three things as the source of our unity: "one Lord, one faith, one baptism; one God and Father of all."

Humility, gentleness, patience, love, the Holy Spirit—that is the prescription for our unity and our peace. It's a package deal, a chain that all hangs together. If we are not at peace with each other, no matter how much we may disagree, that proves that we do not have the Holy Spirit, or that we are blocking him. And if we do not have the Holy Spirit, then we do not have the love that is the very life of God. And if we do not have that love, we will not have the patience that is a part of that love. And if we are not patient with each other, we cannot be gentle with each other. And if we are not gentle with each other, that shows our lack of humility.

So it all begins with humility, with the shocking realization that we are not God, and with the sincere willingness to listen to each other. Even God listens to us; are we more high and mighty than God? Even God, who needs no humility, humbled himself to become our servant. Was God a fool to do that? Would you be a fool if you did that?

Please make a resolution, in prayer, before God himself, to listen, humbly, to others. You just might learn something—unless, of course, you already know everything worth knowing. Ask God for the grace of humility. He is not a bully, so he will not force you to receive that grace if you do not really want it, but he is eager to give that gift if you do really want it. So if you ask him for it, take him seriously enough to expect him to take *you* seriously. Be prepared to leave your comfort zones.

GOSPEL
JOHN 6:1–15 _____

Jesus went across the Sea of Galilee. A large crowd followed him, because they saw the signs he was performing on the sick. Jesus went up on the mountain, and there he sat down with his disciples. The Jewish feast of Passover was near. When Jesus raised his eyes and saw that a large crowd was coming to him, he said to Philip, "Where can we buy enough food for them to eat?" He said this to test him, because he himself knew what he was going to do. Philip answered him, "Two hundred days' wages worth of food would not be enough for each of them to have a little." One of his disciples, Andrew, the brother of Simon Peter, said to him, "There is a boy here who has five barley loaves and two fish; but what good are these for so many?" Jesus said, "Have the people recline." Now there was a great deal of grass in that place. So the men reclined, about five thousand in number. Then Jesus took the loaves, gave thanks, and distributed them to those who were reclining, and also as much of the fish as they wanted. When they had had their fill, he said to his disciples, "Gather the fragments left over, so that nothing will be wasted." So they collected them, and filled twelve wicker baskets with fragments from the five barley loaves that had been more than they could eat. When the people saw the sign he had done, they said, "This is truly the Prophet, the one who is to come into the world." Since Jesus knew that they were going to come and carry him off to make him king, he withdrew again to the mountain alone.

There are many aspects of the story of Jesus' miracle of the feeding of five thousand people with five loaves and two fish—a miracle that is reported in all four Gospels—but there is one very practical question about it that applies to our lives today and can literally change our lives very significantly: What things other than bread and fish does Jesus perform miracles on today by multiplying them?

One ready answer is love, of course. It grows and multiplies, like a good infection, a good virus. Another is wisdom. Truth is like light: it creeps into any place that allows it in. It lives; it multiplies; it creeps in everywhere; you have to stop it with walls or by closing your eyes. All spiritual goods are like that: they all multiply when shared, in contrast to material goods like money and time and energy, which divide when shared. Physicists call that entropy: all forms of physical energy, like heat from a cup of hot coffee, tend to dissipate and die out. If I give you one of my two pieces of pizza, or one of my two cars, I have only one left. But if I give you some joy or love or truth or goodness or beauty, I lose nothing and actually gain. For instance, teaching a subject is the best way to learn it better, and sharing your joys with others always multiplies them.

There is at least one thing in the physical world, however, that also grows instead of diminishing when it's shared with God. That's time.

Let's look at the little boy who gave up his five loaves and two fish to Jesus.

(Notice the little detail that St. John, the youngest of the twelve Apostles, is the only Gospel writer who notes that the loaves and fish came from a little boy.) The boy seemed to have lost them when he gave them away to Jesus, because they were just physical things, and when physical things are given away, the giver has fewer things left. Yet Jesus performed a miracle and transcended that physical law, so the result was that everybody had more than enough to eat, and there were twelve baskets full of scraps, which Jesus commanded his Apostles to gather up. (Notice this little detail too: Jesus took good care of the environment and did not tolerate pollution! This planet is still a Garden of Eden even though it's got snakes and thorns and thistles in it, and we are responsible for caring for our home and keeping it clean and beautiful.)

Jesus still performs miracles today, because "Jesus Christ is the same yesterday, today, and forever" (Heb. 13:8). Most of the miracles Jesus performs today are not sudden and spectacular and public, like the feeding of the five thousand, but subtle and invisible, but they are just as real and just as life changing. They come like the dawn or like the tides, gradually and invisibly but irresistibly and with power. One of these miracles is that he does with time exactly the same thing he did with the five loaves and two fish from the little boy. The more of it you give to him, the more of it you get back from him. He multiplies your time.

Now, that can't be done on a merely physical level. Time multiplication in a literal, physical sense is no more possible than time travel. (Only our mental *awareness* of time can multiply or diminish.) But the multiplication of time is impossible for only one kind of time, physical time, the time that measures the movement of material bodies like the sun and the moon and the stars through the sky, or the radioactive decay of atoms. There is also another kind of time that we all experience, and that is spiritual time, or mental time, or lived time, the kind of time that measures purposes and desires and goods. And that kind of time is not limited to the laws of physical time.

Many languages have two words for these two kinds of time. In Greek, they are *kronos* for clock time or physical time and *kairos* for spiritual time.

Kronos is the source of our English word "chronological," meaning following the order of the clock or chronometer. But when St. Paul wrote that "it is the hour now for you to awake from sleep," "for our salvation is nearer now than when we first believed" (Rom. 13:11), he was not thinking of numbers, of years or months or days or hours or minutes.

Probably no technological invention in history has changed daily life more, and for more people, than the invention of the clock, which dictates that human lives are now to be coordinated by *kronos*, the kind of time that is abstract and contentless, the time measured not by human purposes but by numbers. Before clocks ruled our lives, natural time did: both the natural time of the universe, sunrise and sunset, and the natural time of our bodies, birth and growth and aging and dying; and during each day, the cycles of sleep and waking, hunger and eating; and the movement of generations, first *being* children and then *having* children, first having parents and then being parents.

When you wake up tomorrow morning in obedience to your alarm clock, a thousand little voices will invade your mind: all the things you have to do tomorrow, all the worries you have to worry about tomorrow, all the obligations and duties you are responsible for tomorrow. You will think: I'm going to be so busy today that I don't have much time to pray today, so I'll keep it really short. Or perhaps you won't even think about prayer.

The very first choice you make in the morning is crucial. If you remember God; if you remember whose you are, and who you are; if you remember that neither you nor your many jobs are your God, and that God is the author of all time and life—in other words, if you begin your day by living in the real world, the world in which God is God, instead of living in the dream world in which you are God—then you will not think, "I am too busy today to pray." You will think, "I am going to be so busy today that I need to pray *more* this morning than usual rather than less." In other words, you will be like the little boy in today's Gospel, and you will give your Lord your little loaves and fish of time. You will take time to pray. You will *make* time to pray. And then a miracle will happen. At the end of the day, you will wonder how you accomplished so much. The answer is that you gave a little of your time to the Lord of time, and he multiplied it. And if you don't do that, you will probably wonder at the end of the day why you felt so harried and hassled by the lack of time you had. You will wonder where all the time went and why you did not accomplish more.

How much time each day should be your minimum for prayer? I will not give the safe, comfortable answer that it's all relative, that it's up to you. I will give you a very definite assignment: fifteen minutes. Half of one silly TV show. If you don't pray at all every day, then start with five minutes a day for a week, and then ten the next week, and then fifteen the third week. Fifteen minutes is not the maximum, or the ideal, or the standard; it's the minimum. Two minutes for each of the five loaves and two and a half minutes for each of the two fish. Be sure to include some of the prayers of the Church, like the Psalms, but make them your own; don't just rattle them off like a password. Also include some of your own personal, spontaneous prayers. Just be completely honest.

Methods and choice of content matter much less than you think. Just do it; that's 99 percent of the battle. What you say is less important than just saying it, just being there, being present. That's what you will want the most when you are on your deathbed: the presence of the people you love. That's what God prizes too: your effort, not your success.

This sounds easy and simple, and it is! And it is also guaranteed to make you and your day more delightful, more peaceful, and more productive. But I guarantee that if you do not do this already, it will be a lot harder than you think to do it. It will take weeks, maybe months, to develop the habit.

Why, if it's so reasonable and so fruitful and so productive? Because the devil is terrified of prayer. He will do everything he can to stop you from praying, from opening that line to God so God can pour his graces into your soul and your life and your relationships with others and your world. Life is spiritual warfare. The devil wants you to be miserable, not happy; and God wants you to be happy, not miserable. We are at war. Expect a fight. Nothing really great comes easily.

Can you do that? Can you give God just a few loaves and fish of your time? If you do, I guarantee that he will perform the miracle of multiplication.

EIGHTEENTH SUNDAY
IN ORDINARY TIME

FIRST READING

Exodus 16:2–4, 12–15 _____

The whole Israelite community grumbled against Moses and Aaron. The Israelites said to them, "Would that we had died at the LORD's hand in the land of Egypt, as we sat by our fleshpots and ate our fill of bread! But you had to lead us into this desert to make the whole community die of famine!"

Then the LORD said to Moses, "I will now rain down bread from heaven for you. Each day the people are to go out and gather their daily portion; thus will I test them, to see whether they follow my instructions or not.

"I have heard the grumbling of the Israelites. Tell them: In the evening twilight you shall eat flesh, and in the morning you shall have your fill of bread, so that you may know that I, the LORD, am your God."

In the evening quail came up and covered the camp. In the morning a dew lay all about the camp, and when the dew evaporated, there on the surface of the desert were fine flakes like hoarfrost on the ground. On seeing it, the Israelites asked one another, "What is this?" for they did not know what it was. But Moses told them, "This is the bread that the LORD has given you to eat."

_____

There's a pun in today's reading from the book of Exodus. The word "manna" means literally "What's that?" The line reads: "On seeing it, the Israelites asked one another, 'What is this?' for they did not know what it was." It's like the pun on Staten Island, which constitutes one of the five boroughs of New York City. When the Dutchman Peter Minuit bought the island of Manhattan from the Native Americans, he noticed another island just south of it, and he pointed to it and asked the chief, "Is that an island?" And the chief said, "Yes," so Peter thought that was its name, Staten Island. (The joke sounds better when you understand that a Dutchman can't pronounce the sound "th" so "Is that an island" comes out as "Staten Island.")

There are at least three serious points in the story from Exodus:

The first point is that we, like the ancient Israelites, are ungrateful for the miracles God has already performed for us. In their case it was freeing them from slavery in Egypt by parting the Red Sea for their escape; in our case it is freeing us from the even greater slavery to sin, death, hell, and the devil by sending his Son to free us from our slavery to sin and death by parting the sea of death for us, both physical death and spiritual death, through Jesus' death and Resurrection.

The second point is that even though we are ungrateful complainers, God is merciful and gives us not what we deserve but what we need: another miracle. As he gave the Israelites physical bread from the physical heavens to satisfy their hunger, he gives us Christ, who is our spiritual bread from his own spiritual heaven to satisfy our spiritual hunger, our spiritual need for eternal life, a participation in the very life of God, which is *agape* love. Christ is the food that keeps our souls alive. In today's Gospel, he identifies himself as the real meaning symbolized by the physical manna from heaven that fell on the ancient Israelites.

The third point is that there is a mystery, a hiddenness, to this gift. There is much more there than meets the eye. "What is this?" is a very good question, an honest question, a necessary question to ask if you are honest and sincere. Our eyes tell us the answer to the question "What does that *look like*? What are its appearances?" But our eyes do not tell us the answer to the question "What is that, really? What is its essence, its true nature?" Our eyes do not even tell us the answer to that question about physical things. "Appearances are deceiving." Your shoe does not look like trillions of tiny atoms of electromagnetic energy moving in largely empty space. The sun does not look four hundred times bigger and more massive than the moon. The gray matter of your brain does not look like the world's biggest supercomputer. And Jesus did not look like God to his people, especially while he was dying on the cross.

And the Eucharist, which is Jesus in person, does not look like Jesus; it looks like bread. But it is not. It is manna from heaven; it is the "What is it?" from heaven; it is the great puzzle from heaven, the great mystery from heaven. It is not from earth alone (although it is that, too: Christ was truly the human son of Mary, and she is the literal and biological "Mother of God"). The Eucharist is not bread, even though it looks like bread. It is *not* what it looks like, the stuff we make out of grain from the earth. It is not from earth at all; it is from heaven. It is Jesus, all of him, the whole of him, divinity and humanity; and, within his humanity, body and soul; and, within his body, flesh and blood. Thus the formula "Body and Blood, Soul and Divinity." Well might we ask the question "What is that?"

In fact, if any non-Catholic really asks that question, really pursues that question with an open mind, a truth-seeking mind, and asks that question not only to himself but also to God, in prayer, seeking the truth, he will find it. Jesus himself promised, "Seek and you will find. . . . The one who seeks, finds" (Matt. 7:7–8). He was not referring to winning the lottery or avoiding suffering; he was referring to himself. If you know any non-Catholic Christian who is honestly wondering whether the Catholic Church is Christ's own Church, suggest that they go into a Catholic church, where the Eucharist is reserved in the tabernacle, and pray to Jesus Christ and ask him: "Are you there? Is that really you? Are Catholics right or wrong when they worship that? Is that only a piece of bread, a holy symbol, but not you? Are they bowing down to bread, confusing it with God? If so, don't let me fall into that ridiculous heresy. But if that is really you, please draw me there, where you are; please draw me home."

And if you know anyone who has left the Catholic Church, suggest to them the very same prayer. For if the answer is yes, that that little round thing that looks like bread really is Jesus Christ, God almighty in the flesh, hiding behind the appearances of bread, then no matter what other problems they have with the Catholic Church, if they still have Jesus as their Lord, that is where they should go because that is where he is. They will have to work out all those other problems in light of that, in light of him, in light of the fact that their Lord and their Savior is really present there, fully and personally, Body and Blood, Soul and Divinity, as he is nowhere else in the universe. If they have problems with the Church but not with Jesus, let them start with Jesus and ask Jesus to help them solve all the problems they have with the Church instead of doing it backward and starting with their problems with the Church and then looking at Jesus in light of those personal ideas and issues, rather than vice versa. Perhaps those really are problems in the Church, and perhaps they are really problems in *them*, in their thinking. But in either case, if their absolute is Jesus, and not the Church; if their yes to Jesus is more important than their no to the Church; then let them sit in front of the tabernacle and ask Jesus what to do, praying with total honesty and total open-mindedness. And he will honor his promise that all who truly, sincerely seek him with all their heart will find him.

Of course, he did not promise when or where or how. He's a lover, not an airplane; he does not conform to our schedules.

Thus, the Church has always, from the beginning, seen the Eucharist in the verses of the Psalm that we have in today's liturgy. The Real Presence of Christ her Lord is the absolute center of the whole of the Church's tradition that she has been handing down for two thousand years. Thus, she sings this Psalm.

RESPONSORIAL PSALM
PSALM 78:3–4, 23–24, 25, 54 _____

R. (24b) **The Lord gave them bread from heaven.**

What we have heard and know,
    and what our fathers have declared to us,
We will declare to the generation to come
    the glorious deeds of the LORD and his strength
    and the wonders that he wrought.

He commanded the skies above
    and opened the doors of heaven;
he rained manna upon them for food
    and gave them heavenly bread.

Man ate the bread of angels,
    food he sent them in abundance.
And he brought them to his holy land,
    to the mountains his right hand had won.

"What we have heard and know, and what our fathers have declared to us, we will declare to the generation to come the glorious deeds of the LORD *and his strength and the wonders that he wrought."* The greatest of all the wonders God has wrought is the Incarnation of his Son Jesus Christ, and the continuation of the Incarnation in his real presence in the Eucharist. *"He commanded the skies above and opened the doors of heaven; he rained manna upon them for food and gave them heavenly bread."* Christ himself is that heavenly bread. The manna in the wilderness was the symbol of the Eucharist, not vice versa. *"Men ate the bread of angels, food he sent them in abundance."* Christ's home is in heaven with the angels. Yet even the angels cannot eat his Body in the Eucharist. If angels had jealousy—which they don't—that would be the primary reason for their jealousy. God has given us a privilege even the angels do not have. *"And he brought them to his holy land, to the mountains his right hand had won."* That holy land is heaven, of course. The Eucharist is the bread of heaven. Jesus himself said, "Whoever eats this bread will live forever" (John 6:51). If we eat this bread both with our bodies and with our souls, with our honest faith, we are made part of Jesus' Mystical Body, Jesus' people, Jesus' Church; and Jesus takes his whole Body home to heaven.

If you wonder where the Catholic Church got its teaching about the Eucharist from, or if you have doubts about it—for instance, if you think that perhaps it's only symbolic, not literally true—then please read the whole of chapter six of John's Gospel. Literally. Go home and read that chapter, slowly and thoughtfully and honestly and prayerfully. Ask God to teach you whatever he wants you to learn from it. And mean it. And if you do that, if you are not a convinced Catholic when you read the first verse, you will be when you finish the last, or at least very significantly closer to it and on the road that leads home.

That little red sanctuary lamp that you see burning near the altar in every Catholic church means that there is right now a consecrated, transubstantiated Host in that little gold box called the tabernacle: Jesus the Lord, *your* Lord and Savior and Lover and Friend. The red light is like a candle in the window of your home, and God the Father is like the father of the prodigal son, waiting for his return home.

That light is the fire in the fireplace of your spiritual home, your living room, the room for real living, abundant living, supernatural living—the living he designed you for, the living that is joy and wonder and beauty and hope and love and peace (and also spiritual warfare and challenge and sacrifice and courage and heroism). Because that life means not just living alone, living in yourself, but living in him, in his Body. When we receive the Eucharist, we seem to assimilate him and incorporate him and make him part of our body, but what really happens is that he assimilates us and incorporates us and makes us part of *his* Body, so that all the everyday things that happen to us now happen to him, because we are part of him, part of his Body.

It is life's greatest adventure to eat that manna from heaven.

SECOND READING
Ephesians 4:17, 20–24 _____

Brothers and sisters: I declare and testify in the Lord that you must no longer live as the Gentiles do, in the futility of their minds; that is not how you learned Christ, assuming that you have heard of him and were taught in him, as truth is in

Jesus, that you should put away the old self of your former way of life, corrupted through deceitful desires, and be renewed in the spirit of your minds, and put on the new self, created in God's way in righteousness and holiness of truth.

Today's epistle can be fully understood only in light of today's other readings. The new self, the new life, that St. Paul refers to is not just an abstract set of rules or ideals; it is a new *self*, a new *person*, a new speaker of the word "I." That new person is Jesus Christ. Through the Eucharist and through Baptism you are in him, a member of his Body. And the word "member" here means "organ" in an organism, not a number in a group or a business or a political party. Without the Eucharist you can only imitate Christ, follow Christ, admire Christ, obey Christ, believe in Christ; but with the Eucharist you are now "in" Christ, not outside; you are no longer part of the audience. He is really, truly, literally in you, in your soul, and you are really, truly, literally in him. He is the Head, and you are the Body, and Head and Body are one person. It's like marriage, where the two really, truly, and not just symbolically, become one—and without losing their individuality but fulfilling it.

We have a new lifestyle only because we have a new life. We die to our old lifestyle because we die to our old life, our life of autonomy and loneliness. We called it "freedom," but it was really slavery—slavery to our desires, especially our desire for autonomy, for living out of our own will, our own selfish self, our desire to sing "I did it my way." When we become members of Christ and begin to do it his way, we still very frequently fall back into the habits of our old self and doing it "my way." That's why we have the sacrament of Penance. But that's not our true self anymore; that's the dead old self that's like an albatross still hanging around our neck, giving us trouble—often very serious trouble.

The Greek language in which the New Testament was written has two different words for "life." *Bios* is natural life, and *zoe* is supernatural life. The word translated "flesh," *sarx*, refers to *bios*: fallen, selfish, natural life. The word translated "spirit," *pneuma*, refers to *zoe*, supernatural life, divine life, spiritual life, life from the Holy Spirit. St. Paul's contrast between "the flesh" and "the spirit" does not mean the contrast between the body and the soul but the contrast between *sarx* and *pneuma*, or *bios* and *zoe*.

Thus, St. Paul says in Romans: "For I know that good does not dwell in me, that is, in my flesh. The willing is ready at hand, but doing the good is not. For I do not do the good I want, but I do the evil I do not want. Now if I do what I do not want, it is no longer I who do it, but sin that dwells in me" (Rom. 7:18–20). When we consent to sin, we consent to that old self, that albatross that still hangs around us. Of course, it's our fault because it's our free choice, but it's no longer our deepest, truest identity. Because we are now in Christ.

And we are put there not just by our free choice to believe (that's one necessary part of it, the human half of it) but also by Christ's sacraments, especially the Eucharist, the bread from heaven that nourishes that new life, that *zoe*, in us. That's why we should stop acting like apes and start acting like saints: because we are God's children; we are the King's kids, not King Kong's kids. When we act like apes, we are being what we are not; when we act like the saints, we are being what we are.

Christ is not just an external model for us. Christ is our own identity, for he lives within us. As he is really present in the Eucharist, he is really present in our souls, because our souls are really present in our bodies that consume the Eucharist. The body that eats bread becomes one with the bread. Our bodies that eat the bread from the earth gradually transform that bread into themselves, into parts of the bodies that eat it, and the bread gradually loses its identity as bread. But our body that eats the bread from heaven is gradually transformed into that bread, and instead of losing our identity we gain it.

That's why, behind St. Paul's expectation that we die to our old life*style*, is the insight that we have already died to our old life-*source*, the flesh, our old, fallen human nature, and we have put on a new nature, Christ's nature. The bread from heaven in the Old Testament story of the manna only gave life to bodies, and only for a time; the bread from heaven in the New Testament gives life to our souls, for eternity.

GOSPEL
JOHN 6:24–35 _____

When the crowd saw that neither Jesus nor his disciples were there, they themselves got into boats and came to Capernaum looking for Jesus. And when they found him across the sea they said to him, "Rabbi, when did you get here?" Jesus answered them and said, "Amen, amen, I say to you, you are looking for me not because you saw signs but because you ate the loaves and were filled. Do not work for food that perishes but for the food that endures for eternal life, which the Son of Man will give you. For on him the Father, God, has set his seal." So they said to him, "What can we do to accomplish the works of God?" Jesus answered and said to them, "This is the work of God, that you believe in the one he sent." So they said to him, "What sign can you do, that we may see and believe in you? What can you do? Our ancestors ate manna in the desert, as it is written: *He gave them bread from heaven to eat.*" So Jesus said to them, "Amen, amen, I say to you, it was not Moses who gave the bread from heaven; my Father gives you the true bread from heaven. For the bread of God is that which comes down from heaven and gives life to the world."

So they said to him, "Sir, give us this bread always." Jesus said to them, "I am the bread of life; whoever comes to me will never hunger, and whoever believes in me will never thirst."

_____

To see that today's Gospel is about the Eucharist, let's look at the primary point of it and then connect it with the verses that follow. The primary point is that the bread of life, the bread from heaven that gives eternal life, is Jesus himself, not the physical manna that God gave Israel in the desert or the physical bread that Jesus multiplied from five loaves to feed five thousand people. They were both symbols, but Jesus is not a symbol; Jesus is what these symbols symbolized.

Now, to see that the Eucharist is not just a symbol but Jesus himself, look at the text that follows.

In the last line of today's passage, Jesus says, "I am the bread of life." The Greek word for "life" here is not *bios*, which means natural life, human life, temporal life, but *zoe*, which means supernatural life, divine life, eternal life. Right after Jesus said that, the text says, "The Jews murmured about him because he said, 'I am the bread that came down from heaven.'" So Jesus repeated that claim and then added to it, and added to their reason for murmuring against him, by saying, "And the bread that I will give is my flesh for the life of the world." Shocking. Sounds like cannibalism. The Jews said, "How can this man give us his flesh to eat?" (John 6:41, 51–52).

But Jesus did not soften his claim. He went on to say: "Amen, amen, I say to you, unless you eat the flesh of the Son of Man and drink his blood, you do not have life within you. Whoever eats my flesh and drinks my blood has eternal life, and I will raise him on the last day. . . . Whoever eats my flesh and drinks my blood remains in me and I in him. Just as the living Father sent me and I have life because of the Father, so also the one who feeds on me will have life because of me" (John 6:53–57).

The Gospel goes on to say that "many of his disciples who were listening said, 'This saying is hard; who can accept it?' . . . As a result of this, many of his disciples returned to their former way of life and no longer accompanied him. Jesus then said to the Twelve, 'Do you also want to leave?' Simon Peter answered him, 'Master, to whom shall we go? You have the words of eternal life'" (John 6:60, 66–68).

If Jesus did not mean his words about eating his flesh and drinking his blood to be taken literally, but only symbolically, he surely would have corrected and enlightened those early protesters so that they did not continue in their literalism. But he didn't. And he repeated and reinforced it at the Last Supper.

Those who went away were the first protesters, the first Protestants. Those who stayed, remained faithful to Peter and his words, were the first Catholics. Peter was the first Catholic pope.

Peter and his successors have continued to teach that "hard saying" for two thousand years. And Jesus continues to ask, "Do you also want to leave?" And many say yes. But we continue to answer him, with Peter, "Master, to whom shall we go? You have the words of eternal life. We have come to believe and are convinced that you are the Holy One of God" (John 6:68–69). If you can't trust the words of God incarnate, whose words can you trust?

NINETEENTH SUNDAY
IN ORDINARY TIME

FIRST READING
1 Kings 19:4–8 _____

Elijah went a day's journey into the desert, until he came to a broom tree and sat beneath it. He prayed for death saying: "This is enough, O Lord! Take my life, for I am no better than my fathers." He lay down and fell asleep under the broom tree, but then an angel touched him and ordered him to get up and eat. Elijah looked and there at his head was a hearth cake and a jug of water. After he ate and drank, he lay down again, but the angel of the Lord came back a second time, touched him, and ordered, "Get up and eat, else the journey will be too long for you!" He got up, ate, and drank; then strengthened by that food, he walked forty days and forty nights to the mountain of God, Horeb.

RESPONSORIAL PSALM
Psalm 34:2–3, 4–5, 6–7, 8–9 _____

R. (9a) **Taste and see the goodness of the Lord.**

I will bless the Lord at all times;
   his praise shall be ever in my mouth.
Let my soul glory in the Lord;
   the lowly will hear me and be glad.

Glorify the Lord with me,
   let us together extol his name.

I sought the LORD, and he answered me
  and delivered me from all my fears.

Look to him that you may be radiant with joy.
  And your faces may not blush with shame.
When the afflicted man called out, the LORD heard,
  and from all his distress he saved him.

The angel of the LORD encamps
  around those who fear him and delivers them.
Taste and see how good the LORD is;
  blessed the man who takes refuge in him.

Today's Old Testament reading is an example of today's Psalm, especially about the role of God's angels.

Elijah was one of the greatest prophets of all time. He, like the Blessed Virgin Mary, did not die and decay but was assumed into heaven—in fact, in his case, in a chariot of fire. Yet he was only human, and he had his limits. In today's reading, he is one of the few believers left, and all the powers that be had conspired against him. He is fleeing from them for his life into the desert, and he is exhausted and has given up all earthly hope and prays to God for death. (Notice: death, not suicide. He will not be a murderer.) He has given up hope, but God has not. God saves him.

That drama and that salvation is the most basic plot of the drama of every single human life, whether you are a peasant or a prophet, a loser or a winner, rich or poor. Every human life is full of two things: failure and success, death and life, misery and joy, unhappiness and happiness, poverty and wealth, bad things and good things. No one ever lived who did not experience both. Even people in the most miserable circumstances often find hope and joy in their sufferings, and even people in the most comfortable conditions often find them so unendurable that they are tempted to suicide. The suicide rate is much higher in rich countries than in poor countries, by the way.

What is God's role in all this? He is the Savior, the deliverer, the rescuer. After allowing us to fall, he raises us up. After a time of sorrow, he gives us a time of joy. After every night there is a morning. God did not push us into the pit, but he hoists us out of it. He is not the God of death but of life. He does not have a dark side. The Bible says that "God is light, and in him there is no darkness at all" (1 John 1:5). He is not the author of sin and death and suffering, but he permits these evils, allows them, for a time, and then he saves us from them.

That is the two-act drama of life, the plot of every human life and of every part of life, and that is why it is the plot of every story we tell: problem and solution, challenge and response, fall and rescue. God allows us to fall into darkness for a while, so that he might rescue us and give us light forever.

In this life, the rescues are always followed by other falls; the sunrises are always followed by more sunsets. But the last sunrise lasts forever, because that sun is the eternal Son of God. And that sunrise, that rescue, that salvation, is so full of light and joy that one of the saints, who lived a life full of terrible sufferings, said that when we look at our past earthly life from the viewpoint of heaven, even if it seemed awful and unendurable at the time, it will appear to us to be no worse than one night in an inconvenient hotel.

God is at work in all things. He usually uses intermediaries to do his work. Some of these intermediaries are his angels. They are usually invisible. It was an angel that God used to save Elijah, twice, in our Old Testament story today. Every one of us has a guardian angel. That is not a myth or a hope; that is a definitive dogma that the Church has always taught, because Jesus taught it—for instance, when he said about children that "their angels in heaven always look upon the face of my heavenly Father" (Matt. 18:10). Angels are much more active and involved in our lives than we think.

But so are other people, whom God also uses for the same purposes as he uses his angels: to move us ahead, to help us, even when they seem to be obstacles and hindrances, as they did to Elijah. For, as St. Paul says in Romans 8:28, God works all things together for good to those who love him, the evils that he permits as well as the goods that he performs. He is the author of the whole story.

Until our dying breath, God sends his agents to us to move us on to do his work because we still have work to do: his work. His agents include both angels and humans; and among humans, doctors and nurses and friends and even difficult and inconvenient people. Our faith is an eye that sees the hand of God behind all things in our lives.

God always has some good work for us to do. For we, too, are like his angels; we are instruments, intermediaries, guardians, helpers. And every act we do, every good choice we make, up to and including our last dying breath, if there is faith and hope and love in it, God may use as a link in the long and complex chain that he is using to save some poor soul.

We don't usually see that. But then, we don't see much of what's really going on anywhere, do we? Even in the physical universe, there are countless interactions of energy pulsing through this place and through so-called empty space that we don't see. Why should reality be emptier and less rich and less powerful and less complex and less mysterious when it comes to the relations between spirits and spiritual things—between God and us, and between us and angels, and between one human soul and another that we love and pray for—than it is between the many physical forces in the universe? Why should spiritual gravity be less real than physical gravity?

The author of the drama of our lives and of this whole created universe has full knowledge and full control of every atom and every event in his world, from the Big Bang that created it, through every little event in your life, every hair that falls from your head, to the final end, the end of time, the Last Judgment, and eternity.

Trust him. What else is there to trust, in the end?

SECOND READING

EPHESIANS 4:30–5:2 _____

Brothers and sisters: Do not grieve the Holy Spirit of God, with which you were sealed for the day of redemption. All bitterness, fury, anger, shouting, and reviling must be removed from you, along with all malice. And be kind to one another, compassionate, forgiving one another as God has forgiven you in Christ.

So be imitators of God, as beloved children, and live in love, as Christ loved us and handed himself over for us as a sacrificial offering to God for a fragrant aroma.

Today's epistle tells us, "Do not grieve the Holy Spirit of God, with which you were sealed for the day of redemption." That verse tells us that the Holy Spirit is a divine person, just as the Father and the Son are persons, not impersonal forces. So the right pronoun to translate the ambiguous Greek word *ho* should not be "which" but "whom." St. Paul says, "Do not grieve the Holy Spirit," and you cannot "grieve" a force. Do you "grieve" gravity when you send a rocket into space?

The pronoun for God must be "he," not "it." "He," of course, does not mean biologically male; the image of God, according to Genesis, is "male *and female*" equally. The "he" is the generic he, not the specific he; or as linguists say, the "unmarked" he, not the "marked" he. Our new, so-called "inclusive" language is exactly the opposite of what it claims to be: it is exclusive language instead of inclusive language because it forbids us to use "man" or "he" inclusively or generically, as referring to male and female human beings equally, as was the clear intention of everyone who wrote in the English language for hundreds of years in the past, until radical feminism strangled language for the sake of ideology. But we cannot make just reparation for our past sins against women by present sins against language, any more than we can make reparation for rape by abortion, because two wrongs don't make a right. And we can't use the neutral "it" for God because God is not an abstract, impersonal force but a person. Jesus' name for God was "the Father," not "the Force." I guess we'll have to forgive him for that because he did not have the privilege of seeing the Star Wars movies. But doesn't it feel just a wee bit arrogant to assume that we know how to speak of God better than Jesus does? Does he flunk our theology exam, or do we flunk his?

The Holy Spirit is one of the three divine persons, and because he is the Spirit, he inspires spiritual virtues like the ones St. Paul mentions: kindness and compassion and forgiveness, instead of malice and bitterness and anger. He is the Spirit of love, the infinite love between the Father and the Son. The Spirit proceeds eternally from both, a love so real that he is not just a force but a person.

There are many fruits of the Spirit. The one that St. Paul emphasizes in this passage is forgiveness. It's not easy for us sinful, selfish, fallen fools to practice forgiveness, especially when we've been hurt. But Jesus' strongest words are about the necessity of forgiveness. In the Lord's Prayer, the one and only prayer Jesus himself explicitly gave us, we are commanded to pray for our own damnation if we do not forgive: we are to ask God to "forgive us our trespasses *as we forgive those who trespass against us.*" In other words, we are to pray, "God, if I do not forgive my neighbors' sins against me, then do not forgive my sins against you."

St. Paul says we must be "forgiving one another *as God has forgiven you.*" The Greek word *kathos*, translated "as," means not just an imitation but the very same thing. It could be translated "just as" or "exactly as." In other words, totally and unconditionally.

God has forgiven us many inexcusable sins against his infinite divine goodness. How can we not forgive a comparatively few and comparatively excusable sins from our fellow sinners against our own merely finite human goodness? We owe God a debt that is the equivalent of trillions of dollars; how dare we not forgive each other's debts to us that amount to pennies? When God forgave us, it cost him far more, on the cross, than it could ever cost us to forgive each other. When we refuse to do that, when we clutch the chips on our shoulders and hold them in our heart, we not only burden our shoulders but also harden our heart, which is the very center of our soul, the power in us that is designed to choose love, not hate. When we refuse to love and forgive, we grieve the Holy Spirit, because he is trying to move us to share his very life, to swim in the living waters of his river of love. When we refuse to forgive, we grieve God. He shakes his head sadly at us; he is deeply disappointed with us, because we are harming ourselves, our own souls. St. Augustine says that when we refuse to forgive our enemy, *we* are drinking poison and waiting for *him* to die.

Don't do that. Don't disappoint your heavenly Father and his Son your Savior and his Holy Spirit your saint-maker. What does it cost you to forgive? Only your own pride and temporary misery. But what it costs you to *refuse* to forgive, to refuse to repent of your sin of unforgiveness, is not only your temporal happiness but also your eternal happiness. For if your heart is closed to giving forgiveness to your brothers, it's also closed to receiving it from God. A closed fist can't receive gifts; closed lips can't receive kisses; closed eyes can't receive light; and a closed heart can't receive love.

Don't risk that. Don't wait for a single second more: tell God right now that you want to forgive everyone for everything. Do you say that you can't do that because you still feel hurt and resentment? If you say that, you are misunderstanding what forgiveness is. Forgiveness, like love, isn't a feeling; it's a choice, an act of the will. That's why you're responsible for it. You're not directly responsible for your feelings. But you *are* responsible for choosing to cherish those feelings, for closing your possessive hands on your feelings, for keeping them as if they were precious jewels instead of poisonous snakes. Let the snakes go. Give them up to God. Let his Holy Spirit into your soul, and he will gradually heal it. We're not commanded to feel nice to nasty people; we're commanded to love them.

GOSPEL
JOHN 6:41–51 _____

The Jews murmured about Jesus because he said, "I am the bread that came down from heaven," and they said, "Is this not Jesus, the son of Joseph? Do we not know his father and mother? Then how can he say, 'I have come down from heaven'?" Jesus answered and said to them, "Stop murmuring among yourselves. No one can come to me unless the Father who sent me draw him, and I will raise him on the last day. It is written in the prophets:

They shall all be taught by God.

Everyone who listens to my Father and learns from him comes to me. Not that anyone has seen the Father except the one who is from God; he has seen the Father. Amen, amen, I say to you, whoever believes has eternal life. I am the bread of life. Your ancestors ate the manna in the desert, but they died; this is the bread that comes down from heaven so that one may eat it and not die. I am the living bread that came down from heaven; whoever eats this bread will live forever; and the bread that I will give is my flesh for the life of the world."

The Jews of Jesus' hometown thought they knew him, but they didn't. They thought they knew who his father was, but they didn't. They said, "Is this not Jesus, the son of Joseph? Do we not know his father and mother? Then how can he say, 'I have come down from heaven'?" They thought, "He's only human, for both his parents are only human." A reasonable argument, but with a false premise. *One* of his parents is only human—his mother—but the other is divine. Joseph is not his father. God is his Father. That's the point of the virgin birth: it's not a negation of sex or procreation but an affirmation of Jesus' divine nature.

Why did Jesus' friends disbelieve in him? Part of the answer was their arrogance, their certainty about their false assumption. But another part of the answer was that they were not open to the God they already knew, God the Father, Jesus' Father, and they would not let God draw themselves to him.

Thus, Jesus says to them, "No one can come to me unless the Father who sent me draw him." God does not force us, but he draws us. He does not push us from behind, but he draws us from ahead, by the beauty of his goodness. That's how love works, and "God is love." The Bible never says, "God is irresistible force." Love is resistible because it appeals to free choice. You can remember the difference this way. There are two ways to get a drunk out of a bar. The bouncer can throw him out, or someone can draw him out, lure him out by standing outside and offering free tickets to his favorite sports team to the first person who comes.

The Bible says that God is "not wishing that any should perish but that all should come to repentance" (2 Peter 3:9). Why did many reject Jesus? Not because God stopped loving them, but because they stopped loving him. Not because God stopped drawing them, but because they stopped letting themselves be drawn by him. Divine grace and love, like human grace and love, is resistible. God is always open to us, but we are not always open to him.

Not only does God the Father draw us to his Son, but the Son also draws us to the Father. To say yes to the Son is to say yes to the Father; to say yes to the Father is to say yes to the Son. Equally, to say no to the Son is to say no to the Father, and to say no to the Father is to say no to the Son. The persons of the Trinity never work apart, always together. The three divine persons are one God, not three Gods.

Jesus next goes on to tell us the *effect* of our yes, our faith, our belief in him. That effect is so amazing, so disproportionate to its cause, so generous, that Jesus has to preface what he says about it with the formula "Amen, Amen, I say to you," which means, basically, "I mean this literally and in the strongest possible way, and I solemnly assure you and promise you that it is totally true even though it may seem impossible." The promise is this: "Whoever believes has eternal life"—that is, supernatural life, divine life, immortal life. Our little act of faith lets in the God who is eternal life and eternal joy. Our souls are like water faucets; one little turn of the faucet lets flow an unlimited water supply.

To use another analogy, the one the saints and mystics often use: our souls are like women's wombs, and God wants to impregnate us with new life, his life, eternal life; but he will not force himself upon us; he waits on our free consent, our free love and trust. This is one of the reasons why God is always called "he" and never "she" in all Christian and Jewish and Islamic literature: not because women are bypassed or ignored or inferior but because all souls are feminine to God: he impregnates them, not vice versa. And he is a gentleman; he appeals to faith, not force.

Here is still another image or analogy. In the famous painting of Jesus standing outside a door in the night and holding a lantern, there is no knob on the outside of the door. The house is our soul, and the door is our free will, and the knob is on the inside of the door.

If we let him in, he comes in and gives us his life. If not, not. It's as simple and sharp and concrete as that. That's why faith is necessary for salvation: because salvation does not just mean not going to hell; it means having his divine life, his eternal life, his heavenly life in our soul. Salvation isn't just an eternal-fire insurance policy; it's a spiritual marriage. We have to say "I do."

That "I do," that free consent, permits God to enter our souls and give us eternal life. God awaits our permission, as he awaited Mary's permission when he sent his angel to announce his intention to make her his mother. If she had not freely consented, he would not have forced her but would have gone away, and we all would then have no hope of heaven.

The eternal life that Jesus gives us—what does it look like? Well, two of its properties are sinlessness and deathlessness. The two go together because the soul and body always go together, from the moment of conception to the moment of death. God gave Adam and Eve sinlessness or innocence in their souls and deathlessness or immortality in their bodies. But they rejected him; they divorced themselves from him; and the two results were spiritual death in their souls and physical death in their bodies—because our souls and our bodies always go together. Physical death is the effect of spiritual sin as surely as breaking your bones is the effect of choosing to jump off a cliff, or as surely as scrambling your brains and your life is the effect of choosing to take drugs.

Jesus comes to us with healing for both sin and death, both soul and body. He conquers sin for us by his sacrificial death, and he conquers death for us by his Resurrection.

Jesus says in today's Gospel that he himself is the living bread, the bread of life, and that "the bread that I will give is my flesh for the life of the world." He is speaking of his own literal Body, which he gave us on the cross and which he gives us in the Eucharist.

He says, "Whoever eats this bread will live forever." To "eat" him is a work of both soul and body. It is a work of the soul because it is a work of faith and trust and hope and love; and it is a work of the body because it actually, literally, receives his Body, his Flesh and Blood, into our body in the Eucharist.

That is not a symbol; it is a reality. Bread is a mere symbol of it. All our language about spiritual reality is through physical symbols. We use matter to symbolize spirit; we do not use spirit to symbolize matter. When we say, "I see your point," we use the language of physical sight to symbolize mental understanding. When we say, "That idea never entered my mind," we use the language of physical doors and rooms to symbolize mental doors and rooms, entrances into the mind and places in the mind. When we sing to God, "How great thou art," we use the image of physical size, physical greatness, like a mountain or an ocean or a galaxy, to symbolize, in a very dim and inadequate way, yet a helpful way, the much-greater-than-physical greatness of God. We use physical quantity to symbolize spiritual quality.

God knew what he was doing when he made us creatures of both body and soul, and when he incarnated in a human body and soul, and when he died physically and rose physically, and when he instituted a visible, physical Eucharist and a visible Church. Catholic Christianity is the most physical, most material, most concrete, and most complete religion that ever existed.

When your non-Catholic friends argue that they are "spiritual, not religious," you can tell them that that's not what Jesus said; in fact, that's what the devil says. The devil is spiritual and not religious. He's spiritual because he is a pure spirit, and he hates matter because God created it. And the devil is not religious because religion is a real and personal relationship to God, a relationship of trust and love. Religion is far too concrete and too complete for the devil. The two places he hates and fears the most in all the world are two very concrete physical places: women's wombs and Catholic altars, because those are the two places where God himself makes himself present, miraculously, millions of times every day around the world, creating a new human soul whenever a man and a woman procreate a new human body and miraculously transubstantiating ordinary bread and wine into the Body and Blood of Christ in every Catholic Mass.

Please love and respect those two places above all places in the world.

TWENTIETH SUNDAY
IN ORDINARY TIME

FIRST READING
PROVERBS 9:1–6 _____

Wisdom has built her house,
    she has set up her seven columns;
she has dressed her meat, mixed her wine,
    yes, she has spread her table.
She has sent out her maidens; she calls
    from the heights out over the city:
"Let whoever is simple turn in here;
    to the one who lacks understanding, she says,
Come, eat of my food,
    and drink of the wine I have mixed!
Forsake foolishness that you may live;
    advance in the way of understanding."

Today's Old Testament reading from the Proverbs of Solomon personifies wisdom as a woman who has prepared a house and a meal for us and invites us to partake of her hospitality. It's free. Yet we hang back and prefer foolishness.

How important is wisdom? Without it we cannot be happy, without it we cannot be good, and without it we cannot be saved.

First, without wisdom we cannot be happy because wisdom is the understanding of the road to true happiness. Foolishness, or folly, which is the opposite of wisdom, is not understanding the road and traveling in the wrong direction. You can't get to the Atlantic Ocean by traveling west, or to the Pacific by traveling east, no matter how sincere you are and no matter how much you try. And spiritual roads are just as objectively true and real as physical roads. Wisdom is the discernment between the true and the false, between true food and fake foods, between food and poison. Folly mistakes food for poison and poison for food. The soul as well as the body has its foods and its poisons. Unselfish love, honest love, humble love, is the soul's true food, even when that food may not *taste* sweet at first; and selfish greed, dishonest lust, and proud complacency are the soul's poisons, even when they taste sweet.

Second, without wisdom we cannot be good because wisdom is the knowledge of what goodness truly is, what a truly good person is, what a good life really and truly is. Without wisdom, we trust and imitate wicked fools instead of saints and sages. Wisdom is not just knowledge of facts but of values, of good and evil. Wisdom is knowledge applied to life, theory applied to practice, principles applied to experience.

Third, without wisdom we cannot be saved because to be saved, we must know ourselves as sinners and God as our Savior, and wisdom is above all the understanding of those two most important realities in your life, yourself and God, who are the only two realities you can never, ever escape or avoid for even a second, either in time or in eternity.

Wisdom is like light. Without light, the world's greatest surgeon cannot perform the world's easiest operation. Without light, the world's best pilot cannot safely land the world's simplest plane. Without light, the world's best treasure hunter cannot find the world's easiest treasure. Light was the very first thing God created, because without light no one can see any other created thing. Physical light is a natural symbol of intellectual light, knowledge.

By the language we use, we ourselves implicitly admit that we have not made progress in wisdom today. It is significant that we do not spontaneously speak of "modern wisdom" but of "*ancient* wisdom" and "modern *knowledge*." We know much, much more than our ancestors did, but we are not any wiser for it. In fact, we are probably far less wise. We scorn commonsense proverbs like those in the book of Proverbs in the Bible. They bore us. They feel naïvely simplistic and unfashionably moralistic. It seems that the more we know, the less we understand.

God is the source of all wisdom, and he usually teaches us through his instruments: sages and saints, prophets and popes, and the Church. Satan hates us and feeds us his false food of faithlessness, hopelessness, and lovelessness, instead of faith and hope and love. He is the Lord of death, and he wants to starve our souls to death.

But this war is not between two equal sides. Light one little match in a large dark room. What happens? Light always conquers darkness; darkness does not conquer light.

What is wisdom's cost? Nothing. Wisdom offers herself for free—that's the point of today's reading from Proverbs. What is folly's cost? It costs us our freedom. Satan offers chains of slavery and addiction, disguised as freedom.

How do we get free from folly? How do we attain wisdom? According to the book of Proverbs, wisdom always opens her door to us, to everyone, in every age. She is available. As St. James says in his epistle, "But if any of you lacks wisdom, he should ask God who gives to all generously and ungrudgingly, and he will be given it" (James 1:5). For wisdom is an attribute of God, and God wants nothing more than to give himself to us. But we have to ask. God will not force himself upon us.

Jesus tells us: "Ask and it will be given to you; seek and you will find. . . . For everyone who asks, receives; and the one who seeks, finds" (Matt. 7:7–8). That's a divine promise. Jesus is speaking about God here, of course, and all that God is and has, which includes wisdom. As Solomon says in today's reading from Proverbs, wisdom offers herself for free.

So what's the catch? There is no catch. But there are prerequisites. In fact, there are four of them.

First, in order to ask for wisdom, we have to first of all humbly and honestly acknowledge that we lack it. As Jesus said to the Pharisees, "Those who are healthy do not need a physician, but the sick do" (Luke 5:31). So the first bit of wisdom is the wisdom to know that we lack wisdom. Just as sinners think they are saints while saints know they are sinners, so fools think they are wise while the wise know they are fools. So wisdom's first prerequisite is honest humility.

A second prerequisite for finding wisdom is to love it, to desire it, to care about it, to pursue it with passion. We have to want it, with our heart, before we can understand it with our mind.

A third prerequisite is hope: if we think it is unattainable, we will not seek it. If we are skeptics and cynics and pessimists, we have already lost the war because we have thrown down our weapons.

A fourth prerequisite is faith. If we do not believe there is such a thing as wisdom, or that God wants to give it to us, or that we can receive it, we will not seek it.

So to become wise, we need humility, love, hope, and faith, which are the four most important of all the virtues.

And faith, hope, love, and humility are not only the *prerequisites* for wisdom, the prior *causes* of wisdom: they are also the *consequences* of wisdom, the *effects* of wisdom. For the wiser we are, the more faithful, hopeful, loving, and humble we will be, since that is what wisdom teaches us. Those are the four leading lessons of wisdom, as faithlessness, hopelessness, lovelessness, and pride are the four leading lessons of foolishness.

The height of foolishness can sometimes be found in the places named for the height of wisdom. The word "philosophy" means literally "the love of wisdom," yet 75 percent of all philosophers in Western civilization classify themselves as atheists or agnostics.

The greatest philosopher of all time was a humble peasant woman who never went to college or university. One of the Blessed Virgin Mary's titles is "Seat of Wisdom" because Jesus literally sat on her lap as a baby; and Jesus is Wisdom incarnate, the eternal Wisdom of God, the Mind of God, the Word of God, the complete manifestation or revelation of God. The devil fears Mary more than any other merely human being, and even more than all God's angels. And Mary's deepest desire is to answer our prayer "Show unto us the blessed fruit of thy womb, Jesus." So pray to Mary, the Seat of Wisdom, for the gift of wisdom. She is the one described in the passage from the Proverbs of Solomon. She is the one who has prepared the feast for us.

RESPONSORIAL PSALM
PSALM 34:2–3, 4–5, 6–7

These verses are repeated from last Sunday's Mass. Perhaps there is a Psalm shortage. But because there may be a paper shortage, I will not retype the reflection on it, from last Sunday.

SECOND READING
EPHESIANS 5:15–20

Brothers and sisters: Watch carefully how you live, not as foolish persons but as wise, making the most of the opportunity, because the days are evil. Therefore, do not continue in ignorance, but try to understand what is the will of the Lord. And do not get drunk on wine, in which lies debauchery, but be filled with the Spirit, addressing one another in psalms and hymns and spiritual songs, singing and playing to the Lord in your hearts, giving thanks always and for everything in the name of our Lord Jesus Christ to God the Father.

Today's Old Testament reading from the Proverbs of Solomon was about wisdom. St. Paul, in today's epistle, adds five very specific features of wisdom.

The first and most important piece of wisdom is simply to do it, to practice it, to live it, not just to know it or even just to understand it. Wisdom is not just knowledge, not even deep and profound knowledge; wisdom is not even merely the knowledge of good and evil; it is living according to that knowledge. In fact, we can come to understand wisdom only after we live it. Thus, St. Paul writes, "Watch carefully how you live, not as foolish persons but as wise."

He also adds that this wisdom is especially important in evil times—that is, times that make wise living difficult, times that reward foolishness rather than wisdom, times that encourage pride and greed and lust rather than honest humility, detachment and poverty, and sexual integrity and purity. Times like ours.

Dorothy Day defined a good society as one that makes it easy to be good. By that definition, ours is not a good society, for it is one that makes it easy to be evil. Wisdom is all the more imperative in such times, like our time, when Christians are scorned, and like St. Paul's time, when Christians were persecuted.

The second essential quality of wisdom is a matter of the will: it is willing God's will, aligning our desires and loves with God's, praying and meaning and living the most essential of all prayers, "thy will be done." This is the key to wisdom, for as Jesus told his unbelieving neighbors, "Whoever chooses to do [God's] will shall know whether my teaching is from God or whether I speak on my own" (John 7:17). Only if we will God's will, will we understand it.

And "thy will be done," the most essential of all prayers, does not mean merely a Stoic resignation to whatever sufferings God may see fit to give us, but, much more than that, an active, cheerful trust that in God's perfect wisdom and providence "all things work for good for those who love God" (Rom. 8:28).

Nor does "thy will be done" mean merely our activity. The hymn line "Let us build the city of God" is misleading, for it is God who builds that city, and our role is first of all not our Martha-like busyness and activism but our Mary-like faith in and trust in and love of God who builds it. If you don't remember it, please read the Mary and Martha story in Luke chapter 10 as your reading assignment for today.

The third essential feature of wisdom is a pun on the word "spirit" in English: wisdom is to seek in the Holy Spirit what we usually seek in alcoholic spirits. We are to be "filled with the Spirit" instead of filled with the other kind of spirits. And what is that filling? What do we get from the Holy Spirit that we seek but do not get from drunkenness? Something deeper than mere pleasure or even happiness: it is joy.

Joy is not boring. Pleasures get boring, and sometimes so does contentment or peace or satisfaction or even happiness, but not joy. For joy is a self-forgetfulness, a kind of standing-outside-ourselves (which is the literal meaning of the word "ecstasy").

St. Thomas Aquinas says: "No man can live without joy. That is why one who does not have true spiritual joy goes over to carnal pleasures." If we do not have true joy, we become addicted to false joys. If we do not worship the true God, we inevitably worship false gods, idols, especially the idol of ourselves and our own autonomy or our own feelings. St. Augustine in his *Confessions* imagines God speaking to him in his misspent, wild youth and saying: "Seek what you seek, but it is not where you seek it. You seek happiness of life in the land of death." Augustine famously confessed to God, "You have made us for yourself and our hearts are restless till they rest in you." Wisdom knows where to find the thing we all most deeply seek.

The fourth thing St. Paul mentions about wisdom is also about its joy: it is to sing the joy we have. He does not command us to feel it—feelings cannot be commanded—but to sing it. St. Paul tells us to be "filled with the [Holy] Spirit" instead of with unholy spirits, "singing and playing to the Lord in your hearts" in "Psalms and hymns and spiritual songs."

Notice that St. Paul says "singing and playing." Music is not work; it's play. It's not a practical means to an end; it exists for itself. Play is not practical. Play is not pragmatic. Golfers don't play golf as a means to the end of getting that little ball into that little cup. They could do that much more easily and efficiently by just walking to the cup and dropping the ball in. They play for the sake of playing, just because it's fun. Play is not practical, not useful, not utilitarian, not efficient.

The word "play" also means to play a musical instrument, and the musical instrument St. Paul says we can all play is our hearts. David, the great musician, tells us not to be great musicians but just to be musicians, not professionals but amateurs (the word "amateur" means literally "lover"). He doesn't say "Make perfect music," just "Shout joyfully to God" (Ps. 66:2).

Christian joy is not a feeling. It is a fact. Jesus *is* our joy. And that is our strength. God tells us through his prophet, "Rejoicing in the LORD must be your strength" (Nehemiah 8:10). Our strength is not our feelings. You don't feel the spinach in your stomach giving your body iron and strength, but it is there anyway, because you freely chose to eat it. You don't feel Jesus all the time in your soul, but he is really there anyway. We see him with the eyes of faith, not the eyes of feelings. We must build the house of our life and our hope on the rock of fact, not the sand of feelings. Our faith must rest wholly on him, not on ourselves or on our feelings, or even on our faith. We are not called to have faith in our faith, only in him.

Why don't Catholics sing more? The embarrassingly true reason is because they don't know the joy of Jesus Christ. It's true that some of our hymns feel embarrassingly shallow and silly and sappy and soupy, but that's no excuse. Love sings. If you were in love with mathematics, you would sing the multiplication table. Chesterton wrote: "If reapers sing while reaping, why should not auditors sing while auditing and bankers while banking . . . with a thundering chorus in praise of Simple Addition: 'Up, my lads, and lift the ledgers; sleep and ease are o'er. Hear the Stars of Morning shouting: "Two and Two are Four!" Though the creeds and realms are reeling, though the sophists roar; though we weep and pawn our watches, Two And Two Are Four!'"

St. Augustine said that "he who sings, prays twice," once with the words and once with the music. Music is the language of joy. That is why we all love it so deeply.

The fifth essential feature of wisdom that St. Paul mentions is gratitude, "giving thanks always and for everything in the name of our Lord Jesus Christ to God the Father." All true religion begins with gratitude, cosmic gratitude, gratitude for everything to the Creator of everything, gratitude for sheer existence. Everything is a gift. The whole universe is a gift. Your life is a gift. You are a gift to others. Others are gifts to you.

Gratitude and thanksgiving, like joy, are not feelings. Feelings cannot be commanded, but we are commanded to give thanks always and for everything.

But gratitude for all things? Even sufferings and losses and poverty and frustration? Yes! If God is God, then God works together all things, even bad things, for the greater good. This wisdom is hard to believe, yet it is believable. St. Thérèse of Lisieux, when she was approaching death, said, "Everything is a grace."

A grace is a gift. There is what Archbishop Fulton Sheen called "white grace" and "black grace." White grace is a gift that looks like a gift, that stands in the light. Black grace is also a grace, a gift, but it does not look like a gift. It is mysterious and dark. It does not look like God's love. But it is. Like the sufferings of Job. But God himself assures us that this, too, is a grace, a gift, something we need for our greater good in the end.

We don't see that, but we can believe it because we believe our heavenly Father, who is infinite power, infinite love, and infinite wisdom. We don't worship a God who is weak or wicked or weak-minded. Our wisdom is to trust God's wisdom, totally, and thus to thank him for everything. He turned even our greatest loss, death, into our greatest gain, resurrection. He will do the same to everything else if we only love and trust him. That promise sounds incredible, but the alternative is even more incredible: that God is not God. And to believe that is definitely *not* wisdom.

GOSPEL

JOHN 6:51–58 _____

Jesus said to the crowds: "I am the living bread that came down from heaven; whoever eats this bread will live forever; and the bread that I will give is my flesh for the life of the world."

The Jews quarreled among themselves, saying, "How can this man give us his flesh to eat?" Jesus said to them, "Amen, amen, I say to you, unless you eat the flesh of the Son of Man and drink his blood, you do not have life within you. Whoever eats my flesh and drinks my blood has eternal life, and I will raise him on the last day. For my flesh is true food, and my blood is true drink. Whoever eats my flesh and drinks my blood remains in me and I in him. Just as the living Father sent me and I have life because of the Father, so also the one who feeds on me will have life because of me. This is the bread that came down from heaven. Unlike your ancestors who ate and still died, whoever eats this bread will live forever."

Sometimes the most accurate and true understanding of a controversial saying is to be found in its opponents. For instance, when the Jews tried to stone Jesus for blasphemy when he said, "Before Abraham came to be, I AM" (John 8:58), using the sacred name that God alone can claim, the word spoken to Moses from the Burning Bush, they understood clearly and truly that there were only two possibilities here: either Jesus was God himself and deserved their adoration and worship, or he was the worst blasphemer in human history and deserved to be executed.

Similarly, Jesus' saying in today's Gospel, the thing he says in the first sentence of today's reading and then repeats word for word in the last sentence—namely, that "I am the living bread that came down from heaven; whoever eats this bread will live forever"—is either a most wonderful truth or a most horrible lie. And Jesus' enemies understood that, both his enemies among the Jews who heard him and said, "How can this man give us his flesh to eat?" and his enemies later among the Roman pagans who accused Christians of cannibalism because they took literally Jesus' saying "Unless you eat the flesh of the Son of Man and drink his blood, you do not have life within you."

Both sets of enemies were right! There is no way a mere man can give us his flesh, his body, to eat without making us cannibals. Either that man is insane, or he is not a mere man. If he is not the Lord, he is a liar or a lunatic.

Of course, there is a comfortable middle position: that he didn't really say it, or that he didn't really mean it; that it's only an exaggeration, a figure of speech, a symbol; that of course he cannot literally give us his own Body and Blood and thereby give us eternal life, for no mere man can give us eternal life, and it's easy to think that Jesus is not literally God but only the best of men.

And if we do get eternal life somehow, we think it must be in a purely spiritual way, an interior way, a way in the spirit and mind and will, and not also in the body, not anything like eating something that looks like bread.

How literally did he mean it? Well, if you were one of his disciples, and you stood under his cross, and you had faith in him, and a drop of the Precious Blood of God himself fell on you, you would have the forgiveness of sins and the entrance to heaven and eternal life from that drop of blood. But if you stood under the good thief's cross by mistake and a drop of his blood fell on you, that would not forgive your sins or open to you the gates of heaven or give you eternal life, even if you had just as much faith and goodwill as you had when you stood under the cross of Christ.

Jesus healed the woman with a lifelong hemorrhage of blood because she touched the hem of his garment; but if she had touched the hem of St. Peter's garment instead, even if she had faith, her faith alone would not have healed her.

We need faith, yes, but we also need the reality of the object of faith to be present. In order to get Romeo as her husband, Juliet has to have faith and trust in Romeo and accept his offer to marry her; but she also has to have the real Romeo there to marry her! She can't get married by just having faith without having Romeo.

How do we get Jesus' Body and Blood? Well, he gives it to us in two places: on the cross and in the Eucharist. Bible-believing Protestants believe that we get it literally from the cross but not literally in the Eucharist. In fact, it's almost the opposite. The eating is not literal on the cross, but it is in the Eucharist. In fact, the Greek word Jesus uses for "eat" here, when he is referring to the Eucharist, means "chew" or "chomp" or "masticate." He deliberately chooses the most literal word he can.

Both Protestant Christian believers and non-Christian skeptical unbelievers are right when they are shocked at the Catholic belief that we literally eat the Body of God incarnate and drink his Blood in the Eucharist. Protestants who do not believe in the literal Real Presence of Christ in the Eucharist, the whole Christ, "Body and Blood, Soul and Divinity," interpret the Eucharist as just a holy symbol, and if they are logical they must think Catholics are the world's worst idolaters, because they are bowing down to bread and worshiping wine, adoring the creature as if it were the Creator. That would be so stupid that it would be insane. And unbelievers must think also that we are insane, for a second reason: for believing that this man Jesus, this fully human being, who was born from a mother's womb and who died on a cross, is literally divine, literally God, eternal and all-powerful and perfect.

You see, the two scandals are one: the scandal of the Incarnation and the scandal of the Eucharist—that this man Jesus is literally God, and his death on the cross literally gives us eternal life, and that what we eat in the Eucharist is not bread and wine, as it appears to be, but truly and literally his Body and Blood.

To be outraged at these two shocking claims is at least to understand how shocking they are. If we believe them without being shocked, we are missing something, and we need to learn that something from Jesus' enemies.

And if we believe them only because we first water them down to something only symbolic but not literally true, and if we think we are still Catholic Christians, we are more deluded than those unbelievers. That's like claiming to be a Marxist and not believing in a revolution, or claiming to be a Muslim but not believing Muhammad was a prophet.

Unbelief is not admirable, but there's something admirable in at least understanding what you don't believe; there's nothing admirable in not understanding what you do believe.

What is it that you will eat when you receive Holy Communion? That is not literally bread and symbolically Jesus. It is literally Jesus and only symbolically bread. It is not the literal bread that was made on earth; it is the symbolic "bread" that came down from heaven. What you will literally chew is God. It is not a thing but a person, a divine person: your Savior, your only hope of heaven, your eternal life.

TWENTY-FIRST SUNDAY
IN ORDINARY TIME

FIRST READING

JOSHUA 24:1–2A, 15–17, 18B _____

Joshua gathered together all the tribes of Israel at Shechem, summoning their elders, their leaders, their judges, and their officers. When they stood in ranks before God, Joshua addressed all the people: "If it does not please you to serve the LORD, decide today whom you will serve, the gods your fathers served beyond the River or the gods of the Amorites in whose country you are now dwelling. As for me and my household, we will serve the LORD."

But the people answered, "Far be it from us to forsake the LORD for the service of other gods. For it was the LORD, our God, who brought us and our fathers up out of the land of Egypt, out of a state of slavery. He performed those great miracles before our very eyes and protected us along our entire journey and among the peoples through whom we passed. Therefore we also will serve the LORD, for he is our God."

Today's Old Testament reading is about the gift of free will that God has given us. It is a gift that we sometimes would like to give back, because it gives us an overwhelming responsibility, but we cannot. We are not free to undo this gift of freedom because it is part of our very being, our human nature, our essence.

The historical situation is that Moses has just died, and Joshua, Moses' successor, is about to lead God's chosen people into their promised inheritance, the Holy Land. Joshua bears the same name as Jesus, or Yeshua. It means "Savior" or "God saves."

And Joshua's first words as leader of God's people make the same point as the first words of Jesus in John's Gospel. It is a question. Jesus' formulation of the question is simple. He asks his prospective disciples, "What are you looking for?" (John 1:38). What do you seek? What do you love? What do you choose? He is questioning their hearts. What is the deepest desire of their hearts? Is it God, and all that God is—truth and justice and righteousness and holiness and goodness and mercy and love? Or is it money, sex, power, autonomy, control, comfort, kicks, honor, fame, glory, or any of the many other things that life holds and that many people pursue as their greatest good, their god, their idol? Perhaps their idol is winning the prize on the TV show candidly named *American Idol*.

Joshua asks the same question. The Jews had received God's definitive revelation of his will, the Ten Commandments; and the first commandment, the one Jesus said is the first and greatest commandment, was "You shall not have other gods besides me" (Exod. 20:3). Now Joshua is asking them to choose to obey or to disobey that first and greatest commandment. He says, "Decide today whom you will serve": this God or other gods.

God established a covenant with his people, and the best and fullest example of a covenant is marriage. Joshua now demands an answer to God's spiritual marriage proposal. He gives them many other options besides God: the gods of Egypt, or the many gods of the many religions of the pagans who lived in the land they were about to enter and conquer and cleanse. He does not give them a choice between choosing and not choosing; he gives them a choice between God and everything else, every other god, every idol. "Decide today whom you will serve. . . . As for me and my household, we will serve the LORD."

That is the single most momentous, most important, most fundamental choice that every single human being who ever lives has to make. That is the choice that has total consequences both in this life and afterward, the choice that changes the ultimate point of everything in this life and the one that changes our address for eternity.

Only God sees the choice each of us makes in the deepest depth of our hearts. We do not know what choice any other person makes in the deepest depths of their heart, so we do not know how many will reside in each of the two possible eternal addresses, heaven and hell. When Jesus' disciples asked him, "Lord, will only a few people be saved?" Jesus replied simply, "Strive to enter through the narrow door" (Luke 13:23–24). We can know, however, what choice we make.

There are many aspects of this choice that are not clear. How much knowledge is necessary? How explicit does repentance of sin have to be? How much does God work outside his visible Church and outside his sacraments? How powerful is God's anonymous working in the souls of those who do not know him clearly? That is not clear. But what Joshua says here is clear—it is very, very clear—for us, who are part of the people Joshua is addressing and part of the same people Jesus addressed. It is very clear and very simple—*uncomfortably* clear and simple for those who want to compromise and shuffle and negotiate and "nuance" and relativize and subjectivize and avoid any total and absolute commitment to anything, even God.

Our conscience speaks the same words spoken by Joshua and Jesus: "Decide today whom you will serve." "What are you looking for?" Is it the true God, or is it another god? Is it the God who designed and created you in his image, or is it a god that you designed and created in your image, a "designer god," a god for you to wear like designer jeans? Do you want reality or fantasy? The truth or lies? Light or darkness? Spiritual life or spiritual death? Heaven or hell?

RESPONSORIAL PSALM
PSALM 34:2–3, 16–17, 18–19, 20–21 _____

R. (9a) **Taste and see the goodness of the Lord.**

I will bless the LORD at all times;
   his praise shall be ever in my mouth.
Let my soul glory in the LORD;
   the lowly will hear me and be glad.

The Lord has eyes for the just,
and ears for their cry.
The Lord confronts the evildoers,
to destroy remembrance of them from the earth.

When the just cry out, the Lord hears them,
and from all their distress he rescues them.
The Lord is close to the brokenhearted;
and those who are crushed in spirit he saves.

Many are the troubles of the just one,
but out of them all the Lord delivers him;
he watches over all his bones;
not one of them shall be broken.

Why does the Psalmist bless the Lord and praise the Lord and glory in the Lord? Because "the Lord has eyes for the just, and ears for their cry." Because "when the just cry out, the Lord hears them, and from all their distress he rescues them." Because "the Lord is close to the brokenhearted; and those who are crushed in spirit he saves." Because "many are the troubles of the just one, but out of them all the Lord delivers him." Because "he watches over all his bones; not one of them shall be broken."

But this does not seem to be true. Terrible things happen. Tragedies happen. Injustice is done. Good people are crushed, and bad people crush them. How can the Psalmist ignore the facts? Is this Psalm realism or fantasy?

It's realism, because it admits that "many are the troubles of the just one." It admits that the just cry out in distress. It admits that there are many brokenhearted people in this world, people whose hearts have been broken by their parents or by their children or by their friends or by their enemies. It admits that many people are "crushed in spirit." It does not ignore or deny human injustice and human suffering. Exactly the opposite: it addresses that problem directly. It dares to ask the great and difficult question of where God is in this world so full of injustice and suffering at all times and places in history.

And it answers that question: God is here. He is not an absentee landlord. He is not far away or deaf or blind. He is watching over his people. He is in control. Not a hair falls from our head, not a sparrow falls from the sky, not a person falls out of this world by dying without God's knowledge and permission and control.

God is not doing any of the bad stuff, but he is permitting it. He could stop it. He could stop anything, suddenly and miraculously. But he only does that very rarely, as when he parted the Red Sea for the Israelites to cross it, or when he performs a miraculous healing. Many people have experienced miracles, but no one has ever experienced continuous miracles, a daily diet of miracles. Without miracles, we all get both good things and bad things from life, from this world. Why? If God does not do evil or love evil, why does he allow evil?

God deliberately allows both kinds of evil, the moral evils we commit and the physical evils we suffer. He allows us to commit the moral evils of injustices and sins in order to preserve human free will, and he allows the physical evils of sufferings and tragedies in order to preserve the order of nature instead of performing a miracle a minute to wipe out all suffering on earth.

That is the first thing he is doing about evils. And the second thing he is doing, at the very same time, is delivering us out of all those evils—all evils, both sins and sufferings. But he is doing it gradually and through natural causes, including our own efforts and other people's help as well as through the prayers and intercessions of both our friends who are living and our friends who are dead—namely, the saints. It is God who is behind all our deliverances from evil, from both kinds of evil. He is really there, really present, really acting, even when he is using his intermediaries, just as the general of an army is really acting when he is commanding his soldiers to attack, and just as a writer is really acting when he is using a pen or a keyboard to write, and just as a swordsman is really acting even though it is the sword that is doing the cutting.

God is acting in every good, in every deliverance from evil. Jesus told us to pray for that. The last petition of the Lord's Prayer is "deliver us from evil." There's a lot of stuff before that in the prayer, but all that is also about God delivering us from evil. "Hallowed be thy name" delivers us from the evil of not adoring God. "Thy kingdom come" delivers us from the devil's kingdom. "Thy will be done" delivers us from our short-sighted, self-willed selfishness. "Give us this day our daily bread," which means "give us what we really need," delivers us from our own foolish mistakes about what we really need. "Forgive us our trespasses" delivers us from both self-righteousness and despair—it delivers us from self-righteousness in confessing our trespasses, and it delivers us from despair in hoping for his forgiveness. And it also delivers us from hatred of our neighbors, because we are commanded to pray that God not forgive us if we do not forgive them. Those are all the most serious evils in life, and we are told to pray for God's deliverance from them. Then comes the last petition, which asks God for deliverance from all other evils too.

God promises to answer our prayers if they are in accordance with his will, and we know that all that we ask for in the Lord's Prayer *is* his will because it is he who gave us that prayer. God does not ask us to pray for what he is not intending to give us. He asks us to pray for the things that he is intending to give us.

But why does he wait? Why does he withhold so many good things from us until we pray for them? Because he knows that we need prayer even more than we need the things we pray for.

God is very patient. We are not. We live among instant coffee, instant fast foods, instant internet, and instant obedience from our machines, so we want instant answers from God, instant solutions, instant deliverance. But God is not a machine. God is always working out our deliverance from evil, but he does not do that with the same timing and in the same way that we do most of our work today—namely, by technology, by pushing buttons. God is not a computer or a computer operator, and his world is not a giant computer. He is a father, our heavenly Father, and we are his children, not his machines, and we children, like plants, grow gradually and attain wisdom and maturity through many ups and downs, many mistakes and many bumps in the road. Life is a mystery to be lived, not a puzzle to be solved. God is a dramatist, not a mathematician.

God is patient, and he asks us to be too. God does not run a fast-food restaurant. He is a French chef, and he is preparing an incredibly delicious gourmet dinner for us. Deliverance, like gourmet cooking, is a long process. We need to be patient and faithful here in this world of appetizers for the heavenly banquet. The main course is yet to come. God delivers our deliverance by means of many delivery trucks, and the definitive delivery truck is death, which is the prince's golden chariot that he sends to take Cinderella out of her ashes and into his castle and into a spiritual marriage between Beauty and the Beast, between God and man. Life is indeed a fairy tale, but we don't get to "they all lived happily ever after" here, because we're not at the castle yet, and the road to it is very unpredictable and mysterious. We have to trust the chariot driver, who is our Lord, and his horses, which are his angels, and his chariot, which is the Church.

We grow stronger, holier, wiser, and more mature when we suffer than when we do not. If this were not so, God would certainly not allow the sufferings in the first act of his drama before the deliverance comes in the second act; for his compassion is far greater than ours, not less. C.S. Lewis writes in *A Grief Observed*, "Is it credible that such extremities of torture should be necessary for us? Well, take your choice. The tortures occur. If they are unnecessary, then there is no God or a bad one. . . . For no even moderately good Being could possibly inflict or permit them if they weren't."

St. Augustine says, "Since God is the highest good, he would not allow any evil to exist in his works unless his omnipotence and goodness were such as to bring good even out of evil." Love always seeks the maximum good, the maximum happiness, the maximum joy of the beloved.

The eyes of the body and the eyes of the mind do not see what is happening behind the scenes of act one, and who is allowing our pain, and why, but the eyes of faith do. Doctor God is performing heart surgery on us. In the words of T.S. Eliot, "The Wounded Surgeon plies the steel." Anyone who watched an operation for the first time and knew nothing at all about surgery would conclude that the surgeon was an evil, sadistic torturer. But, in fact, he is a healer, a savior, a deliverer. Our divine surgeon is not a Dracula, the Antichrist who takes our blood; he is the Christ who gives us his own blood. Salvation is a blood transfusion and a heart transplant operation. It's a bloody mess, that horrible sight on Calvary; but it's his kiss of life, not the kiss of death. His five wounds are lips, and they speak the single word behind all the words and deeds of the man whose name is the Word of God. The word is love.

SECOND READING

Ephesians 5:21–32
(or Ephesians 5:2a, 25–32) _____

Brothers and sisters: Be subordinate to one another out of reverence for Christ. Wives should be subordinate to their husbands as to the Lord. For the husband is head of his wife just as Christ is head of the church, he himself the savior of the body. As the church is subordinate to Christ, so wives should be subordinate to their husbands in everything. Husbands, love your wives, even as Christ loved the church and handed himself over for her to sanctify her, cleansing her by the bath of water with the word, that he might present to himself the church in splendor, without spot or wrinkle or any such thing, that she might be holy and without blemish. So also husbands should love their wives as their own bodies. He who loves his wife loves himself. For no one hates his own flesh but rather nourishes and cherishes it, even as Christ does the church, because we are members of his body.

For this reason a man shall leave his father and his mother
  and be joined to his wife,
 and the two shall become one flesh.
This is a great mystery, but I speak in reference to Christ and the church.

_____

There is no passage in the Bible that is more misunderstood and hated and avoided than today's epistle. In fact, the Church even allows us to avoid the single most embarrassing and most disbelieved verse in the entire Bible by offering the option of a shorter version of the passage that does not contain those offensive words: "Wives should be subordinate to their husbands." But before we throw the Bible into the garbage, let's understand just what it is saying.

There are at least seven reasons why this passage definitely does not teach the male chauvinism that so-called feminists accuse it of.

First of all, the translation is misleading. The Greek verb *hypotasso* means to "submit" or "surrender" rather than "be subordinate." It's a "do" word, not a "be" word. Submission or surrender is something you choose to do, but subordination is something you are, your status. It says you are inferior. The Bible does not say that women are inferior. It says, on the contrary, from the very beginning that "the image of God" is "male and female" (Gen. 1:27), not just male. The masculine pronoun for God does not mean God is male, for "male" is a biological term and God has no biological body.

Second—and this is the essential point—St. Paul does not say simply that wives are to submit to husbands. That is only half the picture. The two halves of the picture are, first, St. Paul's instructions to wives, and second, his instructions to husbands. These two parts of the picture come after, and are relative to, the whole picture, which comes first. And that whole "big picture" is that husbands and wives are to submit *to each other*. That is the first thing; that is the context that justifies the wife submitting to her husband. Men are equally commanded to a surrender or submission to their wives. Each of the spouses is not to insist on having his or her own way but is to serve the other.

There are three kinds of marriages, and only one is happy: the one where both spouses serve each other. The other two kinds are the kind where both are selfish, which is unstable and constantly at war, and the kind where one is selfish and the other is unselfish, which may be stable but is unhappy because it is oppressive. Please don't get married if your motive is to find happiness; get married only if your motive is to *give* happiness. And marry someone whose motive is the same as yours.

Third, St. Paul does not say that women in general are to submit to men in general but that wives are to submit to their husbands. Marriage is a unique relationship. It's a God-given invention, a pre-existing thing, like an elephant. We don't have to ride on it, but if we choose to do so, we have to conform to its structure. It's not a car or a boat; God invented it, not us. That's why we can't reinvent it so as to include divorce or spouse swapping or time limits or same-sex marriage or group marriage or polygamy. We can indeed invent all those things, and we have done so; but that's not marriage, any more than a car is an elephant.

Fourth, St. Paul gives equally difficult tasks to both wives and husbands. Husbands are to love their wives "*as Christ loved the church.*" Christ did not oppress or boss around the Church; he sacrificed his life for her. So men, please do not marry any woman you do not want to give your whole self and your whole life to, including not just your love but also your time and your fertility. Hold back nothing; contracept nothing. As a priest must give his whole self to the Church, you must give your whole self to your wife, as Christ gave himself wholly to his spouse, his Church.

Fifth, husbands are to love their wives "as their own bodies. He who loves his wife loves himself." For the two have become "one flesh," one body, one self. It is an altogether unique human relationship. The head is not the *boss* of the body, or the CEO of the body; the head is the *head* of the body, an organ *of* the body, *for* the body, relative to the body. Christ is not the CEO of the Church; Christ is the *Head* of the Church. And the Church is not the business of Christ or the possession of Christ or the organization of Christ; she is the organism of Christ. Christ showed what his headship meant when he washed his disciples' feet and when he died on the cross for them. The Church is not Christ's business but Christ's Body. The wife is not the husband's possession but his body, and the husband is not her owner but her head. And she is his heart.

Sixth, the standard and touchstone of submission is Christ. Wives are to submit to their husbands "*as to the Lord.*" When we submit to Christ, does he demean us or oppress us or enslave us? No, he gives himself to us; he sacrifices himself for us.

Seventh, the word "mission" is in the word "submission." Wives are to submit to their husbands' *mission*, which is to be like Christ to them. If husbands demean and oppress them, wives are *not* to submit to that very un-Christlike mission.

The deepest and fullest point of the whole passage is that this whole picture of Christian marriage makes no sense outside of Christ. Christ is the meaning of marriage. St. Paul concludes his treatise on marriage by saying that "this [that is, human marriage] is a great mystery, but I speak in reference to Christ and the church." Human marriage is relative to divine marriage, not vice versa. The relation between husbands and wives is relative to the relation between Christ and his Church, his Bride, not vice versa. The relation between Christ and his Church is not an image or copy of marriage; marriage is an image or copy of it. The literal and primary and fullest meaning of marriage is the love-relationship between Christ and his Church, his Body—which is us. And that relationship, that marriage, is nothing less than the whole meaning and purpose of life, our greatest good, our final end, and our supreme joy.

The Bible is the only book that begins at the absolute beginning, the first event in history, the creation, and ends at the absolute end; and the absolute end, the last event in history, is the eternal marriage between God and man, between Christ and his Church. Check it out. Read the last chapter of the Bible. You're in it.

And if you're married, you're even now in the world's most complete image of it and the world's most important vocation. Society's success, sanity, and survival does not depend on princes or presidents or philanthropists or philosophers, or even priests, as much as it depends on marriages. Marriage between man and woman was the first sacrament God instituted, in the Garden of Eden, and marriage between God and man, Christ and the Church, is the last and culminating event of human history.

656

GOSPEL
JOHN 6:60–69 _____

Many of Jesus' disciples who were listening said, "This saying is hard; who can accept it?" Since Jesus knew that his disciples were murmuring about this, he said to them, "Does this shock you? What if you were to see the Son of Man ascending to where he was before? It is the spirit that gives life, while the flesh is of no avail. The words I have spoken to you are Spirit and life. But there are some of you who do not believe." Jesus knew from the beginning the ones who would not believe and the one who would betray him. And he said, "For this reason I have told you that no one can come to me unless it is granted him by my Father."

As a result of this, many of his disciples returned to their former way of life and no longer accompanied him. Jesus then said to the Twelve, "Do you also want to leave?" Simon Peter answered him, "Master, to whom shall we go? You have the words of eternal life. We have come to believe and are convinced that you are the Holy One of God."

_____

Jesus is shocking. If you are not shocked by Jesus, you're misunderstanding him. The world's natural response to Christ's teachings is "This saying is hard; who can accept it?" In John's Gospel, these words came not from Jesus' enemies but from many of his disciples. Many of his disciples still protest today against the shocking thing that Jesus said on this occasion about eating his Body and drinking his Blood. These protesters call themselves "Protestants."

Jesus' response to this protest is: "Does this shock you? What if you were to see the Son of Man ascending?" In other words, if I am able to shock you by ascending through the sky to heaven, I am also able to shock you by turning bread and wine into my own Body and Blood. I am "love divine, all loves excelling." Divine love is shocking. It always exceeds our expectations. "What eye has not seen, and ear has not heard, and what has not entered the human heart, what God has prepared for those who love him" (1 Cor. 2:9).

Jesus next said, "It is the Spirit that gives life, while the flesh is of no avail. The words I have spoken to you are Spirit and life." The words Jesus had just spoken were about his Body and Blood, not about his Spirit. So why did he add these words about the Spirit? Because the faith to believe these shocking words is a gift of God the Holy Spirit.

Faith is first of all a gift of grace that comes from God's free will even before it is a choice that comes from our free will. God's grace always comes first. But it does not bypass our free will. It uses our free will; it turns our free will on, not off. Grace does not bypass nature or subvert nature or demean nature; grace perfects nature, especially human nature, and human nature includes free will as part of its very essence. What does not have free will is not human; it is either a machine or an animal.

So we are responsible for the free choice to believe, and we cannot give the excuse that God just has not given us the grace to believe yet. It's not *before* we believe, but *after* we believe, that we need to know that faith is a grace, a gift of God, so that we don't take credit for what is in fact a gift. As St. Thérèse said, "*Everything* is grace." Our very existence is a grace.

God gives each of us the free choice to believe him or to leave him, to be faithful or unfaithful to him. Faith is not a mere idea, a mere opinion. Faith is the trust that says yes to God's proposal of spiritual marriage. Saying yes to that offer changes our whole life, just as earthly marriage does. Faith is not just a belief but a choice, and not just a choice but an act, and not just an act of the mind but also of the body. Many of Jesus' disciples made their choice with their legs: they walked away from Jesus, because they were shocked and scandalized by his words about the Eucharist. That is what Luther and Calvin and many others did. The Twelve also made their choice with their legs: they stayed. When Jesus asked the Twelve, "Do you also want to leave?" Simon Peter, who consistently spoke for all of the twelve Apostles, answered him, "Master, to whom shall we go? You have the words of eternal life." That's the simplest and best reason for being a Catholic.

One of the great Catholic novelists of the twentieth century, Walker Percy, was asked to write an answer to the question why he was a Catholic. He responded, simply, "What else is there?" St. Peter must have inspired that answer.

TWENTY-SECOND SUNDAY
IN ORDINARY TIME

FIRST READING
Deuteronomy 4:1–2, 6–8 _____

Moses said to the people: "Now, Israel, hear the statutes and decrees which I am teaching you to observe, that you may live, and may enter in and take possession of the land which the Lord, the God of your fathers, is giving you. In your observance of the commandments of the Lord, your God, which I enjoin upon you, you shall not add to what I command you nor subtract from it. Observe them carefully, for thus will you give evidence of your wisdom and intelligence to the nations, who will hear of all these statutes and say, 'This great nation is truly a wise and intelligent people.' For what great nation is there that has gods so close to it as the Lord, our God, is to us whenever we call upon him? Or what great nation has statutes and decrees that are as just as this whole law which I am setting before you today?"

RESPONSORIAL PSALM
Psalm 15:2–3, 3–4, 4–5 _____

R. (1a) **The one who does justice will live in the presence of the Lord.**

Whoever walks blamelessly and does justice;
who thinks the truth in his heart
and slanders not with his tongue.

Who harms not his fellow man,
nor takes up a reproach against his neighbor;

by whom the reprobate is despised,
  while he honors those who fear the LORD.

Who lends not his money at usury
  and accepts no bribe against the innocent.
Whoever does these things
  shall never be disturbed.

SECOND READING
JAMES 1:17–18, 21B–22, 27 _____

Dearest brothers and sisters: All good giving and every perfect gift is from above, coming down from the Father of lights, with whom there is no alteration or shadow caused by change. He willed to give us birth by the word of truth that we may be a kind of firstfruits of his creatures.

Humbly welcome the word that has been planted in you and is able to save your souls.

Be doers of the word and not hearers only, deluding yourselves.

Religion that is pure and undefiled before God and the Father is this: to care for orphans and widows in their affliction and to keep oneself unstained by the world.

GOSPEL
MARK 7:1–8, 14–15, 21–23 _____

When the Pharisees with some scribes who had come from Jerusalem gathered around Jesus, they observed that some of his disciples ate their meals with unclean, that is, unwashed, hands.—For the Pharisees and, in fact, all Jews, do not eat without carefully washing their hands, keeping the tradition of the elders. And on coming from the marketplace they do not eat without purifying themselves. And there are many other things that they have traditionally observed, the purification of cups and jugs and kettles and beds.—So the Pharisees and scribes questioned him, "Why do your disciples not follow the tradition of the elders but instead eat a meal with unclean hands?" He responded, "Well did Isaiah prophesy about you hypocrites, as it is written:

> *This people honors me with their lips,*
>   *but their hearts are far from me;*
> *in vain do they worship me,*
>   *teaching as doctrines human precepts.*

You disregard God's commandment but cling to human tradition."

He summoned the crowd again and said to them, "Hear me, all of you, and understand. Nothing that enters one from outside can defile that person; but the things that come out from within are what defile.

"From within people, from their hearts, come evil thoughts, unchastity, theft, murder, adultery, greed, malice, deceit, licentiousness, envy, blasphemy, arrogance, folly. All these evils come from within and they defile."

(Sometimes the four Scripture readings for the day make four quite different points, sometimes there is overlapping of two, sometimes of three, but today all four overlap nicely and can best be explored together in a single reflection.) In today's reading from the Old Testament, Moses is speaking to Israel about the Law that God gave them, and he says, "The nations, who will hear of all these statutes and say, 'This great nation is truly a wise and intelligent people.' For what great nation is there that has gods so close to it as the LORD, our God, is to us whenever we call upon him? Or what great nation has statutes and decrees that are as just as this whole law which I am setting before you today?"

The Ten Commandments are the most admired and influential law in all of human history. Pascal says of the Jews:

> The law by which this people is governed is at once the oldest law in the world,
> the most perfect, and the only one which has been continuously observed in

any state. . . . Even before the word "law" was in use among the Greeks, the Jews had received their Law from God and had been observing it for nearly a thousand years without interruption. I find it strange that the first law in the world should also happen to be the most perfect. . . . But this law is at the same time most severe and rigorous. . . . Thus it is a really amazing thing that this Law has been constantly preserved for so many centuries by a people as rebellious and impatient as this one, while all other states have from time to time changed their laws, although they were very much more lenient. . . . The sincerity of the Jews has lovingly and faithfully handed on this book in which Moses declares that they have been ungrateful toward God throughout their lives, that he knows they will be still more so after his death, and that he calls heaven and earth to witness against them that he told them so often.

In giving the Law, God said through his prophet Moses to his people, "You shall not add to what I command you nor subtract from it." God said the same thing in the last chapter of the last book of the Bible through the prophet St. John: "I warn everyone who hears the prophetic words in this book: if anyone adds to them, God will add to him the plagues described in this book, and if anyone takes away from the words in this prophetic book, God will take away his share in the tree of life and in the holy city described in this book" (Rev. 22:18–19).

Today's Gospel shows us an example of adding to God's law, an example of false prophets saying "Thus says the Lord" for merely human laws. Jesus says to the Pharisees, "You disregard God's commandment but cling to human tradition." Suppose we believed these words of Jesus and dared to apply them to our contemporary lawmakers, who enforce human laws that contradict God's laws, especially, today, God's laws about sexuality. Would we get a hearing in public, or would we be censored and punished for "hate speech"?

Interpreting God's laws and applying them to different situations is not the same as adding to God's laws or subtracting from them. Claiming merely human authority for merely human laws is not adding to God's laws, but claiming divine authority for merely human laws is. And changing or removing bad human laws is not subtracting from God's laws, but changing or removing God's laws is.

The Church clearly distinguishes divine laws from human laws. The Church has many man-made laws, such as laws of fasting and liturgical laws, and laws about whether priests can marry; these laws have changed and can continue to change because they are not divine laws but human laws. But the Church cannot change God's laws, no matter how unpopular they are. That's why she cannot bless any of the sacraments of the "sexual revolution" such as fornication, sodomy, abortion, contraception, divorce, gay marriage, or transgenderism.

In speaking of the "development of doctrine" in the Church, St. John Henry Newman explained the difference between genuine growths from within and changes from without by either additions or subtractions. The growths from within are like leaves on a tree or the natural growth of an organism, while the changes from without are alien, like barnacles on the hull of a ship or cancer cells that add harmful things to the organism (these are both additions), or like amputations or accidents or diseases that take away the organism's natural powers and systems such as walking or breathing or circulation (these are subtractions).

Which are worse, additions or subtractions? Subtractions. Not because they are much more pervasive and popular today but also because additions to divine law only pollute the genuine law, while subtractions destroy it. It's like the difference between polluted water and no water, or between foggy light and darkness, or between adding counterfeit money to genuine money—if someone adds counterfeit money, you may have confusion between the counterfeit and the genuine money, but if someone steals the genuine money, you can't buy anything.

Today's Psalm verses are an example of a natural growth from within. They are not additions but interpretations of the divine law. The Psalmist lists ten specific examples of moral virtues, of obedience to God's commandments. They do not quite correlate one for one to the Ten Commandments, but they can all be derived from the Ten Commandments as immediate, obvious, and natural consequences of them. They describe the person who loves and lives the divine law: "Whoever walks blamelessly and does justice; who thinks the truth in his heart and slanders not with his tongue. Who harms not his fellow man, nor takes up a reproach against his neighbor; by whom the reprobate is despised, while he honors those who fear the LORD. Who lends not his money at usury and accepts no bribe against the innocent." That's ten things (count them), all derived from the Ten Commandments.

St. James, in today's epistle, makes the very practical point that *obeying* the law of God is much more important than *knowing* it. He says, "Be doers of the word and not hearers only, deluding yourselves." We can easily deceive ourselves into thinking we are holy because we know and understand and admire God's law even when we don't live it. We often live in our imagination instead of in the real world, and we think we are obeying God's law simply because we imagine ourselves doing it.

St. James gives two examples of obeying the law and practicing real religion: "Religion that is pure and undefiled before God and the Father is this: to care for orphans and widows in their affliction and to keep oneself unstained by the world."

If we look at today's world and even much of today's religion, we see that half its people specialize in the first of those two things and the other half specialize in the second. Those who focus on caring are usually called the Left, or the "blue states," while those who focus on keeping unstained and pure are called the Right, or the "red states." The first usually follow the donkey, and the second follow the elephant. But the book of Revelation describes Christians as those who "follow the Lamb *wherever* he goes" (Rev. 14:4). That's why they are hospitable to both the unborn and the born, both natives and immigrants, both nationalists and internationalists, both women and men, both black people and white people, both traditionalists and progressivists, both past and future.

TWENTY-THIRD SUNDAY
IN ORDINARY TIME

FIRST READING

Isaiah 35:4–7a _____

Thus says the Lord:
Say to those whose hearts are frightened:
    Be strong, fear not!
Here is your God,
    he comes with vindication;
with divine recompense
    he comes to save you.
Then will the eyes of the blind be opened,
    the ears of the deaf be cleared;
then will the lame leap like a stag,
    then the tongue of the mute will sing.
Streams will burst forth in the desert,
    and rivers in the steppe.
The burning sands will become pools,
    and the thirsty ground, springs of water.

RESPONSORIAL PSALM

Psalm 146:7, 8–9, 9–10 _____

R. (1b) **Praise the Lord, my soul!**
or: R. **Alleluia.**

The God of Jacob keeps faith forever,
  secures justice for the oppressed,
  gives food to the hungry.
The LORD sets captives free.

The LORD gives sight to the blind;
  the LORD raises up those who were bowed down.
The LORD loves the just;
  the LORD protects strangers.

The fatherless and the widow the LORD sustains,
  but the way of the wicked he thwarts.
The LORD shall reign forever;
  your God, O Zion, through all generations. Alleluia.

Today's Old Testament reading is about fear. God tells Isaiah his prophet, "Say to those whose hearts are frightened: Be strong, fear not! Here is your God."

Fear makes us weak. But fear is a natural and normal and necessary human emotion. It is the other side of desire; for the more we desire anything, the more we fear to lose it or miss it. That's true of everything we desire, whether it's a candy bar or a new car, heaven or a hamburger, work or play, material goods or spiritual goods.

In this passage, God tells us that he himself is our reason to be strong and not to fear, because he is real and present. Isaiah writes: "Be strong, fear not! Here is your God, he comes with vindication; with divine recompense he comes to save you."

We don't have to wait for his presence; we only have to wait for his gifts. God is the giver of "all good giving and every perfect gift" (James 1:17), but his gifts do not come on our timetable or on our schedules but on his. Guess whose timetable is wiser and better: ours or God's?

But even before the gifts are here, the Giver is. And he saves us, in the end, from every evil. When Christ commands us to pray "deliver us from evil," he does not add any qualification or limitation on the evils he promises to deliver us from.

Isaiah gives examples of the gifts and deliverances that God can give us that are miraculous: "Then will the eyes of the blind be opened, the ears of the deaf be cleared; then will the lame leap like a stag, then the tongue of the mute will sing. Streams will burst forth in the desert, and rivers in the steppe. The burning sands will become pools, and the thirsty ground, springs of water." If God can give us miraculous goods, he can certainly give us non-miraculous goods.

These miracles that Isaiah prophesies literally happened: either in Old Testament Israel or in the life of Jesus or in the history of the Church and the lives of the saints. God can do *anything*. "For God all things are possible" (Matt. 19:26). There is no limit to his power.

The Psalmist makes the same point as the prophet Isaiah. In fact, he lists ten things God will do for us, some of them in miraculous ways and some in natural ways. First, he "keeps faith forever." Second, he "secures justice for the oppressed." Third, he "gives food to the hungry." Fourth, he "sets captives free." Fifth, he "gives sight to the blind." Sixth, he "raises up those who were bowed down." Seventh, he "loves the just." Eighth, he "protects strangers." Ninth, "the fatherless and the widow the LORD sustains." Tenth, "the way of the wicked he thwarts." All ten of these things God does sometimes miraculously but most often through human instruments.

And then the Psalmist adds that the LORD "shall reign forever . . . through all generations," to make the point that this is not just a nostalgic remembering of the great deeds God did in the past but a promise that he will continue to do the same deeds, or even greater ones, in the future, because he does not change; he is "forever."

There is no limit to these divine gifts. As Mother Teresa of Kolkata loved to say, "God cannot be outdone in generosity." The only limits are in us, in our weak faith and hope and desire to receive them. The only other limit on our receiving them is time. We are in time, and we cannot eat appetizers and meat and dessert all at once. But God's timing, unlike *our* short-sighted timing, is as infallible as God himself. The gifts are complete only in heaven, but even here they begin—as down payments, so to speak, or as appetizers.

Miracles are rare because God prefers to give these gifts through his subordinates, through his creatures, thereby exalting his creatures. Thus, he secures justice for us through human agencies like honest lawyers and wise voters. And he gives food to the hungry through those who work in soup kitchens and food pantries, as well as farmers. And he gives sight to the blind through medical technology and the touch language of braille.

To ask whether these works are our works or God's works is to ask the wrong question. It is like asking whether it was the obedient soldiers or the general who won the battle. All good work is God's work, even when we accomplish it. We are his instruments, his tools. Was it the saw that cut the wood, or was it the carpenter? Both. God is the first cause, the giver of "all good giving and every perfect gift" (James 1:17); but he does not ignore and bypass his human instruments and do the job all by himself, for the same reason parents don't do their kids' homework for them. He's training us; he's cultivating us; he's growing us as farmers grow crops.

That is true for both physical and spiritual work. God instituted physical work in the Garden of Eden, telling Adam to tend the garden of this world, in order to give Adam the dignity of being a gardener; and he also instituted spiritual work, especially prayer, in order to grant to us his creatures the dignity of being real links in the charity chain.

Link up with God's activity in the world and your life will take on new meaning. Pray and live St. Francis' prayer: "Lord, make me an instrument of your peace: where there is hatred, let me sow love; where there is injury, pardon; where there is doubt, faith; where there is despair, hope; where there is darkness, light; and where there is sadness, joy."

I have three pieces of homework for you. They are three things to look at. First, look at our world. Look at all the work to be done. Don't close your eyes to human needs: look for them. Look into the hearts of your family members and your neighbors; look at their sufferings and their needs.

And then, second, open the eyes of your heart and your conscience and look at your Lord face to face; open your heart to the heart of the one who so loved the world that he gave his only begotten Son to save it.

And then, finally, look at yourself and your deepest identity. If you are a baptized Catholic, you are part of his Body. He made you to do his work. Whatever good you do, he does it through you. Offer it to him: all your prayers, works, joys, and sufferings of every day. It takes less than a minute to pray the Morning Offering, and mean it. There is absolutely no excuse for any of us ever to omit it, unless the house is burning down or grandma has fallen into the swimming pool.

SECOND READING
James 2:1–5 _____

My brothers and sisters, show no partiality as you adhere to the faith in our glorious Lord Jesus Christ. For if a man with gold rings and fine clothes comes into your assembly, and a poor person in shabby clothes also comes in, and you pay attention to the one wearing the fine clothes and say, "Sit here, please," while you say to the poor one, "Stand there," or "Sit at my feet," have you not made distinctions among yourselves and become judges with evil designs?

Listen, my beloved brothers and sisters. Did not God choose those who are poor in the world to be rich in faith and heirs of the kingdom that he promised to those who love him?

In today's epistle, St. James sharply criticizes those who discriminate against the poor. The Church has always seen almsgiving, which means all kinds of charity to the poor, as an essential part of the Gospel, not an extra or a specialization for a few.

There are many ways to discriminate against the poor, and your conscience will tell you some of them, if you listen to it, silently and unhurriedly and honestly.

One of the most neglected ways in which we discriminate against the poor is not so much by such blatant sins of commission as James mentions but by sins of omission, by simply not paying attention to their existence and their needs and our ability to help them, often in very simple and easy ways, such as by donating our extra stuff to agencies like the Salvation Army or Goodwill Industries. And we all have lots of extra "stuff."

Another way we ignore and discriminate against the poor is by ignoring the *spiritually* poor and their *spiritual* needs. By that standard, some of the poorest people in our society are people with comfortable houses, jobs, and bank accounts. When Mother Teresa of Kolkata was invited to Harvard University to give the commencement address, she began by reading their invitation to her, which said something like this: "We invite you, Mother Teresa, as the most well-known citizen of India, one of the poorest countries in the world, to share your wisdom with us here in America, one of the richest countries in the world." And Mother said, "That's just not true. India is not a poor country. India is a rich country. India has many kinds of spiritual riches. And America is not a rich country. America is a poor country. Any country that slaughters its own unborn children is a desperately poor country."

The audience in Harvard Yard was totally silent, and totally uncomfortable. We, too, should be silent and listening and uncomfortable. The poor need our charity, and the first and greatest act of charity we can give, writes St. Thomas Aquinas, is to lead our neighbors to the truth, to (as St. Paul put it) speak "the truth in love" (Eph. 4:15).

Truth and love, clarity and charity—we seldom practice both together. Jesus always did.

GOSPEL

MARK 7:31–37 _____

Again Jesus left the district of Tyre and went by way of Sidon to the Sea of Galilee, into the district of the Decapolis. And people brought to him a deaf man who had a speech impediment and begged him to lay his hand on him. He took him off by himself away from the crowd. He put his finger into the man's ears and, spitting, touched his tongue; then he looked up to heaven and groaned, and said to him, "*Ephphatha!*"—that is, "Be opened!"—And immediately the man's ears were opened, his speech impediment was removed, and he spoke plainly. He ordered them not to tell anyone. But the more he ordered them not to, the more they proclaimed it. They were exceedingly astonished and they said, "He has done all things well. He makes the deaf hear and the mute speak."

_____

What the prophets predicted, Jesus fulfilled. Literally. Miraculously. Ears that could not hear began to hear when he commanded them to "be opened!"

When God commands anything, it obeys. In creation, nonbeing obeyed and gave way to being, and darkness obeyed and gave way to light, and chaos obeyed and gave way to order. Nothing in creation can resist its Creator. The only exception is human free will, which is the only thing in the universe that disobeys the divine command. That is why it is a far greater thing for God to make saints out of sinners than for God to make the entire universe out of nothing, for nothingness has no power to resist him, but we do.

Jesus fulfilled all the messianic prophecies literally, both physically and spiritually. For instance, he not only gave physical healing to the physically sick and physical hearing to the physically deaf, but he also gave spiritual hearing to the spiritually deaf and spiritual speech to the spiritually mute. And he continues to perform this miracle in *our* lives today. He opens our deaf ears and our mute mouths. When Jesus says, "Be opened!" not only do deaf ears and hearts obey him, but death itself obeys him, as it did when he raised Lazarus from his tomb. If death itself obeys him and opens its doors, our ears and mouths will obey him too.

The point of Jesus' physical healings was not to put doctors out of business. The point of miracles is to point. They are words. One of the Greek words for "miracles" in the New Testament literally means "signs." A sign points beyond itself to something more important than itself. Since souls are even more important than bodies, Jesus' healing of bodies points to his healing of souls.

And both kinds of healings were meant as signs to point beyond themselves to Jesus himself. Jesus was not all about miracles; the miracles were all about Jesus. Jesus did not come to show us a few miracles. He gave us miracles to show who it was that had come.

And who is that? In the last book in the Bible, the book of Revelation, Jesus appears at the end of time and says, "I am the Alpha and the Omega, the beginning and the end" (Rev. 21:6). The beginning because it was by him, the Word of God, that God created the universe and mankind. The end because it is he with whom we were designed and destined to unite in spiritual marriage forever in heaven in eternal, ecstatic, unimaginable joy.

Jesus is not just a wonder worker; Jesus is the whole meaning of life. The meaning of life is not Jesus plus a few other good things. *All* good things are in him (Phil. 4:19).

And at every Mass, we eat the whole meaning of life and are united with him body and soul, in Holy Communion. It is the most perfect thing you will ever do in your life.

TWENTY-FOURTH SUNDAY
IN ORDINARY TIME

FIRST READING

ISAIAH 50:5–9A _____

The Lord GOD opens my ear that I may hear;
and I have not rebelled,
   have not turned back.
I gave my back to those who beat me,
   my cheeks to those who plucked my beard;
my face I did not shield
   from buffets and spitting.

The Lord GOD is my help,
   therefore I am not disgraced;
I have set my face like flint,
   knowing that I shall not be put to shame.
He is near who upholds my right;
   if anyone wishes to oppose me,
   let us appear together.
Who disputes my right?
   Let that man confront me.
See, the Lord GOD is my help;
   who will prove me wrong?

_____

(See the reflection after the Gospel passage below.)

RESPONSORIAL PSALM
PSALM 116: 1–2, 3–4, 5–6, 8–9 _____

R. (9) **I will walk before the Lord, in the land of the living.**

I love the LORD because he has heard
    my voice in supplication,
Because he has inclined his ear to me
    the day I called.

The cords of death encompassed me;
    the snares of the netherworld seized upon me;
    I fell into distress and sorrow,
And I called upon the name of the LORD,
    "O LORD, save my life!"

Gracious is the LORD and just;
    yes, our God is merciful.
The LORD keeps the little ones;
    I was brought low, and he saved me.

For he has freed my soul from death,
    my eyes from tears, my feet from stumbling.
I shall walk before the LORD
    in the land of the living.

Today's Psalm is not so much theology as drama, because our life is a drama; in fact, it is literally a matter of life and death. In act one, the war begins: "The cords of death encompassed me; the snares of the netherworld seized upon me." In act two, I seem to succumb: "I fell into distress and sorrow. . . . I was brought low." In act three, my last hope arises: "I called upon the name of the LORD, 'O LORD, save my life!'" In act four, I win the war: "He saved me. For he has freed my soul from death, my eyes from tears, my feet from stumbling." In act five, there is the thanksgiving and victory celebration: "I shall walk before the LORD in the land of the living. . . . I love the LORD because he has heard my voice in supplication." Religion is not a dull, abstract formula; religion is concrete drama; religion is real life, and life comes in this five-act drama.

The Fathers of the Church see two meanings in this drama. One meaning interprets these words and experiences as Christ's. They describe his Passion, Death, and Resurrection. The other meaning ascribes the words to us, because we are "in Christ"; we are his Body. And whatever happens to you happens to your body, unless you are out of your body as well as out of your mind.

Notice that God liberates us completely, so he saves us from three things, gives us three freedoms, three dimensions of salvation: "He has freed my soul from death, my eyes from tears, my feet from stumbling." Death is the enemy of life, tears are the enemy of joy, and stumbling is the enemy of sanctity.

God frees our souls from death because souls can die as well as bodies. God is the life of the soul just as the soul is the life of the body. When the body loses its soul, the body dies; and when the soul loses its life in God, the soul dies. You can see many dying souls even in this world.

God also frees our eyes from tears because he is our true joy. That joy is so large that it does not enter into us: we enter into it. Thus, in his parable of the Last Judgment, Jesus has God say to the saved, "Come, share your master's joy" (Matt. 25:21).

And he frees our feet from stumbling. He not only forgives our sins but takes them away. He not only justifies us but also sanctifies us. The process is long, and its completion, for most of us, takes more than a lifetime: that's why purgatory exists. But there is no stumbling, no sin, in heaven. There, "love lifts us up where we belong." If you prefer sin and stumbling to flying on eagles' wings, you won't go to heaven because you wouldn't like it there.

Finally, what is what the Psalmist calls "the land of the living"? What is act five about? "The land of the living" is heaven, of course, because that's the only place where there is no death. But it's also those patches of heaven's light here in our darkness, those heavenly appetizers in our earthly menu, those showers of heavenly water that fall on our deserts, those seeds of heavenly plants that are planted in earthly soil. If heaven's life is not planted in the soil of your soul during life by Baptism and faith, it cannot come to flower after death. If it is, then dying is only transplanting that frail flower into its perfect heavenly flowerpot.

You see, life is a matter of life or death, both for bodies and for souls. In the words of the dark, drug-addicted poet Jim Morrison, "No one here gets out alive." He was right about bodies, but he was wrong about souls. Only souls that choose eternal death don't get out of here alive.

Of course, it takes time for any drama to play out. And this is the answer to the "problem of evil": that it is only temporary, not eternal; that the long defeat that is human history and human hopes will in the end turn into an eternal victory. Aquinas answers the world's most difficult question—why God allows so much evil—by quoting Augustine: "'Since God is the highest good, he would not allow any evil to exist in his works unless his omnipotence and goodness were such as to bring good even out of evil.' This is part of the infinite goodness of God, that he should allow evil to exist and out of it produce good." He brought the greatest of all goods, our eternal salvation, out of the greatest of all evils, the torture and murder of the Son of God on the cross. And if he can do that, he can certainly bring good out of lesser evils.

But we don't see that yet because we're not in act five yet. The drama takes time, both in history and in each individual life. God is patient, like a good chess player. He took almost 13.8 billion years since the Big Bang to produce mankind, and many millennia of mankind after the first Adam fell to prepare for Christ, the Second Adam.

But God is the master of all time because he is the Creator of time itself. He didn't create the universe *in time*; he created time in the universe, as a dimension of the universe together with matter and space. He is the author of all the aspects of his story: the setting, which is the universe; the characters, who are ourselves; the plot, which is our sin and redemption; and the theme, which is the glory and joy and triumph of his love. The story is history, and it is his story, and that is why it is "the greatest story ever told." In fact, since all stories are in it, are part of it, it is the only story ever told.

SECOND READING
JAMES 2:14–18 _____

What good is it, my brothers and sisters, if someone says he has faith but does not have works? Can that faith save him? If a brother or sister has nothing to wear and has no food for the day, and one of you says to them, "Go in peace, keep warm, and eat well," but you do not give them the necessities of the body, what good is it? So also faith of itself, if it does not have works, is dead.

Indeed, someone might say, "You have faith and I have works." Demonstrate your faith to me without works, and I will demonstrate my faith to you from my works.

_____

"If someone says he has faith but does not have works . . . can that faith save him?" The answer is no. Faith will save you, but not that faith. That's dead faith. A tree that produces no fruit is a dead tree. Yes, you absolutely need faith to be saved, but you need good works, too, because living faith always produces good works as a living orange tree always produces oranges.

The most fundamental controversy that produced the Protestant Reformation was about whether faith alone gave you eternal life and eternal salvation or whether it was faith plus good works. That was really as silly a question as whether the life of a plant was in the roots alone or also in the fruits.

Like the roots of a plant, faith is invisible. You can't see faith. How, then, can you know if anyone has faith? Because you can see works. "By their fruits you will know them," Jesus said (Matt. 7:16). How can you know if you have a living orange tree? Because you can see the oranges.

Faith and works are not a two-part ticket to heaven. It's all one thing. The very same spiritual life that begins with faith is the life that grows by hope and produces good works as the works of love. God's life comes into our souls by faith and comes out of our souls by works.

Both faith and works are our free choice. God will not get us into heaven by reducing us to machines and just pushing our passive buttons. He is a lover, not an engineer. He impregnates our souls with his own eternal life, but he is a lover, not a rapist.

Life asks one great question of each of us, and it is the same question God will ask us when we meet him in the next life. The question is this: "Who are you?" We can deceive others about who we are, and we can even deceive ourselves, but we cannot deceive God. Jesus, in today's Gospel, asks a question that is really that same question: "Who do you say that I am?" That question does not mean merely what your religious opinions are. It means "What is your relationship to Christ, who is the source of your very life, the life of your soul?" You will have to answer that question when you die, because hiding and lying will be absolutely impossible then, when we stand face to face with the all-knowing God.

So we'd better practice *here* what we will *have* to do there. We'd better pray.

GOSPEL
MARK 8:27–35 _____

Jesus and his disciples set out for the villages of Caesarea Philippi. Along the way he asked his disciples, "Who do people say that I am?" They said in reply, "John the Baptist, others Elijah, still others one of the prophets." And he asked them, "But who do you say that I am?" Peter said to him in reply, "You are the Christ." Then he warned them not to tell anyone about him.

He began to teach them that the Son of Man must suffer greatly and be rejected by the elders, the chief priests, and the scribes, and be killed, and rise after three days. He spoke this openly. Then Peter took him aside and began to rebuke him. At this he turned around and, looking at his disciples, rebuked Peter and said, "Get behind me, Satan. You are thinking not as God does, but as human beings do."

He summoned the crowd with his disciples and said to them, "Whoever wishes to come after me must deny himself, take up his cross, and follow me. For whoever wishes to save his life will lose it, but whoever loses his life for my sake and that of the gospel will save it."

Today's first reading from the prophet Isaiah says many things about the promised Messiah that are not surprising, such as "I have not rebelled, have not turned back" and "The Lord GOD is my help, therefore I am not disgraced. . . . I shall not be put to shame." But the very same passage also says one thing that seems to contradict that and seems to say he *will* be put to shame: "I gave my back to those who beat me, my cheeks to those who plucked my beard; my face I did not shield from buffets and spitting."

This surprising prediction is also elsewhere in Isaiah. For instance, in chapter 58, the Messiah is described in this way: "Like a lamb led to slaughter or a sheep silent before shearers, he did not open his mouth. Seized and condemned, he was taken away. Who would have thought any more of his destiny? For he was cut off from the land of the living" (Isa. 53:7–8).

In the Acts of the Apostles, that was the passage the Ethiopian eunuch was reading in his chariot when Philip was sent to him to ask him, "Do you understand what you are reading?" He said, "How can I, unless someone instructs me? . . . About whom is the prophet saying this? About himself, or about someone else?" (Acts 8:30–31, 34). So Philip explained to him the Gospel, the Good News about Jesus, the true Messiah. And the Ethiopian was converted and baptized.

Let's put ourselves into the mind of this Ethiopian, this Gentile, this foreigner. He's an open-minded seeker, an inquirer; but there is a problem, a puzzle, an obstacle. God's greatest promise, his Messiah, seems to be described here as a loser, a failure. The one who was supposed to be the great winner, to triumph over evil and injustice, seemingly succumbs to evil and injustice and suffering and shame and disgrace. In today's reading, from Isaiah chapter 50, Isaiah says the Messiah will *not* be put to shame, but eight chapters later, in the passage the Ethiopian was reading, it says he *will* be put to shame. How can both be true? What does it mean?

Perhaps we can understand the answer best if we contrast Jesus with Muhammad. Muhammad was probably the second most influential person who ever lived, next to Jesus, and was the founder of the second largest religion in the world. Muhammad had the same difficulty the Ethiopian probably had with Christ and with Christianity: how could God let his Messiah be disgraced? Muhammad argued, in the Quran, that Jesus was a true prophet and therefore could not possibly have been disgraced and crucified, as the Gospels claim, because Allah would never have allowed one of his prophets to be publicly put to shame. God is a winner, so all his prophets must be winners too, not losers. So either Jesus was put to shame and therefore was not God's prophet, or Jesus was a prophet and therefore was not put to shame. Prophets have to be winners, not losers. Muhammad himself was a winner and not a loser as a warrior, and he spread his religion not only by successful preaching but also by successful warfare. Unlike Jesus, he was never arrested, tried, convicted, or crucified. He was never put to shame.

But sometimes success in the eyes of the world is shame in the eyes of God, and shame in the eyes of the foolish, fallen world is success and glory in the eyes of God. That is why we decorate our crosses with gold, and why Christ kept his wounds in his resurrected body: they were badges of honor.

The mindset of Muhammad is the same mindset St. Peter had in today's Gospel when he tried to correct Christ's course away from the cross. This was one of the stupidest things Peter ever said, and it happened immediately after he said the wisest thing he ever said. These two things happened in rapid succession. First, when Jesus asked his Apostles who they thought he was, Peter answered, "You are the Messiah, the Son of the living God." And Jesus replied (in the words of the more complete account we have in Matthew's Gospel), "Blessed are you, Simon son of Jonah. For flesh and blood has not revealed this to you, but my heavenly Father. And so I say to you, you are Peter, and upon this rock I will build my church" (Matt. 16:16–18).

Peter was brought amazingly high up by this. And then right after that, the second thing happened, the thing that brought Peter as far down as he had just been brought up. Peter's confession of Jesus as the Messiah brought his mind up into contact with the mind of heaven, the mind of God; and now Peter's next words brought Peter's mind into contact with the mind of hell, with the intentions of Satan, and this caused Jesus to say to Peter, "Get behind me, Satan." Jesus addressed Peter as Satan! Jesus had just seen God's inspiration behind Peter's confession, and now he saw Satan's inspiration behind Peter's next words. Why? What did Peter say?

Jesus had just told Peter that he would have to suffer and be rejected and disgraced and crucified. And Peter took him aside and tried to correct him. "Lord, you are the Christ, the Messiah, God's definitive revelation to mankind! This shame cannot happen to you! I cannot let this happen! I will defend you, with the sword, if necessary." Which is exactly what Peter did try to do when Jesus was arrested in the Garden of Gethsemane. He took out his sword and he cut off the left ear of Malchus, the servant of the high priest (John 18:10). Then Jesus ended the most just war in history, healed its one and only casualty, and told Peter to put back his sword because "all who take the sword will perish by the sword" (Matt. 26:52).

Peter had promised Jesus that even if all the other Apostles denied him and fled, Peter would never do that. And then Peter did exactly that, at Jesus' trial, denying him three times because he was ashamed to be associated with Jesus' shame. And when Jesus looked at Peter, Peter "went out and began to weep bitterly" (Luke 22:62).

Where did he go? We don't know, but I have a guess. I think he went to Jesus' mother.

And then, when Jesus met Peter on the shore of the Sea of Galilee after his

Resurrection, he gave Peter three second chances to undo his denial, asking him three times, "Do you love me?" And Peter replied, "Lord, you know everything; you know that I love you" (John 21:17). But Jesus had used the word *agape* for "love"—the kind of love that Jesus had, the kind of love that God is; and Peter had answered with the word *philia* for love, which means friendship, the highest of the merely human loves. Peter had received a lesson in humility, and this time Peter was wise enough to know himself and his limits and his failures. He knew he was not yet ready for true love, Christian love, *agape* love, the costly, sacrificial love that Jesus taught and practiced.

So Jesus then predicted that Peter would come to know that love and live that love and die for that love, and Jesus even predicted Peter's martyrdom. (Read the story in chapter 21 of John's Gospel.)

The Ethiopian, Muhammad, and Peter all made the same mistake: thinking God would never manifest himself in shame and suffering and loss, only in gain and glory and joy. The scandal that God himself would be shamed and suffer and die—that was unthinkable.

What makes it thinkable? Jesus does. He is the final and definitive revelation of both who God is and who man is called to be. He is "the real deal," and the real deal includes his taking up his cross, making light of its shame, and marching up to Calvary and to death. He was a winner, not a loser, but he won the victory not by avoiding the shame and the suffering and the cross and death, but by embracing it and transforming it into redemption and glory.

When God touches anything, he changes it into something more like himself. On the cross, he turned death into life: his death into our life. He turned water into wine at Cana, and he turns wine into his own human Blood in the Eucharist, and he will turn our blood into something glorious in our resurrection.

If we are Christians, we are not only *with* him, but we are *in* him; we are members of his Body. And therefore, we also must take up our cross and follow him through both of the two acts of the great divine drama. Act one is shame and suffering and loss and crucifixion and death; act two is glory and joy and gain and triumph and resurrection and eternal life, a life that makes the world's worst misery and shame look like a tiny speck of dust compared with the ocean of his glory and joy.

We can test this prediction about the next life right here in this life, by experiment. What kind of life leads to glory and joy in the end? *Agape* love. It is a scientific experiment. And so is the opposite philosophy of life, the "I Did It My Way" philosophy. We can observe the results of these two experiments. The "I Did It My Way" experiment is to live for yourself: don't risk suffering and shame. Don't give your heart to anyone else, because if you do, your heart will be broken. But if you live that experiment, what will you find? Suffering and shame. Certainly not joy. But if you live the opposite experiment, if you forget yourself, if you give yourself away to God and your neighbor in love, what will you find? You will find joy.

Jesus says, "Whoever finds his life will lose it, and whoever loses his life for my sake will find it" (Matt. 10:39). This is not a dreamy, abstract ideal; it's a practical, provable fact. It works. It's testable. Life is a laboratory. Life is a kind of scientific experiment. What Jesus says is either true or false, and our experience in the laboratory of life proves it to be true, once we give it a sincere chance.

Why does it work? Because it's God's design for us from the beginning; it's what he made us for. We are made "in his image"; and what does that mean? It means love, because that is what God is: "God *is* love" (1 John 4:8). And what does love do? Love gives itself away; love gives away whatever kind of life it has. God's love gave away his divine life to us, on the cross; and human love gives away our human life to others; and the primary way of doing that is by giving your life to another in marriage and together giving your life to your children. It's done also in other ways, by priesthood or by service in the single life, and sometimes even by martyrdom.

We are given the gift of life, and all the good things in life, and our very self, not to hoard it but to share it, not to fill our coffers but to fill our offers, to offer it up. Life is like money: it's good and happifying only when it's spent. That's testable in practice: Who's happier, an Ebenezer Scrooge or a St. Francis of Assisi?

We are meant to be like the Sea of Galilee, not like the Dead Sea. The same water, the Jordan River, flows into the Sea of Galilee and into the Dead Sea. But the Sea of Galilee is still alive with fish and fishermen today, two thousand years after Jesus was there, while the Dead Sea lives up to its name: it's dead; no fish can live in it. Why? Because the Sea of Galilee not only receives the fresh water of the Jordan River at its inlet, but it also gives it away at its outlet, where it flows south to the Dead Sea. The Dead Sea has an inlet but no outlet. That's why its waters are dead. That's true of souls as well as rivers. That's the difference between spiritual life and spiritual death.

To give yourself away is the only way to live. To grasp your life and the stuff in your life to yourself, to live for yourself, is for your soul to shrivel and die, no matter how rich you are or how healthy your body is. Jesus did not live for himself but for his Father, to love and adore and obey and glorify his Father. And he lived not for himself but for us, to save us, to give himself away to us totally, his whole self, Body and Blood, Soul and Divinity. He embraced suffering and shame because he was bearing *our* shame. As Isaiah prophesied, "By his stripes we were healed" (Isa. 53:5).

And that giving, that offering, is not just noble and holy: it's also the secret of *joy*. That's the great paradox of life: that dying to yourself is truly living, that giving your whole self away is truly gaining your whole self, that the way to get joy is to give joy. Thus, Jesus said not just that it is more *noble* to give than to receive but that it is more *blessed* to give than to receive. Giving is more joyful than receiving. St. Paul says that Jesus, "for the sake of the *joy* that lay before him endured the cross, despising its shame, and has taken his seat at the right of the throne of God" in eternal and infinite joy (Heb. 12:2). If we are Christians, his end is our end too, and his way is our way too.

We all desire joy, and this is not one among many possible ways to it but the only way. Because it is not an "it" but a "who"; it is the one who said, "I am the way and the truth and the life. No one comes to the Father except through me" (John 14:6).

The question Jesus asked his Apostles is the same question he asks us: "Who do you say that I am?" Am I just a holy messenger, just a prophet, like John the Baptist or Elijah? Or am I your Mister Fix-It, your Superman, your superhero? Or am I your obedient servant to all your foolish and fallen desires? Or am I Mister Nice Guy, or Super Social Worker, or Mister Political Correctness? That man you read about in the Gospels—is he a loser? Am I your shame? Are you ashamed of me? Are you ashamed to be called a Christian?

Those are only *my* words. Here are Jesus' own words, from the Gospel of Mark: "Whoever is ashamed of me and of my words in this faithless and sinful generation, the Son of Man will be ashamed of when he comes in his Father's glory with the holy angels" (Mark 8:38).

As the old hymn put it,

> Jesus, and shall it ever be
> A mortal man ashamed of Thee
> Ashamed of Thee whom angels praise
> Whose glories shine through endless days?

> Ashamed of Jesus, that dear Friend
> On Whom my hopes of heaven depend?
> No! When I blush, be this my shame:
> That I no more revere his name.

> Ashamed of Jesus? Yes I may,
> When I've no guilt to wash away,
> No tears to wipe, no good to crave,
> No fears to quell, no soul to save.

TWENTY-FIFTH SUNDAY
IN ORDINARY TIME

FIRST READING

WISDOM 2:12, 17–20 _____

The wicked say:
Let us beset the just one, because he is obnoxious to us;
    he sets himself against our doings,
reproaches us for transgressions of the law
    and charges us with violations of our training.
Let us see whether his words be true;
    let us find out what will happen to him.
For if the just one be the son of God, God will defend him
    and deliver him from the hand of his foes.
With revilement and torture let us put the just one to the test
    that we may have proof of his gentleness
    and try his patience.
Let us condemn him to a shameful death;
    for according to his own words, God will take care of him.

RESPONSORIAL PSALM

PSALM 54:3–4, 5, 6, 8 _____

R. (6b) **The Lord upholds my life.**

O God, by your name save me,
    and by your might defend my cause.
O God, hear my prayer;

hearken to the words of my mouth.

For the haughty men have risen up against me,
the ruthless seek my life;
they set not God before their eyes.

Behold, God is my helper;
the LORD sustains my life.
Freely will I offer you sacrifice;
I will praise your name, O LORD, for its goodness.

Our Old Testament passage from the Wisdom of Solomon would be a perfect addition to C.S. Lewis' classic little masterpiece *The Screwtape Letters,* in which a senior demon is advising a junior demon about how to tempt and corrupt and conquer innocent human victims. It reads like a memo from a strategy session of the War Room in hell.

The Wisdom of Solomon was written before the birth of Christ, so its author did not personally know how perfectly his words would apply to the spiritual warfare between Christ and Satan. He probably meant it simply as the thoughts of wicked human beings concerning righteous human beings, and how to corrupt them and conquer them. The wicked always love to corrupt the righteous because if they succeed it gives them an excuse and a justification for being wicked. They say: "See? This so-called saint is really just like us, a sinner. If we can make him appear no better than us, that makes us no worse than him."

There is also a hidden envy in the desire of the wicked to corrupt the righteous, and they always feel great pleasure when wickedness or even weakness is shown by the righteous. The wicked get a perverse pleasure from seeing others' wickedness and a pain from seeing others' righteousness. The righteous, on the other hand, get genuine pleasure from seeing others' righteousness and genuine pain from seeing others' sins. This is why gossip is a much more serious sin than we usually think: because it reveals a desire to expose and spread the bad news of how wicked supposedly righteous people are. Gossip is harmful not merely because it harms the people gossiped about, but also because that desire to bring others' goodness down a peg, that hidden pleasure in spreading the bad news of others' wickedness, is a serious disease in the soul of the gossiper.

Since there are two authors of every book of the Bible—namely, the human author and the divine author, the Holy Spirit who inspired it—there is, therefore, often a prophetic dimension in the words of the human author that he himself did not consciously understand. And that is clearly the case here, since "the just one" describes not just saints but Christ himself, and "the wicked" describes not just wicked men but the demons who hate him and tempt him and strategize his torture and murder. Their motives and their words in this Old Testament passage are exactly the motives and words of Christ's enemies who crucified him.

Their motive for hating him was that he spoke the truth to them. He was politically incorrect and "judgmental." His enemies say, "He is obnoxious to us; he sets himself against our doings, reproaches us for transgressions of the law." Their motive for crucifying him was to justify themselves by showing the world that God was not on his side, that God did not save him from death, so they say: "Let us find out what will happen to him. For if the just one be the son of God, God will defend him." According to St. Matthew, "Those passing by reviled him, shaking their heads and saying, ' . . . If you are the Son of God, come down from the cross!' Likewise the chief priests with the scribes and elders mocked him and said, 'He saved others; he cannot save himself. So he is king of Israel! Let him come down from the cross now, and we will believe in him. He trusted in God; let him deliver him now if he wants him. For he said, "I am the Son of God."'" (Matt. 27:39–43).

Almost the same words are in this prophetic passage from the Old Testament book of Wisdom: "For if the just one be the son of God, God will defend him and deliver him from the hand of his foes. . . . Let us condemn him to a shameful death; for according to his own words, God will take care of him."

What they said was true in a deeper way than they could understand. God did take care of him. But not by delivering him from the cross and from being condemned to a shameful death, but from succumbing to Satan's temptation to him to avoid that. God did deliver him from his enemies, but his enemies were not the sinners who crucified him—they were the people he died to save—but the evil spirits who tempted him to save himself instead of saving others, to avoid his passion and shame and suffering and death.

Those who crucified him taunted him: "He saved others; he cannot save himself." They did not know how true those words were. It was precisely by not saving himself that he saved others. It was because he saved others that he could not save himself.

Today's Psalm verse is also implicitly about Christ. David the Psalmist's words could have been uttered by Christ: "O God, by your name save me, and by your might defend my cause. O God, hear my prayer; hearken to the words of my mouth. For the haughty men have risen up against me, the ruthless seek my life; they set not God before their eyes. Behold, God is my helper; the LORD sustains my life. Freely will I offer you sacrifice."

David thought of this sacrifice as the sacrifice of thanksgiving he would offer after God would physically save him from his human enemies. He wrote this Psalm when he was being followed by Saul, who was trying to kill him, and he was betrayed to Saul's troops by the Ziphites among whom he was hiding. But the Holy Spirit, who inspired this Psalm, had something else in mind that David could not have understood—namely, Christ's sacrificial death offered to the Father for our salvation.

David wrote, "God is my helper; the LORD sustains my life." He was trusting that God would save his life from Saul. But those words of David also applied to Christ. God sustained Christ's life, but not by having him avoid death, as he did with David, but by having him endure death and transform it into a sacrifice and an offering—not a thanksgiving offering but a sin offering, an atonement for sin; and then God would raise him up in a Resurrection that was made all the more glorious by the death that preceded it. Which is what he will also do for us if only we are "in him"; that is, if we are part of his Mystical Body, his Church, by our faith and Baptism.

There are often many depths and layers of meaning in Scripture that were not consciously intended by the human author, because there is also a divine author, the Holy Spirit, who has many deeper intentions than we do. And this is true not only of the book we call the Bible but also of the book of nature, which God also wrote, and also of the book of our life, which God also writes by his all-inclusive providence. Of all three of these God-inspired books, God can say to us what Hamlet said to Horatio: "Horatio, there are more things in heaven and earth than are dreamt of in your philosophy."

SECOND READING

JAMES 3:16–4:3 _____

Beloved: Where jealousy and selfish ambition exist, there is disorder and every foul practice. But the wisdom from above is first of all pure, then peaceable, gentle, compliant, full of mercy and good fruits, without inconstancy or insincerity. And the fruit of righteousness is sown in peace for those who cultivate peace.

Where do the wars and where do the conflicts among you come from? Is it not from your passions that make war within your members? You covet but do not possess. You kill and envy but you cannot obtain; you fight and wage war. You do not possess because you do not ask. You ask but do not receive, because you ask wrongly, to spend it on your passions.

_____

War and Peace is the title of one of the world's greatest novels. War and peace are two of the most important features of human life. The Epistle of James today tells us where these two things come from.

First of all, it is clear that external, physical, visible war and peace—public, collective wars and peace—come from us, from our own internal, spiritual, invisible war and peace. Even Confucius knew that. He wrote: "If there is peace in the heart, there will be peace in the family. If there is peace in the family, there will be peace in the nation. If there is peace in the nation, there will be peace in the world." We all know that, deep down; that's why we know how wise it is to pray, "Let there be peace on earth and let it begin with me."

So we can trace external, public peace back to internal, spiritual peace as its cause. And the same is true of war. As James says, "Where do the wars and where do the conflicts among you come from? Is it not from your passions that make war within your members?" James is a very good psychologist. He sees the human heart as a zoo, with all the animals, all the selfish passions, hungry for their food and competing for it.

But that fact does not solve the problem; in fact, it makes it even harder to solve. How can we heal our own hearts? How can we end the war in our souls with God and with ourselves and with our neighbors? How can sinners become saints? How can we lift ourselves up by our own bootstraps? How can the blind lead the blind? "Physician, heal thyself."

Our secular prophets, our pop psychologists, tell us we can do that all by ourselves; that we can be whatever we want to be. It's a lie. No one of the animals in the zoo, no one of our passions, can make peace with the other animals. Pop psychologists and commencement speakers are wrong. We are not saints who are repressed by our own lack of self-esteem; we are proud and arrogant sinners who insist that we can make ourselves saints. It is a great big sugar-coated lie.

They omit the first and most important step to peace: external peace comes from internal peace, but internal peace comes from peace with God. Thomas Merton sums up the whole diagnosis and prescription in those two steps when he writes, "We are not at peace with others because we are not at peace with ourselves, and we are not at peace with ourselves because we are not at peace with God."

God is not an addition, a postscript, an extra, for "religious people" only. God is the real cause and source and origin of all real peace, and our war with God is the real cause and source and origin of all war, including the wars within us among our own selfish passions, and the private wars between us and our neighbors, and the wars between races and gangs, and the public wars between nations and ideologies.

Peace is not just the absence of war. Peace is positive. Peace is what happens when we attain our true end, our true identity, our true happiness. And that is God, and our marriage to him.

If God is not our true end and our true peace, then God is not God, God is not real, and our proud and arrogant elitist atheists are the only ones who are wise, and the 99 percent of all human beings who have ever lived, who have believed in some kind of higher being that we are dependent on, are fools. There is no halfway position between these two alternatives. Either it's "the fool" who "says in his heart, 'There is no God'" (Ps. 14:1), or else it's the fool who has said in his heart that there *is*.

If God is real, and if God is God, and if God is the source of peace, then all peace, including world peace, starts with people becoming saints. Saints are people who love God with their whole heart and soul and mind and strength and who love their neighbors as themselves (all of them). And from there peace spreads, like a pandemic, like a virus, like a good infection. But it has to begin with you, and it has to begin not with your relation to others or even with your relation to yourself but with your relation with God. The beginning of peace is prayer.

GOSPEL
MARK 9:30–37 _____

Jesus and his disciples left from there and began a journey through Galilee, but he did not wish anyone to know about it. He was teaching his disciples and telling them, "The Son of Man is to be handed over to men and they will kill him, and three days after his death the Son of Man will rise." But they did not understand the saying, and they were afraid to question him.

They came to Capernaum and, once inside the house, he began to ask them,

"What were you arguing about on the way?" But they remained silent. They had been discussing among themselves on the way who was the greatest. Then he sat down, called the Twelve, and said to them, "If anyone wishes to be first, he shall be the last of all and the servant of all." Taking a child, he placed it in their midst, and putting his arms around it, he said to them, "Whoever receives one child such as this in my name, receives me; and whoever receives me, receives not me but the One who sent me."

Sometimes we are incredibly stupid because we insist on being super smart. Jesus clearly and simply and literally told his Apostles that he would be arrested and killed and rise from death three days later, and they did not understand it. Why not? It could not have been any clearer: because they insisted on interpreting it in some symbolic or mystical or esoteric or allegorical way. Why? Why were they looking for some hidden meaning when the meaning was right out there in front of them? Because they could not believe the obvious, literal meaning of it. This is a good example of how faith often comes first and leads reason, leads the mind, rather than vice versa.

One of the twentieth century's profoundest theologians, Hans Urs von Balthasar, who was one of Pope St. John Paul II's favorite theologians, was once asked what he thought he would ask St. John the Evangelist, author of the profoundest of all the books in the Bible, if he met him in heaven and what John's answer would be. Balthasar answered something like this: "Well, I would probably be stupid enough to ask him what was the significance of the number 153 in the last chapter of his Gospel, when he met Jesus after his Resurrection on the shore after he had been fishing all night and caught nothing and Jesus told him to cast his nets on the other side of the boat, and he caught so many fish that they almost sank the boat, and when he landed and counted the fish there were 153 of them. I am embarrassed to say that I would probably ask him why he wrote that number, and he would probably give me this profound answer: Because there were 153 of them."

Protestants, especially fundamentalists, often accuse Catholic theology of being much too subtle and scholarly and complex and mystical and allegorical and symbolical, but it is the opposite. When Jesus says, in instituting the Eucharist, "This is my Body," Protestants invent all sorts of ways of running away from the plain literal meaning of the words. What did Jesus mean when he said that this is his Body? Catholics have dared to say that Jesus dared to mean exactly what he dared to say: that "this is my Body" really means "this is my Body." And we have been repeating those exact words for two thousand years.

In reaction against fundamentalism, liberal or modernist Protestant theologians refuse to interpret many other passages in the Gospels literally, especially Jesus' miracles and especially his Resurrection. They say it is a resurrection of the Apostles' faith, a resurrection of "Easter faith" instead of a resurrection of Jesus' literal body. So they believe in an "Easter faith" without an Easter. But the earliest Christian creed, the Apostles' Creed, takes the Resurrection so literally, as all Christians have since the beginning, that for the resurrection of the body it uses the Greek words *anastasis nekron*, which mean literally "the standing-up of the corpse."

Good teachers usually mean exactly what they say, and their students are often surprised at that. That's why Jesus often has to add the rabbinic formula "Verily, verily, I say unto you"—which means "Don't nuance this; don't allegorize it; don't dance clever little dances around the straight, clear, plain, and obvious meaning of it. I say exactly what I mean, and I mean exactly what I say."

There are often *many layers* of meaning in Jesus' profound sayings, but they always add to the first and clearest and obvious meaning; they never subtract from it or offer an alternative to it, a way to avoid it. When that meaning is not literal, it is clear and obvious: e.g., when Jesus says, "I am the light of the world," he is obviously not talking about photons and optic nerves and physical light rays. When he says, "I am the door," no one looks for his hinges. And when he says, "I am the way," no one looks for a physical road map with north, south, east, and west. And when he says something that he knows will be misunderstood by taking it literally, he always identifies the misunderstanding; for instance (in John 4:32–34), when he says he has food, and means spiritual food, not physical food, he makes that distinction by first saying, "I have food to eat of which you do not know," and then, when the disciples still think he means hidden physical food, he says, "My food is to do the will of the one who sent me."

Jesus is much more often misunderstood by sophisticated theologians than by simple saints like Mother Teresa of Kolkata, who rarely used words of more than one syllable but who never lost an argument. Her sayings, like Jesus', always cut through the baloney. For instance: "How can there be too many children? That is like saying there are too many flowers." "America is not a rich nation, but a very poor nation—in fact, a desperately poor nation, for she slaughters her own unborn children." A famous Anglican, Malcolm Muggeridge, once said to her, "You know, Mother, God needs some good people outside his Catholic Church too." She replied, simply, "No, he doesn't." Malcolm said there was simply nothing he could possibly say to refute that. And he eventually became a Catholic.

There is a line in an old hymn that says, "If our love were but more simple, we should take him at his word." And if we did that, what would happen? Read the Gospels again with that in mind and find out. Spoiler alert: I'll give you one prediction—if you do that, if you believe everything Jesus says, your life will never be the same again.

TWENTY-SIXTH SUNDAY
IN ORDINARY TIME

FIRST READING

NUMBERS 11:25–29 _____

The LORD came down in the cloud and spoke to Moses. Taking some of the spirit that was on Moses, the LORD bestowed it on the seventy elders; and as the spirit came to rest on them, they prophesied.

Now two men, one named Eldad and the other Medad, were not in the gathering but had been left in the camp. They too had been on the list, but had not gone out to the tent; yet the spirit came to rest on them also, and they prophesied in the camp. So, when a young man quickly told Moses, "Eldad and Medad are prophesying in the camp," Joshua, son of Nun, who from his youth had been Moses' aide, said, "Moses, my lord, stop them." But Moses answered him, "Are you jealous for my sake? Would that all the people of the LORD were prophets! Would that the LORD might bestow his spirit on them all!"

_____

(See the reflection after the Gospel passage below.)

RESPONSORIAL PSALM

PSALM 19:8, 10, 12–13, 14 _____

R. (9a) **The precepts of the Lord give joy to the heart.**

The law of the LORD is perfect,
    refreshing the soul;
the decree of the LORD is trustworthy,
    giving wisdom to the simple.

The fear of the Lord is pure,
    enduring forever;
the ordinances of the Lord are true,
    all of them just.

Though your servant is careful of them,
    very diligent in keeping them,
Yet who can detect failings?
    Cleanse me from my unknown faults!

From wanton sin especially, restrain your servant;
    let it not rule over me.
Then shall I be blameless and innocent
    of serious sin.

The Psalmist prays: "Though your servant is careful of [your laws], very diligent in keeping them, yet who can detect failings? Cleanse me from my unknown faults!"

Our moral character is the sum of our virtues and vices. Virtues are good habits; vices are bad habits. These sinful habits are often easier to hide from ourselves than sinful acts. Another word for sinful habits or vices is "faults." In today's Psalm, the Psalmist prays to God not just to forgive his sinful *acts* but also to cleanse him from his sinful *habits*, his "unknown faults."

The three conditions for any sin are: first, the matter of the deed must be a matter of moral good or evil; second, we must have knowledge of that; and third, it must be done by our free choice or consent. The three conditions for a *mortal* sin, which not only weakens but destroys eternal life in the soul, are: first, a "grave" or very serious moral matter; second, clear knowledge that it is evil; and third, completely free choice or consent.

The second of these three conditions, knowledge, implies that many sinful habits, vices, or faults are unknown, hidden, subconscious. We are all very clever at hiding from ourselves and deceiving ourselves. For instance, the Pharisees were serious sinners, proud and arrogant and self-righteous, but they did not know that; in fact, they thought they were saints! Great sinners often think they are saints, while saints always know they are sinners. Similarly, many fools think they are wise, but all the wise know they are fools. Many proud people think they are humble, and they are proud of their humility; but all who are humble know that they are guilty of pride.

It did not take Sigmund Freud to inform us that most of what goes on in our souls is subconscious, not conscious. The Psalmist knew that too. And therefore he prays, with his conscious mind and will, that God clean up the dirt and darkness in his unconscious mind and will: "Cleanse me from my unknown faults." Sweep my soul's cellar.

We don't have direct knowledge of or access to that cellar, that hidden level of our souls and our characters. The fact that it's hidden or unknown means that it's not known. But that doesn't mean we shouldn't pray about it. Just the opposite—there's all the more need to pray about it if it's there but we don't know it. But God knows it, and has access to it, and works in it, as the sun works on the fog at dawn to gradually but irresistibly dispel it, or as heat works on ice to melt it, or as the tides work on the sand to water it.

So pray to God, who controls the light of the sun and also the light of his only-begotten Son. Pray to God, who controls the heat of the sun and the heat of his love, which is his Holy Spirit. Pray to God, who controls the power of the tides of the sea and the tides of the human heart, and the tides of the spiritual water of his grace.

God is the first cause of every good; and even though we must actively ask for it and cooperate with it, and not just passively wait for it, it's also true that we are totally dependent on God's grace everywhere in our lives, especially in this area of our subconscious, the area where there are hidden sins and unknown faults. We should entrust this dark area to him every day.

He is waiting for our permission to open that door of our soul's cellar, to let his light into our darkness. He will clean our hidden cellar in ways that are usually slow and gradual, like the tides. Wherever he is invited in, he enters, and wherever he enters, there enters with him light and joy.

One of the reasons for praying just before we sleep, even though our minds are less alert and sleepier then than at other times, is to entrust to God the nighttime of our souls, which become more passive and vulnerable and defenseless when we sleep—defenseless both to the devil's evil spirits and to God's good angels, who are stronger. Brother Lawrence, in *The Practice of the Presence of God*, says that "those who have the gale of the Holy Spirit go forward even in sleep."

SECOND READING
JAMES 5:1–6 _____

Come now, you rich, weep and wail over your impending miseries. Your wealth has rotted away, your clothes have become moth-eaten, your gold and silver have corroded, and that corrosion will be a testimony against you; it will devour your flesh like a fire. You have stored up treasure for the last days. Behold, the wages you withheld from the workers who harvested your fields are crying aloud; and the cries of the harvesters have reached the ears of the Lord of hosts. You have lived on earth in luxury and pleasure; you have fattened your hearts for the day of slaughter. You have condemned; you have murdered the righteous one; he offers you no resistance.

_____

Does this passage from the Epistle of James shock you? Listen to what Jesus said about the same subject—namely, riches, money, or wealth.

The first of Jesus' beatitudes was "Blessed are the poor in spirit, for theirs is the kingdom of heaven" (Matt. 5:3). He does not mean "Blessed are those with small bank accounts, even if they are passionately addicted to their money" but "Blessed are those who are detached from their money, no matter how much they have."

The Bible does not say that money is the root of all evil, but it does say that the *love* of money is the root of all kinds of evils. It can easily become an addiction. Money is like alcohol that way. The Bible says that God gave man wine to gladden his heart (Ps. 104:15), but it's easy to become addicted to it, and then it does not gladden but saddens. Wealth, like wine, is not sinful, but it can be dangerous. It can become a more respectable and more hidden addiction than alcohol or other chemicals.

Money is like sex that way: both a good thing and a danger. Greed is to money what lust is to sex: the selfish perversion of a good thing, especially in light of our human weakness, and especially for those who deny or ignore their weakness. Is it *easy* for a man to admire the beauty God created in women without lust? It's possible, but not easy. God created beauty, and sex, and sexual beauty, and these are very good things; but the strength of our selfish passions and the weakness of our will make these very good things also dangerous. The same is true of money. Money is a good, not an evil; but it is dangerous—so dangerous that Jesus says it is very hard for the rich to enter heaven. The disciples were very shocked at this, but Jesus did not water it down at all.

Wise old Aristotle said that money is good only when it is given away, when it is spent for good purposes, not when it's kept and hoarded. That's close to what Jesus says: "It is more blessed to give than to receive" (Acts 20:35).

What James preaches against is the greed for getting and the refusal to give; loving your own wealth more than you love other people; reversing the hierarchy of people over things by *loving* money, and the things money can buy, instead of *using* money and the things money can buy, and loving and serving *people*. We invented money as a useful means, a means of exchange, a means for making people happier and better. Money should serve people; people should not serve money.

It is very easy to turn this upside down and see money as your end and people as your means, and then you start exploiting people, in many dangerously subtle ways. That's why James' warnings are so shrill. They're like an alarm clock, because we're so easily lulled to sleep about our addictions. Money, sex, and alcohol are only three of our most popular addictions. There are many more: smartphones, or shopping, or gossip, or power, especially technological power or political power, or political correctness, or just being thought to be "nice" and "nonjudgmental"—these are only a few of our most popular idols and addictions. All idols enslave us; only Christ frees us, because he is the truth, and only the truth frees us.

GOSPEL
MARK 9:38–43, 45, 47–48 _____

At that time, John said to Jesus, "Teacher, we saw someone driving out demons in your name, and we tried to prevent him because he does not follow us." Jesus replied, "Do not prevent him. There is no one who performs a mighty deed in my name who can at the same time speak ill of me. For whoever is not against us is for us. Anyone who gives you a cup of water to drink because you belong to Christ, amen, I say to you, will surely not lose his reward.

"Whoever causes one of these little ones who believe in me to sin, it would be better for him if a great millstone were put around his neck and he were thrown into the sea. If your hand causes you to sin, cut it off. It is better for you to enter into life maimed than with two hands to go into Gehenna, into the unquenchable fire. And if your foot causes you to sin, cut if off. It is better for you to enter into life crippled than with two feet to be thrown into Gehenna. And if your eye causes you to sin, pluck it out. Better for you to enter into the kingdom of God with one eye than with two eyes to be thrown into Gehenna, where 'their worm does not die, and the fire is not quenched.'"

_____

Today's Old Testament reading and today's Gospel make the same point: that God surprises us by his generosity and not only gives natural gifts to all (he "causes rain to fall on the just and the unjust" [Matt. 5:45]) but gives even supernatural gifts to those we consider "outsiders" or "others." In the Old Testament reading, it was the two elders who were not with Moses when God gave the gift of prophecy to the seventy elders, and in the Gospel reading, it was those who were not with Jesus and his Apostles but were performing miraculous cures in Jesus' name. In both cases, the followers of Moses and of Jesus were surprised and even scandalized at this, and in both cases, Moses, who foreshadowed Jesus, and Jesus, who was the new Moses, corrected them.

We might see the two "outsider" prophets Eldad and Medad as something like Anglicans and Lutherans, who, unlike other Protestants, believe that Christ is really present in the Eucharist, but who have broken apostolic succession, so they do not have a valid priesthood that can consecrate the bread and wine that God promises to transubstantiate into the Body and Blood of Christ and produce the Real Presence. So their sacraments are not valid. But as our own *Catechism* says, God "is not bound by his sacraments."

And we might see those who were not following the Apostles but were performing miracles and healings in Jesus' name, who were mentioned in today's Gospel, as similar to Protestant charismatics and Pentecostals, who tend to expect, and often receive, miracles more often than any other group, but who do not have the authority of the Apostles and their successors, who are the bishops of the Catholic Church.

Jesus gives us the principle by which we are to judge people's deeds: "By their fruits you will know them" (Matt. 7:16). If the fruit is growth in genuine faith, hope, and love of God, even when God is somewhat misunderstood, then God is behind that work. Even when the worker is not Christian, it is Christ, not Antichrist, who is behind all genuinely good works, both natural and supernatural. God is a "big tent" God. God is humble, and often works anonymously. The genuinely selfless love and compassion often shown in the lives of Buddhists, Hindus, Taoists, Confucians, Muslims, and even agnostics is inspired by the God of Jesus Christ, not by the fallen angel whom Jesus calls "the god of this world." Satan wants to advance his own kingdom and harm God's kingdom, and he does not do this by inspiring either the natural virtues of wisdom, justice, courage, and self-control or, much less, the supernatural virtues of faith, hope, and charity, which are God's work, in anyone. As Jesus said on another occasion, when the Pharisees accused him of casting out demons by the power of demons, "If Satan drives out Satan . . . how, then, will his kingdom stand?" (Matt. 12:26).

So when we see these good fruits in the lives of non-Catholics and even non-Christians and even nontheists, we should thank the God who we know inspired them. And at the same time, we should also thank him that out of his grace and through no merit of our own he has given us as Catholics the fullest knowledge of his mind and will. We have been entrusted with the most precious and most complete armory of spiritual weapons, and sometimes those who have inherited much more incomplete and even defective weapons are fighting the good fight more fearlessly and passionately than we are. Our response to that should be to listen and learn what God is teaching us through them, about him and about them and about us.

We should certainly never succumb to the temptation to minimize the special graces and truths that God has entrusted us with as Catholics, so that we thus avoid the special responsibilities and our special obligations as Catholics that these graces and truths also give us. The popular idea of the simple and total equality of all religions is a very convenient fiction that lets us off the hook, so to speak, by denying our special gifts so that we can deny our special duties and our special failures to live up to them.

Immediately after Jesus gave his Apostles their "big tent" lesson, he gave them another lesson, about hell, of all things; and that lesson disturbs many people who call themselves "liberals" or "progressives" as much as his first lesson disturbs many people who call themselves "conservatives" or "traditionalists." We deeply misunderstand Jesus if we are not equally open to *everything* he says, because if we're not, then we are judging him and editing him and correcting him instead of letting him do that to us, as if he were not our Master but our servant, not our teacher but our student.

What he says in the lesson about hell is more terrifying than the popular image of hell, which interprets the biblical symbols like fire and torture literally. Hell is worse than a fire pit or a torture chamber, because there is always hope for deliverance from these, but as Dante said, the sign on hell's gate reads "Abandon all hope, you who enter here."

But don't Jesus' teachings about hell contradict his "big tent" love and compassion? No. There is absolutely no contradiction, or even any tension, between a loving mother's hospitality in welcoming all the kids in the neighborhood into her "big tent" house and that same mother, out of the same love, warning all the kids in the loudest and scariest and most authoritative tone not to skate on the thin ice on the lake behind her house. Love is both shockingly tender and shockingly tough. You'd think we'd learn that by watching mother bears with their cubs. (One of the reasons God made the animals was to teach us things about ourselves.)

Jesus' warning applies to all of us. We are not guaranteed safety. We dare not ignore his warnings. What would Jesus say to pedophile priests? It was something about millstones. He said, "Whoever causes one of these little ones who believe in me to sin, it would be better for him if a great millstone were put around his neck and he were thrown into the sea." These were the words of the most loving and compassionate man who ever lived! He also said: "If your hand causes you to sin, cut it off. It is better for you to enter into life maimed than with two hands to go into Gehenna, into the unquenchable fire. . . . And if your eye causes you to sin, pluck it out. Better for you to enter into the kingdom of God with one eye than with two eyes to be thrown into Gehenna, where 'their worm does not die, and the fire is not quenched.'" Gehenna was the garbage dump outside Jerusalem where garbage was burned perpetually. The Jews would not live there because that was where the Canaanites had murdered their children and offered them up to their demon god Moloch in a great furnace inside the mouth of their great idol.

Of course, our hand or foot or eye does not put us into hell any more than God does; only our own freely chosen and unrepented sins do that. But if those sins did, then what Jesus said would be totally rational. Like Christ himself, we must be merciful to all men, including ourselves, but merciless to our sins. They will all be burned up in an eternal garbage dump, and if we refuse to repent and give them up and dump them, we will go with them.

TWENTY-SEVENTH SUNDAY
IN ORDINARY TIME

FIRST READING
GENESIS 2:18–24 _____

The LORD God said: "It is not good for the man to be alone. I will make a suitable partner for him." So the LORD God formed out of the ground various wild animals and various birds of the air, and he brought them to the man to see what he would call them; whatever the man called each of them would be its name. The man gave names to all the cattle, all the birds of the air, and all wild animals; but none proved to be the suitable partner for the man.

So the LORD God cast a deep sleep on the man, and while he was asleep, he took out one of his ribs and closed up its place with flesh. The LORD God then built up into a woman the rib that he had taken from the man. When he brought her to the man, the man said:

"This one, at last, is bone of my bones
    and flesh of my flesh;
this one shall be called 'woman,'
    for out of 'her man' this one has been taken."

That is why a man leaves his father and mother and clings to his wife, and the two of them become one flesh.

RESPONSORIAL PSALM
PSALM 128:1–2, 3, 4–5, 6_____

R. (cf. 5) **May the Lord bless us all the days of our lives.**

Blessed are you who fear the Lord,
   who walk in his ways!
For you shall eat the fruit of your handiwork;
   blessed shall you be, and favored.

Your wife shall be like a fruitful vine
   in the recesses of your home;
your children like olive plants
   around your table.

Behold, thus is the man blessed
   who fears the Lord.
The Lord bless you from Zion:
   may you see the prosperity of Jerusalem
   all the days of your life.

May you see your children's children.
   Peace be upon Israel!

SECOND READING
Hebrews 2:9–11   _____

Brothers and sisters: He "for a little while" was made "lower than the angels," that by the grace of God he might taste death for everyone.

For it was fitting that he, for whom and through whom all things exist, in bringing many children to glory, should make the leader to their salvation perfect through suffering. He who consecrates and those who are being consecrated all have one origin. Therefore, he is not ashamed to call them "brothers."

GOSPEL
Mark 10:2–16
(or Mark 10:2–12) _____

The Pharisees approached Jesus and asked, "Is it lawful for a husband to divorce his wife?" They were testing him. He said to them in reply, "What did Moses command you?" They replied, "Moses permitted a husband to write a bill of divorce and dismiss her." But Jesus told them, "Because of the hardness of your hearts he wrote you this commandment. But from the beginning of creation, *God made them male and female. For this reason a man shall leave his father and mother and be joined to his wife, and the two shall become one flesh.* So they are no longer two but one flesh. Therefore what God has joined together, no human being must separate." In the house the disciples again questioned Jesus about this. He said to them, "Whoever divorces his wife and marries another commits adultery against her; and if she divorces her husband and marries another, she commits adultery."

And people were bringing children to him that he might touch them, but the disciples rebuked them. When Jesus saw this he became indignant and said to them, "Let the children come to me; do not prevent them, for the kingdom of God belongs to such as these. Amen, I say to you, whoever does not accept the kingdom of God like a child will not enter it." Then he embraced them and blessed them, placing his hands on them.

It is very telling that the thing we fail to notice about the passages we read today about marriage and the family that the Church selects from Scripture is that they all center on the same thing: children. The Genesis account of God creating us male and female, the elaborate blessing of the Psalm, and the story in today's Gospel all center on children as the end and purpose and fruit of God's invention of sex and marriage. The "male and female" exist not just for themselves or even just for each other but for their children. The "one flesh" that both Genesis and Jesus say defines marriage means not just sexual intercourse but its fruit, children. The child is literally the "one flesh," the one body procreated by the two parents—literally and physically, genetically. The real story here, and the real puzzle, is why we forget that. When Jesus says of marriage "the two shall become one flesh," we think of that "one flesh" as only the union of two persons, the man and the woman, but Jesus thinks of three: he thinks also of the child. Shouldn't our thought be more in line with Jesus' thought?

The vast majority in every society in human history except our own—that is, post-Christian modern Western culture—has seen that point, has seen that God's purpose in making us male and female and in instituting marriage was for it to be a mutual self-giving that is total, faithful, monogamous, and heterosexual, and therefore fertile. Children are to marriage what oranges are to orange trees.

Every society except ours has seen children as a blessing and childlessness as a curse. Our contraceptive culture, which Pope St. John Paul II called "the culture of death," has turned this truth upside down and sees children as an "accident," a problem, or even a curse, and childlessness as a blessing, not from God but from our new contraceptive technology.

That is one of the most radical revolutions that has ever happened in all of human history. That is what has made abortion possible. We have aborted not only a million of our own children each year but also our own most powerful natural instinct to cherish and protect our own children at all stages of their development. No other animal species has ever done that. That is why it is the most radical and revolutionary meaning of the "sexual revolution."

What is so revolutionary about it is that it contradicts not just religion and morality but also science. The biological reality that was always seen as "the reproductive system," not only by the Church, the Bible, and Jesus but also by all other cultures, all previous common sense, and modern science, is now seen as the entertainment system, and reproduction and its products, children, are seen as "accidents."

Every society in history until the one we are now living in has spontaneously seen children as a blessing, and a joy, and even a profit. Even selfish people had many children because they were seen as profitable, not only for wealth but also for happiness. Today, selfish people have few or no children because they are seen as a burden, even a martyrdom. That is a change as powerful as the change from flood tide to ebb tide, or from life to death. In fact, that is what it is: the ebbing of life and the coming of cultural death. The Lord of a "culture of death" is no longer the Lord of life.

We have devalued what is literally the most creative thing we can do, pro-creation. Creating children is more creative than creating any art or science or culture or civilization because its product is the only thing in the universe that will outlive the universe itself. It is a person, the only thing in the universe that God loves for its own sake, and that we, too, are to love for its own sake, not just as a means to any other end.

Abortion is backup contraception, backup birth control. They are intrinsically connected. Abortion is the offensive half and contraception is the defensive half of the war against children. The Church has always opposed both, and always will. And almost the whole world used to agree with the Church, instinctively. Even Freud said that "the abandonment of the reproductive function is the common feature of all perversions." Today, no one in our culture sees it that way anymore except the stubborn old Catholic Church. And even within the Church, the vast majority of those who call themselves Catholics neither see it nor believe it nor obey it. In the entire history of the Church, there has never been a doctrine so widely disbelieved, a commandment so widely disobeyed, a holy thing so hated, and a perversion so permitted. That is not a personal opinion or a subjective feeling; that is an objective historical and statistical fact.

Contraception is a triple sin: first of all, against yourself and your own creativity; secondly, against God, whose gift of life is refused by locking the door to his coming and working creation's greatest miracle, the creation of a new immortal soul; and thirdly, against your children, by locking the door against their existence. The Church is pro-children because God himself became a child.

Another consequence of the Church's love of children is her hatred of divorce. Children never love divorce. Scores of scientific statistics prove that children are more emotionally harmed, long-range, by divorce than even by death. In today's Gospel, Jesus clearly forbids divorce. There is no ambiguity here at all, no wiggle room, no lack of clarity and simplicity in his words. No other church stands wholly with Jesus on all the issues of the sexual revolution: lust, fornication, contraception, abortion, divorce, transgenderism, and "test tube babies," which is the flip side of contraception: babies without sex rather than sex without babies.

Divorce always harms children. The Church always calls us to defend the victims, not the victimizers, whether the victims are the enslaved, the poor, the powerless, the small, the unborn, or women.

Christ said, "What God has joined together, no human being must separate." That's why both murder and divorce are wrong: both put asunder what God has joined together, whether that something is a husband and wife in a "one flesh" valid marriage or whether it is the unity of body and soul in a single human being that constitutes his life. The two evils of divorce and murder are connected because suicide is a form of murder, and divorce is the suicide of the "one flesh" union called marriage. There is little hope for the future of any society in which half of all its members commit suicide; families are the fundamental members or units of any society, and in our society we have a more than 50 percent divorce rate.

The reason the Church appears so terribly "judgmental" is because she is so compassionate. The reason she is so "conservative" is because she is so "liberal." She wants to liberate us from harm, to free us; that's why she must conserve and preserve and remind us of her wisdom. That wisdom is not from man but from God. *We* did not invent the Church; Christ did. All of her condemnations are based on his compassion. It is Christ's compassion for sinners that motivates his Church to condemn their sins, just as it was compassion for slaves that motivated the abolitionists' condemnations of slavery. All sins harm the sinner, even though the sinner sometimes sees his poison as food and his chains as freedom.

༄

The epistle for today is also about the family, but not the biological family. It is about the Church family. The Church is a family too, as is the Trinity; and both the Church and the biological family are images of the Trinity. What is common to all three is the gift of self.

In the Bible, the biological family that is made by the marriage between a man and a woman is an image of the family that is made by the marriage between Christ and his Church. St. Paul makes that point when he talks about the relation between husband and wife, their mutual surrender to each other, in which they become one without ceasing to be two. He says: "The two shall become one flesh. This is a great mystery, but I speak in reference to Christ and the church" (Eph. 5:31–32).

In the last two chapters of the last book of the Bible, the book of Revelation, we see the last event in history, the culmination of all of history, the end and point and fulfillment of all history, which is the marriage between Christ and his Church, his people, his Mystical Body and spiritual spouse. All of human history is preparation for that, engagement for that wedding.

The passage from Hebrews that is our epistle for today is also about marriage and the family because it identifies our Christian identity with two family terms: we are Christ's "brothers" and also Christ's "children." We're his biological brothers because he became our brother by the Incarnation, and we're his spiritual children because faith and Baptism give us a second birth into his divine family.

It's family all the way up, because all three levels of self-giving agape love are family relationships. First, at the top, God is not just one person but three. The three persons of the eternal Trinity are like a family that eternally give themselves to each other, holding nothing back. Second, at the bottom, in the biological family, the husband and wife give their whole selves to each other, holding nothing back, including their fertility. Third, our relation to Christ is also a marriage, a spiritual marriage. Christ gives himself to us, his Church, his Mystical Body, his spiritual spouse, and we give ourselves to him. He held nothing back, not one drop of his blood, and we should hold back not one drop of devotion and obedience.

This total self-giving is a sacrifice, of course, a sacrifice of selfishness and egotism and autonomy. But it is also life's most complete joy, and the suffering is swallowed up in the joy as a tiny dust mote is swallowed up in the sunlight. It is nothing less than the fundamental secret of happiness and the meaning life.

TWENTY-EIGHTH SUNDAY
IN ORDINARY TIME

FIRST READING

WISDOM 7:7–11 _____

I prayed, and prudence was given me;
   I pleaded, and the spirit of wisdom came to me.
I preferred her to scepter and throne,
and deemed riches nothing in comparison with her,
   nor did I liken any priceless gem to her;
because all gold, in view of her, is a little sand,
   and before her, silver is to be accounted mire.
Beyond health and comeliness I loved her,
and I chose to have her rather than the light,
   because the splendor of her never yields to sleep.
Yet all good things together came to me in her company,
   and countless riches at her hands.

RESPONSORIAL PSALM

PSALM 90:12–13, 14–15, 16–17 _____

R. (14) **Fill us with your love, O Lord, and we will sing for joy!**

Teach us to number our days aright,
   that we may gain wisdom of heart.
Return, O LORD! How long?
   Have pity on your servants!

715

Fill us at daybreak with your kindness,
    that we may shout for joy and gladness all our days.
Make us glad, for the days when you afflicted us,
    for the years when we saw evil.

Let your work be seen by your servants
    and your glory by their children;
and may the gracious care of the LORD our God be ours;
    prosper the work of our hands for us!
Prosper the work of our hands!

Today's Old Testament reading and today's Psalm are both about wisdom.

Another word for wisdom is "prudence." Prudence does *not* mean being extra careful and not taking any chances. It means simply practical wisdom, wisdom for living.

This is the first of the virtues, because if you are a fool instead of wise, you're unable to move on to any of the other virtues because you don't know where you're going. You have no light, no sight.

In the ancient world, all religions praise wisdom above everything else. In today's reading from the Wisdom of Solomon, the author praises wisdom not just for its practicality but also for its splendor, its glory, its beauty. It is a large, broad, spreading, beautiful, arresting, daring thing, just the opposite of what we today often misunderstand as "prudence" in the sense of a small, narrow, timid, uninspiring, cowardly kind of thing.

The author, a disciple of King Solomon, reputedly the wisest man in the world, claims that wisdom is true riches, true wealth; it is more precious than money. All the money in the world cannot buy it. And if it could, that would be a great investment, worth sacrificing everything else for.

Along with wisdom, ancient cultures praised the virtue of piety, which meant reverence for both the gods and the family and ancestors, because both had wisdom.

And since the old were expected to be wiser than the young, they were envied, not pitied. In Confucian China, to say you looked old was a compliment because it meant you looked wise; to say you looked young was an insult because it meant you looked foolish.

Today we live in the opposite kind of culture, a "cancel culture" that despises its history and its past and its ancestors, a culture that teaches children *not* to revere parents, ancestors, sages, saints, and traditions, to be "yourself," even though you don't know what that means beyond a "whatever." Our children are told the lie that "you can be whatever you want to be," and even told to embrace the lie that you are the gender that you aren't.

Our culture exalts the young because they have more strength and health and pleasure, and most especially more sex, which our materialistic culture prizes far above wisdom.

That's one of the reasons why true religion is necessarily countercultural today. Tradition is the supreme rebellion. If you want to be a countercultural nonconformist and a rebel and a revolutionary today, the only way to do that is to be traditional and religious. Everything else is approved as culturally "progressive."

There is nothing more radically countercultural anywhere in the world today than the Blessed Virgin Mary. Two of her titles are "the Blessed Virgin" and "the Blessed Mother." Our contraceptive culture worships sex without motherhood rather than motherhood without sex. It despises both virginity and motherhood. Mary is the most countercultural force in the world today.

Is Mary wise or foolish? Is our culture supremely foolish or supremely wise? One of Mary's titles is "Seat of Wisdom" because Wisdom itself, Wisdom incarnate, Wisdom himself, the Son of God, literally sat on the seat of her lap.

Wisdom is a deeper *pleasure* than fleeting, external, physical pleasures, because it's your own personal, permanent possession; it's inside you. Everyone who has tasted both the joys of wisdom and the joys of physical pleasures have said the same thing: that there is simply no comparison between the two. If you don't say that, that means you've never tried the higher joys. St. Thomas

Aquinas says, "No one can live without joy. That is why those who are deprived of true, spiritual joys always go over to carnal pleasures."

When we have wisdom, we have truth; and, therefore, we have the true versions of all those other things too. But when we have those other things without having wisdom, we cannot distinguish between their true versions and their false versions, so we do not really have their true versions.

Ironically, all the alternative values that our culture prizes above wisdom can come to us only if we have wisdom, because wisdom is like x-ray vision: it penetrates through deceptive appearances to the true realities behind them.

Thus, wisdom sees that true riches are not money or gold or silver but riches within, riches of the soul, of the self. External riches are not really yours, except legally; internal riches are truly yours.

Wisdom sees that true power is not political power or physical power. In fact, those powers are fleeting and fragile. An ancient cliché, quoted in *Henry IV*, said, "Uneasy lies the head that wears a crown," because kings were often assassinated. Even presidents have no private life, are hated by many, and have to be very, very careful what they say. One of our wisest presidents, Harry Truman, said, "In this great land of ours every baby born an American citizen has an equal opportunity of one day winding up here in the Oval Office. That's just the chance the poor little bastard has to take." Power isn't very powerful.

Where do we get wisdom from? Wisdom comes from God, though he usually gives it to us through other people and through our own internal personal efforts. On the other hand, we have little control over whether we inherit money, health, pleasure, or power, and we can easily lose them once we have them.

How do you get wisdom? There is a very simple answer: Ask for it. St. James writes, "But if any of you lacks wisdom, he should ask God who gives to all generously" (James 1:5). When Solomon inherited the kingship from his father David when David died, God told him, "Ask something of me and I will give it to you." And Solomon asked for wisdom. And God said, "Because you have asked for this—not for a long life for yourself, nor for riches, nor for the life of your enemies, but for understanding so that you may know what is right—I do as you requested. . . . In addition, I give you what you have not asked for, such riches and glory" (1 Kings 3:5, 11–13). God wants to give you wisdom too, and the first proof that you already have wisdom is to realize that you don't have it, and to ask God for it.

The Psalmist also speaks of wisdom today when he asks God to "teach us to number our days aright, that we may gain wisdom of heart." In other words, he knows that the most effective teacher of wisdom is death. It's easy to be a fool when you forget that life's only certainty is that you will die and face the unavoidable truth, the unvarnished truth, the truth, the whole truth, and nothing but the truth, at the Last Judgment.

Suffering also makes us wise. That's one of the reasons God allows it, why in his wise and loving providence there is both affliction and deliverance, both failure and success, both poverty and prosperity. Life is like competitive sports: it's a win-win system because you either win or lose, and winning makes you happier and losing makes you wiser.

Suffering and death also move us to prayer, and to faith and hope and love, which we need more than we need the things we are suffering the loss of. Prayer will make us wiser and happier than any of the things we pray for. That is why God waits to give us many good things until we pray for them. God sees that we need the things we pray for much less than we think we do, and he sees that we need prayer itself much more than we think we do. He sees that we need the virtues that prompt prayer more than we need anything else, and if we can get more of those more precious virtues by getting less of the less precious things that we pray for, God will give us the greater gifts, the better gifts—even at the expense of the lesser gifts, if necessary.

If we had no suffering and no death in this world, we would become insufferably selfish and shallow fools, bored and spoiled brats. We are like eggs: we have to break and hatch. If we don't, we get rotten.

In other words, God so values wisdom that he allows suffering and death because they make us wise. It's a simple chain of reasons: God loves us; and love always seeks the highest happiness of the beloved; and our highest happiness comes only through wisdom; and wisdom comes to us through suffering and death; therefore, God's love gives us suffering and death.

Before the fall, in the innocence of the Garden of Eden, and also after we are in heaven, we had and will have no need of suffering and death to teach us wisdom and true happiness. But between those two places and times, we are fools, and fools need to learn wisdom by experience. That's how we stupid, shallow, and selfish sinners grow into wise, profound, and unselfish saints.

SECOND READING
HEBREWS 4:12–13 _____

Brothers and sisters: Indeed the word of God is living and effective, sharper than any two-edged sword, penetrating even between soul and spirit, joints and marrow, and able to discern reflections and thoughts of the heart. No creature is concealed from him, but everything is naked and exposed to the eyes of him to whom we must render an account.

Today's epistle says something remarkable. It says that "the word of God is living and effective, sharper than any two-edged sword, penetrating even between soul and spirit, joints and marrow, and able to discern reflections and thoughts of the heart."

This is either a miracle, if it's true, or a ridiculous exaggeration, if it's not. And millions of people have said, from their own experience, that it is true.

But how can a book be alive and active?

The translation is misleading when it says "effective" instead of "active." The Greek word is *energés*, from which we get the word "energy." It's alive and active, like heat or light, like the sun; not just "effective," like an economic policy or like a computer. It's like a sharp sword in the hands of a formidable swordsman.

But a book isn't literally alive. It does not move, as we do. When a person reads a book, the person is the actor and the book is the object. How can a book be the actor and the reader be the object? The last sentence of the passage says just that: that to the word of God, "no creature is concealed . . . but everything is naked and exposed."

What the author is saying is that when we read the Bible, we can discover something very unusual: that this is not an ordinary book. It really does read us. When we look at it, it looks at us. It's like looking at a window, thinking you are alone, and then suddenly noticing that there is another person outside looking through that window at you. It's like looking into a mirror and expecting to see only yourself, and suddenly you see another face looking at you from the mirror.

The face is Jesus Christ, of course. The phrase "the Word of God" means the Bible, but it also means Jesus Christ, the Son of God, the second person of the Holy Trinity. He is the primary meaning of the phrase "the Word of God." He is the Word of God in the singular; the Bible is the words of God in the plural. It has many words in it, but God has only one Word in him: Christ. The Word of God is not just a book but a person. That's why when you read the book, you meet the person.

When you read this book, you are praying—in fact, one of the most powerful ways to pray is to read the Bible in the presence of God, in conversation with God. When you pray, you are not alone. Praying is not like being alone and writing a letter to someone who's absent; it's more like having a conversation with someone who's present. And that someone talks back to you and challenges you. He speaks real words. They are the words of the book. The other person is there with you—not bodily, as he is on the cross and in the Eucharist, but spiritually. But spiritual presence is real presence. That face in the window or in the mirror is real; it's not just your imagination.

The book seems to be alive and active and reading you because it is really doing that, and it's doing that because that "it" is a "he." And it cuts into your heart; it cuts into the division between your surface heart and your deep heart, or (in the author's words) between your soul and your spirit. Your soul includes your conscious relation to yourself—to your body and your conscious thoughts and desires and feelings and choices—and to other people, while your spirit includes your relation to God, which is both conscious and subconscious, both clear and mysterious, both rational and mystical. For the human heart, the human spirit, is much deeper and more mysterious than the physical universe.

Elsewhere, the Bible calls itself "the sword of the Spirit," meaning the Holy Spirit (Eph. 6:17). A sword is not active in itself, but it becomes active when a swordsman swings it. So with this book: it is inspired, infused, in-breathed, by God, who is its primary author. The humans who wrote its books are God's instruments. He does not reduce them to machines; he turns them on, not off. But he uses their own minds and personalities to speak to all of us.

Not everyone loves that nakedness before God, that lack of shadows and darkness and hiding. The author writes, "No creature is concealed from him, but everything is naked and exposed to the eyes of him to whom we must render an account."

Psalm 139 begins with this same truth: "O Lord, you have probed me and you know me; you know when I sit and when I stand; you understand my thoughts from afar. My journeys and my rest you scrutinize, with all my ways you are familiar. Even before a word is on my tongue, behold, O Lord, you know the whole of it. Behind me and before, you hem me in and rest your hand upon me. . . . Where can I go from your spirit? From your presence where can I flee?" (Ps. 139:1–7).

David, the saintly Psalmist, confesses this truth in joy, in praise. He wants to be known by God. He wants to stand in the light, even when it exposes him and his sins to God. He loves light; he loves truth, and that is what God is: God is truth (John 14:6).

Great atheists like Sartre and Nietzsche say exactly the opposite: that this all-knowing God would be their supreme torture; that they could not possibly live in a world where there was a God who knew everything in them, including their dark side. That's why they refuse to believe in God; that's the deepest reason for their atheism. It's not intellectual skepticism; it's personal rebellion and fear.

That is the difference between heaven and hell. Some of the saints and mystics say that perhaps heaven and hell in objective reality are the same thing: God's total truth, total light—and that for those who love the light of truth, it is heaven, while for those who hate it, it is hell. Those who love truth and goodness, who hate lies and sins and repent of them, experience this total truth and goodness as heaven; while for the wicked, who love their sins and refuse to repent, this same light is hell. They love darkness, but they can no longer find any, as they could on earth.

That's what Jesus said, in John's Gospel: "This is the verdict, that the light came into the world, but people preferred darkness to light, because their works were evil. For everyone who does wicked things hates the light and does not come toward the light, so that his works might not be exposed" (John 3:19–20).

That is why God gave us the sacrament of Confession. There, we choose light and reject darkness. There, heaven begins. Second only to the altar during the Mass, the devil hates the sacrament of Confession more than any other place in the world.

What about you? Do you hate it too, or do you love it?

Do you want God to speak to you? Do you want to see that face in the window and hear his words? Do you want to know God? If you do, here are the four best ways to do it.

First, read the Bible, especially the Gospels, and meet Jesus Christ.

Second, believe in him, trust him, love him, accept him, receive him, both in your heart and in his sacraments, especially Confession and Communion.

Third, pray, both privately and publicly, both in your own words and in the words of the Mass.

Fourth, live for him; live his will; live his love; give yourself to others as he gave himself to you.

GOSPEL

Mark 10:17–30
(or Mark 10:17–27)

As Jesus was setting out on a journey, a man ran up, knelt down before him, and asked him, "Good teacher, what must I do to inherit eternal life?" Jesus answered him, "Why do you call me good? No one is good but God alone. You know the commandments: *You shall not kill; you shall not commit adultery; you shall not steal; you shall not bear false witness; you shall not defraud; honor your father and your mother.*" He replied and said to him, "Teacher, all of these I have observed from my youth." Jesus, looking at him, loved him and said to him, "You are lacking in one thing. Go, sell what you have, and give to the poor and you will have treasure in heaven; then come, follow me." At that statement his face fell, and he went away sad, for he had many possessions.

Jesus looked around and said to his disciples, "How hard it is for those who have wealth to enter the kingdom of God!" The disciples were amazed at his words. So Jesus again said to them in reply, "Children, how hard it is to enter the kingdom of God! It is easier for a camel to pass through the eye of a needle than for one who is rich to enter the kingdom of God." They were exceedingly astonished and said among themselves, "Then who can be saved?" Jesus looked at them and said, "For human beings it is impossible, but not for God. All things are possible for God." Peter began to say to him, "We have given up everything and followed you." Jesus said, "Amen, I say to you, there is no one who has given up house or brothers or sisters or mother or father or children or lands for my sake and for the sake of the gospel who will not receive a hundred times more now in this present age: houses and brothers and sisters and mothers and children and lands, with persecutions, and eternal life in the age to come."

Today's Gospel tells us the story of the rich young ruler. Matthew tells us that he was young. Luke tells us that he was a ruler and very rich. These three things—money, political and social power, and the enthusiasms of youth—are all good things in themselves; but all three can be misused and idolized, and turn into addictions. All three are good means but bad ends.

This young man was a good man. His passion and enthusiasm are evident from the fact that he "ran" up to Jesus. His piety is evident from the fact that he "knelt down before him." His wisdom is evident from the fact that he called Jesus "good" and "teacher." And the question he asked Jesus was nothing less than the wisest and most important of all questions anyone can ask in this life: "What must I do to inherit eternal life?"

But Jesus always answers the questioner, not just the question. And like all rabbis, he answers a question with another question: "Why do you call me good? No one is good but God alone." (Do you know why a rabbi always answers a question with another question? Here is the answer: Why shouldn't a rabbi answer a question with another question?)

Jesus is testing the young man. He is testing his piety and his wisdom: who does he think Jesus is? God, or mere man? If he thinks Jesus is God, then the young man will accept Jesus' answer, no matter what it is, and not only believe it but also live it, obey it. If he thinks Jesus is a mere man, the young man may disagree with Jesus' answer and disobey it.

And that is what he does, which shows not merely that he gets his ethics wrong but also that he gets his theology wrong. He not only fails to understand himself and his human need, but he also fails to understand Jesus and his divine authority—which is why he fails to understand himself and his own human need. Jesus is the universal touchstone, the standard. If we get him right, we get everything right. If not, not.

So Jesus first tests him as to who he thinks Jesus is, and then he tests him as to who he thinks he is, and who he thinks he should be, how he thinks he should live.

Who he is right now is a young man who is both rich and a ruler, and he is probably using his riches wisely in his ruling, whatever that ruling is, whether it is political or religious or both. But sometimes a good thing can get in the way of a better thing. And Jesus is going to test him, like an x-ray, not so that Jesus can find out what is inside his heart, for Jesus knows that already, but so that the young man can see what is in his own heart. Probably everyone who knew him admired him and thought his heart must be so wise and good that if anyone would deserve eternal life he would. Jesus sees deeper. He always does.

Jesus answers his question about what he must do to inherit eternal life in two steps. Later he is going to tell him something surprising, something that he does not know. But first he tells him what he already knew: God's answer to that question, God's Ten Commandments. Jesus repeats the second part of the Ten Commandments, our duties to our neighbors. That's where we naturally begin: with our natural human relationships. And then we go higher, to our duties to God. The drama here is whether the young man will pass God's test. And it looks like he will, because he replies to Jesus' summary of the second part, "All of these I have observed from my youth."

When we hear that, we suspect this young man is proud and self-righteous, like the Pharisees. But this is not so, for "Jesus, looking at him, loved him." Jesus does not love self-righteousness.

The Greek word for "looking at" implies not just sense perception of external appearances but understanding the heart—not just "looking-at" but "looking-*into*," like an x-ray. Jesus sees his heart, not just his appearance, and he loves his heart. Here is a young man who has obeyed all of the second half of the Commandments completely. Jesus admires him.

But he is not satisfied. He says, "You are lacking in one thing." Matthew's account mentions a significant detail: he tells us that the young man said not merely "All of these I have observed" but also "What do I still lack?" (Matt. 19:20). The young man himself must have felt that something was missing; he must have intuitively known that he was still lacking something. He knew himself well enough not to be self-satisfied. Good for him!

And Jesus then tells him what is missing. He shows him the one piece of himself that is still missing. Like a doctor examining an apparently completely healthy patient, Jesus discovers one little cancer cell, which, if left untreated, can grow and kill his soul.

What Jesus says to him seems cruel, but it is really kind. He seems to make an irrational and impossible demand, one that could only come from God, not from man; and thus, Jesus is now testing him about the first part of the Commandments, the part that is most absolute because it is about the Absolute Being, God, and about his absolute demand on us and about our absolute duty to obey it.

And this is absolutely necessary for this young man because his cancer cell is his addiction to a false god, to his wealth and power. He is probably using this wealth and power very wisely and unselfishly, and doing great good with it. Yet all that good is not God himself, and it is dangerously easy for us to worship very good things as false gods. Few people are tempted to worship evil things, like cruelty, or neutral things, like sand, or very minor goods, like birds or shoes or paper clips, as their gods, as idols. But many people worship major goods that God has given us, like sex or power or their own virtue, as their god, their supreme good. But only God is God, and God will not share his glory with another. God *cannot* share his glory with another, because God cannot lie.

What the young man is missing has to do with the commandment Jesus did not mention, the one Jesus on another occasion called "the greatest and the first commandment" of all (Matt. 22:38), which is this: "You shall not have other gods besides me" (Exod. 20:3).

For this young man, that was his money and power, or, more likely, something much better than that: namely, the very good use that he was making of both. That was his idol. It was a very good idol. He was probably doing many very good things with his money and power. And it seemed utterly unreasonable for Jesus to demand that he give up everything that he had, that he sell all his possessions and give the money to the poor, and that he leave his position and his power and all the good works he was doing with it just to come and follow Jesus, with no guarantees except Jesus' promise that he would have greater treasures in heaven.

Jesus knew what the young man's reaction to that demand would be. He was not surprised that the young man went away sorrowful, "for he had many possessions." And Jesus did not say those words that he knew would disappoint him and make him sorrowful because Jesus *didn't* love him but because he *did*. God gives us sorrows as well as joys for the same reason: out of his love for us, coupled with the wisdom to know what the very best thing for us is, which is not perpetual joy but which includes hard lessons of growth through suffering. They are all necessary. If they were not, God would not allow them, in his perfect wisdom and perfect timing and perfect providence. He always provides what we most need, not what we most want.

We don't know what happened next in this young man's life. But we do know that Jesus loved him and therefore gave him the very best road to his ultimate happiness, a road that included his recognition of his need for detachment from his possessions. We don't know whether he eventually did what Jesus commanded or not, but we know that if he did, he was saved, and if he didn't, he was not. We know that Jesus is the way, the road to heaven; we do not know how many walk that road and how many do not.

This young man is not a special case. He is us. We are all in the same human situation. What we most need is God, and therefore any obstacle to our total love and loyalty to God must be ruthlessly cleared away, no matter how precious it is. On another occasion, Jesus said, "If your right eye causes you to sin, tear it out and throw it away. It is better for you to lose one of your members than to have your whole body thrown into Gehenna" (Matt. 5:29). Of course, having feet and hands and eyes doesn't keep us from heaven, but if it did, it would profit us to lose them, not to keep them. For, as Jesus said, "What profit is there for one to gain the whole world and forfeit his life?" (Mark 8:36).

There is one thing, and one thing alone, that is infinitely and absolutely necessary. And this young man knew it; that's why he chose to ask Jesus about that very question: "What is keeping me back from 'the one thing necessary'?"

This young man's obstacle was his wealth. Wealth—money and the things money can buy—is not everyone's chief obstacle and idol, though it is a very popular one. But money stands for any addictive idol, whether low or high. It could be drugs or pornography; or it could be your own virtues. Our greatest good, our happiness, is neither pleasures nor virtues; it is God.

If that's not true, then God is not God—he is just one thing among many others, like every one of the gods of pagan polytheism. Many people are practicing polytheists. Religion is a good thing, but it has to be balanced by many other things, right? Wrong! Religion is relationship with God, and that is not one thing among many other things any more than your soul is one thing among many other things in you, like your toes.

Just as God often withholds the good things we pray for because he sees that what we need most is to pray, so God often takes away the good things we have because he sees that the attitude toward these things that we most need is detachment. Detachment is freedom. We are enslaved to whatever we cannot part with that is less than ourselves, including our wealth and our possessions and even our human relationships, all of which will be taken away in death. If we are nothing but these things and these relationships, then when we die and they disappear, we will also disappear with them. If there is nobody behind all those relationships and all those appearances, if there is nobody wearing all the masks we wear, then death will reveal that emptiness.

We need detachment from everything that is not God. We need even detachment from our "successes," both our economic successes and our personal achievements, and even our moral successes. Moral virtue alone cannot save us. We are not saved by our own virtues. They are not enough to merit heaven. Only Christ can merit heaven. And he comes to us only when our hands are empty, not grasping. All our this-worldly achievements are toys, and we need to open our grasping hands and let go of our toys before he can put himself into our hands.

Buddha did not know of God, but he knew of man very well, and he taught that the source of all misery is "grasping," or greed (*tanha*), or selfishness.

Jesus' first beatitude is "Blessed are the poor in spirit" (Matt. 5:3). If you have only a penny, but you are grasping it, you cannot receive heaven. If you have a billion dollars, but you are detached from it, you can receive heaven. There is no relationship whatsoever between your salvation and anything in your bank account. There is every relationship between your salvation and everything in your heart.

Jesus uses this occasion to warn his disciples about addiction to riches. He shocks them when he says that is it very difficult for the rich to be saved. In fact, he says that "for human beings this is impossible, but for God all things are possible" (Matt. 19:26). We cannot make ourselves good enough to deserve heaven, or even to endure it and enjoy it, but God can do that for us; he can purge us of our sinful habits and desires perfectly. That's why there is a purgatory, and that's why that's part of the Good News.

Jesus did not say that no one who has riches can be saved. He did not give us statistical information about the size of heaven's population. But he clearly taught that riches are a danger and a temptation.

We will all be rich in heaven because we will get back from God more than all the things we give up to him, all the things we are detached from, and we will get them all in a transformed form, including our own possessions, our own bodies, our pleasures, our virtues, and our very souls. Thus, Jesus ends this shocking and negative lesson with an equally shocking positive promise. When Peter says to him, "We have given up everything and followed you," Jesus promises him that everyone who does that will receive a hundred times more back from the God who simply cannot be outdone in generosity. For, as St. Paul told us, "All belong to you, and you to Christ, and Christ to God" (1 Cor. 3:22–23).

TWENTY-NINTH SUNDAY
IN ORDINARY TIME

FIRST READING

ISAIAH 53:10–11 _____

The LORD was pleased to crush him in infirmity.

If he gives his life as an offering for sin,
    he shall see his descendants in a long life,
    and the will of the LORD shall be accomplished through him.

Because of his affliction
    he shall see the light in fullness of days;
through his suffering, my servant shall justify many,
    and their guilt he shall bear.

The fifty-third chapter of Isaiah is one of literally hundreds of prophecies in the Old Testament about the promised Messiah, and it is probably the one that most clearly points to Jesus as the Christ. ("Christ" means "Messiah," or "the anointed one," "the promised one.")

In the Old Testament, God mandated many different sacrificial offerings for sin, but all of them were sacrifices of animals, not human beings. All the other religions of the world had human sacrifice, at least as a kind of emergency, and sometimes routinely, as with the Canaanites in Old Testament times, and later the Aztecs, both of whom slaughtered a third of their children as offerings to the evil spirits whom they worshiped. But God forbade this practice of human sacrifice for his chosen people in Genesis 11, where he sent his angel to stop Abraham, the father of God's chosen people, from sacrificing his son Isaac in order to dramatically teach Abraham that an animal, in this case a ram, a sheep, a lamb, would be sacrificed instead of an innocent human being.

Judaism was the only religion in the world that taught that all human lives were sacred to God because they were created in God's own image. Nowhere in Scripture does it say that God would be pleased to accept a human life as an offering for sin, except with regard to the Messiah.

Today's passage from Isaiah says that this sin offering would be a joint operation, so to speak, with both God and the Messiah consenting, since the passage says both that God would be pleased to crush his servant the Messiah and also that the Messiah himself would freely give his life as an offering for sin.

Nowhere else does Scripture say that one man's suffering would justify many and bear their guilt. This prophecy applies to the Messiah alone. No other sane man ever claimed to do that. Many people claimed to be the Messiah, especially around the time of Jesus, since the prophecies in the Old Testament are fairly clear about when the Messiah would come. But not one of them fulfilled this prophecy of Isaiah. None of the hundreds of claimants to the title of the promised Messiah, at any time in history, claimed to be the one whose sufferings and death would justify mankind, would save the whole human race from sin and guilt.

Most of the Jews of Jesus' time believed that the Messiah would free the Jews from the totalitarian and tyrannical oppression of the Romans, since the prophecies said that the Messiah would save Israel from her enemies. Those Jews who were wise enough to understand that our real enemies are not flesh and blood but our own sins accepted Jesus as the Messiah; those who did not understand this did not, because they identified their enemies as the Romans, who stole from them what their hearts were most deeply in love with—namely, this-worldly success, political and social and economic and military power. Jesus tested their deepest desires by not being the political messiah they expected, and he tested them even more severely by showing that the way of salvation was not through worldly success but through suffering joined with love, through the love that suffered and gave itself up for the beloved. It was a salvation from sin by means of love and suffering, not a salvation from suffering by means of sins of lovelessness and killing our flesh-and-blood enemies. Our enemies—our sins—were indeed killed by the Messiah, but they were killed by love, not by hate.

RESPONSORIAL PSALM
Psalm 33:4–5, 18–19, 20, 22 _____

R. (22) **Lord, let your mercy be on us, as we place our trust in you.**

Upright is the word of the Lord,
    and all his works are trustworthy.
He loves justice and right;
    of the kindness of the Lord the earth is full.

See, the eyes of the Lord are upon those who fear him,
    upon those who hope for his kindness,
To deliver them from death
    and preserve them in spite of famine.

Our soul waits for the Lord,
    who is our help and our shield.
May your kindness, O Lord, be upon us
    who have put our hope in you.

_____

These Psalm verses are typical, not surprising. But if we look at them carefully, we find a theme that is surprising, though it is also typical. Look at the adjectives that the Psalmist uses to describe the words and works of the Lord. They naturally divide into two different groups. The first group could be called "hard" and the second "soft," or the first "objective and impersonal" and the second "subjective and personal." The first group of adjectives includes words like "upright," "trustworthy," "justice," and "right," and our response to them is described as "fear." "The beginning of wisdom is fear of the Lord" is a truth that is repeated frequently in Scripture. The second group includes "love," "kindness," and "deliverance," and our response to them is described as "hope."

Both what we may call the "hard virtues" like justice and truth and the "soft virtues" like love and kindness are clearly taught by God's revelation in Scripture and also by his voice in our own conscience. But they seem to contradict each other, or at least to contrast sharply with each other, like the two seats on a seesaw. The more one goes up, the more the other goes down. Mercy seems to be a compromise or relaxation of justice, a refusal of justice, a refusal to mete out justice; and justice seems to be a compromise or denial of mercy. If we get justice, we get what we deserve; if we get mercy, we do not get what we deserve but something we don't deserve, either more rewards than we deserve or less punishment than we deserve. So the hard virtues like justice and truth and the soft virtues like mercy and kindness and forgiveness seem not only in contrast to each other but even in contradiction to each other.

And yet God's own inspired word and God's own voice in our conscience demand both of us. Injustice is a sin, and so is mercilessness. How can we combine them without compromise?

If the moral law demands both, and if this law comes to us from God, both through Scripture and through conscience, we must accomplish this combination in God's way, as God does it. So how does God do it?

Christ is the answer. In Christ we are forgiven, but not by ignoring justice. Justice is done. Sin is punished. But it is punished vicariously, in him, the Lamb of God, who suffers the just punishment for our sins while we get the mercy. We exchange places: he takes our place; he is our substitute, our sacrificial lamb.

And now we must do the same thing to our neighbor as he does for us. He made that very clear on the night of the Last Supper when he washed his disciples' feet, a job reserved for the lowest slave. And then he said, "Do you realize what I have done for you? You call me 'teacher' and 'master,' and rightly so, for indeed I am. If I, therefore, the master and teacher, have washed your feet, you ought to wash one another's feet" (John 13:12–14). That's not ignoring justice but going beyond it.

Our mind tells us what justice is, and our heart tells us what love is, and we must ignore neither of these because both are part of God's image in us. The hard virtues of truth and justice and the soft virtues of love and mercy are absolutes because they are attributes of God, who is the absolute.

But how do we practice both in concrete, complex situations? We must find ways. We are not computers or machines or mathematical equations; we are artists and singers and storytellers. We are creative. God created us in his own image, and the image of the Creator must include the ability to create, must include creativity. Compared with all secular alternatives, Christianity is both more "liberal" and more "conservative" than either secular liberalism or secular conservatism. We are more free or "liberal" and creative about applying our absolute and eternal principles to relative and changing situations in ways that we ourselves have to find by using the virtue of practical wisdom, or prudence, *and* at the same time we are more absolutistic and uncompromising, more stick-in-the-mud "conservative" about the principles that God himself has given us, that don't come from ourselves but from him.

God gives us absolute principles and asks us to devise creative ways to apply them. That's what he did in Christ. No one expected what he did there. No one expected the Incarnation, Passion, Death, and Resurrection. That was the most creative solution in all of history to the greatest of all problems—human sin and evil. It was the supreme manifestation of both justice and mercy at once, and at one, on the cross, where the opposing virtues were united, as the two opposing bars of wood, the vertical and the horizontal, were crossed and joined to each other in one. When the Psalmist wrote in another Psalm that "kindness and truth shall meet; justice and peace shall kiss" because righteousness will both "spring out of the earth" and "look down from heaven" (Ps. 85:11–12), he was prophesying that the Messiah would unite mercy and justice by uniting earth and heaven, humanity and divinity, in himself.

That is our concrete model and standard. It's not abstract but concrete. He is not just our impersonal lawgiver but our personal Lord and God, our whole meaning and identity. We must walk in his way because he *is* the way, and the truth, and the life. Not by external imitation, like a photograph, but by creative art, inspired by his real presence and inspiration in our souls, which means not just by our own spirit but by his. That's why we pray not "Please help me establish *my* kingdom, please do *my* will for me" but "*Thy* kingdom come, *thy* will be done on earth as it is in heaven"—that is, in our lives as it was in his. If we mean that prayer, he will answer it in amazingly creative ways that combine truth and love, justice and mercy, righteousness and kindness, toughness and tenderness, as he himself combined them.

SECOND READING

HEBREWS 4:14–16 _____

Brothers and sisters: Since we have a great high priest who has passed through the heavens, Jesus, the Son of God, let us hold fast to our confession. For we do not have a high priest who is unable to sympathize with our weaknesses, but one who has similarly been tested in every way, yet without sin. So let us confidently approach the throne of grace to receive mercy and to find grace for timely help.

_____

The very essence and center of the Christian faith is Christ himself, the God-man, fully divine and fully human at the same time. The two most fundamental heresies against the heart of Christianity are the denial of the full divinity of Christ and the denial of the full humanity of Christ. Both of these heresies have been popular both in the early Church and today, because they are much easier to understand, and less surprising.

On the one hand, so-called "modernist" theology denies the full divinity of Christ and sees him simply as the ideal man, the perfect man, "the man for others," but not, as the Creed claims, "the only begotten Son of God . . . true God from true God . . . consubstantial with the Father." This was called Arianism in ancient times, after the heretical bishop Arius; today it is called "modernism." On the other hand, it is tempting to see Christ as simply God in disguise, timeless and eternal and perfect in every way, not just morally, not subject to human frailties and temptations. That is the error today's epistle corrects.

Jesus shared not just our mortality but also all our weaknesses, sufferings, failures, emotional depressions, and even temptations. (The Greek word that the NAB translates "tested" is more clearly translated as "tempted.") Jesus was tempted by the devil—not just once in the wilderness but repeatedly, just as we are. Every single temptation, every kind of temptation, that is in us, in our human nature, was in him. That included temptations to pride and despair, lust and greed, laziness and stubbornness—everything we have ever felt.

When he assumed human nature, he assumed not the unfallen human nature that the innocent Adam and Eve had before the Fall, with everything perfectly in order, with the passions totally obedient to the reason and will, and with the body totally obedient to the soul, but he assumed our fallen, fragile, imperfect human nature. He felt temptations just as we do. But he did not yield to them. To be tempted you don't have to be a sinner. Eve was not a sinner when she was tempted; she became a sinner only when she yielded to the temptation.

The author first affirms Christ's heavenly divinity, when he writes that "we have a great high priest who has passed through the heavens, Jesus, the Son of God," and then he affirms Christ's full humanity in the next words: "We do not have a high priest who is unable to sympathize with our weaknesses, but one who has similarly been tested in every way, yet without sin."

The author next shows us the *consequence* of this truth, which is very, very practical. It is that because of his closeness to us, we can have a closeness to him: "So let us confidently approach the throne of grace to receive mercy and to find grace for timely help." Christ knows everything about us, and not just from above, as the Father does, but also from within, from his equality with us, from sharing our full humanity. He understands. He can truly say to us, "I know how you feel," without lying or patronizing. He understands us far better than we understand ourselves. St. Augustine calls him "the one who is more intimately present to me than I am to myself." He is the only perfect psychoanalyst. And he doesn't charge anything for his sessions, except our pride and egotism. He is more relentless in extracting our pride than any dentist is in extracting our rotting teeth or any surgeon in cutting away all our cancers. Dentists, doctors, psychologists, lawyers, and politicians ask for our money, not our hearts; it's business, not love. Jesus asks for our hearts, not our money; it's love, not business.

Visit him often. His door is always open. Its name is prayer.

GOSPEL
Mark 10:35–45
(or Mark 10:42–45) _____

James and John, the sons of Zebedee, came to Jesus and said to him, "Teacher, we want you to do for us whatever we ask of you." He replied, "What do you wish me to do for you?" They answered him, "Grant that in your glory we may sit one at your right and the other at your left." Jesus said to them, "You do not know what you are asking. Can you drink the cup that I drink or be baptized with the baptism with which I am baptized?" They said to him, "We can." Jesus said to them, "The cup that I drink, you will drink, and with the baptism with which I am baptized, you will be baptized; but to sit at my right or at my left is not mine to give but is for those for whom it has been prepared." When the ten heard this, they became indignant at James and John. Jesus summoned them and said to them, "You know that those who are recognized as rulers over the Gentiles lord it over them, and their great ones make their authority over them felt. But it shall not be so among you. Rather, whoever wishes to be great among you will be your servant; whoever wishes to be first among you will be the slave of all. For the Son of Man did not come to be served but to serve and to give his life as a ransom for many."

James and John didn't understand that Jesus' kingdom was not of this world (John 18:36). They came to Jesus asking for a piece of the action, a privileged share in his anticipated success, his power and glory. Jesus answered them that they did not know what they were asking for, since his power and glory will come through his passion and death, his self-abandonment. His success would be to die to give us life. He came into the world for that purpose: to die. That is what he meant by "the cup that I drink" and "the baptism with which I am baptized."

Jesus says to James and John that he will indeed answer their request, but not in the way they have in mind, sharing with them the earthly success and power and reign that they expected. They would get a far higher kingdom and power and glory—namely, heaven and holiness. They would become saints, not Caesars. Because that is the only way to true happiness and joy.

When the others heard about the request of James and John, they were envious and angry. So Jesus sat them down and said to them—to all of them equally, both the two who tried to get their feet in the door before the other ten *and* to the other ten—that his kingdom and his power and his glory, the three things we praise God for in the doxology to the Lord's Prayer, are the opposite of what they thought: not being served but serving, not getting but giving, not being first but being last.

They didn't understand that; that's why Jesus had to repeat the lesson many times in many ways. One of those ways was by washing his disciples' feet on Holy Thursday, doing the job of the lowest slave. That action spoke louder than words. It said: "Do you want to be first in my kingdom? Fine. I'll show you how. It's by being last. By serving. By giving up your life, by burning your candle, not hoarding it." His supreme example of this lesson would be literally dying for them, giving them his life, his very body and blood, on the cross and in the Eucharist.

This is life's greatest paradox. A paradox is something that looks like an impossible logical contradiction but isn't. And Jesus proves to them that they need to accept this apparently illogical point by the most logical of arguments: "The Son of Man did not come to be served but to serve" (Matt. 20:28). He made the same argument when he washed their feet; he said, "You call me 'teacher' and 'master,' and rightly so, for indeed I am. If I, therefore, the master and teacher, have washed your feet, you ought to wash one another's feet. . . . Amen, amen, I say to you, no slave is greater than his master" (John 13:13–16). The argument is unanswerable.

The only way to be the greatest in Christ's kingdom is to be the least, to have the least left in your own ego and self-will, to pour out your whole self for others as he did for you.

It is a very strange kingdom that this king invites us into, because it is the kingdom of God, and God is very strange. God is love; God is *agape*, and that means that God is the total gift of self from each of the three persons of the Trinity to each of the other two. In inviting us into his kingdom of *agape*, Jesus is inviting us into *theosis*, which means not imitation but participation, the sharing in the very life of God, who is the source of everything real and true and good and beautiful and joyful.

This truth about God is also a truth about us because we were designed and created in God's image. We were designed to run only on the fuel that God runs on, to live only with God's life. That's why we get joy only by giving joy; we find ourselves only by losing ourselves; we live only by dying to our natural selfishness. It's not an ideal: it's a fact. It's what we are, what we are made for. The reason it looks paradoxical to us is that our selfishness makes us stupid. We are fallen; in fact, we are upside down. If Jesus seems to stand us on our heads, that's because we're really upside down and don't know it; we think *he* is upside down. And which of the two of us do you think is more likely to be right?

THIRTIETH SUNDAY
IN ORDINARY TIME

FIRST READING

JEREMIAH 31:7–9 _____

Thus says the LORD:
Shout with joy for Jacob,
    exult at the head of the nations;
    proclaim your praise and say:
The LORD has delivered his people,
    the remnant of Israel.
Behold, I will bring them back
    from the land of the north;
I will gather them from the ends of the world,
    with the blind and the lame in their midst,
the mothers and those with child;
    they shall return as an immense throng.
They departed in tears,
    but I will console them and guide them;
I will lead them to brooks of water,
    on a level road, so that none shall stumble.
For I am a father to Israel,
    Ephraim is my first-born.

_____

In today's Old Testament passage, through his prophet Jeremiah, God promises deliverance to the Jewish exiles in the Babylonian captivity as something that will happen in the future: "I *will* bring them back. . . . I *will* gather them. . . .

They *shall* return. . . . I *will* lead them." Yet he also refers to this deliverance as something past and already accomplished: "The Lord *has* delivered his people." Is this a confusion of past with future?

From our human point of view, it is; but from the point of view of the God who inspired the Scriptures, it is not, since God is timeless, God is eternal, and to him what we call past and future are both present; what is no longer real or not yet real to us is real and actual and present all at once to God.

If this deliverance is future, if it has not been done yet, how can it be past and already accomplished? How can we thank God for having done it already if it is in the future? It is the same puzzle as Jesus' saying "So I tell you, whatever you ask for in prayer, believe that you have received it, and it will be yours" (Mark 11:24 NRSV-CE). The Greek word for "receive" or "have received," *elabete*, is not in the present progressive tense, which would mean "you are in process of receiving it," but the aorist tense, which means a one-time action, like a slap in the face or a kiss rather than a gradual or habitual process of growth or learning. Here Jesus seems to be confusing the future with the present. When you pray for something to come in the future, Jesus says you should believe that it is already present, fully present, and then it will become present in the future.

That makes little sense as long as we think only of ourselves in time, who live in time; but that forgets that prayer is a relationship between ourselves, who live in time, and God, who does not live in time. God is "eternal," which means "timeless," or "not in time." He is not merely without any beginning and without any ending, but he is not in time at all and does not change at all—although his relationships with us who are in time do change, because the human term of that relationship changes; for instance, when we repent and confess our sins. That God is eternal means that to him all things, including the things that are past or future to us, are present to him.

This is certainly not easy to understand, but here is an analogy to it in our experience. When we read a novel, we are, in our imagination, living in the time of the characters in the novel, and we vicariously share their experiences.

If we are halfway through, half of the characters' experiences are past and gone, and the other half are future and yet to come. But when we finish the novel, if we remember it all, we remember it all at once, even though the events did not occur all at once, because we are no longer in the time of the novel but outside it. We are to the novel something like what God is to us.

How does this relate to Jesus' words about praying for needed graces in our future as if they are already present? Here's how. Our life is divided into past, present, and future. Only the present is actual. The past is dead, and the future is not yet born. Our act of receiving the gifts we have already received from God happened in our past, and our act of receiving the gifts that we are going to receive from God will happen in our future. But to God these are all present.

Here is another way to see it. God giving his gifts and us receiving them are one single action with two dimensions. It's not like the two different actions of my sending you a gift through the mail one day and you getting it the next day. It's like a kiss: the giving and the receiving of the gift are simultaneous; the kiss is one and the same act, with a giver and a receiver, the kisser and a kissed.

In fact, divine grace is very like a kiss, or even like procreation, in which "the two shall become one flesh" (Mark 10:8; see Gen. 2:24). That's why Jesus says, "Believe it and you receive it"—because believing *is* receiving. (Check out John 1:12—the same act is described by those two words, believing and receiving.) It's like the kiss, not like the package in the mail.

God is not only everywhere but also everywhen. He is present in what to us is past and no longer present—we only remember it—and in what to us is future and not yet present—we only desire it or fear it. But God has no past or future, no "no longer" or "not yet." To God, everything is present. To God, our past is still real, and our future is already real. God's eternity is not a *lack* of time, an absence of time, but the presence of all time, what the Bible calls the "fullness of time" (see Gal. 4:4, Eph. 1:10). What is past is lost to us and present only in our memories, our minds, but it is not lost to God. It is not lost in the past but is really present to God. And what is future and not yet real to us, what is only hoped for, is already fully present to God.

That is why God comes to us not only in our present but also in our past and in our future. God is still there in what to us is the past, like someone who is still on the road behind us. All our joys and successes and deliverances and triumphs and glories are to us gone forever, but they are not gone forever to God. And when God takes us up into his own divine life and shares that life with us in heaven, we, too, will recapture all the good in our past. Nothing will be lost; nothing will be dead. And God also comes to us out of our future, like someone who is already there on the road ahead of us. He is also already there with us in what to us is the future, our future glories and joys and successes and triumphs, including our life in heaven. He comes to us out of our past and out of our future.

Think of yourself moving along a road—say, crossing the Hudson River on the George Washington Bridge in a car, from New Jersey to New York. We are at present no longer in New Jersey and not yet in New York. God is present with us in our car, but God is also still with us in New Jersey, and therefore we are also still with him in New Jersey. He keeps our past safe and real for us. And he is also already with us in New York; we see him coming to us not only in the rear-view mirror of our memory but also through the windshield of our hope where we see him in New York with us, and therefore we with him, in what to us is our future. He is still giving us what he gave us in the past, and he is already giving us what we are now asking for and do not yet experience, the deliverance and salvation and joy that we seek.

Of course, this is very difficult to understand and almost impossible to imagine. Did you expect that understanding God would be easy?

Space divides things as time divides events. Space divides things so that no material thing can exist in two places at once. But spirit, or soul, or mind can exist in two places at once. We can think of two places at once, as when we compare New Jersey and New York. The same is true for time. Time divides past events from future events and divides the present from both the past and the future. But God exists as present and actual and active in all times as well as in all places. He is not confined. And he gave us memory and hope as part of his image in us, so that they somewhat transcend time, since memory give us contact with the past and hope gives us contact with the future.

And God reaches out from eternity into time and grasps us to himself and shares something of his eternity with us. He even does that in time, by giving us memory and desire. Memory gives us at least a thin, shadowy unity with the past, and desire does the same with the future.

When we die and leave this world of matter and time and space, we enter God's world, which is not less than this world but more than this world. It is a world where we can be in all places and also in all times. Dying is like finishing a great story and seeing the whole story at once in your mind. A life is like a novel, and when we die, the whole thing goes home to the printer. Nothing is lost. Everything is saved.

We can barely understand time; how can we understand eternity? St. Augustine says, "Obviously when we use [time], we know what we mean, just as when we hear another use it, we know what he means. What then *is* time? If no one asks me, I know; if I want to explain it to a questioner, I do not know." If we do not even understand time, how can we understand eternity? Of course, we can't. But we *can* understand this: that God is more, not less, than we can understand. As St. Paul says, "What eye has not seen, and ear has not heard, and what has not entered the human heart, what God has prepared for those who love him" (1 Cor. 2:9). God is always more, never less, than we can imagine or conceive, hope or desire. That is why there is no boredom in heaven.

This stuff about God and his eternity is extremely hard to understand, but what is easy to understand is its practical human consequence: that it is absolutely and infallibly certain and guaranteed that God always keeps his promises. Just as two plus two cannot possibly not be four, God cannot possibly not keep his promises. Our future is his present, in three senses of that rich word: his present time, not his future time; not just an impersonal fact but his present, or gift, or grace, to us, which is presented and not withheld; and his presence, not his absence.

RESPONSORIAL PSALM

PSALM 126:1–2, 2–3, 4–5, 6 _____

R. (3) **The Lord has done great things for us; we are filled with joy.**

When the LORD brought back the captives of Zion,
    we were like men dreaming.
Then our mouth was filled with laughter,
    and our tongue with rejoicing.

Then they said among the nations,
    "The LORD has done great things for them."
The LORD has done great things for us;
    we are glad indeed.

Restore our fortunes, O LORD,
    like the torrents in the southern desert.
Those that sow in tears
    shall reap rejoicing.

Although they go forth weeping,
    carrying the seed to be sown,
They shall come back rejoicing,
    carrying their sheaves.

SECOND READING

HEBREWS 5:1–6 _____

Brothers and sisters: Every high priest is taken from among men and made their representative before God, to offer gifts and sacrifices for sins. He is able to deal patiently with the ignorant and erring, for he himself is beset by weakness and so, for this reason, must make sin offerings for himself as well as for the people. No one takes this honor upon himself but only when called by God, just as Aaron was. In the same way, it was not Christ who glorified himself in becoming high priest, but rather the one who said to him:

You are my son:
   this day I have begotten you;
just as he says in another place:

You are a priest forever
   according to the order of Melchizedek.

Today's epistle is very clear about three things and very mysterious about a fourth thing. It is very clear, first, that the essential task of priests is to offer sacrifice. Second, it is clear that this task is something priests do not give to themselves or take upon themselves but are chosen and called by God to undertake (for even Jesus became our high priest only because his Father gave him that task). And third, it is clear that human priests, unlike Christ, are members of the class of sinners *for* whom they offer priestly sacrifices. They are not the spotless Lamb of God who takes away the sins of the world; Christ is. That's why Christ offers himself, his own body and blood, to God the Father as the effective sacrifice for our sins, while priests offer not their own body and blood but Christ's.

Priests offer that in literal fact in the New Covenant, and in symbolic and prophetic anticipation in the Old Covenant, or Old Testament. That's why the Old Testament sacrifices were not adequate to really take away sins by themselves; they were only symbols. Protestants who do not believe in the Mass and the Real Presence are in a sense still living in the Old Covenant.

But there is a mysterious point in today's epistle too, which connects with the mysterious point about time in our first two readings. It is the reference to Melchizedek. The words about him in today's epistle are these: "It was not Christ who glorified himself in becoming high priest, but rather the one who said to him: *You are my son: this day have I begotten you; just as he says in another place: You are a priest forever according to the order of Melchizedek."*

What is "the priestly order of Melchizedek"? Who was Melchizedek? The author of Hebrews reminds us: "This 'Melchizedek, king of Salem and priest of God Most High,' 'met Abraham as he returned from his defeat of the kings' and 'blessed him.' And Abraham apportioned to him 'a tenth of everything.' His name first means righteous king, and he was also 'king of Salem,' that is, king of peace. Without father, mother, or ancestry, without beginning of days or end of life, thus made to resemble the Son of God, he remains a priest forever" (Heb 7:1–3).

God instituted three sacred offices in Old Testament Israel: prophets, priests, and kings. No one was ever both a priest and a king, except Melchizedek and Christ, who was the fulfillment of all three offices. Melchizedek is identified with Christ a few verses later, when the author says: "It is clear that our Lord arose from Judah, and in regard to that tribe Moses said nothing about priests. It is even more obvious if another priest is raised up after the likeness of Melchizedek, who has become so, not by a law expressed in a commandment concerning physical descent but by the power of a life that cannot be destroyed. For it is testified [that is, of Christ]: 'You are a priest forever according to the order of Melchizedek'" (Heb. 7:14–17).

Perhaps Melchizedek was literally Christ, the second person of the Trinity, appearing in disguise rather than in a full incarnation. Or perhaps he was just a human being that God called symbolize and anticipate Christ. But what makes Melchizedek most distinctively Christlike is his eternity: he is, as the author of Hebrews says, without human father or mother, without genealogy; in fact, he is the only Old Testament person with no genealogy, no temporal past. If he was the pre-incarnate Christ, that explains his lack of ancestry; if he was only a man whom God chose to symbolize and anticipate Christ, he had human ancestry, but the author of Genesis was inspired by the Holy Spirit to omit it for the sake of the symbolism. Whether literally or symbolically, he transcends time; he is like Christ, God's eternity entering time. That is why he also has no ending: in the words of the text, he is "a priest forever." He is, as Hebrews says, "without beginning of days or end of life." He is eternity entering time.

When Christ enters time and human nature, he enters not human nature as it was in unfallen Adam and Eve, who had no human ancestry and who were created immortal, but fallen, mortal, and weak human nature, so that "he himself is beset by weakness" (Heb. 5:2)—in fact, every human weakness, including temptation, but not sin. Christ was mortal, or able to die, and in fact did die, quite literally. He also had a literal human ancestor—namely, Mary, and, through her, all her ancestors.

So it seems more likely that Melchizedek was not literally Christ himself but only a symbol of Christ, like the Protestant bread and wine. But in either case he is the most mysterious figure in the Old Testament.

GOSPEL
MARK 10:46–52_____

As Jesus was leaving Jericho with his disciples and a sizable crowd, Bartimaeus, a blind man, the son of Timaeus, sat by the roadside begging. On hearing that it was Jesus of Nazareth, he began to cry out and say, "Jesus, son of David, have pity on me." And many rebuked him, telling him to be silent. But he kept calling out all the more, "Son of David, have pity on me." Jesus stopped and said, "Call him." So they called the blind man, saying to him, "Take courage; get up, Jesus is calling you." He threw aside his cloak, sprang up, and came to Jesus. Jesus said to him in reply, "What do you want me to do for you?" The blind man replied to him, "Master, I want to see." Jesus told him, "Go your way; your faith has saved you." Immediately he received his sight and followed him on the way.

_____

Today's Gospel is a simple story, so let's keep it simple and just x-ray it and get its bone structure, so to speak, the fundamental structural stages of its plot. And let's look at them all from Bartimaeus' point of view. It's a story, so these stages are events, actions—some of them spiritual and some of them physical.

Act one of the plot is poor Bartimaeus sitting and begging: his old, pitiful life.

Act two is his awareness that Jesus is coming.

Act three is his immediate crying out to Jesus: "Jesus, son of David, have pity on me." Everyone except Jesus tells him to shut up, but he does not obey them. He's a nonconformist. He's countercultural.

Act four is Jesus stopping and calling him.

But his hearing Jesus' call is act six, not act five. Act five is others telling him that Jesus is calling him. If act five did not happen, act six and the following acts would not have happened either. Perhaps Bartimaeus was a bit deaf, or perhaps the crowd was making so much noise that he could not hear Jesus calling him. Those others, who told him about Jesus, are like the Church, which is the collective prophet to the world. The Church is essentially the chain of witnesses to Jesus.

Act seven is his reaction to this good news that he heard, that Jesus is calling him. The first thing he did was to throw aside his cloak, his old life, just as Peter, Andrew, James, and John all immediately left their fishing nets and their fishing business and their old life to follow Jesus when they heard him call them.

And then—act eight—he sprang up to his feet. As soon as he hears, he acts. He lets no temptation enter the time gap because there is no time gap.

And then—act nine—he uses those feet to move to Jesus. Jesus moved to him, and he responds by moving to Jesus.

Act ten is his listening to Jesus' question. Jesus always asks questions of us, challenges us. Of course, he himself is the answer, but the question is "Are we asking the right question?" That's why the very first thing Jesus says in John's Gospel to his prospective disciples is "What are you looking for?" (John 1:38). In other words, what's in your heart, in your love, in your deepest desire?

The next event, act eleven, is Bartimaeus' honest answer: "Master, I want to see." His using the word "master" or "Lord" for Jesus, like his using the messianic title "Son of David" earlier, reveals his faith, his trust, his hope in Jesus.

Act twelve is Jesus' word of command that miraculously gives Bartimaeus his sight, right? Wrong. That's act thirteen. First, Jesus tells him to act as if he had already received his sight: "Go your way." And only when he does that does he actually receive his sight (act fourteen). It's the same paradox we saw earlier when Jesus said, "All that you ask for in prayer, believe that you will receive it and it shall be yours" (Mark 11:24).

Do you wonder whether you have faith? Act as if you do. Do you wonder whether you have put all your hope in Jesus? Act as if you have. Do you wonder whether your deepest desire is to obey him? Act as if it is. The action is not merely an *expression* of your faith and hope and love; it is also the thing that *produces* your faith, or allows it to happen. Faith and hope and love are not just feelings or thoughts; they are actions.

The very same act of faith, hope, and love is both from us and from God. It is like a mutual kiss. Faith does not merely *cause* salvation as rain causes wet grounds, or as a bat causes a baseball to fly into the air. Our faith *is the act of our receiving* salvation, and God's love is the act of his giving it to us.

And those are not two different acts but the same act, one from our point of view and one from God's point of view. They are simultaneous, like a kiss, not one after the other like the bat moving and then the ball moving. It all happens now, in the present. As St. Paul writes, "*Now* is the day of salvation" (2 Cor. 6:2).

What Christ did to Bartimaeus' physical eyes, he does to our spiritual eyes. We are all spiritually blind; we are all stupid; we are all fools; and the wiser we are, the more readily we admit that. We are also all beggars, like Bartimaeus. That's why God providentially put this story in the Bible for us. This story is about us.

It is us on whom Jesus has pity.

It is us whom Jesus calls, by name. (By name! Not by group, not by a mailing to "dear occupant.")

It is us whom Jesus challenges with his questions: Do you want me? Do you want a new life? Do you want the challenges of seeing, and being responsible for what you see, instead of the comfort of being blind and pitied?

It is us from whom Jesus demands both the faith to call out to him in hope and the good work of coming to him when he calls. (Those two, faith and works, are also two dimensions of one thing, not two different things.)

And it is us who always receive a miracle if we ask for it in faith—in fact, the greatest miracle in the world. We receive it in Baptism and in the Eucharist: it is a share in the very life of God in our souls, the life of Christ who is both God and man, and thus also the life of perfect humanity. It is a new nature, a new double nature, like Christ's, a finite but growing participation in Christ's own eternal nature, both human and divine. It is not just a new lifestyle but a new life. Jesus calls it being reborn, being "born again" or "born from above" (see John 3).

This is the greatest of all miracles, greater than the creation of the universe. For God, to turn nothing into being by creating the universe was easy, because nothingness put up no resistance, but to turn sinners into saints is a greater feat on God's part because sinners, by definition, are those who do put up resistance. And it is a greater feat also because creating the world cost God nothing, but saving the world cost him his own infinitely beloved Son's infinitely precious body and blood, each drop of which has more value than everything else in the universe.

THIRTY-FIRST SUNDAY
IN ORDINARY TIME

FIRST READING

DEUTERONOMY 6:2–6 _____

Moses spoke to the people, saying: "Fear the LORD, your God, and keep, throughout the days of your lives, all his statutes and commandments which I enjoin on you, and thus have long life. Hear then, Israel, and be careful to observe them, that you may grow and prosper the more, in keeping with the promise of the LORD, the God of your fathers, to give you a land flowing with milk and honey.

"Hear, O Israel! The LORD is our God, the LORD alone! Therefore, you shall love the LORD, your God, with all your heart, and with all your soul, and with all your strength. Take to heart these words which I enjoin on you today."

_____

The words of Moses here contain the primary and central prayer of Judaism, the *Shema* (from its first Hebrew word, which means "hear"). This prayer is to Jews what the Lord's Prayer is to Christians. It is this: "Hear, O Israel! The LORD is our God, the LORD alone! Therefore, you shall love the LORD, your God, with all your heart, and with all your soul, and with all your strength."

Notice that this is not just a prayer, but also a commandment. It is God's word to us as well as our word to God. Prayer is essentially a two-way conversation with God, and conversation is dialogue, not monologue. Our adoration, thanksgiving, reparation, and petitions ascend to God; and God's revelation, commandments, and grace descend to us.

And this prayer is also an argument. There is a logical connection between God's "alone," or "one" (Douay), and our "all," between "the LORD is one" and "love the LORD with all your heart." That's why the word "therefore" is in it.

To see this point, reflect that the heart's work is to love, and therefore polytheists, who believe in many gods, cannot have a whole heart because they have many loves, many final ends, many gods, whether these gods are imaginary supernatural beings like Zeus or Jupiter or whether they are things like money and sex and shopping. What you are is determined by what you love, and you can be one great person only if you have one great love, and the only true candidate for that is the true God.

In the words surrounding this prayer, Moses uses five verbs in the imperative mood for its commands. First, "fear" the Lord. Second, "keep" his commandments. Third, "be careful to observe" them. Fourth, "love" your God with all your heart. Fifth, "take to heart these words." Let's look at each of them more carefully.

First comes fear, because fear comes first. The fear of God is not servile fear, the fear that a slave has of a cruel master, but filial fear, the fear of a loving and loyal child, the fear of disappointing its beloved father. It's sometimes said that this fear means "respect," but it is much more than that. It is reverence. It is worship. It is adoration. It is the reaction that God alone deserves. This attitude is the psychological origin and essence of all religion. Almost a synonym for this fear of God is faith, the faith in the perfection of God and his will that motivates the essential prayer that is the heart of all authentic religion, "thy will be done."

And that "thy will be done" is the second command, obedience. Faith is not a mere opinion; faith is not only belief in the mind; faith is fidelity of the will. Faith is a choice, an act, a deed. The eleventh chapter of Hebrews is a list, a roll call, of the great men and women of faith of Old Testament times, and it identifies the faith of each one with their acts of obedience. It tells us what their faith *did*.

Third, this obedience is to be done carefully, which means full of "care." "Be careful" here doesn't mean "be picky" or "be scared," but it means positive passion, attention, and love. "He really *cares* about me" means "he puts me first." When we want to say, "You should care about this totally," we say,

"It's a matter of life or death." God is literally a matter of life or death for us, eternally.

Fourth, the central commandment is to "love" the Lord with your whole heart and soul and strength. That means to put God absolutely first, not merely to add him to your life as the icing on the cake but to let him be the whole cake, the Lord of your whole life, to let God be God. You may think this is impossible for anyone but a saint; but God does not command the impossible. To choose to do that, to try to do that, to want to do that, to will to do that, is to do it.

Fifth, Moses says to "take to heart these words." What does that mean? The Hebrew literally says, "These words shall be upon your heart," or "in your heart." Because we love *God* with our heart, we love these *words* with our heart. We may fail to obey this commandment to love God with all our heart, but we need not fail to love the commandment itself. We may not love God with all our heart, but we can at least *want* to love God with all our heart, and if we do, God will gradually turn our heart into what we want it to be.

In fact, if we don't even *want* to love God with all our heart, that proves that we don't know God. God is supremely lovable because God *is* love, and love always wants to share itself, and God wants nothing more than to give us a share in his heavenly joy, which is a joy that comes only from loving.

RESPONSORIAL PSALM

PSALM 18:2–3, 3–4, 47, 51 ⎯⎯⎯⎯⎯⎯⎯⎯⎯⎯⎯⎯⎯⎯⎯⎯⎯⎯⎯⎯⎯⎯

R. (2) **I love you, Lord, my strength.**

I love you, O LORD, my strength,
    O LORD, my rock, my fortress, my deliverer.

My God, my rock of refuge,
    my shield, the horn of my salvation, my stronghold!

Praised be the LORD, I exclaim,
  and I am safe from my enemies.

The LORD lives! And blessed be my rock!
  Extolled be God my savior.
You who gave great victories to your king
  and showed kindness to your anointed.

In today's Psalm verses, the Psalmist uses no less than eight images or metaphors or analogies for God. They are not *literal*, but they are true; they tell us what God really is to us. The Psalmist uses physical images for spiritual realities. God is called our strength, our rock, our fortress, our deliverer, our refuge, our shield, the horn of our salvation, and our stronghold.

The *meaning* of these eight images is obvious, so I'd like to focus instead on the number and variety of them. They are only a few of the dozens—in fact, hundreds—of images or analogies or metaphors or allegories or symbols for God in Scripture. Why are there so many?

Because there are many kinds of goodness; and every kind of goodness reflects Goodness itself, complete goodness, and that is what God is. God is everything good, everything desirable, everything that we can find our true happiness in, everything that attracts the good will (but not the evil will, the perverted will, the bent will). God is what we all most deeply desire and demand. That's why St. Augustine famously confessed to God that "our hearts are restless until they rest in you": because deep down we want it all, we want everything that is good, and nothing fits that description except God. Everything else has some good in it but also lacks some good in it. Dogs are not as cute as cats, and cats are not as grateful as dogs. Water is not as strong as wine, and wine is not as clear as water. Summer is not as cool as winter, and winter is not as warm as summer. God, the Creator and inventor of everything good in the universe, is the only being that contains all goodness, everything we need, everything we can desire. That's why the one who has God has everything.

Since there is no lack of any kind of goodness in God, there is no lack of any kind of goodness in what God is for us and does for us, and that's why there are so many symbols for God: fire and water, lion and lamb, strength and gentleness, war and peace, offense and defense, justice and mercy, hard and soft, hard to satisfy and easy to please, like a perfectly good parent—and both motherly and fatherly goods, because God invented both mothers and fathers, and both reflect his image in different ways. The story in Genesis of God creating us identifies "the image of God" as "male *and* female" (Gen. 1:27).

The practical lesson here is that since God is the source of our every good, without exception, and the fulfillment of our every need, without exception, therefore it is impossible to waste anything that is offered to God: your heart or your head, your time or your eternity, your life or your death, your joys or your sufferings. That is why each morning we should pray, in the Morning Offering, "O my God, I offer you all my prayers, works, joys, and sufferings of this day." Offer it all up. Keep nothing back.

What we keep back eventually rots, because time rots everything; but what we give away in faith and trust is an investment in eternity. We can trust God to keep everything we give him in trust for us. You can't totally trust any other investment. All human investments can fail. Even the national bank can fail. But whatever is invested in the First Supernatural Bank and Trust Company always pays compound interest.

SECOND READING
HEBREWS 7:23–28 _____

Brothers and sisters: The levitical priests were many because they were prevented by death from remaining in office, but Jesus, because he remains forever, has a priesthood that does not pass away. Therefore, he is always able to save those who approach God through him, since he lives forever to make intercession for them.

It was fitting that we should have such a high priest: holy, innocent, unde-filed, separated from sinners, higher than the heavens. He has no need, as did the high priests, to offer sacrifice day after day, first for his own sins and then for those of the people; he did that once for all when he offered himself. For the law appoints men subject to weakness to be high priests, but the word of the oath, which was taken after the law, appoints a son, who has been made perfect forever.

Jesus is our priest. Parish priests are priests because they share in Jesus' work of priesthood. So what, essentially, is a priest?

A priest is like a prophet in one way, and in another way he is the oppo-site. He is like a prophet in that he is a mediator between God and man. A prophet carries God's words to man. He is God's mouthpiece. A priest is also a mediator between God and man because he carries man's offerings to God. A prophet mediates downwards, so to speak, and a priest mediates upwards. A prophet carries down God's words, God's mind, while a priest carries up man's offerings, man's goods, man's life. A prophet mediates light; a priest mediates life. Both are mediations of love. Light, life, and love are the three greatest things in the world. They are St. John the Evangelist's three favorite words for God.

Jesus is both our prophet and our priest. As prophet, he does not just *carry* God's words; he *is* God's Word, and in the singular, not the plural, as a person, not just a speech. In him God has revealed to us everything that he is. As St. Paul wrote, "In him all the fullness was pleased to dwell" (Col. 1:19), and "in him all things hold together" (Col. 1:17).

Just as Christ the one Word of God is the supreme prophet, so Christ the one high priest is the supreme priest. Human priests are many, sinful, and mortal; Christ is one, perfect, and immortal. His priesthood is as perfect and complete as his prophethood. When he said, on the cross, "It is finished," he left nothing for himself to do, only something for us to do: to accept and receive the work he has finished. He has purchased forgiveness for all the sins of all people in all times and places. He has opened the gates of heaven for all of us. The only obstacle left is our own refusal to repent and believe. Just as the prophetic gift of revelation is given to all, but only some believe it, so the priestly gift of salvation is given to all, but not all accept it.

When your parish priest offers the Mass and offers Christ, really present in the transubstantiated Host, to God the Father for the sins of the world, he becomes Christ's extension, Christ's instrument, as a sword becomes the extension of the swordsman's arm and his instrument. The priest lets Christ use his tongue. When, at the consecration, you hear the words "This is my body," you are not listening to Father Smith: you are listening to Jesus Christ. Because when Fr. Smith says, "This is my body," he does not mean, "This is Fr. Smith's body." It is Christ who is speaking, acting as the one high priest, and simply using Fr. Smith's lips and tongue.

When the priest offers the Mass, he is the representative of the whole congregation, who participate in the Mass, and he is also the representative of Christ himself who is offering himself in the Mass, his whole self, Body and Blood, Soul and Divinity, to God the Father for our salvation. That is why the Mass is by far the greatest and most powerful prayer in the world. It's not Father's Mass; it's Christ's Mass. "Christmas" means "Christ's Mass"; the Mass is Christ's Christmas gift to us. He is both the giver and the gift. He gives himself, first to God the Father in the Mass and then, in Holy Communion, to us.

The offering happened on the cross once for all. Christ is not re-sacrificed, but the sacrifice is re-offered. The very same single event, the very same single offering that happened on the cross, happens again, but not in a bloody manner. Christ does not *die* again, but Christ continues to *offer* his death, to offer his high priestly prayer, again and again in each Mass, for our salvation.

That's why you come to Mass: to come to Mass is to come to Christ. You don't come for the entertainment or the psychoanalysis or the nice, sweet, comfortable, peaceful feelings. You come for him; you come to him; you ride on his back, like a flea riding on the mane of a lion. Here you touch the greatest power in the universe—no, a greater power than all the powers in the universe. And you take that power into your soul, and even into your body, by Holy Communion.

And it is the priest who makes that miracle possible. It is the most important job in the world. Encourage your sons to consider it as their vocation and to pray about it with open mind and will.

GOSPEL
MARK 12:28B–34 _____

One of the scribes came to Jesus and asked him, "Which is the first of all the commandments?" Jesus replied, "The first is this: *Hear, O Israel! The Lord our God is Lord alone! You shall love the Lord your God with all your heart, with all your soul, with all your mind, and with all your strength.* The second is this: *You shall love your neighbor as yourself.* There is no other commandment greater than these." The scribe said to him, "Well said, teacher. You are right in saying, 'He is One and there is no other than he.' And 'to love him with all your heart, with all your understanding, with all your strength, and to love your neighbor as yourself' is worth more than all burnt offerings and sacrifices." And when Jesus saw that he answered with understanding, he said to him, "You are not far from the kingdom of God." And no one dared to ask him any more questions.

This is one of the most important things Jesus ever said. It is also one of the most famous. And it is also one of the clearest. And yet there is a deep mystery to it. When Jesus replied, "You are *not far from* the kingdom of God," what did he mean? Why was the scribe not fully in Christ's kingdom—in fact, in its very center? What more was there?

For Jesus there is always more. "More" is almost his definition. Everything he says suggests something more, like a scent that triggers a distant memory that hovers just beyond your mind's grasp. His words come from a mind that we do not fully comprehend, though we do comprehend that we do not comprehend it, at least if we are wise enough to be humble. God is like the sea, and the words of the Word of God are like the swells and waves on the visible surface of the sea; and there is always more in the sea than what meets the eye on the surface, large leviathans lurking and looming beneath the surface. Similarly, there are large and moving meanings lurking beneath Christ's words. When he is questioned, he sometimes seems to avoid the question, but he never does: he always goes to the very heart of the question, or, rather, to the very heart of the questioner. For he sees that questions are like clothes: they never stand alone, like mountains or trees; there is a person behind them, wearing them, and Jesus sees that person as the real question. He always answers the questioner, not just the question.

And within that questioning person's soul, there are many layers and masks; Jesus always penetrates through all the masks and down to the deepest layer, the person's deepest question and deepest need. For instance, when Nicodemus comes to him, he answers the question Nicodemus had at the center of his heart but never verbalized, when he said, "Amen, amen, I say to you, unless one is born from above, he cannot see the Kingdom of God" (John 3:3).

The scribe in today's Gospel also longs to understand and to enter the kingdom of God, the reign of God, and he understands that that reign must exist in souls, not just in states; within, not just without. Jesus' use of the political term "kingdom" was a sign, a political symbol, not a political reality. As he said to Pilate, "My kingdom does not belong to this world. If my kingdom did belong to this world, my attendants would be fighting to keep me from being handed over" (John 18:36).

Christ spoke about nothing more often than "the kingdom of God." It was his central theme because it was his central purpose. Christ came to earth to establish the "kingdom of God," and his Church is the kingdom of God.

There are many definitions of the Church, but probably the two deepest ones are "the Mystical Body of Christ" and "the People of God."

The two seem opposite: the first, "the Mystical Body of Christ," is invisible, and the second, "the People of God," is visible. The first is mysterious, and the second is clear. The first is cosmic, and the second is personal. The first is divine, and the second is human. But the two definitions should never be separated, but always seen together. The Church of Christ is both invisible and visible, both internal, in souls, and external, in visible reality. It is both very mysterious and very clear, like the Bible. It is both cosmic and personal. It is both divine and human—like Christ himself. It *is* Christ himself, his Body. Your body is you, not one of your possessions. You do not *have* a body: you *are* a body—just as you do not have a soul: you are a soul. "The full Christ" is both Head and Body. As your head and body are one, Christ the Head and the Church his Body are one. He is not the "head" as Bill Gates is the "head" of Microsoft.

He is always more, much more, than we think we have, more than we think we understand. And he will always be that forever in heaven. That is why "when we've been there ten thousand years, bright shining like the sun," we will never, never be bored. Jesus is the only man who ever lived who never bored anybody.

And so even when the best possible answer in words is given to a tremendously important question, as Jesus gave us in today's Gospel, there is always more than the surface. Not less, never less, always more: more truth, more goodness, more beauty; more light, more love, more life; more understanding, more charity, more joy. There's always more in his words because he is the Word of God and there's always more in God, infinitely and forever.

THIRTY-SECOND SUNDAY
IN ORDINARY TIME

FIRST READING

1 KINGS 17:10–16

In those days, Elijah the prophet went to Zarephath. As he arrived at the entrance of the city, a widow was gathering sticks there; he called out to her, "Please bring me a small cupful of water to drink." She left to get it, and he called out after her, "Please bring along a bit of bread." She answered, "As the LORD, your God, lives, I have nothing baked; there is only a handful of flour in my jar and a little oil in my jug. Just now I was collecting a couple of sticks, to go in and prepare something for myself and my son; when we have eaten it, we shall die." Elijah said to her, "Do not be afraid. Go and do as you propose. But first make me a little cake and bring it to me. Then you can prepare something for yourself and your son. For the LORD, the God of Israel, says, 'The jar of flour shall not go empty, nor the jug of oil run dry, until the day when the LORD sends rain upon the earth.'" She left and did as Elijah had said. She was able to eat for a year, and he and her son as well; the jar of flour did not go empty, nor the jug of oil run dry, as the LORD had foretold through Elijah.

A story in the Bible can be both literal and symbolic: both a literal historical event and a divinely designed symbol or sign of something greater, since God writes with real things and events as we write with words, so that these things and events can be both literally, historically true and also symbols of something more, like Jesus' miracles, or the Exodus (an image of salvation) of Israel (symbol of the Church) under Moses (an image of Christ) from Egypt (an image of hell) and Pharaoh (an image of Satan), or the parting of the Red Sea (an image of death), or Israel receiving the Old Covenant of the Law (an image of the New Covenant of the Gospel) in the wilderness (an image of purgatory) on the way to the Promised Land (an image of heaven).

Today's Old Testament story of the prophet Elijah and the miracle of the flour and oil that did not run dry for the starving widow and her son fits that pattern of a historical event that is also an image or symbol. The details in many of the Church Fathers' interpretations of the Christian symbolism in it may seem to us to be a bit of a stretch—or perhaps not—but the principle is valid: First, all of us are widows because we have lost our heavenly Bridegroom by sin. Second, we and our children are starving because the water of grace is not falling on us from heaven. The famine of food and water, the two supports of natural life, is a natural symbol of the famine of supernatural life. Third, we are collecting two sticks to make a fire to cook a last meal before we die in despair. Why did the author specify just two sticks? Because two sticks together make a cross. Fourth, the flour and oil symbolize the food and liquid we need, and they are supplied in the two greatest sacraments, the Eucharist and Baptism. Fifth, Elijah, God's prophet, symbolizes Christ, who gives us the sacraments, symbolized by the flour and oil, which miraculously never run dry, because, like all miracles, they come not just from earth, whose resources are finite and limited, but from heaven, whose resources are infinite and unlimited. Sixth, God promises that the drought will end and heavenly rain will fall on the earth at the end of the story, which symbolizes the coming of Christ, first in Bethlehem and then, at the end of the world, to the whole world.

This symbolic level of interpretation does not do away with the literal one but is based on it. So let's look at the literal level. Elijah, like Christ, meets this widow, like us, deliberately, not by accident. He is God's providential minister of grace to her. He will minister God's compassion on her, but in a demanding way that tests her faith. Before he meets her most obvious need, for earthly food, which is obviously desperately low, he first tests her, because her deepest need is not for the physical food of bread and oil that will keep her body alive but for the spiritual food of faith and hope that will keep her soul alive. So Elijah first asks her to put aside her own desperate needs and give to him the food she was planning to make for herself and her son. She could easily have responded with indignation at this apparent insensitivity and apparent cruelty; but instead she responds with faith and obedience. In return, she gets the miracle she needs.

Christ too, like Elijah, asks us to revere him first, even before our this-worldly needs, because he knows that what we need most of all is faith and hope and love for him, who is our true food. The martyrs gave up literally everything in their lives for him, and that was not foolishness, for, as one martyr, Jim Elliot, said, "He is no fool who gives what he cannot keep to gain that which he cannot lose."

Faith in God *as* God, and not just as one among many good things in our life, is not easy, and it is often tested and made stronger by the test. God's testing trains us to look away from ourselves and our needs and to look to Christ in faith, in trust, in hope. Faith means that instead of judging God's goodness by appearances, we must learn to judge appearances by God's goodness. Faith sees what is invisible to the eyes: the presence and power and wisdom and love of God. But faith is always rewarded, because God is always faithful to his promises. In fact, in the end, he always gives us more, not less, than we ask for or hope for or imagine. And at every moment he is always giving us what we most need, even when he is apparently denying it to us.

In fact, we can even say that everything in life is like the Eucharist: behind the appearances there is the real presence of the God who knows and loves us. Faith hears a voice speaking to us behind all the sufferings and storms in our lives, saying, "It is I. Be not afraid." Pray for the grace to develop the habit of hearing that voice in every aspect of your life. If you do, you will hear those words most clearly when you are dying.

RESPONSORIAL PSALM
PSALM 146:7, 8–9, 9–10 _____

R. (1b) **Praise the Lord, my soul!**

The LORD keeps faith forever,
    secures justice for the oppressed,
    gives food to the hungry.
The LORD sets captives free.

The LORD gives sight to the blind;
    the LORD raises up those who were bowed down.
The LORD loves the just;
    the LORD protects strangers.

The fatherless and the widow he sustains,
    but the way of the wicked he thwarts.
The LORD shall reign forever;
    your God, O Zion, through all generations. Alleluia.

We know anything by its actions. "By their fruits you will know them," Jesus said, as a principle for sizing up people (Matt. 7:16). To put the point in more contemporary language, "If it looks like a duck, walks like a duck, and quacks like a duck, it's probably a duck." And if it flies, it's probably a bird or a plane or Superman. So we know God by what he does. The Psalmist, in four short verses, tells us ten things God does.

First, he "keeps faith forever." He never reneges on his promises. It is impossible for God to lie, because he is truth itself. In the words of the Eucharistic hymn by St. Thomas Aquinas, "Than Truth's own word, there is no truer token."

Second, he "secures justice for the oppressed." We are often oppressed and denied justice from man, but never from God, because God is not just just but justice itself, the higher justice that judges all human justice.

Third, God "gives food to the hungry," both physically (he made food for every species of animal, including man) and spiritually (he himself is our spirit's food, and life).

Fourth, "he sets captives free." There is no slavery worse than the self-slavery of addiction, and sin is our primary addiction. We are not all alcoholics, but we are all sinaholics. And God alone can free us from that self-destructive slavery.

Fifth, he "gives sight to the blind"—not only by occasional physical miracles to the eyes of the body for a select few, but also by healing our spiritual blindness by revealing to the eyes of the soul, which are the eyes of faith, truths about himself that we could not possibly have come to know on our own, especially the truth that God is love itself.

Sixth, God "raises up those who were bowed down" in that he rewards our humility and obedience to him by exalting us and glorifying us and giving us joy. The happiest and completest persons are saints, and saints are made by their humility and obedience, by "thy will be done," by spiritual "bowing down" to God in total love and adoration.

Seventh, God "loves the just." Love, in Scripture, is not a feeling but a choice, a deed, a living, an act, essentially the act of giving one's very self to another. God loves the just, the righteous, the truly good, and gives himself to them. He loves the unjust too, but the just receive more love than the unjust, just as the tropics receive more sunlight than the poles, not because the sun is stingy in giving light to the poles but because the tropics are generous in receiving it.

Eighth, God "protects strangers." He is totally hospitable. We come into this world as strangers to God, as deprived of divine life, as fallen; and God makes us not only his friends but his family, adopting us as his children, by Baptism. We are now no longer strangers to God, or he to us. He is our Father, and we are his children, Christ's brothers and sisters.

Ninth, "the fatherless and the widow he sustains"—literally, since he comforts all the afflicted, and losing a father or a husband is a great affliction, but also spiritually, in that he himself becomes our heavenly Father so that we are no longer fatherless, and he even becomes our husband in spiritual marriage, so that we are not widowed.

Tenth, "the way of the wicked he thwarts." He does this for the sake of the just, since the wicked oppress the just. But he also does this for the sake of the wicked themselves, since they absolutely need to be thwarted and shocked and converted and taught so that they at least learn the hard way, by punishment. Even God's punishments are motivated by his love.

And it is this God, the God of unlimited love and wisdom and power, who "shall reign forever . . . through all generations," both in time and in eternity.

St. Augustine said that he who sings, prays twice. The Psalms are both songs and prayers. In today's Psalm, the Psalmist is singing the hymn "How Great Thou Art," in tenfold detail. He offers us his song not just for our admiration but for our imitation, our use, our own prayer. I hope you all use these and other Psalms as your prayers regularly. The Psalms are the only prayer book that we know was inspired by God himself.

SECOND READING
HEBREWS 9:24–28 _____

Christ did not enter into a sanctuary made by hands, a copy of the true one, but heaven itself, that he might now appear before God on our behalf. Not that he might offer himself repeatedly, as the high priest enters each year into the sanctuary with blood that is not his own; if that were so, he would have had to suffer repeatedly from the foundation of the world. But now once for all he has appeared at the end of the ages to take away sin by his sacrifice. Just as it is appointed that human beings die once, and after this the judgment, so also Christ, offered once to take away the sins of many, will appear a second time, not to take away sin but to bring salvation to those who eagerly await him.

The anonymous author of today's Epistle to the Hebrews compares the symbol with the thing symbolized, the sign with the thing signified, the image with the thing imaged, when he compares the priesthood instituted by God's Old Testament covenant with Christ's priesthood. He mentions ten differences.

First, in the New Covenant there is only one high priest, Christ, not many. There had to be many human priests in the Old Covenant because humans die and are replaced. Christ is never replaced.

Second, Christ's was a finished, one-time sacrifice, "once for all," "at the end of the ages," at one specific time, on Calvary, while the priests of the Old Covenant appeared many times, over and over again. Christ's work was finished when he said "It is finished" on the cross, while the sacrifices of the Old Covenant were repeated many times, like the words of an ongoing prayer.

Christ's work of redemption, and thus our justification, our being made right with God, is finished and complete. The passage does mention Christ's second coming, at the end of the world, but points out that this will be not to take away sin, which he did on the cross, but to make us, who are not yet fully sanctified, not yet saints, finished and complete, rewarded with heavenly glory. That is the future completeness of the salvation that he already won for us once for all on the cross.

Third, the "Holy of Holies" into which the priests of the Old Covenant entered was in the Jerusalem temple, which was made by human hands and made of the material stuff of this universe. That was only an image of the heavenly sanctuary, the true Holy of Holies, into which Christ entered, in heaven. Heaven is not made of earthly matter.

Fourth, Christ continues to appear "on our behalf," but the priests of the Old Covenant are all past and do not continue today. For the Jerusalem temple was destroyed by the Romans in AD 70, never to be rebuilt.

Fifth, Christ's offering is his own body and blood, while the priests of the Old Covenant offered the blood of goats, bulls, oxen, sheep, and lambs, which were only symbols and foreshadowings of the Lamb of God.

Sixth, Christ offered sacrifice for our sins, not his own, since he had none.

The priests of the Old Covenant offered their sacrifices for their own sins as well as for their people's sins.

Seventh, most important of all, the blood of animals could not actually take away our sin, but the blood of Christ did. The sacrifices of the Old Covenant were an icon, a holy picture. A picture, even a holy picture, cannot act. A picture, like a word, cannot change reality. Artists make pictures; pictures don't make artists. That's true of word-pictures too: writers create words; words don't create writers. Pictures, like words, can only mean what they picture, can only *point to* reality, can only *signify* reality. They are only signs. But signs point beyond themselves. These Old Testament signs all pointed to Christ.

In addition to that main point, this passage also clearly teaches that there is no such thing as reincarnation, for it says that "it is appointed that human beings die once, and after this the judgment." Death, like Christ, is final and unique. The closest anyone ever came to reincarnation was Lazarus, who had to die twice. But he was only resuscitated into his old body, not reincarnated into another body or resurrected into an immortal heavenly body.

GOSPEL
MARK 12:38–44
(OR MARK 12:41–44) _____

In the course of his teaching Jesus said to the crowds, "Beware of the scribes, who like to go around in long robes and accept greetings in the marketplaces, seats of honor in synagogues, and places of honor at banquets. They devour the houses of widows and, as a pretext recite lengthy prayers. They will receive a very severe condemnation."

He sat down opposite the treasury and observed how the crowd put money into the treasury. Many rich people put in large sums. A poor widow also came and put in two small coins worth a few cents. Calling his disciples to himself, he said to them, "Amen, I say to you, this poor widow put in more than all the other contributors to the treasury. For they have all contributed from their surplus wealth, but she, from her poverty, has contributed all she had, her whole livelihood."

There is almost always more than meets the eye in the sayings of Jesus. Let's explore some of the deeper meanings in what Jesus tells his disciples (and therefore us) in today's Gospel.

He says that the poor widow who gave a few cents to the temple (and thus to the worship of God, and thus, to God) gave more than the rich who gave very large sums. Why?

The first answer comes from Jesus himself: because they contributed from their surplus, their extra, not their needs, while she gave everything she had. In other words, ten cents is 100 percent of ten cents, while a million dollars is only 10 percent of ten million dollars.

But this is not a mathematical puzzle, so it's not the numbers that define the point here. We might say then that it's not what they gave but what they had left that counts. She had nothing left; the millionaire who gave a million had nine million left. But in a sense zero is a number, so that's a numbers game again, and Jesus isn't playing that game.

But that's closer to the point, because their money was their surplus while hers was her livelihood. They didn't need it or feel its loss. She did. Their large gift was not much of a sacrifice for them; they lost few of the comforts that money can buy, but she lost much.

This explanation is closer to Jesus' point because it focuses not on numbers and calculated quantities but on qualities, not on money itself but on the things money can buy.

But that's still external things. There's a big difference between more and less important external things—for instance, between food and cars, because if you lack food you're suffering a lot, while if you lack a car you're only suffering a little, or maybe even not at all. But food and cars are both external things, and Jesus isn't talking about external things, the things money can buy. He's not an economist. He's talking about people, and people's souls, and about their choices, about their wisdom and morality.

Jesus is criticizing the rich for their personal *motives* in giving expensive and ostentatious amounts of money to the temple treasury. They did it because they loved honor and fame and other people's acclaim, not God and not the worship of God and the spiritual and physical welfare of the people who used the temple to worship God. They appeared to be very loving and generous with their gifts, but their hearts were stingy and selfish. As God said to his prophet Samuel when he chose Jesse's youngest son David to be king rather than any one of his older and taller brothers, "[Man] sees the appearance but the LORD looks into the heart" (1 Sam. 16:7). Because the heart is the power to love, and God looks for hearts because God is love, and love always looks for love. What love is satisfied with is always nothing less than love.

The first and greatest commandment is "You shall love the Lord your God with *all* your heart, with all your soul, with all your mind, and with all your strength" (Mark 12:30). *And* with all your time, and energy, and stuff, and money—some of it directly, like those who gave money to the temple, but all of it at least indirectly. It's all *from* God, the giver of all gifts, the source of all good (most of it indirectly, through others); and it's all *for* God, who is our Omega as well as our Alpha, our end as well as our beginning, our greatest good and end and joy as well as our Creator.

The test of love is sacrifice. We all know that without any doubt when we are on the receiving end of a loving sacrifice, but we can hide from that fact when we are called on to make the sacrifice.

True story: a six-year-old boy had a three-year-old sister who had a disease that she would die of if she did not have a blood transfusion. But she had a very rare blood type, and the only person who could be found with that same blood type was her brother. As soon as he heard this, the brother volunteered to give her the transfusion. While the transfusion was going on, the boy looked sad, and when they asked him why, he said, "How long will it take me to die?"

Salvation is a blood transfusion from Jesus, and he really did die to save us.

THIRTY-THIRD SUNDAY
IN ORDINARY TIME

FIRST READING

DANIEL 12:1–3 _____

In those days, I Daniel,
    heard this word of the Lord:
"At that time there shall arise
    Michael, the great prince,
    guardian of your people;
it shall be a time unsurpassed in distress
    since nations began until that time.
At that time your people shall escape,
    everyone who is found written in the book.

"Many of those who sleep in the dust of the earth shall awake;
    some shall live forever,
    others shall be an everlasting horror and disgrace.

"But the wise shall shine brightly
    like the splendor of the firmament,
and those who lead the many to justice
    shall be like the stars forever."

_____

God gave the prophet Daniel a vision of the last days, the end of the world, the
end of time. Or, more correctly, not just a vision, a picture to be seen with the

eyes, which would leave much room for interpretation, but, more explicitly, words. He says, "I Daniel, heard this word of the LORD."

Five things stand out in this vision.

First, St. Michael the Archangel will arise. He is a "great prince," a ruler over many other angels. He is also the "guardian of your people," of Israel in the Old Testament and also of the Church, the new Israel, in New Testament times. The purpose of a warrior is primarily defense, not offense; thus, Michael's task is to be the "guardian of your people" rather than the destroyer of the people's enemies. God wills these enemies to continue to exist, to test and even tempt the elect, to strengthen them, as he deliberately permitted Satan to torture Job, but in a limited and controlled way: "Thus far shall you come but no farther" (Job 38:11).

God does no evil but permits many evils. Why? For the same reason he does everything that he does. Everything God does is done by his infinite and perfect wisdom, power, and love, including his permitting nature to afflict us with many physical evils and even his allowing our free will to produce many spiritual evils, many sins. He does it all for our very best good, out of his very best and wisest love for us. Of course, we do not see this, or understand it—we are not God—but we can very reasonably believe it.

God uses angels, and also saints, both great and small, as his instruments, because one of the greatest graces he gives us is the grace to be such instruments of his grace to others.

St. Michael is the enemy of Satan. The battle is not between Satan and God but between Satan and Michael. Satan is no match for God, any more than Scrooge is a match for Charles Dickens or Richard III is a match for Shakespeare or Sauron is a match for Tolkien. God is the omnipotent Creator of all angels, both unfallen and fallen. Michael is to Satan what Gandalf is to Sauron.

The angels guard and guide us every day, but this prophecy is about the last days, and the last battle, about the great event described in Revelation chapter 20. It is not a vision of simple upward progress. At the end, before the greatest good, we will see the greatest evil. God's words to Daniel were that it will be "a time unsurpassed in distress since nations began until that time," and Jesus quotes those words to his disciples in speaking of "the tribulation" in the verses just before today's Gospel. He says that "those times will have tribulation such as has not been since the beginning of God's creation until now, nor ever will be. If the Lord had not shortened those days, no one would be saved" (Mark 13:19–20).

That pretty clearly refutes the secular superstition of inevitable and unending "progress"—unless by "progress" the enemies of God and his Church mean simply progress in their technological power and in their moral depravity. We saw a foretaste of what happens when those two things combine in Nazi Germany.

Jesus reveals how awful the last days will be by saying *not* that his disciples will fight and win at least somewhat but only that they should "be vigilant at all times and pray that you have the strength to escape" (Luke 21:36). At that time, as at no other time, Jesus does *not* call upon his disciples to preach and fight and convert the world but to "escape" it, "for it will come upon all who dwell upon the face of the whole earth." The implication is that our only hope will be escape by death.

The next thing God told Daniel about these last days is that the dead will rise. "Those who sleep in the dust of the earth shall awake; some shall live forever, others shall be an everlasting horror and disgrace." Disgrace is not just the opposite of honor—that's dishonor—but dis-grace is the opposite of grace. The Godless will be forever Godless, and therefore without grace, for God is the source of all grace and all goodness.

Daniel is speaking about hell here, for no other evil is "everlasting." Hell is not the state of everlasting life, even painful life; it is the state of everlasting death. For souls can die as well as bodies. Bodies die when they are separated from their source of life, which is the soul; souls die when they separate themselves from their source of life, which is God. Heaven is the presence of *every* good, and hell is the absence of *every* good.

If there were no hell, human life would not offer us any absolute either/or

775

in the end. Jesus clearly taught us that hell is real, and that it is so hopeless that it would profit us to cut off our hands and feet and gouge out our eyes if that was the way to escape it (Matt. 5:29–30). If you don't believe in hell, you don't believe in Jesus—the real Jesus, the one God sent, as distinct from the one your own personal preferences has reinvented.

That's the baddest of the bad news. The best of the good news is that heaven, the grace of God, is free for the taking. You don't have to be good enough to deserve heaven. No one deserves heaven; it's a gift. But a gift has to be freely received as well as freely given. God always freely gives it; not all freely receive it. Freely receiving it means two things: repentance for sin and faith in God's grace through Christ. The God of love and grace throws no one into hell; we throw ourselves there by our own free choice to reject God and his grace. The doors of hell are locked on the inside—on the inside of the souls of the proud and unrepentant.

Daniel's prophecy ends on a note that is supernaturally bright just as the previous point was supernaturally dark: "The wise shall shine brightly like the splendor of the firmament, and those who lead the many to justice shall be like the stars forever." The wise will *shine*, like light. They do that a little bit even now. Look at the eyes of a saint like Mother Teresa or John Paul II. That light does not come up from the earth; it comes down from the heavens.

RESPONSORIAL PSALM
PSALM 16:5, 8, 9–10, 11 _____

R. (1) **You are my inheritance, O Lord!**

O LORD, my allotted portion and my cup,
  you it is who hold fast my lot.
I set the LORD ever before me;
  with him at my right hand I shall not be disturbed.

Therefore my heart is glad and my soul rejoices,
  my body, too, abides in confidence;
because you will not abandon my soul to the netherworld,
  nor will you suffer your faithful one
    to undergo corruption.

You will show me the path to life,
  fullness of joys in your presence,
  the delights at your right hand forever.

Today's Psalm verses teach us at least five things.

First, now as then, God is our only sure hope. David prays, "You it is who hold fast my lot." The last image in Jesus' Sermon on the Mount (Matt. 7:24–27) contrasts those who build the house of their life on Christ the rock, so that it holds fast on its foundation when the storms come, and those who build it on sand. We must be able to say, in the words of the old hymn, "On Christ the solid rock I stand; all other ground is sinking sand."

A second thing this Psalm teaches us is that God is our "inheritance," our "allotted portion." We do not inherit wages; we work for them and deserve them. We do not work for our inheritance; we receive it, and only through a death. Heaven is our inheritance, not our wage. No one deserves heaven. We *receive* it as a gift of grace. When your rich father dies, you inherit his money—not the money you made by your work but the money *he* made by *his* work. What we inherit as Christians is infinitely more precious than money: it is eternal life, life as part of the Mystical Body of Christ. And we inherit it through his death.

A third lesson is in David's confession to God that "you will not abandon my soul to the netherworld," the realm of the dead. If we are in Christ through our faith and Baptism, we resurrect to life with him, in him, as part of his Mystical Body.

Fourth, David prays, "You will show me the path to life." That life is not

777

the natural life we all have already but the supernatural life, the eternal life, that is given to us in Christ. So the path to that life, the way to that life, is not an abstract map but a concrete person, the one who said, "I am the way" (John 14:6). So David's confession "You will show me the path to life" amounts to the faith that "You will show me Christ."

Fifth, this life is called "fullness of joys in your presence." Whatever gives us joy here on earth, whether it is a marriage or a muffin, whether it is a good job or a good joke, is a tiny shadow, an image, an appetizer, a reflection of something in God that will give us infinitely more joy forever. St. Augustine says to his own soul, "What do you seek, O my soul? What do you desire? What do you love? There, there, is everything you seek, everything you desire, everything you love." God is not one among many joys; he is the fullness of joys, and the source of every joy, just as light is not one among many colors but the thing that brings out all colors. God is in every joy, even when the joy is mixed with sorrow or death by his own providential wisdom, or even when the joy is mixed with sin by our own foolishness.

SECOND READING
HEBREWS 10:11–14, 18 _____

Brothers and sisters: Every priest stands daily at his ministry, offering frequently those same sacrifices that can never take away sins. But this one offered one sacrifice for sins, and took his seat forever at the right hand of God; now he waits until his enemies are made his footstool. For by one offering he has made perfect forever those who are being consecrated.

Where there is forgiveness of these, there is no longer offering for sin.

This is the next to last week of the liturgical year. Next Sunday will be the last, the Feast of Christ the King, the universal king, the one true king of the entire universe. Today's epistle is about Christ the Priest, the one universal priest, the priest of all mankind. Christ is also God's universal prophet, the final, total revelation of God, the Word of God in the singular, God's last word. God instituted these three holy offices of prophets, priests, and kings in his covenant with Old Testament Israel, to foreshadow Christ's work as our prophet, our priest, and our king. Today's epistle is about his priesthood.

The essential task and vocation of a priest is to be a mediator, to offer sacrifice to God. Prophets are also mediators, mediators of God's words, God's mind, to us. Kings mediate God's power and authority to us. Priests mediate God's grace and forgiveness and salvation to us. Christ is the one high priest behind all priests. He is also the one true king behind all kings, "the king of kings and Lord of Lords," and the one true prophet behind all prophets.

Today's passage from the Letter to the Hebrews contrasts Christ's priesthood with the priesthood God instituted in Old Testament Israel in six ways. First, they only began the work, but Christ perfected and completed it. Second, they were many, but Christ was one. Third, they offered many sacrifices, but Christ offered only the one sacrifice of himself, which was sufficient. Fourth, their sacrifices did not take away sins, but Christ's did. Fifth, being sinners, they offered sacrifices for their own sins as well as the sins of the people; Christ, being sinless, offered his sacrifice only for us sinners. Sixth, they did not offer themselves as their sacrifice, but animals; Christ offered himself, his own body and blood.

In all of these ways, they were images or symbols or shadows or foreshadowings of Christ. Our priests are that too, but they are aftershadows rather than foreshadows. Yet they are also foreshadows of the gifts Christ will give us in the future, in heaven. The only gift we have on earth that is as great as the gifts we will receive in heaven is the Eucharist, because that is Christ himself, and in him are all gifts, not just some. St. Paul says, "My God will *fully* supply whatever you need, in accord with his glorious riches in Christ Jesus" (Phil. 4:19).

GOSPEL
MARK 13:24–32 _____

Jesus said to his disciples: "In those days after that tribulation
   the sun will be darkened,
      and the moon will not give its light,
   and the stars will be falling from the sky,
      and the powers in the heavens will be shaken.
"And then they will see 'the Son of Man coming in the clouds' with great power and glory, and then he will send out the angels and gather his elect from the four winds, from the end of the earth to the end of the sky.

"Learn a lesson from the fig tree. When its branch becomes tender and sprouts leaves, you know that summer is near. In the same way, when you see these things happening, know that he is near, at the gates. Amen, I say to you, this generation will not pass away until all these things have taken place. Heaven and earth will pass away, but my words will not pass away.

"But of that day or hour, no one knows, neither the angels in heaven, nor the Son, but only the Father."

_____

Two of today's Scripture readings, from the prophet Daniel and from Mark's Gospel, are about the end of the world, the end of time, because the liturgical year ends with these two weeks, this Sunday and next Sunday, the Solemnity of Christ the King; and then the new liturgical year begins with Advent.

What does Jesus tell his disciples (and thus us) about the end of the world?

First, that it will be preceded by a "great tribulation." (See the Daniel reflection for details.)

Second, that the whole universe will be changed, not just life on this little planet. The sun and the moon will be darkened and the stars themselves will fall. The universe is mortal, after all. Even all the stars will eventually die. Entropy, established by the second law of thermodynamics, means that all energy dissipates, like heat escaping from a coffee cup or a room or a star. Nothing here is immortal. Our souls are the only immortal things in the universe. Twenty billion years from now, when all the galaxies have died, we will still be eternally young.

Third, that we will not need the light of sun, moon, and stars because Christ will be our light. His first coming was invisible, in disguise and darkness and the humility of a manger; his second coming will be visible, in total clarity and light and glory to all the world. All of us will see him.

His first coming was in weakness—so weak that he could die, and he did! His second coming will be in power, and then his kingdom will come and his will will be done on earth as it is in heaven.

His first coming was to die. That's why he came. His second coming will bring us life, eternal life.

His first coming was to initiate a new era, a new time. His second coming will end time.

And the new era, the new world, what Revelation calls the new heavens and the new earth, and what Scripture calls the kingdom of God, will itself have no end.

Fourth, that angels will gather the elect and carry us to heaven. This is not a physical "carrying" because angels are pure spirits and have no bodies, and what they will carry to heaven is our souls, not our bodies, which will then be resurrected to join our souls.

Fifth, that "this generation will not pass away until all these things have taken place." But twenty centuries have passed since Jesus said that, and that's much more than one generation. Could Jesus have goofed?

No, God never goofs. There are at least four possible interpretations of this saying.

One is that "this generation" is not meant biologically but historically, as "this era." The word "generation" or "generations" is sometimes used that way in the Bible.

A second possibility is that the first generation of Christians are even now in heaven, not dead and "passed away" but alive and waiting for Christ's second coming on earth.

A third possibility is that what Christ meant by "taken place" is what he was about to do on the cross, which would issue in the last age, or what would happen at Pentecost, the beginning of the only thing that has a beginning but no end.

A fourth interpretation is that in Jesus' divine mind, which judges not by quantity of years but by the importance of events, all the time between the first coming and the second coming is collapsed into relative insignificance. He measures time by quality, not quantity; by importance, not by mathematics. All the time between his first coming and his second coming, even if it's another twenty centuries, is nothing compared to those two events.

It's not certain which of these four interpretations is best, or possibly some fifth one, but what is certain is that God incarnate makes no mistakes.

Sixth, closely connected with the previous question about time, Jesus says that this end of the world is "near." In the last verse in the Bible, in the last chapter of the book of Revelation, Jesus says he is coming "soon" (Rev. 22:20). It is his last word to us. In fact, he says even now, "Behold, I stand at the door" (Rev. 3:20). The door, of course, is death; and that will come quite soon for all of us—it's not twenty centuries away but less than one century away for all of us.

THE SOLEMNITY OF THE
MOST HOLY TRINITY

FIRST READING

DEUTERONOMY 4:32–24, 39–40 _____

Moses said to the people: "Ask now of the days of old, before your time, ever since God created man upon the earth; ask from one end of the sky to the other: Did anything so great ever happen before? Was it ever heard of? Did a people ever hear the voice of God speaking from the midst of fire, as you did, and live? Or did any god venture to go and take a nation for himself from the midst of another nation, by testings, by signs and wonders, by war, with strong hand and outstretched arm, and by great terrors, all of which the LORD, your God, did for you in Egypt before your very eyes? This is why you must now know, and fix in your heart, that the LORD is God in the heavens above and on earth below, and that there is no other. You must keep his statutes and commandments that I enjoin on you today, that you and your children after you may prosper, and that you may have long life on the land which the LORD, your God, is giving you forever."

_____

The word "religion" means literally "binding relationship." A "covenant" is a binding relationship that is freely entered into. Marriage is the most important human covenant. It is between two equal but different humans, one male, one female. It is a "horizontal" covenant. Religion is a "vertical" covenant, with God. Put the two together and you get the shape of the cross.

    Of the thousands of different religions in the world, there is only one that is founded on concrete historical facts rather than abstract principles, truths, and values. These facts, unique in human history, are summarized by Moses in today's first reading.

The first stage of this religion, or covenant, was Judaism, God's covenant with Israel. The second stage, or "new covenant" of this same religion, this same binding relationship with this same God, is Christianity. The Catholic Church, which means literally the Church universal, is the new Israel. Jesus did not found a new religion; he fulfilled the one and only old one. As Jewish converts today confess, a Christian is a completed Jew.

Jesus was a Jew. If God did not create the world, authorize prophets like Moses, miraculously care for his chosen people, and give us the Ten Commandments, Judaism would no longer be a religion, only a culture.

Judaism and Christianity are the only religion that is empirically verifiable, that is based on literal facts of history. It is the only religion that actually happened. The essence of Judaism and Christianity is God's concrete, actual, visible interventions in human history: creation, the Exodus, the prophets, the Incarnation, the Passion and Crucifixion and Resurrection and Ascension of Christ. If you do not believe in these miracles, you do not believe in that religion, even if you believe in all of its abstract truths and values and principles. In fact, most of those principles are similar or identical to those taught by all the other great religions of the world. But Christ is absolutely unique. No other religious founder claimed to be God incarnate, performed miracles, or rose from the dead. The bones of Muhammad, Buddha, Confucius, Zoroaster, and Lao Tzu are in tombs. Jesus' tomb is empty. If the bones of any one of those religious founders were found and conclusively identified, nothing would change; if Jesus' bones were found and identified, Christianity would be totally refuted and dead.

God is an interrupter, an interferer. He is not an ideal, a value, a principle. He barges into history, and he barges into your life. When you receive the Eucharist, Jesus does stuff to you. He does not just stand there smiling and waiting for you to imitate him. Catholic churches should put warning signs on their doors: "Enter this place at your own risk." Bibles should come with warning labels: "This book may be dangerous to your fallen ego's survival."

Our earth has not been visited by other races from other planets, but it has been visited by someone far more formidable who came from a place that is both infinitely farther away than another planet and infinitely closer. And nothing has been the same ever since he has been here. Almost his last words to us, in the book of Revelation, were "Behold, I make all things new" (Rev. 21:5). The first and most important thing he is making new is yourself. And he never stops. He never, never, never gives up on you. And you shouldn't either.

RESPONSORIAL PSALM
PSALM 33:4–5, 6, 9, 18–19, 20, 22 _____

R. (12b) **Blessed the people the Lord has chosen to be his own.**

Upright is the word of the LORD,
    and all his works are trustworthy.
He loves justice and right;
    of the kindness of the LORD the earth is full.

By the word of the LORD the heavens were made;
    by the breath of his mouth all their host.
For he spoke, and it was made;
    he commanded, and it stood forth.

See, the eyes of the LORD are upon those who fear him,
    upon those who hope for his kindness,
To deliver them from death
    and preserve them in spite of famine.

Our soul waits for the LORD,
    who is our help and our shield.
May your kindness, O LORD, be upon us
    who have put our hope in you.

What is it to be religious, to have a religion? It is essentially a relationship of faith and trust and hope and love to God. What is that relationship, what is that faith and trust and hope and love, based on? Is it our needs, our aspirations, our ideals, our ideas, our feelings, our wisdom, our virtues? No. It is not based on us. It is based on God and on what God has done for us. Our relationship to God is based on God's relationship to us. That's the point of today's Psalm.

Who is God? Today's Psalm mentions three of his attributes: goodness, power, and wisdom. Look at the consequences in our life of those three attributes, the difference they make.

First, goodness. God is "upright"—that is, trustworthy, totally trustable. That's why we trust him and believe in him. He "loves justice and right." That's why we love him. He is "full" of "kindness." That's why we hope in him: not because we are good but because he is.

Second, power. This God of trustworthiness and love and justice and kindness has all the power: by his mere word and command the universe was created! "This is my Father's world."

Third, wisdom. He is also all-knowing and makes no mistakes: "The eyes of the Lord are upon those who fear him." God knows exactly what we need. We do not. He makes no mistakes about us. We do.

Put these three divine attributes together: total goodness and kindness, total power, and total wisdom. The consequence of these three attributes, the conclusion of this argument with three premises, changes everything. It conquers all fear, for as St. John says, "perfect love drives out fear" (1 John 4:18). Not our love—that's not perfect love—but God's love. Our religion is not based on our love for God but on God's love for us. That's perfect love. That's the love that casts out our fear.

Perform a little thought experiment to see the difference this makes. Imagine a religion that knew only one of these three divine attributes: total goodness, total power, or total wisdom. What would be the consequences?

If God were only perfect goodness, both justice and mercy, both righteousness and kindness, both the hard virtues and the soft virtues—if God were perfect in goodness but not in wisdom, he might not know us totally; his love might be naïve and not realistic.

If God were perfect in goodness but not in power, he would not be able to rule the world by his goodness; it would be merely an abstract and unattainable ideal far away for us to try to imitate, and of course we would fail terribly.

If God were perfect in power but not in goodness, he might be a devil, a tyrant, an enemy.

If God were perfect in power but not in wisdom, he might be like a blind giant, not knowing how best to use his power. A tyrant or a blind giant does not make a good ruler of the universe or of our lives.

Even if God had two of the three attributes, it would not be enough to ground our faith and hope and love of him.

If he were all-loving and all-powerful but not all-wise, he might have good intentions and be able to do whatever he intended, but he might make mistakes in using his unlimited powers and not succeed in doing good rather than harm.

If he were all-loving and all-wise but not all-powerful, he would be a good ideal but nothing more; he would not have the power to use those two great virtues, wisdom and love, for our benefit.

And if he were all-wise and all-powerful but not all-good, then evil rather than goodness would rule the whole world and all of us.

But in fact, the God who is all-wise and all-powerful is also good and loving and kind. And the God who is all goodness and kindness is also the one who has all the power. And the God who has all the power is also totally wise and knows how best to use it for our good. That is the best news we have ever heard. That is the Gospel.

And that is what Jesus shows us in himself, all three of those divine attributes: the greatest words of wisdom ever spoken, wiser than all the other sages and philosophers, the greatest love in all of human life, the one who sacrificed everything for us, even his own body and blood, and the greatest power in the universe, the one able to conquer death itself. The one who rose from the dead on Easter Sunday morning is also the one who died for our sins out of love and who knows exactly what we need every second of every day of our lives. That is the Christian Gospel already preached in this Jewish Psalm.

Jesus incarnates this God and concretizes this theology.

All three persons of the Trinity totally possess all three of these attributes. But power is especially associated with the Father, the Creator; and wisdom is especially associated with the Son, who is the Logos, the Word or Mind of God, the wisdom that is so real that it is a distinct divine person; and love is especially associated with the Holy Spirit, who is the love between the Father and the Son, the love that is so real that it, too, is a distinct divine person.

And our faith and hope and love are also trinitarian. Their object is all three divine persons, but our faith is especially associated with and directed toward the Father, the Creator and ruler of all things; and our hope is especially associated with and directed toward the Son, our Savior; and our love is especially associated with the Holy Spirit, who quietly and invisibly inspires our best intentions.

SECOND READING
ROMANS 8:14–17 _____

Brothers and sisters: Those who are led by the Spirit of God are sons of God. For you did not receive a spirit of slavery to fall back into fear, but you received a Spirit of adoption, through whom we cry, "Abba, Father!" The Spirit himself bears witness with our spirit that we are children of God, and if children, then heirs, heirs of God and joint heirs with Christ, if only we suffer with him so that we may also be glorified with him.

All three divine persons of the Trinity are mentioned in the short passage from St. Paul's Letter to the Romans that is today's epistle. That is appropriate because they always work not only together but as one God. God is more one than we are! The oneness of the three divine persons is the love among them, and love is a stronger, tighter "glue" than mere quantitative, factual oneness.

St. Paul begins with the Holy Spirit, who is "the Spirit of God" and thus is divine, who is God himself, as our human spirit is our human self itself. This Holy Spirit gives us a share in *zoe*, divine life, supernatural life, eternal life. He makes us children of God, inheritors of God's very life and nature, in a finite way.

We are not born into this; we are born into human nature and human life only. We get this sharing in the divine nature and divine life only by being "born again" by faith and Baptism. We are born into the human race as natural children of Adam but adopted into the divine family as supernatural children of God.

The reason St. Paul says "sons" instead of "children" of God is that in the ancient world it was usually only sons and not daughters who could inherit property from their parents. In fact, it was often only firstborn sons. But all of us equally can inherit eternal life, supernatural life, from God. Thus, we are "heirs of God," that is, of God's own life, "and joint heirs with Christ," who has eternal life eternally while we get it only by God adopting us into his family here in our lifetime. We are now the King's kids!

Thus, God becomes our Father through Christ, so that we can call him not only "God" but "Our Father," and not only "Father" but "Abba," which is the intimate word for "Father," like "Daddy." God is both infinitely holy and transcendent and also infinitely intimate and imminent, so that our relationship with him can be both full of awe and holy fear and also full of total trust and closeness.

It is the Holy Spirit who makes us children of God through faith and Baptism. (Those two, by the way, are almost always mentioned together in the New Testament.) St. Paul calls this the spirit of freedom because we are freed from both the eternal punishment that is deserved by our sins and also from sin itself by the process of gradual sanctification, by which we sinners are transformed into perfect saints so that we can fully enjoy heaven.

St. Paul ends by mentioning two doubles, two sets of opposites that are together in ways that are surprising and wonderful.

One "togetherness" is between our spirit and God's Spirit. The Holy Spirit "bears witness" together with our human spirit, our heart and soul, that we are indeed children of God. The Holy Spirit gives us the gift of faith and the assurance that we are what God says we are, God's beloved children. And even if we do not feel this assurance, we can know that it is so because God has promised it and God cannot lie.

The second "togetherness" is that because Christ has made us like him in making himself like us, therefore our relationship with Christ includes both suffering and glory, because we now participate in all of him, both his sufferings and his glory. Our very sufferings for him are glorious, even though they feel far from glorious. Once again, we must not let our human feelings substitute for our faith in God's revelation. God is like a surgeon who is operating on us, saving our lives and healing our souls as a surgeon heals a body. He indeed is making all things new, as he promised, both our sufferings and our joys. Beware of him; he leaves nothing in us uninterrupted, undisturbed, and alone. Don't try to put him in a cage; he is a lion, not a pussycat.

GOSPEL
MATTHEW 28:16–20 _____

The eleven disciples went to Galilee, to the mountain to which Jesus had ordered them. When they all saw him, they worshiped, but they doubted. Then Jesus approached and said to them, "All power in heaven and on earth has been given to me. Go, therefore, and make disciples of all nations, baptizing them in the name of the Father, and of the Son, and of the Holy Spirit, teaching them to observe all that I have commanded you. And behold, I am with you always, until the end of the age."

Here is Matthew's very short account of the end of Christ's incarnate life on earth. But it contains seven facts that are life-changing, seven of the most important things Christ said and did at the end of his incarnate earthly life, before he ascended back into heaven.

First, the risen Christ was seen by his disciples, literally, with their bodily eyes. In fact, St. Paul mentions in one of his letters (1 Cor. 15:6) that there were more than five hundred people alive at that time who had seen Christ after his Resurrection. Thus, St. Paul is inviting his readers to interview these eyewitnesses and gather the data. The Resurrection is a historical fact, not a fancy or a fantasy or a fiction.

Second, Christ was not only revered and loved but adored and worshiped, as God. For only God can conquer death. The divinity of Christ was not a later invention of the Church; it went back to the earliest disciples and to Christ himself, who claimed it in many ways, one of which was his miracles, especially his own Resurrection from the dead.

Third, they worshiped, but some doubted. For God left us our free choice to believe or not, and we have that choice in every age. In using the plural ("they doubted"), Matthew implies here that it was not only "Doubting Thomas" that doubted.

Fourth, Christ now has all "authority" over everything in heaven and earth, and therefore over everything in our lives, without exception. Authority means not just power but rightful power, the power of right, the right that makes might.

Thus, the first and earliest version of the Christian creed was the three-word formula "Jesus is Lord." Almost every one of the literally hundreds of times St. Paul writes the word "Jesus" he also writes the word "Lord." The word for "Lord," *kyrios* in Greek, was never used by Christians for earthly Lords, kings, and emperors like Herod or Caesar, but for God alone.

Fifth, our job now, both as individuals and as the Church, is to spread the Good News, both by words ("teaching them") and deeds ("to observe"), especially the deed of Baptism, which is the one divine command the Church has obeyed perfectly, always and everywhere for two thousand years.

And seventh, Christ's last solemn and infallible promise to us is that he will never, never leave us alone but will be "with" us always, until the end of

791

time. Christ is "with" his Father always, eternally; and he will no more leave us than he will leave his Father. When we feel desperate, helpless, and hopeless, we must remember this divine and infallible promise. It is our fortress, our anchor, and our lighthouse.

Christ's last words to us are "Behold, I am with you always, until the end of the age." It is a divine promise, and God cannot lie. But we have to "behold" it; we have to remember it; we have to turn our attention to it, and to the one who gave it to us. When we do, and when we confront that promise with what seems to us like his abandonment of us, the lacerating problems of our lives that break our hearts, when we juxtapose the terrifying waves of those storms with this promise from God incarnate, which do we choose to believe: our own foolish, fallen, fearful feelings or the solemn promise of the one who is our Savior and our Lord and who has told us to call God our heavenly Father?

THE SOLEMNITY OF THE MOST HOLY BODY AND BLOOD OF CHRIST

FIRST READING

EXODUS 24:3–8 _____

When Moses came to the people and related all the words and ordinances of the LORD, they all answered with one voice, "We will do everything that the LORD has told us." Moses then wrote down all the words of the LORD and, rising early the next day, he erected at the foot of the mountain an altar and twelve pillars for the twelve tribes of Israel. Then, having sent certain young men of the Israelites to offer holocausts and sacrifice young bulls as peace offerings to the LORD, Moses took half of the blood and put it in large bowls; the other half he splashed on the altar. Taking the book of the covenant, he read it aloud to the people, who answered, "All that the LORD has said, we will heed and do." Then he took the blood and sprinkled it on the people, saying, "This is the blood of the covenant that the LORD has made with you in accordance with all these words of his."

RESPONSORIAL PSALM

PSALM 116:12–13, 15–16, 17–18 _____

R. (13) **I will take the cup of salvation, and call on the name of the Lord.**
or: R. **Alleluia**.

How shall I make a return to the LORD
    for all the good he has done for me?
The cup of salvation I will take up,
    and I will call upon the name of the LORD.

Precious in the eyes of the L\ord
   is the death of his faithful ones.
I am your servant, the son of your handmaid;
   you have loosed my bonds.

To you will I offer sacrifice of thanksgiving,
   and I will call upon the name of the L\ord.
My vows to the L\ord I will pay
   in the presence of all his people.

SECOND READING

H\ebrews 9:11–15 _____

Brothers and sisters: When Christ came as high priest of the good things that have come to be, passing through the greater and more perfect tabernacle not made by hands, that is, not belonging to this creation, he entered once for all into the sanctuary, not with the blood of goats and calves but with his own blood, thus obtaining eternal redemption. For if the blood of goats and bulls and the sprinkling of a heifer's ashes can sanctify those who are defiled so that their flesh is cleansed, how much more will the blood of Christ, who through the eternal Spirit offered himself unblemished to God, cleanse our consciences from dead works to worship the living God.

For this reason he is mediator of a new covenant: since a death has taken place for deliverance from transgressions under the first covenant, those who are called may receive the promised eternal inheritance.

GOSPEL

M\ark 14:12–16, 22–26 _____

On the first day of the Feast of Unleavened Bread, when they sacrificed the Passover lamb, Jesus' disciples said to him, "Where do you want us to go and prepare for you to eat the Passover?" He sent two of his disciples and said to them, "Go into the city and a man will meet you, carrying a jar of water. Follow him. Wherever he enters, say to the master of the house, 'The Teacher says, "Where is my guest room where I may eat the Passover with my disciples?"' Then he will show you a large upper room furnished and ready. Make the preparations for us there." The disciples then went off, entered the city, and found it just as he had told them; and they prepared the Passover.

While they were eating, he took bread, said the blessing, broke it, gave it to them, and said, "Take it; this is my body." Then he took a cup, gave thanks, and gave it to them, and they all drank from it. He said to them, "This is my blood of the covenant, which will be shed for many. Amen, I say to you, I shall not drink again the fruit of the vine until the day when I drink it new in the kingdom of God." Then, after singing a hymn, they went out to the Mount of Olives.

Today we celebrate Christ's institution of the greatest ongoing miracle in the world, the miracle of the Eucharist.

Two questions arise: first, what is the Eucharist? And second, what do we do when we receive this literal miracle? What happens to us?

To answer the first question, I quote two verses from the Song of Solomon. Many of the great Catholic mystics see the Eucharist prophesied in this verse. The storyline is that a girl has been captured and forced into King Solomon's harem. Her true lover comes to her to rescue her. She says of him: "Here he stands behind our wall, gazing through the windows, peering through the lattices. My lover speaks; he says to me, 'Arise, my beloved, my dove, my beautiful one, and come!'" (Song of Sol. 2:9–10).

The captured girl is us; the wall between us and our lover is our sins; and the lattice window through which he calls us and through which we see him is the Eucharist.

It is a door as well as a window, a door in the walls of the world, a door from us to heaven and heaven's free and fresh air, and a door from heaven to us, a door through which heaven's Son shines on us (the pun is deliberate) with his light and heat, the light of his truth and the heat of his love.

As St. Paul wrote, Christ "broke down the dividing wall of enmity" (Eph. 2:14)—the wall between God and man. When he died, "the veil of the sanctuary was torn in two from top to bottom" (Matt. 27:51), because that curtain divided the Holy of Holies, where God himself dwelled in Old Testament times, from the rest of the universe. It was Christ who tore it down by his death. Now there is an open window between heaven and earth until the end of time. It is the Eucharist.

The window is not clear glass. It is a lattice. The light shines through the latticework, like the sun through leaves and branches in the woods, but it is seen only by the eyes of faith and the eyes of love.

A window is a border between the within and the without, between the house and the outdoors. It belongs to two worlds. So does our Lord: he is both divine and human, and his presence in the Eucharist manifests his membership in both the visible and the invisible worlds.

The priest, holding up the consecrated Host, says, "*Behold* the Lamb of God who takes away the sins of the world." The invisible God has become *visible* to us; we are told to "behold" him. The Eucharist is "the extension of the Incarnation." When Jesus was on earth, his divinity was hiding but his humanity was visible. In the Eucharist, both the divinity and the humanity are hiding behind the appearances of bread and wine. In both cases, the eyes of faith pierce the veil and see God. It is a foretaste of heaven, where we will no longer need faith because we will see God face to face, divinity and humanity.

To answer the second question, what do we do when we receive the Eucharist, I want to start by quoting the remarkable first page of a beautiful book about the Eucharist, *The Holy Bread of Eternal Life* by Peter Kwasniewski, published by Sophia Institute Press.

> Imagine eating the sun—and imagine you could do it without perishing.
> What would happen? You would receive into your body the source of light

and warmth. . . . When we receive Jesus in the Most Blessed Sacrament, we receive the source of all supernatural light and warmth, the light of truth, the heat of love. . . . Saint Ephrem the Syrian wrote: ". . . He who eats it with faith, eats Fire and Spirit. . . ." That we are not killed instantly by this contact with eternal and infinite Fire is, in its own way, a greater miracle than would be eating the sun without perishing. Our Lord protects us.

Let's make a kind of thought experiment to surround this one. In fact, let's make seven thought experiments. The first one is easy to imagine, the next five are very difficult to imagine, and the seventh is literally unimaginable.

The first is simply to imagine yourself eating an ordinary piece of bread.

The second is to imagine that by some kind of miracle you eat a lion. The life of the lion enters into you. You are now not just an ordinary human being; you are now a human being who has eaten a lion. The whole lion is in you, and it is still alive, and it is still a lion.

The third is that somehow, by some kind of even greater miracle or magic, you eat the planet earth, all of it. It is still the earth, and you are still you. You do not destroy it, and it does not destroy you, but you have eaten the whole earth.

The fourth is to imagine that you eat the sun. Not just a sunbeam but the sun, the whole sun, in all its solar power and immensity, hundreds of thousands of times greater than the whole planet earth. That would be even more incredible and unimaginable than eating a lion or eating the earth, since just as the earth is millions of times greater than a lion, the sun is hundreds of thousands of times greater than the earth.

The fifth is to imagine that you eat the whole universe, with its trillions of suns. There are literally billions of suns, billions of stars, in our Milky Way galaxy, and there are literally billions of galaxies in the universe.

The sixth is to imagine that you eat the Big Bang, the event that instantly created all the matter, space, and time in the whole universe.

The seventh is to imagine that you eat God himself, the source of that energy, the infinite and eternal Creator. That's literally unimaginable.

Of course, this is just a thought experiment. We do not really eat a lion, or the earth, or the sun, or the universe, or the Big Bang. True. But the real truth is more, not less, than any of these ridiculously exaggerated things we have imagined. The truth is that we eat God.

In the Eucharist, we eat God because we eat Christ, and Christ is God. We eat the whole Christ, the one Christ, divinity as well as humanity. On the cross, his blood was separated from his body, but his humanity was not and cannot be separated from his divinity.

Who could believe that we eat God? Why would anyone ever believe that? There is only one possible reason: that God has said so, that God has told us. Nothing less than God could possibly make that true, and no one less than God could possibly have the authority to tell us that such an incredible thing is true. And in today's Gospel, we have one of the many passages in Scripture where God clearly does tell us that this unbelievable thing is true, and where God asks us to believe this unbelievable thing that the Church has clearly taught for two thousand years.

We believe this is true because Christ says it, and Christ is not a liar; Christ is God. It is God who says this incredible thing.

If we eat Christ himself, and Christ is God, then we eat God.

And if you believe that Christ is not God, then please do not call yourself a Christian, much less a Catholic Christian, and please stop being a hypocrite and a liar by reciting the Creed when you come to church.

And if you *do* believe that Christ is God and that the Eucharist is Christ, the Real Presence of Christ, the whole Christ, Body and Blood, body and soul, humanity and divinity, then what? Then tremble. Tremble with amazement and gratitude and joy and love and holy fear and honor and glory and adoration. Because nothing—nothing in all the universe, nothing in all of time and history, nothing in your life—can come even remotely close to that.

And that is literally what you will do, what you will receive, the next time you receive the Eucharist. You are not going to eat the sun; you are going to eat more, not less, than the sun; you are going to eat the Son of God.

THE SOLEMNITY OF OUR
LORD JESUS CHRIST,
KING OF THE UNIVERSE

FIRST READING
DANIEL 7:13–14 _____

As the visions during the night continued, I saw
    one like a Son of man coming,
      on the clouds of heaven;
    when he reached the Ancient One
      and was presented before him,
    the one like a Son of man received dominion, glory, and kingship;
      all peoples, nations, and languages serve him.
    His dominion is an everlasting dominion
      that shall not be taken away,
      his kingship shall not be destroyed.

RESPONSORIAL PSALM
PSALM 93:1, 1–2, 5 _____

R. (1a) **The Lord is king; he is robed in majesty.**

The LORD is king, in splendor robed;
    robed is the LORD and girt about with strength.

And he has made the world firm,
    not to be moved.

Your throne stands firm from of old;
    from everlasting you are, O Lord.

Your decrees are worthy of trust indeed;
    holiness befits your house,
    O Lord, for length of days.

SECOND READING

Revelation 1:5–8 _____

Jesus Christ is the faithful witness, the firstborn of the dead and ruler of the kings of the earth. To him who loves us and has freed us from our sins by his blood, who has made us into a kingdom, priests for his God and Father, to him be glory and power forever and ever. Amen.

    Behold, he is coming amid the clouds,
        and every eye will see him,
        even those who pierced him.
    All the peoples of the earth will lament him.
        Yes. Amen.

"I am the Alpha and the Omega," says the Lord God, "the one who is and who was and who is to come, the almighty."

GOSPEL

John 18:33b–37 _____

Pilate said to Jesus, "Are you the King of the Jews?" Jesus answered, "Do you say this on your own or have others told you about me?" Pilate answered, "I am not a Jew, am I? Your own nation and the chief priests handed you over to me. What have you done?" Jesus answered, "My kingdom does not belong to this world. If my kingdom did belong to this world, my attendants would be fighting to keep me from being handed over to the Jews. But as it is, my kingdom is not here." So Pilate said to him, "Then you are a king?" Jesus answered, "You say I am a king. For this I was born and for this I came into the world, to testify to the truth. Everyone who belongs to the truth listens to my voice."

Today's reading from the Old Testament prophet Daniel is a vision of Christ, the Son of Man, receiving from the Father total, universal, and everlasting kingship, Lordship, over all people and nations.

Today's Psalm verse, which is also a prophecy, also announces that the Lord is King, from of old and from everlasting to everlasting, forever.

The prophecy from the book of Revelation calls Jesus the "ruler of the kings of the earth." He is the "king of kings"—not only the greatest of all kings, but the ruler over all kings. And the passage says that his kingdom is *us*! He has made us into his kingdom. His kingdom is not just abstract power but people, his spiritual family, children of our Father who is in heaven.

In today's Gospel, it is ironic that it is Pontius Pilate who asks Jesus, "Are you the King of the Jews?" Jesus does not look like a king. He has just been tortured, scourged, and crowned with thorns, not with gold, and Pilate is about to sentence him to be crucified. And Jesus answers Pilate's question by affirming that his kingdom is not of this world. He is a greater king, not a lesser one, than Caesar, Lord of the world. He is the king of all earthly rulers, including Pilate.

Jesus gave a strange answer to Pilate's question. Pilate asked, "Then you are a king?" and Jesus answered, "You say I am a king." But Pilate did *not* say that Jesus was a king; Pilate *asked* Jesus whether he was a king. What's going on here?

I think we can find the answer to that question if we read a little further. When Pilate had Jesus crucified, he had a sign made to go on the cross that said, "Jesus the Nazorean, the King of the Jews." The Jews who asked Pilate to crucify Jesus complained, "Do not write 'The King of the Jews,' but that he said, 'I am the King of the Jews.'" But Pilate refused to change the sign, saying, "What I have written, I have written" (John 19:19–22). Why did Pilate say that? Because Pilate knew that Jesus really was a king. Pilate was not ignorant; he was wicked and dishonest. He may have not known that Jesus was divine, but he did know that Jesus was innocent, yet he sinned against the truth he knew, against his own conscience. That's why Jesus said to Pilate, "*You* say I am a king. [In other words, your own conscience tells you that I am a true king, a spiritual king.] For this I was born and for this I came into the world, to testify to the truth. Everyone who belongs to the truth listens to my voice" (John 18:37). Pilate deliberately sinned against the truth that he knew. He sneeringly and scornfully said, "What is truth?" (John 18:38). In other words, "Truth be damned." He did not merely condemn Christ; he condemned truth. And that is a mortal sin. It kills the soul. If not repented of, it prevents you from going to heaven.

And for two thousand years, every time Christians repeat their most basic creed, every Sunday, all around the world, Pilate is mentioned by name as the one responsible for Jesus' murder: "Crucified under Pontius Pilate."

As usual, Jesus was reversing the roles of questioner and answerer. Every time anyone asked Jesus a question to test him, Jesus always turned the situation around so that the questioner was being questioned, being challenged, being tested. God always does this. For instance, Job was prepared to ask God the greatest of all questions, why he allowed so much evil to happen to good people: Who was God, anyway? Wasn't he just? And when God showed up, he didn't answer Job's question but instead he *asked* Job a question: Who do you think *you* are? Did you design the universe and human life? I didn't see you there advising me when the angels sang together at the creation.

Whenever we ask God "Who are you?" God replies, "Who are *you*?" We have to answer that question every time we make a choice between good and evil, or between truth and falsehood, between light and darkness, between the true God and false gods, idols. All sins are idolatries. We all need to pray, in the words of the old hymn, "The dearest idol I have known, whate'er that idol be, help me to tear it from thy throne and worship only thee."

That is our life's task, because God is real, and there is only one God, and only God is God, and nothing else is God, and God is the king of all creation, the king of the universe, and the king of every human person, and of every human life. And Jesus Christ is God; Jesus Christ is Lord. That is the first and shortest of all Christian creeds. We find it stated twice in St. Paul's epistles, the three-word formula "Jesus is Lord."

If we really believe that and practice that in our lives, then the kingdom of God will come and God's will will be done on earth by us as it is in heaven by the angels. That is the ultimate meaning of our lives: to be honest, unlike Pilate; to love and seek and acknowledge and live the truth; to be sane, to live in reality, to live in the real world, to live out the ultimate fact that Jesus Christ is Lord.